SEXUAL ORIENTATION

AND GENDER EXPRESSION

IN SOCIAL WORK PRACTICE

SEXUAL ORIENTATION
AND GENDER EXPRESSION
IN SOCIAL WORK PRACTICE

WORKING WITH GAY, LESBIAN, BISEXUAL, AND TRANSGENDER PEOPLE

EDITED BY
Deana F. Morrow and Lori Messinger

COLUMBIA UNIVERSITY PRESS   NEW YORK

COLUMBIA UNIVERSITY PRESS
Publishers Since 1893
New York Chichester, West Sussex

Library of Congress Cataloging-in-Publication Data

Sexual orientation and gender expression in social work practice : working with gay, lesbian,
    bisexual, and transgender people / Deana F. Morrow and Lori Messinger, editors.
        p.   cm.
    Includes bibliographical references and index.
ISBN 978-0-231-12728-8 (cloth : alk. paper) - ISBN 978-0-231-12729-5 (pbk. : alk. paper)
0–231–50186–2 (electronic)
    1. Social work with gays. 2. Gay culture. I. Morrow, Deana F. II. Messinger, Lori.
HV1449.S49   2006
362.8—dc22   2005045564

∞

Columbia University Press books are printed on permanent
    and durable acid-free paper.

Printed in the United States of America

This book is dedicated to

Frankie Tack, MS, LPC, CCAS

 —DFM

and

all of the brave lesbian, gay, bisexual,
and transgender social work scholars who
have enriched the field of social work research

 —LM

CONTENTS

VOLUME EDITORS

DEANA F. MORROW, PHD, LPC, LCSW, ACSW, is an associate professor of social work at Winthrop University in Rock Hill, South Carolina. She received her doctorate in counselor education from North Carolina State University, the master of social work degree and a graduate-level certificate in gerontology from the University of Georgia, and a master's degree in counseling from Western Carolina University. Dr. Morrow teaches micro and mezzo practice courses at both the graduate and the undergraduate levels. Her practice background is in clinical practice in the fields of mental health, aging, and health care. Her research focus is in the areas of social work practice with sexual minority populations and social work education. She is a licensed professional counselor and a licensed clinical social worker in North Carolina and a member of the Academy of Certified Social Workers at the national level. She holds memberships in the National Association of Social Workers and the Council on Social Work Education, where she holds a national appointment to the Council on Sexual Orientation and Gender Expression. She is also a member of the Educators and Friends of Lesbians and Gays, sponsored by the Social Worker Baccalaureate Program Directors Association. In addition, Dr. Morrow holds a gubernatorial appointment to the North Carolina Social Work Certification and Licensure Board. She is also a certified site visitor for the reaccreditation of social work education programs through the Council on Social Work Education.

LORI MESSINGER, PHD, MA, MSW, is an assistant professor and Director of the BSW Program at the University of Kansas School of Social Welfare. She received her doctorate in social work, as well as her master of social work degree, from the University of North Carolina at Chapel Hill, and she also holds a master of arts in political science from Rutgers University. An award-winning teacher, Dr. Messinger teaches courses in social welfare policy, political advocacy, multicultural social work, qualitative research, human sexuality, and program planning. Her practice background is in the fields of sexual assault and domestic violence services, public health education, and social program planning. Dr. Messinger's primary areas of research include comprehensive community planning processes, cultural competence in social work education, feminist theories and research methodologies, and lesbian and gay studies. She holds memberships in the Council on Social Work Education and the Social Work Baccalaureate Program Directors Association, where she is a founding member of Educators and Friends of Lesbians and Gays (EFLAG). She has served as a board member for Equality Alabama, an organization working to advance full equality and civil rights for all the people of Alabama through education and action.

CONTRIBUTORS

VERONICA C. ARAVENA, MA, earned a bachelor of arts degree in English literature and a master of arts degree in sociology from Louisiana State University. She is presently pursuing doctoral study in sociology at the University of Texas at Austin, where she is affiliated with the Population Research Center. Her research focus is in demography, specializing in Mexico–United States-US migration and immigrant health in the United States.

HARRIET L. COHEN, PHD, LMSW-ACP, is an assistant professor and director of the social work program in the Department of Rehabilitation, Social Work, and Addictions at the University of North Texas in Denton. She received a doctorate in adult education and a master's in social work from the University of Georgia. In addition, she holds a certificate in women's studies and qualitative research from the University of Georgia and in Jewish communal studies from the Hebrew Union College–Jewish Institute of Religion, Los Angeles. Dr. Cohen teaches in the areas of macro practice, human behavior in the social environment, and aging. Her research/training interests include spirituality, midlife and older women, lesbian and gay issues, reflective practice, and intergenerational service learning. Dr. Cohen is a trainer with the National Coalition Building Institute and the Ally training program on campus. She is a member of the steering committee of the National Association of Social Workers, North Texas Chapter, and a member of the Texas Department on Aging Policy Resource Group. She is a member of the Council on Social Work Education, AGE-SW, and the Social Work Baccalaureate Program Directors (BPD) Association, where she serves on the Educators and Friends of Lesbian and Gays (EFLAG) Committee and the Gerontology Committee. Dr. Cohen is a licensed master social worker–advanced clinical practitioner and a registered massage therapist and certified neuromuscular therapist in the state of Texas.

MASEN S. DAVIS, MSW, is the president and founder of FTM Alliance of Los Angeles, a community-based nonprofit agency dedicated to empowering the female-to-male transgender community. His current research explores bicultural socialization among transsexual adults. He also works as a macro practitioner in the area of child welfare in Los Angeles, California.

DIANE E. ELZE, PHD, is an assistant professor in the George Warren Brown School of Social Work at Washington University in St. Louis, Missouri. She received her doctorate in social work from Washington University in St. Louis and earned a master of science in social administration degree from the Mandel School of Applied Social Sciences at Case Western Reserve University in Cleveland, Ohio. Dr. Elze teaches foundation courses in human behavior and human diversity, as well as clinical practice with adolescents and with GLBT populations. Her research focuses on the well-being of gay, lesbian, bisexual, and transgender youths, and HIV prevention interventions. Her practice background is in adolescent services; HIV prevention, case management, and community education; and services specifically for GLBT youth. Dr. Elze is cochair of the Council on Social Work Education's Council on Sexual Orientation and Gender Expression, and she also holds memberships in the National Association of Social Workers, the Society for Social Work and Research, the American Public Health Association, the Society for Research on Adolescence, and the Missouri Association for Social Welfare.

ELISE M. FULLMER, PHD, is professor and chair of the School of Social Work at Spaulding University, Louisville, Kentucky. She received her doctorate in social work with an emphasis in gerontology from the State University of New York at Albany and the master of social work degree from the University of Utah. Dr. Fullmer has published several articles on aging and mental retardation and on the aging of lesbians and gay men, and she is presently developing a book on death and dying. She has also taught a variety of human behavior and practice courses at both the graduate and the undergraduate levels. Her practice background is in state social services, aging, and health care. Her research focus is principally centered in gerontology and disenfranchised populations. She is also a certified site visitor for the reaccreditation of social work education programs through the Council on Social Work Education.

PATRICIA L. GREER, MSW, completed the master of social work degree at the University of North Carolina at Charlotte. She earned her bachelor of social work degree magna cum laude at UNC Charlotte, with minors in religious studies and sociology. As a student, she was president of the Social Work Club and received the Outstanding BSW Senior award. She is a member of Phi Kappa Phi National Honor Society, Alpha Delta Mu (a national social work honor society), Key International Honor Society, and Alpha Sigma Lambda National Honor Society. For her work with inner-city at-risk boys, Ms. Greer was honored with the national Whitney Young Award from the Boy Scouts of America and the Paul Harris Award from Rotary International. Ms. Greer is presently pursuing licensure as a clinical social worker (LCSW). Her clinical practice interests center on women with anxiety, depression, abuse issues, and post-traumatic stress disorder.

ELISABETH GRUSKIN, DRPH, is a public health research scientist in the Division of Research at Kaiser Permanente in Oakland, California. She conducts qualitative and epidemiological research on the alcohol, tobacco, and illicit-drug use of lesbians, gay men, and bisexual people.

KRISTINA M. HASH, MSW, PHD, is an assistant professor in the Division of Social Work at West Virginia University in Morganton, where she received her MSW and graduate certificate in gerontology. Dr. Hash received a doctorate in social work from Virginia Commonwealth University. Her research interests include caregiving, gay and lesbian issues in aging, and geriatric education. She teaches human diversity, social work practice, research methods, and human behavior in the social environment. Her practice background includes positions in home health care, social work continuing education, and research and program evaluation. Additionally, she has been involved in several volunteer activities with community-based agencies serving older adults. She holds memberships in the National Association of Social Workers, the Association for Gerontology Education in Social Work, the Lesbian and Gay Aging Issues Network of the American Society on Aging, the Rural Social Work Caucus, and the Council on Social Work Education Caucus on Sexual Orientation and Gender Expression. Her own experience as a caregiver for her grandmother was the driving force behind her interest in social work and aging.

NANCY A. HUMPHREYS, DSW, is professor of policy practice and director of the Institute for the Advancement of Political Social Work Practice at the University of Connecticut School of Social Work. She is the school's former dean and served as director of the Michigan State University School of Social Work in the mid-1980s. She is a former president of the National Association of Social Workers and a former vice president of the Council on Social Work Education. In 2002 Dr. Humphreys was awarded an honorary doctorate from Yerevan State University in the Republic of Armenia in recognition of her work in assisting the development of the social work profession and social work education in the newly independent country. In 2003 she was honored with a lifetime achievement award from the National Association of Social Workers.

ARLENE ISTAR LEV, CSW-R, CASAC, is a social worker, family therapist, and educator addressing the unique therapeutic needs of lesbian, gay, bisexual, and transgender people. She is the founder of Choices Counseling and Consulting (info@choicesconsulting.com and www.choicesconsulting.com) in Albany, New York, providing family therapy for LGBT people. She is also on the adjunct faculties of the State University of New York, Albany, School of Social Welfare, and Vermont College of the Union Institute and University. Ms. Lev's expertise is in issues related to sexual and gender identity issues, as well as trauma recovery, addictions, adoption, and parenting in alternative families. She is the founder and project manager for Rainbow Access Initiative, a training program on LGBT issues for therapists. Lev is the author of *Transgender Emergence: Therapeutic Guidelines for Working with Gender-Variant People and Their Families* (Haworth Press, 2004) and *How Queer: Lesbian, Gay, Bisexual, and Transgender Parenting* (Penguin). She writes a "Dear Ari" column on parenting in alternative families. Lev is a member of the National Association of Social Workers, the Harry Benjamin International Gender Dysphoria Association, the American Psychological Association, and she is a board member of the Family Pride Coalition.

EMILIA LOMBARDI, PHD, is an assistant professor in the Graduate School of Public Health, Department of Infectious Diseases and Microbiology, University of Pittsburgh, Pittsburgh, Pennsylvania. She received her doctorate in sociology from the University of Akron in Ohio. She served as the principal investigator in a National Institute of Drug Abuse study titled "Substance Use and Treatment Experiences of Transgender/Transsexual Men and Women," and she served as a collaborator on a UCLA School of Nursing project on Latino HIV medication adherence. Dr. Lombardi also served as the principal investigator of a CDC National Network for Tobacco Prevention and Control contract, for which she developed materials and planned, supervised, and analyzed focus group data. In addition, Dr. Lombardi supervises needs assessments and program evaluations for a CDC and state department of health project studying HIV-prevention knowledge, attitudes, and access to service of people at risk for HIV infection. Dr. Lombardi is also a member of the University of Pittsburgh's Center for Research on Health and Sexual Orientation.

JAMES I. MARTIN, PHD, CSW, ACSW, is an associate professor at the New York University School of Social Work. He received a doctoral degree in social work from the University of Illinois at Chicago and a master of social work degree from the University of Michigan. Dr. Martin teaches graduate courses in clinical practice, research methods, and GLBT issues, and doctoral courses in dissertation research and statistical analysis. His scholarship focuses on HIV prevention, the relationship between sexuality and spirituality, research methods with GLBT populations, and GLBT identities. He is the coauthor of *Research Methods with Gay, Lesbian, Bisexual, and Transgender Populations* (Harrington Park, 2003) and *Lesbian, Gay, and Bisexual Youths and Adults: Knowledge for Human Services Practice* (Sage, 1998), and the coeditor of *Lesbian, Gay, Bisexual, and Transgender Issues in Social Work: A Com-*

prehensive Bibliography with Annotations (CSWE, 2001). Dr. Martin is chair of the Caucus of LGBT Faculty and Students in Social Work and a member and former cochair of the CSWE Council on Sexual Orientation and Gender Expression, and he serves on the editorial advisory board of the *Journal of Gay and Lesbian Social Services*.

DAPHNE L. MCCLELLAN, PHD, MSW, LSW, ACSW, is an assistant professor in the Department of Social Work at the University of Maryland, Baltimore County. She received her doctorate in social policy from the Florence Heller School of Social Welfare at Brandeis University and the master of social work degree from the University of Oklahoma. Dr. McClellan has taught social policy courses at both the graduate and the undergraduate levels. Her practice background is in the fields of domestic violence, sexual assault, and aging, and her research focus has centered primarily on gay and lesbian family issues. Dr. McClellan has worked as an activist and organizer in the GLBT community for many years. She cofounded the Dignity/Integrity organization in Tulsa, Oklahoma, in the early 1980s and serves today on the national board of directors of the Family Pride Coalition, an organization serving GLBT-headed families. She holds memberships in the Council on Social Work Education, the Social Work Baccalaureate Program Directors Association, and the National Association of Social Workers, where she has served as the vice president of the Maryland chapter.

ROBIN E. MCKINNEY, PHD, LPC, ACSW, is an assistant professor and coordinator of the BSW program at Western Michigan University. He completed his doctoral degree at Michigan State University. His research and practice interests include sexual orientation and race/ethnicity, parenting and family issues and sexual orientation, and race/ethnicity and special-needs children.

YOLANDA C. PADILLA, PHD, LMSW-AP, is an associate professor in the School of Social Work at the University of Texas at Austin. She received a joint doctoral degree in social work and sociology from the University of Michigan and a master of science in social work degree from the University of Texas at Austin. Dr. Padilla teaches courses in policy, community, and organizational practice as well as a specialized course on policy and clinical practice with gay, lesbian, bisexual, and transgender populations. Dr. Padilla is the editor of *Gay and Lesbian Rights Organizing: Community-Based Strategies*. Her course syllabus "Gays and Lesbians in American Society: Policy and Practice Issues" was selected for inclusion in *Teaching Social Policy: Model Course Outlines and Modules* (Council on Social Work Education, 2003). Her research interests focus on gay rights and policy development and GLBT youth in family, organization, and community contexts. She serves on the Council on Sexual Orientation and Gender Expression of the Council on Social Work Education and the Committee on Gay/Lesbian/Bisexual Issues of the National Association of Social Workers/Texas. Dr. Padilla is a licensed master social worker–advanced practitioner in the state of Texas. She specializes in gay and lesbian studies, Latino studies, poverty, and social welfare policy.

CHERYL A. PARKS, PHD, ACSW, is an associate professor at the University of Connecticut School of Social Work. She completed her doctorate in social work at Bryn Mawr College in 1997 and the master of social work degree at the University of Washington in 1978. Dr. Parks teaches in both the MSW and the PhD programs, primarily courses in research design, substance abuse, data analysis, and foundation practice. Her direct practice experience spans eighteen years, including eight years as a private practitioner working in agency-based practice settings as a social work clinician and an administrator in mental health, substance abuse, and child welfare. Dr. Parks's primary research focus is on issues related to lesbian identity and alcohol use, lesbian parenting, and gender differences in alcohol use patterns and problems across diverse populations. In 2003 she received a four-year National Institute on Alcohol Abuse and Alcoholism (NIAAA) grant to examine cohort differences in identity development and drinking among lesbians. She is a member of the National Association of Social Workers, the Academy of Certified Social Workers, the Society for Social Work and Research, and the Research Society on Alcoholism. She is also a member of the Council on Social Work Education, where she holds an appointment to the Council on Sexual Orientation and Gender Expression.

CAITLIN RYAN, MSW, ACSW, a clinical social worker and an organizer, helped develop community-based services at the beginning of the AIDS epidemic. A graduate of Hunter College and Smith College School for Social Work, Ryan is a founder and past president of the National Lesbian and Gay Health Foundation and a founder of the National Association of People with AIDS. In 1981 she initiated and was co-investigator of the National Lesbian Health Care Survey, the first major study to identify lesbian health and mental health needs and concerns. She coauthored the first book on AIDS policy, *AIDS: A Public Health Challenge*, which was distributed to all members of Congress, governors, and state health officials and served as the basis for many of the recommendations of the first Presidential Commission on AIDS. Her more recent research has focused on health concerns of LGBT youth in family, community, and institutional settings. Ryan's work has been acknowledged by many groups, including the American Association of Physicians for Human Rights and the National Association of Social Workers, which named her Social Worker of the Year in 1998. She is presently the director of adolescent health initiatives at the César Chávez Institute at San Francisco State University.

MARY E. SWIGONSKI, PHD, LCSW, ACSW, is an associate professor in the Department of Social Work at Monmouth University in West Long Branch, New Jersey. She received her doctorate in social work from Rutgers University, New Brunswick, New Jersey. She also holds a master of social work degree and a bachelor's degree in politics. Dr. Swigonski teaches courses in human behavior and the social environment, diversity, and research at both the graduate and the undergraduate levels. Her areas of interest include the intersection of social justice and care, human rights, and cultural diversity, especially as these inform hate crime prevention and lesbian issues; she also publishes in the areas of empowerment, cultural diversity, feminist theory, and lesbian and gay issues. She holds memberships in the National Association of Social Workers; the Association of Social Work Baccalaureate Program Directors, where she is a member of Educators and Friends of Lesbians and Gays; and the Council on Social Work Education, where she holds an appointment to the Council on Sexual Orientation and Gender Expression.

BOO TYSON, MDIV, BSW, serves as the Assistant Director of the MAINstream Coalition, a nonprofit organization in Kansas that promotes the principles and practices of the separation of religion and state. In that role, Ms. Tyson has worked to organize a clergy-led effort called Mainstream Voices of Faith that seeks to be an alternative faithful voice to religious extremists. She received a Master of Divinity degree from Wake Forest University, a Certificate in Nonprofit Management from Duke University, and a Bachelor of Social Work degree from North Carolina State University. Her work experience also includes organizing people of faith around issues of full inclusion for LGBT persons and working directly with persons who are homeless.

D. R. YONKIN, MSW, CSW, is a psychotherapist at Harris Rothenberg International, an employee assistance program in New York City. He received a master of clinical social work degree from the Shirley M. Ehrenkranz School of Social Work at New York University. His private practice and research focus on gender identity and sexual orientation in LGBTQ communities, with a specialization in mental health care, relationships, spirituality, and substance abuse among gay and transgender individuals. He is a licensed social worker in New York State and holds memberships in the National Association of Social Workers, the American Psychological Association Division 44, the International Foundation for Gender Education, and the Intersex Society of North America.

PART ONE

A CONTEXT FOR SOCIAL WORK PRACTICE

1

SEXUAL ORIENTATION AND GENDER IDENTITY EXPRESSION

Deana F. Morrow

NASW encourages adoption of laws that recognize inheritance, insurance, same-sex marriage, child custody, property, and other rights in lesbian, gay, and bisexual relationships.... NASW encourages the adoption of laws that will facilitate individuals in identifying with and expressing their gender choice without discrimination against them and their civil rights in education, housing, inheritance, health and other types of insurance, child custody, property, and other areas.

—NATIONAL ASSOCIATION OF SOCIAL WORKERS, 2003

MANY SOCIAL workers and related human services professionals have had minimal preparation for serving gay, lesbian, bisexual, and transgender (GLBT) clients. Most social work professionals trained before the mid-1990s had no academic preparation for working with sexual minority populations, and many social workers trained since then have had minimal, if any, academic exposure to these populations. Thus, it is not uncommon to encounter even seasoned practitioners who perpetuate misinformation and negative bias in their services to GLBT clients. The purpose of this book is to help social work and human services students and practitioners to develop a theoretical and methodological knowledge base for understanding and working with sexual minority people. This first chapter serves as a basic introduction to the remainder of the book, providing a general foundation. The rest of the chapters will, in turn, examine particular topics in greater depth. This chapter will address some of the negative myths commonly associated with GLBT people. In addition, it examines the question of whether GLBT people constitute their own culture. The chapter establishes a foundation for social work values and ethics-based service to GLBT clients and presents a context for social work practice with GLBT people. Finally, it gives an overview of topics that are addressed in the book and ends with practice suggestions to help workers better serve GLBT clients.

COMMON MYTHS

Numerous myths and stereotypes about GLBT people operate to perpetuate mis-information and negative social attitudes about them. Consider, for example, the following:

1. *Homosexuality is a lifestyle choice rather than an innate orientation.* Many people perceive gay, lesbian, and bisexual (GLB) people as having made a choice to go "against the grain" of society. They view GLB people as deliberately undermining society by selecting a renegade "lifestyle" that runs counter to moral tradition and the general well-being of society. In reality, research strongly suggests that biological genetic influences contribute significantly to a person's sexual orientation—whether gay, lesbian, bisexual, or heterosexual (Bailey & Benishay, 1993; Bailey & Pillard, 1991; Bailey, Pillard, Neale, & Agyei, 1993; Hamer, Hu, Magnuson, Hu, & Pattatuci, 1993; LeVay, 1991). Thus, the term *sexual orientation* is more appropriate than the term *sexual preference*. *Preference* implies ease and simplicity of choice or selection, while *orientation* more accurately connotes the innate essence of a person's intimate and affectional nature. Perhaps the best way to understand the role of choice in relation to sexual orientation is that people must choose whether to embrace or reject whatever is their essential orientation.

2. *Homosexuality is not a normal aspect of human diversity.* Human diversity is encompassing and can be represented by differences among people in areas such as race, ethnicity, sex, gender expression, culture, age, sex, and *sexual orientation*. Homosexuality is a naturally occurring phenomenon that has existed throughout history (Boswell, 1980). It is more socially accepted—and not nearly so controversial—in many countries (e.g., Canada, Denmark, Sweden, The Netherlands) other than the United States. Additionally, research has established that gay and lesbian people are physically, mentally, and emotionally as normal as heterosexual people (Friedman & Downey, 1994; Gonsiorek, 1991; Hooker, 1957). In recognizing that homosexuality in itself is not pathological, the American Psychiatric Association declared in 1973 that homosexuality would no longer be included as a psychiatric disorder in the *Diagnostic and Statistical Manual of Mental Disorders*.

3. *GLBT people are immoral.* A person's sexual orientation and gender expression are, in themselves, morally neutral. It is by individuals' actions toward others—not by virtue of their sexual orientation—that judgments are to be made about their moral character. There are those who claim the Bible as their basis for judging GLBT people as immoral. Yet the Bible was written by humans in a cultural, social, and historical period when scientific knowledge of sexual orientation and gender expression was nonexistent:

The Gospel writers and the missionary Paul did not possess the psychological, socio-logical, and sexological knowledge which now inform[s] our theological reflections about human sexuality. They knew nothing of sexual orientation or of the natural heterosexual-bisexual-homosexual continuum that exists in human life. They did not postulate that people engaging in same-sex sex acts could have been expressing their natural sexuality.

(JOHNSON, 1992, PP. 145–146)

The biblical writers never addressed the concept of committed, loving, same-sex relationships. The biblical passages often cited as condemning same-sex relationships addressed, instead, exploitative behaviors that did not involve loving relationships (Gomes, 1996; McNeill, 1993; Spong, 1988, 1991, 1998). Furthermore, nowhere in the Bible did Jesus address homosexuality or gender expression variances as inappropriate or immoral.

4. *Gay and lesbian people are more likely to abuse children and/or convert them from heterosexuality to homosexuality.* Gay and lesbian people are no more likely to abuse children than are heterosexual people (Berger & Kelly, 1995; McCammon, Knox, & Schact, 1998). In fact, the vast majority of child sex abuse cases involve men molesting female children (Berger & Kelly, 1995). There is no evidence that exposure of heterosexual children to gay and lesbian people changes their orientation to gay or lesbian any more than exposure of gay and lesbian children to heterosexual people changes their orientation to heterosex-ual (Patterson, 1994). Indeed, most people who are gay or lesbian were them-selves reared by heterosexual parents. Research indicates that children growing up in gay and lesbian parent households are as well adjusted and as psycho-logically healthy as children who are reared in heterosexual parent households (Patterson, 1995; Strickland, 1995; Tasker & Golombok, 1997). The quality of parenting—rather than the sexual orientation of the parents—is what most sig-nificantly influences the well-being of children.

5. *Two people of the same sex in a relationship play out masculine and femi-nine roles.* This myth is based on the stereotype that one person has to adopt "the male role" and the other "the female role" whenever two people are in a relationship together and on the heterosexist assumption that only a man and a woman can form an intimate relationship. Same-sex couples tend to be far less likely than heterosexual couples to adopt specialized gender-defined roles within their relationships (Hyde, 1994; McCammon, Knox, & Schact, 1998). They tend to place high value on equality and the sharing of power in their relationships.

6. *Transgender people are gay or lesbian in sexual orientation.* It is an error to assume that all transgender people are gay or lesbian in sexual orientation. The sexual identity of a transgender person could be gay, lesbian, bisexual, or hetero-sexual. *Gender identity does not dictate sexual orientation.* Transgender people

are often included with GLB people in the literature because, like GLB people, they constitute a sexual minority group and encounter discrimination because of their sexual minority status.

7. *Same-sex couples do not develop long-term, committed relationships*. There are those who maintain long-term committed relationships and those who have a series of relationships without significant long-term commitments among heterosexual as well as among GLBT people. Same-sex relationships in the United States are not afforded the same legal and social supports offered to other-sex relationships. The lack of legal recognition of same-sex relationships is an example of unequal rights under the law. There are more than one thousand legal rights and benefits accorded to legally married people that are unavailable to same-sex couples—no matter how many years they have been a committed couple (Human Rights Campaign, 2003).

8. *The "gay agenda" is a plan for undermining family values and for affording "special rights" to GLBT people*. In response to the movement toward equality for GLBT citizens, conservative political pundits coined the term *gay agenda*, which became a code phrase for stereotyping GLBT people as seeking to dismantle the structure of American values and seeking to garner special privileges not afforded to other groups in society. This so-called agenda is, to the contrary, an effort by GLBT people and their allies to secure the same civil rights and responsibilities (for example, legal sanction of their relationships, legal sanction of their parenthood, freedom from job discrimination on the basis of sexual orientation and gender expression, spousal inheritance rights) already afforded to all non-GLBT Americans. Thus, there is no "special rights" agenda for GLBT people; rather, there is a strong political movement on behalf of equal rights for them.

GLBT CULTURE

Is there a GLBT culture? What is culture and how might it be related to GLBT people? Healey (1997) describes culture as consisting of "all aspects of the way of life associated with a group of people. It includes language, religious beliefs, customs and rules of etiquette, the values and ideas people use to organize their lives and interpret their existence" (18).

Sheafor and Horejsi (2003) describe culture as patterns of thought and behavior in families and communities that are passed from generation to generation. They further describe it as "a set of interrelated beliefs, values, patterns of behavior, and practices that strongly influence how a group of people meet their basic needs, cope with the ordinary problems of life, make sense out of their experiences, and negotiate power relationships, both within and outside their own group" (174). Similarly, Lum (1999) suggests that culture includes institutions, language, artistic expressions, and patterns of social and interpersonal relationships that are passed on from generation to generation within a group of people.

Given these descriptions of culture, the claim can be made that there is such a thing as GLBT culture. Members of the respective groups (gay, lesbian, bisexual, and transgender) that constitute the GLBT community have commonalities indicative of the development of culture. They are bounded by the challenges of coping with social oppression in the forms of heterosexism, homophobia, and rigid interpretations of gender expression. There are GLBT-focused social institutions such as churches, civil rights groups, social groups, and community centers. There are literature forms, music forms (e.g., women's music), and artistic expressions that uniquely represent GLBT people. Patterns of social expression (e.g., coming out, dating, forming relationships and families, coping with GLBT-based discrimination) are passed from generation to generation among those who are GLBT.

While these commonalities bind GLBT people as a cultural group, it is important as well to honor the characteristics that make each group distinct. As the reader will see throughout this book, certain characteristics and experiences are unique to gay male culture, lesbian culture, bisexual culture, and transgender culture. Thus, while the argument is made here that these sexual minority groups, collectively, constitute culture based on their common experiences, the reader is reminded as well that each of the groups also constitutes its own unique subculture within the overall GLBT culture.

PRINCIPAL TERMS

This section identifies and defines the principal terms used throughout the book. For a more complete listing, as well as GLBT-related symbols and resources, see appendix A and appendix B.

▪ *Gay, lesbian, bisexual, transgender (GLBT)*. *Gay* refers to people (male or female) whose principal intimate attractions and romantic relationships are toward other people of the same sex. *Lesbian* refers specifically to women whose principal intimate attractions and romantic relationships are toward other women. Some women prefer to describe themselves as gay, while others prefer to describe themselves as lesbian. *Bisexual* refers to men or women whose principal intimate attractions and romantic relationships are toward other women or men. *Transgender* refers to people whose gender identity is different from the gender commonly socially assigned to them on the basis of their biological sex (e.g., a biological male with a feminine gender identity). The acronym *GLBT* is used in this book when referring to all of these groups, which, collectively, are also referred to as *sexual minority populations*.

▪ *Gender, gender identity, and gender expression. Gender* refers to the behavioral, cultural, and psychological characteristics that are socially constructed to express femininity (associated with females) and masculinity (associated with males). *Gender identity* refers to an individual's personal sense of identity as masculine or feminine, or some combination thereof. *Gender expression* relates to how a person outwardly manifests, or expresses, gender.

▪ *Homophobia* is the fear and hatred of GLBT people or those presumed to be GLBT. Homophobia can be *external*, imposed on GLBT people by others, or *internal*, which relates to the internalization of GLBT-negative biases and prejudices by GLBT people.

▪ *Heterosexism* is the belief in the superiority of heterosexuality over other forms of sexual orientation. Like racism and sexism, heterosexism is ingrained in American society and serves to systematically privilege heterosexual people and oppress GLBT people.

▪ *Ally.* An ally is a person who is not GLBT but is an advocate for GLBT equal rights. Heterosexual allies are some of the most effective and powerful advocates for GLBT civil rights (Human Rights Campaign, 2003).

SOCIAL WORK VALUES AND ETHICS

The material presented in this textbook will help the reader address two central questions with regard to services to sexual minority people: (1) "As a practicing social worker, what is my professional ethical obligation in serving GLBT clients?" and (2) "What is the social work profession's ethical obligation in responding to issues of sexual orientation and gender expression?" Both the National Association of Social Workers (NASW), which is the national association for professional social workers, and the Council on Social Work Education (CSWE), which is the national accrediting body for social work education programs in colleges and universities, have taken affirmative and inclusive positions with regard to sexual minority populations.

The NASW *Code of Ethics* (National Association of Social Workers, 1996) prohibits social workers from discriminating against clients on the basis of "race, ethnicity, national origin, color, sex, sexual orientation, age, marital status, political belief, religion, or mental or physical disability" (Standard 4.02). The code also challenges social workers to "promote policies and practices that demonstrate respect for difference" (Standard 6.04) and to take social and political action to "prevent and eliminate ... discrimination against any person, or group, or class on the basis of race, ethnicity, national origin, color, sex, sexual orientation, age, marital status, political belief, religion, or mental or physical disability" (Standard 6.04). The code espouses the professional social work values of honoring the dignity and worth of all people and seeking social justice on behalf of vulnerable and oppressed people. Because of the impact of heterosexism and homophobia,

JANE ADDAMS (1860–1935)

Jane Addams, the principal founder of the social work profession, was a lesbian. Addams was born in Cedarville, Illinois, and graduated from Rockford College (Illinois) in 1881. She then entered medical school, but had to withdraw because of failing health. Thereafter, she traveled Europe extensively with her female partner, Ellen Gates Starr, whom she had met while they were in college together. Addams and Starr visited Toynbee Hall, a settlement house in London where socially conscientious upper-class young women lived among the poor, studied social conditions, and worked for reform. Addams and Starr were so impressed with the settlement house concept that they returned to the United States to establish a settlement house themselves. They found a location in an impoverished area of Chicago and in 1889 christened it Hull House in honor of its original builder. The mission of Hull House was to provide cultural and service opportunities for neighborhood working-class people. Another part of its mission was to train young women workers who would become the early pioneers of the social work profession. Services offered at Hull House included a playground and gymnasium, a day nursery, a community kitchen, college courses, training in music and the arts, and a boarding place for young women workers. Hull House expanded over time to include thirteen buildings and a camp near Lake Geneva, Wisconsin. Even though Ellen Starr continued to work at Hull House, she and Addams eventually broke off their intimate relationship. In 1890 Mary Rozet Smith joined Hull House, and she and Addams became life partners for the next forty years. They shared a bed, and they bought a house together in Maine in 1904. Addams was bold for the time period in always requesting a double bed whenever she and Smith traveled together.

A pacifist, Jane Addams was bold on many fronts. She campaigned for the first juvenile court law in the United States, the eight-hour workday, improved working conditions in factories, workers' compensation laws, and voting rights for women. In 1910 Addams became the first woman president of the National Conference of Social Workers. In 1915 she chaired the International Congress of Women at The Hague, Netherlands. This event led to the formation of the Women's International League for Peace and Freedom in 1919. Addams helped found the American Civil Liberties Union in 1920; and, in 1931 she became the first American woman to win the Nobel Peace Prize. Addams also authored a number of books, including Democracy and Social Ethics (1902), Newer Ideals of Peace (1907), The Spirit of Youth and the City Streets (1909), Twenty Years at Hull House (1910), and The Second Twenty Years at Hull House (1930).

Jane Addams is frequently mentioned in social work textbooks as the "founding mother" of social work. Yet seldom is she also noted to be a lesbian. It is time to recognize Addams for the whole person she was—activist, pacifist, feminist, author, and lesbian in a long-term committed relationship.

SOURCE: ADAPTED FROM RUSSELL (1994).

including social, political, and legal marginalization, GLBT people constitute a vulnerable and oppressed group.

NASW has also issued policy statements in support of domestic partnership and marriage legislation for GLBT people, and for their full civil rights with regard to nondiscrimination in employment, parental rights, inheritance rights, and insurance benefits. Furthermore, NASW has issued policy statements in opposition to reparative/conversion therapy with GLBT people, in support of the adoption of laws that support people in identifying with and expressing their gender of choice, and in favor of nondiscrimination against transgender people with respect to full civil rights, including employment, housing, health care, and child custody (National Association of Social Workers, 2003).

The CSWE Educational Policy and Accreditation Standards (Council on Social Work Education Commission on Accreditation, 2003), the educational standards to which all accredited social work education programs must adhere, require that programs "provide a learning context in which respect for all persons and understanding of diversity (including age, class, color, disability, ethnicity, family structure, gender, marital status, national origin, race, religion, sex, and sexual orientation) are practiced" (Standard 6.0). Social work education programs are required to integrate content on diversity (Educational Policy 4.1) and populations at risk (Educational Policy 4.2) into their social work educational curricula. Knowledge and understanding of GLBT people and the issues that affect them is a component of diversity and populations-at-risk content.

Thus the national professional organizations for both social work practice and social work education honor the value of affirmative service to and knowledge building about GLBT people. From these perspectives, it is clear that practicing social workers have an ethical obligation to affirmatively serve sexual minority clients and their families and to be a voice for social justice on their behalf, and it is also clear that social work educators have an obligation to include GLBT content in educational curricula.

A CONTEXT FOR SOCIAL WORK PRACTICE

A feature of effective social work practice is that it can be applied across a variety of client populations, system sizes, and practice settings. This section presents a context for social work practice that is applicable for working with GLBT clients. Six principles of effective social work practice will be discussed in relation to their applicability for serving GLBT people.

1, *Values-based and ethics-based practice*. Social work values and ethics (National Association of Social Workers, 1996) establish that workers should treat GLBT people with respect, honor their worth and dignity as individuals, and work affirmatively on their behalf.

2. *The ecological systems perspective*. The ecological systems perspective in social work recognizes that a person's social environment, including the legal, political, social, familial, religious, and school or work systems contained in that environment, has a significant impact on personal well-being. Given the pervasiveness of anti-GLBT religious, political, and social attitudes, the social environment for many sexual minority people can frequently be a source of strain and thus is often a point of intervention.

3. *Diversity*. While GLBT people are sometimes described as a collective group because of the sexual minority status and social oppression that they hold in common, it is important to understand that each of the subgroups within the overall GLBT community possesses its own distinctive characteristics, concerns, and needs. In addition, there is tremendous diversity among the individuals within these subgroups (e.g., diversity related to race, ethnicity, sex, sexual orientation, gender expression, personal politics, socioeconomic status, age, regional location, and ability level). In providing services, it is important to acknowledge the individuality and uniqueness of each client.

4. *Empowerment*. GLBT people can be considered a population at risk in that they have a greater probability of encountering discrimination and social oppression because of their sexual minority status. Populations at risk tend to be socially and politically marginalized. It is important to work toward empowering clients—particularly those who are disempowered. One way to work from an empowerment perspective with GLBT people is to identify and honor their strengths and to build on those strengths in planning intervention strategies.

5. *Research-based knowledge*. Effective social work practice is based on sound research evidence with respect to building a knowledge base of one's practice population and knowing which interventions are most applicable, given the client and his or her situation. Many social workers have minimal knowledge of issues pertaining to GLBT people, and therefore they operate from older paradigms that do not reflect the current scientific understanding of sexual orientation and gender expression. This book will help the reader develop a knowledge base about GLBT people and the necessary practice considerations for structuring affirmative intervention with them.

6. *Social justice*. Social justice relates to the value of all citizens having the same basic rights, protections, and obligations under the law (Kirst-Ashman & Hull, 2002). According to the NASW *Code of Ethics*, social workers should "pursue social change, particularly with and on behalf of vulnerable and oppressed individuals and groups of people" (National Association of Social Workers, 1996, p. 5). A number of social injustices affect GLBT people and their families, including the following: the lack of legal recognition of their relationships and families; religious persecution; denial of survivorship benefits in government programs such as Social Security; and denial of inheritance rights to spousal survivors of deceased partners.

OVERVIEW OF TEXT

The chapters of this textbook are ordered into four broad sections. Part 1, "A Context for Social Work Practice," focuses on establishing a sociohistorical context for understanding social work practice with GLBT people. Chapter 1, "Sexual

Orientation and Gender Identity Expression," describes an essential context for social work practice with GLBT people. Chapter 2, "A Historical Perspective," provides a history of GLBT people and the GLBT civil rights movement in the United States. As the final chapter in this section, chapter 3, "Oppression, Prejudice, and Discrimination," provides an in-depth examination of heterosexism and the social oppression of GLBT people.

Part 2, "Identity Development and Coming Out," focuses on issues of identity and disclosure for GLBT people. Chapter 4, "Gay, Lesbian, and Bisexual Identity Development," discusses an array of models that have been proposed to describe the process of gay, lesbian, and bisexual (GLB) identity development. Chapter 5, "Transgender Identity Development," focuses specifically on identity development among transgender people. Chapter 6, "Coming Out as Gay, Lesbian, Bisexual, and Transgender," discusses disclosure, or coming out, and its personal and social impact.

In Part 3, "Relationships and Families," chapter 7, "Psychosocial Support for Families of Gay, Lesbian, Bisexual, and Transgender People," explores the family perspective of having a loved one who is GLBT. Chapter 8, "Gay, Lesbian, Bisexual, and Transgender Youth," provides insight into the experiences of sexual minority young people, including the risks associated with being a GLBT teen. Chapter 9, "Gay Male Relationships and Families," offers an examination of gay male couples and families. In like fashion, chapter 10, "Lesbian Relationships and Families," chapter 11, "Bisexual Relationships and Families," and chapter 12, "Transgender Emergence Within Families," deal with relationships and families in relation to each of the identified populations. Chapter 13, "Gay, Lesbian, Bisexual, and Transgender Older People," addresses the importance of understanding older GLBT people within an appropriate generational context.

Part 4, "Society and Culture," focuses on macro issues that affect the well-being of GLBT people. Chapter 14, "Gay, Lesbian, and Bisexual Health Issues," focuses on health care concerns pertinent to GLB people, ranging from HIV disease and other sexually transmitted diseases to mental health and access to affirmative health care. Chapter 15, "Transgender Health Issues," discusses an array of health concerns specific to transgender people, including the issues of hormone therapy and sex reassignment. Chapter 16, "Hate Language and Violence," examines the research on the incidence of hate and violence against GLBT people. Chapter 17, "Religion and Spirituality," addresses religion as both a tool of oppression and a tool of liberation for GLBT people. It also discusses the value that religious and spiritual expression holds for many GLBT people. Chapter 18, "Workplace Issues," examines the impact of heterosexism and homophobia in work settings (including domestic partner benefits) and the importance of establishing safe, nondiscriminatory, and inclusive work environments. Chapter 19, "Social Policy and Advocacy," addresses social and legal policies and legislation that affect the civil rights of GLBT people. Chapter 20, "Toward Affirmative Practice," offers a synthesis of affirmative practice approaches presented in earlier chapters, moving the reader toward an integration of social justice, professional use of self, social work ethics, and knowledge and skills for working with GLBT populations.

This book also has two appendixes. Appendix A sets forth definitions and explanations of words and symbols related to GLBT culture; appendix B provides a list of resources pertinent to working with sexual minority populations.

In addition to offering a review of the research and current issues that affect GLBT people, this book also details specific practice suggestions in each chapter. Thus, practitioners who read this text should be able to develop a theoretical, empirical knowledge base about GLBT people and the issues that affect their psychosocial well-being, as well as practice methodology content on how best to function effectively as a social worker in engaging affirmative practice with GLBT people.

GUIDELINES FOR PRACTICE

Social work practice with GLBT people is not some mysterious, esoteric specialty. In reality, practice with GLBT people is similar to good social work practice with other populations. There are, however, some special issues and concerns of which the practitioner must be mindful in intervening with this population. The following are some general suggestions for social work practice with GLBT people. Subsequent chapters will provide practice suggestions for specific topics.

1. *Develop a GLBT content knowledge base.* To work effectively with GLBT people, social work practitioners must develop a knowledge base about issues pertinent to sexual minority populations. Workers need to understand the psychosocial, political, and legal manifestations of heterosexism and how those factors affect GLBT people. They also need to understand identity development for GLBT people and how it affects coming out (disclosure), self-esteem, and socialization. They need to know the difference between sexual orientation and gender expression and how each is manifested. And they need to have knowledge of particular risk factors for GLBT people, such as depression, substance abuse, suicide, and school performance problems.

2. *Challenge personal biases about sexual minority people and practice in accordance with social work values and ethics.* This book will challenge readers to examine their personal biases and misinformation about GLBT people. In their practice with sexual minority populations, social workers must go beyond developing "tolerance" to embracing affirmative practice in accordance with NASW values and ethics.

3. *Do not presume the sexual orientation or gender identity of clients.* To presume that all clients are heterosexual and that they express traditional gender roles unless they inform the worker otherwise is a manifestation of heterosex-

ism. Openness and inclusivity with regard to the development of intake forms, as well as worker statements during interviews, are typically well received by clients. Such actions communicate a climate of respect, safety, and acceptance.

4. *Use accurate and respectful language in all communications to and about clients.* The term *sexual orientation* is more appropriate than the term *sexual preference*. *Preference* implies choice, while *orientation* recognizes the innate aspect of sexual identity and expression. The phrase *gay and lesbian* is preferred to the term *homosexuals* in describing people whose sexual orientation is to same-sex people. Describing people as homosexuals has come to be perceived by some as having negative connotations. Some clients may describe themselves using other terms, such as *queer, queen, fag,* or *dyke.* Workers are encouraged to exercise caution in their use of such terms with clients in order to assure that they are not perceived as being disrespectful or derogatory in addressing or describing clients.

5. *Avoid assuming that the characteristics and needs of all sexual minority groups—gay, lesbian, bisexual, transgender—are the same.* While all these groups do have issues in common, such as coping with coming out and combating heterosexism, they all also have needs and issues specific to their unique group experience. In addition, within-group distinctions must be considered, among them race, ethnicity, sex, sexual orientation, gender expression, age, ability, and socioeconomic status.

6. *Approach cases from an ecological systems perspective.* The social environment can be oppressive for GLBT people. Because social systems have such a significant impact on the treatment and civil rights of sexual minority populations, it is critical to consider their influence on clients' lives. It may be necessary to establish social supports to help clients cope with issues such as family rejection, workplace discrimination, and faith community marginalization. A number of GLBT-affirmative social systems exist and may be utilized in developing intervention plans. For more information on affirmative social systems, see the list of resources in appendix B.

7. *Honor diversity among GLBT people.* A richness of diversity exists among GLBT people. In honoring diversity across sexual minority populations, the "rainbow flag" is often used as a symbolic expression to represent sexual minority people and their wide-ranging diversity. Effective practice requires that workers honor that diversity and plan intervention accordingly (i.e., there is no "one size fits all" formula for working with GLBT people). Workers must also recognize the stress of social oppression across many levels. For example, being a person of color, a female, an older person, or a person with a disability means encountering added layers of oppression (e.g., racism, sexism, ageism, ableism) in addition to the oppression encountered by one's status as a sexual minority person. Workers must respond to the added vulnerability that layer upon layer of social oppression can create for clients.

8. *Honor client self-determination regarding disclosure.* Workers should honor "where clients are" with regard to coming out, or disclosure, to others. Workers may seek to empower clients in their choices about coming out, yet the actual decision making regarding disclosure—to whom and under what circumstances— is best left to the clients.

9. *Honor clients' rights to privacy regarding their sexual orientation and gender identity.* Seeking to know a client's sexual orientation and/or gender identity is pertinent only when that information is relevant to the case. Asking about sexual orientation and gender identity simply out of worker curiosity is an inappropriate invasion of client privacy. Also avoid unnecessary "outing" of clients to other workers and staff. It is important to ensure the privacy of client information to the greatest extent allowable. Unfortunately, information about a client's sexual orientation and gender identity may be used by others for harmful means— especially in legal proceedings such as child custody cases.

10. *Advocate for GLBT-affirmative work environments and GLBT-affirmative agency services.* In honoring the social work value of social justice, social work practitioners should be a voice for GLBT-affirmative work environments. Creating an affirmative work environment includes developing agency non-discrimination policies that include sexual orientation and gender expression, advocating for insurance benefits for domestic partners, developing ongoing diversity training for employees, nurturing a GLBT-affirmative work climate, and hiring openly GLBT workers. Establishing GLBT-affirmative agency services for clients can include displaying GLBT-supportive literature (e.g., newsletters and magazines) and symbols (e.g., rainbow flag emblems and pink triangle stickers) in worker offices and client waiting areas. Affirmative agency service also includes the development of programs that specifically address the needs of GLBT clients.

CONCLUSION

The importance of knowledge-based affirmative practice with GLBT people is a theme that is woven throughout this book. Accurate knowledge is a critical tool in the dismantling of social prejudice and oppression that subjugates GLBT people. In its role as a liberating voice for the oppressed, the social work profession must be at the forefront in affirming full civil rights for GLBT people. It is, after all, simply a matter of social justice.

REFERENCES

Bailey, J. M., & Benishay, D. S. (1993). Familial aggregation of female sexual orientation. *American Journal of Psychiatry, 150*(2), 272–277.

Bailey, J. M., & Pillard, R. C. (1991). A genetic study of male sexual orientation. *General Psychiatry, 48,* 1089–1095.

Bailey, J. M., Pillard, R. C., Neale, M. C., & Agyei, Y. (1993). Heritable factors influence sexual orientation in women. *Archives of General Psychiatry, 50*, 217–223.

Berger, R. M., & Kelly, J. J. (1995). Gay men overview. In R. L. Edwards (Ed.), *Encyclopedia of social work* (19th ed., vol. 2) (pp. 1064–1075). Washington, DC: NASW Press.

Boswell, J. (1980). *Christianity, social tolerance, and homosexuality: Gay people in Western Europe from the beginning of the Christian era to the fourteenth century.* Chicago: University of Chicago Press.

Council on Social Work Education Commission on Accreditation (2003). *Handbook of accreditation standards and procedures* (5th ed.). Washington, DC: Council on Social Work Education.

Friedman, R. C., & Downey, J. I. (1994). *Male homosexuality: A contemporary psychoanalytic perspective.* New Haven, CT: Yale University Press.

Gomes, P. J. (1996). *The Good Book: Reading the Bible with heart and mind.* New York: William Morrow.

Gonsiorek, J. C. (1991). The empirical basis for the demise of the illness model of homosexuality. In J. C. Gonsiorek & J. D. Weinrich (Eds.), *Homosexuality: Research implications for public policy* (pp. 115–136). Newbury Park, CA: Sage.

Hamer, D. H., Hu, S., Magnuson, V. L., Hu, N., & Pattatuci, A. M. (1993). A linkage between DNA markers on the X chromosome and male sexual orientation. *Science, 261*, 321–327.

Healey, J. F. (1997). *Race, ethnicity, and gender in the United States: Inequality, group conflict, and power.* Thousand Oaks, CA: Pine Forge Press.

Hooker, E. (1957). The adjustment of the male overt homosexual. *Journal of Projective Techniques, 21*, 18–31.

Human Rights Campaign. (2003). *Rights and protections denied same sex partners.* Available at: http://www.hrc.org/familynet/chapter.asp?article = 675.

Hyde, J. S. (1994). *Understanding human sexuality* (5th ed.). New York: McGraw-Hill.

Johnson, W. R. (1992). Protestantism and gay and lesbian freedom. In B. Berzon (Ed.), *Positively gay: New approaches to gay and lesbian life* (2d ed.) (210–232). Berkeley, CA: Celestial Arts.

Kirst-Ashman, K. K., & Hull, G. H. (2002). *Understanding general practice* (3rd ed.). Pacific Grove, CA: Brooks/Cole.

LeVay, S. (1991). A difference in hypothalamic structure between heterosexual and homosexual men. *Science, 253*, 1034–1037.

Lum, D. (1999). *Culturally competent practice.* Pacific Grove, CA: Brooks/Cole.

McCammon, S., Knox, D., & Schact, C. (1998). *Making choices in sexuality: Research and applications.* Pacific Grove, CA: Brooks/Cole.

McNeill, J. J. (1993). *The church and the homosexual* (4th ed.). New York: Beacon.

National Association of Social Workers. (1996). *Code of ethics of the National Association of Social Workers.* Washington, DC: NASW Press.

——. (2003). *Social work speaks: National Association of Social Workers policy statements 2003–2006* (6th ed.). Washington, DC: NASW Press.

Patterson, C. J. (1994). Lesbian and gay couples considering parenthood: An agenda for research, servic, and advocacy. *Journal of Gay and Lesbian Social Services, 1*(2), 33–56.

——. (1995). Lesbian mothers, gay fathers, and their children. In A. R. D'Augelli & C. J. Patterson (Eds.), *Lesbian, gay, and bisexual identities over the lifespan* (pp. 262–290). New York: Oxford University Press.

Russell, P. (1994). *The gay 100: A ranking of the most influential gay men and lesbians, past and present*. Secaucus, NJ: Carol Publishing Corporation.

Sheafor, B. W., & Horejsi, C. R. (2003). *Techniques and guidelines for social work practice* (6th ed.). Boston: Allyn & Bacon.

Spong, J. S. (1988). *Living in sin? A bishop rethinks sexuality*. Nashville: Abingdon.

———. (1991). *Rescuing the Bible from fundamentalism*. San Francisco: Harper & Row.

———. (1998). *Why Christianity must change or die*. San Francisco: Harper.

Strickland, B. R. (1995). Research on sexual orientation and human development: A commentary. *Developmental Psychology, 31*(1), 137–140.

Tasker, F. L., & Golombok, S. (1997). *Growing up in a lesbian family: Effects on child development*. New York: Guilford.

2

A HISTORICAL PERSPECTIVE

Lori Messinger

What was once a secret, despised identity had become the basis for ... community, sharing many of the characteristics of more traditional ethnic groupings. And the community had, in turn, spawned a vigorous politics that gave it unusual national influence and served as a beacon of hope for others.

—D'EMILIO, 1983, P. 473

A CAREFUL look at research and writing about American social welfare history reveals absences. While many of these histories discuss presidents and other politicians, white upper-class social reformers, and the occasional grassroots movement beyond the Civil Rights Movement, the histories and perspectives of members of oppressed populations have been largely ignored. Though recent histories and supplemental materials have been more inclusive (Carlton-LaNey, 2001; Day, 2000), even these textbooks in social welfare history have little to offer about the experiences of GLBT people. If one relied only on these texts, it would seem that GLBT people did not exist until the Stonewall Rebellion of 1969. But didn't gay men, lesbians, bisexuals, and transgender people live and love before they gathered to fight for their rights?[1]

Fortunately, the most recent movement in historical research has focused on hidden populations—people of color, low-income people, immigrants, women, and GLBT people. GLBT activists and historians have struggled to uncover evidence of GLBT people and the communities they created (Duberman, Vicinus, & Chauncey, 1989, p. 2). Several books (D'Emilio, 1983; Duberman, Vicinus, & Chauncey, 1989; Faderman, 1991, 1999; Katz, 1978, 1983; Sears, 1997, 2001) give us more insight into the histories of GLBT people in the United States.

As John D'Emilio notes in the quote that opened this chapter, the history of GLBT people reveals a persistent theme: the establishment, dissolution, and reestablishment of communities. Communities serve a variety of purposes for members of oppressed populations: connection, safety, resistance, support, comfort, change. Research has shown that GLBT people who have stronger ties to GLBT communities exhibit better mental and physical health (Crocker & Major, 1989; Kurdek, 1988; Levy, 1989, 1992; Meyer, 1993). Yet community building has been especially difficult for GLBT people in the United States, who, as members of hidden and stigmatized populations, are often invisible to one another. Members of these populations have lacked knowledge of their rich history, traditions, and cultural heritage upon which to build a sense of community (D'Augelli & Garnets, 1995). Thus the history of GLBT community development has been a story of struggle, especially when there was no definition of sexual orientation and gender expression as such, as was the case before the late 1800s; when GLBT gathering places were raided, as were the gay bars of the 1920s–1960s; when laws are enacted that limit protections of sexual and gender expression, as they have been since the 1970s; and when GLBT people are at risk of being the targets of hate crimes, as they are now.

This chapter will focus specifically on the establishment of local, regional, and national GLBT communities in the United States from colonial times until the present. The GLBT communities discussed here existed in separate spheres created by time, geography, class, job, race, sexual orientation, and gender; they also sometimes comprised people who transcended these boundaries. These communities were influenced by and themselves influenced larger social movements for civil rights. They produced leaders, developed formal and informal

---

SETTING SOCIAL WELFARE HISTORY A LITTLE TOO STRAIGHT

There have been many GLBT leaders in social change and social welfare in the United States, though their sexual orientations and gender expressions often are unacknowledged in social welfare history textbooks. While many of these individuals may not have conceptualized sexual orientation or gender identity as we now know them, details of their intimate relationships and expressions help us to apply the terms retroactively. Perhaps foremost among such leaders is Jane Addams, often called one of the mothers of social work (see sidebar in chapter 1). Other important bisexual and lesbian white women who began social justice work during the Progressive Era include social reformer Frances Kellor and her partner Mary Drier, child welfare workers Jessie Taft and her partner Virginia Robinson, labor activist Molly Dewson, and cabinet official Frances Perkins. First lady Eleanor Roosevelt was another advocate for social justice whose intimate relationships with both men and women marked her as bisexual. These women built on the work of lesbian and bisexual white women's suffrage activists Susan B. Anthony, Frances Willard, and Anna Howard Shaw. Another important historical figure is Bayard Rustin, an African American gay man who as a leader in the Civil Rights Movement was primarily responsible for organizing the 1963 March on Washington. Other African American GLBT Civil Rights figures include feminist lawyer Pauli Murray, author James Baldwin, and playwright Lorraine Hansberry. More-recent history reveals important activists fighting for GLBT rights, including Mattachine founder Harry Hay, Daughters of Bilitis founder Barbara Grier, Supreme Court litigant Frank Kameny, author/poet Audre Lorde, transsexual activist Christine Jorgensen, city councilman Harvey Milk, feminist global activist Charlotte Bunch, US congressman Barney Frank, and national GLBT organization director Urvashi Vaid.

organizations, and created and maintained movements for social justice and civil rights for GLBT people. The stories recounted here are selected from in-depth histories of GLBT people and are intended to supplement general histories of social welfare and social work in the United States.

THE SETTLING OF THE AMERICAS

Transgender expression and same-sex intimacies have been documented in the United States from the time of the first European explorers. Spanish and French accounts dating from the early 1500s describe Native American men dressing and working as women and engaging in erotic activities with other men (Katz, 1983). While most European observers condemned this behavior, "some, like Marquette, noted that cross-dressing Illinois Indians were often regarded as persons of consequence who oversaw religious ceremonies" (p. 26).

Katz (1983) documents almost twenty cases involving charges of "sodomy" or other same-sex erotic acts between 1607 and 1740, using legal records in the English and Dutch colonies. The statutes in the 1600s "established and strictly enforced social organization of procreation and family life [as] ... the major productive institutions of early colonial society" (p. 31). Colonial statutes forbade or set limits for men living alone or establishing a household with another man. The legal focus on men and their procreative duties was indicative of the agricultural culture of the times; men were seen as farmers who "planted their seed" to create babies, while women were simply the "ripe" or "unripe" vessel (p. 33). Expending sperm by masturbating or by engaging in nonprocreative sexual activities, including same-sex activities, was seen as wasteful and not supporting the family. The capital laws of Massachusetts Bay prescribed death for blasphemy, being a witch, worshiping any God but the Lord God, and sodomy, among other crimes (p. 76). Homosexuality, therefore, was defined as acts—specific behaviors by men—that were forbidden.

Evidence of intersex people can also be found in the early American colonies. In 1629 the Virginia magistrate resolved the case of Thomas/Thomasine Hall's gender identity by allowing Hall to wear both men's and women's clothing in public without censure, recognizing Hall's intersex status as both "a man and woman" (Katz, 1983, p. 50). It is important to note that gender identity was so strictly regulated at that time that such a matter was brought to the courts.

AMERICA THROUGH THE CIVIL WAR (1750–1865)

Procreation was still the basis for the regulation of sexuality for North American settlers who emigrated from England in the seventeenth and eighteenth centuries. Judeo-Christian perspectives shaped the attitudes toward homosexuality and same-sex eros. "Though criminal records, church sermons, and other evidence reveal homoerotic activity among the residents of the colonies, nothing indicates that men and women thought of themselves as 'homosexual'" (D'Emilio, 1983, p. 10). Colonial legal codes prescribed death for sodomy and characterized other same-sex behavior as "lewd."

During that time the Cult of True Womanhood (or Manhood) was a philosophical stance that established the mental, moral, and emotional traits of each sex. Those who did not fit those molds of womanhood or manhood were seen as "false-sexed mutants." Women who criticized the female role, such as Mary Wollstonecraft, Frances Wright, and Harriet Matineau, were condemned in 1838 by a minister as "only semi-women, mental hermaphrodites" (Katz, 1983, p. 140).

The Civil War provided opportunities for women who chose to dress in masculine garb. One woman who "passed" as a man in order to fight in the war was Sarah Edmonds Seelye, who called herself Frank Thompson and served as a soldier and a nurse. Seelye went on to marry a man and publish a book about her adventures (Katz, 1983). The memoirs of a Union Army general reveal the story of two other cross-dressing women in his command, "between whom an intimacy had sprung up" (Katz, 1978, p. 227). It is clear, though, that no matter whether women who dressed as men had same-sex desires or not, they were freed from "the bondage with which woman is oppressed" (1855 quote from Lucy Ann Lobdell, a cross-dressing woman, cited in Katz, 1978, p. 220).

THE PRIVILEGES OF CLASS AFTER THE CIVIL WAR (1866–1880)

The Industrial Age, with its establishment of a workplace outside the home, created opportunities for men, and some women, to seek financial support and sustenance outside of the family structure. The growing urban centers facilitated the development of emotional and sexual relationships outside of one's small community (D'Emilio, 1983). There was a corresponding rise in "working class women who 'passed' as men in the public sphere while constructing a private life with a female-centered erotic and emotional focus" (p. 94).

Same-sex loving relationships were also increasingly common among middle-class women working in education, nursing, and other helping professions, as these women trained together at the new institutions of higher education. "By 1880, forty thousand women, over a third of the higher education student population in America, were enrolled in [single-sex] colleges and universities and there were 153 American colleges that they could attend" (Faderman, 1991, p. 13). Young college women developed romantic social cultures in the single-sex environments, where attractions between the women were called "smashes," "crushes," and "spoons" (p. 19). Many of the women "who graduated paired with other female college graduates to establish same-sex households—'Boston Marriages,' as they were sometimes called in the East where they were so common" (p. 15). These relationships were very loving and intimate, and some might have been sexual as well. Perhaps the most famous of these Boston marriages was between Virginia Robinson and Jessie Taft, two child welfare social workers who adopted children in the 1930s. Many of these women went on to create long-lasting circles of friends who worked together for social change.

SCIENCE, PROGRESSIVES, AND THE DEVELOPMENT OF HOMOSOCIAL COMMUNITIES (1881–1913)

In the 1880s and 1890s, a scientific interest in the causes of homosexuality emerged. "A new medical idea of 'normal' and 'abnormal' love began to be formulated by physicians" (Katz, 1983, p. 141). Doctors spoke of "sexual perverts," who felt the erotic attraction to the same sex, as well as identifying individuals who "wished, believed, or claimed themselves to be, the other sex" (p. 145). Sexual orientation and gender expression were thus conflated, seen as elements of the same "illness." Most believed that this condition was hereditary and congenital. Homosexuality was a disease, either of the body or of the psyche (e.g., Freud) (D'Emilio, 1983, p. 16). This conflation of sexual orientation and gender expression changed in 1910 when the term *transvestism* was created by Dr. Magnus Hirshfeld to describe cross-dressing behaviors as separate from sexual behaviors (Katz, 1983, p. 146).

The publication and dissemination of these scientific opinions had an effect on the larger society. D'Emilio (1983) writes:

> In America's cities, there [was emerging] a class of people who recognized their erotic interest in members of their own sex, interpreted this interest as a significant characteristic that distinguished them from the majority, and sought others like themselves. Case histories compiled by doctors, vice commission investigations, … newspaper accounts, … and, more rarely, personal correspondence and diaries testify to the wide social variety of these gay [and lesbian] lives.
>
> (P. 11)

Individual relationships were developing into small networks and larger communities, with their own institutions, norms, and practices.

D'Emilio (1983) describes the development of a number of gay, lesbian, and transgender institutions: cruising areas in large cities like New York and San Francisco, where gay men could find one another; bars and saloons in a number of big and smaller cities and towns; and annual drag balls for African American men in St. Louis and Washington, DC. Social Progressives, many of whom were active in social welfare movements, established gay and lesbian literary societies and developed circles of gay and lesbian friends. Many faculties at women's colleges, settlement houses, and professional associations and clubs for college-educated women formed webs of lesbian friendships. These social groups were seen as sources of support and friendship, as well as serving as a barrier against an unfriendly and unwelcoming world. "By about June 1895, according to Earl Lind, the effeminate male homosexual cross-dressers who frequented the New York City club known as 'Paresis Hall' had formed the *Cercle Hermaphroditos*, 'to unite for defense against the world's bitter persecution'" (Katz, 1983, p. 158).

Lillian Faderman (1991) argues that close female-female relationships, previously ignored or characterized as harmless, started to be spoken of as a threat at this time, when economic conditions made it possible for significant numbers of women to act on their feelings and set up homes together, independent of men and the traditional family. The public acceptance of Freudian and sexologists' theories changed the acceptance of romantic friendships between college women, sexualizing these relationships in the eyes of others in such a way that they came to be regarded as unacceptable.

WORLD WAR I, THE ROARING TWENTIES, AND THEIR AFTERMATH (1914–1940)

The end of World War I saw significant changes for GLBT people. Dr. Alan L. Hart was diagnosed as a transsexual person and treated using a method much like that accepted today. Hart, born female, was treated with psychotherapy and surgery in 1918 to thereafter live as a male. Gay men and lesbians were beginning to find one another in cities and to work for social and political change. Katz (1983) notes the establishment of the Chicago Society for Human Rights, a homosexual emancipation group, as a private nonprofit in Chicago in 1924. The "Roaring Twenties" would become a time of sexual experimentation for people of diverse sexual orientations and gender expressions. Nowhere was this more apparent than in Harlem, in New York City.

As a result of the mass influx of black men and women coming north for industrial jobs, Harlem was a thriving black community. "During the Harlem Renaissance period, roughly 1920 to 1935, black lesbians and gay men were meeting each other on street corners, socializing in cabarets and rent parties, and worshiping in church on Sundays, creating a language, a social structure, and a complex network of institutions" (Garber, 1989, p. 318). Black GLBT poets, blues singers and musicians, artists, writers, and others found a community in the Harlem atmosphere. Famous bisexual and lesbian entertainers of that time included Bessie Smith, Gladys Bentley, Jackie "Moms" Mabley, Alberta Hunter, Gertrude "Ma" Rainey, Josephine Baker, and Ethel Waters. Other famous GLBT people in

Harlem artistic circles were poet Langston Hughes, sculptor Richmond Barthe, painter Aaron Douglas, and writers Wallace Thurman, Arna Bontemps, and Zora Neale Hurston. "With its sexually tolerant population and its quasi-legal nightlife, Harlem offered an oasis to white homosexuals" as well (p. 329).

White lesbians found another source of solace in the U.S. publication of *The Well of Loneliness* in 1928. Authored by English lesbian Radclyffe Hall, this book presented a main character, Stephen Gordon, who was characterized as a congenital lesbian, "a man in a woman's body," a butch lesbian (Faderman, 1991, p. 173). Many lesbian readers saw themselves in the characters and found hope in the existence of others like themselves.

The stock market crash of 1929 and the end of Prohibition in 1933 brought an end to the Harlem Renaissance, as the white pleasure-seekers had neither the money nor the need to make the trip uptown to Harlem. However, "the Harlem lesbian and gay community survived, though it became smaller, less 'spectacular,' and less racially integrated" (Garber, 1989, p. 331). After Prohibition, bars became central meeting places for working-class lesbians, though the number of bars that attracted lesbians would never be as high as those that served gay men (D'Emilio, 1983).

GLBTS FIGHTING THE TWO WARS IN WORLD WAR II (1941–1944)

World War II brought young single men and women into cities to do defense work and into the military and military support. Most found themselves in sex-segregated settings, away from families and familiar structures. During the 1940s, exclusively gay bars, once found only in the largest cities, like New York, Los Angeles, and Chicago, appeared for the first time in smaller cities as diverse as San Jose, Denver, Kansas City, Cleveland, and Worcester, Massachusetts (D'Emilio, 1983). These bars were routinely harassed and denied their liquor licenses, and some states and localities passed laws forbidding the congregation of homosexuals.

Allan Berube (1990) described how the military lifestyle provided an opportunity for communities of gay men and lesbians to develop. "Army canteens witnessed men dancing with one another.... Men on leave or those waiting to be shipped overseas shared beds in YMCAs and slept in each other's arms in parks or in aisles of movie theaters that stayed open to house them" (D'Emilio, 1983, p. 25). Similarly, the Women's Army Corps (WAC) and the Women's Army Auxiliary Corps (WAAC) kept female personnel segregated from men and produced training manuals that praised the desire for "intense comradeship" in service as "one of the finest relationships" possible for women (p. 27). Though official policies of the military forces were established to keep gay men and lesbians out, these policies were sometimes overlooked, as the need for soldiers and support staff was great. In one well-publicized story from World War II, General Eisenhower requested that his assistant, WAC sergeant Johnnie Phelps, identify the lesbians in her battalion and create a list for removal. Sergeant Phelps responded that she would be happy to provide him a list of names, but that he should know that her name would be at the top of the list, along with the names of all of the file clerks, the section heads, most of the commanders, and the motor pool. General Eisenhower rescinded the order (Faderman, 1991). Yet such stories were the anomalies; more often the stories were of persecution, witch hunts, and dishonorable discharges of lesbians and gay men in the military during the war, and especially after the war ended. In fact, as president, Eisenhower went on to issue an executive order in 1953 making homosexuality a sufficient reason to terminate a federal employee.

LIFE UNDER THE GOVERNMENT EYE (1945–1955)

In the ten years after World War II, the American public stopped seeing same-sex behaviors as individual transgressions and focused more on men and women as being homosexuals (D'Emilio, 1983, p. 4). Legislatures of more than half the states passed sexual psychopath laws that officially recognized homosexuality as a socially threatening disease. Doctors experimented on lesbians and gay men using psychotherapy, hypnosis, castration, hysterectomy, lobotomy, electroshock, aversion therapy, and the administration of untested drugs (p. 18).The McCarthy-driven anti-communist movement emerged, made manifest by the House Un-American Activities Committee's search for traitors, and became a way to attack homosexuals. "Sexual perverts" were seen as risks to national security. "During the 1950s, the FBI engaged in widespread surveillance of the gay [and lesbian] world" (p. 124). The U.S. Postal Service put tracers on suspected homosexuals' mail in order to gather enough evidence for dismissal from federal positions and possible arrest. Public disclosure of homosexuality was enough to get most people fired from their jobs and ostracized from families and communities (McWhorter, 1996).

The homophile movement emerged at this time as a response to these oppressive practices. McCarthyism "inadvertently helped to foster self-awareness and identity among" lesbians and gay men who supported this organizing (Faderman, 1991, p. 190). Books such as *The Homosexual in America*, Donald Webster Cory's 1951 subjective account of living as a homosexual man in the United States, argued for acceptance (D'Emilio, 1983).

The Mattachine Society, the first advocacy organization of the new Homophile Movement, was established in Los Angeles in 1951 by left-wing or Communist gay men (D'Emilio, 1983). The purpose of the society was to "unify isolated homosexuals, educate homosexuals to see themselves as an oppressed minority, and lead them in a struggle for their own emancipation" (p. 67). The society, made up of male and (some) female members, offered discussion groups and conferences. The group organized local homosexuals to fight police entrapment in 1952 and also formally incorporated as a nonprofit educational foundation in California that same year. By May 1953, membership in the society stood at approximately two thousand people. As the group grew, the membership grew increasingly diverse, including gay men, lesbians, businesspeople, factory workers, and university faculty members (p. 72). In 1953 members of Mattachine launched a homophile magazine, titled *ONE*, which eventually became an independent organization. Chapters of Mattachine emerged in New York City and San Francisco as well.

Mattachine was most often the bastion of men, with few lesbians participating in the organization. The male members tended to focus on their own concerns and issues and often conceptualized gay life through gendered lenses, ignoring the perspectives of lesbian members. As a result, Daughters of Bilitis (DOB) was established in 1955 by Del Martin and Phyllis Lyon and three other lesbian couples in San Francisco (D'Emilio, 1983, p. 102). The DOB, which saw itself as part of the larger homophile movement, maintained a focus on the needs and concerns of lesbians. In 1956 the group published the first issue of *The Ladder*, its magazine for lesbians. The DOB appealed predominantly to white-collar, semi-professional lesbians who preferred more feminine dress; as a result, upper-class women and more "butch" (masculine-appearing) women were not welcome or comfortable in the organization (p. 106).

Daughters of Bilitis, the Mattachine Society, and ONE, Inc., together became the backbone of the homophile movement. D'Emilio characterizes this movement as focused predominantly on helping gay men and lesbians fit into society; these homophile organizations of the 1950s were not focused on fighting for legal and political change.

GLBTS IN THE CIVIL RIGHTS ERA (1956–1968)

The Civil Rights Movement of the late 1950s and 1960s, fighting for the rights of African Americans, challenged the boundaries and structures of American culture. Similar social changes were taking place for GLBT people as psychological and legal scholars were undermining entrenched notions about homosexuality, while judicial rulings on pornography and obscenity allowed the creation and distribution of fiction, theater, and photographs with gay and lesbian themes. In 1962 Illinois became the first state to decriminalize same-sex behavior between adults (D'Augelli & Patterson, 1995).

The overarching impact of civil rights organizing could be seen in strategies employed by the new gay rights activists. Frank Kameny, fired from the federal government for his sexual orientation, argued against the homophile strategy of accommodation to heterosexual culture and biases. Instead, he advocated a gay civil rights movement on the model of the National Association for the Advancement of Colored People (NAACP) and the Congress on Racial Equality (CORE). He worked with the Mattachine Society in Washington, D.C., to challenge the discriminatory policies of the U.S. Civil Service Commission, the armed forces, and the Pentagon (D'Emilio, 1983, p. 154). In 1964, in an action reminiscent of early Civil Rights Movement activists, conservatively dressed lesbians and gay men picketed the White House, the Pentagon, and all government installations, protesting the treatment of homosexuals by the government (Faderman, 1991).

Soon thereafter, new gay rights activists in New York, Washington, and other East Coast cities gathered to form the East Coast Homophile Organizations (ECHO), "a loosely structured coalition" that "exchanged information, debated tactics, and concocted schemes for pushing their groups towards great militancy" (D'Emilio, 1983, p. 161). "In 1966, the North American Conference of Homophile Organizations (NACHO) took the example of the militant black movement to heart and adapted the slogan 'Gay is Good' from 'Black is Beautiful'" (Faderman, 1991, p. 193).

Southerners were not left out of the homophile organizing. In 1963 Richard A. Inman of Florida formed the first state-chartered homophile organization in the South, publishing the *Atheneum Review* and eventually allying himself with the Mattachine Society. Inman was the first Southerner to challenge anti-gay laws in the courts (one case went to the U.S. Supreme Court), to write in the popular press about the homosexual, and to appear on local television and radio programs. Membership in NACHO also included small groups started in the late 1960s in the South, such as the Circle of Friends, a social group in Dallas; the Promethean Society, a more political Houston group formed to address police raids; and the Tidewater Homophile League of Norfolk, Virginia (Sears, 2001).

Student activism in civil rights and antiwar protests sparked homophile organizing on campus. Student homophile organizations emerged during the late 1960s and early 1970s at Columbia University, the University of Houston, the University of Florida, the University of Kentucky, and the University of Alabama. Many of these student groups had to fight their schools to be allowed to meet on university grounds and be officially recognized as student organizations (Sears, 2001).

Distinct cultural changes were occurring during this time period among lesbian communities. Kennedy (1994) outlines the development of working-class lesbian bar cultures in the 1950s, when the "butch/femme" lesbian dynamic could be found. Women identifying as butch lesbians were more likely to wear masculine dress and pass as men in public. Faderman (1991) identified attempts by "working-class and young lesbians in the 1950s and 60s to build institutions other than the gay bars"—specifically, softball teams (p. 162). These teams, and the leagues of which they were a part, provided ways for lesbians to meet one another outside of bars. Sears (2001) found similar institutions—bars, softball teams, private parties—in the 1950s and 1960s lesbian communities in Louisville, Kentucky (pp. 60–61).

Butch and femme roles were less common among lesbians of the middle and upper classes. A 1962 study found that lesbians "in the upper financial brackets who owned homes in affluent neighborhoods, generally appeared in feminine clothes and demonstrated no marked emphasis on roles" (Prosin, cited in Faderman, 1991, p. 181). These women were more likely to host private parties in their homes. Class and racial distinctions clearly divided these lesbian communities, as well as those of their gay, bisexual, and transgender counterparts. GLBT people were creating new businesses to cater to their communities. The first gay bookstore, the Oscar Wilde Bookshop, was opened in 1967 in New York City's Greenwich Village. In the next ten years, other bookstores and businesses would emerge across the country.

The sexual revolution of the 1960s "ushered in an unprecedented sexual permissiveness, characterized by mini skirts, the pill, group sex, mate swapping, a skyrocketing divorce rate, and acceptance of premarital sex" (Faderman, 1991, p. 201). The culture of sexual openness among heterosexuals opened the door for more acceptance of homosexuality. The hippie culture of "free sex, unisex haircuts and clothes, love-ins, challenge to authority and conventional morality" (p. 203) and the leftist antiwar movement of the late 1960s provided the backdrop for a radical new challenge to the norms of heterosexist morality.

THE STONEWALL REBELLION AND GAY LIBERATION: TENSIONS AND DIVISIONS (1969–1979)

It was in this more politicized and culturally permissive atmosphere that the Stonewall Rebellion occurred in Greenwich Village on June 27, 1969. The Stonewall Inn, a private GLBT club, was raided shortly before midnight by local police, who were ostensibly checking to see if liquor was being served without a license. After being questioned, the two hundred "working-class patrons—drag queens, third world gay men, and a handful of butch lesbians—congregated in front of the Stonewall and, as blacks and other oppressed groups had done before them in the course of a decade, commenced to stage a riot" (Faderman, 1991, p. 194). The rioting continued the next night, with hundreds of rioters, gay power graffiti, and condemnation of police. Though not the first bar raid to be protested, nor the first riot after a raid of a GLBT bar, it was an event that occurred in the midst of an organized homophile movement, in a city with a large GLBT population, during a time when "rebellion was the rhetoric of the day" (D'Emilio, 1983, pp. 231–232).

1970s in large U.S. cities: the National Bisexual Liberation Group in New York in 1972, which published a newsletter called *The Bisexual Expression*; New York City's Bi Forum in 1975; the San Francisco Bisexual Center in 1976; and Chicago's BiWays in 1978. Though these early groups were predominantly run by men, Highleyman explains that bisexual women began to establish their own groups, "experiencing alienation from lesbian communities as separatism and polarization around sexual orientation increased in the late 1970s. For many bisexual women, bisexuality was an integral part of their feminist politics and they wanted their groups to reflect this emphasis. The Boston Bisexual Women's Network (formed in 1983) and the Seattle Bisexual Women's Network (founded in 1986) are based on these principles"(¶ 5).

GLBT activists were not focused solely on the political; they also addressed their spiritual and religious lives. The Metropolitan Community Church, a Christian denomination that would welcome GLBT people, was founded in 1969 (Smith, 2000). The earliest GLBT religious group in a mainstream denomination, Dignity/USA, began in 1969 in San Diego under the leadership of Father Patrick Nidorf, first as a Catholic counseling group and then a support group. It became a national organization in 1973. Other GLBT religious support and advocacy groups created during this time period include American Baptists Concerned (1972); Integrity, a group for GLBT Episcopalians (1974); Lutherans Concerned (1974); Gay United Methodists (1975), which later became Affirmation and Reconciling United Methodists; More Light Presbyterians (1978); AXIOS, a GLBT organization for Eastern Orthodox people (1980); and a number of Jewish GLBT organizations.

All of this political, religious, and social activism coalesced in the first National March on Washington in October 1979. A national advisory group was established to plan the march with representatives of the various segments of the GLBT communities: youth, older people, physically challenged people, and transgender people. Interestingly, even after a protracted floor fight among planners, transgender people were not included in the official name of the march. The advisory group required a minimum of 50% women and 20% people of color to be included in all march planning and leadership. More than 100,000 participants attended the march (Smith, 2000).

It is important to remember that not all lesbians, gay men, bisexuals, and transgender people were activists. Many of those who sought out and developed lesbian and gay communities were searching for social outlets and personal freedom of expression, rather than political change (Hunter, Shannon, Knox, & Martin, 1998). Bisexuality as a distinct identity had not yet been acknowledged by most of the members of these communities, and transgenderism also was not well recognized or well understood. The AIDS epidemic of the 1980s would change these perspectives.

AIDS AND THE DEVELOPMENT OF SUPPORTIVE COMMUNITIES (1980–1990)

"While studies have documented human infections with HIV prior to 1970, available data suggest that the current pandemic started in the mid-to-late 1970s" (Mann, 1989). In early 1981 several cases of Kaposi's sarcoma and a rare pneumonia called *Pneumocystis carinii* pneumonia (PCP) were discovered in gay men in New York and California, and as a result, the Centers for Disease Control (CDC) became aware of what would eventually be known as AIDS. The spread of HIV was rapid: "By the beginning of July 1982, a total of 452 cases, from 23 states, had been reported to the CDC" (AVERT, 2003). Unfortunately, political officials were slow to acknowledge the epidemic. President Reagan did not even mention the word *AIDS* in public until well into his second term in office, several years into the epidemic. "Public health officials cite the slowness of the Reagan Administration's response as the central reason for AIDS becoming an epidemic in America" (League@NCR, 2003).

In the face of inaction by the federal government, a number of AIDS-specific voluntary organizations were created by 1982, including the San Francisco AIDS Foundation, AIDS Project Los Angeles, and Gay Men's Health Crisis (AVERT, 2003). These organizations, rooted in GLBT social networks and administered by GLBT people, developed information and referral systems, support networks of "buddies" for people who needed help, counseling services, sexual health education and training models, and other resources. AIDS services agencies and organizing efforts were most successful in white, middle-class communities. "Few HIV/AIDS programs in White lesbian and gay communities addressed the cultural needs of racial and ethnic groups" (Hunter et al., 1998, p. 41).

These medical and social services were complemented by a growing political advocacy and the establishment of new advocacy groups. AIDS Coalition to Unleash Power (ACT-UP), a radical activist organization, used guerrilla theater and civil disobedience to raise awareness about AIDS. On the other side of the political spectrum, the Human Rights Campaign Fund (HRCF) was established in 1980 as a mainstream organization to raise money for gay-supportive congressional candidates. HRCF reorganized in 1989, becoming a membership organization (HRC) with a connected PAC, in recognition of the group's expanded efforts at lobbying and political organizing (Human Rights Campaign, 2003).

Though AIDS was often considered a gay man's disease, the issue had a profound effect on the bisexual movement. Highleyman (1993) explains:

[Bisexual] men were stigmatized as spreaders of HIV from homosexuals to the "general population." In the late 1980s, as awareness of AIDS in women increased, bisexual women began to be stigmatized as spreaders of HIV to lesbians. These developments spurred discussions about the distinction between sexual behavior and sexual identity (for example, many self-identified bisexual women did not have sex with men, while many self-identified lesbians did).

¶ 7

These tensions challenged the alliances among people with different sexual orientations, spurring continued formation of bisexual groups throughout the 1980s.

> Washington DC's bisexual group began in the early 1980s. Philadelphia's Bi Unity, the Wellington Bi Women's Group in New Zealand & groups in Germany & Australia formed in the mid-1980s. Umbrella groups were formed to facilitate regional organizing, including the East Coast Bisexual Network in 1985 (now the Bisexual Resource Center) and the Bay Area Bisexual Network in 1987. At the same time, the first groups devoted specifically to bisexual political activism were formed, including San Francisco's BiPol (1983), Boston's BiCEP (1988) & New York City's BiPAC (1989).
>
> HIGHLEYMAN, 1993, ¶ 6

The 1980s were a time of social and cultural progress and regression regarding GLBT people. Wisconsin became the first state to ban employment discrimination on the basis of sexual orientation in 1982, and a year later Representative Gerry Studds of Massachusetts disclosed his sexual orientation in a speech to the House of Representatives to become America's first openly gay member of Congress. In 1986 the U.S. Supreme Court issued a 5–4 decision upholding the right of states to enforce laws against homosexual sodomy in *Bowers v. Hardwick*, while Pope John Paul II released a fourteen-page letter calling gays "intrinsically disordered" and "evil" and ordering Catholic Church officials to ensure that "all support" be withdrawn from gay Catholic organizations such as Dignity. Over the next several years Catholic churches across the United States systematically enforced the order and ejected Dignity chapters, which had been allowed to hold meetings in their buildings ("The 80s in review," 1989). This movement in the Catholic Church was mirrored by the growth of anti-gay Christian activism by the Moral Majority, the Christian Coalition, and the Family Values Councils.

Such rejections of GLBT people and the continuing fight for federal recognition and funding for HIV/AIDS provided the impetus for the second National March on Washington for Lesbian and Gay Rights on October 11, 1987. A bisexual contingent of 75 people joined more than 600,000 others to march in what proved to be the largest U.S. nationwide GLBT gathering, though once again transgender people were left out of the official title of the march (Highleyman, 1993; Smith, 2000). The AIDS quilt, a memorial to people who had died from the disease, was displayed on the National Mall that weekend, covering a space larger than a football field and including 1,920 panels (Aids Memorial Quilt, n.d.). Two days later, more than 600 GLBTs were arrested at the largest civil disobedience event ever held at the U.S. Supreme Court ("The 80s in Review," 1989).

The 1990s sparked a new movement within GLBT politics that found ways to connect members of lesbian, gay, bisexual, and transgender communities: the queer movement. This movement, using developments in social theories of sexuality and gender expression, emphasized the inclusion of bisexuals, transgender people, and other sexual minorities under the "queer" umbrella. This philosophy and movement were embodied in a new organization, Queer Nation, which embraced a radical politic, challenging established notions of gender and hierarchy, and utilized direct action to work for justice for GLBT people (D'Augelli & Garnets, 1995; Highleyman, 1993).

WE ARE EVERYWHERE: A TIME OF VISIBILITY AND CHIC (1991–2003)

Whereas the political and social organizing of the 1980s raised the visibility of GLBT people in the United States, the 1990s would witness the public's recognition of GLBTs as a potential force in mainstream politics. The election of William Jefferson "Bill" Clinton as president in 1992 marked the first time that a winning candidate had sought out and received the support of GLBT communities. Clinton had promised that he would lift the gay ban in the military and support gay-affirmative federal legislation; neither of these promises later materialized, though Clinton did end the federal ban on security clearances for gay and lesbian people (League@NCR, 2003). Nevertheless, the excitement of Clinton's election provided the momentum for the 1993 March on Washington for Lesbian, Gay, and Bi Equal Rights and Liberation. After a bitter debate, the transgender community was included in the march's purpose and goals, if not in the title of the march (Frye, 2000). Highly charged media covered the record-breaking one million GLBTs and allied people who converged on the nation's capital (Smith, 2000).

More and more public figures disclosed their sexual orientations as gay, lesbian, or bisexual in the 1990s; among them tennis star Martina Navratilova, golfer Muffin Spencer-Devlin, diver Greg Louganis, *Essence* magazine editor Linda Villarosa, journalist Steven Gendel, singer Melissa Etheridge, and comedian Ellen Degeneres, who disclosed her own sexual orientation at the same time that her television character "came out" on her sitcom. The media even talked about a growing public acceptance of lesbians, calling it "lesbian chic," a phenomenon probably best exemplified by the 1993 *Vanity Fair* cover that showed model Cindy Crawford pretending to shave lesbian singer/actress k. d. lang, who was dressed in drag. Unfortunately, any emerging "lesbian chic" did not translate into better social and political opportunities for lesbians. The disclosure of public figures in the media was accompanied, however, by increasing "outness" of GLBT people to their families, friends, and coworkers throughout the United States.

New GLBT organizations developed in the 1990s, and already existing ones took on new roles, to combat the growing political and social advocacy of the conservative Christian Right. The Center for Lesbian and Gay Studies (CLAGS) was established at City University of New York in 1991 as the first university-based research center dedicated to fostering research and scholarship about lesbian and gay lives and social institutions, as well as about homophobia and oppression (Center for Lesbian and Gay Studies, n.d.). In 1993 the Human Rights Campaign Fund adopted the National Coming Out Day event, held annually every October 11 in honor of the first National March on Washington, and developed educational and promotional materials about homophobia and disclosure for the event (Human Rights Campaign, 2003).

In October 1998 the death of Matthew Shepard—a young college student beaten and left tied to a fence for eighteen hours because he was gay—prompted nationwide vigils and demonstrations. More outrage ensued when religious extremists picketed Shepard's funeral carrying anti-gay placards. Shepard's death, and the lesser-known murder of another gay man, Billy Jack Gaither, sparked a Washington, D.C., march, discussions in the media about homophobia, and a renewed push for gay hate crime legislation.

The 1990s also gave rise to significant developments in the realm of gay and lesbian relationships and families. Numerous legal cases proceeded in state courts across the country regarding adoption and foster care, child custody, and marriage rights. While some states created bans on gay parenting, others successfully challenged or eliminated such legislation. Hawaii and Vermont saw challenges to their restriction of marriage to opposite-sex couples; while an amendment to the state constitution maintained the status quo in Hawaii, the Vermont Supreme Court ruled that the state must grant gay and lesbian couples the same rights as heterosexual couples, and its legislature instituted civil unions as an alternative for same-sex couples.

Transgender communities were developing new national and international organizations to recognize the needs and diversity of its members, while fighting for recognition by established lesbian and gay groups. The International Conference on Transgender Law and Employment Policy was formed in 1991 to redress the absence of transgender legal issues in national lesbian and gay legal groups. This was followed by the establishment of FTM International in 1993 (Frye, 2000). In 1994 Cheryl Chase worked with others to found the Intersex Society of North America (ISNA), an organization "devoted to systemic change to end shame, secrecy, and unwanted genital surgeries for people born with an anatomy that someone decided is not standard for male or female" (Intersex Society of North America, 2003). After years of advocacy, many lesbian and gay groups began to include bisexual and transgender people in their purposes and goals, if not in their names; among the groups to make such changes were Parents and Friends of Lesbians and Gays (PFLAG), the National Gay and Lesbian Task Force (NGLTF), and the National Lesbian and Gay Legal Association (NGLTA) (Frye, 2000).

The Internet and e-mail emerged as organizing tools for GLBT communities. For example, "national [and] international bisexual networking was aided by the creation of electronic computer mailing lists such as the BISEXU-L & BIFEM-L lists, the soc.bi newsgroup on Usenet & numerous private bulletin boards" (Highleyman, 1993, ¶ 11). The Internet also was heavily used to promote a fourth National GLBT March on Washington, held in 2000. This march, however, was more contested than previous marches. Critics thought that the march was poorly timed, given the upcoming election, and that activists should have been focused on local and state organizing (Smith, 2000). Regardless of its divisiveness, the march showed that the Internet and e-mail were cutting-edge tools that would continue to shape GLBT communities into the next century.

CURRENT GLBT COMMUNITIES

Perhaps one measure of how far GLBT communities have come is the inclusion of questions about same-sex cohabiting partners in the U.S. 1990 and 2000 Censuses. While the census counts vastly underestimate the true numbers of GLBT people in the United States (see Badgett & Rogers, 2003), they do provide a glimpse of the increasing presence of GLBT communities that are becoming ever more willing to claim themselves. While the 1990 Census reported only slightly more than 145,000 same-sex cohabiting couples, the 2000 Census reported just over 600,000 in the United States and Puerto Rico. The representation of same-sex couples ranged from a low of 0.47% of all couples living together in North Dakota to a high of 5.14% in Washington, D.C. In the largest cities, such as New York, Chicago, Los Angeles, San Francisco, Dallas, Atlanta, and Seattle, same-sex couples are found in abundance, continuing a trend that began during World War II. The census also identified smaller pockets of same-sex couples in the artistic towns of Asheville, North Carolina, and New Hope, Pennsylvania; college towns of Ithaca, New York; Madison, Wisconsin; Northampton, Massachuetts; and Tacoma Park, Maryland; and resort towns such as Provincetown, Massachusetts; Rehoboth Beach, Delaware; and Key West, Florida.

When GLBT communities are large enough, businesses and social groups targeting these populations are more likely to emerge. GLBT-owned businesses are found in many cities and towns. In addition to GLBT-oriented bars and restaurants, there are insurance companies, legal firms, accountants, counseling centers, clothing stores, realtors, art studios, and other businesses owned and op-erated by and/or for GLBT people. Gay-affirmative spiritual communities exist throughout the United States, some within mainstream denominations and oth-ers in small nondenominational settings. More than sixty GLBT bookstores can be found in cities and towns across the country, though many more have closed in the last ten years as a result of the growth of larger chains and online distribu-tors that carry GLBT-related books, movies, and magazines. A wide variety of social groups have been established for GLBTs, including bowlers, bikers, singers and musicians, jugglers, hikers, skiers, folk dancers, car enthusiasts, Olympians, and nudists (Appelby & Anastas, 1998, p. 98). This GLBT institution building will surely continue in small and large communities alike.

Colleges and universities have also seen an increase in GLBT student, faculty, and staff members' presence and have developed institutions to address their needs. GLBT student resource centers have been developed at more than thirty-five institutions, with many more administrators assigned to oversee GLBT re-sources, needs, and services. Undergraduate and graduate degrees, minors, and certificate programs also have developed in GLBT studies at more than thirty colleges and universities throughout the nation, researching and theorizing about the histories, cultures, and development of GLBT individuals, institutions, and communities.

GLBT people today have better connection to information about their com-munities through more than twenty national magazines and two hundred state and local newspapers and newsletters on GLBT issues, many of which are avail-able online. Online information providers like gay.com offer up-to-the-minute national news coverage (GLINN Media Corporation, 2003). Rural, young, el-derly, and disabled GLBT people frequently use the Internet to connect with other community members and break out of their isolation. Even mainstream civic organizations, such as local chambers of commerce, have added informa-tion about GLBT events and businesses to their Web sites.

Gay Pride events have proliferated and are now held in towns and cities, pri-vate businesses, and public organizations. Usually scheduled in June to honor the Stonewall Rebellion, these events provide forums for GLBT people to gather, celebrate their cultures, and organize for social and political change. Indepen-dent professional organizations and caucuses within established professional or-ganizations offer information and support for GLBT teachers, psychologists, sci-entists, computer programmers, law enforcement officers, athletes, pilots, nurses, engineers, architects, postal workers, accountants, and veterans, among others.

National, state, and local advocacy organizations are fighting for GLBT civil rights across the United States. In the field of social work, the National Association of Social Workers (NASW), the Council on Social Work Education (CSWE), and the Baccalaureate Program Directors Association (BPD) have subcommittees on GLBT concerns. These groups advise social workers on appropriate practice and educational methods with these populations, while actively working to support social and legal activism on behalf of GLBT people.

BUILDING AND STRENGTHENING GLBT COMMUNITIES IN THE FUTURE

Five strategies have been identified through which social workers can facilitate the development of GLBT communities and strengthen the connections of GLBT people to already established communities. First, social workers can conduct research about GLBT communities (D'Augelli & Garnets, 1995). Given "the lack of knowledge among GLBT persons about their histories and cultures, and the importance of this knowledge to building a strong sense of identity and pride" (p. 305), social workers should conduct research on the histories of their local GLBT communities and disseminate their findings. Clinicians can use oral history techniques with their clients, helping them to recognize and revalue their own history as part of their local GLBT community. Social workers should also conduct needs assessments with the local GLBT populations, identifying gaps in services and emerging areas of need. Current services to GLBT people should also be assessed for their appropriateness, thoroughness, and quality, with the findings used to improve the effectiveness of these services.

Second, social workers can offer community education on historical and current issues facing GLBT populations, including HIV and AIDS, homophobia and heterosexism, and GLBT rights. Using workshops, training, seminars, pamphlets, flyers, and the local media, social workers can dispel myths and provide accurate information about GLBT people. Information from the Human Rights Campaign's National Coming Out Day project would be useful in this effort. These interventions should be targeted to the needs and cultures of specific communities. Such education would be useful to people of all sexual orientations and gender expressions, helping those in the majority and those in minority populations to appreciate their similarities and differences. The information would also be useful to practitioners working directly with GLBT clients, helping them to build a positive self-image and address their internalized oppression.

Community outreach is a third strategy that social workers can use to connect GLBT people to necessary resources in their neighborhoods or regions. Many service providers and community organizations advertise at local GLBT-oriented bars and bookstores and sponsor GLBT events, such as concerts, Gay Pride events, and dances. Since some GLBT people hide their sexual orientations and/or gender expressions and might not frequent these venues, it is necessary to use a variety of methods to provide more closeted GLBTs with information about local resources. GLBT organization Web sites, community listservs, newsletters, and newspapers are important mechanisms for advertising available services, as

GLBT people can gain access to such sources in the privacy of their own homes. Social workers can also make sure that their clients are aware of existing resources by making appropriate referrals, displaying informative materials about local resources in waiting areas, and building official linkages between their own agencies and organizations offering GLBT services.

In those areas where such resources do not already exist, social workers can use a fourth community practice strategy: community development. They can establish new programs to meet the needs of GLBT people, such as community centers, lending libraries, youth centers, retirement communities, coming out support groups, and advocacy and research organizations. Established organizations, such as women's resource centers, battered women's programs, and other agencies serving low-income, elderly, and disabled people, can also develop services specifically targeting these GLBT subpopulations. Private and public funding can be identified to support these services; examples of possible private funders include the Billy Jean King Foundation, the Gill Foundation, and the Ford Foundation, while the federal Violence Against Women Act (VAWA) and the Centers for Disease Control have money designated for programs with GLBT people.

Finally, social workers can be activists, working as part of the GLBT rights movements in their local communities, states, as well as nationally. These movements have been developing in the United States for more than a hundred years now, beginning locally and becoming stronger and better organized on a national level. The NASW calls on social workers to support civil rights for gay and lesbian people, acceptance of gay and lesbian identities as normal sexual orientations, and the empowerment of gay and lesbian clients. Only in joining the movements for GLBT rights can social workers meet the needs of their individual clients, improve services in our communities, and work, as we should, for social and economic justice.

REFLECTIONS ON THE RAINBOW: GLBT SOCIAL WELFARE HISTORY

The rainbow is one of the main symbols of GLBT community pride, displayed on flags, T-shirts, jewelry, and bumper stickers. It serves as a symbol of the diversity and unity within the GLBT community (HRC, 2003). Yet, reflecting on GLBT American history of the last two hundred years, the rainbow as a symbol of hope is perhaps an even more appropriate metaphor. The experiences of GLBT people in the United States have changed dramatically, moving from isolation in the seventeenth and eighteenth centuries, to the establishment of small networks in the late nineteenth century, and then to the establishment of more diverse communities in the twentieth century. During that time, GLBT people and communities have fought discrimination in legal, medical, religious, and social settings and greatly progressed in their struggle for civil rights and social acceptance. Perhaps the arc of history, like the arc of the rainbow, will see GLBT people in the next century winning full legal rights and acceptance in all parts of society. The strength, vision, and successes detailed in this chapter offer hope for this future. Perhaps as social workers learn and share this history with their clients, the promise of the rainbow will be fulfilled.

NOTE

1. The terms *lesbian, gay, bisexual,* and *transgender* are social constructions whose histories do not date back further than the late 1800s. Yet, in order to enable readers to see the continuity of this history, these terms are used throughout this chapter, in which readers will learn about their development and their related identities.

REFERENCES

Adoption History Project. (2003). *Jessie Taft, 1880–1960*. Eugene, OR. Department of History, University of Oregon. Retrieved August 23 from http://www.uoregon.edu/~adoption/people/taft.htm.

AIDS Memorial Quilt. (n.d.). *A history of the quilt*. Retrieved June 28, 2003, from http://www.aidsquilt.org/history.htm.

Appelby, G. A., & Anastas, J. W. (1998). *Not just a passing phase: Social work with gay, lesbian, and bisexual people*. New York: Columbia University Press.

AVERT. (2003). *The history of AIDS: 1981–1986*. Retrieved June 28, 2003, from http://www.avert.org/his81_86.htm

Badgett, M. V. L., & Rogers, M. A. (2003). *Left out of the count: Missing same-sex couples in Census 2000*. San Francisco: Institute for Gay and Lesbian Strategic Studies. Retrieved June 30, 2003, from http://www.iglss.org/media/files/c2k_leftout.pdf.

Bedford, K., & Wilson, A. (1999). *Lesbian feminist chronology: 1963–1970*. Retrieved June 30, 2003, from http://www.womens-studies.ohio-state.edu/araw/chrono1.htm.

Berube, A. (1990). *Coming out under fire: The history of gay men and women in World War Two*. New York: Free Press.

Carlton-LaNey, I. (2001). *African American leadership: An empowerment tradition in social welfare history*. Washington, DC: NASW Press.

Center for Lesbian and Gay Studies. (n.d.). *Then, now, and tomorrow*. Retrieved June 30, 2003, from http://web.gsuc.cuny.edu/clags/history.htm.

Crocker, J., & Major, B. (1989). Social stigma and self-esteem: The self-protective properties of stigma. *Psychological Review, 96,* 608–630.

D'Augelli, A. R., & Garnets, L. D. (1995). Lesbian, gay, and bisexual communities. In A. R. D'Augelli & C. J. Patterson (Eds.), *Lesbian, gay, and bisexual identities over the lifespan: Psychological perspectives* (pp. 293–320). New York: Oxford University Press.

D'Augelli, A. R., & Patterson, C. J. (Eds.). (1995). *Lesbian, gay, and bisexual identities over the lifespan: Psychological perspectives*. New York: Oxford University Press.

Day, P. J. (2000). *A new history of social welfare* (3d ed.). Needham Heights, MA: Allyn & Bacon.

D'Emilio, J. (1983). *Sexual politics, sexual communities: The making of a homosexual minority in the United States, 1940–1970.* Chicago: University of Chicago Press.

Duberman, M. B., Vicinus, M., & Chauncey Jr., G. (Eds.). (1989). *Hidden from history: Reclaiming the gay and lesbian past.* New York: New American Library.

The 80s in review. (1989, December 12). *Washington Blade.* Retrieved June 30, 2003, from http://www.glinn.com/news/h122989a.htm.

Faderman, L. (1991). *Odd girls and twilight lovers: A history of lesbian life in twentieth-century America.* New York: Columbia University Press.

———. (1999). *To believe in women: What lesbians have done for America—A history.* Boston: Houghton-Mifflin.

Frye, P. R. (2000). Facing discrimination, organizing for freedom: The transgender community. In J. D'Emilio, W. B. Turner, & U. Vaid (Eds.), *Creating change: Sexuality, public policy, and civil rights* (pp. 451–468). New York: St. Martin's.

Garber, E. (1989). A spectacle in color: The lesbian and gay subculture of Jazz Age Harlem. In M. B. Duberman, M. Vicinus, & G. Chauncey, Jr. (Eds.), *Hidden from history: Reclaiming the gay and lesbian past* (pp. 318–331). New York: New American Library.

GLINN Media Corporation. (2003). *Gay media database.* Retrieved June 30, 2003, from http://www.gaydata.com/gmd2.htm.

Highleyman, L. A. (1993). *A brief history of the bisexual movement.* Retrieved June 30, 2003, from http://www.ncf.ca/ip/sigs/life/gay/bi/bi.

Human Rights Campaign. (2003). *Human rights campaign.* Retrieved June 30, 2003, from http://www.hrc.org.

Hunter, S., Shannon, C., Knox, J., & Martin, J. I. (1998). *Lesbian, gay, and bisexual youths and adults: Knowledge for human services practice.* Thousand Oaks, CA: Sage.

Intersex Society of North America. (2003). *The Intersex Society of North America.* Retrieved June 30, 2003, from http://www.isna.org.

Katz, J. (1978). *Gay American history: Lesbians and gay men in the U.S.A.* New York: Harper and Row.

———. (1983). *Gay/lesbian almanac: A new documentary.* New York: Harper and Row.

Kennedy, E. L. (1994). *Boots of leather, slippers of gold: The history of a lesbian community.* New York: Penguin.

Kurdek, L. A. (1988). Perceived social support in lesbians and gays in cohabiting relationships. *Journal of Personality and Social Psychology, 54,* 504–509.

Lambda Legal. (2003). *Strength—strategy—success: Shaping the future since 1973.* Retrieved June 28, 2003, from http://www.lambdalegal.org/cgi-bin/iowa/documents/record? record = 1207.

League@NCR. (2003). *GLBT history in the United States: A timeline.* Retrieved June 30, 2003, from http://www.league-ncr.com/library/history/timeline.html.

Levy, E. F. (1989). Lesbian motherhood: Identity and social support. *Affilia, 4*(4), 40–53.

———. (1992). Strengthening the coping resources of lesbian families. *Families in Society: The Journal of Contemporary Human Services, 73*(1), 23–31.

Mann, J. M. (1989). AIDS: A worldwide pandemic. In M. S. Gottlieb, D. J. Jeffries, D. Mildvan, A. J. Pinching, T. C. Quinn, & R. A. Weiss (Eds.), *Current topics in AIDS* (Vol. 2). New York: John Wiley.

McWhorter, L. (1996). *A brief history of homosexuality in America.* Retrieved June 29, 2003, from http://www.salp.wmich.edu/lbg/GLB/Manual/abrief.html.

Meyer, I. H. (1993). *Prejudice and pride: Minority stress and mental health in gay men.* Unpublished doctoral dissertation, Division of Sociomedical Sciences, School of Public Health, Columbia University, New York.

Morris, B. J. (1999). *Eden built by Eves: The culture of women's music festivals.* Los Angeles: Alyson Books.

National Gay and Lesbian Task Force. (2003). *About NGLTF: Three decades of fighting for freedom, justice, and equality.* Retrieved June 30, 2003, from http://www.ngltf.org/about/ highlights.htm.

Sears, J. T. (1997). *Lonely hunters.* New York: HarperCollins-Westview.

———. (2001). *Rebels, rubyfruits, and rhinestones: Queering space in the Stonewall South.* New Brunswick, NJ: Rutgers University Press.

Smith, N. (2000). Three marches, many lessons. In J. D'Emilio, W. B. Turner, & U. Vaid (Eds.), *Creating change: Sexuality, public policy, and civil rights* (pp. 438–450). New York: St. Martin's.

Torres, V. (2003). *Gay events timeline: 1970–1999.* Sexual Orientation Issues in the News. Retrieved June 29, 2003, from http://www.usc.edu/schools/annenberg/asc/projects/soin/ enhancingCurricula/timeline.html.

Transhistory. (1998). *TransHistory ... Timeline of significant events.* Retrieved June 28, 2003, from http://www.transhistory.org/history/index.html.

3

OPPRESSION, PREJUDICE, AND DISCRIMINATION

Diane E. Elze

For Harry Hay (1912–2002)

As a Black, lesbian, feminist, socialist, poet, mother of two including one boy and a member of an interracial couple, I usually find myself part of some group in which the majority defines me as deviant, difficult, inferior, or just plain "wrong."

From my membership in all of these groups I have learned that oppression and intolerance of differences comes in all shapes and sizes and colors and sexualities; and that among those of us who share the goals of liberation and a workable future for our children, there can be no hierarchies of oppression.

—LORDE, 1983, P. 9

THE HISTORY of gay, lesbian, bisexual, and transgender people in America is a history of oppression and resistance. Since colonial times, gender-variant people, and people who love and sexually desire those of the same sex, have been imprisoned, executed, witch-hunted, pilloried, confined in asylums, fired, excommunicated, disinherited, evicted, extorted, entrapped, censored, declared mentally ill, drugged, and subjected to castration, hormone injections, clitoridectomy, hysterectomy, ovariectomy, lobotomy, psychoanalysis, and aversive therapies such as electroshock and pharmacologic shock (Haldeman, 1994; Israel & Tarver, 1997; Katz, 1976; Silverstein, 1991).

GLBT people have documented their long-standing resistance to such condemnation and discrimination in their diaries, letters, journals, novels, poems, and essays. Their resilience is evidenced in the narratives of women who passed as men and men who passed as women, in the creation of private and public gathering places, and in early organizing on behalf of homosexual rights (D'Emilio & Freedman, 1988; Feinberg, 1996), such as that conducted in the 1920s by the short-lived Chicago-based Society for Human Rights, which sought to reform the laws criminalizing homosexual acts (Katz, 1976).

Harry Hay, the founder of the Mattachine Society, was the first to call "homosexuals" an oppressed minority (Goldstein, 2002). Although the cultural landscape for GLBT people has shifted dramatically since the Stonewall Rebellion of 1969, with the emergence of a visible and vocal GLBT civil rights movement, the election of openly GLBT public officials, and significant changes in social policies and laws, personal hostility and institutional intolerance persist. Prejudice, discrimination, and oppression on the basis of sexual orientation and gender identity permeate our sociocultural context, affecting everyone in deleterious ways, not just GLBT people (Blumenfeld, 1992). GLBT people must, however, manage the stigmatization that accompanies their sexual minority or gender-variant status throughout their life course. The oppression they experience will vary, depending upon their age, gender, race/ethnicity, class, physical and mental abilities, and religious affiliation.

Lee (1994) noted that social workers should hold a historical view of oppression and be knowledgeable about social policy affecting oppressed groups. This chapter describes the multiple forms of oppression experienced by GLBT people, how discrimination based on sexual orientation and gender identity intersects with other forms of oppression (e.g., racism, sexism, classism), the impact of oppression on GLBT people and society; and social work practice suggestions for eradicating or attenuating oppression.

SEXUAL ORIENTATION AS A SOCIAL CONSTRUCT

Heterosexuality and homosexuality (Katz, 1995), like race (Ferrante & Brown, 1998) and gender (Lorber, 1994), are socially constructed categories, created and assigned meaning within specific historical periods and maintained through socialization, reinforcement, and punishment. Historically, social inequalities based on categories of race, gender, and sexual orientation have been given biological rationales and legitimated by societal norms and values, as well as by political, economic, religious, legal, educational, and scientific institutions (Ferrante & Brown, 1998; Katz, 1995; Lorber, 1994).

The terms *heterosexuality* and *homosexuality* did not exist until 1868, when Karl Maria Kertbeny, a German-Hungarian sex law reformer, used them (Katz, 1995). Katz (1995) chronicled the historical evolution of heterosexuality as an invented social institution, illustrating how heterosexuality and homosexuality signified "historically specific ways of thinking about, valuing, and socially organizing the sexes and their pleasures" (p. 12). Into the twentieth century, heterosexual sexual activity was considered by many as normal if practiced for creative (child-producing) purposes and as perverted if practiced for nonprocreative purposes.

With the help of Freud and emerging sexologists, nonprocreative sexual practices were eventually accorded more legitimacy (Katz, 1995). Throughout different historical periods, same-sex sexual behavior was defined as a sin by ecclesiastical authorities, then as a crime by legal authorities, and then, in the 1800s, as a medical problem requiring treatment (Katz, 1976, p. 130).

THE DEFINING CHARACTERISTICS OF OPPRESSION

Systems of oppression (e.g., racism, sexism, classism, ableism, ageism, and heterosexism) share common elements (Pharr, 1988; Tinney, 1983; Young, 2000). Young (2000) delineated five characteristics, or what she called the five faces of oppression: exploitation, powerlessness, systemic violence, cultural imperialism, and marginalization. Pharr (1988) noted that across all forms of oppression, inequities in institutional and economic power and threats of individual and institutional violence function to enforce behavioral norms established by the dominant group. Members of subordinate social groups are rendered invisible, defined as "Other," stereotyped, blamed for their own victimization, and they internalize society's negative attitudes and stereotypes (i.e., internalized oppression) (Pharr, 1988).

EXPLOITATION

Exploitation refers to structural relationships of power and inequality that enable some people to profit from the labor of others, transferring the fruits of one social group's labor to another social group (Young, 2000). Although GLBT people pay into the Social Security system, should they die, their same-sex partners are denied survivor and spousal benefits, regardless of the longevity of their relationship, costing GLBT seniors in same-sex relationships approximately $124 million a year. Unlike married heterosexual couples, who can roll over their deceased partner's 401(k) benefits into a tax-exempt individual retirement account, surviving partners of same-sex couples pay a 20% federal withholding tax on any 401(k) distribution left to them by their partner, denying them hundreds of thousands of dollars in retirement wealth (Cahill, South, & Spade, 2000).

POWERLESSNESS

Powerlessness refers to people's lack of decision-making power in the workplace or other institutions, their exposure to disrespectful treatment because of their subordinate status in the social hierarchy, and their diminished opportunities to develop talents and skills (Young, 2000). Various studies indicate that between 16% and 30% of gay men and lesbians report experiences of work-related discrimination (Badgett, 2001). People in same-sex relationships may face diminished prospects for career advancement in occupations that require socialization with colleagues, or they may avoid or leave occupations where discrimination is likely or where passing is more difficult (Badgett, 2001). Transgender people report high rates of unemployment, underemployment, and involuntary job terminations and reassignments (Frye, 2000; Gagne & Tewksbury, 1998; Lombardi & van Servellen, 2000).

Multiple forms of oppression interact to limit people's life chances. GLBT people vary in both the powerlessness and the opportunities they experience as a result of their membership in other social groups. Because of the exorbitant expense of genital reassignment surgery, that opportunity is available primarily to middle- and upper-class transgender people (Bornstein, 1994). Domestic partnership benefits help only same-sex couples who are privileged enough to receive employee benefits such as health insurance (Bernstein, 2001). GLBT people who desire children find that adoption, second-parent adoption, surrogacy arrangements, alternative insemination, and other reproductive technologies are prohibitively expensive, beyond the means of those who are less economically privileged (Boggis, 2001).

The intersection of racism, sexism, and heterosexism means that ethnic minority lesbians live in "triple jeopardy" because they are members of three oppressed social groups (Greene & Boyd-Franklin, 1996). In a multisite longitudinal study of cardiovascular risk factors in black and white adults (Krieger & Sidney, 1997), one-third of the women of color and more than half (56%) of the white women who had at least one same-sex sexual partner reported experiences with sexual orientation discrimination; nearly all (85%) of the black women also reported racial discrimination; and 89% of the women in the study reported gender-based discrimination. Box 3.1 describes how multiple structural oppressions influenced the private and the public sectors' responses to AIDS.

SYSTEMATIC VIOLENCE

Systematic violence, directed at members of subordinate groups simply because of their group membership (Young, 2000), is exemplified by the prevalence of verbal abuse and physical assaults against GLBT people (Berrill, 1990). When same-sex couples violate what Tinney (1983) called the socially created "defined public space" (p. 6), for example, by holding hands while walking down the street, thereby refusing to restrict themselves to gay bars or pride festivals, they are often threatened with serious harm, physically attacked, and accused of being "too blatant." The omnipresent threat of harm keeps many same-sex couples from venturing beyond the socially ordained public space. Transgender people are at heightened risk for victimization, including harassment, sexual assault, and physical violence (Gagne & Tewksbury, 1998; Gainor, 2000; Sember, Lawrence, & Xavier, 2000).

BOX 3.1

WHEN MULTIPLE OPPRESSIONS INTERSECT: AIDS-RELATED DISCRIMINATION

Perhaps no issue better illustrates the interaction between multiple, institutionalized oppressions than the private and public sectors' response to AIDS. The stigmatization of homosexuality and other marginalized groups, socially conservative positions about sex and sexuality, fear of an infectious disease, and misinformation all contributed to the snail's pace at which policymakers responded in the early years of the epidemic (Shilts, 1987). Although African Americans represent 12% of the population, they account for nearly 38% of all reported AIDS cases and more than 50% of all new HIV infections, with same-sex sexual contact accounting for the highest proportion of cases among African American men. African American and Hispanic women account for more than 75% of all AIDS cases among women (Centers for Disease Control and Prevention, 2001).

The onset of the AIDS epidemic ushered in a new wave of discrimination at the local, state, and federal levels against gay and lesbian communities, affecting not only people with HIV but also their caretakers and people perceived to have HIV. The first national survey of HIV-related discrimination conducted by the AIDS Project of the American Civil Liberties Union found that 13,000 discrimination complaints were fielded by 260 agencies across the country between 1983 and 1988 (ACLU-AIDS Project, 1990). Discriminatory practices excluded people with HIV from emergency shelters, schools, substance abuse treatment programs, hospitals, and nursing homes. They were barred from airplanes, restaurants, and hotels and were denied housing, employment, child visitation, funeral home services, bail, and medical procedures such as dental services, dialysis, and abortion (ACLU-AP, 1990; Hunter, 1989; Kelly, 1989; Schatz, 1987). The U.S. Department of Justice legitimated such discrimination in 1986 when it issued a memorandum declaring that federal disability rights legislation did not cover HIV-related discrimination (Schatz, 1987), although this policy was later reversed (Kelly, 1989).

Anti-gay discrimination in the insurance industry also flourished in response to the HIV epidemic, though it should be understood as part of a long history of race-, religious- and gender-based discrimination by that industry (Schatz, 1987). The insurance industry canceled policies; denied or delayed payments for valid claims; excluded HIV-related conditions from coverage; rejected applicants perceived to be gay or bisexual, sometimes basing these decisions on occupation, living arrangements, or zip code; and stopped issuing group policies to employers believed to employ many gay people (ACLU-AP, 1990; Schatz, 1987). Schatz (1987) reported on a health insurance company that distributed a memorandum directing its agents to flag applications from "single males without dependents that are engaged in occupations that do not require physical exertion ... restaurant employees, antique dealers, restaurant workers, interior decorators, consultants, florists, and people in the jewelry or fashion business" (p. 1787).

CULTURAL IMPERIALISM

Cultural imperialism (Young, 2000), or what Tinney (1983) called collective oppression, is the process by which the dominant group renders invisible the history of subordinate groups, universalizes its own experiences and worldview as the norm against which all others should be judged, and stereotypes and defines as deviant or "Other" the subordinate groups. Institutions practice cultural imperialism through a conspiracy to silence, the denial of culture (Tinney, 1983), the distortion of events, and the presentation of false information (Pharr, 1988).

Particularly in the educational sector, societal institutions go to great lengths to enforce the conspiracy to silence and the denial of culture, evident in the absence of GLBT issues from health education, social studies, and other curricula; the lack of openly GLBT role models; bitter battles over GLBT-affirmative student organizations; and policies and norms against GLBT student visibility at school events (Button, Rienzo, & Wald, 2000; Friend, 1993). The Salt Lake City School Board, in 1996, initiated a nearly five-year-long controversy, which cost the district $250,000, when it banned *all* noncurricular clubs in order to block the East High Gay/Straight Alliance without violating the federal Equal Access Act (Lambda Legal Defense and Education Fund, 2000). North Carolina passed legislation in 1996 that bans schools from teaching about homosexuality in a positive manner (Button et al., 2000). During the mid-1990s, nearly a hundred high school libraries in the Greater St. Louis, Missouri, area refused to display *Becoming Visible*, a book about gay and lesbian history, after receiving a complimentary copy from the Gay, Lesbian, Straight Education Network in celebration of Gay and Lesbian History Month (Little, 1995).

The Public Broadcasting System (PBS) has, on several occasions, refused to air gay and lesbian content, such as *Out at Work*, a documentary about workplace discrimination, and many local affiliates declined to show Marlon Riggs's *Tongues Untied*, an award-winning film about black gay men, and *It's Elementary: Talking About Gay Issues in School*, another award-winning documentary (Gross, 2001).

The conspiracy to silence is also evidenced by policies barring the use of federal funds to produce sexually explicit, culturally sensitive HIV-prevention materials targeting men who have sex with men (Patton, 1996; Vaid, 1995). In 1987, when 73% of all Americans diagnosed with AIDS were men who reported same-sex sexual experiences, disproportionately men of color (Centers for Disease Control and Prevention, 1987), Congress passed the Helms Amendment, which continues to prohibit federal funding of HIV-prevention materials that "promote" or "encourage" same-sex sexual behaviors (Bailey, 1995), a vague standard that is subject to personal prejudices. Conservative legislators quickly used this new law to harass AIDS services organizations by demanding multiple audits (Patton, 1996). Nearly a decade into the epidemic, in 1992, the AIDS Action Council reported that no federal dollars were funding HIV-prevention education aimed at gay, lesbian, and bisexual people (Vaid, 1995). More recently, the Bush administration announced another round of audits to ensure that federally funded HIV-prevention materials do not encourage sexual activity or incorporate "obscene content" (Osborne, 2001), a move criticized by AIDS activists and service organizations for undermining effective prevention messages and diverting valuable agency time from prevention activities.

MARGINALIZATION

Marginalization—what Young (2000) referred to as "perhaps the most dangerous form of oppression" (p. 41)—is the exclusion of particular people from full citizenship, their expulsion from useful participation in social life, and their disrespectful and demeaning treatment by societal institutions and services. Pharr (1988) and Tinney (1983) called this the lack of prior claim to rights and privileges.

Branded as morally weak, emotionally unstable, and therefore as national security risks, gay men and lesbians, until 1974, were systematically excluded from federal civil service employment, a practice that set an unfortunate standard for private employers (D'Emilio & Freedman, 1988). Until 1990, gay men and lesbians were barred as visitors and immigrants to the United States (Rubenstein, 1990). Not until 1995 did sexual orientation cease to be a factor in the issuance of government security clearances (Kameny, 2000). Currently, discrimination based on sexual orientation and gender-variant expression in employment, housing, public accommodations, and access to credit is perfectly legal in most states (Bennett, 2002). As recently as June 2000, the U.S. Supreme Court held that the Boy Scouts of America could legally exclude gay men from serving as scoutmasters (*Boy Scouts of America et al. v. Dale*, 2000).

The extreme marginalization of transgender people is reflected in a recent Kansas Supreme Court decision that denied a transsexual woman's claim to her deceased husband's estate by voiding the marriage and ruling that she was still a man for purposes of marriage, even though she had undergone genital reassignment surgery years earlier (Lamoy & Downs, 2002).

Systems of oppression tokenize some members of stigmatized groups and hold them up for others to emulate, increasing the marginalization of other group members (Pharr, 1988). Gamson (2001) argued, for example, that despite the explosion of cultural visibility for GLBT people, daytime talk television normalizes white, middle-class families headed by gay men and lesbians but marginalizes bisexual and transgender people, as well as gay men and lesbians who are less educated, poor or working class, or people of color. Bisexual people are represented as threats to monogamous family relationships, caught in love triangles, sexually voracious, and unable to commit, and transgender people are attacked for confusing or traumatizing their children with their transition (Gamson, 2001).

MARGINALIZATION WITHIN GLBT COMMUNITIES Marginalization also occurs within oppressed groups, rendering women, people of color, and bisexual and transgender people invisible and universalizing the experience of white gay males. Greene (1996) noted, "The very act of defining the experiences of all lesbians and gay men by the characteristics of the most privileged and powerful members of that group is an act of oppression" (p. 62). The devaluation of African American gay men within white-dominated gay communities is well documented (Hemphill, 1991; Icard, 1996). Viewed as inferior members of the gay community, black gay men are denied the psychological benefits of community affiliation (Icard, 1986).

For women and people of color who experience intersecting oppressions, gender, race, and class may be mitigating factors in the process of disclosing sexual orientation (Snider, 1996). Within Euro-American gay and lesbian communities, not coming out is usually viewed as a reflection of internalized homophobia rather than as an exceedingly rational decision in response to multiple vulnerabilities (Snider, 1996). Because family plays such a central role in the lives of many ethnic minority people, providing a protective refuge from racist oppression (Greene & Boyd-Franklin, 1996; Smith, 1997), the fear of familial rejection because of cultural heterosexism is particularly salient for ethnic minority GLBT people (Greene, 1997; Liu & Chan, 1996).

Although bisexuality is now accepted as a valid sexual orientation (Fox, 2000), bisexual people often encounter discomfort, suspicion, devaluation, and antagonism from gay and lesbian people (Ochs & Deihl, 1992; Rust, 1996). Transgender people have long faced discrimination and marginalization within gay and lesbian communities (Bornstein, 1994; Gainor, 2000; Wilchins, 1997). For years, lesbian feminists have debated whether transsexual women are, in fact, women and, if partnered with women, lesbians, and whether they should be allowed in women-only or lesbian-only spaces (Raymond, 1979; Wilchins, 1997). Organizers of the 1993 March on Washington for Lesbian, Gay, and Bi Equal Rights and Liberation voted to include transgender issues in the goals but to exclude the word *transgender* from the name of the event (Bornstein, 1994). For years, the Human Rights Campaign (HRC) refused to add transgender to the Employment Non-discrimination Act (ENDA) for fear of losing congressional votes. Gay and lesbian organizations, however, are increasingly expanding the scope of their work to include transgender issues, for example by promoting statutes dealing with inclusive nondiscrimination, hate crimes, and safe schools (Currah & Minter, 2000) and by incorporating bisexual and transgender people in their mission statements (Frye, 2000). In response to persistent advocacy from transgender activists, the HRC voted in August 2004 to support a version of ENDA that includes gender identity and gender expression (HRC, 2004).

DEFINITIONS: PREJUDICE, STEREOTYPES, HOMOPHOBIA, BIPHOBIA, AND TRANSPHOBIA

Systems of oppression are bolstered by prejudice, cultural myths, and stereotypes that privilege one group over another and assign a stigmatized identity and lesser value to the subordinate groups. *Prejudice* refers to an individual's attitude or evaluative stance, usually negative, toward a social group, or preconceived opin-

ions or judgments, usually made on the basis of limited information, such as stereotypes, distortions, and omissions. *Stereotypes* are exaggerated, overly general,
and fixed beliefs about members of a social group, imposed by the dominant
group, which function to justify the subjugation of subordinate groups (Allport,
1954; Herek, 1991), as illustrated by the concurring opinion of Alabama Supreme
Court justice Roy Moore, issued in February 2002, that denied child custody to
a lesbian mother:

> Homosexual conduct is, and has been, considered abhorrent, immoral, detestable,
> a crime against nature, and a violation of the laws of nature and of nature's God
> upon which this Nation and our laws are predicated. Such conduct violates both
> the criminal and civil laws of this State and is destructive to a basic building block
> of society—the family.... It is an inherent evil against which children must be pro-
> tected.
>
> (EX PARTE H.H., 2002 ALA. LEXIS 44)

The media often project gay men as white, sexually obsessed, flamboyant, sar-
castic, moneyed, and materialistic, and lesbians as masculine, swaggering man-
haters. African American gays and lesbians are stereotyped as "finger-snapping,
wig-wearing, drag queens who work in beauty parlors" and "man-hating, masculine butches preying on naïve and unsuspecting heterosexual women" (Jones &
Hill, 1996, p. 550). Cultural myths that gay men and lesbians recruit, corrupt,
and molest children, are incapable of being good parents, impair children's gender role and sexual identity development, and expose children to unhealthy role
models are used to legitimate the systemic discrimination faced by gay men and
lesbians in judicial processes related to child custody and visitation, adoption,
and foster parenting (Falk, 1993; Herek, 1991; Polikoff, 2000).

The dichotomous categories of sexual orientation (heterosexual-homosexual)
and gender (male-female) in Euro-American cultures stigmatize bisexual and
transgender individuals in unique ways, marginalizing them within both the
dominant culture and the gay and lesbian communities. Bisexual people are assumed to be going through an immature, transitional phase on their way to a gay
or lesbian identity. They are also stereotyped as sexually insatiable; promiscuous; shallow; unable to make commitments; indecisive fence-sitters who cannot
make up their minds; betrayers of gay or lesbian partners; opting for heterosexual
privilege; and suffering from internalized homophobia (Ochs & Deihl, 1992).
Transgender individuals are assumed to be psychopathological (Israel & Tarver,
1997).

The term *homophobia* is frequently used to identify prejudice toward gay men
and lesbians. Weinberg (1973) popularized the word, defining it as a revulsion
toward and dread of being in close proximity with gays and lesbians. Other common definitions are "the fear of feelings of love for members of one's own sex

and therefore the hatred of those feelings in others" (Lorde, 1984, p. 45) and "the irrational fear and hatred of those who love and sexually desire those of the same sex" (Pharr, 1988, p. 1).

Biphobia and *transphobia* entered the lexicon more recently with increased activism among bisexual and transgender people. These two terms refer to attitudes, beliefs, and behaviors that devalue, stigmatize, or render invisible bisexual people and bisexuality as a sexual orientation (Ochs & Deihl, 1992) or transgender people and gender-variant modes of expression, respectively (Blumenfeld, 2000).

FROM HOMOPHOBIA TO HETEROSEXISM

Herek (2000), a scholar of anti-lesbian and anti-gay prejudice, challenged the use of the term *homophobia* because it implies that these attitudes are expressions of irrational fears rather than potentially motivated by multiple factors. Herek (2000) proposed instead the term *sexual prejudice*, defined as negative attitudes toward individuals because of their sexual orientation, because it allows for the multiple motivations that underlie prejudicial attitudes. He posited a model distinguishing several types of anti-gay or anti-lesbian attitudes on the basis of their psychological function; each requires, therefore, a different intervention for change to occur: (a) experiential (i.e., categorizing social reality by past interactions with gay men and lesbians), (b) ego-defensive (i.e., coping with inner conflicts or anxieties by projecting them onto gay men and lesbians), (c) value-expressive (i.e., expressing values or ideological positions to consolidate one's personal identity), and (d) social-expressive (i.e., expressing values or ideological positions to connect with a social network or reference group) (Herek, 1995).

Additionally, *homophobia*, *biphobia*, and *transphobia* fail to convey the pervasiveness and institutionalized nature of oppression against GLBT people, locating the aversion toward same-sex love or gender-variant expression in the psychopathology of individuals rather than in the larger sociocultural context and social institutions that actively teach people to dislike GLBT people (Herek, 1995). Kitzinger and Perkins (1993) provided a more radical critique of the term *homophobia*, rejecting it not only for replacing political explanations of oppression with individual explanations but also for undermining radical lesbian politics by denying the revolutionary potential of lesbianism as a threat to heterosexist and male supremacist institutions.

The term *heterosexism* expresses both the institutional and the individual nature of prejudice that targets gay, lesbian, and bisexual people or people who are perceived to be gay, lesbian, or bisexual. Heterosexism has been defined as "the belief in the inherent superiority of one pattern of loving and thereby its right to dominance" (Lorde, 1984, p. 45) and "an ideological system that denies, denigrates, and stigmatizes any nonheterosexual form of behavior, identity, relationship or community" (Herek, 1990, p. 316). Current thinking about heterosexism as a system of oppression, based in socially constructed ideologies of gender and gender expression, emerged from early lesbian feminist scholarship that critiqued heterosexuality as a historically embedded social and political institution that is made compulsory through multiple layers of social coercion (Myron & Bunch, 1975; Rich, 1980). These early theorists viewed heterosexuality as the cornerstone of male supremacy and women's oppression. Small (1975) used the term *heterosexual hegemony* to reflect the pervasiveness of the culture's heterosexual assumptions and rigid gender role prescriptions.

THE INTERPLAY BETWEEN SEXISM AND HETEROSEXISM

Because normative gender role prescriptions dictate sexual object choice *and* gender expression, societal intolerance for gender-variant behavior is an integral component of heterosexism, affecting anyone who transgresses normative gender role expectations. Oppressions that are based on gender, sexual orientation, and gender expression are inextricably linked, for people, regardless of their sexual orientation or gender identity, are stigmatized if they are gender-variant in their appearance or behavior. Youths and adults exhibiting gender-variant behavior are assumed, oftentimes wrongly, to be gay or lesbian. Masculine-appearing females and feminine-appearing males, regardless of their sexual orientation, are more visible and more frequently targeted for abuse (Feinberg, 1998). Gay men and lesbians are targeted for their gender-variant sexual object choice and, if applicable, their gender-variant expression. Transgender people report being denied treatment by gender clinics unless they profess a heterosexual orientation (Green & Brinkin, cited in Gainor, 2000).

Pharr (1988) conceptualized homophobia as a weapon of sexism that reinforces traditional gender roles and institutional male supremacy. Homophobia lies at the core of Euro-American constructions of masculinity (Herek, 1986; Kimmel, 1994). Cultural norms for men not only include expectations that they be "powerful, masculine, independent, emotionally reserved, career motivated and sexually driven" (Cabaj, 2000, 16) but also that they dominate women. This means that all men perceived to be more feminine, regardless of their sexual orientation, are targeted for abuse (Cabaj, 2000). Men and boys live in fear of being viewed as a "sissy" (Kimmel, 1994). Children exhibiting gender atypicality or nonconformity, particularly boys, suffer from ridicule, physical and emotional abuse, and other forms of mistreatment from peers and adults (Brooks, 2000; Savin-Williams, 1998). Herek (1986) theorized that heterosexual masculinity, as a socially constructed gender identity, is strengthened through the expression of hostility toward gay men. This hostility becomes central to the cultural script of heterosexual masculinity and reduces the likelihood that heterosexual men will interact with gay men, thereby minimizing opportunities for positive attitudes to develop through interpersonal contact with gay men and lesbians (Herek & Capitanio, 1996).

CULTURAL AND PSYCHOLOGICAL HETEROSEXISM

Herek (1990) distinguished between cultural and psychological heterosexism. Cultural heterosexism is manifested in systemic discrimination in political, economic, educational, legal, medical, social services, religious and cultural institutions (e.g., legal prohibitions against same-sex marriage and the insurance industry's exclusion of sexual reassignment services from coverage),and cultural norms, standards, and values that devalue, stigmatize, or render invisible people of diverse sexual orientations, gender identities, and gender expressions (e.g., the invisibility of same-sex couples in mainstream cultural images of long-term relationships). Psychological heterosexism, comprising stereotypes and negative attitudes, is the individual expression of cultural heterosexism (e.g., prejudices, fears, stereotypes, hostility, disgust, name-calling, and acts of violence) (Herek, 1990).

PSYCHOLOGICAL HETEROSEXISM

Despite growing support for an end to discrimination on the basis of sexual orientation (Herek, 2002; Yang, 1997), the majority of Americans still hold negative attitudes toward homosexual behavior (Herek & Capitanio, 1996; Yang, 1997) and gay and lesbian individuals (Herek, 1994). People endorsing heterosexist attitudes are more likely than people with positive attitudes to support traditional gender roles, perceive similar attitudes among their peers, report less personal contact with gay men and lesbians, hold strong religious beliefs, be older and less well educated, and live in geographic locales where negative attitudes predominate (Herek, 1995). Research suggests that attitudes toward gay men are more negative than attitudes toward lesbians, particularly among heterosexual men (Herek & Capitanio, 1996). Little is known about people's attitudes toward bisexual (Fox, 2000) or transgender people. Many heterosexual adults persist in equating homosexuality or bisexuality with AIDS, an association that is positively related to higher levels of sexual prejudice (Herek & Capitanio, 1999). However, existing research demonstrates that personal contact with gay men or lesbians is the most effective way to reduce heterosexist attitudes and behaviors (Herek & Glunt, 1993).

Psychological heterosexism exercised at the voting booth can have far-reaching consequences on the lives of gay men and lesbians. Public initiatives and referendums in the 1990s overturned Maine's nondiscrimination legislation (Donovan,

Wenzel, & Bowler, 2000) and secured a constitutional amendment allowing the Hawaii legislature to restrict marriage to heterosexual couples (Lewis & Edelson, 2000). Colorado's Amendment 2 passed in 1992, but it was later overturned by the U.S. Supreme Court. Its purpose was to amend the state constitution to ban any governmental agency from prohibiting discrimination on the basis of sexual orientation. This measure would have eliminated all local nondiscrimination ordinances and barred future civil rights protections for gay, lesbian, and bisexual people (Donovan et al., 2000).

CULTURAL HETEROSEXISM

Cultural heterosexism (Herek, 1995) permeates every sector of society, limiting the life chances of people inclined toward same-sex love or gender-variant expression. Because of the structural nature of oppression, members of dominant social groups benefit from the oppression of others, regardless of their own personal intentions or belief systems. In her classic essay on white privilege, McIntosh (1990) delineated the multiple ways in which white people benefit and gain real advantages from racism, what she called "the invisible package of unearned assets" (p. 31). Heterosexual privilege bestows unearned rewards and opportunities upon heterosexual people.

Same-sex couples, for example, are excluded from certain provisions under the Family and Medical Leave Act of 1993 (FMLA). The FMLA requires businesses with more than fifty employees to provide up to twelve weeks of unpaid leave to certain eligible workers for the birth of a child or the placement of a child through adoption or foster care; to care for dependents, spouses, or aged parents with a serious health condition; or for their own health condition (Trzcinski, 1994). People in same-sex relationships are not eligible for leave to care for their partner, or for their partner's child or aged parent.

The legal prohibition on same-sex marriage denies same-sex couples access to benefits, rights, privileges, and obligations granted on the basis of marital status in more than one thousand federal laws (General Accounting Office, 1997). Benefits and protections granted to married couples but denied to same-sex couples involve medical decision making and hospital visitation, security for children, employee benefits for families, income and estate tax benefits, Social Security and disability benefits, inheritance, and immigration (Gay and Lesbian Advocates and Defenders [GLAD], 2001).

MAJOR EXAMPLES OF CULTURAL HETEROSEXISM Cultural heterosexism is most evident in the denial of equal protection under the law, sodomy statutes, family law and benefits, and child custody, adoption, and foster parenting. Although detailed discussions of these issues are found elsewhere in this book, they warrant mention in this chapter on oppression.

Denial of Equal Protection Under the Law Although tremendous achievements in legal protections for GLBT people distinguish the post-Stonewall
era from the pre-Stonewall years, GLBT people are excluded from basic civil
rights protections embodied in most federal and state laws. Not yet considered
a "suspect class" warranting heightened scrutiny for equal protection claims
under the U.S. Constitution, GLBT people are excluded from federal civil
rights legislation (Donovan et al., 2000) and thus lack recourse when they suffer
discrimination because of their sexual orientation or gender identity. Further,
with no federal protection, civil rights protections granted at the state and local
levels can be overturned through citizen initiatives and referendums (Donovan
et al., 2000).

Sodomy Statutes Sodomy laws originally proscribed nonprocreative sex and
applied to sexual acts between opposite-sex and same-sex partners (D'Emilio &
Freedman, 1988). During the 1900s, sodomy as a social construct became increasingly associated with same-sex sexual liaisons (Bernstein, 2001), to the point that
eight states decriminalized sodomy between opposite-sex partners while continuing to criminalize same-sex sexual acts (Bernstein, 2001). The U.S. Supreme
Court legitimated sodomy laws in 1986 when it upheld a state's right to prosecute
adults for engaging in consensual same-sex sexual acts in the privacy of their
homes (*Bowers v. Hardwick*, 1986). Fortunately, the U.S. Supreme Court revisited
and overturned that ruling on June 26, 2003, in the landmark *Lawrence and Garner v. Texas* decision, striking down the sodomy statutes in the thirteen states that
still retained them. Although rarely enforced, sodomy laws provided gay, lesbian,
and bisexual people with a constant reminder of their marginalized status, encapsulated by Mohr's (1987) statement. that "unenforced sodomy laws are the chief
systematic way that society as a whole tells gays they are scum" (p. 13). Sodomy
statutes were frequently invoked to deny child custody and visitation rights to gay
and lesbian parents, to prohibit gay-lesbian adoptions (Polikoff, 2000), and to justify employment discrimination (Vaid, 1995). Oklahoma used the state's sodomy
law as recently as 1998 in an attempt to ban gay men and lesbians from teaching
in the public schools (Haider-Markel, 2000).

Family Law and Benefits Perhaps nowhere are heterosexist attitudes more intran-
sigent, and institutionalized oppression of GLBT people more evident, than in
cultural definitions of family and matters related to family benefits and family
law. Federal public policy marginalizes GLBT family structures by defining a
family as two or more people residing together who are related by birth, marriage,
or adoption (U.S. Census Bureau, 2000). By representing GLBT people as threats
to children and traditional family values, as if GLBT people did not belong to
families, social conservatives generate public opposition to GLBT visibility, social
acceptance, and equal protection. Although most Americans oppose employment

discrimination (Herek, 2002) and the military's exclusionary policy (Yang, 1997), fewer support same-sex marriage (Herek, 2002; Yang, 1997) and gay/lesbian adoption (Yang, 1997). Heterosexual marriage remains the cultural norm denied to same-sex couples, with domestic partnership benefits and Vermont's civil unions constituting a "separate but equal" system (Bernstein, 2001, p. 436).

In the 1990s, the full force of government was harnessed to maintain heterosexual relationships as the only legally sanctioned mode of intimate relationships. When it appeared that Hawaii might legalize same-sex marriage, Congress passed the Defense of Marriage Act (DOMA) in 1996. DOMA denies federal recognition to same-sex marriages and permits states to refuse to recognize legally sanctioned same-sex marriages performed in other states (Polikoff, 2000). By 2001, thirty-four states had passed laws banning same-sex marriages (National Gay and Lesbian Task Force, 2001).

Recently, significant victories on behalf of same-sex marriage guarantee that this issue will remain the focus of national debate, legislative initiatives, and court battles for years to come. On November 18, 2003, the Massachusetts Supreme Judicial Court, in *Goodridge v. Department of Public Health*, declared unconstitutional any ban on same-sex marriage. The following February, the Supreme Judicial Court reaffirmed that only full marriage rights, as opposed to civil unions, would meet the equality guarantees of the state's constitution. Thus, just after midnight on May 17, 2004, the day the ruling went into effect, the city clerk's office in Cambridge, Massachusetts, started issuing marriage license applications to same-sex couples while hundreds of people celebrated in the streets (Gay and Lesbian Advocates and Defenders, 2004).

Massachusetts governor Mitt Romney made visible the interconnections between racism and heterosexism when he resurrected an archaic state law in an attempt to deny out-of-state same-sex couples the right to marry, using a system of white privilege to promote heterosexual privilege. Senate Bill 234, passed in 1913, barred nonresidents from marrying in Massachusetts if their marriage would be illegal in their home state, a law that many believe was originally aimed at interracial couples (Greenberger, 2004).

Meanwhile, on the other side of the country, San Francisco mayor Gavin Newsom directed city workers to issue marriage licenses to same-sex couples. A flurry of municipalities and counties across the country followed suit. Between February 12 and March 11, 2004, San Francisco issued more than 4,000 marriage licenses to same-sex couples, but the California Supreme Court invalidated those marriages on August 12. Multiple lawsuits challenging same-sex marriage bans are making their way through state courts across the country. As in the previous decade, a backlash is afoot. President George W. Bush endorsed a constitutional amendment banning same-sex marriage, and voters in eleven states added same-sex marriage bans to their state constitutions in the November 2004 elections (Belluck, 2004).

Child Custody, Adoption, and Foster Parenting Despite some successes in the courts and abundant research demonstrating that children raised by gay and lesbian parents develop as well psychosocially as the children of heterosexual parents (Patterson, 1995; Stacey & Biblarz, 2001), biases against gay men and lesbians as children's caretakers persist. Judicial decisions on child custody, visitation, and adoption vary widely among the states, among jurisdictions within states, and from judge to judge (Stein, 1996). Gay men and lesbians are still unlikely to retain custody in many parts of the country. As Polikoff (2000) noted,

> neither the increased visibility of lesbian and gay families, nor the mental health research on the well-being of children raised by lesbian and gay parents, nor the successes in the areas of adoption and foster parenting have decreased the risks to a lesbian mother or gay father battling a heterosexual former spouse over custody or visitation.
>
> (P. 334)

Although adoption policies have become increasingly more inclusive over the past two decades, allowing for a more diverse array of adoptive parents, including gay men and lesbians (Sullivan, 1995), attacks against gay and lesbian adoption and foster parenting escalated during the mid-1990s, with several states waging legislative attempts to ban these practices (Stacey & Biblarz, 2001). For international adoptions, many countries now require written certification from agencies that the prospective adoptive parent is not gay or lesbian (Buell, 2001).

When parental roles are not legally sanctioned, as in the case of same-sex couples, the rights of the nonbiological or second adopting parent are unprotected and at the whim of the court (Morton, 1998). Without protective legislation or supportive state higher court rulings, judicial jurisdictions favorable toward second-parent adoptions could easily become unsympathetic as judges are replaced (Dalton, 2001). The failure of the courts to legally recognize same-sex couples as co-parents denies children continuity in their attachments with significant adults and financial benefits available to the children of heterosexual couples (e.g., health insurance, property transfer, and Social Security should the second parent die) (Dalton, 2001).

HETEROSEXISM IN EDUCATION AND SERVICE DELIVERY SYSTEMS

EDUCATION

For some GLBT adolescents, their educational experiences are marked by stigmatization, prejudice, isolation, and discrimination (e.g., Bochenek & Brown,

2001; Elze, 2003; Pilkington & D'Augelli, 1995). Transgender students have been prohibited from attending school wearing clothing congruent with their gender identity but deemed inappropriate for their biological sex (GLAD, 2000). Gay, lesbian, and bisexual students are significantly more likely than their heterosexual peers to experience threats with a weapon, property damage, and fighting at school (Garofalo, Wolf, Kessel, Palfrey, & DuRant, 1998). Despite the pervasiveness of students' victimization, however, research suggests that many school personnel are ill equipped, and sometimes unmotivated, to handle the challenges that they confront when faced with students of diverse sexual orientations and gender expressions (Telljohann & Price, 1993).

In a historic, precedent-setting lawsuit against a school district, a federal appellate court awarded nearly $1 million to Jamie Nabozny in 1996, finding the school administration liable for violating his constitutional rights to equal protection from harm in repeatedly failing to protect him from homophobic abuse (Bennett, 2002; Logue, 1997). Transgender youths are also beginning to demand their rights to nondiscrimination in educational settings. The Supreme Court of Massachusetts, in a precedent-setting case, ruled that a middle school could not prohibit a transgender student from expressing her female gender identity (GLAD, 2000).

SERVICE DELIVERY SYSTEMS

Gay, lesbian, bisexual, and transgender people encounter similar barriers to the receipt of mental and physical health care and other social services as other people do, as well as additional barriers related to heterosexism. Existing empirical research points to an overall lack of knowledge, skills, and sensitivity on the part of social workers (Berkman & Zinberg, 1997), substance abuse counselors (Eliason, 2000), psychologists (Garnets, Hancock, Cochran, Goodchilds, & Peplau, 1991; Greene, 1994), health care providers (O'Hanlan, Cabaj, Schatz, Lock, & Nemrow, 1997; Stevens, 1992), and educators (Sears, 1991), which hinders their ability to effectively address the needs of GLBT adults and adolescents, contributing to service delivery that is, at best, ineffective and at worst, harmful. Clinical training programs in psychology, social work, and medicine offer limited information on sexual orientation, gender identity, and GLBT people (Greene, 1994; Hellman, 1996; Tesar & Rovi, 1998). Research consistently finds the persistence of negative attitudes about gay men and lesbians among mental health care providers, including social workers and psychologists (e.g., Garnets et al., 1991; O'Brien, Travers, & Bell, 1993; Rothblum, 1994). Fear of stigmatization, mistreatment, and poor quality of care deter many GLBT adults and adolescents from seeking help for mental and physical health problems (Mercier & Berger, 1989; Sember et al., 2000; Solarz, 1999; Stevens & Hall, 1988) and prevent clients from disclosing their sexual orientation to their providers, potentially compromising the quality and comprehensiveness of their care (Stevens & Hall, 1988; White & Dull, 1997).

Despite the well-documented neglect and abuse of GLBT adolescents within the foster care system (Mallon, 1998), no state child welfare agency recently surveyed had in place policies prohibiting discrimination against youths on the basis of sexual orientation or required training for agency staff and foster parents on the needs of GLBT youths (Sullivan, Sommer, & Moff, 2001). GLBT elders report mistreatment related to their sexual orientation and gender identity status in nursing homes, including the devaluation of their relationships and abusive remarks by staff (Cahill et al., 2000; Kimmel, 1993). Domestic violence workers and law enforcement officials often make assumptions that because same-sex partners may be similar in size and strength, battering in same-sex relationships must involve mutual violence (Ristock, 2002). Transgender people experience difficulty in accessing social services because their gender identity and expression may be different from the gender documented on their birth certificate, driver's license, passport, and other official documents (Currah & Minter, 2000). Keegan (2001) reported on a transgender woman living with AIDS who was denied admission to a homeless shelter because shelter staff would not consider placing her in the women's section, yet also refused her a bed in the male section because of safety considerations.

MENTAL HEALTH SERVICES

Historically, the mental health field has legitimated and perpetuated cultural intolerance of sexual orientation diversity and gender-variant behavior. The American Psychiatric Association (APA) removed homosexuality from its list of mental disorders in 1973 only after concerted advocacy throughout the 1960s and early 1970s by gay and lesbian clinicians, their heterosexual allies within the APA, and gay and lesbian activists who orchestrated protests at psychiatric and medical conventions (Bayer, 1981; Brewer, Kaib, & O'Connor, 2000). The controversy continued, however, when the APA added ego-dystonic homosexuality to its list of disorders in 1980 (later removed, in 1986). This diagnosis essentially labeled as a mental illness the consequences of cultural stigmatization (Krajeski, 1996) as it was applied to people who experienced distress or conflict over their same-sex sexual feelings.

Some social workers and other mental health professionals persist in treating gay men and lesbians under the assumption that homosexuality is a mental disorder and the client should change (Henetz, 1998; Socarides, Kaufman, Nicolosi, Satinover, & Fitzgibbons, 1997). Psychiatric treatment facilities assume heterosexuality, marginalizing and alienating gay, lesbian, and bisexual people (Hellman, 1996). Although not all bisexual people are involved in nonmonogamous relationships, polyamorous bisexual people experience oppression from the "cultural idealization of monogamy" (Rust, 1996, p. 130) and encounter mental health clinicians who assume that all nonmonogamous relationships are unhealthy, irresponsible, and immature (Dworkin, 2001).

Currently, the diagnoses of gender identity disorder (GID) and transvestic fetishism stigmatize gender-variant self-identification, feelings, and/or behaviors (Israel & Tarver, 1997) and reflect a societal reluctance to acknowledge gender variance and cross-gendered identifications as congruent with mental health (Gainor, 2000). Behaviors diagnosed as symptomatic of GID may not be problematic to individual children; in fact, these behaviors may predict an adult homosexual orientation, given the correlation between adult homosexuality and childhood GID behaviors (Menvielle, 1998). Transvestic fetishism applies only to heterosexual males, ignoring cross-dressing by gay men, lesbians, and heterosexual women and reflecting, transgender activists note, the sexist bias inherent in the diagnosis.

Not only are transgender people required to seek mental health services in order to proceed with the physical process of gender transitioning, a prerequisite that many transgender people find patronizing, but they must also accept a mental illness diagnosis in order to access genital reassignment surgery, no matter their emotional stability and psychological health (Bornstein, 1994). Mental health clinicians often encourage transsexual people to keep their transsexual status secret except in physically intimate relationships, causing Bornstein (1994) to admonish, "Transsexuality is the only condition for which the therapy is to lie" (p. 62). Transgender people have reported discrimination and cultural insensitivity in substance abuse treatment programs, including verbal and physical abuse by staff, requirements that they dress as their biological gender, and room assignments based on their biological gender, even if they underwent genital reassignment surgery (Lombardi & van Servellen, 2000).

HEALTH CARE SERVICES

The Gay and Lesbian Medical Association surveyed its membership and found that 88% of the respondents reported hearing colleagues make disparaging remarks about GLB patients; 64% believed that GLB patients risked receiving poorer care if they disclosed their orientation; and 52% had observed GLB patients receiving substandard care, or being denied care, because of their sexual orientation (Schatz & O'Hanlan, cited in Council on Scientific Affairs, 1996).

An extensive literature documents negative reactions from health care providers when GLB patients disclose their sexual orientation, such as moralizing, hostility, disgust, and roughness in physical examinations (e.g., Denenberg, 1995; O'Hanlan et al., 1997; Stevens & Hall, 1988). Lesbians and bisexual women of color, who may be less inclined than white women to disclose their orientation to service providers (Cochran & Mays, 1988), report both racial epithets and heterosexist assumptions from health care professionals (Stevens, 1994). Older lesbians, in particular, who may need to interface more frequently with health care providers, fear receiving poor quality of care or losing a long-term physician should they disclose (Quam & Whitford, 1992).

Heterosexist biases in women's health care services are readily apparent in their focus on reproductive health care needs (Stevens, 1995; White & Dull, 1997), public funding centered on family planning and prenatal care (Solarz, 1999), and intake forms and counseling protocols that assume patients' heterosexuality (Stevens, 1995). Lesbians face discrimination from some physicians and fertility clinics when attempting to access alternative insemination or other reproductive technologies (Robinson, 1997).

Transgender people report ridicule, discrimination, hostility, physical abuse, and life-threatening denials of emergency medical care at the hands of health care providers (Feinberg, 1998; Graff, 2001; Lawrence, Shaffer, Snow, Chase, & Headlam, 1996); the exclusion of medical and mental health services related to genital reassignment from most public and private health insurance programs; arbitrary denials of other health care procedures (Gainor, 2000; Israel & Tarver, 1997); and a paucity of resources to meet their needs (Sember et al., 2000). Without sufficient financial resources and lacking access to health care providers, transgender people frequently resort to underground suppliers for hormones and silicone injections, increasing their risk for severe health complications and morbidity (Sember et al., 2000).

THE IMPACT OF HETEROSEXISM: INTERNALIZED OPPRESSION AND INTERNALIZED DOMINANCE

Internalized oppression "refers to the acceptance and internalization by members of oppressed groups of negative stereotypes and images of their groups, beliefs in their own inferiority, and concomitant beliefs in the superiority of the dominant group" (Smith, 1997, p. 289). Internalized oppression not only influences coming out and identity formation processes among GLBT people but also affects them throughout the life course (see chapter 6). Cabaj (2000) asserted the universality of internalized homophobia among gay, lesbian, and bisexual people, given their socialization in a homophobic society.

Less often discussed is the impact of internalized heterosexism or dominance on heterosexual people. Sexual orientation is what Allport (1954) called a label of primary potency that "distracts our attention from concrete reality. The living, breathing, complex individual ... is lost to sight" (p. 179). Heterosexism distorts people's perceptions of reality when they learn only about the lives of heterosexuals. Heterosexism destroys families when GLBT members are rejected for their sexual orientation or gender expression. Heterosexism also prevents people, particularly men, from developing emotional intimacy with same-sex friends (Thompson, 1992).

Heterosexism discourages men from entering occupations that are considered unmanly or feminine, and it targets women entering nontraditional occupations with lesbian baiting, regardless of their sexual orientation (Blumenfeld, 1992). Heterosexism and racism interact to create cultural stereotypes of black men as hypermasculine and sexually aggressive (Kimmel, 1994).

Unless social workers understand their own privileged statuses, including heterosexual privilege if they are heterosexual, they may pathologize their clients, engage in blaming the victims, and underestimate the impact of environmental stressors on their less privileged clients (Simoni & Walters, 2001).

THE MENTAL AND PHYSICAL HEALTH CONSEQUENCES OF HETEROSEXISM

Despite the pervasiveness of heterosexism, no significant differences exist in the overall psychological adjustment of gay men and lesbians compared to that of heterosexuals (e.g., Bradford, Ryan, & Rothblum, 1994; Gonsiorek, 1991; Hughes, Haas, Razzano, Cassidy, & Matthews, 2000). Heterosexism, however, has mental and physical health consequences for GLBT people.

Brooks (1981) introduced the term *minority stress* to identify chronic psychosocial stress related to stigmatization and minority status. Research findings consistently point to an association of stigmatization, discrimination, and victimization with psychological distress in the lives of GLBT adults (Garnets, Herek, & Levy, 1990; Herek, Gillis, & Cogan, 1999; Meyer, 1995; Otis & Skinner, 1996) and adolescents (Hershberger & D'Augelli, 1995; Lock & Steiner, 1999). The prominence of bars in the lives of many gay men and lesbians, as social, cultural, and romantic centers, coupled with the stress of living in a hostile society, have been implicated in higher rates of substance use among gay men and lesbians (Cabaj, 2000), though the association of victimization and stigmatization with substance use is unclear (Hughes & Eliason, 2002). Among gay and bisexual male adolescents, gay-related stressful life events have been associated with conduct problems, substance use, risky sexual behaviors, and symptoms of anxiety and depression (Elze, 2002; Rosario, Rotheram-Borus, & Reid, 1996; Rotheram-Borus, Rosario, Van Rossem, Reid, & Gillis, 1995). Grossman (1994) suggests that, for young gay and bisexual males, societal stigmatization leads to isolation, alienation, and surreptitious sexual liaisons with older males, making heterosexism a factor in HIV infection.

Cochran and Mays (1994) found higher rates of depression among homosexually active African American men and women than would be expected solely because of gender, ethnicity, or sexual orientation, suggesting the interactive effects of racism, sexism, and heterosexism on people's psychological well-being. More recently, using data from the National Survey of Midlife Development in the United States, a nationally representative sample of adults aged 25 to 74, Mays and Cochran (2001) found that the relationships between mental health indicators and sexual orientation were attenuated when controlling for differences in discriminatory encounters, providing evidence that encounters with discrimination explain psychological distress.

Compared to other crime victims, lesbian and gay male survivors of hate crimes report significantly more symptoms of depression, anxiety, anger, and post-traumatic stress; greater fear of crime and perceived vulnerability; lower self-mastery; less belief in people's benevolence; and increased likelihood of attributing personal setbacks to sexual prejudice (Herek, Gillis, & Cogan, 1999). Internalized oppression can resurface as one's sexual orientation becomes linked with the pain and punishment of victimization (Garnets et al., 1990).

Chronic stress associated with heterosexism pervades the lives of GLBT individuals and families. Gay men and lesbians report work-related stress such as vigilance around coworkers, homophobic jokes and comments, fear of job loss, and fear and anxiety related to hiding one's sexual orientation (Gonsiorek, 1993). The fear of stigmatization and discrimination keeps gay, lesbian, and bisexual people silent with colleagues about the dissolution of intimate relationships, depriving them of potential sources of comfort (Morton, 1998). The management of self-disclosure, particularly in the workplace, is associated with psychological difficulties (Morgan & Brown, 1993). Visibility increases the likelihood that GLBT people will be victimized (Herek, 1991), and those who remain hidden may experience chronic stress associated with fear of discovery (DiPlacido, 1998). Lesbian mothers worry about heterosexism directed at their children and family—from unsupportive day care providers and health professionals to concerns about legally protecting their family unit with wills, powers of attorney, and co-parent adoptions (Gartrell et al., 1999). Children of gay and lesbian parents may experience stress related to the negative attitudes they encounter from people outside their family, public expressions of anti-gay attitudes, and fears of ridicule or discrimination against their parents (Tasker & Golombok, 1997).

Gender role expectations vary cross-culturally (Greene, 1997) and place added stress on GLBT people from ethnic minority groups. GLBT people of color hold membership in at least three cultures: the white, heterosexist dominant culture, a GLBT culture, and their racial or ethnic culture. The norms, values, and expectations of these cultures conflict, and GLBT people from ethnic minority groups often feel they must choose between their ethnic community and GLBT communities for support (Greene, 1997; Smith, 1997), a conflict that may contribute to HIV risk behaviors, substance abuse, and other deleterious outcomes (Icard, Schilling, El-Bassel, & Young, 1992).

Studies with transgender people have found a high prevalence of substance use, including intravenous drug use, and HIV infection (Clements et al., cited in Hughes & Eliason, 2002). The profound stigmatization, discrimination, and victimization experienced by transgender people, and their economic marginalization, push many to the streets, where they have limited options other than engaging in survival sex (Sember et al., 2000).

ANTI-OPPRESSIVE SOCIAL WORK PRACTICE

Social workers are well positioned to actively confront prejudice, discrimination, and oppression against GLBT people at micro, mezzo, and macro levels of practice. Tully (2000) developed a comprehensive list of guidelines for social workers preparing for practice with, and on behalf of, GLBT people. The elimination of heterosexism requires interventions that generate individual and institutional change. Because subsequent chapters will address intervention strategies for specific life course challenges, this section offers general principles for anti-oppressive social work practice.

McClintock (2000) conceptualized a continuum of strategies for confronting oppression that advance social justice: (a) educating oneself, (b) interrupting oppressive behavior, (c) interrupting oppressive behavior *and* educating the perpetrator(s) to prevent future oppression, (d) supporting the proactive responses of others, and (e) initiating proactive responses. On this continuum, interventions range from interrupting a colleague's anti-gay joke to testifying before legislative committees on behalf of civil rights legislation to engaging in civil disobedience to protest discriminatory judicial decisions (box 3.2). School social workers, for example, are uniquely positioned to provide counseling, information, and referral services to sexual minority adolescents; help GLBT youths establish school-based support groups; and provide education and training to teachers, support staff, administrators, and school boards on how to effectively create harassment-free schools (Elze, 2003). Sears and Williams (1997) edited a groundbreaking collection of essays delineating effective strategies for reducing heterosexism in educational settings, law enforcement agencies, corporations, religious institutions, the media, and multicultural communities. The most effective interventions integrate cognitive, affective, and behavioral domains; reflect cultural competency; and address the specific functions of heterosexist beliefs, attitudes, and behaviors (Sears, 1997).

To challenge heterosexism, social workers must first examine their own beliefs, attitudes, and knowledge base about GLBT people, avoiding myths and stereotypes and educating themselves about cultural and psychological heterosexism and about the diversity among GLBT people. Mullaly (2001) called for social

BOX 3.2

SOCIAL WORK INTERVENTIONS FOR ERADICATING OPPRESSION

- A high school social worker agrees to serve as faculty advisor for a gay-straight alliance.
- Employed by a neighborhood redevelopment agency, a social worker talks with neighborhood residents about vandalism targeting the home of a household headed by a gay male. With the agency's support, the residents convene a neighborhood meeting to discuss the problem and develop a plan of action.
- Social workers join GLBT activists in an action of civil disobedience outside the U.S. Department of Health and Human Services to protest the agency's withdrawal of funds for a conference on lesbian health issues.
- A state NASW chapter officially endorses an amendment to the state's human rights act that would protect GLBT people from discrimination in employment, housing, education, public accommodations, and access to credit.
- A social worker at a community mental health agency advocates with the board of directors to include sexual orientation and gender identity as protected categories in the equal employment opportunity policy.
- A social worker in a group home for people with developmental disabilities interrupts a colleague's anti-gay joke, telling her that she finds the joke offensive, hurtful, and disrespectful of the agency's GLBT clients, staff, and board members.
- A social worker in a hospital-affiliated oncology clinic realizes that several lesbians are currently receiving chemotherapy treatments at the clinic. She approaches them individually to explore if they would like to participate in a support group for lesbian cancer survivors.
- A social worker testifies before a state legislative committee about the need for increased funding for HIV-prevention education programs for men who have sex with men.

workers to engage in critical self-reflection about their position within the social order, as both oppressor and oppressed, in order to avoid reproducing relations of domination-subordination in their social work practice. Becoming an ally to GLBT people requires that social workers understand how heterosexual privilege and internalized heterosexism operate in their personal and professional lives.

At all levels of practice, social workers should create a safe space for GLBT clients, eliminate heterosexist language from assessments and other documents, address heterosexism with clients and colleagues, know community resources for GLBT people, and educate and advocate to eliminate heterosexism from service delivery systems, institutions, and public policies.

MICRO-LEVEL PRACTICE

GLBT people seek mental health services for reasons similar to those of heterosexual people who seek services, including problems in personal relationships, personal growth issues, work-related stress, and treatment for substance abuse and other mental disorders (Bradford et al., 1994; Cabaj, 2000; Gainor, 2000), but they may also seek mental health services for reasons associated with oppression. Micro practice with GLBT people should include an exploration of the stigmatization and victimization in the life of the client, the strategies used to cope with bias, and the contribution of past coping to the person's current resiliency and functioning (Cabaj, 2000). Micro-level, anti-oppressive social work practice links personal problems with structural causes, insights with actions that create changes in social conditions, and individual frustrations over the denial of rights and privileges with the necessity of collective action to secure these rights and privileges (Mullaly, 2001). Such practice aims to repair the intrapsychic damage associated with oppression and build an individual's strengths for developing solidarity with others and for taking action against oppression (Mullaly, 2001).

MEZZO- AND MACRO-LEVEL PRACTICE

Strategies for creating GLBT-affirming agencies and organizations include hiring supportive employees; providing in-service training for boards, staff, and volunteers; creating a physical environment that welcomes GLBT clients (e.g., through GLBT-oriented posters and reading materials in agency waiting areas); and developing nondiscrimination and anti-harassment policies for the protection of GLBT staff and clients (Metz, 1997; Phillips, McMillen, Sparks, & Ueberle, 1997).

At the structural level, anti-oppressive social work practice challenges social, economic, and political institutions that benefit the dominant group at the expense of subordinate groups (Mullaly, 2001). Gil (1998) noted that reforms aimed at alleviating suffering and reducing the severity of injustice constitute necessary interim goals for social movements committed to pursuing more fundamental social transformation. Social workers have long been involved in community organizing, coalition building, advocacy, and lobbying for social justice on behalf of GLBT people at the local, state, and federal levels. Local, state, and national GLBT organizations include social workers among their members. Intense political battles continue to be waged for antidiscrimination legislation, hate crimes laws, domestic partnership benefits, funding for HIV prevention and treatment services, the educational rights of GLBT youths, and the legalization of same-sex marriage (Button et al., 2000). Social workers can contribute to public policy development in multiple ways, such as through letter writing, providing testimony, lobbying, and running for office.

SUMMARY

Gay, lesbian, bisexual, and transgender people live their lives within a heterosexist sociocultural context that stigmatizes and denies opportunities on the basis of sexual orientation, gender identity, and gender expression. The twentieth century witnessed remarkable forward movement in securing greater cultural visibility and institutional gains for gay and lesbian people. GLBT people and their allies achieved these advances through education, community organizing, coalition building, creation of alternative community structures, lobbying, legal remedies, advocacy, public demonstrations, and coming out in interpersonal relationships. Germain and Gitterman (1986) remind us that the core function of social work is to strengthen the fit between people and their environments. Anti-oppressive social work practice directs us to challenge psychological and cultural heterosexism dialectically, simultaneously intervening at individual and structural levels (Mullaly, 2001), with the goal being the eradication of systemic injustice and oppression.

REFERENCES

ACLU AIDS Project. (1990). *Executive summary. Epidemic of fear: A survey of AIDS discrimination in the 1980s and policy recommendations for the 1990s.* Washington, DC: American Civil Liberties Union.

Allport, G. W. (1954). *The nature of prejudice.* New York: Addison-Wesley.

Badgett, M. V. L. (2001). *Money, myths, and change: The economic lives of lesbians and gay men.* Chicago: University of Chicago Press.

Bailey, W. A. (1995). The importance of HIV prevention and programming to the lesbian and gay community. In G. M. Herek & B. Greene (Eds.), *AIDS, identity, and community: The HIV epidemic and lesbians and gay men* (pp. 210–225). Thousand Oaks, CA: Sage.

Bayer, R. (1981). *Homosexuality and American psychiatry: The politics of diagnosis.* New York: Basic Books.

Belluck, P. (2004, November 7). Maybe same-sex marriage didn't make the difference. *New York Times,* sec. 4, p. 5.

Bennett, L. (2002). *The state of the family: Laws and legislation affecting gay, lesbian, bisexual, and transgender families.* Washington, DC: Human Rights Campaign Foundation.

Berkman, C. S., & Zinberg, G. (1997). Homophobia and heterosexism in social workers. *Social Work, 42,* 319–332.

Bernstein, M. (2001). Gender transgressions and queer family law: Gender, queer family policies, and the limits of law. In M. Bernstein & R. Reimann (Eds.), *Queer families, queer politics: Challenging culture and the state* (pp. 420–446). New York: Columbia University Press.

Berrill, K. (1990). Anti-gay violence and victimization in the United States: An overview. *Journal of Interpersonal Violence, 5,* 274–294.

Blumenfeld, W. J. (1992). Introduction to W. J. Blumenfeld (Ed.), *Homophobia: How we all pay the price* (pp. 1–19). Boston: Beacon.

——. (2000). Heterosexism. In M. Adams, W. J. Blumenfeld, R. Castañeda, H. W. Hackman, M. L. Peters, & X. Zuniga (Eds.), *Readings for diversity and social justice* (pp. 261–266). New York: Routledge.

Bochenek, M., & Brown, A. W. (2001). *Hatred in the hallways: Violence and discrimination against lesbian, gay, bisexual, and transgender students in U.S. schools.* New York: Human Rights Watch.

Boggis, T. (2001). Affording our families: Class issues in family formation. In M. Bernstein & R. Reimann (Eds.), *Queer families, queer politics: Challenging culture and the state* (pp. 176–181). New York: Columbia University Press.

Bornstein, K. (1994). *Gender outlaw: On men, women, and the rest of us.* New York: Vintage.

Bowers v. Hardwick, 478 U.S. 186 (1986).

Boy Scouts of America et al. v. Dale, (99–699) 530 U.S. 640 (2000).

Bradford, J., Ryan, C., & Rothblum, E. D. (1994). National Lesbian Health Care Survey: Implications for mental health care. *Journal of Consulting and Clinical Psychology, 62,* 228–242.

Brewer, S. E., Kaib, D., & O'Connor, K. (2000). Sex and the Supreme Court: Gays, lesbians, and justice. In C. A. Rimmerman, K. D. Wald, & C. Wilcox (Eds.), *The politics of gay rights* (pp. 377–408). Chicago: University of Chicago Press.

Brooks, F. L. (2000). Beneath contempt: The mistreatment of non-traditional/gender atypical boys. *Journal of Gay and Lesbian Social Services, 12*(1/2), 107–115.

Brooks, V. R. (1981). *Minority stress and lesbian women.* Lexington, MA: Lexington Books.

Buell, C. (2001). Legal issues affecting alternative families: A therapist's primer. *Journal of Gay and Lesbian Psychotherapy, 4*(3/4), 75–90.

Button, J. W., Rienzo, B. A., & Wald, K. D. (2000). The politics of gay rights at the local and state level. In C. A. Rimmerman, K. D. Wald, & C. Wilcox (Eds.), *The politics of gay rights* (pp. 269–289). Chicago: University of Chicago Press.

Cabaj, R. P. (2000). Substance abuse, internalized homophobia, and gay men and lesbians: Psychodynamic issues and clinical implications. In J. R. Guss & J. Drescher (Eds.), *Addictions in the gay and lesbian community* (pp. 5–24). New York: Haworth.

Cahill, S., South, K., & Spade, J. (2000). *Outing age: Public policy issues affecting gay, lesbian, bisexual, and transgender elders.* Washington, DC: National Gay and Lesbian Task Force Policy Institute.

Centers for Disease Control and Prevention. (1987, February 16). AIDS *weekly surveillance report.* Atlanta: Author.

——. (2001). *HIV/AIDS surveillance report: Midyear edition.* Atlanta: Author.

Cochran, S. D., & Mays, V. M. (1988). Disclosure of sexual preference to physicians by black lesbian and bisexual women. *Western Journal of Medicine, 149,* 616–619.

——. (1994). Depressive distress among homosexually active African American men and women. *American Journal of Psychiatry, 151*(4), 524–529.

Council on Scientific Affairs, American Medical Association. (1996). Health care needs of gay men and lesbians in the United States. *Journal of the American Medical Association, 275,* 1354–1359.

Currah, P., & Minter, S. (2000). *Transgender equality: A handbook for activists and policymakers.* Washington, DC: National Lesbian and Gay Task Force. Retrieved April 15, 2002, from http://www.ngltf.org/downloads/transeq.pdf.

Dalton, S. E. (2001). Protecting our parent-child relationships: Understanding the strengths and weaknesses of second-parent adoption. In M. Bernstein & R. Reimann (Eds.), *Queer families, queer politics: Challenging culture and the state* (pp. 201–220). New York: Columbia University Press.

D'Emilio, J., & Freedman, E. B. (1988). *Intimate matters: A history of sexuality in America.* New York: Harper and Row.

Denenberg, R. (1995). Report on lesbian health. *Women's Health Issues, 5*(2), 1–11.

DiPlacido, J. (1998). Minority stress among lesbians, gay men, and bisexuals: A consequence of heterosexism, homophobia, and stigmatization. In G. M, Herek (Ed.),

Stigma and sexual orientation: Understanding prejudice against lesbians, gay men, and bisexuals (pp. 138–159). Thousand Oaks, CA: Sage.

Donovan, T., Wenzel, J., & Bowler, S. (2000). Direct democracy and gay rights initiatives after Romer. In C.A. Rimmerman, K.D. Wald, & C. Wilcox (Eds.), *The politics of gay rights* (pp. 161–190). Chicago: University of Chicago Press.

Dworkin, S.H. (2001). Treating the bisexual client. *Journal of Clinical Psychology/In Session: Psychotherapy in Practice, 57*, 671–680.

Eliason, M.J. (2000). Substance abuse counselors' attitudes regarding lesbian, gay, bisexual, and transgender clients. *Journal of Substance Abuse, 12*, 311–328.

Elze, D. (2002). Risk factors for internalizing and externalizing problems among gay, lesbian, and bisexual adolescents. *Social Work Research, 26*, 65–128.

——. (2003). Gay, lesbian, and bisexual adolescents' perceptions of their high school environments and factors associated with their comfort in school. *Children and Schools, 25*, 225–239.

Ex parte H.H. 2002 Ala. LEXIS 44 (February 12, 2002).

Falk, P.J. (1993). Lesbian mothers: Psychosocial assumptions in family law. In L.D. Garnets & D.C. Kimmel (Eds.), *Psychological perspectives on lesbian and gay male experiences* (pp. 420–436). New York: Columbia University Press.

Feinberg, L. (1996). *Transgender warriors: Making history from Joan of Arc to RuPaul.* Boston: Beacon.

——. (1998). *Trans liberation: Beyond pink or blue.* Boston: Beacon.

Ferrante, J., & Brown, P. (Eds.) (1998). *The social construction of race and ethnicity in the United States.* New York: Longman.

Fox, R.C. (2000). Bisexuality in perspective: A review of theory and research. In B. Greene & G.L. Croom (Eds.), *Education, research, and practice in lesbian, gay, bisexual, and transgendered psychology* (pp. 161–206). Thousand Oaks, CA: Sage.

Friend, R.A. (1993). Choices, not closets: Heterosexism and homophobia in schools. In L. Weis & M. Fine (Eds.), *Beyond silenced voices: Class, race, and gender in United States schools* (pp. 209–235). Albany: State University of New York Press.

Frye, P.R. (2000). Facing discrimination, organizing for freedom: The transgender community. In J. D'Emilio, W.B. Turner, & U. Vaid (Eds.), *Creating change: Sexuality, public policy, and civil rights* (pp. 451–468). New York: St. Martin's.

Gagne, P., & Tewksbury, R. (1998). Conformity pressures and gender resistance among transgendered individuals. *Social Problems, 45*, 81–101.

Gainor, D.A. (2000). Including transgender issues in lesbian, gay, and bisexual psychology: Implications for clinical practice and training. In B. Greene & G.L. Croom (Eds.), *Education, research, and practice in lesbian, gay, bisexual, and transgendered psychology* (pp. 131–160). Thousand Oaks, CA: Sage.

Gamson, J. (2001). Talking freaks. Lesbian, gay, bisexual, and transgender families on daytime talk TV. In M. Bernstein & R. Reimann (Eds.), *Queer families, queer politics: Challenging culture and the state* (pp. 68–86). New York: Columbia University Press.

Garnets, L., Hancock, K.A., Cochran, S.D., Goodchilds, J., & Peplau, L.A. (1991). Issues in psychotherapy with lesbians and gay men: A survey of psychologists. *American Psychologist, 46*, 964–972.

Garnets, L., Herek, G., & Levy, B. (1990). Violence and victimization of lesbians and gay men: Mental health consequences. *Journal of Interpersonal Violence, 5*, 366–383.

Garofalo, R., Wolf, C., Kessel, S., Palfrey, J., & DuRant, R. (1998). The association between health risk behaviors and sexual orientation among a school-based sample of adolescents. *Pediatrics, 101*, 895–902.

Gartrell, N., Banks, A., Hamilton, J., Reed, N., Bishop, H., & Rodas, C. (1999). The National Lesbian Family Study. 2. Interviews with mothers of toddlers. *American Journal of Orthopsychiatry*, 69, 362–369.

Gay and Lesbian Advocates and Defenders (GLAD). (2000, December). GLAD breaks new ground for students. *GLAD briefs: Year-end 2000*. Available from GLAD, 294 Washington Street, Suite 740, Boston, MA 02108.

———. (2001). *Protections, benefits, and obligations of marriage under Massachusetts and federal law: Some key provisions of a work-in-progress*. Boston: Author.

General Accounting Office. (1997). *Categories of laws involving martial status*. GAO/ OGC-97- 16. Washington, DC: Author.

Germain, C. B., & Gitterman, A. (1986). The life model approach to social work practice. In F. J. Turner (Ed.), *Social work treatment* (3d ed.) (pp. 618–644). New York: Free Press.

Gil, D. G. (1998). *Confronting injustice and oppression*. New York: Columbia University Press.

Goldstein, R. (2002, July 1). Attack of the homocons. *The Nation*, 275(1), 11–15.

Gonsiorek, J. C. (1991). The empirical basis for the demise of the illness model of homosexuality. In J. C. Gonsiorek & J. D. Weinrich (Eds.), *Homosexuality: Research implications for public policy* (pp. 115–136). Newbury Park, CA: Sage.

———. (1993). Threat, stress, and adjustment: Mental health and the workplace for gay and lesbian individuals. In L. Diamant (Ed.), *Homosexual issues in the workplace* (pp. 243–264). Washington, DC: Taylor and Francis.

Graff, E. J. (2001, December 17). The m/f boxes: Transgender activists may force us to rethink basic assumptions about sex. *The Nation*, 273, 20.

Greene, B. (1994). Lesbian and gay sexual orientation: Implications for clinical training, practice, and research. In B. Greene & G. M. Herek (Eds.), *Lesbian and gay psychology: Theory, research, and clinical applications* (pp. 1–24). Thousand Oaks, CA: Sage.

———. (1996). Lesbians and gay men of color: The legacy of ethnosexual mythologies in heterosexism. In E. D. Rothblum & L. A. Bond (Eds.), *Preventing heterosexism and homophobia* (pp. 59–70). Thousand Oaks, CA: Sage.

———. (1997). Ethnic minority lesbians and gay men: Mental health and treatment issues. In B. Greene (Ed.), *Ethnic and cultural diversity among lesbians and gay men* (pp. 216–239). Newbury Park, CA: Sage.

Greene, B., & Boyd-Franklin, N. (1996). African American lesbian couples: Ethnocultural considerations in psychotherapy. *Women and Therapy*, 19(3), 49–60.

Greenberger, S. S. (2004, May 21). History suggests race was the basis. *Boston Globe*. Retrieved May 25, 2004, from http://222.boston.com/.

Gross, L. (2001). *Up from invisibility: Lesbians, gay men, and the media in America*. New York: Columbia University Press.

Grossman, A. H. (1994). Homophobia: A cofactor of HIV disease in gay and lesbian youth. *Journal of the Association of Nurses in AIDS Care*, 5(1), 39–43.

Haider-Markel, D. P. (2000). Lesbian and gay politics in the states: Interest groups, electoral politics, and policy. In C. A. Rimmerman, K. D. Wald, & C. Wilcox (Eds.), *The politics of gay rights* (pp. 290–346). Chicago: University of Chicago Press.

Haldeman, D. C. (1994). The practice and ethics of sexual orientation conversion therapy. *Journal of Consulting and Clinical Psychology*, 62, 221–227.

Hellman, R. E. (1996). Issues in the treatment of lesbian women and gay men with chronic mental illness. *Psychiatric Services*, 47, 1093–1098.

Hemphill, E. (1991). Introduction. In E. Hemphill (Ed.), *Brother to brother: New writings by black gay men* (pp. xv–xxxi). Boston: Alyson Publications.

Henetz, P. (1998, March 28). Utah social workers practice reparative therapy: Social workers oppose therapy to change gays. *Salt Lake Tribune.* Retrieved March 28, 1998, from http://www.sltrib.com.

Herek, G. M. (1986). On heterosexual masculinity: Some psychical consequences of the social construction of gender and sexuality. *American Behavioral Scientist, 29*(5), 563–577.

———. (1990). The context of anti-gay violence: Notes on cultural and psychological heterosexism. *Journal of Interpersonal Violence, 5*(3), 316–333.

———. (1991). Stigma, prejudice, and violence against lesbians and gay men. In J. C. Gonsiorek & J. D. Weinrich (Eds.), *Homosexuality: Research implications for public policy* (pp. 60–80). Newbury Park, CA: Sage.

———. (1994). Assessing attitudes toward lesbians and gay men: A review of empirical research with the ATLG scale. In B. Greene & G. M. Herek (Eds.), *Lesbian and gay psychology: Theory, research, and clinical applications* (pp. 206–228). Thousand Oaks, CA: Sage.

———. (1995). Psychological heterosexism in the United States. In A. R. D'Augelli & C. J. Patterson (Eds.), *Lesbian, gay, and bisexual identities over the lifespan: Psychological perspectives* (pp. 321–346). New York: Oxford University Press.

———. (2000). The psychology of sexual prejudice. *Current Directions in Psychological Science, 9*(1), 19–22.

———. (2002). Gender gaps in public opinion about lesbians and gay men. *Public Opinion Quarterly, 66*(1), 40–66.

Herek, G. M., & Capitanio, J. P. (1996). "Some of my best friends": Intergroup contact, concealable stigma, and heterosexuals' attitudes toward gay men and lesbians. *Personality and Social Psychology Bulletin, 22*(4), 412–424.

———. (1999). AIDS stigma and sexual prejudice. *American Behavioral Scientist, 42,* 1126–1143.

Herek, G. M., Gillis, J. R., & Cogan, J. C. (1999). Psychological sequelae of hate-crime victimization among lesbian, gay, and bisexual adults. *Journal of Consulting and Clinical Psychology, 67,* 945–951.

Herek, G. M., & Glunt, E. K. (1993). Interpersonal contact and heterosexuals' attitudes toward gay men: Results from a national survey. *Journal of Sex Research, 30*(3), 239–244.

Hershberger, S. L., & D'Augelli, A. R. (1995). The impact of victimization on the mental health and suicidality of lesbian, gay, and bisexual youths. *Developmental Psychology, 31,* 65–74.

Hughes, T. L., & Eliason, M. (2002). Substance use and abuse in lesbian, gay, bisexual, and transgender populations. *Journal of Primary Prevention, 22*(3), 263–298.

Hughes, T. L., Haas, A. P., Razzano, L., Cassidy, R., & Matthews, A. K. (2000). Comparing lesbians' and heterosexual women's mental health: Findings from a multi-site study. *Journal of Gay and Lesbian Social Services, 11*(1), 57–76.

Human Rights Campaign. (2004). *Human Rights Campaign adopts policy supporting modernized workplace legislation.* Retrieved December 6, 2004, from http://www.hrc.org.

Hunter, N. (February 8, 1989). *AIDS policy updates.* New York: American Civil Liberties Union Foundation.

Icard, L. D. (1986). Black gay men and conflicting social identities: Sexual orientation versus racial identity. In J. Gripton & M. Valentick (Eds.), *Social work practice in sexual problems* (pp. 83–93). New York: Haworth.

—— (1996). Assessing the psychosocial well-being of African American gays: A multi-dimensional perspective. In J. F. Longres (Ed.), *Men of color: A context for service to homosexually active men* (pp. 25–49). New York: Harrington Park.

Icard, L. D., Schilling, R. F., El-Bassel, N., & Young, D. (1992). Preventing AIDS among black gay men and black gay and heterosexual male intravenous drug users. *Social Work, 37,* 440–445.

Israel, G. E., & Tarver, D. E. (1997). *Transgender care: Recommended guidelines, practical information, and personal accounts.* Philadelphia: Temple University Press.

Jones, B. E., & Hill, M. J. (1996). African American lesbians, gay men, and bisexuals. In R. P. Cabaj & T. S. Stein (Eds.), *Textbook of homosexuality and mental health* (pp. 549–561). Washington, DC: American Psychiatric Press.

Kameny, F. E. (2000). Government v. gays: Two sad stories with two happy endings, civil service employment and security clearances. In J. D'Emilio, W. B. Turner, & U. Vaid (Eds.), *Creating change: Sexuality, public policy, and civil rights* (pp. 188–207). New York: St. Martin's.

Katz, J. (1976). *Gay American history: Lesbians and gay men in the U.S.A.* New York: Thomas Y. Crowell.

Katz, J. N. (1995). *The invention of heterosexuality.* New York: Dutton.

Keegan, A. (2001, July 13). Trans PWA turned away. *Washington Blade.* Retrieved May 13, 2002, from http://www.washblade.com/national/010713a.htm.

Kelly, J. F. (1989, May). *AIDS information exchange.* Washington, DC: United States Conference of Mayors.

Kimmel, D. C. (1993). Adult development and aging: A gay perspective. In L. D. Garnets & D. C. Kimmel (Eds.), *Psychological perspectives on lesbian and gay male experiences* (pp. 517–534). New York: Columbia University Press.

Kimmel, M. S. (1994). Masculinity as homophobia: Fear, shame, and silence in the construction of gender identity. In H. Brod & M. Kaufman (Eds.), *Theorizing masculinities* (pp. 119–141). Thousand Oaks, CA: Sage.

Kitzinger, C., & Perkins, R. (1993). *Changing our minds: Lesbian feminism and psychology.* New York: New York University Press.

Krajeski, J. (1996). Homosexuality and the mental health professions: A contemporary history. In R. P. Cabaj & T. S. Stein (Eds.), *Textbook of homosexuality and mental health* (pp. 17–31). Washington, DC: American Psychiatric Press.

Krieger, N., & Sidney, S. (1997). Prevalence and health implications of anti-gay discrimination: A study of black and white women and men in the CARDIA cohort. *International Journal of Health Services, 27,* 157–176.

Lambda Legal Defense and Education Fund. (2000, October 6). Students and Salt Lake City School Board end feud over gay-supportive clubs. *Lambda Legal News Releases.* Retrieved June 10, 2002, from http://www.lambdalegal.org/cgi-bin/iowa/documents/record?record = 721.

Lamoy, A., & Downs, S. (2002, March 16). Kansas Supreme Court rules against transsexual in estate case. *Kansas City Star* [Electronic version]. Retrieved June 14, 2002, from http://www.kansascity ... ascity/2002/03/16/news/2869589.htm.

Lawrence, A. A., Shaffer, J. D., Snow, W. R., Chase, C., & Headlam, B. T. (1996). Health care needs of transgendered patients. *Journal of the American Medical Association, 276,* 874.

Lee, J. A. B. (1994). *The empowerment approach to social work practice.* New York: Columbia University Press.

Lewis, G. B., & Edelson, J. L. (2000). DOMA and ENDA: Congress votes on gay rights. In C. A. Rimmerman, K. D. Wald, & C. Wilcox (Eds.), *The politics of gay rights* (pp. 193–216). Chicago: University of Chicago Press.

Little, J. (1995, November 23). New book on history of gays left unshelved at most schools. *St. Louis Post-Dispatch*, p. 2B.

Liu, P., & Chan, C. S. (1996). Lesbian, gay, and bisexual Asian Americans and their families. In J. Laird & R. Green (Eds.), *Lesbians and gays in couples and families* (pp. 137–152). San Francisco: Jossey-Bass.

Lock, J., & Steiner, H. (1999). Gay, lesbian, and bisexual youth risks for emotional, physical, and social problems: Results from a community-based survey. *Journal of the American Academy of Child and Adolescent Psychiatry, 38,* 297–304.

Logue, P. M. (1997). Near $1 million standard for settlement raises protection of gay youth. *Lambda Update, 14*(1), 1. Available from Lambda Legal Defense and Education Fund, 120 Wall St., Suite 1500, New York, NY, 10005.

Lombardi, E. L., & van Servellen, G. (2000). Building culturally sensitive substance use prevention and treatment programs for transgendered populations. *Journal of Substance Abuse Treatment, 19,* 291–296.

Lorber, J. (1994). *Paradoxes of gender.* New Haven, CT: Yale University Press.

Lorde, A. (1983). There is no hierarchy of oppressions. *Interracial Books for Children Bulletin, 14*(3–4), 9.

——. (1984). *Sister Outsider.* Trumansburg, NY: Crossing Press.

Mallon, G. P. (1998). *We don't exactly get the welcome wagon: The experiences of gay and lesbian adolescents in child welfare systems.* New York: Columbia University Press.

Mays, V. M., & Cochran, S. D. (2001). Mental health correlates of perceived discrimination among lesbian, gay, and bisexual adults in the United States. *American Journal of Public Health, 91,* 1869–1876.

McClintock, M. (2000). How to interrupt oppressive behavior. In M. Adams, W. J. Blumenfeld, R. Castaneda, H. W. Hackman, M. L. Peters, & X. Zuniga (Eds.), *Readings for diversity and social justice* (pp. 483–485). New York: Routledge.

McIntosh, P. (1990). White privilege: Unpacking the invisible knapsack. *Independent School, 49,* 31, 33–36.

Menvielle, E. J. (1998). Gender identity disorder. *Journal of the American Academy of Child and Adolescent Psychiatry, 37,* 243–244.

Mercier, L. R., & Berger, R. M. (1989). Social service needs of lesbian and gay adolescents: Telling it their way. *Journal of Social Work and Human Sexuality, 8*(1), 75–95.

Metz, P. (1997). Staff development for working with lesbian and gay elders. In J. K. Quam (Ed.), *Social services for senior gay men and lesbians* (pp. 35–45). New York: Harrington Park.

Meyer, I. H. (1995). Minority stress and mental health in gay men. *Journal of Health and Social Behavior, 36,* 38–56.

Mohr, R. (1987). Dignity vs. politics: Gay strategy after the Supreme Court case. *Christopher Street, 12*(105), 10–20.

Morgan, K. S., & Brown, L. S. (1993). Lesbian career development, work behavior, and vocational counseling. In L. D. Garnets & D. C. Kimmel (Eds.), *Psychological perspectives on lesbian and gay male experiences* (pp. 267–286). New York: Columbia University Press.

Morton, S. B. (1998). Lesbian divorce. *American Journal of Orthopsychiatry, 68,* 410–419.

Mullaly, B. (2001). *Challenging oppression: A critical social work approach.* Ontario: Oxford University Press.

Myron, N., & Bunch, C. (Eds.). (1975). *Lesbianism and the women's movement.* Baltimore: Diana Press.

National Gay and Lesbian Task Force. (2001). *Specific anti-same-sex marriage laws in the U.S.–June 2001.* Retrieved January 8, 2002, from http://www.ngltf.org.

——. (2002).[the 2002 article is not cited in text; please add citation there] *The right to privacy in the U.S.* Retrieved July 9, 2002, from http://www.ngltf.org.

O'Brien, C., Travers, R., & Bell, L. (1993). *No safe bed: Lesbian, gay, and bisexual youth in residential services.* Toronto: Central Toronto Youth Services.

Ochs, R., & Deihl, M. (1992). Moving beyond binary thinking. In W. J. Blumenfeld (Ed.), *Homophobia: How we all pay the price* (pp. 67–75). Boston: Beacon.

O'Hanlan, K., Cabaj, R. B., Schatz, B., Lock, J., & Nemrow, P. (1997). A review of the medical consequences of homophobia with suggestions for resolution. *Journal of the Gay and Lesbian Medical Association, 1,* 25–40.

Osborne, D. (2001). AIDS Advocates worry AIDS audits may signal new culture war. *Lesbian and Gay New York Newspaper Online.* Retrieved June 10, 2001, from http://www.lgny.com/0173web/NewsAIDSAudits173.html.

Otis, M. D., & Skinner, W. F. (1996). The prevalence of victimization and its effect on mental well-being among lesbian and gay people. *Journal of Homosexuality, 30,* 93–121.

Patterson, C. J. (1995). Lesbian mothers, gay fathers, and their children. In A. R. D'Augelli & C. J. Patterson (Eds.), *Lesbian, gay, and bisexual identities over the lifespan: Psychological perspectives* (pp. 262–290). New York: Oxford University Press.

Patton, C. (1996). *Fatal advice: How safe-sex education went wrong.* Durham, NC: Duke University Press.

Pharr, S. (1988). *Homophobia: A weapon of sexism.* Little Rock, AK: Chardon Press.

Phillips, S., McMillen, C., Sparks, J., & Ueberle, M. (1997). Concrete strategies for sensitizing youth-serving agencies to the needs of gay, lesbian, and other sexual minority youths. *Child Welfare, 76,* 393–409.

Pilkington, N. W., & D'Augelli, A. R. (1995). Victimization of lesbian, gay, and bisexual youth in community settings. *Journal of Community Psychology, 23,* 34–56.

Polikoff, N. (2000). Raising children: Lesbian and gay parents face the public and the courts. In J. D'Emilio, W. B. Turner, & U. Vaid (Eds.), *Creating change: Sexuality, public policy, and civil rights* (pp. 305–335). New York: St. Martin's.

Quam, J. K., & Whitford, G. S. (1992). Adaptation and age-related expectations of older gay and lesbian adults. *Gerontologist, 32,* 367–374.

Raymond, J. G. (1979). *The transsexual empire: The making of the she-male.* Boston: Beacon.

Rich, A. (1980). Compulsory heterosexuality and lesbian existence. *Signs, 5,* 631–660.

Ristock, J. L. (2002). *No more secrets: Violence in lesbian relationships.* New York: Routledge.

Robinson, B. E. S. (1997). Birds do it. Bees do it. So why not single women and lesbians? *Bioethics, 3/4,* 217–227.

Rosario, M., Rotheram-Borus, M. J., & Reid, H. (1996). Gay-related stress and its correlates among gay and bisexual male adolescents of predominantly black and Hispanic background. *Journal of Community Psychology, 24,* 136–159.

Rothblum, E. D. (1994). "I only read about myself on bathroom walls": The need for research on the mental health of lesbians and gay men. *Journal of Consulting and Clinical Psychology, 62,* 213–220.

Rotheram-Borus, M. J., Rosario, M., Van Rossem, R., Reid, H., & Gillis, R. (1995). Prevalence, course, and predictors of multiple problem behaviors among gay and bisexual male adolescents. *Developmental Psychology, 31,* 75–85.

Rubenstein, B. (1990, December 28). *Memorandum: Lesbian and Gay Policy Network*. Washington, DC: American Civil Liberties Union.

Rust, P.C. (1996). Monogamy and polyamory: Relationship issues for bisexuals. In B.A. Firestein (Ed.), *Bisexuality: The psychology and politics of an invisible minority* (pp. 127–148). Thousand Oaks, CA: Sage.

Savin-Williams, R.C. (1998). " ... *And then I became gay*": *Young men's stories*. New York: Routledge.

Schatz, B. (1987). Commentary. The AIDS insurance crisis: Underwriting or overreaching. *Harvard Law Review*, 100(7), 1782–1805.

Sears, J.T. (1991). Educators, homosexuality, and homosexual students: Are personal feelings related to professional beliefs? *Journal of Homosexuality*, 22(3/4), 29–79.

———. (1997). Thinking critically/intervening effectively about heterosexism and homophobia: A twenty-five-year research retrospective. In J.T. Sears & W.L. Williams (Eds.), *Overcoming heterosexism and homophobia: Strategies that work*. New York: Columbia University Press.

Sears, J.T., & Williams, W.L. (Eds.). (1997). *Overcoming heterosexism and homophobia: Strategies that work*. New York: Columbia University Press.

Sember, R., Lawrence, A., & Xavier, J. (2000). Transgender health concerns. *Journal of the Gay and Lesbian Medical Association*, 4, 125–134.

Shilts, R. (1987). *And the band played on: Politics, people, and the AIDS epidemic*. New York: St. Martin's.

Silverstein, C. (1991). Psychological and medical treatments of homosexuality. In J.C. Gonsiorek & J.D. Weinrich (Eds.), *Homosexuality: Research implications for public policy* (pp. 101–114). Newbury Park, CA: Sage.

Simoni, J.M., & Walters, K.L. (2001). Heterosexual identity and heterosexism: Recognizing privilege to reduce prejudice. *Journal of Homosexuality*, 41, 157–172.

Small, M. (1975). Lesbians and the class position of women. In N. Myron & C. Bunch (Eds.), *Lesbianism and the women's movement* (pp. 49–61). Baltimore: Diana Press.

Smith, A. (1997). Cultural diversity and the coming-out process: Implications for clinical practice. In B. Greene (Ed.), *Ethnic and cultural diversity among lesbians and gay men* (pp. 279–300). Newbury Park, CA: Sage.

Snider, K. (1996). Race and sexual orientation: The (Im)possibility of these intersections in educational policy. *Harvard Educational Review*, 66, 294–302.

Socarides, C., Kaufman, B., Nicolosi, J., Satinover, J., & Fitzgibbons, R. (1997, January 9). Don't forsake homosexuals who want help. *Wall Street Journal*, A12.

Solarz, A.L. (Ed.). (1999). *Lesbian health: Current assessment and directions for the future*. Washington, DC: National Academy Press.

Stacey, J., & Biblarz, T.J. (2001). (How) does the sexual orientation of parents matter? *American Sociological Review*, 66, 159–183.

Stein, T.J. (1996). Child custody and visitation: The rights of lesbian and gay parents. *Social Service Review*, 70, 435–450.

Stevens, P.E. (1992). Lesbian health care research: A review of the literature from 1970 to 1990. *Health Care for Women International*, 13, 91–120.

———. (1994). Protective strategies of lesbian clients in health care environments. *Research in Nursing and Health*, 17, 217–229.

———. (1995). Structural and interpersonal impact of heterosexual assumptions on lesbian health care clients. *Nursing Research*, 44, 25–30.

Stevens, P.E., & Hall, J.M. (1988). Stigma, health beliefs, and experiences with health care in lesbian women. *Image: Journal of Nursing Scholarship*, 20, 69–73.

Sullivan, A. (1995). Policy issues. In A. Sullivan (Ed.), *Issues in gay and lesbian adoption: Proceedings of the Fourth Annual Peirce-Warwick Adoption Symposium* (pp. 1–9). Washington, DC: Child Welfare League of America.

Sullivan, C., Sommer, S., & Moff, J. (2001). *Youth in the margins: A report on the unmet need of lesbian, gay, bisexual, and transgender adolescents in foster care.* Washington, DC: Lambda Legal Defense and Education Fund.

Tasker, E., & Golombok, S. (1997). *Growing up in a lesbian family: Effects on child development.* New York: Guilford.

Telljohann, S. K., & Price, J. H. (1993). A qualitative examination of adolescent homosexuals' life experiences: Ramifications for secondary school personnel. *Journal of Homosexuality, 26*(1), 41–56.

Tesar, C. M., & Rovi, S. L. D. (1998). Survey of curriculum on homosexuality/bisexuality in departments of family medicine. *Family Medicine, 30,* 283–287.

Thompson, C. (1992). On being heterosexual in a homophobic world. In W. J. Blumenfeld (Ed.), *Homophobia: How we all pay the price* (pp. 235–248). Boston: Beacon.

Tinney, J. S. (1983). Interconnections. *Interracial Books for Children Bulletin, 14*(3–4), 4–6, 27.

Trzcinski, E. (1994). Family and medical leave, contingent employment, and flexibility: A feminist critique of the U.S. approach to work and family policy. *Journal of Applied Social Sciences, 18*(1), 71–87.

Tully, C. (2000). *Lesbians, gays, and the empowerment perspective.* New York: Columbia University Press.

U.S. Census Bureau. (2000). *Current population survey.* Retrieved March 29, 2002, from http://www.census.gov/population/www/cps/cpsdef.html.

Vaid, U. (1995). *Virtual equality: The mainstreaming of gay and lesbian liberation.* New York: Doubleday.

White, J. C., & Dull, V. T. (1997). Health risk factors and health-seeking behavior in lesbians. *Journal of Women's Health, 6,* 103–112.

Wilchins, R. A. (1997). *Read my lips: Sexual subversion and the end of gender.* Ithaca, NY: Firebrand Books.

Yang, A. (1997). Trends: Attitudes toward homosexuality. *Public Opinion Quarterly, 61,* 477–507.

Young, I. M. (2000). Five faces of oppression. In M. Adams, W. J. Blumenfeld, R. Castaneda, H. W. Hacksmn, M. L. Peters, & X. Zuniga (Eds.), *Readings for diversity and social justice* (pp. 35–49). New York: Routledge.

PART TWO

IDENTITY DEVELOPMENT AND COMING OUT

4

GAY, LESBIAN, AND BISEXUAL IDENTITY DEVELOPMENT

Deana F. Morrow

Not all things are black nor all things white. It is a fundamental taxonomy that nature rarely deals with discrete categories. Only the human mind invents categories and tries to force facts into separated pigeon-holes. The living world is a continuum in each and every one of its aspects. The sooner we learn this concerning human sexual behavior the sooner we shall reach a sound understanding of the realities of sex.

—KINSEY, POMEROY, & MARTIN, 1948, P. 639

THIS CHAPTER will explore the concept of gay, lesbian, and bisexual identity. What does it mean to formulate an identity as a GLB person? How does that process unfold? And what can social workers do to help clients navigate the process? The chapter will begin with an examination of the etiology, or cause, of sexual orientation—specifically that of a GLB sexual orientation. Is sexual orientation genetic? Is it the result of social influences? Or could it result from some combination of genetics and the environment? Then, the remainder of the chapter will focus on the process of identity development for GLB people. In particular, a number of models of identity development from the research literature will be presented. While models cannot always account for every person's individual journey toward developing a positive GLB identity, they can serve as useful road maps with which to consider the identity development process in general. The chapter will conclude with practice guidelines useful for helping to facilitate the identity development process for GLB clients.

ETIOLOGY OF SEXUAL ORIENTATION

A common question that arises is, "What is the cause of homosexuality and bisexuality?" Perhaps the more appropriate question is, "What is the cause of sexual orientation in general?" While researchers have postulated reasons why people may be gay, lesbian, or bisexual, there has been no equivalent focus on discovering the causes of heterosexuality. That heterosexuality is presumed to be normative—and therefore the unquestioned "natural" state—is an example of heterosexism in science.

The famous Kinsey studies of the late 1940s and early 1950s were ground-breaking in establishing that sexual orientation can exist along a continuum. After interviewing more than 5,000 men (Kinsey, Pomeroy, & Martin, 1948) and nearly 6,000 women (Kinsey, Pomeroy, Martin, & Gebhard, 1953), Kinsey and his associates developed what came to be known as the Kinsey Scale (figure 4.1). This scale depicts seven different points of classification relative to sexual orientation. At one end of the scale are those who are exclusively heterosexual and at the other end are those who are exclusively gay or lesbian. There are also five points in between these two bipolar endpoints of the scale. Point 3 on the scale represents bisexuality, and the points from 0 to 2 represent a predominantly heterosexual orientation, while the points from 4 to 6 represent a predominantly gay or lesbian orientation.

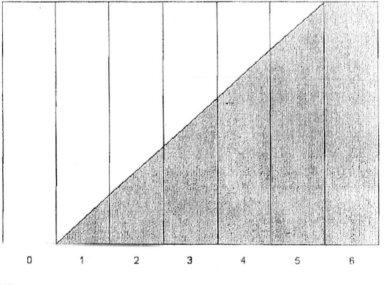

Heterosexual   Homosexual

FIGURE 4.1 THE KINSEY SCALE

Note: 0 = Exclusively heterosexual; 1 = Predominantly heterosexual, incidental homosexuality; 2 = Predominantly heterosexual, more than incidental homosexuality; 3 = Bisexual; 4 = predominantly homosexual, more than incidental heterosexuality; 5 = Predominantly homosexual, incidental heterosexuality; 6 = Exclusively homosexual

SOURCE: KINSEY, POMEROY, & MARTIN, 1948.

Theorists have debated the impact of both biological and environmental influences in relation to the formation of a gay, lesbian, or bisexual orientation. The *essentialist perspective* suggests that sexual orientation is primarily genetically or biologically determined. That is, a predisposition toward sexual orientation is basically biologically hardwired. Conversely, the *social constructionist perspective* suggests that sexual orientation is primarily environmentally determined. Social constructionists argue that sexual orientation unfolds within a context of environmental or social influences. The *interactionist perspective* acknowledges the influence of both biology and the environment in determining sexual orientation. From an interactionist perspective, Herron and Herron (1996) describe sexual orientation as being "produced by a mixture of complementary genetic and learned influences ... a genetic predisposition to sexual orientation that is environmentally activated" (p. 129). Similarly, Stein (1997) describes sexual orientation as a "set of multiply determined individual, interpersonal, and cultural phenomena that are derived from a wide and diverse range of biological features, personal histories, and cultural forces" (p. 84).

Early hypotheses about the so-called cause of homosexuality originated from the psychodynamic perspective that men (women were virtually ignored) became gay because of a dysfunctional family system in which they were emotionally enmeshed with their mothers and had distant relationships with their fathers (Bene, 1965a; Bieber et al., 1962; Evans, 1969; Fenichel, 1945; Freud, 1938). As a result, men who were gay were believed to have developed an over-identification with their mothers, including their mothers' choice of love objects—other men (Vreeland, Gallagher, & McFalls, 1995). Despite the social popularity of this perspective, empirical data to support it have not been established.

Because it is virtually impossible to completely separate biological versus environmental influences over the course of a person's development, the factors that determine sexual orientation in full are not all completely known. However, a number of studies in the latter part of the twentieth century significantly advanced the scientific understanding of biological and genetic influences in sexual orientation. For example, LeVay (1991) studied autopsied brain tissue from 41 people: 19 gay men who had died from AIDS complications, 16 deceased heterosexual men (6 of whom had died from AIDS complications); and 6 heterosexual women (one of whom had died from AIDS complications). LeVay examined the interstitial nuclei of the anterior hypothalamus (INAH). Four sections of the INAH were examined, and no differences were found among sections 1, 2, and 4. However, LeVay discovered that the INAH3 section of the brains was more than twice as large in the heterosexual men compared to the gay men and the heterosexual women. That is, the INAH3 was significantly larger in those with an attraction to women (i.e., heterosexual men) when compared to those with an attraction to men (i.e., gay men and heterosexual women).

The variable of AIDS was controlled for in LeVay's study in that there was no significant difference in the size of the INAH3 when comparing the brain tissue of those who died from AIDS and those who died from other causes. And the variable of biological sex was controlled for in that there were no significant INAH3 size differences between the gay men and the women. The results of the study could not, however, reveal whether the size of the INAH3 in a person is a cause or a consequence of sexual orientation. Nor could it determine if the size of the INAH3 and sexual orientation co-varied under the influence of some other unknown third variable.

In another study to investigate the possibility of a genetic influence in sexual orientation, Hamer, Hu, Magnuson, Hu, and Pattatuci (1993) examined 114 families of gay men through pedigree analysis and family DNA linkage studies. They found a significant correlation between the inheritance of genetic markers on chromosomal region Xq28 and sexual orientation among gay men. Of the families studied, there was a greater likelihood of increased same-sex orientation on the maternal, rather than paternal, side of the families. The researchers reported a "statistical confidence level of more than 99% that at least one subtype of male sexual orientation is genetically influenced" (p. 321). That is, at least one form of male homosexuality was preferentially transmitted through the maternal side of families and was genetically linked to chromosomal region Xq28. Next steps for research in this area would be the development of "chromosomal mapping of the loci and isolation of the relevant DNA sequences" (p. 325) that inform sexual orientation.

Michael Bailey and Richard Pillard are the two principal researchers who have investigated the possibility of a genetic link to sexual orientation by studying gay, lesbian, and bisexual people and their siblings. They investigated whether the siblings of gay and bisexual men would be more likely themselves to be gay or bisexual (Bailey & Pillard, 1991). Their study sampled monozygotic (identical) cotwins, dizygotic (fraternal) cotwins, nontwin biological siblings, and adoptive brothers of gay and bisexual men. They found that the more genetic material that was shared between the siblings, the more likely it was that the co-siblings would also be gay or bisexual. Of 56 monozygotic cotwins, 29 (52%) were gay or bisexual; of 54 dizygotic cotwins, 12 (22%) were gay or bisexual; of 142 nontwin biological siblings, 13 (9.2%) were gay or bisexual, and among 57 adoptive brothers, 6 (11%) were gay or bisexual.

In a similar study of women, Bailey, Pillard, Neale, and Agyei (1993) found that of 71 monozygotic cotwins, 34 (48%) were lesbian or bisexual; of 37 dizygotic cotwins, 6 (16%) were lesbian or bisexual; and of 35 adoptive sisters, 2 (6%) were lesbian or bisexual. In yet another study, Bailey and Benishay (1993) investigated the extent to which a group of lesbians and bisexual women, in comparison to a group of heterosexual women, would have lesbian or bisexual siblings. Of 84 lesbian and bisexual women, 21% of their siblings were also lesbian or bisexual. In the comparison group of 79 heterosexual women, only 2% of their siblings were lesbian or bisexual. Again, heredity appears to be a factor in sexual orientation. As Pillard (1998) states, "One can hardly escape concluding that there must be some hereditary bias toward a homosexual orientation—and thus, also toward a heterosexual orientation" (p. 81).

Although these studies provide evidence that sexual orientation is at least somewhat inherited, the question of exactly what is inherited remains. Science has yet to precisely explain the factors that might actually predict sexual orientation—whether gay, lesbian, bisexual, or heterosexual. Nor can science, so far, explain the factors that constitute—for some people—individual variability in sexual orientation expression over time. What can be inferred from the research at this point is the probability of a genetic predisposition toward sexual orientation that is likely also influenced by environmental variables (e.g., meeting the "right" person, existing in a more versus a less open and accepting environment, and so on). Clearly the social environment is overwhelmingly reinforcing for those who have a heterosexual predisposition, but far less so for those who have a gay, lesbian, or bisexual predisposition. For example, a woman with a genetic predisposition toward a lesbian or bisexual orientation may be more likely to fully actualize that orientation in an environment that is open and accepting of her as a lesbian or bisexual woman, whereas another woman with a similar genetic predisposition living in a more homophobic environment may never openly live as a lesbian or bisexual.

IDENTITY

Because images of heterosexuality are so ubiquitous and dominant in American culture, it is implicitly assumed that a person is heterosexual unless demonstrated or expressed to be otherwise. Because of heterosexuality's social dominance as the norm, people who are heterosexual in orientation do not have to deliberately ponder how to develop a heterosexual identity. In contrast, gay, lesbian, and bisexual people have as their task the development of an identity that runs counter to the heterocentric culture in which they are socialized. They must come to terms with having a sexual orientation that is socially ridiculed, and they must formulate a sense of identity as a gay, lesbian, or bisexual person. Doing so is a process that requires time—usually years. *Identity*, as the term is used here, relates to "organized sets of characteristics an individual perceives as definitively representing the self" (Troiden, 1985, p. 102). A gay, lesbian, or bisexual identity refers to a life process that eventually leads to the development of a self-image as a gay, lesbian, or bisexual person.

MODELS OF GAY AND LESBIAN IDENTITY DEVELOPMENT

A number of models for describing the process of developing a gay or lesbian identity have been proposed (Cass, 1979; Coleman, 1982; Minton & McDonald, 1984; Plummer, 1975; Troiden, 1979). In general, these models have in common a process that leads from an initial awareness of having a gay or lesbian orientation—in contrast to a socially presumed and expected heterosexual orientation—to a growing acceptance of oneself as a sexual minority person. Table 4.1 depicts a variety of gay and lesbian identity development models that have been proposed. The stages, or phases, of each model are depicted in relation to the other stages in the table. The Cass model (Cass, 1979, 1984), which has received the most empirical support to date, will be explained more fully in the next section.

THE CASS MODEL

On the basis of her years of clinical work with lesbians and gay men, Vivian Cass (1979, 1984a, 1984b) proposed a six-stage model of gay and lesbian identity development. She attached both personal and social components to the conception of identity, describing it as "organized sets of self-perceptions and attached

TABLE 4.1 Models of Gay and Lesbian Identity Development

CASS (1979)	COLEMAN (1982)	MINTON & McDONALD (1984)	PLUMMER (1975)	TROIDEN (1979)
Identity confusion	Pre–coming out	Egocentric interpretation of homoerotic feelings	Sensitization	Sensitization
Identity comparison				Dissociation and signification
Identity tolerance	Coming out	Sociocentric-internalization of normative, conventional assumptions about homosexuality	Signification and disorientation	
Identity acceptance	First relationship	Universalistic post-conventional phase—positive gay identity achieved	Coming out	Coming out
Identity pride				
Identity synthesis	Integration		Stabilization	Commitment

feelings that an individual holds about self with regard to some social category ... the synthesis of [one's] own self-perceptions with views of the self perceived to be held by others" (Cass, 1984a, p. 110). Cass (1984b) views homosexual identity as being formed by lesbian and gay individuals after they realize that their sexual orientation is in contrast to that of the dominant heterosexual culture:

> In essence, the process involved in the acquisition of a homosexual identity is one of identity *change* in which a previously held image of sexual orientation is replaced with a homosexual image. In most cases, the former image is likely to have been heterosexual, since the promotion of an ideal heterosexual image is one of the most prominent features of socialization in industrial societies.
>
> (CASS, 1984B, P. 145)

A gay or lesbian identity, according to Cass (1984a), ultimately includes "the presentation of a homosexual self-image to both homosexual and heterosexual others" (p. 111). She further states that "where presentation is to one but not the other of these groups [gays and lesbians but not to heterosexuals], a homosexual identity cannot completely evolve" (p. 111). Hence Cass emphasizes the need for disclosure, or coming out, as an essential component of positive gay and lesbian identity development. It is in this sense that coming out (to be more fully discussed in chapter 6) is viewed as a crucial component to fully actualizing a gay or lesbian identity.

The Cass model of gay and lesbian identity development is based on interpersonal congruency theory (Secord & Backman, 1961, 1964, 1974; Secord, Backman, & Eachus, 1964), a theory that assumes an interaction between the person and the environment. Cass (1984a) relates, "Stability and change in human behavior are dependent on the congruency or incongruency that exists within an individual's interpersonal environment" (p. 220). She indicates that movement through the stages of her developmental model is facilitated by incongruence that exists in an individual's environment as a result of experiencing gay or lesbian self-perceptions. "Growth occurs when P [the person] attempts to resolve the inconsistency between perception of self and others" (Cass, 1979, p. 220).

Two basic assumptions underlie the six-stage Cass model: (1) Identity is acquired through a developmental process, and (2) the locus for stability of, and change in, behavior lies within the interaction of the person and the environment (Cass, 1979, p. 219).

Cass suggests that the length of time required to progress through the stages of the model varies depending on the person and that people of differing ages may cope with various stages differently. She also suggests that identity foreclosure— becoming stalled or shutting down in the developmental process—can occur at any point in the model. The likelihood of foreclosure is increased whenever the lesbian or gay individual encounters extreme negativity within self or within the environment in response to homosexuality. Cass further suggests that individuals tend to develop both public and private gay/lesbian identities. She views these public and private identities as separate but related: "It is possible for P [the person] to hold a private identity of being homosexual while maintaining a public identity of being heterosexual" (Cass, 1979, p. 220). This phenomenon is commonly known as "passing" for heterosexual (Berzon, 2001), and it can occur whenever gay or lesbian people feel personally or socially threatened about their sexual orientation.

The following is an overview of the stages of the Cass model of gay and lesbian identity development (Cass, 1979, 1984b):

STAGE 1: IDENTITY CONFUSION Individuals in Stage 1 develop a conscious awareness that a same-sex orientation has personal relevance in thoughts, emotions, and behaviors. They come to an awareness that their behavior "may" be termed gay or lesbian. These individuals may begin to experience dissonance between their heretofore presumed heterosexuality and a burgeoning awareness of self as possibly gay or lesbian. Cass (1979) reports that "Who am I?" and "Am I gay/lesbian?" are burning questions at this stage of development. If individuals in Stage 1 perceive their same-sex behavior, thoughts, and feelings to be highly undesirable, they may adopt a foreclosed status in an effort to shut off further awareness of same-sex cognitions and behaviors. Cass posits that males and females may have differing perceptions of themselves regarding their same-sex orientation awareness:

> For males, showing emotion, mouth kissing, and repeated contacts with the same person may be perceived as homosexual, whereas genital contact is simply "fooling around." For females, genital contact is considered homosexual, but strong emotional feelings for another woman are not.
>
> (CASS, 1979, P. 224)

It is rare that individuals in Stage 1 would share their thoughts and feelings with others because the growing awareness of self at this stage is a somewhat confusing and highly personal matter. If foreclosure does not occur, individuals' growing dissonance about sexual orientation may propel them into Stage 2.

STAGE 2: IDENTITY COMPARISON Individuals in Stage 2 accept the *possibility* that they "may" be lesbian or gay. It is in Stage 2 that they begin to compare themselves to others and experience incongruence, or dissonance, in realizing that they are different from the dominant and socially accepted heterosexual culture. A sense of social alienation ensues, and as a result, people in this stage are likely to experience a lack of belonging. Those in Stage 2 typically still do not want to tell others of their perceived sexual orientation, and they commonly continue to present a public image of heterosexuality ("passing"). Yet, at the same time they feel a growing urge to interact with other lesbian and/or gay people — to connect with others like themselves. At times they may think, "I am the only person in the world like this." These ambivalent feelings and thoughts can lead to internal incongruence (dissonance).

There are several ways individuals may deal with these thoughts and feelings, as well as with the perceived alienation of this stage of identity development. Some people may perceive that theirs is a "special case:" "If it were not for this special person I would be a heterosexual" (Cass, 1979, p. 227). Also, some people may define themselves as bisexual, perceiving bisexuality to be a less stigmatizing label than homosexuality. Others may view themselves as only "temporarily gay or lesbian," with an intention of returning to a heterosexual identity at some appointed time in the future (e.g., "I will assume a heterosexual lifestyle after graduating from college"). Still others may adopt a reaction formation means of coping by devaluing homosexuality, believing that if they devalue that identity harshly enough, their own same-sex desires will be extinguished. If the sense of social alienation is perceived strongly enough, identity foreclosure can occur. If the dissonance experienced is not too personally overwhelming and an acceptance of being different is developed, people may continue into the next stage of development.

STAGE 3: IDENTITY TOLERANCE   Individuals in Stage 3 feel rather sure they are gay or lesbian. A sense of social isolation has heightened to the point where they begin to seek out other lesbian and/or gay people — not so much from a positive perspective but rather from a need to counter feelings of isolation and the social stigmatization of homosexuality. It is important to note that identity tolerance implies just that — a tolerance of sexual orientation rather than an acceptance of it. Upon socializing with other gay and/or lesbian people, those in Stage 3 have the opportunity to experience lesbian and gay individuals who feel positive about their sexual orientation as well as ones who feel negative about it. Positive contacts can enhance individuals' sense of self as gay or lesbian and can facilitate movement into the fourth stage of identity development. Negative contacts, on the other hand, may serve to reinforce heterosexist stereotypes about homosexuality that Stage 3 individuals have acquired over time, thereby facilitating the possibility of foreclosure. Thus, the social contacts made at this stage of identity development can be crucial in facilitating or inhibiting continued positive gay or lesbian identity development. Cass (1984b) discusses the importance of Stage 3 individuals' increasing contact with other lesbian and/or gay people:

> Mixing with the gay subculture offers P [the person] the chance to observe that it [the lesbian/gay community] offers several positive features such as opportunity to meet a partner, provision of role models who present homosexuality as acceptable,

the chance to learn techniques for better management of a homosexual identity, practice in feeling more at ease by socialization to subculture behavior, and a ready-made support group.... At the same time, P [the person] is made aware of the negative aspects of these contacts: the demand for greater commitment to a homosexual identity; the possibility, by disclosure to homosexuals, that P's [the person's] identity may be made known to those outside the gay subculture.

(P. 231)

It is not unusual for Stage 3 individuals to adopt a lesbian or gay identity when among other gay and lesbian people and to adopt a heterosexual identity when among presumed heterosexual others, thus continuing their "passing" strategy within the heterosexual culture.

STAGE 4: IDENTITY ACCEPTANCE Stage 4 lesbian and gay individuals are quite sure of their sexual orientation and have a positive acceptance of that aspect of themselves. "The questions, 'Who am I?' and 'Where do I belong?' generated in the early stages of development have how been answered" (Cass, 1979, p. 232). Individuals in this stage continue to mix with others in the gay and/or lesbian community, and the quality of these interactions continues to influence their identity development as gay or lesbian. Stage 4 individuals are more open about their sexual orientation with others—with gay and lesbian people as well as with heterosexual people. However, they remain acutely aware of the potential negative reactions they may encounter when being more open, and they remain selective about to whom they disclose their sexual orientation. Stage 4 individuals may continue to choose a passing strategy in many arenas where they are likely to encounter rejection and negativity because of their sexual orientation. According to Cass (1979), many people may comfortably foreclose their identity development process at Stage 4: "With incongruency low, a homosexual identity positively formulated, and considerable stability existing in the interpersonal environment, P [the person] is able to 'fit in' both with gay and with established institutions. For many homosexuals this proves to be a satisfactory way to live their lives" (p. 232).

Entering into a positive gay and lesbian community that fully legitimates a lesbian or gay orientation can propel individuals onward toward Stage 5 of the Cass identity development model.

STAGE 5: IDENTITY PRIDE Gay and lesbian individuals enter Stage 5 with an awareness of the differences that exist between their positive sense of self as lesbian or gay and the social stigma assigned to them by the dominant heterosexist society. This incongruence between self-perspective and social perspective creates emotional and cognitive dissonance for gay and lesbian individuals. It is typical for those in Stage 5 to feel anger toward the dominant heterosexist culture that oppresses them. Cass (1979) relates that they "use strategies to devalue the

importance of heterosexual others and to revalue homosexual others more positively" (p. 233). They may dichotomize their world into gays and lesbians (credit-
able) and heterosexuals (discreditable). They may immerse themselves in the gay
and/or lesbian community more fully than ever before. It is during this stage that
lesbian and gay individuals develop a strong sense of pride in their sexual orientation. It is not unusual for some in this stage to take an activist stance to confront
heterosexism and to advocate on behalf of gay and lesbian civil rights. As Cass
(1979) relates, disclosure (coming out) is a heightened interest for lesbians and
gays in Stage 5 of identity development:

> Disclosure has two positive effects: a) it creates more situations in which P's [the
> person's] homosexual identity is known and so lends support to P's public identity
> in line with P's private identity. On the other hand, disclosure leads P into situations
> in which incongruency is likely to be heightened. Where this becomes unmanage-
> able, P may choose to disclose on some occasions, but not on others.
>
> (PP. 233–234)

Cass (1979) indicates that for individuals in Stage 5 foreclosure can occur
when they experience the heterosexual culture as consistently negative toward
gay and lesbian people. Such a situation might result in enduring anger and
hostility toward heterosexual people rather than a working-through of anger.
Movement toward Stage 6 is more likely to occur when at least some of the heterosexual contacts are perceived as positive and accepting.

STAGE 6: IDENTITY SYNTHESIS Lesbian and gay individuals entering Stage
6 begin to relinquish the dichotomized "them and us" perspective of Stage 5.
Those in Stage 6 acknowledge that there are some heterosexual people who
approve of them as gay or lesbian and others who do not. They increase their
trust in heterosexual people who are accepting and further devalue those who
are unaccepting. Although feelings of pride are still present and individuals may
remain active in lesbian and gay causes, they seem less angry than they may
have appeared in Stage 5. In comparison to Stage 5 individuals, whose sexual
orientation may be central to their sense of identity, Stage 6 individuals might be
more likely to experience sexual orientation as one component of a multifaceted
personal identity. Their public and private identities become synthesized into
one image rather than maintained as two different images. For those in Stage 6,
disclosing their sexual orientation to others can become more of a by-product of
their identity and less a critical personal issue.

CASS MODEL RESEARCH

Cass (1984b) conducted research to test the validity of her proposed model of gay
and lesbian identity development. She tested two hypotheses: (1) Across-Profiles

Hypothesis: That subjects at each stage would obtain highest scores on the profile of their particular stage compared with other stage profiles, and that scores on these latter profiles would decrease progressively as predicted. (2) Across-Groups Hypothesis: That subjects at each stage would obtain highest scores on the profile of their particular stage compared with subjects at other stages, whose scores would be expected to decrease progressively as predicted.

The nonrandom sample for the study was derived through various resources: private social functions, personal acquaintances, a lesbian and gay counseling service, client referrals from other agencies, newspaper advertisements, and a gay and lesbian rights march. A total of 227 questionnaires were mailed to respondents. Of the questionnaires mailed, 178 (78.4%) were returned. Of that number, 12 were excluded from analysis because those respondents completed the questionnaire incorrectly. The final sample consisted of 166 respondents (103 males and 63 females).

An analysis of biographical data revealed no significant differences between subjects with regard to gender, occupation, religious upbringing, birth order, birthplace, age of first awareness of homosexual feelings, or age of first labeling of self as homosexual (Cass, 1984b, p. 155).

Two instruments were used to assess the validity of Cass's model. The first instrument, which she developed, is the Stage Allocation Measure (SAM), which was derived as a self-report measure of stage allocation. The SAM consists of one-paragraph descriptions of ideal profiles for each stage. In addition, a description of a pre–Stage 1 person is added.

The second instrument, also developed by Cass, is the Homosexual Identity Questionnaire. Initially, Cass delineated sixteen dimensions that she then related to lesbian and gay identity: commitment, disclosure, generality, identity evaluation, group identification, social interaction, alienation, inconsistency, sexual orientation activity, acculturation, deference to others, dichotomization, personal control, strategies, personal satisfaction, and professional contact. She then developed cognitive, behavioral, and affective characteristics for each dimension in accordance with how certain characteristics might fit with the various stages of development. In developing the Homosexual Identity Questionnaire, Cass constructed multiple-choice and checklist items designed to measure the various aspects of the sixteen dimensions. The following are examples of questionnaire items:

Example 1. Commitment
I am quite certain I am not a homosexual.
I am fairly certain I am not a homosexual.
I believe I may be a homosexual.
I am fairly certain I am a homosexual.

Example 2. Group Identification: How much do you feel you fit into homosexual groups?

Not at all.
A little.
Some.
A fair amount.
Totally.

Scoring was based on Cass's predictions of how subjects at each stage of identity development would respond to each item. Predicted responses were then considered to be correct responses for each of the six identity stages. Six separate scoring keys were generated, one for each stage. In total, 364 items were included in the scoring format.

The procedure for the study consisted of examining respondents' self-allocated stages on the SAM profile in conjunction with their scores on the Homosexual Identity Questionnaire.

Results revealed Stage 4 (Acceptance) to be the modal stage on the SAM, with 71 of the 166 respondents (42.77%) classifying themselves in that category. Eleven people classified themselves at Stage 1, 13 at Stage 2, 11 at Stage 3, 16 at Stage 5, and 44 at Stage 6.

With regard to the across-profiles hypothesis, an analysis for comparison of means under order restrictions was utilized over profile scores for each stage group. The hypothesis was supported at the $p < .001$ level for Stages 1, 5, and 6. Cass (1984b) reports that Stages 2 and 4 were "very nearly significant at the .05 level" (pp. 158–159). Stage 3 did not reach statistical significance. "The stage three group indicated the predicted ordering of means on five of the six occasions, but differences between means were too small to be significant" (Cass, 1984b, p. 160).

The across-groups profile was assessed similarly to the first hypothesis. All stages were supported at the $p < .001$ level, with the exception of Stage 3, which was supported at $p < .05$. Small cell frequencies precluded an examination of gender differences in scores.

To examine whether the differences found between subject groups were an artifact of researcher bias in constructing the questionnaire and scoring keys, a discriminant analysis was utilized. Results revealed 97.0% of the cases to be correctly classified, suggesting that (a) it is possible to distinguish among the six groups and (b) the scoring keys might have been limiting in maximizing group differences as well as limiting the discriminant analysis. Cass further indicated that "where results are not clear-cut, this is almost always due to a blurring of adjacent stages rather than a more dramatic repatterning of stages" (1984b, p. 162).

In sum, initial analyses revealed there may be some blurring between Stages 1 and 2 and between Stages 5 and 6, suggesting that identity formation may involve four rather than six stages. In contrast, the discriminant analysis provides support for all six stages, including a sequential ordering of stages.

Further study of the Cass model of lesbian and gay identity development has been done by Kahn (1988, 1989, 1991). Kahn (1988) completed a study comparing the SAM with the Openness Questionnaire (Graham, Rawlings, & Girten, 1985), which is a nonstandardized measure of openness for lesbian and gay individuals. In having a nonrandom sample of 62 primarily European American professional lesbians complete the questionnaires, Kahn found the SAM to be positively correlated with the Openness Questionnaire, $r = .50$, $p < .001$. In the same study, Kahn also found the SAM to be negatively correlated with a measure of internalized homophobia, $r = -29$, $p < .01$. Regarding the SAM, Kahn found that lesbians fitting the descriptions of Stages 5 and 6 were more receptive to these categories whenever a statement about political activism supportive of gay and lesbian rights was included in the respective descriptions. She suggested that the SAM stage descriptions be modified in these two stages by adding a statement of political activism that would more accurately describe the profile of lesbians in Stages 5 and 6.

In subsequent research, Kahn (1989) utilized this modified SAM in a study of 290 lesbians (nonrandom sample, 92% European American, 4.1% African American, 1.4% Latino, and 0.4% Asian American). She found the modified SAM (with Stages 5 and 6 modified to include a statement supporting political activism) to be positively correlated with all measures of openness on the Openness Questionnaire at the $p <. 0001$ level (correlations ranging from .44 to .58). Also, the SAM showed a small positive correlation with the Attitudes Toward Women Scale (AWS), Short Form (Spence, Helmreich, & Stapp, 1973), $r = .15$, $p < .01$ level. "Those women reporting more advanced stages of development on the SAM also indicate a faster rate of development ($r = -35$, $p < .001$) and openness with family of origin ($r = -29$, $p < .0001$)" (Kahn, 1989, p. 159).

In regard to the stage progression of respondents within the Cass model itself, Kahn found that 21.1% of respondents did not find the early stages of the model to be applicable to them: 26.3% of the sample reported skipping the "early and middle stages" of the model, 10.4% reported skipping one or more of the middle stages, and 26.3% reported progressing sequentially through all stages as outlined in the model.

In yet another study of a nonrandom sample of 81 lesbians (93.5% European American and 6.5% African American), Kahn (1991) again examined the sequential ordering of stages in the Cass model. Although 40% of the sample reported sequential progression through all the stages in their identity formation process, just under 4% reported bypassing the early stages, 14.8% reported not experiencing Stage 3 (Identity Tolerance), 11.1% reported skipping one or more of the middle stages, and 17.3% reported a heterosexual identity until they were in their twenties.

In another study, Morrow (1992) examined the relationship between ego development, Cass model identity development, and empowerment in a nonrandom sample of 96 lesbian women (94.79% European American, 4.16% African American, and 1.04% Latino; mean age 31.5). Measurements used in this correlation study were the Sentence Completion Test (SCT) (Loevinger, 1985; Loevinger & Wessler, 1970; Loevinger, Wessler, & Redmore, 1970), short form, for measuring level of ego development, the SAM (Cass, 1984b) for measuring lesbian identity development, and the Lesbian Empowerment Scale (LES) (Morrow, 1992) for measuring degree of empowerment among lesbians. Pearson Product Moment Correlations were performed on the variables. The findings revealed no statistically significant relationship between ego development and lesbian identity development, nor between ego development and lesbian empowerment. However, statistical significance was found between lesbian identity and level of empowerment ($r = 46$, $p < .0001$). That is, respondents at higher stages of the Cass model were more likely to perceive themselves as empowered lesbian women. In a subsequent group intervention study, Morrow (1993) found a significant correlation between Cass model identity development and degree of disclosure among a group of Caucasian adult lesbians participating in a "coming out issues" group. Thus, lesbians at higher stages of the Cass model were more likely to disclose their sexual orientation to others.

In sum, perhaps no one model can truly encompass the wholeness of gay and lesbian identity development in any absolute prescriptive way. Cass herself does not proclaim her model to be universal for all lesbian and gay individuals:

> The model is presented as a broad guideline for understanding how an individual comes to adopt a homosexual identity. It is not intended that it should be true in all respects for all people since individuals and situations are inherently complex. Further, it is expected that over time, changes in societal attitudes and expectations will require changes in the model.
>
> (CASS, 1979, P. 235)

Thus, while one should not approach the Cass model—nor the other models noted in this chapter—as absolute in describing identity development for all gay and lesbian people, models can nonetheless be useful general frameworks from which to consider the overall process of gay and lesbian identity development.

LESBIAN IDENTITY DEVELOPMENT

A number of theorists have developed models focused specifically on lesbian identity development (Chapman & Brannock, 1987; McCarn & Fassinger, 1996;

TABLE 4.2 Models of Lesbian Identity Development

MCCARN & FASSINGER (1996)	CHAPMAN & BRANNOCK (1987)	PONSE (1978)	RAPHAEL (1974)	SOPHIE (1986)
Awareness	Incongruence	Sense of difference	Awareness	First awareness
Exploration	Self-questioning/ exploration	Understanding of same-sex feelings and significance	Testing	Testing and exploration
Deepening/ Commitment	Self-identification	Acceptance and socialization	Compartmentalization	Identity acceptance
Integration/ Synthesis	Choice of lifestyle	Relationship	Decompartmentalization	Identity integration

Ponse, 1978; Raphael, 1974; Sophie, 1986). Table 4.2 provides an overview of those models and their corresponding stages/phases.

This section will focus in particular on the model of lesbian identity development proposed by Susan McCarn and Ruth Fassinger (McCarn & Fassinger, 1996). The McCarn and Fassinger model includes four phases of lesbian identity development, or identity progression. McCarn and Fassinger use the term *phases*, rather than *stages*, in order to emphasize the flexibility they believe is needed in addressing identity development. They state: "Although we outline phases in a progression, we conceptualize the process as continuous and circular" (pp. 521–522). Their model is also unique in that identity development is recognized as occurring in a twofold parallel format: personal development and group membership development. Each of the four phases of their model is characterized in terms of individual sexual identity and group membership identity. The phases of the McCarn and Fassinger model are (1) Awareness, (2) Exploration, (3) Deepening/Commitment, and (4) Internalization/Synthesis.

AWARENESS A woman in Phase 1, Awareness, becomes increasingly aware of feeling different from the dominant heterosexual culture. Her prior assumptions of heterosexuality for others and for herself are called into question. This questioning does not, however, imply self-labeling in terms of sexual orientation at this point. Group membership identity in this phase includes the development of an awareness that heterosexuality is not universal—that there are other forms of sexual orientation besides heterosexuality.

EXPLORATION Phase 2 of individual sexual identity, Exploration, involves active examination of the questions that arose in Phase 1. It would be common for women in this phase to demonstrate strong feelings for women or relationships with women or another woman. Group membership identity in Phase 2 is "characterized by [the] active pursuit of knowledge about lesbian/gay people, in terms of both the group as a whole and the possibility of one's belonging in the group" (McCarn & Fassinger, 1996, p. 524).

DEEPENING/COMMITMENT Individual sexual identity in Phase 3, Deepening/Commitment, is characterized by further clarity and self-understanding with regard to one's sexual identity. McCarn and Fassinger state: "The emerging lesbian is likely to recognize her desire for other women as within herself and, with deepening self-awareness, will develop sexual clarity and commitment to her self-fulfillment as a sexual being" (p. 523). Group membership identity in Phase 3 is characterized by an increased awareness of social oppression against lesbians and gays, as well as a growing interest in identifying with lesbian culture. It is also not uncommon for people in Phase 3 to reject a heterosexist culture that oppresses lesbians and gays.

INTERNALIZATION/SYNTHESIS Phase 4 of individual sexual identity development, Internalization/Synthesis, includes a deepening self-acceptance of same-sex desire and love as a part of one's overall identity. The woman in Phase 4 makes choices about where and how to disclose her sexual identity. She is quite sure of who she is internally, and it is in this phase that she demonstrates an integration of her internal self with her external self. Group membership identity in Phase 4 involves moving away from the dichotomized view of the world ("lesbians and gays versus oppressive heterosexuals") that was common in Phase 3 and toward a greater integration or synthesis of the person's sexual identity with the external world.

While McCarn and Fassinger proposed their model as applicable to lesbians, it has also been applied to a group of gay men. Fassinger and Miller (1996) tested the model, using a modified Q-sort methodology, on a sample of 34 gay men. Their findings indicated support for the model in describing gay male identity across all phases and in terms of both individual identity and group membership identity.

BISEXUAL IDENTITY DEVELOPMENT

While numerous models of gay and lesbian identity development have been proposed, that is not the case for bisexual identity. Bisexuality has, in general, received far less research attention than homosexuality and heterosexuality. A literature review did reveal one model of bisexual identity development, proposed by Weinberg, Williams, and Pryor (1994). Theirs is a four-stage model describing a "years long" process whereby one comes to understand oneself as having a predominantly bisexual identity. The stages of the Weinberg et al. model are as follows: (1) Initial Confusion, (2) Finding and Applying the Label, (3) Settling Into the Identity, and (4) Continued Uncertainty.

INITIAL CONFUSION It is common that bisexual people experience "considerable confusion, doubt, and struggle regarding their sexual identity before defining themselves as bisexual" (Weinberg et al, 1994, p. 27). For some people, the notion of having sexual feelings for people of either sex can be unsettling and frightening. They may feel uncertain about how to respond to seemingly conflicting feelings, and they may experience dissonance over an inability to declare either a gay/lesbian or a heterosexual orientation. The stress and dissonance of the first stage can last for years.

FINDING AND APPLYING THE LABEL Stage 2 signifies the resolution of the initial confusion of Stage 1 by finding and applying the label, bisexuality, to one's sexual orientation identity. Heretofore, people may have experienced frustration at trying to categorize themselves into dichotomous categories of gay/lesbian or heterosexual. Their discovery and understanding of bisexuality as a legitimate sexual orientation in itself brings relief and validation.

SETTLING INTO THE IDENTITY While the previous stage related to discovering and applying bisexuality as an identity, this stage entails a settling-in time during which self-acceptance as a bisexual person increases and concerns about socially disapproving attitudes from others diminish. Individuals demonstrate increasing comfort with self-identifying as bisexual in this stage.

CONTINUED UNCERTAINTY This final stage of the model seems, in a sense, to contradict the progress made in the three previous stages. Weinberg et al. describe this final stage as reflecting an ultimate uncertainty that bisexual people experience regarding their sexual orientation: "Even after having discovered and applied the label 'bisexual' to themselves, and having come to the point of apparent self-acceptance, they still experienced continued intermittent periods of doubt and uncertainty regarding their sexual identity" (1994, pp. 34–35). Reasons for some degree of continued uncertainty include a lack of social validation for their bisexual orientation as well as persistent social pressures to label oneself as either gay/lesbian or heterosexual. Thus, even though a bisexual identity has been well formulated and the person has reached a state of self-acceptance as bisexual, this model asserts that some degree of uncertainty is apt to continue over time. Furthermore, Weinberg et al. point to the possibility that the bisexually identified person may come to identify as gay/lesbian or heterosexual over time when in the context of a long-term monogamous relationship with a man or a woman. It is important, however, to work against the erroneous notion that bisexual identity is nothing more than a possible pathway toward eventually declaring a gay/lesbian or heterosexual identity. Such a narrow perception of bisexuality unfairly minimizes those for whom bisexuality is long-standing and sustainable in the same way that a same-sex or other-sex orientation is for others.

DIVERSITY CONSIDERATIONS

GLB people of color possess a "minority within a minority" status (Morales, 1989) as sexual minority people within a racial or ethnic minority group. They are commonly challenged by discrimination on several fronts: race, ethnicity, gender in the case of lesbians and bisexual women, and sexual orientation. These multiple layers of jeopardy can create significant psychological stress. Greene (1997) points out that ethnic, gender, and sexual orientation oppression are interrelated. One affects the other, and the effects are compounded. GLB people of color also face the challenges of not being accepted for their GLB identity in their racial or ethnic communities, which are often heterosexist, and of not being fully embraced for their racial identity by the white-dominated GLB communities, where racism persists. Thus GLB people of color commonly have as their task the development of multiple identities, which can include a minority racial and/or ethnic identity, a minority gender identity, and a minority sexual identity.

GUIDELINES FOR PRACTICE

A number of practice considerations pertain to assessing and understanding GLB identity formation among clients. The formation of a positive GLB identity is a process that may take years to unfold. The extent to which that identity develops in a positive form—or not—can significantly influence client self-worth, disclosure, socialization with others, and coping abilities. In general, the farther along GLB people are in the process of identity development, the better able they are to accept themselves and cope effectively with the daily challenges of living in a heterocentric society. This section identifies a number of practice guidelines for working with clients relative to issues of GLB identity development.

PEOPLE AT LOWER LEVELS OF IDENTITY DEVELOPMENT ARE AT HIGHER RISK

In relation to the Cass model, Stages 1 through 3 may be thought of as a "red zone" area of risk in that clients in these early stages have not yet arrived at the point of accepting themselves as gay or lesbian. As a result of the emotional dissonance involved in this process, individuals at these earlier stages of the Cass model may be at a greater risk for low self-esteem, substance abuse, depression, and even suicide. Correspondingly, bisexual clients who are not yet at a place of self-acceptance in their respective journey toward developing a positive bisexual identity may also be at higher risk. It is important here to emphasize that the risks referred to do not develop because GLB people are somehow inherently less able to cope in life or are less emotionally stable because of their sexual orientation. Rather, the risks relate to the psychosocial stress of coming to terms with a highly stigmatized identity and coping within a social environment where—because of their sexual orientation—people are in jeopardy of losing the support of family and friends, losing their employment because of sexual orientation discrimination, having their relationships socially and legally invalidated, and being physically and mentally assaulted because of hate-related violence.

HIGHER LEVELS OF IDENTITY DEVELOPMENT LEAD TO GREATER DISCLOSURE

Generally those who are farther along in GLB identity development are more likely to disclose their identity as GLB (Cass, 1979; Coleman, 1982; Minton & McDonald, 1984; Plummer, 1975; Troiden, 1985). Thus, social workers can anticipate that clients who have developed a positive GLB identity will be more likely to disclose that identity to others. In contrast, those who are at an earlier stage in the process of coming to terms with a GLB identity may be less likely to disclose their sexual identity to others (they may even conceal their sexual identity, depending on the circumstances). It is important that social workers honor client self-determination in relation to disclosure. It is especially a mistake to pressure clients toward disclosure when they are early in their own process of GLB identity development. Furthermore, even clients with well-developed GLB identities may choose not to disclose in certain situations, for emotional or physical safety reasons. Disclosure is, in many cases, a situation-specific event even for those with well-developed GLB identities (Whitman, Cormier, & Boyd, 2000).

ACCURATE INFORMATION CAN FACILITATE THE IDENTITY DEVELOPMENT PROCESS

Knowledge is a powerful tool for understanding oneself and one's society. Most people—including GLB people—have not been educated about sexual orientation diversity and sexual minority people. Public schools typically do not offer education on sexual orientation in health education or diversity curricula. Therefore, old myths and other misinformation about sexual orientation and sexual minority people tend to be perpetuated generation after generation. Social workers can intervene with GLB clients by helping them build an accurate knowledge base on such topics as sexual orientation diversity, GLB identity development, heterosexism, and GLB political issues. This knowledge is powerful in helping GLB clients move toward understanding and self-acceptance as sexual minority people.

POSITIVE ROLE MODELS CAN BE HELPFUL

Visible positive role models for GLB people are few, and their value is significant. Social workers can seek to connect GLB clients with positive community role models whenever possible. It can be valuable for agencies and schools to have openly GLB employees who can be available as role models for clients. Interaction with positive GLB role models can facilitate GLB client self-acceptance and identity development among GLB people (Cass, 1979; Morrow, 1993, 1996).

CONCLUSION

This chapter began with a discussion of the etiology of sexual orientation, including the presentation of the essentialist, social constructionist, and interactionist perspectives. A review of research on genetic influences in sexual orientation suggests that sexual orientation is likely formed by a combination of genetic influences supplemented by social environment triggers.

The concept of developing a positive GLB identity was discussed, with an emphasis on the Cass model of gay and lesbian identity development, the McCarn and Fassinger model of lesbian identity development, and the Weinberg, Williams, and Pryor model of bisexual identity development. No one model can always predict every individual's movement through identity development, yet models such as these can be helpful for understanding the general process.

The chapter concluded with several guidelines for working with GLB clients on issues pertaining to GLB identity development. Social workers should keep in mind that individuals at lower levels of identity development may be at higher risk for stress-related problems such as substance abuse, depression, and suicide. Workers should also be aware that GLB people at higher levels of identity development may be more likely to disclose their sexual orientation to others, while GLB people at lower levels may be less likely to disclose. And finally, the chapter emphasized the importance of providing clients with accurate information on such topics as sexual orientation diversity, GLB identity development, heterosexism, and GLB political issues, with the recognition that building such a knowledge base can facilitate the identity development process for clients, as can exposure to positive GLB role models who themselves have well-developed GLB identities.

REFERENCES

Bailey, J. M., & Benishay, D. S. (1993). Familial aggregation of female sexual orientation. *American Journal of Psychiatry, 150*(2), 272–277.

Bailey, J. M., & Pillard, R. C. (1991). A genetic study of male sexual orientation. *Archives of General Psychiatry, 48,* 1089–1095.

Bailey, J. M., Pillard, R. C., Neale, M. C., & Agyei, Y. (1993). Heritable factors influence sexual orientation in women. *Archives of General Psychiatry, 50,* 217–223.

Bene, E. (1965a). On the genesis of male homosexuality: An attempt at clarifying the role of the parents. *British Journal of Psychiatry, 111,* 803–813.

Berzon, B. (Ed.). (2001). *Positively gay: New approaches to gay and lesbian life* (3d ed.). Berkeley, CA: Celestial Arts.

Bieber, I., Dain, H. J., Dince, P. R., Drellich, M. G., Grand, H. G., Gundlach, R. H., Kremer, M. W., Rifkin, A. H., Wilbur, C. B., & Bieber, T. B. (1962). *Homosexuality: A psychoanalytic study.* New York: Basic Books.

Cass, V. C. (1979). Homosexual identity formation: A theoretical model. *Journal of Homosexuality, 4*(3), 219–235.

——. (1984a). Homosexual identity: A concept in need of definition. *Journal of Homosexuality, 9*(2/3), 105–126.

——. (1984b). Homosexual identity formation: Testing a theoretical model. *Journal of Sex Research, 20*(2), 143–167.

Chapman, B. E., & Brannock, J. C. (1987). Proposed model of lesbian identity development: An empirical examination. *Journal of Homosexuality, 14*(3/4), 69–80.

Coleman, E. (1982). Developmental stages of the coming out process. *Journal of Homosexuality, 7*(7), 31–43.

Evans, R. B. (1969). Childhood parental relationships of homosexual men. *Journal of Consulting Clinical Psychology, 33,* 129–135.

Fassinger, R. E., & Miller, B. A. (1996). Validation of an inclusive model of sexual minority identity formation on a sample of gay men. *Journal of Homosexuality, 32*(2), 53–78.

Fenichel, O. (1945). *Psychoanalytic theory of neurosis.* New York: Norton.

Freud, S. (1938). *The basic writings of Sigmund Freud.* New York: Modern Library.

Graham, D., Rawlings, E., & Girten, A. (1985). *Are closets healthy?* Unpublished manuscript, University of Cincinnati.

Greene, B. (1997). Family, ethnic identity, and sexual orientation: African American lesbians and gay men. In B. Greene (Ed.), *Ethnic and cultural diversity among lesbians and gay men* (pp. 40–52). Thousand Oaks, CA: Sage.

Hamer, D. H., Hu, S., Magnuson, V. L., Hu, N., & Pattatuci, A. M. (1993). A linkage between DNA markers on the X chromosome and male sexual orientation. *Science, 261,* 321–327.

Herron, W. G., & Herron, M. J. (1996). The complexity of sexuality. *Psychological Reports, 78,* 129–130.

Kahn, M. J. (1988). *Factors affecting the coming out process.* Paper presented at the annual conference of the Association of Women in Psychology, Bethesda, MD.

——. (1989). Factors related to the coming out process for lesbians. *Dissertation Abstracts International, 51*/07B, 3590.

——. (1991). Factors affecting the coming out process for lesbians. *Journal of Homosexuality, 22*(3), 47–70.

Kinsey, A. C., Pomeroy, W. B., & Martin, C. E. (1948). *Sexual behavior in the human male.* Philadelphia: W. B. Saunders.

Kinsey, A. C., Pomeroy, W. B., Martin, C. E., & Gebhard, P. H. (1953). *Sexual behavior in the human female.* Philadelphia: W. B. Saunders.

LeVay, S. (1991). A difference in hypothalamic structure between heterosexual and homosexual men. *Science, 253,* 1034–1037.

Loevinger, J. (1985). Revision of the sentence completion test for ego development. *Journal of Personality and Social Psychology, 48,* 420–427.

Loevinger, J., & Wessler, R. (1970). *Measuring ego development. 1. Construction and use of a sentence completion test.* San Francisco: Jossey Bass.

Loevinger, J., Wessler, R., & Redmore, C. (1970). *Measuring ego development. 2. Scoring manual for women and girls.* San Francisco: Jossey-Bass.

McCarn, S. R., & Fassinger, R. E. (1996). Revisioning sexual minority identity formation: A new model of lesbian identity and its implications for counseling and research. *Counseling Psychologist, 24,* 508–534.

Minton, H. L. S., & McDonald, G. J. (1984). Homosexual identity formation as a developmental process. *Journal of Homosexuality, 9*(2/3), 91–104.

Morrow, D. F. (1992). *An exploration of the relationship between ego development, lesbian identity development, and lesbian empowerment.* Unpublished manuscript, North Carolina State University, Raleigh, NC.

———. (1993). Lesbian identity development through group process: An exploration of coming out issues. *Dissertation Abstracts International, 54–*02, 0428.

———. (1996). Coming out issues for adult lesbians: A group intervention. *Social Work, 41*(6), 647–656.

Pillard, R. C. (1998). Biologic theories of homosexuality. *Journal of Gay and Lesbian Psychotherapy, 2*(4), 75–85.

Plummer, L. (1975). *Sexual stigma.* Boston: Routledge and Kegan Paul.

Ponse, B. (1978). *Identities in the lesbian world.* Westport, CT: Greenwood.

Raphael, S. (1974). Coming out: The emergence of the movement lesbian. *Dissertation Abstracts International, 35/*08-A, 5536.

Secord, P. F., & Backman, C. W. (1961). Personality theory and the problem of stability and change in individual behaviour: An interpersonal approach. *Psychological Review 68,* 21–32.

———. (1964). Interpersonal congruency, perceived similarity, and friendship. *Sociometry 27,* 115–127.

———. (1974). *Social psychology* (2d ed.). Tokyo: McGraw-Hill.

Secord, P. F., Backman, C. W., & Eachus, H. T. (1964). Effects of imbalance in the self-concept on the perception of persons. *Journal of Abnormal and Social Psychology, 68,* 442–446.

Sophie, J. (1986). A critical examination of stage theories of lesbian identity development. *Journal of Homosexuality, 12*(2), 39–51.

Spence, J., Helmreich, R., & Stapp, J. (1973). A short version of the Attitudes Towards Women scale (AWS). *Bulletin of the Psychodynamic Society, 2,* 219–220.

Stein, T. S. (1997). Deconstructing sexual orientation: Understanding the phenomena of sexual orientation. *Journal of Homosexuality, 34*(1), 81–85.

Troiden, R. R. (1979). Becoming homosexual: A model of gay identity acquisition. *Psychiatry, 42,* 362–373.

———. (1985). Self, self-concept, identity, and homosexual identity: Constructs in need of definition and differentiation. *Journal of Homosexuality, 10*(3/4), 97–109.

Vreeland, C. N., Gallagher, B. J., & McFalls, J. A. (1995). The beliefs of members of the American Psychiatric Association on the etiology of male homosexuality: A national survey. *Journal of Psychology, 120*(5), 507–517.

Weinberg, M. S., Williams, C. J., & Pryor, D. W. (1994). *Dual attraction: Understanding bisexuality*. New York: Oxford University Press.

Whitman, J. S., Cormier, S., & Boyd, C. J. (2000). Lesbian identity management at various stages of the coming out process: A qualitative study. *International Journal of Sexuality and Gender Studies, 5*(1), 3–18.

5

TRANSGENDER IDENTITY

James I. Martin and D. R. Yonkin

And just as chaos theory in the nineteenth century disrupted reductionistic and mechanistic views of the universe, transgender theory as we near the twenty-first century is shaking up reductionistic and mechanistic ideas of the "known" body we live in. Fixed ideas of gender bipolarism are wavering, forging a revolution on bodies and consciousness that embraces their complexity. From this new vantage the emergence of at least 50 billion galaxies of gender becomes a distinct possibility.

—MACKENZIE, 1999, P. 193

THERE IS evidence of gender-variant experience throughout history and across cultures (Green, 1998). People of gender-variant experience are found throughout the world today. Some examples include *hijras* and *sādhins* in India; *travetís*, *bichas*, and *viados* in Brazil; *mahus* in Hawaii/Polynesia; and *kathoeys* in Thailand. Because conceptions about gender are socially constructed, manifestations of gender variance and their meanings are shaped by social and cultural influences (Nanda, 2000). Accordingly, gender-variant people have been understood in a variety of ways among cultures and across history.

Although the United States is often mythologized as a melting pot of many ethnic and religious groups, acceptance and integration have seldom been simple. Gender variance has faced significant challenges in this country, even during the earliest days of settlement. Among North America's First Nations worldviews arose from multiple perspectives based upon varied life and spiritual experiences, creating an extraordinary constellation of gender role systems. For Native Americans the Anglo-Western view of a fixed gender/sexual identity, which was imposed upon them, was considered unnatural and discordant (Kehoe, 1997).

Transgender is the term that is often held up as the designated "umbrella" over the many self-identifying phrases and labels manifesting from within and outside the various gender-variant cultures. However, it is quickly giving way to the simpler and more impartial *trans*, by itself and in conjunction with other terms. There is still little standardization of the language around trans experiences, which also tend to be complicated by various political, medical, and personal agendas in academic literature. Also, transpeople may have their own understandings of terms and phrases that differ from those used by academics and other professionals.

Self-identifying terms that trans individuals and communities use may include *transgendered* (TG), *transgenderist*, *gender-variant*, *gender different*, *bi-gendered*, *gender-queer*, and *multi-gendered*. *Male-to-female* (MTF or M2F) and *transwoman* refer to people who are male-bodied and female-gendered. *Female-to-male* (FTM or F2M) and *transman* refer to those who are female-bodied and male-gendered. *Transition* refers to the process of bringing the body in line with the internal gender experience through surgery and/or hormones. Elkins and King (1998) asserted that terms such as *transsexual* and *transvestite* presume pathology, narrow the range of trans phenomena, and promote the study of characteristics while ignoring behavior. The term *two-spirit* is used by some Native Americans who do not identify with traditional Western gender roles or heterosexual sexual orientation. *Cross-dresser* (CD) refers to individuals who dress in the clothing of the "opposite" gender. Although the term *hermaphrodite* is still used sometimes for those with atypical reproductive anatomies, it is rapidly being replaced by *intersex*. Gender-variant experience is not related to sexual orientation, as transpeople and intersex people experience the same variety of sexual orientation identities as other people do.

CROSS-DRESSERS

Dressing in the clothing typically associated with the opposite gender was considered either illegal or pathological during much of the last hundred years in the United States. The American Psychiatric Association (APA) still considers such activity to be a mental illness if it is accompanied by sexual arousal (APA, 2000). However, cross-dressing has often been accepted across cultures and throughout history, especially in the context of the performing arts.

Hirschfeld (1910), writing in German, first coined the label *transvestite* for those who obtained erotic pleasure from cross-dressing, noting that such people could be either homosexual or heterosexual. Until fairly recently, most of those who today might consider themselves transgender were labeled either transvestites or transsexuals, using a variety of classification schemes (Cole, Denny, Eyler, & Samons, 2000). In general, those who enjoyed cross-dressing but did not wish to feminize their male bodies or masculinize their female bodies were labeled transvestites. Further differentiations were sometimes made between those who obtained sexual pleasure from cross-dressing and those who did not, and between those who encapsulated their cross-dressing activity and those who wished to cross-dress in public (Bullough & Bullough, 1997). Nearly all of the attention and concern about transvestism was focused on cross-dressing men; little was written about women who cross-dressed. However, today there is an increasingly visible culture of cross-dressing among lesbians who may self-identify as drag kings or butches (Warren, 2001).

Benjamin (1997) claimed that most male transvestites are heterosexual, and in many cases married. In one study of cross-dressing men (Docter & Prince, 1997), 87% of the participants self-identified as heterosexual, with 60% married at the time the survey was conducted. Eighty percent reported that cross-dressing allowed them simply to express a different part of themselves, and three-quarters felt themselves to be "a man with a feminine side" (p. 597). Sixty percent considered their gender identity to be equally masculine and feminine. More than 80% reported that their wives knew about their cross-dressing, with nearly a third knowing about it before they married. Only 19% of the wives reported feeling "completely antagonistic" (p. 595) about the cross-dressing. Beginning in the 1950s, some cross-dressing men began to organize support organizations such as the early Hose and Heels Club and Tri-Ess: The Society for the Second Self, which continues to exist today (Cole et al., 2000).

Cross-dressing is also found among men with same-gender sexual orientation, who are more likely to cross-dress for entertainment or sexual purposes (Whitam, 1997). Within gay male culture, dressing up in outrageous female drag is commonly done for fun, particularly on special occasions like Halloween or Gay Pride celebrations. According to Chauncey (1994), dressing in drag long predates the construction of contemporary gay male identities. For example, as early as the 1920s, Harlem was the site of numerous drag balls drawing hundreds, even thousands, of extravagantly dressed men. In the late nineteenth century, it was common for some men to seek sex with masculine-identified — often heterosexual — men by dressing and acting like women. Although this aspect of gay culture gradually disappeared in the second half of the twentieth century (Chauncey, 1994), it may still be found among some men engaged in sex work in major cities (Boles & Elifson, 1994).

INTERSEXED PEOPLE

Intersexed people are born with genetic and/or hormonal attributes of both males and females, with atypical external genitalia and/or internal reproductive systems. Intersex support and advocacy groups that seek to destigmatize and depathologize intersexed conditions widely reject the older term *hermaphrodite*. These groups also promote the term *atypical genitalia* to describe their reproductive features (AIS Support Group Australia, 2002). Estimates of intersexed births range from

2 per 1,000 (Intersex Support, 2001) to 17 per 1,000 (Fausto-Sterling, 2000). Intersexed people may not necessarily identify as trans. However, like transpeople, they experience maltreatment and discrimination because their existence challenges the binary assumptions of sex and gender (Dreger, 1999).

According to American medical practice, sex is conditionally assigned at birth according to whether there is a penis of acceptable size. If there is, the child is assigned male sex; otherwise the child is assigned female sex (Hubbard, 1998). Scientists can now determine a child's chromosomal and hormonal sex, but these factors are often preempted by sociocultural factors (Kessler, 2000). Medical teams often treat an intersex birth as an emergency, although the child's health is seldom in danger. When a child classified as female is born with an atypically large (masculinized) clitoris, it is often surgically reduced or removed as soon as possible. Additional surgical procedures are often needed, which can cause painful scarring (Fausto-Sterling, 2000). Sex reassignment is forced upon some children later in their lives, and they are coerced into undergoing surgeries and abandoning the gender in which they may already feel secure (Dreger, 1999).

Parents are not always fully informed about their child's intersexed condition, and genital surgery may be performed without their consent (Fausto-Sterling, 2000). They usually comply with doctors' requests to raise the child without ambiguity, keeping the circumstances secret from the child (Kipnis & Diamond, 1998). Consequently, some adults have no knowledge that they were born intersexed.

As intersexed individuals have increasingly come together and shared their common experiences, organizations such as the Intersex Society of North America (1994) seek the adoption of a new medical model. For example, they state that surgery should be avoided unless it is medically necessary. They advocate for qualified mental health care for the child and family and for the empowerment of intersexed people toward understanding their status and their ability to choose or reject medical intervention.

GENDER AND THEORIES OF ITS DEVELOPMENT

Gender typically refers to the subjective, social status of a person as a woman or a man (Devor, 1998). Originally a linguistic term to designate masculine, feminine, or neuter nouns, the term *gender* was adapted in 1955 by sexologist John Money (1994) in order to better convey the relationship between biological and social influences on male and female identities. Gender is a social construct, and a culture's social systems are grounded in gender-based concepts (Kessler, 2000). Members of social systems learn *gender roles* that are consistent with these cultural beliefs, along with the signs and symbols of these roles, such as names and pronouns, appropriate ways to speak, move, and dress, and occupational choices.

Gender identity is the innate sense of being a man, woman, or other gender such as trans. Being internally felt, it is private and invisible. Gender expression is the communication of one's gender. Only if people choose to disclose their gender identity is it possible to know whether it matches their gender expression (Brown & Rounsley, 1996). People are seen as gender-congruent if their gender identity, gender role, and all its associated symbols are in agreement (Bullough, 2000) and gender-variant when any of these aspects of self-identity or self-expression seem incongruent with each other or with the person's sex (Devor, 1998).

Although there are numerous theories on the development of gender identity in general, very few examine transgender identities. Attempts during the last forty years to identify the biopsychosocial processes that explain how and why transgenderism/transsexualism occurs have yielded inconclusive results (Cole et al., 2000; Michel, Mormont, & Legros, 2001). Gagné and Tewksbury (1998) noted that one limitation of much of the research on trans individuals is that it has come from medical, psychiatric, or deviance perspectives, with limited consideration given to the social contexts in which these people live. Another shortcoming of this research is that most has focused only on MTF individuals (Devor, 1997).

In addition, studies that seek to explain why transgenderism occurs assume that this is an important question to answer. Cole et al. (2000) challenge this assumption, asserting, "Why should it matter if someone wishes to crossdress, change sex, or engage in same-sex sexual behavior? It is one's right to do so. Etiologic investigation (or speculation) has tended to obscure this central truth" (p. 151). Unlike the theories summarized below, sociological theories hold that gender is a social construction (Bussey & Bandura, 1999) and that gender role behaviors are maintained through social structures and practices that reinforce the greater power and status of male gender (Eagly, 1987). In addition, conceptualizations of gender as dichotomous tend to be gross overgeneralizations that ignore vast differences within the categories of male and female (Bussey & Bandura, 1999).

BIOLOGICAL THEORIES

These theories propose that differences between male and female gender developed over the course of human evolutionary history because they were adaptive, especially in ensuring reproductive success. Biological theories assume that gender should be consistent with biological sex and that there are only two genders and two sexes; some propose that hormones regulate gender differences. None of these theories has been strongly supported by empirical research, however, since studies testing them have found conflicting results or results with low explanatory power. Thus the degree of influence that genetics and hormones have on gender development (especially among individuals rather than populations) is likely to be small (Bussey & Bandura, 1999). Research on transgenderism has assumed that it expresses either a genetic abnormality or an abnormal fetal environment. However, another possibility is that transgenderism is not abnormal; it exists among humans because it too has served an evolutionary purpose. Research has not examined this alternative biological perspective.

PSYCHOLOGICAL THEORIES

PSYCHOANALYTIC THEORY Freud theorized that people become gendered in childhood as part of a developmental process of psychosexual stages. Freudian psychoanalytic theory focuses on the unconscious psychic conflicts of children whose awareness of their genitals around age three or four gives rise to erotic fantasies concerning their other-sex parent and feelings of rivalry with their same-sex parent. Freud labeled a son's inevitable erotic attraction to his mother and hostility and jealousy toward his father as the Oedipus complex; attraction of a daughter to her father and rivalry with her mother was labeled the Electra complex. Children could resolve these situations only by identifying with their same-sex parent and repressing their desire for their other-sex parent. The result would be a male gender identity among boys, a female gender identity among girls, and a heterosexual sexual orientation for both (Brannon, 2002).

A number of alternate versions of this theory have been proposed by other psychoanalytic writers, such as Horney (1939) and Chodorow (1978); however, there is no empirical evidence supporting either Freud's original theory or these alternatives (Brannon, 2002; Bussey & Bandura, 1999). According to such theories, when transgenderism develops it would presumably indicate an abnormal or unsuccessful resolution of the Oedipus complex.

SOCIAL LEARNING THEORY This formulation views the development of gender from the perspective of Skinner's (1969) principles of operant conditioning. According to Skinner, children learn to adopt gender role behaviors that have reinforcing consequences. For example, if a young girl plays with a doll and her parent joins in, she is likely to play with a doll again; similarly, if she is scolded for playing with a truck, she might avoid trucks as toys in the future (Brannon, 2002). In addition to operant conditioning, learning through observation of modeled behavior, as described by Mischel (1966), is also important in this theory. Children are most likely to learn behaviors modeled by others whom they regard as having power or prestige, or as being similar to them in some way, especially if the behavior is rewarded (Brannon, 2002). In addition to parents, children's teachers, their peers, and the media are also important sources of gender role behavior modeling (Hardy, 1995).

Social learning theory is primarily concerned with behavior; it does not seek to explain how a core sense of gender, or gender identity, develops. In addition, there is little evidence of widespread reward of gender-variant behavior in the childhoods of transpeople. On the contrary, such behaviors are often harshly rejected (Grossman & D'Augelli, in press). Nevertheless, this theory would predict that children learn gender-variant behaviors that are modeled by others who are seen as powerful or prestigious, especially if they receive reinforcement when they display such behaviors.

COGNITIVE-DEVELOPMENTAL THEORY Kohlberg (1981) theorized that children's gender identity (called *gender constancy* in this theory) structures and regulates the development of appropriate gender role behavior through a series of stages. According to this theory, children develop gender awareness (called *gender identity*) by the age of three from what they see and hear from people around them, and they are then led by their developing cognitive processes to form gender stability (belief that one's gender does not change over time) and gender consistency (belief that one's gender does not change with clothes, hairstyle, or play activities). They then fit their behavior to these concepts, negotiating gender consistency by age seven. The theory also proposes that because cognitive consistency is inherently gratifying, appropriate gender role behaviors are rewarding (Bussey & Bandura, 1999).

Although there is some empirical support for components of this theory (e.g., Kuhn, Nash, & Brucken, 1978), the major tenets have not been supported (Bussey & Bandura, 1999). According to this theory, children whose parents or other influential adults reflect back to them a gender that is inconsistent with their biological sex might develop a variant gender identity. If such children are rejected or punished for displaying gender-variant behaviors, as they often are (Mallon, 1998), they might adopt gender-conforming behaviors. However, they might also retain a core sense of being gender-variant.

THE MEDICAL MODEL OF GENDER VARIANCE

The medical model usually assumes that disorders represent an underlying bodily dysfunction or disease process. Although psychiatric classification is based on the medical model, it has not always clearly followed this assumption (Wakefield, 1992). Labels such as *transvestite, transsexual, gender dysphoria,* and *gender identity disorder* represent a medicalized understanding of gender variance. Physicians and psychiatrists created these labels in order to classify those whose experience of gender does not conform to the presumption of binary gender as determined by anatomy, and who suffer distress as a result. Assigning pathological meaning to such experience through classification provides justification for medical or psychiatric treatment.

The medical model of gender variance is controversial among contemporary trans communities. When this model's conceptualization changed from psycho-analytic to biomedical in the 1950s, many transpeople welcomed its pathological labeling because it allowed them to receive the hormones and surgery that they desired. However, an increasing number of transpeople reject the medical model and its central assumption that gender variance is pathological (e.g., Nangeroni, 1997).

The two most important applications of the medical model of gender variance are the Harry Benjamin International Gender Dysphoria Association's (HBIGDA) (2001) Standards of Care for Gender Identity Disorders and the American Psychiatric Association's (APA) diagnostic categories contained in the *Diagnostic and Statistical Manual of Mental Disorders* (DSM-IV-TR) (2000), both of which are used to guide treatment of transpeople.

THE STANDARDS OF CARE (SOC)

HBIDGA was formed in the late 1970s by a group of professionals in order to formulate and articulate ethical standards for treating transpeople. Until then, hormones and surgery were available either on the black market or through extremely selective and rigid university-based gender programs. Such services were not widely available, and there were no ethical guidelines for their provision. Since their release in 1979, the SOC have always outlined constraints on professionals and consumers in the provision of services, especially in setting minimum standards for access to hormone replacement therapy (HRT) and gender-confirming surgery (GCS) (Denny & Roberts, 1997). The standards have little to say about treatment of transpeople who are not seeking hormones or surgery. The most recent version of the SOC was released in 2001. Its goal is to promote "lasting personal comfort with the gendered self in order to maximize overall psychological well-being and self-fulfillment" (HBIGDA, 2001, p. 1).

Strict eligibility and readiness criteria are set forth in the SOC. Only adults over age eighteen can receive HRT, after showing an understanding of the consequences and documentation of either a real life experience (living full-time for three months as their desired gender) or three months of psychotherapy. Adults of legal age are eligible for genital surgery after twelve months of both continuous HRT and full-time real life experience; sometimes psychotherapy is required. An understanding of the phases, requirements, and potential complications of surgical treatment is required. Letters from mental health professionals are also needed for HRT and for genital and breast surgery (HBIGDA, 2001).

There is concern that free access to medical transition options might do more harm than good (Denny, 2001). According to Hale (2001), the constraints that the Standards of Care place on consumers cast mental health professionals as gatekeepers, conflicting with their role as therapists. This point is highly relevant for social workers, since the National Association of Social Workers (NASW) (1996) *Code of Ethics* forbids dual-role relationships with clients. The SOC restrictions may also exaggerate patient medical risks and undervalue patient autonomy (Hale, 2001). Although many transpeople strongly object to the gatekeeping aspects of the SOC, others have expressed satisfaction (Denny & Roberts, 1997).

PSYCHIATRIC CLASSIFICATION

The two major categories in the *DSM-IV-TR* (APA, 2000) that are used for psychiatric diagnosis of transpeople are Gender Identity Disorder, either in Adolescents and Adults (302.85) or in Children (302.6), and Transvestic Fetishism (302.3). The current version of the *DSM* places these categories in the section "Sexual and Gender Identity Disorders." The central feature of gender identity disorder is an intense and persistent self-identification with the opposite gender, combined with an enduring discomfort with the sex one is assigned. Among adolescents and adults, self-identification with the opposite gender manifests itself through a variety of symptoms that include "a stated desire to be the other sex, frequent passing as the other sex, desire to live or be treated as the other sex, or the conviction that he or she has the typical feeling and reactions of the other sex" (p. 537). Discomfort with the assigned sex manifests itself in "preoccupation with getting rid of primary and secondary sex characteristics … or belief that he or she was born the wrong sex" (p. 538). The diagnosis may also note whether the person is sexually attracted to men or women, both, or neither.

Among children, the symptoms are somewhat different. In particular, children do not have to be preoccupied with removal of their primary or secondary sex characteristics. They might express either an aversion to them or a fantasy or wish that they will change or disappear. Children's cross-gender identification and discomfort with the assigned gender manifest primarily as preferences for the clothing, activities, roles, and/or playmates of the opposite gender.

Transvestic fetishism is one of the paraphilias, which have to do with sexual urges, fantasies, or behaviors involving objects, activities, or situations considered unusual. It is diagnosed only in heterosexual men. In transvestic fetishism, the urges, fantasies, or behaviors of concern involve cross-dressing accompanied by sexual arousal. To be diagnosable, these characteristics must persist for more than six months, and they must interfere significantly in the person's functioning in any area of life or result in substantial distress. In addition, the diagnosis can specify whether gender dysphoria, or "persistent discomfort with gender role or identity" (p. 531), is also present. In such cases the person would not meet the full criteria for gender identity disorder.

Social workers should not reify these or any of the *DSM's* diagnostic categories, since they are all social constructions strongly shaped by social and political forces (Martin, 1997). As noted previously, the *DSM* does not conceptualize disorders as bodily dysfunctions that cause distress to the individual. Instead, it substitutes statistically unexpected or deviant responses for bodily dysfunctions (Wakefield, 1992). Wakefield asserted that this substitution results in diagnostic categories of questionable validity. In the case of gender variance, the problem with this conceptualization is that the experience of distress could be a normal reaction to oppressive social, economic, or political conditions, and a lack of empowerment. Thus assigning the distressed gender-variant person a pathological label would constitute blaming the victim. As noted by Corbett (1998), the medicalized concept of gender conflates conformity with mental health.

HORMONAL REPLACEMENT THERAPY AND ALTERNATIVES

HRT has several goals: to eliminate undesired secondary sex characteristics, to induce and enhance those of the desired sex (Gooren, 1999), and to provide a sense of psychological and emotional fulfillment (Israel & Tarver, 1997). HRT can greatly assist a person's *presentation* (appearance to the outside world), which is important for transpeople who wish to *pass* (appear as the gender they feel themselves to be). Some pass well enough to be *stealth* (when others do not perceive them as trans). When transpeople do not pass, they are considered *read* or *clocked*. An increasing number of trans individuals are choosing not to pass. They embrace and openly present their trans identity as valid and worthy, with or without HRT. In most cases, public and private health insurance programs in the United States deny coverage to transpeople for HRT, viewing it as elective and unnecessary (Middleton, 1997).

HRT is often preliminary to genital-confirming surgery (GCS), and some providers require provisional psychotherapy and real life experience before proceeding (Bockting et al., 2001). However, not all transpeople feel the need for surgery; some are comfortable with the changes achieved by HRT alone. In addition, the physical and psychological transformations brought about by HRT may be profound enough to eliminate the need for any psychiatric medications that were prescribed before the initiation of HRT (Bockting et al., 2001; Ettner, 1999).

As with all steroids, the use of sex hormones has significant side effects, including risks to liver function and blood pressure. People should use only hormones that are prescribed for them by a doctor, and they should also have blood levels and health changes monitored regularly. Transpeople who are geographically isolated or without financial resources may self-medicate with black market hormones or another's prescriptions or syringes; such practices present serious risks for HIV, hepatitis, and other diseases.

MASCULINIZING HORMONAL THERAPY

Testosterone is an androgenic hormone produced by the testes, although minute quantities are also present in female bodies. It is generally known as *T* in trans communities. A common method of administration used in the United States is intramuscular injection (Morton, Lewis, & Hans, 1997). Many clients eventually learn how to self-inject. T can also be administered via transdermal patches, topical gel, or pellets periodically implanted in the lower abdomen. Pills taken orally can severely compromise liver function as they metabolize, preventing adequate levels from reaching the bloodstream.

In a female-bodied person, an adequate course of HRT will typically result in menstrual cessation, permanent lowering of the vocal pitch, acne, permanent hair growth on the face and body, an increase in muscle mass and strength, increased sex drive, and permanent clitoral enlargement (Kirk, 1996). Because testosterone is likely to increase sexual arousal (Slabbekoorn, Van Goozen, Gooren, & Cohen-Kettenis, 2001), consumers could be more susceptible to impulsive and potentially risky sex.

FEMINIZING HORMONAL THERAPY

Estrogen and progesterone are sex hormones produced by the ovaries, with minute amounts also present in male bodies. For a male-bodied person who seeks feminization, HRT generally begins with estrogen and/or progesterone pills, often with anti-androgens to lessen or reverse existing masculine qualities. Intramuscular injections, transdermal patches, and skin creams may also be used. Medical evaluation, periodic blood monitoring, and complete and accurate disclosure of other medications used are important for a healthy transition. Depending on genetic disposition, feminizing HRT will result in maximum breast development within two years, while body hair diminishes or disappears. The skin noticeably softens, body fat redistributes toward a smaller waist and larger hips, and muscle mass decreases. The penis, testes, and prostate gland may shrink. Sexual desire and frequency of erection often diminish, which some consider a welcome relief (Bland, 1999). Long-term estrogen use may cause impotence and permanent infertility (Heather, 2001).

Time-consuming, costly, and painful, electrolysis or laser hair removal is often necessary for successful female presentation. Because HRT does not feminize the voice, great effort may go into learning how to raise the vocal pitch and change speech manners and inflections. Vocal cord surgery remains experimental, unpredictable, and risky (James, 2002).

ALTERNATE HORMONAL APPROACHES AND SOCIAL TRANSITION

In spite of the societal and medical pressures to conform, not all transpeople and intersex people recognize or want the binary experience of sex and gender. Not taking hormones, or NoHo, is an alternative option in which presentation relies solely on combinations of dress, speech, mannerisms, and behavior (Barlow, 2002). Social transition may integrate these elements in an unlimited number of ways, utilizing personal preferences for names and self-referencing pronouns (Wahng, 2002). Social transition is increasingly being explored as a means of self-empowerment, with or without surgery. It may also be enhanced through lower HRT, or LoHo (Barlow, 2002). Some consumers might self-adjust the initially prescribed dosage to increase or decrease bodily changes, or to reduce discomfort about health risks. Self-adjustment might feel empowering, but it is risky. Concerns about hormones should be discussed with a knowledgeable physician before making any adjustments to prescribed dosages (Ettner, 1999).

Some individuals feel that being perceived as trans or gender-different is an important part of their identity. An FTM person who values his feminine past might use a LoHo or NoHo approach to retain a meaningful connection with it; an MTF person might use it if she cannot accept the anti-androgenic effects of impotence or lowered libido.

NONMEDICAL, STREET, AND HERBAL SUBSTANCES

Geographic isolation, lack of finances or insurance, limited or no access to sensitive health care, desire for anonymity, or consumer ignorance may lead some trans individuals to obtain hormones from nonmedical sources. Using such substances without appropriate monitoring can be damaging to the user's health, and the desired effects are usually minimal and temporary. Black market hormones, including herbal substances, may contain unknown ingredients that could compromise one's health or even threaten one's life. Studies have shown that these chemicals could compete with or obstruct pharmaceutical HRT (Tampa Stress Center, 2002). Because they are not medically regulated, it is difficult to establish correct and safe dosages (Israel, 1996).

Anabolic steroids obtained by female-bodied persons who desire masculinizing changes have severe, damaging effects that may include depression, heart attack, cancer, HIV from shared needles, and physical and psychological addiction. Their nonmedical use is illegal in the United States (National Institute on Drug Abuse, 2002).

GENDER-CONFIRMING SURGERY

For sex reassignment surgery (SRS), the term *gender-confirming surgery* is increasingly being used worldwide because of the recognition that such surgery acts to confirm, rather than establish anew, one's gender status. Some individuals may utilize various surgical procedures in order to bring the body in line with their gender, with or without HRT. The social, psychological, and physical consequences of such procedures must be carefully considered by the consumer, especially since such surgery tends to be expensive, is often not covered by insurance, and has relatively permanent results that are often painful or otherwise disappointing (Israel & Tarver, 1997).

AESTHETIC SURGERY

Aesthetic or nongenital cosmetic surgery is used to enhance a person's appearance. A transwoman might have a tracheal shave (Adam's apple removal), and other gender-confirming procedures. Breast augmentation with saline implants, a common procedure to simulate or enhance natural breasts, is available to all women with few questions asked. However, people from lower socioeconomic backgrounds, sex workers, and those who are prone to higher rates of victimization and unemployment may be likely to seek out more easily obtainable silicone breast injections that are unsafe and now illegal in the United States (Israel & Tarver, 1997)

Among transmen, appearance is often hampered by the breasts, which they may hide through binding. However, this approach can cause skin rashes, breathing difficulties, and even tissue damage. Many seek freedom and relief through various procedures used to achieve a masculinized chest, including breast reduction or a double mastectomy. Known as top surgery, these procedures are often considered the most important step in transition.

GENITAL REASSIGNMENT SURGERY

Genital reassignment surgery (GRS) enables many transwomen to bring the body into line with their gender identity. No longer considered experimental, GRS is now recognized to be part of a healthy process toward the desired psychological and physical results (Israel & Tarver, 1997). After an orchidectomy (removal of the testes), vaginoplasty (construction of a vagina and vulva) and labiaplasty (inner and outer labial shaping) are used to construct the neovagina, neoclitoris, and neolabia without removal of the penis (Carlisle, 1998). Infection and tissue death may be serious complications, and revisions may be needed later (Israel & Tarver, 1997). There is some empirical evidence of satisfaction with surgical outcomes among MTFs, including improvement in important domains of daily life (Walworth, 1997).

Among transmen, GRS may involve removal of the ovaries and uterus (oophorectomy and hysterectomy) to prevent cancer associated with HRT, though others may never have these procedures. Phalloplasty, or bottom surgery, constructs a penis through a series of surgeries. A skin flap with arteries and nerves is removed from the thigh or arm, and the neophallus is microsurgically attached to the pubis. The urethra is lengthened, and erection devices are sometimes implanted. Costly and risky, phalloplasty may result in deep scarring and a penis of debatable aesthetics that is not sexually functional. An alternative, metoidioplasty, surgically releases the testosterone-enlarged clitoris from ligaments to increase its length; the urethra is also lengthened. In either procedure, a scrotum may be formed from labial tissue, with testicular implants (Morton, Lewis, & Hans, 1997).

The Internet is widely used to obtain information about GCS. Clients and social workers should make sure that such information comes from reliable and legitimate sources, since much misinformation may also be found on the Internet.

RECOMMENDATIONS FOR AFFIRMATIVE SOCIAL WORK PRACTICE

Health changes, aging, substance abuse, relocation to a city, relationships, adult children leaving home or parents dying, economic issues, and depression resulting from struggles around gender identity are among the experiences that bring trans and gender-questioning people into treatment (Cook-Daniels, 2002). Many seek information about, or support for, HRT and GCS, but difficulties in accessing health care and inadequate legal protection are frequent barriers (Connors, Durkee, Kammerer, & Mason, 2001). Anxiety about self-disclosure, shame from stigmatizing diagnoses, and transphobic reactions are major obstacles in their search for help (Hill, 2003). Disempowerment and social marginalization are frequently among the dynamics underlying the experiences of transpeople and intersex people (Dreger, 1998). Isolation is often a driving force, and transpeople of color may be even more disenfranchised, lacking support from both the dominant, majority culture and their culture of origin (Israel & Tarver, 1997).

There are several models of trans-affirmative practice. For example, Raj (2001) developed a transpositive therapeutic model that is client-centered and useful for training purposes. It promotes affiliation between trans and non-trans professionals. This model adapts the Standards of Care, encouraging additional guidelines and input from trans-health practitioners. It recommends multidisciplinary teamwork based on a structure of at least two clinicians. In particular, a physician/assessor and a therapist/healer work together, monitoring and assessing each other's work with the client. All clinical work should be transpositive and culturally competent (Raj, 2001).

Lev (2004) proposed a six-stage normative, developmental model of practice called emergence. In this model, transition, with therapeutic support, becomes a process of acquiring a healthy, authentic sense of gender identity by "coming out" from a world of pain and confusion. The model includes continued support for losses associated with transition experienced by both clients and their significant others, family, friends, and allies (SOFFAs).

Recognizing that some people are unable to negotiate the SOC, or have been traumatized in some way by their experience with them, Callen-Lorde Community Health Center in New York City has developed an innovative protocol for providing HRT to trans adults and youth. Departing from the SOC, it stresses self-determination, minimizes gatekeeping, and promotes partnership between clients and providers. Referral letters, real life experiences, and psychotherapy are not required in order to receive HRT. However, the protocol does follow a "do no harm" ethic by emphasizing consumer psychoeducation that enables clients' understanding of medical and health consequences, and counseling and psychotherapy for support and problem solving. Whenever suicide ideation, psychosis, or serious health problems present, they receive priority attention (Douglass & McGowan, 2002).

A growing number of gender identity programs, many of them peer-supported, provide nonpathologizing, client-centered services throughout North America. For example, the Gender Identity Project at New York's Gay, Lesbian, Bisexual and Transgender Community Center offers multidisciplinary professional assessment, referrals, counseling, and support groups. Trans and transpositive workers provide outreach services to sex workers and workshops on trans issues for organizations, schools, and social work agencies (Lesbian, Bisexual, and Transgender Community Center, 2002).

More specifically, social workers can ensure that their practice with transpeople is affirmative at each step in the helping process by using the following recommendations as a guide. Drawn from a variety of models, they emphasize ecosystems and narrative approaches, a strengths perspective, and avoidance of pathologizing trans experiences. According to the NASW, people of diverse gender should be supported nonjudgmentally toward self-empowerment through all phases of the healing process, while promoting comprehensive psychological and social support services for them and their families (NASW, 2000).

ENGAGEMENT

When initiating work with trans clients, social workers should always ask about their reasons for seeking services and the reasons for seeking them at this time. Israel and Tarver (1997) suggested that the professional assume nothing about the client. Workers should be familiar with using affirming, transpositive language. Unsure of their physical safety in unfamiliar surroundings, clients may introduce themselves with their birth name instead of the name that is their own choice. The worker should ask them how they would prefer to be addressed and thereafter use the preferred name and pronouns (Pazos, 1999). Because these clients are often nervous about which restrooms they can safely use, they should be assured that they can use the ones they feel are most appropriate (Brown & Rounsley, 1996); social workers must make sure that agency staff understand and support trans clients' needs in this matter.

Trans clients may be hypervigilant for the most subtle of negative responses to their presentation and discussion about GCS, HRT, or sex work, and practitioners must use disciplined self-awareness to recognize and control their own reactions. In order to engage and work successfully with these clients, practitioners should utilize supervision for managing their countertransference (Anderson, 1998). Those who are unaware of their own internalized transphobia may unconsciously prevent productive exploration of a client's gender concerns (Cope & Darke, 1999) or misinterpret a client's desire for surgery as self-mutilation or suicidal ideation (Vitale, 1997). People of gender-variant experience must often interact with providers who do not identify as trans and who have little or no accurate information about their issues (Israel & Tarver, 1997). Practitioners may find themselves the focus of mistrust and discriminatory remarks and behavior from clients because of the *practitioners'* perceived non-trans status (Carroll & Gilroy, 2002). While this might be an uncomfortable situation, it provides a valuable opportunity for engagement with clients, inviting them to share their feelings around this experience and from there to continue exploration together.

Social workers should elicit clients' feelings about discussing their bodies and sex and encourage them to raise issues and concerns at any time during the working relationship (Israel & Tarver, 1997). Since social workers should always start where the client is, during the engagement phase they should avoid questions about clients' surgical status or HRT, or their body's physical state, unless those topics are initiated by the clients themselves (Xavier, 2001). When discussing safer sex and other sexual issues, if there is uncertainty about clients' anatomy, practitioners should avoid specific references and terms based on biology or natal genitalia (Gender Education and Advocacy, 2001). For example, they could ask, "Do you have unprotected genital-genital (manual-genital, oral-genital, oral-anal, genital-anal) contact?" or "Is there an exchange of body fluids?"

ASSESSMENT

Trans clients may present suicidal ideation and a variety of self-destructive behaviors, including substance abuse and unprotected sex (Leslie, Perina, & Maqueda, 2001). These behaviors may occur because of low self-esteem and feelings of guilt and shame (Xavier, 2001), but gender variance by itself does not constitute a mental illness. FTMs in particular may lack knowledge of safer sex, and they generally do not consider themselves at risk for HIV (Namaste, 1999). Often lacking empathic support during childhood and adolescence, socially isolated transpeople may present as adults with poor interpersonal skills, frequently at levels fixated below their chronological age (Anderson, 1998). External transphobic experiences, exacerbated by isolation, may result in varying degrees of internalized fear and loathing (Cope & Darke, 1999). This internalized transphobia may manifest as discomfort with gender and/or sexual orientation, intense aversion to the genitals, shame about compulsive cross-dressing, and beliefs of being perverted, mentally ill, or evil (Anderson, 1998).

In the assessment phase, social workers should avoid pathologizing trans clients' gender variance. They should not assume that trans clients are necessarily seeking help with their gender identity, since they might want help with problems that are unrelated to it. Social workers should be careful in not moving too quickly toward asking specific questions about clients' gender experiences or their bodies. However, they should ask whether clients have any health needs or problems, or if they have ever received social work or counseling services previously. In order to develop an ecosystems perspective, they should ask about clients' living situation, social supports, and relationships with other systems. Sometimes trans clients may not be aware of their strengths. Social workers can help to empower them in the assessment phase by identifying and reflecting the strengths that become evident, both within clients and in their environments. For example, they might have been able to survive on the streets since an early age, take care of aging parents, or overcome substance abuse problems on their own. Or they might have supports among other sex workers (if they are engaged in sex work themselves) or homeless people, or have family-like relationships within certain clubs and bars.

GOAL SETTING AND CONTRACTING

An overall goal for trans clients should be the realization of a self-empowered, productive, and meaningful life through the relief of symptoms and recovery or establishment of a state of psychological homeostasis (Anderson, 1998). Specific goals should be set in collaboration with clients. Sometimes trans clients may already have specific goals when they come in for service. In these cases practitioners should work with clients to determine the clarity and safety of the goals and whether they are within the domain of the agency's function. The contract might include actions that practitioners will take to advocate for their clients in obtaining other services, especially when providers may lack cultural competence with this population.

INTERVENTION

In order to intervene effectively, practitioners should continuously work to increase their knowledge about transpeople. No one model of practice is likely to be best in work with trans clients, although models that assume the normality of binary gender and the greater value of traditional gender roles may be inappropriate. Mallon (1999) suggested using a narrative approach in which practitioners encourage clients to tell their story. Trans stories are acts of empowering self-revelation, and they reveal the languages, values, and beliefs that clients may have (Boenke, 1999). The narrative process may reveal the extent of disempowerment derived from destructive relationships between clients and their environment (Mallon, 1999). This approach assumes that clients are the experts about themselves and that they have developed coping strengths through a lifetime of inner searching (Brown & Rounsely, 1996). Practitioners should encourage the flow of narrative by reflecting it back without substituting or negating content. They should, however, ask for clarification about unfamiliar words and phrases and affirm clients' strengths and skills (Carroll & Gilroy, 2002).

The narrative approach may be nested within an ecosystems model (Mallon, 1999), which can help to reveal the quality of the interface between individuals

---

FOUR PEOPLE WHO WORKED TO CHANGE THEIR ENVIRONMENT

Louis Graydon Sullivan was a cofounder of the FTM community. In the mid-1970s he was one of the earliest known FTM persons, if not the only one, who openly identified as a gay man. An activist, speaker, and prolific writer, he pioneered methods to obtain peer support, professional counseling, hormone therapy, and gender-confirming surgery outside of institutional gender identity clinics. After being diagnosed with AIDS in 1986, and until his death five years later at the age of 39, Sullivan continued to devote his work to the FTM and gay communities. The San Francisco Public Library now holds his vast collection of short stories, poems, essays, correspondence, diaries, photographs, and file clippings, which document his search for, and struggle with, his gender and sexual identities (Gay and Lesbian Historical Society of Northern California, 1999).

Reed Erickson was a successful business-transman and philanthropist who funded the Erickson Educational Foundation, which supported nearly every aspect of work on trans issues in the United States in the 1960s and 1970s. It developed and maintained an extensive referral list of service providers throughout the world, and it sponsored educational films, radio and television appearances, and newspaper articles that brought transsexualism to the attention of the general public. Erickson was also an early supporter of the Harry Benjamin Foundation and the Johns Hopkins Clinic, and he sponsored many symposia and research projects on homeopathy, acupuncture, dreams, and dolphin communication systems. Erickson led an eccentric life and used his wealth surreptitiously, improving the lives of many people who never even heard of him (Devor, 2002; MacIntosh, 1999).

Cheryl Chase was the founding director of the Intersex Society of North America. Influenced in part by Chase's 10,000-word amicus brief, the Supreme Court of Colombia issued a historic decision establishing human rights protections for intersexed infants in 1999. Her efforts to improve the social and medical treatment of intersexed people were recognized with the Felipa de Souze Human Right Award in 2000. Her presentation to the Pediatric Endocrine Society in 2000 is considered an unprecedented patient-led breakthrough in medical reform (Intersex Society of North America, 2004).

Sylvia Lee Rivera was a lifelong trans activist. Some claim that she initiated the Stonewall riots in 1969 by throwing a high-heeled shoe at police officers who were attempting to arrest cross-dressers and gay men. In collaboration with her trans sister Marsha P. Johnson, Rivera established Street Transgender Action Revolutionaries, an action group that provided food, clothing, and shelter to trans homeless, sex workers, and youth, and promoted their rights. Often thorny and never soft-spoken, she struggled with addiction and homelessness throughout her life. As the New York State legislature considered including trans rights in the Sexual Orientation Nondiscrimination Amendment in 2002, Rivera lobbied and negotiated with officials from her hospital deathbed. A few months after she died at age 51, the New York City Council voted to include trans people in its human rights law (Adam aka Ruby Lips, 2002; Transgender Law and Policy Institute, 2002).

and their environment (Saleebey, 2001). Acknowledging institutional and environmental sources of oppression and the role of these factors in traumatizing transpeople is very important (Cromwell, Denny, & Green, 2001). However, practitioners should avoid encouraging clients simply to adapt to these oppressive environmental forces. Instead, they should help clients to change them (Saleebey, 2001).

Practitioners should be familiar with skilled gender specialists and transpositive health care, HIV-prevention providers, and sexual-assault-prevention providers, in order to make appropriate referrals when needed (Carroll & Gilroy, 2002). Gender specialists should be licensed psychotherapists or counselors, or gender identity educators, with appropriate training and supervision (Israel & Tarver, 1997). They should also have an understanding of relevant psychiatric classification according to the *DSM* (Vitale, 1997).

Practitioners should also be prepared to intervene at the macro level. Attending vigils, writing letters to editors, and professional writing can serve advocacy purposes. Practitioners can provide HIV-prevention information, safer-sex kits, and police safety guidelines to trans sex workers and the homeless. Advocacy for trans eldercare is needed to address challenges around health, relationships, and retirement and nursing homes. Community organizing with strategies for collective empowerment and self-esteem is also important. A strong sense of community promotes self-respect and pride among its members, which may also lead to positive changes in societal attitudes toward them (Connors et al., 2001).

REFERENCES

Adam aka Ruby Lips. (2002). *Obituary for Sylvia Lee Rivera*. Retrieved June 4, 2002, from www.dainna.com/tss/sylvia.html.

AIS Support Group Australia. (2002). *Intersex Q. & A.* Retrieved May 20, 2002, from http://home.vicnet.net.au/~aissg/intersexq&a.htm.

American Psychiatric Association. (2000). *Diagnostic and statistical manual of mental disorders (DSM-IV-TR)* (4th ed. rev.). Washington, DC: Author.

Anderson, B.F. (1998). Therapeutic issues in working with transgendered clients. In D. Denny (Ed.), *Current concepts in transgender identity* (pp. 215–226). New York: Garland.

Barlow, J.Z. (2002, February). *Occupying the middle: The no/low hormone, non-operative transsexual*. Symposium conducted at True Spirit Conference 2002, Washington, DC.

Benjamin, H. (1997). *The transsexual phenomenon* [electronic version]. Düsseldorf, Germany: Symposion Publishing. Obtained March 19, 2002, from www.symposion.com/ijt/benjamin.

Bland, J. (1999). *About gender: Estrogens and androgens*. Retrieved May 25, 2002, from http://www.gender.org.uk/about/06encrn/62_hormn.htm.

Bockting, W., Cohen-Kettenis, P., Coleman, E., DiCeglie, D., Devor, H., Gooren, L., Joris Hage, J., Kirk, S., Kuiper, B., Laub, D., Lawrence, A., Menard, Y., Meyer III, W., Patton, J., Schaefer, L., Webb, A., & Wheeler, C. (2001). The standards of care for gender identity disorders, 6th version. *International Journal of Transgenderism*, 5(1). Retrieved May 24, 2002, from http://www.symposion.com/ijt/soc_2001/index.htm.

Boles, J., & Elifson, K.W. (1994). The social organization of transvestite prostitution and AIDS. *Social Science and Medicine*, 39, 85–93.

Brannon, L. (2002). *Gender: Psychological perspectives* (3d ed.). Boston: Allyn and Bacon.

Brown, M.L., & Rounsely, C.A. (1996). *True selves: Understanding transsexualism*. San Francisco: Jossey-Bass.

Bullough, B., & Bullough, V. (1997). Men who cross-dress: A survey. In B. Bullough, V. Bullough, & J. Elias (Eds.), *Gender blending* (pp. 174–188). Amherst, NY: Prometheus Books.

Bullough, V.L. (2000). Transgender and the concept of gender. *International Journal of Transgenderism*, 4(3). Retrieved May 9, 2002 from http://www.symposion.com/ijt/gilbert/bullough.htm.

Bussey, K., & Bandura, A. (1999). Social cognitive theory of gender development and differentiation. *Psychological Review*, 106, 676–713.

Carlisle, D.B. (1998). *Human sex change and sex reversal*. Lewiston, NY: Edwin Mellen Press.

Carroll, L., & Gilroy, P.J. (2002). Transgender issues in counselor preparation. *Counselor Education and Supervision*, 41, 233–242.

Chauncey, G. (1994). *Gay New York*. New York: Basic Books.

Chodorow, N. (1978). *The reproduction of mothering: Psychoanalysis and the sociology of gender*. Berkeley: University of California Press.

Cole, S.S., Denny, D., Eyler, A.E., & Samons, S.L. (2000). Issues of transgender. In L.T. Szuchman & F. Muscarella (Eds.), *Psychological perspectives on human sexuality* (pp. 149–195). New York: John Wiley.

Connors, M., Durkee, R., Kammerer, N., & Mason, T. (2001). Transgender health and social service needs in the context of HIV risk. In W. Bockting & S. Kirk (Eds.), *Transgender and HIV* (pp. 39–57). New York: Haworth.

Cook-Daniels, L. (2002). *Growing old transgendered*. Retrieved June 20, 2002, from http://www.forge-forward.org/handouts/growingoldtg.htm.

Cope, A., & Darke, J. (1999). *Trans accessibility project: Transphobia and discrimination*. Retrieved June 15, 2002, from www.queensu.ca/humanrights/tap/3discrimination.htm.

Corbett, K. (1998). Cross-gendered identification and homosexual boyhood: Toward a more complex theory of gender. *American Journal of Orthopsychiatry*, 68, 352–360.

Cromwell, J., Denny, D., & Green, J. (2001, October). *The language of gender variance*. Paper presented at the 17th HBIGDA International Symposium on Gender Dysphoria, Galveston, TX.

Denny, D. (2001). *Some notes on access to medical treatment. A position paper*. Retrieved March 23, 2002, from www.firelily.com/gender/resources/dallas.soc.html.

Denny, D., & Roberts, J. (1997). Results of a questionnaire on the Standards of Care of the Harry Benjamin International Gender Dysphoria Association. In B. Bullough, V.L. Bullough, & J. Elias (Eds.), *Gender blending* (pp. 320–336). Amherst, NY: Prometheus Books.

Devor, H. (1997). *FTM: Female-to-male transsexuals in society*. Indianapolis: Indiana University Press.

———. (1998). Sexual-orientation identities, attractions, and practices of female-to-male transsexuals. In D. Denny, (Ed.), *Current concepts in transgender identity* (pp. 249–275). New York: Garland.

———. (2002). Reed Erickson: How one transsexed man supported ONE. In V. Bullough, J. Saunders, & S. Valente (Eds.), *Before Stonewall: Activists for rights of gays and lesbians* (pp. 738–756). New York: Haworth.

Docter, R. F., & Prince, V. (1997). Transvestism: A survey of 1032 cross-dressers. *Archives of Sexual Behavior, 26,* 589–605.

Douglass, K., & McGowan, H. (2002, February). *Callen-Lorde's approach to hormone therapy.* Presentation conducted at the True Spirit Conference 2002, Washington, D.C.

Dreger, A. D. (1998). *Hermaphrodites and the medical invention of sex.* Cambridge, MA: Harvard University Press.

———. (1999). *Intersex in the age of ethics.* Hagerstown, MD: University Publishing Group.

Eagly, A. H. (1987). *Sex differences in social behavior: A social role interpretation.* Hillsdale, NJ: Erlbaum.

Elkins, R., & King, D. (1998). Blending genders: Contributions to the emerging field of transgender studies. In D. Denny (Ed.), *Current concepts in transgender identity* (pp. 97–115). New York: Garland.

Ettner, R. (1999). *Gender loving care: A guide to counseling gender-variant clients.* New York: Norton.

Fausto-Sterling, A. (2000). *Sexing the body: Gender politics and the construction of sexuality.* New York: Basic Books.

Gagné, P., & Tewksbury, R. (1998). Conformity pressures and gender resistance among transgendered individuals. *Social Problems, 45*(1), 88–101.

Gay and Lesbian Historical Society of Northern California. (1999). *Louis G. Sullivan papers.* Retrieved June 4, 2002, from www.oac.cdlib.org/dynaweb/ead/glhs.

Gender Education and Advocacy. (2001). *Basic tips for health care and social service providers working with transgendered people.* Retrieved June 16, 2002, from http://gender.org/resources/dge/gea01006.pdf.

Gooren, L. (1999). Hormonal sex reassignment. *International Journal of Transgenderism, 3*(3). Retrieved May 24, 2002, from http://www.symposion.com/ijt/ijt990301.htm.

Green, R. (1998). Mythological, historical, and cross-cultural aspects of transsexualism. In D. Denny (Ed.), *Current concepts in transgender identity* (pp. 3–14). New York: Garland.

Grossman, A. H., & D'Augelli, A. R. (in press). Transgender youth: Invisible and vulnerable. *Journal of Homosexuality.*

Hale, C. J. (2001). *Medical ethics and transsexuality.* Obtained May 29, 2002, from www.symposion.com/ift/hbigda/2001/69_hale.htm.

Hardy, M. S. (1995). The development of gender roles: Societal influences. In L. Diamant & R. D. McAnulty (Eds.), *The psychology of sexual orientation, behavior, and identity: A handbook* (pp. 425–443). Westport, CT: Greenwood.

Harry Benjamin International Gender Dysphoria Association. (2001). *Standards of care for gender identity disorders* (6th version). Obtained June 12, 2002, from www.hbigda.org.

Heather, K. (2001). *Reproductive options for transsexuals.* Retrieved June 4, 2002, from www.genderpsychology.org/reproduction/index.html.

Hill, D. B. (2003). Genderism, transphobia, and genderbashing: A framework for interpreting anti-transgender violence. In B. Wallace & R. Carter (Eds.), *A multicultural approach for understanding and dealing with violence: A handbook for psychologists and educators* (pp. 118–136). Thousand Oaks, CA: Sage.

Hirschfeld, M. (1910). *Die transvestiten: Ein Untersuchung über den erotischen Verkleidungstrieb.* Berlin: Pulvermacher.

Horney, K. (1939). *New ways in psychoanalysis*. New York: Norton.

Hubbard, R. (1998). Gender and genitals: Constructs of sex and gender. In D. Denny (Ed.), *Current concepts in transgender identity* (pp. 3–14). New York: Garland.

Intersex Society of North America. (1994). *ISNA's recommendations for treatment*. Retrieved May 18, 2002, from http://www.isna.org/library/recommendations.html.

——. (2004). *Cheryl Chase, executive director*. Retrieved December 5, 2004, from www.isna.org/drupal/about/staff/cheryl.

Intersex Support. (2001). *Intersex defined*. Retrieved May 18, 2002, from http://www.intersexsupport.org/intersex_defined.htm.

Israel, G. E. (1996). *Talking with your doctor (#4)*. Retrieved May 25, 2002, from http://indigo.ie/~transgen/talk.htm.

Israel, G. E., & Tarver, D. E. (Eds.) (1997). *Transgender care: Recommended guidelines, practical information, and personal accounts*. Philadelphia: Temple University Press.

James, A. (2002). Vocal feminization: Surgery. *TS road map*. Retrieved May 25, 2002, from http://www.tsroadmap.com/physical/voice/voicesurg.html.

Kehoe, A. B. (1997). On the incommensurability of gender categories. In S. Jacobs, W. Thomas, & S. Lang (Eds.), *Two-spirit-people: Native American gender identity, sexuality, and spirituality* (pp. 265–271). Urbana: University of Illinois Press.

Kessler, S. J. (2000). *Lessons from the intersexed*. New Brunswick, NJ: Rutgers University Press.

Kipnis, K., & Diamond, M. (1998). Pediatric ethics and the surgical assignment of sex. *Journal of Clinical Ethics, 9*(4), 398–410.

Kirk, S. (1996). *Masculinizing hormonal therapy for the transgendered*. Blawnox, PA: Together Lifeworks.

Kohlberg, L. (1981). *The meaning and measurement of moral development*. Worcester, MA: Clark University Press.

Kuhn, D., Nash, S. C., & Brucken, L. (1978). Sex role concepts of two- and three-year olds. *Child Development, 49*, 445–451.

Lesbian, Gay, Bisexual, and Transgender Community Center. (2002). *The Gender Identity Project*. Retrieved June 2, 2002, from http://gaycenter.org/programs/mhss/gip.html.

Leslie, D. R., Perina, B. A., & Maqueda, M. C. (2001). Clinical issues with transgender individuals. In *A provider's introduction to substance abuse treatment for lesbian, gay, bisexual and transgender individuals* (pp. 91–98). Retrieved June 14, 2002, from http://www.health.org/govpubs/BKD392/index.pdf.

Lev, A. I. (2004). *Transgender emergence: Counseling gender variant people and their families*. Binghamton, NY: Haworth.

MacIntosh, J. (1999). *Reed Erickson and the Erickson Educational Foundation*. Retrieved June 4, 2002, from http//web.uvic.ca/~erick123.

Mackenzie, G. O. (1999). 50 billion galaxies of gender: Transgendering the millennium. In K. More & S. Whittle (Eds.), *Reclaiming genders: Transsexual grammars at the fin de siècle* (pp. 193–218). New York: Cassell.

Mallon, G. P. (1998). *We don't exactly get the welcome wagon: The experiences of gay and lesbian adolescents in child welfare systems*. New York: Columbia University Press.

——. (1999). Knowledge for practice with transgendered persons. In G. P. Mallon (Ed.), *Social services with transgendered youth* (pp. 1–18). Binghamton, NY: Haworth.

Martin, J. I. (1997). Political aspects of mental health treatment. In T. R. Watkins & J. W. Callicutt (Eds.), *Mental health policy and practice today* (pp. 32–48). Thousand Oaks, CA: Sage.

Michel, A., Mormont, C., & Legros, J. J. (2001). A psycho-endocrinological overview of transsexualism. *European Journal of Endocrinology, 145*, 365–376.

Middleton, L. (1997). Insurance and the reimbursement of health care. In G. E. Israel & D. E. Tarver (Eds.), *Transgender care: Recommended guidelines, practical information, and personal accounts* (pp. 215–224). Philadelphia: Temple University Press.

Mischel, W. (1966). A social-learning view of sex differences in behavior. In E. E. Maccoby (Ed.), *The development of sex differences* (pp. 56–81). Stanford, CA: Stanford University Press.

Money, J. (1994). The concept of gender identity disorder in childhood and adolescence after 39 years. *Journal of Sex and Marital Therapy, 20,* 163–177.

Morton, S., Lewis, Y., & Hans, A. (1997). Notes on gender transition. *FTM 101 — The invisible transsexuals.* Retrieved May 24, 2002, from http://www.avitale.com/FTM_101.html.

Namaste, V. K. (1999). HIV/AIDS and female to male transsexuals and transvestites: Results from a needs assessment in Quebec. *International Journal of Transgenderism, 3*(1/2). Retrieved June 20, 2002, from http://www.symposion.com/ijt/hiv_risk/namaste.htm.

Nanda, S. (2000). *Gender diversity: Crosscultural variations.* Prospect Heights, IL: Waveland Press.

Nangeroni, N. R. (1997). SRS tomorrow: The physical continuum. In B. Bullough, V. L. Bullough, & J. Elias (Eds.), *Gender blending* (pp. 344–351). Amherst, NY: Prometheus.

National Association of Social Workers (NASW). (1996). *Code of ethics.* Washington, DC: Author.

——— . (2000). Policy statement on transgender and gender identity issues. *Social work speaks* (5th ed.) (pp. 300–304). Washington, DC: Author.

National Institute on Drug Abuse. (2002). *Research report — Steroid abuse and addiction.* NIH Publication No. 00–3721. Retrieved April 26, 2002, from www.nida.nih.gov/ResearchReports/Steroids/anabolicsteroids3.html.

Pazos, S. (1999). Practice with female-to-male transgendered youth. In G. Mallon (Ed.), *Social services with transgendered youth* (pp. 65–82). Binghamton, NY: Haworth.

Raj, R. (2001). *Towards a transpositive therapeutic model: Developing clinical sensitivity and cultural competence in the effective support of transsexual and transgendered clients.* Unpublished manuscript, Adler School of Professional Psychology, Toronto, Ontario.

Saleeby, D. (2001). *Human behavior and social environments: A biopsychosocial approach.* New York: Columbia University Press.

Skinner, B. F. (1969). *Contingencies of reinforcement: A theoretical analysis.* New York: Appleton-Century-Crofts.

Slabbekoorn, D., Van Goozen, S., Gooren, L., & Cohen-Kettenis, P. (2001). Effects of cross-sex hormone treatment on emotionality in transsexuals. *International Journal of Transsexualism, 5*(3). Retrieved May 25, 2002, from www.symposion.com.

Tampa Stress Center. (2002). Herbal hormones. In *TransGenderCare.* Retrieved May 25, 2002, from www.transgendercare.com/medical/herbal_hormones.htm.

Transgender Law and Policy Institute. (2002). *New York City Council votes to include transgender people in its human rights law.* Retrieved June 6, 2002, from www.transgenderlaw.org/nycapril02.htm.

Vitale, A. (1997). The therapist versus the client: How the conflict started and some thoughts on how to resolve it. In G. E. Israel & D. E. Tarver (Eds.), *Transgender care: Recommended guidelines, practical information, and personal accounts* (pp. 251–256). Philadelphia: Temple University Press.

Wahng, S. (2002, February). *LoHo FTMs and other hormonal alternatives.* Presentation conducted at the True Spirit Conference 2002, Washington, DC.

Wakefield, J. C. (1992). Disorder as harmful dysfunction: A conceptual critique of DSM-III-R's definition of mental disorder. *Psychological Review, 99,* 232–247.

Walworth, J. (1997). Sex reassignment surgery in male-to-female transsexuals: Client satisfaction in relation to selection criteria. In B. Bullough, V. L. Bullough, & J. Elias (Eds.), *Gender blending* (pp. 352–369). Amherst, NY: Prometheus.

Warren, B. E. (2001). Sex, truth, and videotape: HIV prevention at the Gender Identity Project in New York City. In W. Bockting & S. Kirk (Eds.), *Transgender and HIV: Risks, prevention, and care* (pp. 145–151). New York: Haworth.

Whitam, F. L. (1997). Culturally universal aspects of male homosexual transvestites and transsexuals. In B. Bullough, V. Bullough, & J. Elias (Eds.), *Gender blending* (pp. 189–203). Amherst, NY: Prometheus.

Xavier, J. M. (2001). A primer by Transgender Nation. *TGS-PFLAG Virtual Library.* Retrieved June 15, 2002, from www.critpath.org/pflag-talk/tgprimer.htm.

6

COMING OUT AS GAY, LESBIAN, BISEXUAL, AND TRANSGENDER

Deana F. Morrow

Visibility strikes a powerful blow for the demand that certain realities be accepted and integrated into society. There is no going back from the reality of a gay presence in American life.... We have a voice now and it is distinctive. Our message is clear. We are in this fight for respect, for understanding, for equality, and for acknowledgment of the humanity we share with all ... others.

—BERZON, 2001, P. 15

COMING OUT (also known as disclosure) is defined as the acknowledgment of a gay, lesbian, bisexual, and/or transgender (GLBT) identity—initially to oneself and then to others. It is a central feature in the experience of being GLBT. Practicing social workers will observe great variability in the degree of openness, or "outness," among their GLBT clients. Such openness is affected by numerous factors, including the GLBT person's own internalized oppression, external oppression, and the GLBT person's trust in any particular person to whom he or she may disclose. Because most people tend to automatically assume that others are heterosexual (an example of heterosexism), GLBT people are constantly confronted with whether to disclose their sexual orientation or transgender identity. This chapter will explore the dynamics surrounding coming out and how social workers can work affirmatively with GLBT clients in relation to that process. The terms *coming out* and *disclosure* will be used interchangeably throughout the chapter.

DISCLOSURE AND IDENTITY

GLBT identity development is discussed at length in chapters 4 and 5 of this book. Identity development for GLBT people is a comprehensive process whereby a person comes to terms in understanding and claiming his or her identity as a sexual minority person. As GLBT people engage that elaborate and complex process, they must also make decisions relative to issues of disclosure. While disclosure is not synonymous with identity development, it is a salient feature that typically arises in the course of the identity formation process. For example, in the Cass model (Cass, 1979, 1984a, 1984b) discussed in chapter 4, we see that the farther along people are in the identity development process, the more likely they are to disclose to others. Coming out is also identified as one of the central components in other identity development models as well (see Coleman, 1982; Minton & McDonald, 1984; Troiden, 1979). Thus disclosure is centrally connected to—though not the same as—identity development for GLBT people.

COMING OUT AS AN ONGOING PROCESS

Coming out is often thought of as a milestone in the lives of GLBT people (Ben-Ari, 1995a; Berzon, 2001; Morrow, 1993, 1996; Signorile, 1995). It represents their giving voice to who they are, internally as well as externally to others, and it is often marked by events such as coming out initially to oneself and then to significant others (e.g., family members, coworkers, faith community). Yet disclosure is more realistically viewed as a continuous daily and ongoing process that never really ends. Social environments are constantly evolving and presenting new contexts in which GLBT people have to make new decisions relative to disclosure (Morrow, 2000). Some people may elect to be out in virtually every aspect of their lives; other people may be out in some contexts but not in others.

REASONS FOR AND AGAINST DISCLOSURE

Berzon (2001) suggests there are two principal reasons for disclosure. The first is the personal growth that can accompany being honest about oneself. There is something very empowering about openly and honestly portraying oneself—even if that identity is socially stigmatized, as is the case for GLBT people. The second reason Berzon cites is the political power in being part of a visible GLBT citizenry. She states: "The changes that are needed in social policies and in laws in order to improve the quality of life for gay people have come only when there was a political and economic gay and lesbian constituency that was visible and identifiable" (2001, p. 28). Other motives cited as reasons for disclosure include a desire to maintain a sense of integrity and honesty within oneself in interacting with others (Harry, 1993), an interest in increasing closeness and open communication with others (Ben-Ari, 1995b; Cramer & Roach, 1998), an interest in increasing self-confidence and developing an improved self-image (Rhoads, 1995), and a desire to avoid the social and psychological costs associated with maintaining secrecy or falsehoods about one's identity (Ben-Ari, 1995b; Cain, 1991; Harry, 1993).

Reasons that people give for avoiding disclosure include the following: fear of rejection (Elliott, 1996; Harry, 1993); fear of being physically harmed (Elliott, 1996); fear of discrimination and harassment (Rhoads, 1995); and a desire to protect loved ones from the stress that disclosure may cause (Ben-Ari, 1995a; Boon & Miller, 1999). GLBT people seem to fear coming out to their parents more than to any other audience (Boon & Miller, 1999). While friends and even lovers may be replaced, a person has only one set of parents. The loss of parents because of rejection is, for many, irreplaceable. Franke and Leary (1991) found that the greatest predictor of openness among a sample of sexual minority people was their perception of others' attitudes toward sexual minorities. That is, the more accepting the lesbians and gay men in the study perceived people to be, the more likely they were to disclose to them.

Coming out can result in feelings of loss and relationship upheaval (Rhoads, 1995). Magee and Miller (1994) suggest that coming out carries with it not only a potential for empowerment but also the risk of relationship damage. Coming out requires that GLBT people confront the socially constructed and personally internalized anti-gay shame and negativity—as well as gender role rigidity—that is perpetuated by society and lived out in families and communities. Thus, despite their growing visibility, GLBT people remain largely a socially despised group (Chekola, 1994; Hartman, 1996; Herdt, 1989; Magee & Miller, 1994). As a result, disclosure remains a potentially emotionally charged issue for both GLBT people and their loved ones.

THE HUMAN RIGHTS CAMPAIGN: NATIONAL COMING OUT PROJECT

The Human Rights Campaign (HRC) is a national political advocacy organization that works to advance equality based on sexual orientation and gender expression. HRC lobbies Congress, mobilizes grassroots action in diverse communities, invests strategically to elect a fair-minded Congress, and increases public understanding through innovative education and communication strategies. It is the largest and most visible national organization working on behalf of GLBT people and their families. The national HRC Web site, located at www.hrc.org, is an excellent resource for accessing an array of GLBT-focused information, including information about coming out.

The HRC National Coming Out Project is a public education and outreach program that has as its purpose the promotion of honesty and openness about being GLBT on campus, in the workplace, and at home. The Coming Out Project's Web site is located at www.hrc.org/ncop. It provides a rich resource for information on coming out.

SOURCE: HUMAN RIGHTS CAMPAIGN WEB SITE, www.hrc.org.

DIVERSITY CONSIDERATIONS

Members of racial and ethnic minority groups who disclose as GLBT encounter not only the broad-based heterosexism common to United States social culture in general but also the negativity and potential rejection of the racial or ethnic group with which they identify (Greene, 1997; Thompson, 1992). The African American community has strong historic religious ties that value heterosexuality, traditional gender roles, and procreation and devalue same-sex relationships and nontraditional gender roles (Greene, 1994a, 1994b). African American GLBT people may risk rejection from central systems of support—their racial communities and church communities—if they disclose their sexual minority status (Cohen, 1996; Simmons, 1991). One study that compared disclosure among gay and bisexual men (Kennamer, Honnold, Bradford, & Hendricks, 2000), found that African American men were far less likely than Caucasian men to disclose their sexual orientation to others.

Similarly, traditional gender roles and procreation-based heterosexuality are highly valued in many Latino households where conservative Catholicism is a common form of religious practice (Wall & Washington, 1991). And in Asian American culture, being GLBT is often equated with shaming one's family and rejecting Asian culture, which values traditional roles for men and women, including the responsibility to carry forth the family line (Chan, 1989, 1995).

Thus, holding multiple minority identities (for example, being GLBT, female, and a person of color) can result in layers of jeopardy—racism, heterosexism, sexism—and rejection by one's racial or ethnic community. In addition, GLBT people of color report that not only do they risk rejection by their racial and ethnic communities because of their sexual orientation or transgender status, they also many times encounter racism in the Caucasian-dominated GLBT community. As a result, they are at risk of marginalization on a number of fronts.

An interesting contradiction to the pattern of rejection by ethnic communities is that in some Native American cultures GLBT people have historically been thought of as gifted with special spiritual powers, including the possession of both female and male spirits within the same person (Tafoya, 1996). Thus in many situations Native American GLBT people have been honored for their "two-spirit" special status.

Disclosure may also present special challenges for GLBT people from small towns and rural communities compared to those residing in urban and suburban settings where GLBT-supportive resources are more available. Many cities have a network of formal GLBT social supports such as youth groups, GLBT film festivals, and GLBT-oriented faith communities. It may be more challenging for those who reside in small towns and rural areas to connect with other GLBT people, and the social culture in these areas is often more conservative and traditional. For people who have computer and Internet access, however, options for support, information, and making connections with others are readily available. Many GLBT people—no matter their regional location—are choosing to come out online before coming out in their own communities (Human Rights Campaign Foundation, 2002).

DISCLOSURE IN ADOLESCENCE

While the age at which people choose to come out is highly variable, research offers clear evidence that many sexual minority people engage the coming-out process during their teen years. Coleman (1982) found the average age for coming out in a sample of gay males to be age 15 and for lesbian females to be age 20. Remafedi (1987) identified the average age of coming out in a sample of gay and lesbian youth to be 14 years. D'Augelli, Hershberger, and Pilkington (1998b) found an initial age of self-awareness among a sample of GLB youth to be around age 10, with first disclosure to a friend by age 16. And in another study of GLB youth, Maguen, Floyd, Bakeman, and Armistead (2002) found an average age of self-awareness as GLB at around age 11, with first disclosure to a friend by age 16. While there are no comparable data regarding age of disclosure for transgender youth, the available literature suggests that transgender people tend to report early childhood self-awareness that their gender identity does not conform to traditional expectations (Burgess, 1999; Swann & Herbert, 1999).

Given that the vast majority of GLBT youth are reared in families where heterocentric ideals and traditional gender role divisions are the norm, they typically have neither family support nor guidance on how to express their identities as sexual minority people. In fact, one of the greatest risks for adolescents in coming out is rejection by family. Worst-case scenarios could include parents' withdrawal of emotional and financial support from their GLBT child, ousting the child from the home and even committing acts of violence against the child because of his or her sexual orientation or transgender identity. Pilkington and D'Augelli (1995) found that more than 30% of the GLB youth they surveyed had been verbally abused at home and 10% had been assaulted by a family member because of their sexual orientation.

Coming out as GLBT means facing the stigma associated with being identified as a sexual minority person. That stigma can be particularly acute during adolescence, a time when peer pressure to fit in with a heterocentric norm is enormous. School environments are generally not supportive of sexual minority youth. Sexual orientation and gender identity diversity are typically not included in health education and diversity education curricula in schools, and school employees are ill prepared to effectively support the needs of GLBT youth. Because of the social stress GLBT youth encounter at school and among peers, they are at high risk for academic difficulties, being ridiculed by their peers, isolating themselves in school settings, absenteeism, and dropping out (Elia, 1993; Rotheram-Borus & Fernandez, 1995; Tharinger & Wells, 2000).

While GLBT youth are coming out more frequently these days—in their families, in their peer groups, and at school—it remains important to recognize the stress involved in coming out as a teen in a highly heterosexist social culture. GLBT youth are at higher risk for depression and suicide compared to their presumed heterosexual counterparts. An alarming 30% to 40% of sexual minority youth have attempted suicide (compared to a rate of 8% to 13% for presumed heterosexual youth) (D'Augelli & Hershberger, 1993; D'Augelli et al., 1998a; Friedman, Asnis, Boeck, & DiFiore, 1987; Garland & Zigler, 1993; Gibson, 1989; Martin & Hetrick, 1988; National Lesbian and Gay Health Foundation, 1987; Schneider, Farberow, & Kruks, 1989; Smith & Crawford, 1986). Supportive and understanding family members, peers, and teachers can be crucial if GLBT youth are to successfully navigate disclosure issues.

COMING OUT TO PARENTS

Disclosure to parents and significant family members can be considered as among the most significant of all coming out events (Ben-Ari, 1995a; Berzon, 2001; D'Augelli, 1991; Morrow, 1993, 1996, 2004b; Signorile, 1995). Whether one is out to one's parents and, if so, how well that process went, is a common discussion topic in GLBT friendship networks. Ben Ari (1995a) found that the greatest fear associated with coming out to families was parental rejection. She also discovered that the weeks or months prior to disclosure, known as pre-disclosure, were a time in which lesbians and gays felt distant and alienated from their parents. This pre-disclosure period can be a time for making a final decision about whether to disclose, determining how to handle the disclosure, and pondering how the recipient will respond.

A person's first disclosure is rarely made to parents (Savin-Williams, 1998). Rather, it is more often made to an age-similar peer (D'Augelli & Hershberger, 1993). Furthermore, siblings often know about a sexual minority brother's or sister's status before parents know (Murray, 1994). Disclosers are likely to come out to their mother before their father, in the belief that mothers will be more understanding and accepting than fathers (Maguen et al., 2002; Savin-Williams, 1998; Savin-Williams & Dube, 1998). Researchers have found that mothers tend to be more accepting of their sexual minority children initially after disclosure (Pilkington & D'Augelli, 1995; Rotheram-Borus, Rosario, & Koopman, 1991). Paradoxically, however, it has also been found that mothers are more likely than fathers to verbally abuse their GLBT child—especially if the child is a lesbian daughter (Savin-Williams, 1998).

PARENTS, FAMILIES, AND FRIENDS OF LESBIANS AND GAYS (PFLAG)

Parents, Families, and Friends of Lesbians and Gays (PFLAG) is a national nonprofit organization located in Washington, DC, with almost 500 affiliate organizations located throughout the United States. PFLAG affiliates can be found in most urban areas throughout the country. The mission of PFLAG is to promote the health and well-being of gay, lesbian, bisexual, and transgender people, and their families and friends. The organization seeks to support GLBT people in coping with societal heterosexism, to provide education to the public about GLBT concerns, and to advocate for the civil rights of GLBT people. Local PFLAG meetings are typically safe places where parents, family, and friends of GLBT people can come together to engage in dialogue. GLBT people themselves are also welcome at PFLAG meetings. For many GLBT people and their families, PFLAG becomes a common connecting point of information, understanding, support, and advocacy.

SOURCE: NATIONAL PFLAG WEB SITE, www.pflag.org.

Disclosure often creates a family crisis. Parents may be ill prepared to understand, much less embrace, the concept of having a sexual minority child. They need time to adjust to the change in their assumptions about the sexual orientation or gender identity of the child. They need to mourn the loss of their heterosexual-based dreams for their child—"traditional" marriages and families. And parents commonly experience an initial sense of guilt for having "done something wrong" that resulted in their child's being GLBT (Fairchild & Hayward, 1998; Jung & Smith, 1993). Given time, as well as accurate educational information, many parents can come to better accept and understand their GLBT son or daughter. Many even become empowered enough to become social justice advocates on behalf of sexual minority people through organizations such as Parents, Families, and Friends of Lesbians and Gays (PFLAG).

GLBT PARENTS COMING OUT TO CHILDREN

Disclosure to one's children is a significant issue in the lives of GLBT parents. For parents to keep their sexual orientation or gender identity a secret from their children is an arduous task—and one that often is not in their children's best interests. Such family secrets nearly always produce communication difficulties and psychological barriers that are problematic (Appleby & Anastas, 1998). Parental disclosure while children are young (early childhood) is generally most successful for families (Barret & Robinson, 1990; Lynch & Murray, 2000; McDonald, 1990). From this early point in the development of the family, having sexual minority parents becomes intertwined with the essence of the family system. It can be more difficult for children to adjust to the news of having a sexual minority parent when the disclosure occurs during adolescence (Bigner,

1996; O'Connell, 1993; Patterson, 1992). Peer pressure toward conformity to a heterosexual family norm—as well as heterosexist prejudices—is more likely to be formed by adolescence. In addition, adolescence is the developmental period when teens themselves are taking on the tasks of coming to terms with their own sexual identity. This process in itself is overwhelming without also facing the task of adjusting to the news that a parent is GLBT. In some situations, however, adolescence may the time when parents disclose to their children because it has taken parents themselves a number of years to come to terms with their own sexual minority identity. In general, being honest and keeping the lines of communication open—no matter the age of the children—is a strategy worth pursuing.

In studying families of lesbian and gay parents and co-parents, Lynch and Murray (2000) found that parental coming out decisions were based on two concerns: (1) parents' fears of losing custody of their children if they disclosed their sexual orientation and (2) parents' concerns about how their disclosure would affect their children's lives. In another study of more than 2,000 lesbian and bisexual mothers and nonmothers, Morris, Balsam, and Rothblum (2002) found that women who had children before coming out were likely to be older when they first thought of themselves as being lesbian or bisexual and older when they first disclosed to another person. On the whole, the lesbian and bisexual women in the study who had children were less likely to be out to others compared to the lesbian and bisexual women without children. Thus it would seem that women with children may feel a greater need for discretion regarding their sexual identity in order to protect their families from possible legal entanglements (e.g., custody disputes with an ex-husband) and external heterosexism.

Barret and Logan (2002) offer a number of suggestions for parents who are considering coming out to their children. A central point they make is that parents must come to terms with their own sexual (or transgender) identity before disclosing to their children. Parents who are not yet clear on their own identity are unprepared to clearly inform their children of what it means to be a sexual minority person and how that status might affect the family system. Barret and Logan also suggest that once a parent is clear about his or her identity, children are never too young to be told. Information should be disclosed in an age-appropriate format, and parents need to keep the lines of communication open so that they can help their children process and understand the information as they continue to grow and develop over time. They also note that disclosure should be phrased not as a confession but as a deliberate sharing of information about oneself with one's children.

Ultimately, parents' decisions about coming out to children are theirs alone to make. Some parents feel the need to withhold information in order to avoid the threat of losing custody of their children. Others experience a need to protect their children from the hostility of external heterosexism. It is important for social workers to help parents process their thoughts and feelings about disclosure and how it may affect the overall family system. Social workers can provide valuable assistance to parents as they prepare to disclose to children and help them to identify educational and support resources for themselves and their children (e.g., reading materials, support groups, connections with other GLBT families).

DISCLOSURE AMONG OLDER ADULTS

In understanding disclosure among older adults, it is important to have a historical perspective. Adults who are 65 and older came of age during the pre-Stonewall era—before the gay and lesbian civil rights movement began. They grew through adolescence and into adulthood at a time when being lesbian or gay was identified as a mental illness and transgenderism was not yet differentiated from sexual orientation. Research on sexual orientation and the psychological health of sexual minority people was in its infancy, and opportunities for social supports and meeting other GLBT people were few (Morrow, 2001). Gayness was considered to be moral depravity, and its occurrence was largely blamed on dysfunctional parenting. Thus a lifetime of overt anti-GLBT social and cultural oppression has informed the existence of older GLBT people.

In order to protect themselves, GLBT people of that generation virtually had to be less forthcoming about their sexual orientation and/or gender identity. Many kept their GLBT identity secret in order to avoid being shunned by family and friends, losing their jobs, being physically assaulted, and even being forced into psychiatric treatment targeted toward "changing" their identity to heterosexuality. In sum, many led clandestine lives in an effort to avoid the harm and violence that could befall them because of their sexual orientation and/or gender identity (Adelman, 1990; Appleby & Anastas, 1998; Deevey, 1990), and they learned to conceal their sexual minority status as a means of survival (Grossman, 1995; Martin & Lyon, 2001; McLeod, 1997; Shenk & Fullmer, 1996). As a result, it is not uncommon for the secrecy and discretion formed during those earlier years to carry over into their senior years for many older GLBT people. In contrast, there are also members of this generational cohort who became early pioneers in what would eventually become the "modern" GLBT civil rights movement. These were the people who dared to push the envelope of visibility by coming out in order to challenge the societal heterosexism that defined them as sick, sinful, and criminal (Morrow, 2001). As a group, however, many older GLBT people may tend to be less forthcoming regarding disclosure than post-Stonewall generations. In understanding the context in which older GLBTs came of age, it is important to respect their right to self-determination regarding disclosure.

COMING OUT IN COMMUNITY ENVIRONMENTS

People involve themselves in an array of community environments and social systems throughout their lives. These environments and systems evolve and change as people's lives unfold. Thus new social situations constantly arise in which decisions about disclosure must be made. This section examines three common community settings where GLBT people must decide the degree to which they will be out: the workplace, health care systems, and faith communities.

Disclosure in the workplace can be risky for many GLBT people. There are no federal laws to protect against job discrimination on the basis of one's sexual orientation or gender identity (Human Rights Campaign Foundation, 2002). Neither sexual orientation nor gender identity is included in the Civil Rights Act. Therefore, people can—and do—lose their jobs or are denied promotion because of their sexual minority status. A prime example is the U.S. military service. With its discriminatory "don't ask, don't tell" policy, the U.S. government has enacted a nondisclosure requirement of sexual minority people who serve in the military. Those who come out while in the military are guaranteed dismissal from service—regardless of their job performance. People who work in fields serving children (e.g., teachers, day care workers, adoption workers) are also at risk of losing their employment because of the heterosexism centered in the unfounded stereotype that GLBT people are somehow detrimental to the healthy development of children.

Researchers have found that approximately 60% of gay men and lesbians report having experienced job discrimination because of their sexual orientation (National Gay and Lesbian Task Force, 1991; Waldo, 1999). Lab-based research demonstrates that discrimination in the hiring of lesbian and gay job applicants remains prevalent (Griffith & Quinones, 2001). Thus disclosure in the workplace presents a dilemma.

Some GLBT people remain closeted at work in order to avoid heterosexist repercussions that might negatively affect their career. Researchers have found that workplace disclosure is related both to job satisfaction and to job anxiety (Driscoll, Kelley, & Fassinger, 1996; Griffith & Hebl, 2002). That is, people who are out at work are likely to be more satisfied with their employment, and out workers also experience greater anxiety related to the fear of workplace discrimination because of their sexual minority status. Griffith and Hebl (2002) found that sexual minority workers were more likely to disclose at work when their employing organization had nondiscrimination policies that included sexual orientation, when employers demonstrated active support for sexual minority workers, and when employers offered workplace diversity training that specifically included sexual orientation content.

Health care systems present another disclosure dilemma for GLBT people. Health care workers commonly presume that all patients are heterosexual unless patients disclose otherwise. Medical forms—an ever-present component of health care treatment—tend not to incorporate options for people who have same-sex partners. For example, most forms depict relationship categories only as *single, married,* or *divorced*—nothing to represent domestic partners. It is not surprising, then, that many GLBT people tend to avoid health care because of provider negativity toward sexual minority concerns (Eliason & Shope, 2001; Schilder, Kennedy, Strathdee, Goldson, Hogg, & O'Shaughnessy, 1999). Disclosure to health care providers entails some degree of risk, depending on how the provider responds. Yet nondisclosure means accepting the frustrating assumption that one is heterosexual and traditionally gender-identified.

Disclosure within one's faith community can be a special challenge for GLBT people. Institutional religion has a long history of heterosexist intolerance and oppression of sexual minority people (Davidson, 2000; Hilton, 1992; McNeill, 1993), and many mainstream religions continue to depict sexual minorities as immoral and spiritually corrupt. Because of religious oppression on the basis of sexual orientation and gender identity, many GLBT people have suffered shame, family rejection, social rejection, and the loss of their faith communities as places of support (Morrow, 2004a, 2004b).

While traditional religion has been a source of oppression against GLBT people, newer theological interpretations of the Bible (Gomes, 1996; McNeill, 1993; Spong, 1998) have resulted in a growing demand for the full inclusion of sexual minorities in many socially progressive faith communities. GLBT people take on a calculated risk in coming out to their communities of faith. They must anticipate the likely response of their faith community in deciding whether to disclose in that setting. For some, the potential pain of negative repercussions is too great, and they either live their true lives in secrecy or reject their community of faith completely. For others, coming out in their community of faith becomes a bold step toward claiming their goodness and value as human beings and challenging institutional religion to accept and affirm all people regardless of their sexual orientation or gender identity.

THE STRESS OF THE CLOSET

While every person's right to disclose or not disclose in any given situation is to be respected and honored, the stress of "the closet"—of keeping a central part of one's identity secret and hidden from others—cannot be dismissed. Silence is a tool of oppression. When a person's voice is silenced, when the liberation of claiming personal identity is denied, then that person—as well as all people like him or her—is silenced and made invisible. Remaining in the closet requires living a double life—one part as a GLBT person and another part as a member of the presumed dominant group. Closeted people live in constant fear of being discovered, of being "outed" by another against their will. They live in fear of the potential repercussions of their sexual orientation or transgender identity being revealed. They learn to compartmentalize their lives, to avoid the use of pronouns that would reveal the gender of those they love, and to keep their personal lives hidden from view. As a result of this concealment, they are at risk of seeming aloof and one-dimensional to others.

In some situations nondisclosure is a healthy choice if one is to remain safe from the harmful consequences of discovery (e.g., violence, job loss, rejection). In other situations, nondisclosure represents internalized oppression—a person having internalized the negative social, religious, and political messages propagated to keep their group in its "place." Internalized oppression for GLBT people means internalizing a belief in the negative stereotypes and the harmful rhetoric perpetuated by a heterosexist society. It means internalizing a sense of shame about one's sexual orientation or gender identity and about one's own personal worth, and it means being filled with self-doubt about one's full value as a human being. The secrecy of the closet, fueled by internalized oppression, can leave GLBT people at higher risk for low self-esteem, depression, substance abuse, and suicide.

GUIDELINES FOR PRACTICE

Social workers can play a key role in helping clients address issues of disclosure. They can explore with clients the costs and benefits of coming out, and they can help clients make decisions about disclosure across a variety of social contexts. In addition, they can help clients gain necessary knowledge and interpersonal relationship skills that will facilitate their decisions and actions on disclosure. This section provides guidelines for practice in facilitating client exploration of and preparation for disclosure. The goal is not necessarily that all clients will choose disclosure in every context. Rather, the goal is to offer a systematic means for helping clients explore whether disclosure is desirable and, if it is, to provide a process for helping them prepare for that task. Above all, client self-determination regarding disclosure should be honored. The guidelines below are adapted in part from those presented in Morrow (2000).

1. *Assess the client's social context.* An evaluation of the social context of coming out becomes the foundation for client decision making about whether to disclose in a variety of contexts. At issue is the purpose to be served by disclosure, juxtaposed with the expected outcomes of doing so. What does the client hope to accomplish through coming out in a selected social context? What are the cultural values and political views regarding sexual orientation and gender diversity of the potential recipients of the news? Are there safety concerns for the cli-

ent relative to disclosure? In situations where clients are considering coming out to family members who provide them financial support, what is the risk of losing that support upon disclosure?

According to Herek (1985), one can expect negative reactions to be more likely among those who are older, less educated, and more conservative toward sexuality in general. In addition, Herek found that those who subscribe to conservative political and religious ideologies, support traditional and restrictive gender roles, and manifest high levels of authoritarianism and related personality characteristics (dogmatism, rigidity, and intolerance of ambiguity) are more likely to be GLBT-negative. After thoroughly assessing the social context of coming out, the social worker and the client can collaborate on the anticipated safety as well as the costs and benefits of disclosure. In cases where the anticipated costs outweigh the benefits, clients may wish to defer coming out until the social context changes.

2. *Assess the client's level of GLBT identity development.* Assessing the client's level of GLBT identity development relates to determining the degree to which the client has established a positive and secure personal identity as a sexual minority person. The primary concern here is that if clients are not sure of and comfortable with their sexual orientation or transgender identity, they may not yet be ready to help others become comfortable with it.

Clearly, determining the degree to which identity as a GLBT person has been formed is a challenging process that can vary from person to person. In an effort to better explain and predict this process, a number of models of identity development have been proposed (Cass, 1979; Chapman & Brannock, 1987; Coleman, 1982; McCarn & Fassinger, 1996; Minton & McDonald, 1984; Plummer, 1975; Ponse, 1978; Sophie, 1986; Troiden, 1979; Weinberg, Williams, & Pryor, 1994). GLBT identity development and these models are addressed more fully in chapter 4 of this book.

It should be noted that identity is an elusive construct to capture in any "absolute" fashion and models offer but one aspect of considering identity development. Nonetheless, they can be useful tools for assessing a client's progress in establishing a positive identity as a sexual minority person. In general, the farther along clients are in developing a positive GLBT identity, the better prepared they are internally to engage the coming out process. Those who have not yet developed a secure GLBT identity would potentially benefit from furthering that process before focusing their energy on external disclosures.

3. *Develop a client knowledge base related to gay and lesbian issues.* One way to help GLBT clients prepare for coming out to others is to help them become educated about issues pertinent to sexual orientation and gender identity. Social workers can help clients brainstorm questions and concerns that they would likely encounter in coming out in various social contexts. Workers can assist clients in developing an accurate knowledge base of information to address identi-

fied questions and concerns. Common issues of concern that might be raised by people unfamiliar with accurate information on GLBT issues can include the following: HIV/AIDS risk, sexual orientation versus sexual "preference," misinformation and stereotypes regarding sexual perversion and child molestation, religious rhetoric commonly used to oppress gay and lesbian people, and the value of loving, committed GLBT relationships versus stereotypes of sexual promiscuity.

4. *Develop a social support system.* Clients who are considering making significant disclosures (e.g., to family, at work) will benefit from having an identified social support system in place as they approach the time of coming out. Social supports are critical, in particular, for GLBT youth. They generally have minimal personal and financial resources (Rotheram-Borus & Fernandez, 1995), and family rejection can leave them homeless and without financial support. Furthermore, GLBT youth, as well as older GLBT people, are at risk for suicide, anxiety, and depression because of the stress of being gay in a homophobic and heterosexist culture (Gibson, 1989; Schneider, 1991). Rejection by family members can especially exacerbate this risk. Social workers can be significant sources of therapeutic support for clients during this time. Other sources of support can include GLBT-related community services such as adult and adolescent groups, GLBT-affirmative faith communities, partners, friends, and colleagues.

5. *Engage in practice experiences before coming out to families.* Because major coming out events (disclosures to family, coworkers, etc.) can be significantly stressful for many GLBT people (Ben-Ari, 1995a; Eichberg, 1990), practice experience in coming out to trusted others beforehand can be helpful preparation (Signorile, 1995). Workers can help clients identify those who they expect will respond to their coming out in an accepting manner. Having at least one successful experience before disclosure to families can be a vital confidence builder for clients. Even if a practice experience results in a negative reaction, that too can serve as grist for the therapeutic mill in the worker–client relationship. In such cases, further practice experiences with positive results might be especially needed.

6. *Determine the availability of supportive family allies.* In the case of coming out to family members, it may be helpful to determine the availability of family allies—well-respected GLBT-affirmative friends or relatives who can be supportive both to the GLBT person who is coming out and to family members who receive the news. In such situations, family members and their GLBT family member can have a third party with whom they can process information. Effective allies can become additional sources of education, emotional support, and encouragement for all parties in the coming out process. It is important that an ally, if chosen, be a person who is trustworthy (the coming out news should come from the GLBT person, not from the ally), GLBT-affirmative, and respected by the family as well as by the GLBT person. If the involvement of an ally is planned, the social worker can facilitate the client's preparation for effec-

tively utilizing that support and for negotiating agreed-upon roles and boundaries related to the ally's role in the process.

7. *Choose language and terminology appropriate for the receiver of the news.* Social workers can support clients in coming out in various social contexts by helping them to determine the language and terminology that would be most appropriate and understandable for the recipients of the news. In general, the language of coming out should be phrased in positive rather than negative terms (Ben-Ari, 1995a; Signorile, 1995). That is, recipients are more likely to receive the news positively if they perceive the GLBT person is happy and secure rather than upset about his or her sexual orientation or transgender identity. The social worker and client can collaborate on language options considered most acceptable for the client and the recipients of the news. In general, workers should encourage clients to use terms that will be most comfortable and understandable for both them and their family members.

8. *Select the method of information delivery.* Clients preparing for disclosure must select the method through which the news will be communicated. Typical options include person-to-person sharing, phone communication, letters, and e-mail correspondence. Workers can help clients explore these communication options. In a study of 32 gay and lesbian people who had come out to parents, Ben-Ari (1995a) found that the majority (60%) chose to communicate the information in person. Other information delivery options reported in the study were by phone (20%) and through letters (20%). Social workers can utilize role play and rehearsal exercises to help clients prepare their method of information delivery.

In social contexts where clients perceive that their verbal communication will be frequently interrupted or distorted by recipients, they may prefer to consider communicating through writing. Possible benefits of using a written form of communication include the following: the message can be formulated exactly as the client prefers; the client will not be interrupted before communicating the entire message; the recipient will have time to read and reread the information, and thereby distortion might be minimized; and the recipient has time to process the information before responding to the news (Eichberg, 1990).

In some instances, a client may wish to make the disclosure to significant people (e.g., family members) in the presence of the social worker. If that is the case, the worker can serve as a facilitator of the process and as therapeutic support and intervention for both the client and the family members.

9. *Structure the timing of coming out.* It is vital that clients have control over the timing of the coming out event. If at all possible, disclosure should be planned and deliberate—not reactive (e.g., in the midst of an argument). Ideally, coming out should be an act of care and relationship building (Eichberg, 1990) rather than an act of argumentative confrontation. In general, it is better to avoid coming out to family members during a family crisis (e.g., illness, accident, or

death of a family member). It may also be better to avoid coming out on or just before major holidays, since such times are often stressful events in themselves for families (Signorile, 1995). The days following a holiday may be a less stressful time if coming out to families must occur close to a holiday.

10. *Prepare the client for possible negative reactions.* In some situations, people respond negatively to disclosure. For example, adjusting to the news that a family member is gay or lesbian generally involves some degree of family upheaval or crisis (Cramer & Roach, 1998; Harry, 1993; Magee & Miller, 1994; Morrow, 1993; Savin-Williams & Dube, 1998). Given that the greatest fear reported among sexual minority people in coming out is fear of rejection (Ben-Ari, 1995b; Elliott, 1996), it is important to prepare clients for unanticipated negative responses—in case the unexpected occurs. In general, social workers can help clients develop skills to de-escalate hostility, and they can help clients develop a safety plan for themselves should it be needed. In the best cases, such plans will not be needed. Yet preparation for the unexpected is effective social work practice.

CONCLUSION

The visibility of sexual minority people is central to the achievement of equal rights for the GLBT community. Whenever any group remains invisible to society at large, it is more difficult for them to be socially acknowledged and politically validated as fully functioning human beings. There is greater openness and visibility of GLBT people than ever before, yet many remain closeted for fear of the repercussions that would come with disclosure. Social workers have a responsibility to assist GLBT people in their journey of coming out—both to themselves and to other people.

REFERENCES

Adelman, M. (1990). Stigma, gay lifestyles, and adjustment to aging: A study of later-life gay men and lesbians. *Journal of Homosexuality, 20*(3–4), 7–32.

Appleby, G. A., & Anastas, J. W. (1998). *Not just a passing phase: Social work with gay, lesbian, and bisexual people.* New York: Columbia University Press.

Barret, R. L., & Logan, C. (2002). *Counseling gay men and lesbians.* Pacific Grove, CA: Brooks/Cole.

Barret, R. L., & Robinson, B. E. (1990). Gay fathers. In F. Bozett (Ed.), *Gay and lesbian parents* (pp. 39–57). New York: Praeger.

Ben-Ari, A. (1995a). Coming out: A dialectic of intimacy and privacy. *Families in Society: The Journal of Contemporary Human Services, 76*(5), 306–314.

——— (1995b). The discovery that an offspring is gay: Parents', gay men's, and lesbians' perspectives. *Journal of Homosexuality, 30*(1), 89–111.

Berzon, B. (Ed.). (2001). *Positively gay: New approaches to gay and lesbian life* (3d ed.). Berkeley, CA: Celestial Arts.

Bigner, J. J. (1996). Working with gay fathers' developmental, postdivorce, parenting, and therapeutic issues. In J. Laird & R. J. Green (Eds.), *Lesbians and gays in couples and families* (pp. 370–403). San Francisco: Jossey-Bass.

Boon, S. D., & Miller, R. J. (1999). Exploring the links between interpersonal trust and the reasons underlying gay and bisexual males' disclosure of their sexual orientation to their mothers. *Journal of Homosexuality, 37*(3), 45–68.

Burgess, C. (1999). Internal and external stress factors associated with the identity development of transgendered youth. *Journal of Gay and Lesbian Social Services, 10*(3/4), 35–47.

Cain, R. (1991). Relational contexts and information management among gay men. *Families in Society, 72,* 344–352.

Cass, V. C. (1979). Homosexual identity formation: A theoretical model. *Journal of Homosexuality, 4*(3), 219–235.

———. (1984a). Homosexual identity: A concept in need of definition. *Journal of Homosexuality, 9*(2/3), 105–126.

———. (1984b). Homosexual identity formation: Testing a theoretical model. *Journal of Sex Research, 20*(2), 143–167.

Chan, C. S. (1989). Issues of identity development among Asian-American lesbians and gay men. *Journal of Counseling and Development, 68,* 16–20.

———. (1995). Issues of sexual identity in an ethnic minority: The case of Chinese American lesbians, gay men, and bisexual people. In A. R. D'Augelli & C. J. Patterson (Eds.), *Lesbian, gay, and bisexual identities over the lifespan* (pp. 87–101). New York: Oxford University Press.

Chapman, B. E., & Brannock, J. C. (1987). Proposed model of lesbian identity development: An empirical examination. *Journal of Homosexuality, 14*(3/4), 69–80.

Chekola, M. (1994). Outing, truth-telling, and the shame of the closet. *Journal of Homosexuality, 27*(3/4), 67–90.

Cohen, C. J. (1996). Contested membership: Black gay identities and the politics of AIDS. In S. Seidman (Ed.), *Queer theory/sociology* (pp. 362–394). Cambridge, MA: Blackwell.

Coleman, E. (1982). Developmental stages of the coming out process. *Journal of Homosexuality, 7*(7), 31–43.

Cramer, D. W., & Roach, A. J. (1998). Coming out to mom and dad: A study of gay males and their relationships with their parents. *Journal of Homosexuality, 15*(3/4), 79–91.

D'Augelli, A. R. (1991). Gay men in college: Identity processes and adaptations. *Journal of Student Development, 32,* 140–146.

D'Augelli, A. R., & Hershberger, S. L. (1993). Lesbian, gay, and bisexual youth in community settings: Personal challenges and mental health problems. *American Journal of Community Psychology, 211,* 421–448.

D'Augelli, A. R., Hershberger, S. L., & Pilkington, N. W. (1998a). Lesbian, gay, and bisexual youth in community settings: Personal challenges and mental health problems. *American Journal of Community Psychology, 21,* 421–448.

———. (1998b). Lesbian, gay, and bisexual youth and their families: Disclosure of sexual orientation and its consequences. *American Journal of Orthopsychiatry, 68*(3), 361–371.

Davidson, M. G. (2000). Religion and spirituality. In R. M. Perez & K. A. DeBord (Eds.), *Handbook of counseling and psychotherapy with lesbian, gay, and bisexual clients* (pp. 409–433). Washington, DC: American Psychological Association.

Deevey, S. (1990). Older lesbian women: An invisible minority. *Journal of Gerontological Nursing, 16*(5), 35–39.

Driscoll, J. M., Kelley, F. A., & Fassinger, R. A. (1996). Lesbian identity and disclosure in the workplace: Relation to occupational stress and satisfaction. *Journal of Vocational Behavior*, 48(2), 229–242.

Eichberg, R. (1990). *Coming out: An act of love*. New York: Plume.

Elia, J. P. (1993). Homophobia in the high school: A problem in need of resolution. *High School Journal*, 77, 177–185.

Eliason, M. J., & Shope, R. (2001). Does "don't ask don't tell" apply to health care? Lesbian, gay, and bisexual people's disclosure to health care providers. *Journal of the Gay and Lesbian Medical Association*, 5(4), 125–134.

Elliott, M. (1996). Coming out in the classroom: A return to the hard place. *College English*, 58(6), 693–708.

Fairchild, B., & Hayward, N. (1998). *Now that you know: A parents' guide to understanding their gay and lesbian children* (3d ed.). San Diego: Harcourt Brace.

Franke, R., & Leary, M. R. (1991). Disclosure of sexual orientation by lesbians and gay men: A comparison of private and public processes. *Journal of Social and Clinical Psychology*, 10(3), 262–269.

Friedman, J. M., Asnis, G. M., Boeck, M., & DiFore, J. (1987). Prevalence of specific suicidal behaviors in a high school sample. *American Journal of Psychiatry*, 144, 1203–1206.

Garland, A. F., & Ziegler, E. (1993). Adolescent suicide prevention: Current research and social policy implications. *American Psychology*, 48, 169–182.

Gibson, P. (1989). Gay male and lesbian youth suicide. In ADAMHA, *Report of the Secretary's Task Force on Youth Suicide*. DHHS Publication No. ADM 89–1623, 3:110–142. Washington, DC: U.S. Government Printing Office.

Gomes, P. J. (1996). *The Good Book: Reading the Bible with heart and mind*. New York: William Morrow.

Greene, B. (1994a). Lesbian and gay sexual orientations: Implications for clinical training, practice, and research. In B. Greene & G. Herek (Eds.), *Psychological perspectives on lesbian and gay issues*, Vol. 1, *Lesbian and gay psychology: Theory, research, and clinical applications* (pp. 1–24). Thousand Oaks, CA: Sage.

—— (1994b). Lesbian women of color: Triple jeopardy. In L. Comas-Diaz & B. Greene (Eds.), *Women of color: Integrating ethnic and gender identities in psychotherapy* (pp. 389–427). New York: Guilford.

—— (1997). Family, ethnic identity, and sexual orientation: African American lesbians and gay men. In B. Greene (Ed.), *Ethnic and cultural diversity among lesbians and gay men* (pp. 40–52). Thousand Oaks, CA: Sage.

Griffith, K. H., & Hebl, M. R. (2002). The disclosure dilemma for gay men and lesbians: "Coming out at work." *Journal of Applied Psychology*, 87, 1191–1199.

Griffith, K. H., & Quinones, M. A. (2001). *Lesbian construction workers and gay flight attendants: The effects of sexual orientation, gender, and job type on job applicant ratings*. Unpublished manuscript, Rice University.

Grossman, A. H. (1995). At risk, infected, and invisible: Older gay men and HIV/AIDS. *Journal of Association of Nurses in AIDS Care*, 6(6), 13–19.

Harry, J. (1993). Being out: A general model. *Journal of Homosexuality*, 26(1), 25–39.

Hartman, A. (1996). Social policy as a context for lesbian and gay families. In J. Laird & R. J. Green (Eds.), *Lesbians and gays in couples and families*. San Francisco: Jossey-Bass.

Herdt, G. (1989). Gay and lesbian youth, emergent identities, and cultural scenes at home and abroad. *Journal of Homosexuality*, 17(1/2), 1–42.

Herek, G. M. (1985). Beyond homophobia: A social psychological perspective on attitudes toward lesbians and gay men. In J. P. DeCecco (Ed.), *Bashers, baiters, and bigots: Homophobia in American society* (pp. 1–21). New York: Harrington Park.

Hilton, B. (1992). *Can homophobia be cured?* Nashville: Abingdon.

Human Rights Campaign Foundation. (2002). *Resource guide to coming out*. Washington, DC: Author.

Jung, P. B., & Smith, R. F. (1993). *Heterosexism: An ethical challenge*. Albany: State University of New York Press.

Kennamer, J. D., Honnold, J., Bradford, J., & Hendricks, M. (2000). Differences in disclosure of sexuality among African American and white gay/bisexual men: Implications for HIV/AIDS prevention. *AIDS Education and Prevention, 12*(6), 519–531.

Lynch, J. M., & Murray, K. (2000). For the love of the children: The coming out process for lesbian and gay parents and stepparents. *Journal of Homosexuality, 39*(1), 1–24.

Magee, M., & Miller, D. C. (1994). Psychoanalysis and women's experiences of coming out: The necessity of becoming a bee charmer. *Journal of the American Academy of Psychoanalysis, 22*(3), 481–504.

Maguen, S., Floyd, F. J., Bakeman, R., & Armistead, L. (2002). Developmental milestones and disclosure of sexual orientation among gay, lesbian, and bisexual youths. *Applied Developmental Psychology, 23*(2), 219–233.

Martin, A. D., & Hetrick, E. S. (1988). The stigmatization of the gay and lesbian adolescent. *Journal of Homosexuality, 15*, 163–184.

Martin, D., & Lyon, P. (2001). The older lesbian. In B. Berzon (Ed.), *Positively gay: New approaches to gay and lesbian life* (3d ed.) (pp. 111–120). Berkeley, CA: Celestial Arts.

McCarn, S. R., & Fassinger, R. E. (1996). Revisioning sexual minority identity formation: A new model of lesbian identity and its implications for counseling and research. *Counseling Psychologist, 24*, 508–534.

McDonald, H. B. (1990). *Homosexuality: A practical guide to counseling lesbians, gay men, and their families*. New York: Continuum.

McLeod, B. (1997). Yvonne and Helen: Finding a way to trust. *Journal of Gay and Lesbian Social Services, 6*(1), 105–107.

McNeill, J. J. (1993). *The church and the homosexual* (4th ed.). New York: Beacon.

Minton, H. S., & McDonald, G. J. (1984). Homosexual identity formation as a developmental process. *Journal of Homosexuality, 9*(2/3), 91–104.

Morris, J. F., Balsam, K. F., & Rothblum, E. D. (2002). Lesbian and bisexual mothers and nonmothers: Demographics and the coming out process. *Journal of Family Psychology, 2*, 144–156.

Morrow, D. F. (1993). Social work with gay and lesbian adolescents. *Social Work, 38*(6), 655–660.

——. (1996). Coming out issues for adult lesbians: A group intervention. *Social Work, 41*(6), 647–656.

——. (2000). Coming out to families: Guidelines for intervention with gay and lesbian clients. *Journal of Family Social Work, 5*(2), 53–66.

——. (2001). Older gays and lesbians: Surviving a generation of hate and violence. *Journal of Gay and Lesbian Social Services, 13*(1/2), 151–169.

——. (2004a). Cast into the wilderness: The impact of institutionalized religion on lesbians. *Journal of Lesbian Studies, 7*(4), 109–123..

——. (2004b). Social work practice with gay, lesbian, bisexual, and transgender adolescents. *Families in Society, 85*(1), 91–99.

Murray, C. I. (1994, November). *Siblings of gay and lesbian people: Coming out, identity, and caregiving issues.* Paper presented at the annual meeting of the National Council on Family Relations, Minneapolis.

National Gay and Lesbian Task Force. (1991). *National Gay and Lesbian Task Force Survey (National Gay and Lesbian Task Force records, 1973–2000).* Division of Rare and Manuscript Collections, Cornell University.

National Lesbian and Gay Health Foundation. (1987). *National lesbian health care survey: Mental health implications.* Unpublished report, Atlanta.

O'Connell, A. (1993). Voices from the heart: The developmental impact of a mother's lesbianism on her adolescent children. *Smith College Studies in Social Work,* 63(3), 281–300.

Patterson, C. J. (1992). Children of lesbian and gay parents. *Child Development,* 63, 1025–1042.

Pilkington, N. W., & D'Augelli, A. R. (1995). Victimization of lesbian, gay, and bisexual youth in community settings. *Journal of Community Psychology,* 23, 33–56.

Plummer, L. (1975). *Sexual stigma.* Boston: Routledge and Kegan Paul.

Ponse, B. (1978). *Identities in the lesbian world.* Westport, CT: Greenwood.

Remafedi, G. (1987). Adolescent homosexuality: Psychosocial and medical implications. *Pediatrics,* 79, 331–337.

Rhoads, R. A. (1995). Learning from the coming out experiences of college males. *Journal of College Student Development,* 36(1), 67–74.

Rotheram-Borus, M. J., & Fernandez, M. I. (1995). Sexual orientation and developmental challenges experienced by gay and lesbian youths. *Suicide and Life-Threatening Behavior,* 25, 26–34.

Rotheram-Borus, M. J., Rosario, M., & Koopman, C. (1991). Minority youths at high risk: Gay males and runaways. In M. E. Colten & S. Gore (Eds.), *Adolescent stress: Causes and consequences* (pp. 181–200). New York: deGruyter.

Savin-Williams, R. C. (1998). The disclosure to families of same-sex attractions by lesbian, gay, and bisexual youths. *Journal of Research on Adolescence,* 8(1), 49–68.

Savin-Williams, R. C., & Dube, E. M. (1998). Parental reactions to their child's disclosure of same-sex attractions. *Family Relations,* 47, 1–7.

Schilder, A. J., Kennedy, C., Strathdee, S. A., Goldson, I. L., Hogg, R. S., & O'Shaughnessy, M. V. (1999). A lot of things I hide: Understanding disclosure in the care of HIV-positive men. *Journal of the Gay and Lesbian Medical Association,* 3(4), 119–126.

Schneider, M. (1991). Developing services for lesbian and gay adolescents. *Canadian Journal of Community Mental Health,* 10(1), 133–151.

Schneider, S. G., Farberow, N. L., & Kruks, G. N. (1989). Suicidal behavior in adolescents and young adult gay men. *Suicidal and Life-Threatening Behavior,* 19, 381–394.

Shenk, D., & Fullmer, E. (1996). Significant relationships among older women: Cultural and personal constructions of lesbianism. *Journal of Women and Aging,* 8(3–4), 75–89.

Signorile, M. (1995). *Outing yourself.* New York: Simon and Schuster.

Simmons, R. (1991). Some thoughts on the challenges facing black gay intellectuals. In E. Hemphill (Ed.), *Brother to brother: New writings by black gay men* (pp. 211–228). Boston: Alyson.

Smith, K., & Crawford, S. (1986). Suicidal behavior among "normal" high school students. *Suicidal and Life-Threatening Behavior,* 19, 381–325.

Sophie, J. (1986). A critical examination of stage theories of lesbian identity development. *Journal of Homosexuality,* 12(2), 39–51.

Spong, J. S. (1998). *Why Christianity must change or die*. San Francisco: Harper.

Swann, S., & Herbert, S. E. (1999). Ethical issues in the mental health treatment of gender dysphoric adolescents. *Journal of Gay and Lesbian Social Services, 10*(3/4), 19–34.

Tafoya, T. N. (1996). Native two-spirit people. In R. P. Cabaj & T. S. Stein (Eds.), *Textbook of homosexuality and mental health* (pp. 603–617). Washington, DC: American Psychiatric Press.

Tharinger, D., & Wells, G. (2000). An attachment perspective on the developmental challenges of gay and lesbian adolescents: The need for continuity of caregiving from family and schools. *School Psychology Review, 29*(2), 158–173.

Thompson, C. A. (1992). Lesbian grief and loss issues in the coming out process. *Women and Therapy, 1/2*, 175–185.

Troiden, R. R. (1979). Becoming homosexual: A model of gay identity acquisition. *Psychiatry 42*, 362–373.

Waldo, C. R. (1999). Working in a majority context: A structural model of heterosexism as minority stress in the workplace. *Journal of Counseling Psychology, 46*, 218–232.

Wall, V. A., & Washington, J. (1991). Understanding gay and lesbian students of color. In N. J. Evans & V. A. Wall (Eds.), *Beyond tolerance: Gays, lesbians, and bisexuals on campus* (pp. 67–78). Alexandria, VA: American Association of Counseling and Development.

Weinberg, M. S., Williams, C. J., & Pryor, D. W. (1994). *Dual attraction: Understanding bisexuality*. New York: Oxford University Press.

PART THREE

RELATIONSHIPS AND FAMILIES

7

PSYCHOSOCIAL SUPPORT FOR FAMILIES OF GAY, LESBIAN, BISEXUAL, AND TRANSGENDER PEOPLE

Harriet L. Cohen, Yolanda C. Padilla, and Veronica C. Aravena

[PARENTS OF GAYS: UNITE IN SUPPORT FOR OUR CHILDREN]

THE THEME of this now famous sign carried by Jeanne Manford in support of her gay son in the 1972 Christopher Street Liberation Day March in New York (McGarry & Wasserman, 1998) resonates as loudly today. The reaction of parents, spouses and intimate partners, children, and other family members to their coming out is a primary concern of gay, lesbian, bisexual, and transgender individuals and affects their ability to embrace their sexuality, by enabling self-acceptance or by evoking earlier feelings of self-doubt (Appleby & Anastas, 1998; D'Augelli & Hershberger, 1993; Savin-Williams, 1990). It is essentially from this family foundation that GLBT people, as members of a socially marginalized group, are able to negotiate other personal relationships, as well as organizational, community, and larger societal barriers and opportunities (Van Voorhis, 1998).

Yet American educational, religious, and other social institutions for the most part do not adequately prepare families to support and affirm their GLBT family members. Gay, lesbian, bisexual, and transgender content is absent from school curricula (Lipkin, 1999), and major religious denominations send families mixed messages, teaching them to love their gay and lesbian family members but to refuse to condone their homosexual relationships (Davidson, 2000). For example, the official Catholic guide on helping parents of gay children, *Always Our Children: A Pastoral Message to Parents of Homosexual Children*, characterizes a child's coming out as an unfortunate family crisis and counsels parents to help their children understand the immorality of same-sex sexual behavior (United States Conference of Catholic Bishops, 1997). Thus, for parents, children, and spouses, embracing their gay, lesbian, bisexual, or transgender family members often means questioning deep-seated and fundamental beliefs and societal expectations.

This chapter will focus on helping families of GLBT people respond to the news that a loved one is gay, lesbian, bisexual, or transgender. It will begin with a discussion of the role that family plays in the lives of GLBT people. The literature related to family responses to coming out will be reviewed, including models of expected reactions. Separate sections will be devoted to supporting particular groups, including families of origin, heterosexual spouses and intimate partners, and children of GLBT people. Suggestions for practice will focus on assessing and intervening with family-focused cases and on empowering family members to become allies who can help change organizations and communities to become more responsive to the GLBT population.

WHAT DOES FAMILY MEAN?

In Western culture, heterosexuality or reproductive sexuality is assumed to be the norm, and both parents and children are assumed to be heterosexual, with little consideration of healthy non-heterosexual alternatives. *Family* is a term that has traditionally been used to denote this system composed of heterosexual members. Only recently has there been a recognition of the lives of gay, lesbian, bisexual, and transgender people as members of heterosexual families of origin or other heterosexual family structures. Clearly, however, these individuals have lived, at least part of their lives, as members of a heterosexual family system and partici-pated in a heterosexual community. Of particular concern are the experiences of heterosexual families of origin, spouses, or intimate partners of individuals who recognize or reveal their gay, lesbian, bisexual, or transgender identity after they are already in a heterosexual relationship, and children of GLBT parents.

The family is recognized as the primary group to which individuals turn for emotional and financial security as well as safety and comfort when facing nega-tive pressures from the larger society. However, for many GLBT individuals, the family does not act as a safe haven. Indeed, often the first closet in which GLBT individuals hide is inside their own families—within families of origin, within the larger extended family, with their spouses and intimate partners, or with their own children. They may believe that they have failed their families because they cannot meet the expectation of forming heterosexual families and engaging in re-productive sexuality. As a result, they often fear rejection and experience shame, guilt, and anger. They are, therefore, reluctant to view their home as a safe haven against a hostile world. The family provides only a tenuous shelter from the dis-counting and intimidating world (Simpson, 1976).

Research suggests, however, that the ways in which GLBT members are inte-grated within the family vary widely. In families of color, for example, the lesbian or gay family member is not usually rejected, although other family members may disapprove of his or her sexual orientation (Greene, 1997a, 1998). A study conducted by Mays, Cochran, and Rhue (1993) with African American gay and lesbian participants found that African American lesbians maintained closer relationships with their families and were more likely to turn to their families for support and assistance than were their heterosexual counterparts. On the other hand, they were also less likely to seek professional help, although they experienced more stressors and were less likely to be a part of the broader gay and lesbian community. Despite significant variations in family dynamics, available research that addresses the interaction of sexual orientation, class, and ethnic and cultural diversity is very limited (Carroll & Gilroy, 2002; Greene, 1994a, 1994b, 1997a, 1997b, 1998; Leslie, 1995; Neissen, 1987; Smith, 1997; Sue, Arredondo, & McDavis, 1992; Sue & Sue, 1999). As the case of African Americans suggests, it is important for practitioners to understand the stressors and developmental tasks of GLBT people of different backgrounds and their families, so that they may respond in culturally appropriate ways (Allen & Demo, 1995; Carroll & Gilroy, 2002; Clark & Serovich, 1997; Greene, 1997a, 1998; Leslie, 1995; Sue et al., 1992).

Despite the tenacity of traditional concepts of family, patterns of family structure are not static but are being deconstructed, and new definitions of family are emerging (Laird, 1998; Shernoff, 1984). In the GLBT community, the word *family* has been appropriated to refer to intimate partners, friends, and the GLBT community itself. "Is she/he family?" is an expression used to determine whether someone identifies as gay, lesbian, bisexual, or transgender. These chosen support systems and friendship networks become the family of choice for many individuals who feel rejected and alienated from their family of origin. In reality, however, most GLBT people are engaged in many family systems, including their family of origin, their family of choice, the gay community, and the non-gay community (Tully, 2000).

FAMILY RESPONSES TO A LOVED ONE'S COMING OUT

In exploring the relationships of families with their GLBT children, spouses, or parents, perspectives of families concerning homosexuality and gender identity first need to be clarified. Families including gay, lesbian, bisexual, and transgender members exist in the same homophobic, heterosexist, and transphobic environment as does the rest of society (Barret & Logan, 2002; Greene, 1997a; Israel, 1996; Laframboise & Long, n.d.; Mengert, 1990; Patterson & D'Augelli, 1998; Serovich, Kimberly, & Greene, 1998; Serovich, Skeen, Walters, & Robinson, 1993). Often family members have internalized oppressive cultural stereotypes without ever having challenged or deconstructed the prejudicial attitudes and limiting beliefs represented by those labels and statements. Political and religious leaders, the media, and the educational system all provide negative images of non-heterosexual lifestyles. The messages often emphasize that the gay, lesbian, bisexual, and transgender culture is sexually deviant, immoral, and sexually driven (Barret & Logan, 2002). Just as the GLBT person straddles both the heterosexual and the homosexual cultures, so too does the family walk in the world of both subcultures.

Families may hold differing beliefs about why a family member is gay, lesbian, bisexual, or transgender, and those beliefs may affect their ability to reconcile values about homosexuality and gender identity with the reality of having a GLBT loved one (Crosbie-Burnett, Foster, Murray, & Bowen, 1996). Parents and spouses sometimes react with guilt or a sense of failure, believing that somehow they "caused" the homosexuality (Strommen, 1989a). Families may struggle to resolve the tension between negative cultural stereotypes of homosexuality and transgender identity and their previous relationship with the family member who has now disclosed that he or she is gay, lesbian, bisexual, or transgender (DeVine, 1984; Strommen, 1989b). Furthermore, families need time to accept their new identity as parents, intimate partners or spouses, or children of people who identify as GLBT (Laframboise & Long, n.d.; Mengert, 1990; New York City Parents and Friends of Lesbians and Gays, 1995; Tuerk, 1998; Williamson, 1998). This adjustment involves rejecting society's view of homosexuality and transgender identity as deviant and finding new roles for, and ways of relating to, the GLBT family member within the family structure.

Given the social and family context, families of origin, spouses, and children of GLBT people respond in a variety of ways to the announcement that a family member is gay, lesbian, bisexual, or transgender (Neissen, 1987). Some families may respond with love and acceptance, while others may withdraw and become angry and disappointed. Still others may choose to deny the news altogether and simply continue their daily activities as if nothing had happened. Even within the same family, responses may vary from person to person. Devine (1984) demonstrates how family values affect family responses. He identifies three family values that are related to how family members may react when a loved one comes out. The first is the extent to which they wish to "maintain respectability at all costs," which implies keeping up an external appearance and buying into society's negative images of the GLBT community. The second is whether they believe that "as a family we can resolve our own problems," which limits their access to educational information or resources that might help to challenge misinformation and constricted attitudes. The third value is related to how strictly they adhere to certain religious beliefs—"be as the religion teaches us." Strong religious beliefs can provide a rationale to reject homosexuality and transgenderism and sometimes the GLBT family member as well. The level of acceptance of any of these values may indicate to the professional some of the barriers and obstacles the family will face in moving to a place of acceptance with their loved one (Neissen, 1987; Strommen, 1990).

In assessing families, therefore, it is important not to assume that the problem is with the gay, lesbian, bisexual, or transgender member, but rather to look at the whole family system. For example, it is important to first explore communication styles, problem-solving skills, and previous patterns of accepting difference and change within the family system (van Wormer, Wells, & Boes, 2000). What has been the nature of the relationships between family members in the past? How have family members adjusted to other changes within the family system, from the birth of a child, to a child leaving for college, to the death of a parent? Who in the family manages change well? Who has been reluctant or resistant to change? How has the family dealt with the resistant family member? What coping skills and resources have they used in the past that could be employed to assist them in this situation?

The literature makes clear that even if the family suspects that a family member is gay, lesbian, bisexual, or transgender, confirmation of that suspicion may be a shock and require an initial period of adjustment (Savin-Williams, 2001; Strommen, 1989a; Williamson, 1998). The fact that the family's acceptance is an ongoing and sometimes complex process is demonstrated by the existence of support groups not only for GLBT individuals but for families as well. For example, Parents and Friends of Lesbians and Gays (PFLAG) is a grassroots national organization with more than 80,000 members and 450 chapters located throughout the United States and the world. The mission of PFLAG is to promote the physical and mental health of GLBT people and their families and friends through support, education, and advocacy (PFLAG, n.d.). In particular, PFLAG literature addresses many of the questions parents ask when they first find out that their child is gay, lesbian, bisexual, or transgender.

Smith (1997, p. 285) emphasizes that the individual is part of a family system and the "family part of a culturally diverse context." Thus the dynamics of family expectations associated with the coming out process may vary significantly across families. The case of African American families provides a clear illustration:

> For African Americans who are gay, lesbian, or bisexual, not talking about sexual partners with parents, relatives, or even close friends may be a respectful way of maintaining needed privacy rather than an indication of self-hatred, denial of sexuality, or a sign of struggle with self-acceptance due to shame.
>
> (SMITH, 1997, P. 292)

The costs of and opportunities for coming out are not the same for all individuals or all families. People of color confront the impact of multiple oppressions. Although GLBT people may face discrimination, threats, and exclusion based on sexual orientation, people of color, and especially women of color, are vulnerable to additional burdens because of race and gender (Greene, 1994b; Smith, 1997).

The multiple and overlapping identity issues experienced by people of color may require creative interventions.

In sum, beyond examining their own views about homosexuality and gender identity, families of gay, lesbian, bisexual, and transgender people must learn to navigate the coming out process themselves, just as their GLBT family members do. This process can be complex, nonlinear, and at times more emotional than rational. Initially, the coming out process for individuals and families was described as a linear process that involved coming to terms with one's sexual identity (Cass, 1979, 1984). In effect, however, for individuals and their families, coming out is not a stepwise linear model or an outcome but rather an ongoing process that involves deciding whom to tell, when to tell, and what to tell in a variety of new and different situations with family members, coworkers, neighbors, friends, and others (Dempsey, 1994; Martin, 1991; Smith, 1997). Thus families face many of the same issues in the coming out process as do gay, lesbian, bisexual, and transgender people themselves.

FAMILIES OF ORIGIN

It is estimated that gays and lesbians and their parents constitute at least one-third of the population (Woodman, 1985), making the issue of how families adjust to disclosure of their children's sexual or gender identity and how they interact with their GLBT children an important concern for practitioners and researchers. Families need time to let go of the old role that the GLBT person as a child played within the family system, to allow old hopes, dreams, images, and expectations to die, and to give birth to new dreams and the recognition of a changed relationship and different roles for their child (Robinson, Walters, & Skeen, 1989; Tuerk, 1998). Accepting a child who is gay, lesbian, bisexual, or transgender involves rejecting cultural definitions and values related to social deviancy (Strommen, 1989a, 1989b).

Virtually all models characterizing the response of families of origin to the coming out of a GLBT child indicate that some of the first feelings they experience are those of shock and disbelief (Laframboise & Long, n.d.; Mengert, 1990; New York City Parents and Friends of Lesbians and Gays, 1995; Tuerk, 1998; Williamson, 1998). Initial disclosure may lead to a period of strain, tension, and internal or external conflict within the family as the family begins to confront its negative, internalized cultural stereotypes and values about GLBT people. Strommen (1989b, p. 10) states that families have a double challenge, to "both create a positive identity for the homosexual member *and* create a place for this identity within the family." As will be discussed, the resolution reached by the family of origin has a profound influence on the well-being of GLBT children.

Crosbie-Burnett and colleagues (1996) identify three stages in the process of adjustment for heterosexual families of origins: (a) performing incremental disclosure to others, (b) adjusting to the new role of parent or sibling of a gay or lesbian child, and (c) coming out as family members. The first stage involves deciding whom to tell first and what responsibility that person has either for telling other family members or for making sure that other family members do not find out. This sometimes leads to a conspiracy of silence between some of the family members. Maintaining family secrets can cause tension and stress in any family system as it defines in-group and out-group boundaries that serve to divide and alienate family members.

During the second stage of adjustment, family members often look for someone or something to blame. Parents often wonder whether they did or did not do something that caused their son or daughter to become gay, lesbian, bisexual, or transgender. They may question whether they were unfit as parents and as role models for their children. Research on how long it takes family members to adjust to their new identity as the parent or sibling of a GLBT person, as well as variations across race, ethnicity, and class (Greene, 1994a, 1994b), is limited. This lack of information about the experiences of heterosexual family members "is a reflection of their near invisibility, closeted status, and marginalization in the society in general" (Crosbie-Burnett et al., 1996, p. 397). Nevertheless, some research indicates that the best predictor of the family's adjustment response is the quality of the relationship between parent and child prior to the disclosure (Cohen & Savin-Williams, 1996; Patterson, 2000; Patterson & D'Augelli, 1998; Savin-Williams & Cohen, 1996; Serovich et al., 1998).

Sometimes family members can move past their feelings of blame, confusion, anger, and failure as parents to accept and affirm their love for their gay, lesbian, bisexual, or transgender child. For some families it takes years, and for some it never happens (Gillespie, 1999; Griffin, Wirth, & Wirth, 1996). Families must also come to terms with the reality that they have lost their real or perceived status as a "normal" family and that they may be confronted with homophobia in the workplace, in the larger family system, within the religious community, and in their own social network.

The third, and final, stage of the coming out process for families is characterized as "emotionally complex" (Crosbie-Burnett et al., 1994), as families of origin weigh the consequences of their own disclosure as the family of a gay, lesbian, bisexual, or transgender child. Just as GLBT individuals must struggle with decisions about who, what, where, when, and how to tell, so family members must also wrestle with these decisions in relation to other family members, friends and neighbors, members of their faith community, coworkers, and others. Social workers can help families during this time by letting them know that gays and lesbians form satisfying relationships (Peplau and Cochran, 1990) and may choose to create their own families within same-sex relationships (Patterson, 1996, 2000; Patterson & D'Augelli, 1998; Tasker and Golombok, 1995).

DeVine (1984) offers an alternative model of family adjustment that describes the process through which the family moves as a series of stages. The first stage is *subliminal awareness*, when the family suspects that a family member may be homosexual, bisexual, or transgender. *Impact* is the second phase, when the truth is exposed and families must confront their own reactions to this revelation. The third phase involves the families' *adjustment* as they begin to adapt to the news; it might include an attempt on the part of the family to get the loved one to change or to go back into the closet so that the family does not have to change. Some families move to the fourth phase of *resolution*, in which family members begin to identify and confront their own values and modify them in light of new information or a new perspective. Not all families are able to achieve the final phase, *integration*, when family members change their values and accept a new relationship with their gay, lesbian, bisexual, or transgender child.

Research shows that the success of the integration phase is related to parental attitudes and background. A study by Serovich et al. (1993) of 347 parents of lesbians and gay men found that parents' favorable attitude toward homosexuality is a significant factor in their acceptance of their gay or lesbian child and of his or her partner. Their openness to homosexuality also affects their comfort with external displays of affection (Griffin et al., 1996). In addition, they found a significant relationship between parental socioeconomic status and their attitudes toward homosexuality (i.e., the higher the level of education and income, the more accepting the family).

The adjustment process for families of transgender children is similar to that experienced by families of GLB children. Parents may experience feelings of denial, grief, shame, and confusion. However, the process is often more difficult because of the complex and intense changes characterizing the gender transformation of their children (Wren, 2000). Families of transgender children often do not recognize that their children are experiencing a difficult time as they become aware of their gender identity, although some begin to realize their child's preference for the other gender as young as age three (Xavier, Sharp, & Boenke, 2001). Furthermore, parents also have to deal with very real issues that their children may confront as they become older, issues related to safety, discrimination within the health care system, sex reassignment surgery, and obstacles to employment (Xavier et al., 2001). At the same time, because of the taboo associated with gender identity and the neglect of transgender issues in schools, health settings, and social services, families are likely to lack adequate information, support networks, and role models to help them deal with the developmental and health concerns of their transgender children (Chen-Hayes, 2001). Despite the barriers that families of transgender children face, case studies reveal that families of origin have the capacity to successfully adjust to the profound changes that occur when a transgender child comes out (Boenke, 1999).

As suggested in the dynamic nature of these models, family adjustment is an ongoing process, rather than a single event, and there is no set length of time for family members to move through their individual adjustment processes toward affirmation. A family's emotional responses can vary greatly, depending on many factors (Serovich et al., 1998), and may change in response to various events. For example, a family may be very accepting of an adult son's disclosure about his sexuality until he brings his partner/lover/significant other to a family function or about a daughter's disclosure until she announces that she and her partner are planning to have a child through artificial insemination. The social worker will need to be able to assess the family's level of emotional readiness and support them where they are (Williamson, 1998). Clearly family members need both education and emotional support as they learn to incorporate their child's sexual and gender identity into their concept of themselves as parents.

CONSEQUENCES OF FAMILY RELATIONSHIPS FOR GLBT CHILDREN

Because children depend on their parents for nurturance and support, the adjustment process of parents to their children's homosexuality or transgender identity has significant consequences for their children. The manner in which parents respond to their child's homosexuality or gender identity—be it a real or a perceived reaction—profoundly affects the development and well-being of their children. The reaction to their coming out can significantly influence the extent to which GLBT children are able to come to terms with their sexuality, by enabling them to accept themselves or by increasing their feelings of self-doubt. Thus, learning about the way that GLBT children deal with their families and their perspectives about their family's reactions to their homosexuality or gender identity provides important information about relationships between families of origin and their GLBT children (D'Augelli, Hershberger, & Pilkington, 1998) and is essential in thinking about psychosocial support for families of GLBT people.

According to research by Savin-Williams (2001), children are disclosing their sexual orientation to parents at younger ages, while still living at home, than in earlier generations. As a result, the process of parental adjustment has more immediate and longer-term consequences for the children than when disclosure occurs during adulthood. The vast majority of youth do disclose to parents, but parents are rarely the first to know about their children's homosexuality (youth typically first come out to their friends) (D'Augelli et al., 1998). This means that youth struggle with their sexuality for several years before opening up to their parents. However, once youth have disclosed to their parents, they feel significantly more comfortable in disclosing their sexual orientation to their heterosexual friends and to others in the community, including their schools, compared to those who have not told their parents. Not surprisingly, most of those who do not disclose expect that their parents will not be accepting, and many worry about verbal and physical abuse (Savin-Williams, 1989, 1990).

Although the findings on the degree to which parents respond positively to their children's homosexuality vary widely according to different studies (D'Augelli et al., 1998; Hammelman, 1993; Savin-Williams, 1989, 1990), empirical evidence shows that parental acceptance can serve as an important protective factor for GLBT youth. For example, one study found that gay and lesbian youth whose parents were accepting were generally more likely to feel comfortable with their sexuality (Savin-Williams, 1989, 1990). Furthermore, parental acceptance — in particular maternal acceptance — is highly predictive of self-esteem among gay and lesbian youth.

On the other hand, children who face parental rejection are more vulnerable to a variety of psychosocial problems. Negative interpersonal relationships and low levels of attachment with parents partly explain higher levels of psychological distress among sexual minority youth, a condition that can sometimes develop into clinical depression (Ueno, 2002). Some studies show that a high proportion of youth who have been rejected by family members attempt or seriously consider suicide (Hammelman, 1993). Indeed, according to at least one study, next to feelings of isolation, the second most common presenting problem for youth between the ages of 12 and 21 participating in social service agencies serving gay and lesbian youth and their families is difficulties with family (Hetrick & Martin, 1987). Youth indicated that they lacked attachment to their families and feared rejection, violence, and expulsion from home because of their homosexuality. Of the clients who came to the center because of violence or suicidal ideation, almost half had suffered violence at the hands of their families.

Although there is little research that directly links non-affirming relationships with family with poor outcomes for gay, lesbian, and bisexual adolescents, a negative response by significant others in the adolescent's family environment is often associated with several problematic outcomes, including school-related problems, running away from home, conflict with the law, substance abuse, prostitution, and suicide (Savin-Williams, 1994). Sometimes the effects manifest themselves well into adulthood. For example, findings from a study based on a probability sample of 912 Latino adult gay men in their twenties and thirties in four large urban centers (Díaz & Ayala, 2001) revealed a significant relationship between feelings of family rejection and high-risk behaviors. Specifically, Latino gay men who felt that their homosexuality had hurt or embarrassed their families were more likely to engage in high-risk sexual behaviors as adults. Conversely, parental acceptance led to higher self-esteem and lower levels of psychological distress, social isolation, and substance abuse, which in turn decreased the likelihood of involvement in high-risk sexual behaviors for this group.

What is known about the consequences of the quality of family relationships for transgender children is more limited, and because no data are available, conclusions usually cannot be drawn on the basis of on empirical analyses. Unlike sexual orientation, disclosure is not a choice for children who enter a gender transition, given that gender is so visible (Wren, 2000). Thus transgender children have a more difficult time remaining closeted and often confront greater emotional crises on the part of their families when they disclose. As expected, transgender children experience a variety of responses from their families, from acceptance to total rejection, and the parental response has significant consequences in terms of intensifying the child's problems or easing his or her developmental processes. When parents and other family members reject their transgender children, those children face some of the same risks as do gay, lesbian, and bisexual youth, including running away, substance abuse, and suicide (Xavier et al., 2001).

HETEROSEXUAL SPOUSES AND INTIMATE PARTNERS

"In at least 2 million marriages, a spouse has come out or will disclose being gay, lesbian, bisexual, or transgender," according to the Straight Spouse Network (n.d.), an international support network of heterosexual spouses and partners, current or former, of gay, lesbian, bisexual, and transgender mates. For spouses and intimate partners the revelation often, but not always, means the end of a marriage or a relationship. Knowledge about the motivation of gay, lesbian, and bisexual people to enter into marriage with heterosexual people can provide social workers with a better understanding of the trajectories of mixed-orientation marriages and the effects on spouses.

Some studies based on clinical samples suggest that gay men marry women as a way of denying their sexuality, because they have come to internalize views that homosexuality is sinful and sick (Isay, 1998). Some do realize their homosexuality, but marry in hopes that those desires will disappear in the context of marriage. In approximately one-third of cases, however, men and women who enter into mixed-orientation marriages considered themselves heterosexual before marriage (Matteson, 1987; Ross, 1990). Among those who come out to themselves, the desire to maintain their family and children motivates some to remain married. However, the research clearly demonstrates that remaining in a marriage does not decrease homosexual desires (Bozett, 1987; Gochros, 1985). It is important to note, however, that several of the studies of gay and lesbian individuals in mixed-orientation marriages were conducted in the 1980s. Matteson (1987) suggests that with the development of more accepting attitudes toward homosexuality, gays and lesbians are likely to have come to terms with their sexual orientation before marriage and to experience less crisis even as they decide to marry.

The process of adjustment for spouses of GLBT people involves three general stages: shock, anger and confusion, and finally reintegration (Beeler & DiProva, 1999; Gochros, 1985, 1989). The research on spouses has focused on the experiences of wives of gay men and shows that the first stage involves an initial period of distress, even if the wife has begun to suspect her husband's homosexuality. The wife may feel anger, guilt, blame, and shame. Like the first stage, the second, or interim, stage may range from mild to extreme stress. While it usually begins shortly after hearing the news of disclosure, it may last from weeks to years. The reintegration, or third stage, occurs when the wife has come to terms with her feelings and the larger family system has adjusted to the change and learned new ways of coping. During this time, which often involves a divorce, the wife must begin to make plans for her future (Barret & Robinson, 2000; Gochros, 1985, 1989). This stage may last from three to five years or more after divorce. According to Crosbie-Burnett et al. (1996), throughout this process wives report that they sometimes fail to seek support or assistance for fear of disapproval or rejection by family, friends, and professionals, as they progress through their own coming out process.

An in-depth study of 103 women married to gay men that included, in addition to interviews with the wives, interviews with husbands, other family members, relatives, and friends, reveals some information relevant to providing psychosocial support to this population (Gochros, 1985). According to the study, the response of wives to their husband's news is affected by a variety of contextual factors in the marriage and varies according to their previous relationship. For example, the response depends on whether the revelation is viewed as a betrayal or as a demonstration of trust between the two. It also depends on the current circumstances, such as whether they are under stress because of other events, such as childbirth, and the availability of support for each of them. Regardless of the circumstances, however, wives are less deeply affected by the issue of their husband's homosexuality per se than by resulting problems of isolation, stigma, loss, cognitive confusion and dissonance, and the lack of knowledgeable, empathic support or help in problem solving.

Earlier research indicates that between one- and two-thirds of these mixed-orientation marriages end in divorce (Smith & Allred, 1990). Smith and Allred (1990) attempted to discern the experiences of women formerly married to gay men by conducting a comparative analysis with women divorced from heterosexual men. Measured on a series of psychological assessment instruments, women who have been divorced from gay men do not differ from women who have been divorced from heterosexual men on measures of self-worth, emotional separation, grief, social trust, and self-worth. There was no significant difference in the adjustment to the divorce. Furthermore, little distinction was found between the two groups in terms of level of anxiety or depression. Wives divorcing gay men did, however, display significantly more anger than did women divorcing heterosexual men.

Intimate partners of transgender people go through a complex process of making sense of their partner's gender transitions. In the case of transsexuality, the expectations and conceptions that intimate partners hold concerning the identities of their transsexual partners are deeply challenged as they see their physical and other transformations. As with partners of gay and lesbian individuals, the manner in which partners of transsexual people deal with the transitions depends on the history and current circumstances of the relationship (Cole, 2000). On the basis of in-depth interviews with 40 transsexual men and women and 16 partners, Davis (2002) reported that those who lived with their partners during the pre-transition period found the transition process confusing. Thus they frequently continued to see their partner in their gender of birth or in some unique combination of masculine and feminine characteristics. While many view the process as a form of gender transgression, some begin to question the rigid social definitions of gender performance and become more accepting of the fluidity of gender. The intimate partners also must reexamine their own sexuality in light of the revelation of their partners' transsexuality. For example, a woman who identifies as heterosexual may now find herself with a man who defines himself as female. Ultimately, while some relationships dissolve, many non-transsexual partners remain involved as co-parents, non-intimate partners, or intimate partners.

CHILDREN OF GLBT PEOPLE

Forming a family and raising children is an important part of life for many gay, lesbian, bisexual, and transgender people (Green, 1998; Patterson, 2000). While many gays and lesbians have children within their same-sex families, through either adoption or birth, many have borne children in the context of previous heterosexual relationships, before coming out. It is estimated that between 6 million and 14 million children in the United States live with at least one gay parent (Patterson & Redding, 1996). The successful adjustment of children of GLBT parents is primarily related to the extent to which they experience family stability. Perhaps the biggest concern raised about children in GLBT families is how their normal development is affected. Children who are part of GLBT families grow up to be healthy individuals, despite the discrimination that often legally limits the rights of their parents.

Research on the psychosocial process of adjustment for children of GLBT parents upon hearing about their parent's disclosure shows that they tend to respond favorably. Children of lesbian or gay parents often initially respond with an apparent lack of concern about the news; however, other feelings may emerge with time (O'Connell, 1999; Turner, Scadden, & Harris, 1990). Gay fathers indicate that their children's initial responses included a range of emotions, including closeness, confusion, shame, relief, blame, and lack of understanding (Harris & Turner, 1986).

However, most fathers in the study felt that their children were accepting of their gayness. Some studies suggest that the child's response is related to his or her stage of development; younger children and young adults have fewer problems with acceptance than do adolescent children (Bozett, 1987; O'Connell, 1999).

More important, however, according to Wallerstein and Blakeslee (1989), is that many of the issues experienced by children of gay and lesbian parents are a result of going through a difficult divorce, rather than of the parent's sexual orientation. Children of gay and lesbian parents may be dealing with conflicting feelings about a parental divorce, a new living situation, or meeting their parents' new partners for the first time. The findings from these studies are consistent with extensive analyses of research on children of GLBT parents (Allen & Demo, 1995; Clark & Serovich, 1997; Patterson, 2000), which show that the sexual orientation of parents is less of an issue for children than is the quality of the relationship and interaction between parents and children.

There is no evidence of differences in psychosocial development between children of parents in these various relationships compared to children in heterosexual families (Patterson, 1996, 2000; Stacey & Biblarz, 2001). In a comprehensive review of 21 studies, Stacey and Biblarz (2001) found that the developmental outcomes of children of GLB parents do not differ from those of children of heterosexual parents in terms of self-esteem and psychological well-being, despite the social stigma that these children are likely to face. Furthermore, children who grow up with GLB parents receive the same quality of parenting as do children who grow up with heterosexual parents. The authors found no significant differences in terms of quality of parent-child relationships, parent's self-esteem or psychological well-being, or parental behaviors and expectations toward children's sexual development. Finally, children of GLB parents were not more likely to self-identify as lesbian, gay, or bisexual but tended to be more accepting of diversity.

The same patterns are evident among children of transgender parents, although the very minimal research that does exist is based solely on clinical samples. The available research suggests that the normal development of children of transsexual parents is not disrupted by a parent's disclosure (Green, 1998). According to Green, children of transsexual parents do not experience gender identity confusion. Furthermore, the majority of children do not suffer detrimental consequences as a result of their parent's gender transitions. Children as young as seven are able to reasonably understand and accept their parent's gender transitions according to their developmental levels. Most children are able to negotiate their family's experience among their peers; although some do not disclose to all their peers, among those who do so, teasing is usually temporary and eventually resolved. Thus counselors working with transgender families agree that it is not primarily the parent's gender transition that affects children as much as it is disruptions in the relationship between the transsexual parent and the non-transsexual parent (Ettner & White, 2000). Children who are able to maintain contact with their transsexual parent, whose parents cooperate on parenting issues, and who have the support of extended families are less likely to be at risk for adjustment difficulties.

Just as parents and spouses of GLBT individuals have to deal with their own coming out process, children of GLBT parents may struggle with the problem of coming out to peers, fearing rejection or even violence. A study of young adults between the ages of 17 and 35 reared in lesbian homes revealed a sense of pride in their mothers' sexual identity. In most cases, respondents did not recall feeling ostracized by peers during adolescence or feeling uncomfortable about revealing their family background. As expected, however, they did not feel as positively as adolescents about their lesbian family identity as they did as adults, but that was because of their fears of social ostracism rather than to problems with family relations. Although adolescents often choose to keep the secret, one in-depth study (O'Connell, 1999) showed that children of lesbian parents who have contact with children of other lesbians have fewer problems with isolation. In addition, these children, as do gays and lesbians themselves in this society, may feel "different" (O'Connell, 1999). Psychosocial intervention may involve enabling children to explore the feeling of being unlike their playmates regarding family structure and supporting them as they develop new ways of coping.

Although growing up in a GLB family does not negatively affect the psychosocial well-being of children, the lives of children of GLB parents are clearly subject to disruption because they live in a context in which basic rights to marriage and parenting are denied their parents (Patterson & Redding, 1996). Illegal sexual conduct as defined by sodomy laws is often used to deny visitation rights and child custody to GLB parents. Often GLB parents are granted the right to remain a part of their children's lives only on condition that they refrain from same-sex relationships or from exposing their children to gay or lesbian influences. Furthermore, as a result of restrictions on parental marriage and adoption, children of same-sex partners are denied a series of benefits—such as medical insurance coverage, the ability of both parents to make decisions on their behalf, and the legal right to remain with the nonbiological parent should the biological parent die.

Therefore gay and lesbian parents have some important concerns about raising their children in a world filled with homophobia, and they often engage in efforts to protect their children. According to a study of lesbian mothers with toddlers (Gartrell et al., 1999), to minimize their children's exposure to homophobia, lesbian mothers attempted to place their children in day care centers staffed by lesbians and gay men. They also planned to send their children to schools that reflected diversity along socioeconomic class, racial, gender, and cultural lines. In addition, lesbian mothers attempted to reduce homophobia in their communities by becoming politically involved. Finally, in order to protect their children from discrimination, most took steps within the legal system. Many had wills, powers of attorney for the child's medical care, co-parenting agreements, and co-parent adoptions where available.

IMPLICATIONS FOR PRACTICE

FAMILY-FOCUSED PRACTICE

Psychosocial intervention with parents, spouses, and children of gay, lesbian, bisexual, or transgender people requires a family-focused approach. One of the challenges for social workers in assessing families of GLBT people is helping them address the question of how their internalized stereotypes affect their behavior and their ability to see their family member as the same person that he or she was before coming out. By exploring the meaning of these attitudes and the values associated with them as part of the initial family assessment, the social worker can determine what interventions will work more effectively with the family. After ascertaining family beliefs and attitudes, social workers need to assess patterns in family relationships as well as the stage at which various family members are in the adjustment process. Psychosocial intervention for some families may focus on providing information; for others, it may involve helping them move to acceptance; and for yet other families, it may mean enabling them to move beyond acceptance to affirmation of their GLBT family member.

It is also important to explore families' attitudes and beliefs about gender and gender role expectations, about masculinity and femininity. Social workers need to be knowledgeable about the meaning of sex in the family's culture and the acceptable range of sexual expression. How do families understand the meaning of sexual orientation and gender expression in their culture? What fears do family members hold? Do families believe they are "responsible" and feel blame and shame? Have they received accurate information on issues such as the origins or "causes" of gender or sexual orientation? What are their specific concerns about their child's, spouse's, or parent's gender identity or sexual orientation? To help families explore their values, Smith (1997) suggests the practice of psychoeducational family sessions to provide family members with the opportunity to share and listen to each other's stories and experiences.

Varying family structures, such as single-parent families, blended families, and multigenerational families, as well as ethnically and culturally diverse family systems, may affect how families respond to the news of a loved one's coming out (Greene, 1994a; Julie, 2001; Serovich et al., 1993; Smith, 1997). In addition to family structure, the chronological age and developmental stage of the individual at the time of disclosure may influence the family's response. In the case of families of origin, for example, most parents do want to stay connected with their children and will work hard to find some level of acceptance (Williamson,

1998). However, a 17-year-old son living at home who is questioning his gender identity and a 33-year-old daughter living in a separate community who discloses that she is a lesbian may evoke different reactions. Working with families can be quite complex and challenging, given that families move along the spiral of adjustment at different speeds.

In addition, the question of changing family dynamics and support emerges as one views relationships of GLBT people with their families across the life cycle. In their study of families with gay children, Serovich et al. (1993) found that the younger generation perceived family relationships more negatively than did the older generation. Changes in the level of acceptance of GLBT family members by parents, spouses or intimate partners, and children can also occur depending on their stage in the life course. Possible shifts in feelings regarding acceptance and affirmation for the gay or lesbian child may occur when parents age and look to their adult children for assistance with caregiving tasks, recognizing them as simply their children, not their gay or lesbian children (Herdt & Beeler, 1998; Hoffman, 1994; Raphael & Meyer, 2000).

In sum, psychosocial intervention may include providing families with accurate information about gender identity and sexual orientation, helping families to deconstruct negative stereotypes about sexual orientation and gender identity, and assisting families of various cultural backgrounds in negotiating their values and beliefs regarding sexual and gender identity vis-à-vis the well-being of their GLBT family member. Finally, intervention may also involve providing resources to family members, including information on how to access local agencies and other support organizations that offer services for families of gay, lesbian, bisexual, and transgender people and their families.

EMPOWERING FAMILY MEMBERS TO BECOME ALLIES

Beyond direct practice approaches, psychosocial intervention with marginalized groups involves helping clients to seek changes in the conditions that oppress them (Van Voorhis, 1998). According to Van Voorhis, practice that is relevant to victims of oppression involves "building on clients' strengths and mobilizing resources, and aiding clients to increase their access to power" (p. 126). According to this model, when oppressed people engage in social action to challenge conditions that violate their freedom, they regain a sense of self-esteem and control. Although families of GLBT people may endure the effects of discrimination only indirectly, this group is in a unique position in that oppression based on sexual orientation and gender identity directly affects their children, spouses, parents, or other family members. Research shows that people who have a gay or lesbian family member, friend, or acquaintance are more likely to have positive attitudes toward gays and lesbians and support gay and lesbian rights than are those who do not have such relationships (Lewis & Rogers, 1999). Thus family members of gay, lesbian, bisexual, and transgender people can be empowered to become allies who can help change organizations and communities to advance the well-being of the GLBT community.

In addition to providing acceptance and support, as allies family members can redirect the distress and frustration they feel as a result of seeing their GLBT family members suffer discrimination. On a macro level, such activities can include becoming involved in increasing public awareness and advocating for improved conditions of GLBT populations in a variety of settings, including the political arena, the workplace, schools, and religious organizations, among others. Biographical accounts from parents, children, spouses, other relatives, and friends of GLBT people clearly demonstrate the empowering and healing effects of participating in such actions (Woog, 1999). Accordingly, opportunities for ally activism to end discrimination and to secure equal civil rights are an important component of many support organizations for family members of GLBT people, such as Parents and Friends of Lesbians and Gays (PFLAG, n.d.) and Children of Lesbians and Gays Everywhere (COLAGE, n.d.).

Indeed, support provided by heterosexual allies, individuals who advocate on behalf of GLBT people, can be a very real and effective source of strength. Unlike other minority populations, such as racial and ethnic minorities, gay, lesbian, bisexual, and transgender individuals do not bring with them the strength of a common family and community experience. That is, their families and neighbors do not share their identity and experience as members of sexual minorities. This is considered to be a major factor in their lack of political power, because not only are GLBT people small in numbers across the population, but they are also geographically dispersed (Sherrill, 1996). With very few exceptions, such as the Castro district in San Francisco and Montrose in Houston, GLBT people do not constitute the majority in their communities; thus it is impossible for them to independently influence political campaigns in their favor (Button, Rienzo, & Wald, 1997; Wald, 2000). The same is true across all mainstream organizational settings. Gay, lesbian, bisexual, and transgender individuals constitute a very small, often invisible minority. Despite the disadvantaged social and political position of the GLBT population, heterosexual family members have a unique opportunity to serve as a link between their GLBT children, spouses, or parents and mainstream social institutions.

Family members can be educated about strategies for political mobilization in collaboration with the gay, lesbian, bisexual, and transgender community. Studies show that having a broad base of support outside the lesbian and gay community increases the likelihood for success of gay rights reforms (Button et al., 1997; D'Emilio, 2000; Riggle & Tadlock, 1999; Rimmerman, Wald, & Wilcox, 2000). Allies play an important role in the advancement of gay civil rights by facilitating the formation of coalitions between gay rights groups and a broad range of other groups, including women's, religious, African American, university, business, and environmental groups (Button et al., 1997). Another way to help families mobilize resources to support their GLBT relatives is to make them aware of ways in which they can influence the organizations around them to become more accepting. The task of allies at an organizational level is to create safe and affirming environments for gay, lesbian, bisexual, and transgender members. Allies can help in the development of support groups and services, inclusive employment policies, educational forums, and policies against sexual harassment (Mann, 1997; Sears & Williams, 1997; Unks, 1995).

REFERENCES

Allen, K. R., & Demo, D. H. (1995). The families of lesbian and gay men: A new frontier in family research. *Journal of Marriage and Family, 57*(1), 111–128.

Appleby, G. A., & Anastas, J. W. (1998). *Not just a passing phase: Social work with gay, lesbian, and bisexual people.* New York: Columbia University Press.

Barret, B., & Logan, C. (2002). *Counseling gay men and lesbians: A practice primer.* Pacific Grove, CA: Brooks/Cole.

Barret, R. L., & Robinson, B. E. (2000). *Gay fathers: Encouraging the hearts of gay dads and their families.* San Francisco: Jossey-Bass.

Beeler, J., & DiProva, V. (1999). Family adjustment following the disclosure of homosexuality by a member: Themes discerned in narrative accounts. *Journal of Marital and Family Therapy, 25,* 443–459.

Boenke, M. (Ed.). (1999). *Trans forming families: Real stories of transgendered loved ones.* Imperial Beach, CA: Walter Trook Publishing, 1999.

Bozett, F. W. (1987). Children of gay fathers. In F. W. Bozett (Ed.), *Gay and lesbian parents* (pp. 39–57). New York: Praeger.

Button, J. W., Rienzo, B. A., & Wald, K. D. (1997). *Battles over gay rights in American communities.* Washington, DC: CQ Press.

Carroll, L., & Gilroy, P. J. (2002). Transgender issues in counselor preparation. *Counselor Education and Supervision, 41,* 233–242.

Cass, V. (1979). Homosexual identity formation: A theoretical model. *Journal of Homosexuality, 4,* 219–236.

—— . (1984). Homosexual identity formation: Testing a theoretical model. *Journal of Sex Research, 20,* 143–167.

Chen-Hayes, S. F. (2001). Counseling and advocacy with transgendered and gender-variant persons in schools and families. *Journal of Humanistic Counseling, Education, and Development, 40*(1), 34–49.

Clark, W. M., & Serovich, J. M. (1997). Twenty years and still in the dark? Content analysis of articles pertaining to gay, lesbian, and bisexual issues in marriage and family therapy journals. *Journal of Marital and Family Therapy, 23*(3), 239–253.

Cohen, K. M., & Savin-Williams, R. C. (1996). Developmental perspectives on coming out to self and others. In R. C. Savin-Williams & K. M. Cohen (Eds.), *The lives of lesbians, gays, and bisexuals: Children to adults* (pp. 113–151). New York: Harcourt Brace.

COLAGE. (n.d.). *About COLAGE.* Retrieved September 17, 2002, from http://www.colage.org/ about.html.

Cole, S. (2000). A transgender dilemma: The forgotten journey of the partners and families. *International Journal of Transgenderism*, 4(1). Retrieved September 10, 2002, from http://symposion.com/ijt/ greenpresidental /greem0.htm.

Crosbie-Burnett, M., Foster, T. L., Murray, C. I., & Bowen, G. L. (1996). Gay and lesbians' families of origin: A social-cognitive-behavioral model of adjustment. *Family Relations*, 45(4), 397–403.

D'Augelli, A. R., & Hershberger, S. L. (1993). Lesbian, gay, and bisexual youth in community settings: Personal challenges and mental health problems. *American Journal of Community Psychology*, 21(4), 421–448.

D'Augelli, A. R., Hershberger, S. L., & Pilkington, N. W. (1998). Lesbian, gay, and bisexual youth and their families: Disclosure of sexual orientation and its consequences. *American Journal of Orthopsychiatry*, 68(3), 361–371.

D'Emilio, J. (2000). Cycles of change, questions of strategy: The gay and lesbian movement after fifty years. In C. A. Rimmerman, K. D. Wald, & C. Wilcox (Eds.), *The politics of gay rights* (pp. 31–53). Chicago: University of Chicago Press.

Davidson, M. G. (2000). Religion and spirituality. In R. Perez, K. A. DeBord, & K. Bieschke (Eds.), *Handbook of counseling and psychotherapy with lesbian, gay, and bisexual clients* (pp. 409–433). Washington, DC: American Psychological Association.

Davis, E. C. (2002, August). *Negotiating gender and sexual boundaries: Examining how intimate partners make sense of gender transitions.* Paper presented at the meeting of the American Sociological Association, Chicago.

Dempsey, C. L. (1994). Health and social issues of gay, lesbian, and bisexual adolescents. *Families in Society*, 75(3), 160–167.

DeVine, J. L. (1984). A systemic inspection of affectional preference orientation and the family of origin. *Journal of Social Work and Human Sexuality*, 2, 9–17.

Díaz, R. M., & Ayala, G. (2001). *Social discrimination and health: The case of Latino gay men and HIV risk.* Washington, DC: National Gay and Lesbian Task Force.

Ettner, R. C., & White, T. J. H. (2000). Children of a parent undergoing a gender transition: Disclosure, risk, and protective factors. *International Journal of Transgenderism*, 4(1). Retrieved September 10, 2002, from http://symposion.com/ijt/greenpresidental /green17.htm.

Gartrell, N., Banks, A., Hamilton, J., Reed, N., Bishop, H., & Rodas, C. (1999). The National Lesbian Family Study. II. Interviews with mothers of toddlers. *American Journal of Orthopsychiatry*, 69(3), 362–369.

Gillespie, P. (Ed.). (1999). *Portraits of lesbian, gay, bisexual, and transgender parents and their families.* Amherst: University of Massachusetts Press.

Gochros, J. S. (1985). Wives' reactions to learning that their husbands are bisexual. *Journal of Homosexuality*, 11(1/2), 101–113.

——. (1989). *When husbands come out of the closet.* New York: Harrington Park.

Green, R. (1998). Transsexuals' children. *International Journal of Transgenderism*, 2(4). Retrieved September 10, 2002, from http://www.symposion.com/ijt/ijtc0601.htm.

Greene, B. (1994a). Lesbian and gay sexual orientations: Implications for clinical training, practice, and research. In B. Greene & G. M. Herek (Eds.), *Lesbian and gay psychology: Theory, research, and clinical applications* (pp. 1–24). Thousand Oaks, CA: Sage.

——. (1994b). Lesbian women of color: Triple jeopardy. In L. Comas-Diaz & B. Greene (Eds.), *Women of color: Integrating ethnic and gender identities in psychotherapy* (pp. 387–427). New York: Guilford.

——. (Ed.). (1997a). *Ethnic and cultural diversity among lesbian and gay men.* Thousand Oaks, CA: Sage.

——. (Ed.). (1997b). *Lesbian women of color: Triple jeopardy*. New York: Haworth.

——. (Ed.). (1998). *Family, ethnic identity, and sexual orientation: African American lesbians and gay men*. New York: Oxford University Press.

Griffin, C. W., Wirth, M. J., & Wirth, A. G. (1996). *Beyond acceptance: Parents of lesbians and gays talk about their experiences*. New York: St. Martin's Griffin.

Hammelman, T. L. (1993). Gay and lesbian youth: Contributing factors to serious attempts or consideration of suicide. *Journal of Gay and Lesbian Psychotherapy, 2*(1), 77–89.

Harris, M. D., and Turner, P. H. (1986). Gay and lesbian parents. *Journal of Homosexuality 12*, 101–113.

Herdt, G., & Beeler, J. (1998). Older gay men and lesbians in families. In C. J. Patterson & A. R. D'Augelli (Eds.), *Lesbian, gay, and bisexual identities in families: Psychological perspectives*. New York: Oxford University Press.

Hetrick, E. S., & Martin, A. D. (1987). Developmental issues and their resolution for gay and lesbian adolescents. *Journal of Homosexuality, 14*, 25–43.

Isay, R. A. (1998). Heterosexually married homosexual men: Clinical and developmental issues. *American Journal of Orthopsychiatry, 68*(3), 424–432.

Israel, G. (1996). *A parent's dilemma: The transgender child*. Retrieved August, 2002, from http://www.firelily.com/gender/gianna/dilemma.html.

Julie. (2001, June 21). *An open letter to the parents, family, and friends of a transsexual*. Gender Web Project. Retrieved August 30, 2002, from http://www.genderweb.org/family /tsfam.html.

Laframboise, S., & Long, B. (n.d.). *An introduction to: Gender, transgender, and transphobia*. Retrieved August 30, 2002, from http://mypage.direct.ca/h/hrp/gendertr.html.

Laird, J. (1998). Invisible ties: Lesbians and their families of origin. In C. J. Patterson & A. R. D'Augelli (Eds.), *Lesbian, gay, and bisexual identities in families: Psychological perspectives* (pp. 197–228). New York: Oxford University Press.

Leslie, L. A. (1995). The evolving treatment of gender, ethnicity, and sexual orientation in marital and family therapy. *Family Relations, 44*, 359–367.

Lewis, G. G., & Rogers, M. A. (1999). Does the public support equal employment rights for gays and lesbians. In E. D. B. Riggle & B. L. Tadlock (Eds.), *Gays and lesbians in the democratic process: Public policy, public opinion, and political representation* (pp. 118–145). New York: Columbia University Press.

Lipkin, A. (1999). *Understanding homosexuality, changing schools: A text for teachers, counselors, and administrators*. Boulder, CO: Westview.

Mann, W. (1997). Portraits of social services programs for rural sexual minorities. *Journal of Gay and Lesbian Social Services, 7*(3), 95–103.

Martin, H. P. (1991). The coming-out process for homosexuals. *Hospital and Community Psychiatry, 42*, 158–162.

Matteson, D. R. (1987). The heterosexually married gay and lesbian parent. In F. W. Bozett (Ed.), *Gay and lesbian parents* (pp. 139–159). New York: Praeger

Mays, V. M., Cochran, S. D., & Rhue, S. (1993). The impact of perceived discrimination on the intimate relationships of black lesbians. *Journal of Homosexuality, 25*(4), 1–14.

McGarry, M., & Wasserman, F. (1998). *Becoming visible: An illustrated history of lesbian and gay life in twentieth-century America*. New York: Penguin Studio.

Mengert, S. (1990, June 21, 2001). *An open letter to the parents of transsexual children*. Gender Web Project. Retrieved August 30, 2002, from http://www.genderweb.org/family/gfam3.html.

Neissen, J. H. (1987). Resources for families with a gay/lesbian member. *Journal of Homosexuality, 14*(1/2), 239–251.

New York City Parents and Friends of Lesbians and Gays. (1995). *For parents of gay children.* OutProud (adapted with permission). Retrieved August 30, 2002, from http://www. outproud.org/brochure_for_parents.html.

O'Connell, A. (1999). Voices from the heart: The developmental impact of a mother's lesbianism on her adolescent children. In J. Laird (Ed.), *Lesbians and lesbian families: Reflections on theory and practice* (pp. 261–280). New York: Columbia University Press.

Patterson, C. J. (1996). Lesbian mothers and their children: Findings from the Bay Area Families study. In J. Laird & R. J. Green (Eds.), *Lesbians and gays in couples and families* (pp. 420–437). San Francisco: Jossey-Bass.

——. (2000). Family relationships of lesbians and gay men. *Journal of Marriage and Family, 62*(4), 1052–1070.

Patterson, C. J., & D'Augelli, A. R. (Eds.). (1998). *Lesbian, gay, and bisexual identities in families: Psychological perspectives.* New York: Oxford University Press.

Patterson, C. J., & Redding, R. E. (1996). Lesbian and gay families with children: Implications of social science research for policy. *Journal of Social Issues, 52*(3), 29–50.

Peplau, L. A., & Cochran, S. D. (1990). A relationship perspective on homosexuality. In D. P. McWhirter, S. A. Sanders, & J. M. Reinisch (Eds.), *Homosexuality/heterosexuality: Concepts of sexual orientation* (pp. 321–349). New York: Oxford University Press.

PFLAG. (n.d.). *PFLAG's Vision and Mission.* Retrieved September 13, 2002, from http://www.pflag.org/about/mission.html.

Raphael, S. M., & Meyer, M. K. (2000). Family support patterns for midlife lesbians: Recollections of a lesbian couple 1971–1997. In M. R. Adelman (Ed.), *Midlife lesbian relationships: Friends, lovers, children, and parents.* New York: Harrington Park.

Riggle, E. D. B., & Tadlock., B. L. (Eds.). (1999). *Gays and lesbians in the democratic process: Public policy, public opinion, and political representation.* New York: Columbia University Press.

Rimmerman, C. A., Wald, K. D., & Wilcox, C. (Eds.). (2000). *The politics of gay rights.* Chicago: University of Chicago Press.

Robinson, B. E., Walters, L. H., & Skeen, P. J. (1989). Response of parents to learning that their child is homosexual and concern over AIDS: A national study. *Journal of Homosexuality, 18*(1–2), 59–80.

Ross, M. W. (1990). Married homosexual men: Prevalence and background. In F. W. Bozett & M. B. Sussman (Eds.), *Homosexuality and family relations* (pp. 35–58). New York: Harrington Park.

Savin-Williams, R. C. (1989). Coming out to parents and self-esteem among gay and lesbian youths. *Journal of Homosexuality, 18*(1/2), 1–35.

——. (1990). *Gay and lesbian youth: Expressions of identity.* New York: Hemisphere Publishing.

——. (1994). Verbal and physical abuse as stressors in the lives of lesbian, gay male, and bisexual youths: Associations with school problems, running away, substance abuse, prostitution, and suicide. *Journal of Consulting and Clinical Psychology, 62*(2), 261–269.

——. (2001). *Mom, Dad. I'm gay. How families negotiate coming out.* Washington, DC: American Psychological Association.

Savin-Williams, R. C., & Cohen, K. M. (1996). *The lives of lesbians, gays, and bisexuals: Children to adults.* New York: Harcourt Brace.

Sears, J. T., & Williams, W. L. (Eds.). (1997). *Overcoming heterosexism and homophobia: Strategies that work.* New York: Columbia University Press.

Serovich, J. M., Kimberly, J. A., & Greene, K. (1998). Perceived family member reaction to women's disclosure of HIV-positive information. *Family Relations, 47*(1), 15–22.

Serovich, J. M., Skeen, P., Walters, L., & Robinson, B. (1993). In-law relationships when a child is homosexual. *Journal of Homosexuality, 26,* 57–76.

Shernoff, M. J. (1984). Family therapy for lesbian and gay clients. *National Association of Social Workers, 29*(4), 393–396.

Sherrill, K. (1996). The political power of lesbians, gays, and bisexuals [Electronic version]. *PS: Political Science and Politics, 29*(3), 469–473. Retrieved August 30, 2002, from http://www.apsanet.org /PS/sept96/sherrill.cfm.

Simpson, R. (1976). *From the closet to the courts: The lesbian transition.* New York: Viking.

Smith, A. (1997). Cultural diversity and the coming-out process: Implications for clinical practice. In B. Greene (Ed.), *Ethnic and cultural diversity among lesbians and gay men* (pp. 279–272–300). Thousand Oaks, CA: Sage.

Smith, D. F., & Allred, G. H. (1990). Adjustment of women divorced from homosexual men: An exploratory survey. *American Journal of Family Therapy, 18*(3), 273–284.

Stacey, J., & Biblarz, T. (2001). (How) Does the sexual orientation of parents matter? *American Sociological Review, 66,* 159–183.

Straight Spouse Network. (n.d.). *Who we are.* Retrieved August 30, 2002, from http://www.ssnetwk.org/purpose.htm.

Strommen, E. F. (1989a). "You're a what?" Family member reactions to the disclosure of homosexuality. *Journal of Homosexuality, 18*(1–2), 37–58.

—— (1989b). Hidden branches and growing pains: Homosexuality and the family tree. *Marriage and Family Review, 14,* 9–34.

Sue, D. W., Arredondo, P., & McDavis, R. J. (1992). Multicultural counseling competencies and standards: A call to the profession. *Journal of Counseling and Development, 70,* 477–486.

Sue, D. W., & Sue, D. (1999). *Counseling the culturally different: Theory and practice* (3d ed.). New York: Wiley.

Tasker, F. L., & Golombok, S. (1995). Adults raised as children in lesbian families. *American Journal of Orthopsychiatry, 65*(2), 203–215.

Tuerk, C. (1998). Stages parents go through when a child comes out. *In the Family, 16*(4), 1, 16.

Tully, C. T. (2000). *Lesbians, gays, and the empowerment perspective.* New York: Columbia University Press.

Turner, P. H., Scadden, L., & Harris, M. B. (1990). Parenting in gay and lesbian families. *Journal of Gay and Lesbian Psychotherapy, 1*(3), 55–56.

Ueno, K. (2002, July). *Sexual orientation and psychological distress in adolescence: Examining interpersonal stressor and social support processes.* Paper presented at the Add Health Users Workshop, Bethesda, MD.

United States Conference of Catholic Bishops. (1997). *Always our children: A pastoral message to parents of homosexual children and suggestions for pastoral ministers.* A statement of the Bishops' Committee on Marriage and Family. Washington, DC: United States Conference of Catholic Bishops. Retrieved August 30, 2002, from http://www.usccb.org/laity/always.htm.

Unks, G. (1995). *The gay teen: Educational practice and theory for lesbian, gay, and bisexual adolescents.* New York: Routledge.

Van Voorhis, R. M. (1998). Culturally relevant practice: A framework for teaching the dynamics of oppression. *Journal of Social Work Education, 34,* 121–133.

van Wormer, K., Wells, J., & Boes, M. (2000). *Social work with lesbians, gays, and bisexuals: A strengths perspective.* Boston: Allyn and Bacon.

Wald, K. D. (2000). The context of gay politics. In C. A. Rimmerman, K. D. Wald, & C. Wilcox (Eds.), *The politics of gay rights* (pp. 1–30). Chicago: University of Chicago Press.

Wallerstein, J. S., and Blakeslee. S. (1989). *Second chances: Men, women, and children a decade after divorce.* New York: Tickor and Fields.

Williamson, D. S. (1998). An essay for practitioners: Disclosure is a family event. *Family Relations, 47,* 23–25.

Woog, D. (1999). *Friends and family: True stories of gay America's straight allies.* Los Angeles: Alyson Books.

Wren, B. (2000). Patterns of thinking and communication of families where an adolescent shows atypical gender identity organization. *International Journal of Transgenderism, 4*(1). Retrieved September 10, 2002, from http://symposion.com/ijt/greenpresidental/green52.htm.

Xavier, J., Sharp, C., & Boenke, M. (2001). *Our trans children: A publication of the Transgender Special Outreach Network of Parents, Families, and Friends of Lesbians and Gays (PFLAG).* Washington, DC: PFLAG. Retrieved September 18, 2002, from http://www.youth-guard.org/pflag-t-net/booklet.pdf.

8

GAY, LESBIAN, BISEXUAL, AND TRANSGENDER ADOLESCENTS

Deana F. Morrow

Gay and lesbian [and transgender] youth are an isolated silent population that has generally been abandoned by society and overlooked by the counseling professions.

—ROBINSON, 1994, P. 326

THIS CHAPTER will explore social work practice issues with GLBT youth, defined here as young people from the ages of 12 to 21. Adolescence, in general, is a challenging time of development, and it is all the more challenging for young people who are GLBT. The challenge of developing a positive GLBT identity as a sexual minority youth will be discussed, and questions of disclosure, or coming out, will be examined in conjunction with identity development. Challenges encountered in the family system and the school environment will be addressed. In addition, issues pertaining to the emergence of sexuality, as well as the consideration of diversity when working with this population, will be reviewed. Particular emphasis will be given to a number of risk factors that GLBT youth encounter: emotional distress, isolation, internalized homophobia/transphobia, depression, substance abuse, suicide, violence/victimization, family conflict, school performance, and sexually transmitted diseases and pregnancy. The chapter will conclude with a section on guidelines for social work practice with GLBT youth.

ADOLESCENT DEVELOPMENT

Adolescence is a transition period from childhood to adulthood. Accordingly, adolescents actively engage the process of figuring out who they are as "no-longer-

Portions of this chapter appeared as D. F. Morrow (2004), Social work practice with gay, lesbian, bisexual, and transgender adolescents, *Families in Society* 85(1), 91–99.

children, but not-yet-adults," throughout this transition process. Perhaps the most salient developmental task of adolescence is that of developing a sense of identity (Erikson, 1950, 1963, 1968). Included in this process are such tasks as thinking about a career, fitting into a peer group, developing social skills, coping with increasing independence, and dealing with emerging sexuality. Developing a positive identity within a heterocentric social environment can be especially challenging for GLBT youth in that there are often severe social penalties, such as ostracism, taunting, and even violence, for not conforming to socially approved dating practices and gender expression norms.

GLBT ADOLESCENT DEVELOPMENT

Adolescent development for GLBT youth can be a perilous journey. Peer pressure to fit in socially is tremendous during the adolescent years. The stress of feeling different from the majority of their peers—whether with regard to sexual orientation or gender expression—can be daunting (Morrow, 1993a). Thus, a primary task in identity development for GLBT adolescents is that of adjusting to a socially stigmatized role (Hetrick & Martin, 1987). GLBT adolescents must cope with developing a sexual minority identity in the midst of negative comments, jokes, and often the threat of violence because of their sexual orientation and/or transgender identity. To develop an overall positive identity in the midst of such negative social stigma requires courage and resilience.

It is important to note that GLBT youth typically enter adolescence with no preparation for the social identity that comes with being a sexual minority person. In contrast, other minority youth (e.g., African Americans, Latinos/as, Jewish youth) have numerous social supports, such as their families, neighborhoods, and faith communities, to help prepare them for life as a member of their respective group. For GLBT youth, however, these supports are generally not available. GLBT youth commonly do not see themselves reflected in their families, among their neighbors, or within their faith communities. Positive role models are not nearly so easily visible and available for them as they are for heterosexual youth. GLBT youth may, indeed, witness numerous episodes of GLBT-negative language, jokes, and actions as the result of growing up in their family environment. Thus the internalization of homophobic and heterocentric messages begins very early—often before GLBT youth fully realize their sexual orientation and gender identity.

Adolescent development typically includes some degree of sexual exploration. Not all youth who demonstrate a history of same-sex sexual behaviors are necessarily GLB. And those who have a history of other-sex sexual behaviors are not necessarily heterosexual. Research suggests that the majority of gay- and lesbian-oriented people report a past history of heterosexual behaviors (Coleman & Remafedi, 1989). This is not surprising, given that the social mandate for heterosexually oriented sexual behaviors is overwhelming. The process of exploring sexuality is especially stressful for GLB youth in that such exploration takes place in a "context and ecology of cultural denial, distorted stereotypes, rejection, neglect, harassment, and sometimes outright victimization and abuse" (Tharinger & Wells, 2000, p. 159). A similar point can be made for transgender youth in reference to their exploring a gender identity that is construed as inconsistent with who they "should" be according to socially constructed gender expectations based on biological sex determinants (Burgess, 1999).

The process of developing a GLBT identity in adolescence is usually a fairly lengthy one. Many youth go through a questioning period before arriving at an understanding of a GLB sexual orientation or a transgender identity. In a study of more than 100 gay and lesbian youth (D'Augelli, Hershberger, & Pilkington, 1998), the average age of awareness of having a gay or lesbian sexual orientation was 10, the average age of labeling oneself as gay or lesbian was 14, the average age of first disclosure of sexual orientation (coming out) to a friend was 16, and the average age of first disclosure to family was 17. Ryan and Futterman (1997) found that most gay and lesbian adolescents disclose their sexual orientation to other people in the following order: other GLB peers, close heterosexual peers, close non-parental family members, and finally parents. Thus parents are among the last to know about their child's GLB sexual orientation. This finding is not surprising, given the power and control parents have over their underage children. GLBT youth who disclose their sexual orientation or transgender identity to their parents are at risk of parental rejection, withdrawal of financial support, authoritative restrictions to their social lives, forced counseling, and even violence and removal from the home.

For GLBT youth, developing a positive identity specifically includes coming to terms with their sexual minority status. Those who have acquired a positive identity as GLBT have negotiated the challenges of being socially stigmatized because of their sexual orientation or gender identity. They have become able to inwardly acknowledge and own who they are, and they have navigated disclosing that identity to trusted others. Developing self-acceptance, as well as having positive family support and supportive school relationships can facilitate this positive identity development process (Cass, 1979, 1984a; Hershberger & D'Augelli, 1995; Proctor & Groze, 1994; Tharinger & Wells, 2000). A lack of social supports can contribute to internalized homophobia and a negative self-concept, which can hinder the development of a positive GLBT identity.

FAMILY ISSUES

GLBT youth fear disapproval and rejection from their families. Because of the social stigma assigned to a GLB orientation or transgender identity, GLBT youth may believe that something is "wrong" with them and that they must keep their sexual orientation or transgender identity secret so as not to disappoint the family. Some youth may withdraw from their families as a way of coping (Green, 1994), while others may manage the stress of keeping their secret by indulging in self-destructive behaviors such as substance abuse, risky sexual behaviors, running away, or attempting suicide (Gonsiorek, 1988; Proctor & Groze, 1994; Savin-Williams, 1994).

How open to be with the family about their sexual orientation or transgender identity is a major issue for GLBT youth (Morrow, 2000). Those who come out to their families hope for support and validation, yet they are also at risk for disapproval, maltreatment, and disownment (Teague, 1992). These risks can be especially high in ethnic minority families where being GLBT is viewed as deviant and an "aberration of Caucasian society" (Newman & Muzzonigro, 1993, p. 216). Some research suggests that youth who get along well with their families may be more reluctant to disclose their sexual orientation or transgender identity because of a greater fear of disapproval (Waldner & Magruder, 1999). Thus, GLBT youth who are more strongly identified with their families may be more likely to try and meet the heterocentric and traditional gender role expectations of their families.

Of those who come out to family, the greater likelihood is that they will elect to disclose to mothers rather than fathers (D'Augelli et al., 1998). More-conservative and traditional families are less likely to be accepting and validating upon disclosure (Teague, 1992). And those who come out to parents are at risk of disapproval and rejection. In a study of more than 100 gay and lesbian youth who had disclosed to their parents (D'Augelli et al., 1998), only half of the mothers and siblings were accepting of the news, and fewer than 25% of the fathers were accepting. In the same study, more than half of the disclosers reported thoughts or actions related to suicide, while 12% of the nondisclosers reported similar suicidal tendencies. The disclosers were at greater risk of physical violence from family members, with the brothers of gay male youth being the most likely perpetrators of violence against their gay or lesbian sibling. There was virtually no incidence of family member attacks among the nondisclosers. Thus there does appear to be some element of risk for those who disclose their GLBT status to family.

THE SCHOOL ENVIRONMENT

School is a central component in virtually every adolescent's life. It is the primary social setting where friends are made, social skills are learned, and self-efficacy is developed. Healthy psychosocial development in adolescence is fundamentally connected to the quality of the social interactions that take place within the school setting (Black & Underwood, 1998). Yet the school environment can be among the most dangerous of places for GLBT youth. The school social environment is filled with anti-GLBT rhetoric. Pejorative words like *fag*, *dyke*, *queer*, *lezzie*, and *homo* are common, and those terms often go unchallenged by teachers and administrators in ways that similar pejorative terms against other groups of students would never be tolerated.

It is not surprising then that many GLBT youth remain closeted in the school setting. Some react to the stress of the school environment by socially isolating themselves, being reluctant to participate in school-related activities, frequently being absent, and dropping out (Hunter & Schaecher, 1987). Others cope through overachieving academically or athletically, or by adopting the defense mechanism of reaction formation, which consists of taking on an exaggerated heterosexual image (Smith & Smith, 1998).

GLBT adolescents who are more open, or more visible in terms of their sexual minority status, face the prospect of negativity and harassment from other students and, in some instances, even from teachers and school administrators. In one study, nearly half of LGB youth who had disclosed their sexual orientation reported losing friends because of their disclosure (D'Augelli et al., 1998). In the same study, 27% also reported having been physically assaulted by other students because of their sexual orientation.

The education curriculum in most schools does not prepare students and teachers to cope with anti-GLBT rhetoric. Most diversity and health education curricula omit GLBT content because it can be a politically controversial spark plug among parents and community members. Silence and ignorance thus perpetuate misinformation, lack of understanding, intolerance, and hatred. Openly GLBT teacher role models are minimal in school settings because teachers can still lose their jobs if they present themselves as openly GLBT (Morrow, 1993a). Anti-GLBT harassment too often goes unaddressed by teachers and administrators who fear for their own job security should they become identified as GLBT-affirmative.

EMERGING SEXUALITY

During adolescence, young people begin to discover and actualize their emerging sexual identities. Heterosexual youth learn about their form of sexuality through sex education classes in school. The broader social culture is replete with images of heterosexual sexuality for youth to emulate. But GLBT sexuality is typically not addressed in sex education classes, and there are very few cultural images of positive GLBT sexual expression. Therefore, GLBT youth are left to seek out their emerging sexuality in a culture of limited knowledge, social stigma, and secrecy.

Sexual exploration is a normal part of developing a sexual identity. More than 70% of all adolescents have engaged in sexually intimate behaviors by age

18 (Guttmacher Institute, 1994). While some adolescents may be clear about their sexual orientation and gender identity during their teen years, many do not achieve such clarity until adulthood (Appleby & Anastas, 1998). Gay male youth tend to focus initially more on the physical aspects rather than the relational aspects of sexuality, while lesbian youth tend to focus initially on developing an emotional relationship before engaging in the physical aspects of sexual expression (Hunter & Schaecher, 1987). GLB youth express a range of sexual behaviors, and stereotypical adherence to particular roles is relatively uncommon (Bell & Weinberg, 1978; Roth, 1985).

Transgender youth tend to be less sexual in relationships than nontransgender youth. Some transgender youth may be uncomfortable with having their sex organs touched, especially if their sex organs are perceived as personally undesirable, as might be the case for those interested in transitioning to the other sex (Brown & Rounsley, 1996). In some situations transgender youth who date people of the same biological sex may view themselves as having a heterosexual orientation while their partners may be GLB. For example, a male-to-female transgender person who possesses a female gender identity may date a gay male and view that relationship as heterosexual—even though the partner may identify himself as gay.

DIVERSITY AMONG GLBT YOUTH

Diversity in the form of sexual orientation and gender expression is also accompanied by other areas of diversity, including sex, race, ethnicity, class, and physical ability. GLBT youth live multicultural lives. In addition to navigating the dominant heterocentric culture as sexual minority people, they must also navigate the other areas of their cultural lives, such as ethnicity and class, within the overlapping context of their GLBT status.

African American and Latino communities—both of which are dominated by relatively conservative religious traditions—are considered less accepting of sexual orientation and gender expression diversity than the Anglo community (Diaz et al., 1993, Icard, 1996). Latino males who have sex with other males are less likely to identify as gay because of the machismo tradition of their culture (Appleby & Anastas, 1998). Asian cultures also frequently view same-sex relationships as a rejection of the vital role of parenthood—an affront to Asian tradition (Chan, 1993). Thus GLBT youth in ethnic minority cultures are often especially vulnerable and invisible.

Additionally, urban and suburban GLBT youth may be more open about their sexual orientation and gender identity than their rural counterparts (Fellows, 1996). Youth in small towns and rural areas are likely to have fewer social options for meeting other GLBT youth; there may be fewer social service supports available, and fewer opportunities for anonymity in exploring their sexual and gender identities.

Garnets and Kimmel (1993) identified a number of themes from the literature that can be useful to social workers in assessing the impact of diversity in working with GLBT youth:

1) The importance of religion within the culture and the relevance of sexuality to central beliefs;
2) The significance of distinctions between male and female gender roles;
3) The nature and influence of the family structure;
4) The process of reconciling one's ethnicity, gender, and sexual orientation; and,
5) The degree of interaction with and integration into the lesbian and gay community

(PP. 331–337)

RISK FACTORS

There are a host of risk factors pertaining to GLBT youth for which social workers need to be aware. Risk factors are defined here as situations or circumstances that, when they occur, have the potential to compromise the bio-psycho-social well-being of individuals. This section will identify a number of risk factors for GLBT youth.

EMOTIONAL DISTRESS

In a study by Savin-Williams (1994) more than 95% of gay and lesbian teens reported that they frequently felt separated and emotionally isolated from their peers. GLBT youth commonly voice feeling "different" from their peers, and this experience of differentness, in itself, can create distress and a sense of not belonging. GLBT youth encounter the stress of deciding whether to disclose their sexual minority status to friends and family. Many live with the fear that their orientation or transgender identity will be discovered before they are ready to share that information, and they also live with the constant fear of social ridicule, lack of acceptance, harassment, and potential violence.

ISOLATION

GLBT youth are often isolated from peers, family, adult role models, and other social supports. Those who do not disclose their orientation or transgender identity may isolate from peers and family in order to avoid calling undue attention to their sexual orientation or transgender identity status. Others isolate in order to avoid ridicule and rejection. In a study of GLB teens, more than half reported being ridiculed by their peers (Rotheram-Borus, Rosario, & Koopman, 1991). Isolation can lead to other problems as well, such as low self-esteem, limited social skill development, substance abuse, and depression.

INTERNALIZED HOMOPHOBIA/TRANSPHOBIA

Internalized homophobia and internalized transphobia represent the state in which GLB people and transgender people, respectively, internalize the negative messages perpetrated by society relative to their sexual orientation or transgender identity status. Being GLBT does not automatically make a person immune to the pejorative terms and misinformation used to construct images and stereotypes of GLBT people. GLBT people tend to internalize those messages, and they have to "unlearn" much of that harmful rhetoric. Doing so can be difficult in a social context that is overwhelmingly heterocentric and traditional in the appointing of rigid gender roles. Unaddressed internalized homophobia or transphobia can place GLBT youth at risk for other problems, including depression, substance abuse, and even suicide.

DEPRESSION

Because of the multiple stressors encountered by GLBT youth, they are at risk for depression (Proctor & Groze, 1994). These youth must cope on a daily basis with the painful experience of being different from the majority of their peers (Black & Underwood, 1998), with making decisions about whether to disclose their sexual minority status to others, and with the fear of rejection and abuse. Transgender youth may become repelled by or ashamed of their developing physical sex characteristics (Burgess, 1999), and since they are underage for medical decision making, those who would desire intervention such as hormone therapy may feel helpless in engaging parental support for treatment. Feelings of self-worth and a positive sexual orientation or transgender identity are critical to the mental health of GLBT youth (Hershberger & D'Augelli, 1995), and when there are deficits in these areas, their mental health may be at risk. In particular, if family support is lacking, the risk for depression may be higher (D'Augelli et al., 1998; Proctor & Groze, 1994; Savin-Williams, 1994; Tharinger & Wells, 2000).

SUBSTANCE ABUSE

Substance abuse is a particular risk for GLBT youth (Dempsey, 1994; Hunter & Schaecher, 1994; Proctor & Groze, 1994; Savin-Williams, 1994; Tharinger & Wells, 2000). Abusing substances can be a means of coping with the stress of social ostracism, fear of rejection, and internalized homophobia/transphobia. In addition, the bar scene has historically been an entrée into adult GLBT socializing. An estimated 20% to 30% of GLBT people have substance abuse problems (Amico & Neisen, 1997).

SUICIDE

Because of the significant amount of psychosocial stress they must endure, it is not surprising that an alarming 30% to 40% of GLBT youth have attempted suicide (D'Augelli & Hershberger, 1993; Gibson, 1989; Martin & Hetrick, 1988; National Lesbian & Gay Health Foundation, 1987). These data compare with a suicide rate of 8% to 13% for presumed heterosexual youth (Friedman, Asnis, Bock, & DiFiore, 1987; Garland & Zeigler, 1993; Schneider, Farberow, & Kruks, 1989; Smith & Crawford, 1986). Ben-Ari and Gill (1998) cite the following themes as contributors to suicidality in gay and lesbian youth: negative personal conceptions of homosexuality, conflicted family relationships, and negative social relationships. Swann and Herbert (1999) suggest that transgender youth may be at risk for harm to themselves through self-mutilation in a desperate effort to further their cross-gender identification. Suicide assessment should always be a part of effective social work practice with GLBT youth. Those youth who already have problems with depression or substance abuse and those who have a history of past suicidality should be considered at particularly high risk.

VIOLENCE/VICTIMIZATION

It is not uncommon for GLBT youth to be victimized through verbal abuse and physical violence. Martin and Hetrick (1988) found that more than 40% of the GLBT youth served at the Institute for the Protection of Lesbian and Gay Youth in New York City had suffered violence because of their sexual minority status. Violence and victimization against GLBT youth occur not only within schools and communities but also at home. Pilkington and D'Augelli (1995) found that 33% of the GLB youth they surveyed had been verbally abused at home and that 10% had been physically assaulted by a family member. Hunter (1990) also found that more than 60% of the violence perpetrated against a sample of gay and lesbian youth had been inflicted by family members.

Another area of victimization for GLBT youth is through the practice of conversion therapy, also known as reparative therapy. Conversion therapy is a systematic means for attempting to change a person's sexual orientation from lesbian, gay, or bisexual to heterosexual. Such therapies often occur in religious contexts and can include techniques such as prayer, exorcism, religious-based guilt inducement, and punishment-oriented forms of behavior modification (Tozer & McClanahan, 1999; White, 1995). Parents who are uncomfortable with having a gay or lesbian child may seek out conversion therapy practitioners under the mistaken assumption that their child's sexual orientation can be changed through such therapy. There is no credible empirical support for the success of conversion therapy in actually changing sexual orientation (Haldeman, 1994; Mills, 1999; Tozer & McClanahan, 1999). Conversion therapy practice can cause psychological harm to GLBT youth by reinforcing negative stereotypes and misinformation and inducing internalized homophobia. The National Committee on Lesbian, Gay, and Bisexual Issues (1999) of the National Association of Social Workers has taken the stance that the practice of conversion therapy by social workers is unethical and harmful to clients. Effective social work practice with GLBT youth must consider the emotional and psychological well-being of clients, as well as their physical safety.

FAMILY CONFLICT

Families are commonly ill prepared to deal with having a GLB or transgender child. Parents tend to have minimal accurate knowledge—yet lots of culturally transmitted misinformation and stereotypes—about sexual minority groups. Many GLBT youth keep their sexual orientation or gender identity secret from their families for fear of disappointing them. Others avoid disclosing for fear of rejection, abuse, or parental withdrawal of all emotional and financial supports. Nearly all families go through some type of conflict or crisis when it becomes known that a child is GLB or transgender (Borhek, 1994; Morrow, 2000). Some families weather the crisis and are able to effectively incorporate the news into the ongoing life and development of the family, while other families are never able to reach resolution. Accurate information about sexual orientation diversity and gender expression may be useful. Also, GLBT-affirming clergy may be helpful resources for families whose religious values may conflict with understanding sexual orientation and gender identity (Morrow, 2003).

SCHOOL PERFORMANCE

Because the school environment is so stressful for GLBT youth, it is not unusual that many of them would have academic difficulties. Rotheram-Borus et al, (1991) report that more than 50% of sexual minority youth are ridiculed by their peers. The most frequent abusers of GLBT youth are other teens (Savin-Williams, 1994). It is difficult for GLBT youth to perform well academically when they are schooled in a climate where they must fear for their safety and emotional well-being. Those who feel fearful and alienated at school are more likely to isolate themselves, have high absenteeism rates, or drop out of school as a means of coping (Burgess, 1999). In a study of gay and lesbian youth, Elia (1993) found that 80% demonstrated declining school performance, 40% had problems with truancy, and 30% had dropped out of school. In a study of 36 LGBs, Sears (1991) found that

97% reported negative attitudes among their classmates and more than 50% feared being harassed should they disclose their sexual orientation at school.

SEXUALLY TRANSMITTED DISEASES AND PREGNANCY

Regardless of their sexual orientation, adolescents seek to actualize their sexual identities and learn how to develop intimate relationships (Zastrow & Kirst-Ashman, 2004). GLBT youth must figure out how to master these rites of passage in a virtual vacuum, for there are few adult role models to help them learn about socially responsible sexual expression. Those who do not practice heterosexual relationship patterns are often viewed with disdain. Thus some GLBT youth cope by displaying socially expected and rewarded heterosexual behaviors—even though doing so does not correspond with their true sexual orientation. Some gay male teens father children, and some lesbian teens become pregnant in seeking social validation by "passing" for heterosexual. Some GLBT youth become sexually promiscuous in seeking to find the boundaries around their socially stigmatized sexual expression; they are at greater risk for HIV and other sexually transmitted diseases (Governor's Commission on Gay and Lesbian Youth, 1994).

PROTECTIVE FACTORS

While the previous section examined risk factors for GLBT youth, it is important as well to identify protective factors that serve to enhance and support the bio-psycho-social well-being of GLBT youth. Positive and supportive family relationships can be central in this regard (Tharinger & Wells, 2000). A validating family system can be crucial for youth who, on a daily basis, encounter shame and ridicule from the broader society because of their sexual orientation or transgender identity. Other protective factors include stable intellectual functioning, self-confidence, high self-esteem, a socially appealing disposition, a supportive and validating faith, special talent (e.g., athletic or musical skills), sustainable hope, and supportive school relationships (Cicchetti & Toth, 1998; Masten, 1994; Masten & Coatsworth, 1998; Rutter, 1998). Identifying and utilizing these protective factors as client strengths are important strategies in social work practice with GLBT youth.

GUIDELINES FOR PRACTICE

This section will address practice considerations in working with GLBT youth, including both direct (micro and mezzo) and indirect (macro) services.

ASSESS THE DEGREE OF GLBT IDENTITY DEVELOPMENT

The extent of positive identity development as a GLBT person can be crucial to a youth's overall sense of efficacy and well-being. The Cass model (Cass, 1979, 1984a, 1984b) was introduced in chapter 4 as one means of assessing the identity development of gay and lesbian people. A brief review of that model appears in table 8.1. Youth who are assessed to be in Stages 1 through 3 (i.e., those stages that precede Identity Acceptance) may be at higher risk for problems such as low self-esteem, depression, substance abuse, and even suicide as a result of the stress they experience in coming to terms with being gay or lesbian. Stages 1 through 3 represent what may be termed a "red zone" of concern, in which gay and lesbian youth are experiencing the dissonance of who they are discovering themselves to be in contrast to a culture that denigrates homosexuality. Those who appear to be at Stage 4 or higher on the model are far more likely to have developed a positive gay or lesbian identity.

There are no similar models for bisexual and transgender identity development. Yet a worker may assess, in a fashion similar to the Cass model, the extent to which bisexual and transgender youth have achieved positive self-acceptance. Those who have internalized negative societal messages and developed a sense of shame about themselves are at higher risk than are those who are moving progressively toward self-acceptance.

ASSESS LEVEL OF DISCLOSURE

It can be expected that the farther along GLBT youth are in identity development, the more likely they will be to disclose their sexual orientation or transgender identity to others (Cass, 1979). Conversely, the less far along they are, the more likely they are to remain closeted. It is crucial that workers respect clients' level of outness and not push clients to disclose beyond their own reasonable level of safety and comfort. It can be helpful to systematically explore with clients the costs and benefits of their disclosure to significant others, such as parents, siblings, friends, and teachers (Morrow, 2000). In some situations (e.g., at home or at school), it may even be safer for youth to remain closeted than to disclose their sexual orientation or transgender identity (D'Augelli et al., 1998; Tharinger & Wells, 2000). Client self-determination should be encouraged and respected with regard to disclosure decisions.

ASSESS FOR SAFETY

Because GLBT youth are at risk for depression, substance abuse, suicide, and victimization, workers should always assess client safety when working with this population. It is not unusual to find GLBT youth presenting for services at a

TABLE 8.1 The Cass Model of Gay and Lesbian Identity Development

Stage 1: Identity Confusion. Conscious awareness that homosexuality has personal relevance in thoughts, emotions, or behaviors. Dissonance regarding one's heretofore presumed heterosexuality contrasted with a burgeoning awareness of self as possibly gay/lesbian.

Stage 2: Identity Comparison. Recognition of the probability that one is gay/lesbian. Dissonance in the realization of being different from the dominant and socially valued heterosexual culture. Feelings of social alienation.

Stage 3: Identity Tolerance. Reasonable certainty of a personal gay/lesbian identity. Tolerance, rather than acceptance, of that identity (based on anti-gay socialization). Seeks out other gay/lesbian people to counter social alienation.

Stage 4: Identity Acceptance. Positive acceptance of self as gay/lesbian. Social interaction with other gay/lesbian people grows. Emerging interest in being more open and honest with others regarding sexual identity.

Stage 5: Identity Pride. Immersion in learning about and experiencing gay/lesbian culture. Interest in associating primarily with gay/lesbian people, and a growing concern/frustration with a dominant heterosexual culture that overtly oppresses gays/lesbians.

Stage 6: Identity Synthesis. Integration of being gay/lesbian with other aspects of overall identity. Social interactions likely include both gay/lesbian and gay-affirmative heterosexual people. Disclosing one's gay/lesbian sexual identity to others becomes more a by-product of interaction and less a major personal issue.

Sources: Cass, 1979, pp. 105–126; Morrow, 1993b.

point where they have been rejected by family, become homeless, or suffered violence because of their sexual orientation or transgender identity. Initial service may need to be in the form of crisis intervention to stabilize a presenting crisis situation.

PROVIDE ACCURATE EDUCATIONAL INFORMATION

Because content on sexual orientation and gender identity expression is typically not included in health education or diversity education curricula in schools, GLBT youth and youth who are questioning their sexual orientation and gender identities have minimal access to accurate factual information about these issues. Workers should keep on hand basic materials that will assist GLBT and questioning youth — as well as all youth, regardless of sexual orientation or gender identity — in having access to accurate information on the range of sexual orientation and gender identity expression. For more information on educational materials, the reader is referred to Bass and Kaufman (1996), Berzon (2001), Brown and Rounsley (1996), Ettner (1999), Gray (1999), and Harris (1998).

ESTABLISH A GLBT-SUPPORTIVE WORK MILIEU

GLBT youth learn quickly to be vigilant of their surroundings for signs of acceptance and rejection. Workers can communicate their openness and acceptance of GLBT youth by displaying GLBT-supportive literature (e.g., newsletters and magazines) and symbols (e.g., pink triangle or rainbow flag sticker) in their offices and waiting areas (Phillips, McMillen, Sparks, & Uberle, 1997). They can also demonstrate openness to diversity in sexual orientation and gender identity expression by making sure the language on agency forms is inclusive and nonbiased. In addition, social work agencies can nurture the development of a GLBT-affirming staff and work environment by including sexual orientation and gender identity in agency nondiscrimination policies, by offering in-service training on GLBT youth issues for staff, and by hiring openly GLBT workers.

ADVOCATE FOR ENHANCED SOCIAL SERVICES

In virtually every human services agency, save for those few dedicated specifically to serving GLBT youth, services to sexual minority youth are minimal to nonexistent. Social workers need to advocate for services that specifically include and respond to the needs of sexual minority youth. Examples include the need for GLBT-oriented support groups dealing with issues such as coming out, forming healthy relationships, and coping with heterosexism; GLBT-oriented substance abuse recovery groups and treatment programs; educational programs for GLBT youth and their families; and, services to meet the needs of GLBT youth in child welfare agencies.

ADVOCATE FOR MORE SUPPORTIVE SCHOOL ENVIRONMENTS

The school setting is a hostile environment for GLBT youth, and significant reformation is needed in order for them to be emotionally and physically safe there. Sexual orientation and gender identity should be included in school nondiscrimination policies, and those policies must be fully enforced. There must be zero tolerance for anti-GLBT language and behaviors in the same way that other hate language and behaviors are not tolerated. Teachers and staff must be educated, through in-service training, about the needs of GLBT youth, and administrators must support school personnel in establishing an inclusive environment for GLBT students. Schools need to hire openly GLBT teachers as role models for students in the same manner in which they seek ethnic minority teachers and both men and women teachers as role models. And children need to be educated about GLBT people as part of the spectrum of diverse groups of people that are to be respected and valued. Diversity education curricula would be an appropriate place to include GLBT content, along with other diversity-oriented content.

THE HETRICK-MARTIN INSTITUTE

The Hetrick-Martin Institute, located in New York City, is a social services agency that serves GLBT and questioning youth. It was founded in 1979 by Drs. Emery S. Hetrick and A. Damien Martin in response to the beating of a 15-year-old gay male youth in a New York City group home. Administrators at the group home handled the incident by discharging the victim and claiming that the abuse would never have happened had the victim not been gay. The Hetrick-Martin Institute serves nearly 8,000 youth each year with an array of services, including individual and family counseling, housing and services to homeless youth, case management, youth initiatives, and public policy advocacy. The institute also administers the Harvey Milk School, the first and largest accredited public school devoted to the educational needs of GLBT and questioning youth.

The Hetrick-Martin Institute
and the Harvey Milk School
2 Astor Place
New York, NY 10003
(212) 674–8695
website: http://www.hmi.org
email: info@hmi.org

ADVOCATE FOR SOCIAL CHANGE

There are no federal civil rights laws that protect against discrimination on the basis of sexual orientation and gender expression. Although many progressive businesses (e.g., Bank of America, Levi Strauss, Microsoft Corporation) have added domestic partnership benefits for same-sex couples, most businesses—including most social services agencies—do not offer such benefits. Conservative political forces continue to perpetuate heterosexism by seeking to deny same-sex couples the legal recognition, including all the accompanying responsibilities and benefits, that their unions deserve. Social workers should advocate for the constitutional principle of equal protection under the law—in their own agencies as well as at the community, state, and national levels—so that today's GLBT youth will grow into adulthood in a nation that is more equitable and just.

SUMMARY

Adolescent development was discussed and identity development for GLBT youth in particular was examined. GLBT youth who have difficulty forming a positive identity are at greater risk for problems such as low self-esteem, depression, substance abuse, and suicide. Issues pertaining to disclosure, the family, and the school environment were explored, and issues of emerging sexuality and consideration of diversity were addressed. The following risk factors were identified and discussed: emotional distress, isolation, internalized homophobia/transphobia, depression, substance abuse, suicide, violence/victimization, family conflict, school performance, and sexually transmitted diseases and pregnancy. Protective factors that serve to enhance the well-being of GLBT youth were identified, and the following guidelines for social work practice with GLBT youth were discussed: assess the degree of GLBT identity development, assess level of disclosure, assess for safety, provide accurate educational information, establish a GLBT supportive work milieu, advocate for enhanced social services, advocate for more supportive school environments, and advocate for social change.

REFERENCES

Amico, J. M., & Neison, J. (1997, May–June). Sharing the secret: The need for gay-specific treatment. *Counselor*, 12–15.

Appleby, G. A., & Anastas, J. W. (1998). *Not just a passing phase: Social work with gay, lesbian, and bisexual people*. New York: Columbia University Press.

Bass, E., & Kaufman, K. (1996). *Free your mind: The book for gay, lesbian, and bisexual youth and their allies*. New York: HarperCollins.

Bell, A. P., & Weinberg, M. S. (1978). *Homosexualities: A study of diversity among men and women*. New York: Simon and Schuster.

Ben-Ari, A. T., & Gill, S. (1998). Perceptions of life and death among suicidal gay adolescents. *Omega*, 37(2), 107–119.

Berzon, B. (Ed.). (2001). *Positively gay: New approaches to gay and lesbian life* (3d ed.). Berkeley, CA: Celestial Arts.

Black, J., & Underwood, J. (1998). Young, female, and gay: Lesbian students and the school environment. *Professional School Counseling*, 1(3), 15–21.

Borhek, M. V. (1994). *Coming out to parents: A two-way survival guide for lesbians and gay men and their parents*. New York: Pilgrim.

Brown, M. L., & Rounsley, C. A. (1996). *True selves: Understanding transsexualism*. New York: Jossey-Bass.

Burgess, C. (1999). Internal and external stress factors associated with the identity development of transgendered youth. *Journal of Gay and Lesbian Social Services*, 10(3/4), 35–47.

Cass, V. C. (1979). Homosexual identity formation: A theoretical model. *Journal of Homosexuality*, 4(3), 219–235.

———. (1984a). Homosexual identity: A concept in need of definition. *Journal of Homosexuality*, 9(2/3), 105–126.

———. (1984b). Homosexual identity formation: Testing a theoretical model. *Journal of Sex Research*, 20(2), 143–167.

Chan, C. S. (1993). Issues of identity development among Asian American lesbian and gay men. In L. D. Garnets & D. C. Kimmel (Eds.), *Psychological perspectives on lesbian and gay male experiences* (pp. 376–387). New York: Columbia University Press.

Cicchetti, D., & Toth, L. L. (1998). The development of depression in children and adolescents. *American Psychologist*, 53, 221–242.

Coleman, E., & Remafedi, G. (1989). Gay, lesbian, and bisexual adolescents: A critical challenge to counselors. *Journal of Counseling and Development*, 68(1), 36–40.

D'Augelli, R. R., & Hershberger, S. L. (1993). Lesbian, gay, and bisexual youth in community settings: Personal challenges and mental health problems. *American Journal of Community Psychology, 211*, 421–448.

D'Augelli, R. R., Hershberger, S. L., & Pilkington, N. W. (1998). Lesbian, gay, and bisexual youth and their families: Disclosure of sexual orientation and its consequences. *American Journal of Orthopsychiatry, 68*(3), 361–371.

Dempsey, C. (1994). Health and social issues of gay, lesbian, and bisexual adolescents. *Families in Society, 75*(3), 160–167.

Diaz, T., Chu, S., Frederick, M., Hermann, P., Levy, A., Mokotoff, E., Whyte, B., Conti, L, Herr, M., Checko, P., Rietmeijer, C., Sorvill, R., & Quaiser, M. (1993). Sociodemographics and HIV risk behaviors of bisexual men with AIDS: Results from a multistate interview project. *AIDS, 7*(9), 1227–1232.

Elia, J. P. (1993). Homophobia in the high school: A problem in need of resolution. *High School Journal, 77*, 177–185.

Erikson, E. H. (1950). *Childhood and society.* New York: Norton.

——. (1963). *Childhood and society* (2d ed.). New York: Norton.

——. (1968). *Identity: Youth and crisis.* New York: Norton.

Ettner, R. (1999). *Gender loving care: A guide to counseling gender-variant clients.* New York: Norton.

Fellows, W. (1996). *Farm boys: Lives of gay men from the rural Midwest.* Madison: University of Wisconsin Press.

Friedman, J. M., Asnis, G. M., Boeck, M., & DiFore, J. (1987). Prevalence of specific suicidal behaviors in a high school sample. *American Journal of Psychiatry, 144*, 1203–1206.

Garland, A. F., & Zeigler, E. (1993). Adolescent suicide prevention: Current research and social policy implications. *American Psychology, 48*, 169–182.

Garnets, L. D., & Kimmel, D. C. (Eds.). (1993). *Psychological perspectives on lesbian and gay male experiences.* New York: Columbia University Press.

Gibson, P. (1989). Gay male and lesbian youth suicide. In ADAMHA, *Report of the Secretary's task force on youth suicide.* DHHS Publication No. ADM 89–1623, 3:110–142. Washington, DC: U.S. Government Printing Office.

Gonsiorek, J. C. (1988). Mental health issues of gay and lesbian adolescents. *Journal of Adolescent Health Care, 9*, 114–122.

Governor's Commission on Gay and Lesbian Youth. (1994). *Prevention of health problems among gay and lesbian youth: Making health and human services accessible and effective for gay and lesbian youth.* Boston: State House.

Gray, M. E. (1999). *In your face: Stories from the lives of queer youth.* New York: Haworth.

Green, B. (1994). Lesbian and gay sexual orientations. In B. Green & G. M. Herek (Eds.), *Psychological perspectives on lesbian and gay issues.* Vol. 1, *Lesbian and gay psychology: Theory, research, and clinical applications.* Thousand Oaks, CA: Sage.

Guttmacher Institute. (1994). *Sex and America's teenagers.* New York: Alan Guttmacher Institute.

Haldeman, D. C. (1994). The practice and ethics of sexual orientation conversion therapy. *Journal of Consulting and Clinical Psychology, 62*(2), 221–227.

Harris, M. G. (Ed.). (1998). *School experiences of gay and lesbian youth.* New York: Haworth.

Hershberger, S. L., & D'Augelli, A. R. (1995). The impact of victimization on the mental health and suicidality of lesbian, gay, and bisexual youths. *Developmental Psychology, 31*(1), 65–74.

Hetrick, E. S., & Martin, A. D. (1987). Developmental issues and their resolution for gay and lesbian adolescents. *Journal of Homosexuality, 14*(1/2), 25–42.

Hunter, J. (1990). Violence against lesbian and gay male youths. *Journal of Interpersonal Violence, 5,* 295–300.

Hunter, J., & Schaecher, R. (1987). Stresses on lesbian and gay adolescents in schools. *Social Work in Education, 9*(3), 180–189.

——. (1994). AIDS prevention for lesbian, gay, and bisexual adolescents. *Families in Society, 75*(6), 346–354.

Icard, L. D. (1996). Black gay men and conflicting social identities: Sexual orientation versus racial identity. In J. Gripton and M. Valentich (Eds.), *Journal of Social Work and Human Sexuality: Social work practice in sexual problems, 4*(1–2), 83–93.

Martin, A. D., & Hetrick, E. S. (1988). The stigmatization of the gay and lesbian adolescent. *Journal of Homosexuality, 15,* 163–184.

Masten, A. S. (1994). Resilience in individual development: Successful adaptation despite risk and adversity. In M. C. Wang (Ed.), *Educational resilience in inner-city America: Challenges and prospects* (pp. 3–25). Hillsdale, NJ: Erlbaum.

Masten, A. S., & Coatsworth, J. D. (1998). The development of competence in favorable and unfavorable environments: Lessons from research on successful children. *American Psychologist, 53,* 205–221.

Mills, K. I. (1999). *Mission impossible: Why reparative therapy and ex-gay ministries fail.* Human Rights Campaign. Retrieved February 5, 2002, from http://www.hrc.org/publications/exgay_ministries/change.asp.

Morrow, D. F. (1993a). Social work with gay and lesbian adolescents. *Social Work, 38*(6), 655–660.

——. (1993b). Lesbian identity development through group process: An exploration of coming out issues. *Dissertation Abstracts International, 54–02*(0428).

——. (2000). Coming out to families: Guidelines for intervention with gay and lesbian clients. *Journal of Family Social Work, 5*(2), 53–66.

——. (2003). Cast into the wilderness: The impact of institutionalized religion on lesbians. *Journal of Lesbian Studies, 7*(4), 109–124.

National Committee on Lesbian, Gay, and Bisexual Issues, National Association of Social Workers. (1999). *Position statement on reparative and conversion therapies for lesbians and gay men.* Washington, DC: National Association of Social Workers.

National Lesbian and Gay Health Foundation. (1987). *National lesbian health care survey: Mental health implications.* Unpublished report. Atlanta.

Newman, F. S., & Muzzonigro, P. G. (1993). The effects of traditional family values on the coming out process of gay male adolescents. *Adolescence, 28*(109), 213–226.

Phillips, S., McMillen, C., Sparks, J., & Uberle, M. (1997). Concrete strategies for sensitizing youth-serving agencies to the needs of gay, lesbian, and other sexual minority youths. *Child Welfare, 76*(3), 393–409.

Pilkington, N. W., & D'Augelli, A. R. (1995). Victimization of lesbian, gay, and bisexual youth in community settings. *Journal of Community Psychology, 23,* 33–56.

Proctor, C. D., & Groze, V. K. (1994). Risk factors for suicide among gay, lesbian, and bisexual youths. *Social Work, 39*(5), 504–513.

Robinson, K. E. (1994). Addressing the needs of gay and lesbian students: The school counselor's role. *School Counselor, 41,* 326–332.

Roth, S. (1985). Psychotherapy with lesbian couples: Individual issues, female socialization, and the social context. *Journal of Marriage and Family Therapy, 11*(3), 173–286.

Rotheram-Borus, M. J., Rosario, M., & Koopman, C. (1991). Minority youths at high risk: Gay males and runaways. In M. E. Colten & S. Gore (Eds.), *Adolescent stress: Causes and consequences* (pp. 181–200). New York: Aldine.

Rutter, M. (1998). *Studies of psychosocial risk.* New York: Cambridge University Press.

Ryan, C., & Futterman, D. (1997). Lesbian and gay youth: Care and counseling. *Adolescent Medicine: State of the Art Review, 8*(2), 94–99.

Savin-Williams, R. C. (1994). Verbal and physical abuse as stressors in the lives of lesbian, gay male, and bisexual youths: Associations with school problems, running away, substance abuse, prostitution, and suicide. *Journal of Consulting and Clinical Psychology, 62,* 261–269.

Schneider, S. G., Farberow, N. L., & Kruks, G. N. (1989). Suicidal behavior in adolescents and young adult gay men. *Suicide and Life-Threatening Behavior, 19,* 381–394.

Sears, J. T. (1991). *Growing up gay in the South: Race, gender, and journeys of the spirit.* New York: Harrington Park.

Smith, G. W., & Smith, D. E. (1998). The ideology of "fag": The school experience of gay students. *Sociological Quarterly, 39*(2), 309–336.

Smith, K., & Crawford, S. (1986). Suicidal behavior among "normal" high school students. *Suicide and Life-Threatening Behavior, 16,* 313–325.

Swann, S., & Herbert, S. E. (1999). Ethical issues in the mental health treatment of gender dysphoric adolescents. *Journal of Gay and Lesbian Social Services, 10*(3/4), 19–34.

Teague, J. B. (1992). Issues relating to the treatment of adolescent lesbians and homosexuals. *Journal of Mental Health Counseling, 14*(4), 422–439.

Tharinger, D., & Wells, G. (2000). An attachment perspective on the developmental challenges of gay and lesbian adolescents: The need for continuity of caregiving from family and schools. *School Psychology Review, 29*(2), 158–173.

Tozer, E. E., & McClanahan, M. K. (1999). Treating the purple menace: Ethical considerations of conversion therapy and affirmative alternatives. *Counseling Psychologist, 27*(5), 722–743.

Waldner, L. K., & Magruder, B. (1999). Coming out to parents: Perceptions of family relations, perceived resources, and identity expression as predictors of identity disclosure for gay and lesbian adolescents. *Journal of Homosexuality, 37*(2), 83–100.

White, M. (1995). *Stranger at the gate: To be gay and Christian in America.* New York: Simon and Schuster.

Zastrow, C., & Kirst-Ashman, K. K. (2004). *Understanding human behavior and the social environment* (6th ed.). Belmont, CA: Brooks/Cole.

9

GAY MALE RELATIONSHIPS AND FAMILIES

Robin E. McKinney

Civilization is a process whose purpose is to combine single human individuals, and after that families, and then races, peoples and nations, into one great unity, the unity of mankind.

—DEFORD, SPEICHER, AND LAFLOUR, 1997, P. 94

MANY MYTHS surrounding the etiology of same-sex orientation have confused and distorted meaningful understanding of gay men, their relationships with domestic partners, extended family, and, of more recent interest, their children (Barret & Robinson, 2000). The study of gay men in families is further complicated by lack of precise definitions of homosexuality and the fact that many gay men lead heterosexual lifestyles with intermittent homosexual activity (Isay, 1989). A popular notion that 10% of the population is composed of gay males arose from Kinsey, Pomeroy, and Martin's (1948) study of male sexuality. Their study focused on sexual behavior rather than emotional attachments and relationships. In this chapter, gay men are defined as those men who have emotional attachments and sexual interaction with other men. Gagnon, Micheal, and Micheal (1994) estimated that perhaps 5% of the U.S. population is composed of gay males. Spada (1979) believed that 20% of gay men have been previously married, while Miller (1979) believed the estimate to be between 20% and 50%. The number of children fathered by gay men has been estimated as between two and four million (Patterson & Chan, 1996). The discrepancies regarding the number of gay men and what constitutes a gay man limit the ability to accurately study this population.

Equally challenging is the definition of family. Most definitions assume a heterosexual configuration, namely a mother, father, and their offspring (Laird, 1993). However, in 1996, only 25.2% of U.S. families matched this description (Ryan, 2000). With family formation drastically changing, it is ironic that gay men and lesbians are struggling for recognition of family with legal rights consistent with those of heterosexual families. Strong social and political forces have prevented legal recognition of gay and lesbian families in most states (Rofes, 2000).

As shown by van Wormer, Wells, and Boes (2000), early research focused upon sexual behavior rather than emotional and psychological aspects of gay men and their relationships. While sexual behavior is an important aspect of gay relationships, how gay men establish and maintain emotional and psychological attachments is perhaps of greater importance in dispelling myths associated with them. The first portion of this chapter addresses social, political, legal, and religious doctrines pertaining to the establishment and maintenance of gay relationships. The second section is devoted to gay couples and the third section to gay fathers and their children. Various avenues to parenthood are explored, as well as current social and legal ramifications of gay parenthood, including relationships with grandparents, former spouses, and siblings. Finally, suggestions for social work practice and education are presented, as well as directions for future research.

SOCIAL FACTORS AFFECTING GAY COUPLE DEVELOPMENT

ORIGINS OF NEGATIVE PERCEPTIONS OF GAY RELATIONSHIPS: RELIGION, SCIENCE, AND THE LAW

Research on gay couples is often incomplete and invalidating toward gay men and their partners (LaSala, 1998). Laird (1993) noted that many early studies considered homosexuality as both dysfunctional and deviant social behavior. Such negative perceptions of gay men led to a proliferation of stereotypes and myths of gay men as inherently flawed and psychologically disturbed. It was not until 1973 that homosexuality was removed from the *Diagnostic and Statistical Manual of Mental Disorders* (Isay, 1989).

The depiction of gay men as hedonistic, depraved, and amoral has historical importance stemming from early Greek and Roman association of homosexuality with sexual perversions and orgies. Despite the romanticized accounts of homosexual relationships between men and adolescent boys in ancient Greece, gay relationships beyond those parameters were considered unnatural (van Wormer et al., 2000).

Western cultures dominated by Christianity deemed same-sex behavior immoral and sinful (O'Neill & Naidoo, 1990). Consistent with religious edicts, civil laws were enacted prohibiting same-sex behavior, and the practice became criminal and punishable by the state. Those caught engaging in such behavior could be imprisoned or executed. The consolidation of civil and religious condemnation of homosexuality further diminished recognition of gay relationships as viable.

Conrad and Schneider (1992) noted that the advent of medical theories of sexual deviance placed homosexuality within the realm of mental pathology. It was thought that same-sex behavior was merely a manifestation of mental disturbance. Physicians believed that feminine behaviors exhibited by men and masculine behaviors displayed by women were symptomatic of physiological and psychological disorders (Faderman, 1991). With the addition of medical condemnation of gay relationships, a monolithic view of homosexuality as pathological emerged (Mondimore, 1996). Homophobia, the irrational fear of homosexuality, became a social institution supported by religion, the medical community, and the state (Zastrow & Kirst-Ashman, 2001). As suggested by Isay (1989), the existing social structures forced many gay men to reject and/or conceal their orientation and adopt lifestyles consistent with secular and sacred expectations. Many gay men married and functioned as heterosexuals. Relationships engaged in with other men were secretive and fleeting. For fear of persecution, the practice of engaging in impersonal, oftentimes anonymous sexual liaisons emerged. Others internalized the social condemnation of homosexuality, accepting it and rejecting themselves. This self-rejection adversely affected the establishment of stable, lasting relationships (Laird, 1993). The apparent preference among gay men for fleeting sexual encounters rather than lasting relationships was more a function of social constraints than personal selection.

CULTURAL AND ETHNIC FACTORS

There is a paucity of literature regarding sexual orientation and ethnic/racial identity (Isay, 1989; van Wormer et al., 2000; Zastrow & Kirst-Ashman, 2001). Gay men from ethnic/racial minority groups face potential dual marginalization and social isolation based upon sexual orientation and ethnic/racial identification. In some ethnic and racial groups, same-sex behavior is condemned. If a member of an ethnic/racial minority group experiences hostility or discrimination from those outside the group, members and nonmembers of the ethnic/racial group may rally to the support of the harmed individual. However, if discrimination is on the basis of sexual orientation, there can be an erosion of support from within and outside the ethnic/racial group (Icard, 1996).

SUBSTANCE ABUSE

Cabaj (1997) noted that a greater percentage of gay males (30%) than heterosexual males (12%) deal with substance use disorders. He suggested that the pressures of coping with "coming out" and negative societal reception of gay males have contributed to the elevation of substance abuse among them. However, it is further indicated that many studies on substance abuse and sexual orientation have poorly constructed definitions of substance abuse and sexual orientation, thereby rendering the findings of limited use. Nevertheless, the stereotypical depiction of gay men as a hedonistic, substance-abusing community has persisted.

DE-PATHOLOGIZING GAY MEN AND THEIR RELATIONSHIPS

Kinsey, Pomeroy, and Martin's (1948) landmark study of human sexuality articulated the fact that men engaged in same-sex behavior with more frequency than was once thought. The notion that approximately 10% of the adult male population may be gay arose from perhaps overinterpretation of the Kinsey et al. report (Laird, 1993). While some men engage in same-sex behavior, a smaller number, perhaps 4%, would classify themselves as exclusively gay. That is, integrating sexual behavior with emotional and psychological attachment toward another man (Zastrow & Kirst-Ashman 2001) defines orientation to a greater extent than does sexual activity alone. Nevertheless, Kinsey et al.'s report signaled the expansion of homosexuality from study of sexual behavior to study of sexual behavior within an emotional and psychological context.

The fields of genetics and biology offered additional support for de-pathologizing same-sex behavior (Zastrow & Kirst-Ashman, 2001). Some scientists have suggested that there may be a biological predisposition for same-sex attraction (Bailey & Pillard, 1991). Furthermore, sexual orientation may be determined early in life and remain relatively fixed (Isay, 1989). Supporters of the biological theories hold that sexuality is biologically determined and therefore does not represent any type of moral depravity and should not be viewed as pathological.

Because scientists challenged the pathology perspective of homosexuality, gay men began forming communities supportive of their sexual orientation (Herdt, 1992). Socializing in gay-friendly bars and bathhouses became avenues for meeting and pairing with other gay men. Within the confines of gay establishments, men were free to explore their sexual and emotional attraction toward other men. As suggested by Isay (1989), gay men still exercised great caution, as most states had laws forbidding same-sex activity and social condemnation remained stringent. For fear of negative repercussions, many gay men remained in secretive, fleeting sexual arrangements.

The 1969 Stonewall riots involving police entry into a gay bar in New York City's Greenwich Village marked a transition from a secretive, cloistered gay community to a gay community that actively rejected social condemnation on the basis of sexual orientation (Vaid, 1995). By coming out and/or publicly displaying same-sex orientation, gay men hoped that public sentiment toward homosexuality would shift, much as it had done with African Americans and civil rights and the women's movement. Defiance of civil and religious opposition to gay life afforded the opportunity to pursue gay relationships, establish couples, and seek equal treatment, which had not been seen before Stonewall. A cohesive sense of community emerged, and for many with same-sex orientation, liberation from oppressive social structures was at hand (van Wormer et al., 2000).

HIV/AIDS

The onset of the AIDS epidemic in the 1980s fueled the rebirth of waning public disdain toward homosexuality (Vaid, 1995). Some religious leaders sought to exploit the plight of those affected by the AIDS epidemic by labeling the epidemic as the wrath of God on those who engaged in immoral sex acts (Isay, 1989). This notion was dispelled when the modes of acquiring and transmitting the disease were discovered. Many people who were not associated with homosexuality also contracted AIDS and ultimately died.

The impact of AIDS resulted in significant and dramatic changes in the sexual behaviors of gay men. Before the AIDS epidemic, some gay men continued to engage in anonymous sex with multiple partners rather than establish stable, lasting relationships. Because it was known that one method of transmission of the AIDS virus was through casual, unprotected sex with multiple partners, gay men began limiting sexual contact and increasingly participating in committed relationships (Herdt, 1992; Isay, 1989). The disease, which at one time decimated the gay male population, helped to establish public visibility of gay male couples.

Although advances in medicine and the social sciences are indicative of the "normality" of gay men, religious and civil institutions have been slow to recognize gay relationships as viable. Much of the religious and civil marginalization of gays is inherently wedded to antiquated notions surrounding the morality of gay men. These institutions tend to suggest that sexual orientation is a matter of choice. In-group marginalization has also precluded acceptance of gay men within ethnic/racial minority groups, which in their endeavors to legitimate themselves with majority groups have often failed to support gay men within their ranks. Native American communities, however, have made efforts to welcome gay men in their communities. The AIDS epidemic, which disproportionately affected gay men, further stigmatized them as a community. The overwhelming condemnation of gay men has led some of them to substance abuse as a means of coping with such social pressure. Gay men are thought to have a higher incidence of substance abuse issues than heterosexual men.

Despite overwhelming odds, some gay men are able to overcome societal restrictions and form committed relationships. Within that context, gay men are free to express both sexual and emotional intimacy with other men. As will be discussed in the next section, gay men have developed relationship styles that contrast with those of heterosexual relationships. The contrasts are both satisfying and, in some cases, vital to maintenance of gay male relationships.

THE GAY MALE COUPLE

A variety of factors affect formation and functioning of gay male couples, among them relationship type (monogamous or nonmonogamous), emotional intimacy, and legal recognition of gay relationships.

MONOGAMOUS AND NONMONOGAMOUS COUPLINGS: FUNCTIONAL CONSIDERATIONS

The modern gay couple is more complex and varied than previous writings on the subject may have implied (LaSala, 2001). Much of the early literature emphasized either causal factors leading to adult homosexuality or social, religious, and legal aspects of homosexuality. When relationships were discussed, it was in the context of value-laden terms referencing promiscuity and instability of gay male relationships (Laird, 1993). Furthermore, there was little mention of how social condemnation, via enactment of civil laws punishing known gay men, shaped the content and formation of gay male relationships. As suggested by Isay (1989), in the past some gay men assumed heterosexual lifestyles while engaging in intermittent homosexual liaisons. Sexual interactions in this context were usually of very little emotional interest. Rather, casual sexual encounters were opportunities to express suppressed desires for sexual interaction with other men. Unfortunately, these random, oftentimes anonymous encounters were believed by some to be the only context in which gay men interacted.

In contrast, researchers in the 1970s (Bell, Weinberg, & Hammersmith, 1978; Harry, 1984; McWhirter & Mattison, 1984) found that gay relationships in that decade thrived and were quite diverse. The function of extra-couple sexual relationships emerged as a central theme in gay male relationships. It appeared that some couples were content with monogamous (closed) gay relationships, in which sexual encounters outside of the couple were viewed as a betrayal of trust. Gay men in closed relationships developed lifestyles and households similar to those of many heterosexuals.

In nonmonogamous or open relationships, extra-couple sexual encounters were not viewed as betrayals and were not indicative of failure of the primary couple relationships. Peplau and Cochran (1981) found no difference in relationship satisfaction, commitment, and security when comparing open and closed couples who remained together for more than three years. In addition, those in open relationships reported greater relationship longevity than those in closed relationships. Similar observations were made by LaSala (2001). In his study concerning open and closed gay relationships, he found that, with increasing relationship longevity, the likelihood of establishing open relationships increased.

Previous studies indicated that men are more willing than women to separate sexual activity from emotional intimacy (Laird, 1993). Blumstein and Schwartz

(1983) suggested that men in general were inclined to have more extra-couple and extramarital sexual relationships whether they are gay or heterosexual than women who are either heterosexual or lesbian. They found that 33% of heterosexual men and 82% of gay men had been nonmonogamous within the context of a committed relationship, compared to 26% for cohabitating heterosexual women, 21% for married women, and 28% for lesbians. Zastrow and Kirst-Ashman (2001) noted that socialization differences with regard to sexual activity may account for higher levels of sexual activity in gay and heterosexual men when compared to all women. Whereas women are taught that sexual fidelity is an essential component of a committed relationship, men are not taught such values to a similar degree. Laird (1993) echoed this observation and further indicated that for gay men the history of anonymous sexual encounters and the number of men engaged in both heterosexual and homosexual encounters may account for increased extra-couple relationships. Sexual encounters with strangers, or "tricking," has been a social institution within the gay male community for many years and is often detached from emotional involvement.

The above discussion illustrates the complexity of gay male relationships. Numerous studies have shown that sexual fidelity alone is not indicative of relationship satisfaction and functionality. Some prefer closed relationships, while others prefer open relationships. The personal preferences of the participants, rather than culturally defined expectations of sexual fidelity, determine the functionality and satisfaction of gay male relationships. It may be, however, that emotional intimacy and support, which may not include sexual fidelity, are perhaps more vital in establishing and maintaining a gay male relationship than in heterosexual and lesbian relationships.

EMOTIONAL INTIMACY AND SUPPORT

By virtue of nontraditional relationship formation—namely, nonmonogamous versus monogamous—gay men have developed additional means by which to stabilize and maintain relationships (Johnston & Bell, 1995), among them self-acceptance, mate selection, and extended family.

SELF-ACCEPTANCE A key aspect of emotional intimacy has to do with self-acceptance (van Wormer et al., 2000). Gay men who are secure in their sexual orientation may develop more-stable relationships than those who are less secure. As suggested by LaSala (2001), self-acceptance is key to coming out as well as to establishing and maintaining positive gay relationships. Striking a balance between support and overreliance on the relationship is a significant task in gay male relationships. Those with a fragile self-concept may expect that a sense of self will emerge from involvement in a relationship. However, relying too much upon the relationship for a sense of self can overtax the relationship, resulting in its failure. Furthermore, boundary issues related to how "out" the couple is to extended family and the community are related to personal comfort and self-acceptance of partners (LaSala, 2001).

MATE SELECTION In heterosexual couples, mate selection is based upon the obvious attraction to a member of the other sex, and socialized gender-specific behaviors are instrumental in providing avenues for complementarity of roles. In contrast, gay men, by having many gender-similar behaviors, may seek greater psychological complementarity than do heterosexual couples.

Many of the roles and tasks undertaken by heterosexual couples are consistent with gender and social expectations (Laird, 1993). In gay couples, however, there may be greater freedom in role selection, since both people are the same gender. It is perhaps this freedom from gender role stereotypes that enhances stability in gay male relationships. Johnston and Bell (1995) noted in their study of 49 gay and 84 heterosexual male college students that heterosexual males were less likely to engage nongender role behavior than were gay males. Furthermore, the gay men in this study reported having engaged in behaviors associated with the female gender when they were younger and of being teased by peers for doing so. The willingness to abandon gender-role-prescribed behavior was predictive of later homosexual orientation. Herdt (1992) reported that many adult gay men indicated feeling and acting differently than other boys did when they were young, which resulted in isolation and teasing by other boys.

Johnston and Bell (1995) suggested that among gay males opposites do attract. They found that gay men were more likely to have partners who were quite different from themselves in terms of role expectations. Nontraditional role expectation difference in gay men may serve a function similar to that of gender role expectation in heterosexual relationships. Role freedom and enhanced opportunity for self-expression, and acceptance of self-expression within the context of a couple, may be vital in maintaining emotional fidelity within the gay couple (Barret & Robinson, 2000). The element of choice in terms of role expectation may be less prominent in heterosexual relationships. In addition, egalitarian decision making was related to role freedom rather than to gender expectations (Johnston & Bell, 1995).

EXTENDED FAMILY As suggested by Fredriksen (1999), openly gay couples may experience rejection from family and friends because of their sexual orientation. To be an openly gay couple, both partners must be comfortable with their sexual orientation. LaSala (1998) found that many parents of openly gay men in couples may not acknowledge the relationship or may disapprove of the relationship. Siblings of participants in a gay couple may also shun the couple. In the face of familial rejection, the couple may serve as an emotional buffer for each other. Cabaj (1997) and LaSala (1998) reiterate the importance of extended-family boundaries in maintaining harmony within the gay couple in the presence of familial rejection or lack of acknowledgment of the relationship. A positive sense of self and a clear differentiation from family-of-origin issues regarding sexual orientation can enhance the gay couple's mutual support in the face of familial rejection.

LEGAL RECOGNITION OF GAY COUPLES

As more gay men have formed committed relationships than in the past (Herdt, 1992), the issue of legal recognition of gay couples has reached the forefront of political thought. Some have argued that gay relationships are on par if not superior to others in that participation in such relationships is, for the most part, voluntary (Blumstein & Schwartz,1983). However, debating the merits of hetero-sexual versus gay relationships when partner rights are involved is irrelevant. In many states, domestic partner rights in terms of job benefits, medical decisions, medical benefits, and personal assets apply exclusively to heterosexual, cohabiting couples (Fetto, 2000; Martel, 2000; Muhl, 1999; Rofes, 2000). The United States lags behind some other industrialized nations with regard to rights for same-sex partners. Several European nations, including the Netherlands, France, Spain, Italy, and Norway, have enacted laws protecting the rights of same-sex domestic partners (Curry, Clifford, & Hertz, 2002). Canada has recently granted to same-sex couples rights having to do with same-sex marriages. To date, only one state, Vermont, has enacted legislation protecting the rights of same-sex couples on a par with those of heterosexual married couples (Curry et al., 2002; Fetto, 2000). In reaction to Vermont and other states' consideration of granting rights to same-sex couples, the federal government enacted the Defense of Marriage Act (DOMA) in 1996 (Curry et al., 2002). DOMA mandated that only heterosexual marriages would be recognized within and among states. The issue of same-sex marriage has also been debated within the gay and lesbian community. Marriage, although granted by the state, has long been associated with organized religious ceremo-nies. Given the long-standing religious opposition to homosexuality, it is doubtful that marriage in many traditional religious institutions would become open for gays. It should be noted (van Wormer et al., 2000), that some priests and pastors have nonetheless chosen to ignore religious dogma and perform same-sex mar-riages. This practice has resulted in expulsion and other disciplinary actions for those who perform such ceremonies. While participation in a religious ceremony may provide a measure of psychological legitimacy to same-sex couples, it does not provide legal protection of rights.

Other arguments for insistence upon legal protections pertain to medical deci-sions, personal assets, and health care benefits. With respect to a partner's health care eligibility, sexual orientation must be disclosed in order for the nonemployed partner to receive benefits. While some employers have granted domestic partner status to same-sex partners (Muhl, 1999), the potential for discrimination is also a risk once a disclosure of sexual orientation is made. In some instances, it may be advantageous to conceal sexual orientation in the workplace.

With regard to medical decisions and personal assets in states without domestic partner protection for gays, extended family may be granted authority to make medical and personal asset decisions rather than a gay partner in cases of incapacitation and/or death of a partner. Even when there is a will, parents of partners have challenged—and in some cases won—the right to make decisions for an incapacitated adult child or upon the death of an adult child. Without legal protections, a hostile extended family could preclude hospital visitation in emergencies and, in the case of death, could deprive the surviving partner of assets intended for him. Given these circumstances, it is likely that same-sex partners will continue to strive for legal recognition of gay relationships.

SOCIAL WORK PRACTICE WITH GAY COUPLES

ENHANCING GAY COUPLES Because of the potential for sexual relationships outside of the primary relationship among some gay couples, clinicians may have to work with couples to address this issue. The decision about sexual exclusivity or not is couple-specific and requires much discussion and planning. Social workers unfamiliar with the potential for nonmonogamous gay relationships may mistakenly represent the existence of sexual relationships beyond the couple relationship as dysfunctional. Rather, social work practice surrounding extra-couple sexual relationships requires a focus upon each partner's values pertaining to sexual exclusivity in couple relationships. For such arrangements to work, both partners must agree on the context and the parameters of extra-couple liaisons. If one partner truly does not approve of such arrangements, there could be disastrous complications within the relationship. Jealousy, mistrust, and intimacy issues can arise from conflicts surrounding nonmonogamous relationships.

In working with couples who wish to address sexual non-exclusivity, it is important that the social worker assess client values and the overall impact of non-exclusivity. If such activities adversely affect stability and intimacy within the couple relationship, then it may be in the couple's best interest to renegotiate their boundaries. As noted by LaSala (2001), transitions from monogamous and nonmonogamous relationships are possible. Gay couples need to be aware that they can renegotiate the parameters of relationships without destroying the existing relationships. Normalizing renegotiation can enhance the couple's transitions regarding extra-couple sexual involvements and the viability of such involvements.

Of paramount importance relative to nonmonogamous couples is the issue of safe sex and HIV/AIDS. Couples engaging in sexual activities beyond the couple relationship must agree on safe sex practices. Not only does each partner have increased individual potential for contracting sexually transmitted diseases in nonmonogamous relationships, but so does the couple. It is vital that partners in nonmonogamous relationships be completely honest with each other regarding extra-couple sexual activities. Failure to accurately portray such activities could result in danger to partners and perhaps death related to HIV infection.

SELF-ACCEPTANCE AND THE GAY COUPLE The social worker interacting with gay couples must see that each partner's contentment and comfort with his sexual orientation is addressed. If there are wide differences in the levels of self-acceptance between the partners, there may be conflict about how open the couple can be regarding sexual orientation. Closely aligned with self-acceptance is emotional support. Partners who are self-assured have less difficulty in supporting partners with respect to roles and expectations within the relationship. Social work practitioners may need to assist both partners in building a positive attitude toward sexual orientation.

As noted by LaSala (2001), partners suffering from internalized homophobia may have impaired ability in establishing and maintaining long-term relationships. For gay couples, lack of an internal sense of well-being has been linked to relationship failure, primarily related to intimacy issues.

EXTENDED FAMILY As previously stated, extended-family approval or disapproval can have a profound impact upon the gay couple. Gay couples with extended-family support may have less couple distress regarding interactions with extended family. However, social work practitioners may need to help the couple maintain a strong couple relationship if the extended family disapproves. When extended-family support is absent, workers may need to assist gay couples in seeking and maintaining support systems independent of familial support, thereby strengthening the legitimacy and stability of the gay relationship. Building a support network of "surrogate" family and friends can buffer the couple from adverse reactions by members of the extended family. The primacy of the gay couple relationship must be maintained.

LEGAL STATUS Legal status of the relationship can present challenges. Some couples want legal recognition. In such cases support will be needed in selecting the best avenue for the couple to pursue legitimating the relationship. Extended-family concerns may also be addressed. Lastly, some male couples want to have children. If neither partner has children already, it might be necessary to explore options such as adoption and foster care. As most states have instituted barriers to gay couples' becoming parents, couples will need support as they endeavor to secure a child.

The discussion of gay male relationships addressed structure/function, emotional fidelity, and legal ramifications of gay male relationships. Gay male relationships are diverse, ranging from monogamous to nonmonogamous. The success or failure of gay male relationships in many cases does not rest only on sexual fidelity. Rather, the amount of role flexibility and emotional fidelity found within gay male couples might more adequately reflect satisfaction and functionality of the couple relationship. In a hostile social environment that is unreceptive to the gay male relationship, the support found within the relationship may act as a buffer against oppressive social forces that could include extended-family members of one or both partners. And lack of legal status in most states creates particularly stringent challenges to relationships. Despite these and other barriers, gay men are succeeding in establishing and maintaining couple relationships.

GAY FATHERS AND THEIR CHILDREN

Although a growing number of gay men are fathers, relatively few studies of gay fathers and their children have been undertaken (Patterson & Chan, 1996). As gay issues become more mainstreamed, awareness of issues specific to gay parents and their children will require further exploration (van Wormer et al., 2000). This section addresses needs of gay fathers and their children within the context of gay couples. Included in the discussion are legal issues, custodial and noncustodial fathers, stepfathers, adoption, and foster parenting, as well as blended families and extended-family issues.

LEGAL ISSUES

In the past, gay parents often failed to disclose their sexual orientation for fear of legal repercussions (Zastrow & Kirst-Ashman, 2001). In some instances, parents who disclosed their sexual orientation ultimately lost custody of children because of it (Barret & Robinson, 2000). One popular definition of family is, "the basic unit in society having at its nucleus, two or more adults living together and cooperating in the care and rearing of their own or adopted children" (Curry et al., 2002). While this is a broad definition, rarely is it extended to include gay fathers and their children. As suggested by Laird (1993), most of what we know about families is related to heterosexual families. Much of the exclusion of gay families is interwoven with myths regarding same-sex parents (Barret & Robinson, 2000). Examples of these myths include: gay parents teach children to be gay; gay parents expose children to harassment from others; gay parents molest children; and, gay fathers are "sex fiends" (Barret & Robinson, 2000). While these myths seem incredible, fears associated with them have been responsible for legal sanctions against gay parents and couples. In reality, children reared by gay couples tend to be no different in social development, academic and occupational achievement, and satisfaction with life than children reared in heterosexual families (Brooks & Goldberg, 2001; Zastrow & Kirst-Ashman, 2001). Children from gay and lesbian families tend to be more tolerant of others, less judgmental, and more open to new experiences than children reared in heterosexual families. In addition, children from these families are less likely to have gender biases, since they have parents of the same gender sharing the responsibilities within the home (Brooks & Goldberg, 2001).

Fortunately, biological parents who are gay or lesbian are now in less danger of having parental rights terminated solely on the basis of sexual orientation than in the past (van Wormer et al., 2000). As will be discussed, adoption and foster care by gay couples can be hampered by a legal system that still discriminates against gay partners.

GAY BIOLOGICAL FATHERS

The most common manner in which gay males become fathers is through past heterosexual relationships (Laird, 1993). When a gay father is not the custodial parent, tensions between the gay father and his children who reside with the biological mother may not be as great. However, children will need to understand the father's sexual orientation. Coming out to children in a noncustodial situation depends on several factors. The father's relationship with the child's mother is of great importance, as is the mother's acceptance of the father's sexual orientation. When mothers are accepting and the relationship between the mother and father is positive, children may accept disclosure of the father's sexual orientation more readily than when the relationship is poor (Barret & Robinson, 2000). The father's acceptance of his own sexual orientation is also important. Fathers should not disclose their sexual orientation until they themselves are comfortable with it. And finally, the age of the child is important. Children need not be burdened with sexual orientation issues until they have reached an age where the information becomes meaningful. That age depends upon the child's own development. The keys are providing education and support to children and understanding that this situation may be confusing and complex to them. Specifically addressing issues such as homophobia and causes of homosexuality with children can ease their fears regarding homosexuality.

In gay relationships where one partner is the custodial parent of his biological children, several factors are of importance in facilitating a child's adjustment to the father's sexual orientation (van Wormer et al., 2000). In addition to maintaining relationships with biological mothers, custodial gay couples must decide on the type of relationship they want between themselves. An issue in gay male relationships is that of monogamous versus nonmonogamous relationships. If partners engage in sexual activities beyond the couple relationship, great care must be taken to avoid complicating the child's life with such an arrangement.

Second, fathers generally become custodial parents as a result of divorce and/ or death of the biological mother (Barret & Robinson, 2000). Thus children residing with a custodial gay father may be adjusting to the father's sexual orientation while they are also dealing with issues related to divorce and/or the death of a parent. Either of these issues can cause distress for children, and the introduction of parental sexual orientation may be overwhelming. Gay fathers have to provide support while children adjust to all circumstances, including the father's sexual orientation.

As in all blended-family situations, the child's relationship with a stepparent is important (Berger, 2002). Great care is needed in addressing gay fathers' and partners' relationships with children. Explanation of the father's relationship with his partner may require swifter and more direct intervention when the child resides with the father. It has been suggested (Barret & Robinson, 2000) that strategies used in most stepfamilies are effective in same-sex families. These strategies include fostering communication and trust between the stepparent and the child and support in the face of torn loyalties and confusion over the split of biological parents. While these items are challenges in heterosexual families, the added dimension of sexual orientation complicates the tensions found in some gay blended families.

In addition, care must be taken to shield children from teasing and ridicule by others. Some children who reside in gay-affirming areas such as the Castro district in San Francisco (Laird, 1993) may encounter less social stigma regarding parents' sexual orientation than children residing in areas devoid of gay families. However, those who reside in areas where there are no other same-sex families may need parents' assistance in developing a positive perception of their family system. In some instances, exposing children to videos and other popular venues that feature gay and lesbian families may help them to adjust to membership in a same-sex family.

EXTENDED FAMILY

Extended-family issues also become very important (Berger, 2002). In many cases, grandparents may not approve of children residing with gay parents. Strains in parents' relationships with grandparents can result in the exclusion of grandparents from children's lives. As noted by LaSala (1998), intergenerational discord can cause conflict within the gay couple. When children are involved, boundaries must be maintained while simultaneously preserving children's relationships with grandparents when possible. At times, grandparents may hold homophobic beliefs and express them to grandchildren. The gay couple may need to supervise children with grandparents and or limit interactions with grandparents. Attempts to preserve relationships with grandparents and other extend family should be made, unless doing so damages family integrity.

Gay men's family of origin may also be important in providing opportunities for children to interact with significant females in their lives (Barret & Robinson, 2000). As previously mentioned, gay fathers typically become custodial parents through divorce or death of the biological mother. Aunts and grandmothers can be an important influence and provide gender balance in the absence of a mother figure.

GAY FOSTER AND ADOPTIVE PARENTS

In the past, gay men and couples were overlooked as potential foster and adoptive parents. As a growing number of children are in need of stable homes, however, many states have begun questioning restrictions against gay foster and adoptive parents (Brooks & Goldberg, 2001; Ryan, 2000), though some continue to maintain that gay men and couples are not suitable as foster or adoptive parents. In the international arena, countries that provide protections for gay couples do not necessarily extend these protections to adoption (Martel, 2000). Since the list of specific countries and states that allow same-sex adoptions and foster arrangements fluctuates constantly, it is a good idea either to seek legal assistance regarding these matters for a particular state or country or to visit one of the many gay Web sites devoted to these issues. One particularly useful Web site is www. lambdalegal.org, which is the official site for Lambda Legal.

Two separate issues must be explored when addressing gay adoption. The first is second-parent adoption (stepparent adoption), and the second is joint adoption (Curry et al., 2002). In second-parent adoptions, one parent is the biological parent and the second parent is the mate of the biological parent. In most states, heterosexual stepparents are allowed to adopt the biological child or children of a spouse provided either that the absent parent gives consent or that that parent's rights have been legally terminated (Crawford, 1999). While this is a rather routine procedure for heterosexual couples, it can be an exasperating and complex experience for gay couples. In the case of gay couples, the absent parent merely has to deny the adoption. If there is no cause for termination of the absent parent's rights, then the adoption is halted. If homophobia is a factor for the absent parent, she may not permit the adoption. Most states refuse to allow second-parent adoptions in gay couples.

The second type of adoption is joint adoption, a more difficult adoption to secure. In this situation, neither partner is a biological parent (Crawford, 1999). Florida, Utah, and Missouri are the only states with laws prohibiting gay and lesbian couples from adopting (Curry et al., 2002). Many states have adopted a policy of "in the best interest of the child." The same is true for many foreign countries. What the stated policy means is that workers, judges, and other personnel make a decision based upon the perceived best interests of the child. This is a precarious situation at best (Ryan, 2000). In the absence of statutes and laws expressly prohibiting joint adoptions by gay couples, the personal beliefs of workers, judges, and welfare workers may preclude same-sex partners from adopting.

SOCIAL WORK PRACTICE WITH GAY COUPLES AND THEIR CHILDREN

Many of the issues addressed in the discussion of practice with gay couples are also applicable to couples with children. However, additional dimensions need attention when gay couples are custodial parents. Gay fathers who become custodial parents through divorce from the biological mother or because of her death may face severe challenges. In such cases, fathers will need to provide support to children who may be coping with divorce or death issues. In addition, fathers will have to gauge wisely their coming out to the children. In the face of other pressures associated with divorce or death, it may be overwhelming to a child to address a parent's sexual orientation at the same time. Therefore, the timing of disclosure will be important. Extended-family issues are also of concern. If grandparents disapprove of the family relationship, they may become estranged from the children. It is important for the couple to ensure that children have adequate interaction with grandparents whenever possible, provided the interaction is not detrimental to family relationships. Homophobia can also be a problem. Others who are aware of their fathers' sexual orientation may tease children, and the family may need to buffer children against such teaching. Finally, when children reside with a gay father who is in a committed relationship, legal measures must be pursued to ensure that the stepparent has rights relative to the children. This is extremely important should the biological parent become incapacitated or die. If legal precautions are not taken, the extended family may be awarded custody of the children in such circumstances.

SOCIAL WORK PRACTICE WITH CHILDREN OF GAY MEN

Children residing with gay fathers and their partners present unique challenges for the social work practitioner. Depending upon the circumstances that bring children to reside with fathers, work with such children may need to address several items simultaneously. In cases of the father's divorce from a mother or the death of the mother, children will need support with the grieving process. Clinicians will need to separate grief issues from sexual orientation with children. This may be quite a challenge. Depending upon a child's age, the child's feelings about sexual orientation may pose a concern. Some children negatively perceive sexual orientation and will need assistance in developing a positive understanding of gay fathers. Clinicians may also need to facilitate the father's coming out process. Some children may have less difficulty with this if they are exposed to other children with gay fathers. In the absence of such models, the social worker can provide, through video or other media, opportunities for children to see positive portrayals of gay men and their children. Finally, children from gay families exist in two cultures, as do most children from minority groups. They will require assistance in navigating between the heterosexual world and the gay world and in learning the strengths of both worlds.

Gay male couples with children often present with complex issues. Besides the issue of parental sexual orientation, children also face issues pertaining to adoption, divorce, and in some cases, teasing about their parents' sexual orientation. Within the context of the gay male couple, parents may need to buffer children from homophobic attitudes portrayed by society and extended family. Fathers' comfort with their own sexual orientation is predictive of the emotional availability they will have for their children. Fathers who are comfortable with their sexual orientation are in a better position to assist their children than are fathers who struggle with accepting their sexual orientation issues. Also, the dyadic relationship in families headed by gay male couples, as in all two-parent families, is vital in shaping children's attitudes and adjustment toward sexual orientation issues. When the dyadic relationship is cohesive and supportive, the home environment can provide positive perceptions of gay life in the face of hostile heterosexist social attitudes.

SOCIAL WORK RESEARCH ON GAY MALE FAMILIES AND ROLES OF SOCIAL WORKERS

This final section addresses salient issues in social work research on gay men and their families, highlighting some areas in which research in this area could expand.

SOCIAL WORKERS AS ADVOCATES

As noted throughout this chapter, many policies exist that either discount gay families or limit their ability to function as a family with protections by the law. These include lack of marriage or other institutions granting status to same-sex couples and the inability of gays to adopt as stepparents or joint parents in many states and foreign countries (Martel, 2000; Ryan, 2000). Many of these exclusions are predicated on antiquated notions of homosexuality as bad, sick, and/or immoral. Social workers have traditionally championed the causes of oppressed populations. Gays and lesbians are the only minority group for which legalized discrimination remains in effect (Appleby, 2001; Zastrow & Kirst-Ashman, 2001).

Appleby (2001) suggests that the helping professions suffer from homophobia just as the general public does. Many social policies and accepted legal standards have not considered same-sex couples and their children. Social workers in policy positions must work with the gay and lesbian communities in efforts to remove barriers that preclude full societal participation by gays and lesbians.

SOCIAL WORK RESEARCH ON GAY MEN AND FAMILIES

The final area of concern is research. As noted earlier, little is actually known about gay men and their children. Relatively few studies have been conducted with this population. As more fathers—heterosexual and gay—become primary caregivers, however, research will need to address the impact of custodial fathers' rearing children. The imperative for such research is especially strong in the case of gay male fathers. One of the difficulties in studying gay families is that some gay men fear discrimination and bias on the part of researchers. Past research tended to portray gay men in a negative light. Given that most states do not protect the rights of gays, gay men may be reluctant to participate in research for fear of exposure and other negative ramifications that could arise from their participation.

Second, definitions of the family have traditionally been biased against same-sex parents. Much of what is considered normal family development excludes gay men, their partners, and their children. Researchers studying gay families commonly attempt to apply heterosexual expectations and outcomes to them. As noted above, however, some kinds of interactions are unique to gay families, and therefore it is necessary to study gay families on their own terms rather than through the lens of heterocentric expectations. Until the definition of the family is expanded to include gay men and their families, they will remain marginalized.

REFERENCES

Appleby, G. (2001). Lesbian, gay, bisexual, and transgender people confront heterocentrism heterosexism, and homophobia. In G. Appleby, E. Colon, & J. Hamilton (Eds.), *Diversity, oppression, and social functioning: Person-in-environment assessment and intervention.* Boston: Allyn and Bacon.

Bailey, J. M., & Pillard, R. C. (1991). A genetic study of male sexual orientation. *General Psychiatry, 48,* 1085–1095.

Barret, R. L., & Robinson, B. E. (2000). *Gay fathers* (2d ed.). San Francisco: Jossey-Bass.

Bell, A., Weinberg, S., & Hammersmith, S. (1978). *Homosexualities: A study of diversity among men and women.* New York: Simon and Schuster.

Berger, R. (2002). Gay stepfamilies: A triple-stigmatized group. *Families in Society, 81*(5), 504–516.

Blumstein, P., & Schwartz, P. (1983). *American couples: Money, work, sex.* New York: William Morrow.

Brooks, D., & Goldberg, S. (2001). Gay and lesbian adoptive and foster care placements: Can they meet the needs of waiting children? *Social Work, 46*(2), 147–157.

Cabaj, R. (1997). Gays, lesbians, and bisexuals. In J. Lowenson, P. Ruiz, R. Millman, & J. Langrod (Eds.), *Substance abuse: A comprehensive textbook* (3d ed.) (pp. 725–733). Baltimore: Williams and Wilkins.

Conrad, P., & Schneider, J. (1992). *Deviance and lexicalization: From bad to sickness.* Philadelphia: Temple University Press.

Crawford, J. (1999). Co-parent adoptions by same-sex couples: From loophole to law. *Families in Society, 80*(3), 271–278.

Curry, H., Clifford, D., & Hertz, F. (2002). *A legal guide for lesbian and gay couples* (11th ed.). Berkeley, CA: Nolo.

Deford, D., Speicher, J., & LaFlour, M. (1997), *Quotable quotes* (3d ed.) (p. 202). New York: Readers Digest.

Faderman, L. (1991). Odd girls and twilight lovers: A history of lesbian life in twentieth-century America. New York: Columbia University Press.

Fetto, J. (2000) With this ring. *American Demographics, 22*(6), 14–15.

Fredriksen, K. (1999). Family caregiving responsibilities among lesbians and gay men. *Social Work, 44*(2), 142–155.

Gagnon, J., Laumann, E., Micheal, R., & Micheal, S. (1994). *The social organization of sexuality.* Chicago: University of Chicago Press.

Harry, J. (1984). *Gay couples.* New York: Praeger.

Herdt, G. (1992). *Gay culture in America: Essays from the field.* Boston: Beacon.

Icard, L. (1996). Assessing the psychosocial well-being of African American gays: A multidimensional perspective. *Journal of Gay and Lesbian Social Services, 5*(2), 25–49.

Isay, R. (1989). *Being homosexual: Gay men and their development.* New York: Farrar-Straus-Giroux.

Johnston, M., & Bell, A. (1995). Romantic emotional attachment: Additional factors in the development of sexual orientation of men. *Journal of Counseling and Development, 73*(6), 612–625.

Kinsey, A., Pomeroy, W., & Martin, C. (1948). *Sexual behavior in the human male.* Philadelphia: W. B. Saunders.

Laird, J. (1993). Lesbian and gay families. In F. Walsh (Ed.), *Normal family processes* (2d ed.) (pp. 283–238). New York: Guilford.

LaSala, M. (1998). Coupled gay men, parents, and in-laws: Intergenerational disapproval and the need for a thick skin. *Families in Society, 79*(6), 585–595.

——. (2001). Monogamous or not: Understanding and counseling gay male couples. *Families in Society, 82*(6), 605–611.

Martel, F. (2000). Gay rights and civil unions. *Dissent, 47*(4), 20–23.

McWhirter, D., & Mattison, A. (1984). *The male couple: How relationships develop.* Englewood Cliffs, NJ: Prentice-Hall.

Miller, B. (1979). Gay fathers and their children. *Family Coordinator, 28,* 544–552.

Mondimore, F. (1996). *A natural history of homosexuality.* Baltimore: Johns Hopkins University Press.

Muhl, C. (1999). Extension of job benefits. *Monthly Labor Review, 122*(4).

O'Neill, B., & Naidoo, J. (1990). Social services to lesbians and gay men in Ontario: Unrecognized needs. *Social Worker, 58*(3), 101–104.

Patterson, C., & Chan, R. (1996). Gay fathers. In M. E. Lamb (Ed.), *The role of the father in child development* (3d ed.) (pp. 245–260). New York: John Wiley.

Peplau, L., & Cochran, S. (1981). Value orientations in the intimate relationships of gay men. *Journal of Homosexuality, 6*(3), 1–19.

Rofes, E. (2000). After California votes to limit marriage: A call for direct action and civil disobedience. *Social Policy, 30*(4), 31–35.

Ryan, S (2000). Examining social workers' placement recommendations of children with gay and lesbian adoptive parents. *Families in Society*, 81(5), 517–528.

Spada, J. (1979). *The Spada Report*. New York: New American Library.

Thomas, W., & Jacobs, S. (1999). "... And we are still here": From Berdache to two-spirited people. *American Indian Culture and Research Journal*, 23(2), 91–107.

Vaid, U. (1995). Virtual equality: The mainstreaming of gay and lesbian liberation. New York: Anchor.

van Wormer, K., Wells, J., & Boes, M. (2000). *Social work with lesbians, gays, and bisexuals: A strengths perspective*. Boston: Allyn and Bacon.

Zastrow, C., & Kirst-Ashman, K. (2001). *Understanding human behavior and the social environment* (5th ed.). Chicago: Brooks/Cole.

10

LESBIAN RELATIONSHIPS AND FAMILIES

Cheryl A. Parks and Nancy A. Humphreys

The irony of gay and lesbian mainstreaming is that more than fifty years of active effort to challenge homophobia and heterosexism have yielded us not freedom but "virtual equality," which simulates genuine civic equality but cannot transcend the simulation.

—VAID, 1995, P. 4

LESBIAN COUPLES—the character and dynamics of their relationships as well as their visibility and marginalization within mainstream society—have received little research attention over the last several decades. In contrast, lesbian parents and the children they rear have commanded the interest and attention of researchers, the media, and politicians as well. Some of that interest has been driven by very publicly contested child custody decisions and some by the growing visibility and possibilities of a "lesbian baby boom." Considered within the context of continuing, often heated, state and national debates surrounding the Defense of Marriage Act (DOMA), legalized civil unions between same-sex partners, and legal sanctioning of second-parent adoptions, there exists a compelling need to accurately represent the women and children who live in and identify themselves as members of this alternative family form.

As one consequence of this public debate, a foreboding sense of uncertainty bears down on the personal and social well-being, legal status, and economic security of lesbian families. The protections afforded lesbian partners, parents, and their children are highly variable, and media coverage of "lesbian and gay rights" initiatives often fails to include a comprehensive discussion of the inconsistencies. Consequently, social workers and the public at large may lack a clear and complete understanding of the barriers and challenges faced by lesbian and gay families as they attempt to carry out the most basic functions assumed "by right" among heterosexuals.

Social workers engaged in practice with lesbian couples and families require knowledge and understanding of the interpersonal, social, and political realities of their lives. This chapter reviews findings of lesbian family research conducted since the early 1980s and places it within the context of the current legal and political climate surrounding lesbian family formation. The research describes the characteristics and strengths of lesbian partners and families as well as the obstacles and challenges that they confront in living within a heterosexist society. The highly charged, conflicting views and exposure generated by the political debate and consequent media coverage serve to further illuminate those strengths and challenges.

CAVEATS AND LIMITATIONS

The information presented here cannot be generalized to "all lesbians," nor should it be interpreted as a complete representation of "the lesbian experience." Lesbians are a diverse group, and there is not one experience that is uniquely lesbian. Research has been constrained by the lack of consistent or standardized definitions of "who is lesbian?" (Solarz, 1999) and "what is a lesbian family?" (Allen & Demo, 1995) and by the "invisibility" of the population overall. Despite some positive changes in public attitudes, lesbians continue to be stigmatized within our society and remain hidden and unavailable or unwilling to participate in research. Consequently, in most lesbian-focused studies, sample sizes are small and participants are typically young, white, middle to upper class, well educated, living in urban areas, and open about their identity. Little is known about other lesbians (e.g., those who are older, nonwhite, non-urban, closeted, or of lower socioeconomic status), and this void in our understanding of lesbian experiences must be acknowledged in any interpretation or application of the information presented.

Definitions used by researchers to qualify participants as "lesbian," "family," "parent," or "co-parent" also affect all aspects of the research process as well as the reported findings. The term *lesbian* typically is used to refer to a respondent who self-identifies as lesbian or reports either a present exclusive interest or a primary affectional bond with a same-sex partner. *Lesbian family* may include only those qualified by a legally defined relationship between a biological or adoptive mother and her child(ren), or it may be expanded to include the legal mother's partner, former partner, and possibly others as well. References of *second parent*, *co-parent*, and *stepparent* are used to identify current and former partners of the biological or adoptive mother. Second or co-parent identification typically refers to a partner with whom the decision to have or adopt a child was reached, while a partner who joined an existing mother-child(ren) dyad is referred to as a stepparent. Interpretation and comparability (between studies or with heterosexual family studies) of findings reported is affected by the use of these legal versus voluntary criteria of family inclusion.

Definitions of *family* within state and federal legislative and policy initiatives provide yet another layer of complexity to understanding and appreciating "lesbian family" experiences. Hartman (1996) notes that within federal legislation there are no fewer than 2,086 separate and often competing references to *family*. The presence of more than 2,000 references to *family* in state statutes is not uncommon; in fact, California, with more than 4,000, exceeds all other states (Hartman, 1996). These references are used to determine membership; establish relationships and obligations of family members to one another; authorize a variety of benefits, provisions, and protections for family members; set tax obligations and breaks; and confer numerous other benefits and obligations as well. They often constitute differing definitions of family, many of which conflict with one another, creating dilemmas for individual families as well as for those who must carry out public policy. It is not uncommon for a family to meet the definition of family in one program or statute but not to satisfy the criteria of another closely related program. Of particular concern for purposes of the present discussion, lesbian couples and children are systematically excluded from most official definitions of family, particularly those used by government. The most commonly applied definitions require a legal and/or biological relationship between all members. Even when a lesbian partner is permitted to adopt her partner's biological child(ren), this new family unit does not meet the traditional definition of a family because there is no legal relationship between the adult partners.

Finally, although attention to the experiences of lesbian couples and families has increased, published research in professional journals (other than specialized LGBT venues) remains limited and narrowly focused. Allen and Demo (1995) calculated that less than one half of one percent of all articles published in three leading family research journals between 1980 and 1993 focused on LGB families. More recently, Van Voorhis and Wagner (2001) reviewed 3,787 articles published in twelve social work journals between 1988 and 1997. Just 3.2% (121) contained substantive LGB content; of those, two-thirds ($N = 80$) focused on HIV/AIDS, while just 10 addressed LGB parenting (6) or partners and families (4) as topics. Further, much of the reported research draws comparisons between heterosexual and LGB respondents and their children, often with an intent to demonstrate the absence of pathology among children raised in LGB families (Patterson, 1992; Perrin & Kulkin, 1996). Although used successfully in arguments supporting child custody for lesbian parents, this comparative approach in research and in practice also serves to reinforce the "privileged" position of heterosexuality and the oppressive view of LGB families as "normal" only insofar as they are *just like* heterosexuals (Clarke, 2000).

LESBIAN COUPLES

Anecdotal accounts suggest that lesbians may have difficulty initiating dating relationships, that relationships proceed rapidly from friendship to intimacy, and that lesbian friendship circles are heavily populated with ex-partners who constitute an "extended family of choice" (Weston, 1991). However, little empirical evidence exists to either support or refute these perceptions. Lesbian friendships and patterns of dating have received little research attention; personal reflections and theorizing about the nature and meaning of lesbian friendships and communities in the lives of individuals are much more prevalent (for a review, see Weinstock, 2000). Relatively speaking, lesbian couple relationships—including examination of valued characteristics, levels of conflict and satisfaction, boundary and role definitions, social supports, and "coming out" or visibility concerns—have received more attention, but research in this area is also fairly limited.

ARE WE DATING OR JUST FRIENDS?

Friendships are an important source of validation, support, and satisfaction for lesbian individuals and couples. In "coming out," most lesbians first disclose their identity to other lesbians and to same-sex heterosexual friends before disclosing to family members (Radonsky & Borders, 1995), and in general lesbians are more likely to be "out" with gay and heterosexual friends than with family (Bradford, Ryan, & Rothblum, 1994; Morris, Waldo, & Rothblum, 2001). Most lesbians who participate in research report strong social connections and supports within an extended network of friends—female and male, gay and straight, in lesbian communities and not (Bradford et al., 1994). However, the availability, and accessibility, of supportive communities and friendship networks is also highly variable, depending on the geographic area (Friedman, 1997) and the historic era in which lesbians have been located (Weinstock, 2000).

As women, lesbians are generally socialized to value intimacy and connectedness in relationships rather than sexuality, which may contribute to a blurring of the boundary between "friendship" and "relationship" among some of them. Rose and Zand (2000), in an effort to add clarity to our understanding of lesbian dating and romance, examined the dating and "courtship" experiences of 38 predominantly white lesbians (ages 22–63). On average, these women had been involved in four to six romantic relationships with other women during their lifetimes. A majority (74%) reported at least one romantic relationship that had evolved out of a preexisting friendship ("friendship script"). However, 55% had also followed a "romance script" (characterized by dating, emotional intensity, sexual attraction, and rapid progression to sexual contact), and 63% followed a "sexually explicit" script (sexual attraction and sexual contact without an expectation to sustain an enduring commitment) on at least one occasion. Respondents were equally divided in their preferences for the friendship versus romance scripts; none favored the sexually explicit script. Freedom from gender roles, a high degree of intimacy, and "quick to develop" were unique characteristics ascribed to lesbian dating by most of the women in this study; constraints on where dating can occur, because of societal prejudice, was another. Although younger lesbians (ages 20–29) were more likely than older or midlife women to report they "waited to be asked" on a date, most of these women were direct in using verbal declarations of interest as a primary means to convey (and learn of) a romantic attraction. Lacking public rituals to identify transitions in their relationships (Slater & Mencher, 1991), most determined a change in status from friendship to romance by the presence of sexual energy or contact.

INTIMACY OR INDEPENDENCE OR BOTH?

Lesbian couples, once formed, do not differ significantly from other couples in either the quality of their relationships or the challenges they face in coming together as a family unit (Laird & Green, 1996; Roth, 1985; Schneider, 1986). What sets them apart are three salient characteristics: (1) both partners are women; (2) they are not a socially sanctioned family unit; and (3) full commitment by both partners to the couple requires acceptance of a stigmatized identity (Roth, 1985).

Personal autonomy (independence) and dyadic attachment (intimacy) are convergent values held by individuals within lesbian couples (Eldridge & Gilbert, 1990; Peplau, Cochron, Rook, & Padesky, 1978). Although highly valued, autonomy is negatively correlated with stability and permanence in the relationship (Schneider, 1986), with dependency (Schreurs & Buunk, 1996), and with relationship satisfaction (Eldridge & Gilbert, 1990; Kurdek, 1988). Conversely, intimacy is positively correlated with both stability and satisfaction (Eldridge & Gilbert, 1990; Peplau et al., 1978; Schreurs & Buunk, 1996).

Researchers have explored the boundary and role definitions of lesbian couples and families, particularly in reference to fusion in the relationship (Krestan & Bepko, 1980; Laird, 1993; Roth, 1985) and to the absence of social sanction from outside others (Roth, 1985; Schneider, 1986). Lacking social sanction, partners may become enmeshed or fail to differentiate (fusion) within the relationship as they attempt to define boundaries and to maintain the family unit (Kreston & Bepko, 1980). Most U.S. researchers have found that legitimation of the couple relationship by friends and family serves to diminish fusion and enhance both couple satisfaction and psychological adjustment (Caron & Ulin, 1997; Eldridge & Gilbert, 1990; Kurdek, 1988; Kurdek & Schmitt, 1986; Roth, 1985). However, a study of 119 Dutch lesbian couples found that social support and participation in lesbian subcultures played no role in relationship satisfaction (Schreurs & Buunk, 1996), but this may reflect an effect of the greater social tolerance available to lesbians in the Netherlands as well. By way of contrast, while not measuring social support directly, Sarantakos (1996) suggests that the level of conflict and instability found among same-sex couples in Australia is likely attributable, at least in part, to the social conditions of discrimination and oppression under which they live. In a 2001 report on data compiled from two ongoing longitudinal studies in the United States, Kurdek (2001) found lower levels of parental support and higher levels of support from friends among lesbian versus heterosexual couples, and lesbians reported higher levels of relationship satisfaction. Taken as a whole, these findings suggest that the availability of friendship or community support may act to buffer the negative effects of low family support for lesbian couples.

Roles, power, and division of labor within lesbian couple relationships have received some research attention. In the absence of affirmative lesbian role models and norms, women in same-sex relationships exercise a strong egalitarian value in defining family roles flexibly, on the basis of preference rather than upon a prescribed gender standard (Peplau et al., 1978; Schneider, 1986). Matthews, Tartaro, and Hughes (2003) found that lesbians were more likely than heterosexual women to report that their partners shared equally in household tasks, and Kurdek and Schmitt (1986) reported that lesbian couples evidenced higher levels of shared decision making than did either gay male or heterosexual couples.

"Coming out" and differences between partners in their comfort with the visibility of their relationship are issues of considerable concern to many couples. Individuals within the couple may be at different points in their acceptance of and willingness to disclose a lesbian identity (Berger, 1990). Disclosure, whether voluntary or otherwise, can have negative consequences in the individual's friendship, family, and work environments (Day & Schoenrade, 1997; Franke & Leary, 1991). It also may have a positive potential to enhance the network from which individuals and the couple receive support for and sanction of their relationship (Caron & Ulin, 1997). With such conflicting potentials, the decision to disclose usually is viewed as a prerogative of the individual. As individuals act according to their own positions along this continuum, behaviors may be perceived as either threatening to the more closeted partner or as limiting and controlling to the more open mate (Roth, 1985). Thus the couple is challenged to negotiate accommodations to the needs and sensitivities of both partners, and they must do so within the "surround" of public policies and social attitudes that both condemn and affirm their very right to exist.

THE (PERSONAL) POLITICAL AND ECONOMIC REALITIES OF CIVIL UNION VERSUS MARRIAGE

In attempting to capture the recent sea change in public policy and social attitudes regarding lesbian and gay families, D'Emilio, Turner, and Vaid (2000) note that as recently as 1966 a *Time* magazine essay described homosexuality as a "pathetic little second-rate substitute for reality, a pitiable flight from life" (p. vii). More than three decades later, lesbians and gays are recognized, and their relationships are validated by a few states, some localities, and many of the country's leading corporations, which provide domestic partnership benefits to their employees. Perhaps even more important in terms of social attitudes, gay themes are now a regular part of television programming (e.g., they constitute the main plot line in *Will and Grace*, one of the most popular sitcoms in 2002). The authors marvel at the fact that this change has occurred during a period of increasing conservatism in U.S. politics. "Somehow lesbians and gays have managed to effect a political transformation of gargantuan scope in the face of dauntingly unfavorable political conditions" (D'Emilio et al., 2000, p. viii).

Of course, not all changes have been favorable. The infamous Defense of Marriage Act (DOMA)—a federal law initiated by the ultraconservative Republican-controlled House of Representatives, agreed to by the Republican-controlled Senate, and signed by Democratic president Bill Clinton during the most heated period of the 1996 presidential campaign—expressly forbids federal recognition of any same-sex marriage. DOMA defines marriage as a legal union between one man and one woman. This law further holds that any marriage-type recognition of lesbian or gay partnerships allowed in one state does not require recognition by any other state. This provision violates the "full faith and credit" principle of the U.S. Constitution, whereby states recognize the laws of other states even when specific provisions of the two state laws differ.

It was in response to the possibility that a single state (Hawaii) was about to recognize lesbian and gay partnerships that the federal DOMA was enacted. Yet it wasn't until 2000 that Vermont became the first state to permit lesbian and gay couples to enter into a marriage-type relationship known as a civil union. However, only lesbian and gay citizens of Vermont can have their partnerships legally recognized. If residents of another state complete the procedures for a civil union, as many have, their union will not be recognized in the home state, given the provisions of the federal DOMA. In addition to Vermont, two other states have recognized lesbian and gay partnerships as "legal" relationships: California and Connecticut both passed limited domestic partnership legislation, in 2001 and 2002, respectively. These laws grant limited benefits, such as access to health insurance, bereavement leave, visitation, and other employer-regulated benefits. Most recently, in 2004 Massachusetts became the first and only state to provide legal recognition of same-sex marriage.

For many and varied reasons, there has been controversy about the quest for marriage and access to domestic partnership benefits within the LGB community as well (Bolte, 2001; Lewin, 2001; Vaid 1995). Not all lesbians and gays support the quest for marriage, and many do not access the benefits to which they may be entitled. For example, many radical feminists/lesbians oppose the institution of marriage, which they associate with the oppression of women. Others argue against marriage as a church-sanctioned institution and in favor of state-sanctioned recognition (such as civil unions), but with *all* the same rights, responsibilities, benefits, and protections that come to married couples. Some want the blessing of the church in their relationship, and others reject all forms of legal recognition by the state. In terms of domestic partnership benefits, many refuse to access those benefits on principle (e.g., in most instances, LGBs are required to present documentation not required of heterosexuals) or because doing so requires "coming out" and publicly acknowledging their relationship. While living in the closet may be less likely today, especially among young people, untold numbers of lesbian and gay couples may not be out to their employers for fear of subtle forms of discrimination, especially in terms of promotion and career advancement (Day & Schoenrade, 1997).

Andrew Sullivan (1995), editor of the *New Republic* and a noted gay activist, argues that recognition of marriage will be a sign of maturity of the gay and lesbian civil rights movement. More practically, such recognition would automatically entitle same-gender partners to a host of financial benefits, among them the same tax protections that are currently available to straight couples. Another obvious advantage would be the fact that legally sanctioned couples would have to have their relationships terminated through a legal procedure that would recognize the rights of each partner and any children. Currently, except in the three instances of statewide recognition of lesbian and gay partnerships, ending a same-gender relationship happens informally. Any protections the couple may have constructed to protect themselves and their futures are open to challenge by other "real" family members. For example, the homophobic family of a deceased partner may contest a will that designates the surviving partner as the primary beneficiary and executor. Under current law, such cases must go to court, where the outcome will depend on the whim or will of a single judge or jury. Because the courts have traditionally been hostile to the interests of lesbians, the surviving partner may decide to capitulate to the challenges of the family, believing that an expensive court fight will not likely prevent a negative outcome.

These controversies within and surrounding the lesbian and gay community will continue, just as public policy will continue to change and build on what has happened in the last decade. Social workers need to be aware of the policies, the changes, and their potential effects on the well-being and security of lesbian couples and families.

LESBIAN-PARENT FAMILIES

Estimating the number of women and children who constitute lesbian-parent families is constrained by problems of both definition (e.g., what is a lesbian family?) (Dean et al., 2000; Sell, 1997) and homonegativity (e.g., fear of discrimination; failure to include data on sexual orientation in population-based surveys) (Dean et al., 2000; Sell & Becker, 2001). Employing a variety of assumptions, researchers have projected numbers ranging from 2 million to 8 million families (Dew & Myers, 2000) raising between 6 million and 14 million children (Patterson,1992). The number of women choosing to have children after "coming out" as lesbian was estimated in 1990 as 5,000 to 10,000 (Patterson, 1992), but that number is believed to have increased radically over the last decade (McClellan, 2001). In one large-scale study that directly measured the presence of lesbian-parent families, Bradford et al. (1994) reported that 9% of the 1,925 respondents to the National Lesbian Health Care Survey were living with their children.

Embedded in these estimates is an acknowledgment that not only are lesbian-parent families not "new" but neither are they "all the same." In addition to religious, ethnic, economic, and other forms of diversity used to describe families, lesbian-parent families are also distinguished by their "route of creation." Lesbians may have become parents in the context of previous heterosexual unions, through assumption of a stepparent role with the children of a new lesbian partner, or through known or unknown donor insemination or adoption, as a single or a co-parent. Their children may live full-time with the biological or adoptive mother alone; with mother and partner; in a shared-custody arrangement with mother, father, or mother's former partner; or in a variety of other arrangements that may include other relatives or friends of the lesbian parent at different points in time. Each family origin or living arrangement imposes different role definitions and relationships on individual members. Many of the challenges that lesbian parents and their children confront reflect these differences in family origin. It is that distinction—between children conceived or adopted within a heterosexual union that has dissolved and those born or adopted into a lesbian family—that has received the most research attention.

PATHWAYS TO PARENTHOOD

VIA HETEROSEXUAL UNIONS Lesbian parent families that originate following the dissolution of a heterosexual relationship confront, often simultaneously, a change in family structure and a redefinition, at least by the mother, of one aspect of personal identity. These changes provoke several necessary adaptations on the part of both mothers and children, not unlike those required of heterosexuals in similar circumstances (Erera & Fredriksen, 1999). A mother's identification as lesbian presents additional challenges, and benefits, to which she and her children must respond (O'Connell, 1993; Van Voorhis & McClain, 1997; Wright & Schmitz, 2001).

Researchers (Green, Mandel, Hotvedt, Gray, & Smith, 1986; Levy, 1989; Lewin, 1993; Lewin & Lyons, 1982) and the authors of several reviews (Dew &

Myers, 2000; Parks, 1998; Patterson, 2000; Perrin, 2002) have reached the same conclusion: divorced lesbian mothers cannot be distinguished from heterosexual mothers on measures of psychological health, child-rearing, or commitment to their maternal role. Lesbians and heterosexuals are similarly motivated in their decision to divorce and view that decision as a positive step toward increased autonomy, independence, and competence. Among lesbians, "coming out" occurred simultaneously with divorce only sometimes and did not necessarily influence the divorce directly. Yet divorced lesbian mothers report more fears about loss of child custody than divorced heterosexual moms do.

Lesbian mothers describe their "coming out" in positive terms—as a discovery or affirmation of their "true self," a liberating experience, a step toward wholeness. Although they identify the disadvantages of being both lesbian and divorced, they do not accentuate them. Rather, they address such factors as stigma, threats to child custody, economic insecurity, and difficulties with intimate relationships from within a framework of competence and achievement. Strategies used in responding to these challenges are most often crafted out of an identification with motherhood and the meaning that it, not lesbianism, gives to their lives (Lott-Whitehead & Tully, 1993).

AFTER COMING OUT Dew and Myers (2000) describe the desire to parent as "a normal developmental need, regardless of sexual orientation," affirming that lesbians choose to become parents for many of the same reasons as their heterosexual counterparts do. In their comparison of 51 lesbian and heterosexual mothers' responses to the Value of Children Scale, Siegenthaler and Bigner (2000) provide empirical support for this belief. Their findings indicate that lesbian and heterosexual mothers are more similar than different in their reasons for wanting a child and in how they value children in adult life. However, lesbians also face two issues that do not affect heterosexuals: internalized homophobia (e.g., "Is it okay for lesbians to have kids?") and a societal or religious attitude of "compulsory childlessness" (e.g., "God made man and woman to procreate"). These questions can provoke self-doubt, ambivalence, and a sense that a lesbian mother, if she chooses to parent anyway, must be prepared to somehow be more than just an "ordinary" mom.

The decision to have a child is followed by consideration of different avenues by which parenthood may be achieved. Donor insemination, single and co-parent adoption, stepparenting, and foster parenting are the primary options available. Each involves practical, financial, legal, and emotional questions that the prospective mother, and her partner, must consider. Whether and how these issues are addressed will affect not only the process of having a child but the long-range consequences of that decision (Dunne, 2000).

Donor insemination, sometimes but not always followed by the nonbiological mother obtaining a co-parent adoption after the child's birth (McClellan,

2001), is believed to be the preferred method of lesbian family formation (Dew & Myers, 2000), but several legal issues remain unexplored or unresolved. Although access to medically assisted insemination procedures is legally available and used by lesbians in the United States (Gartrell et al., 1996; Parks, 1998), Great Britain (Tasker & Golombok, 1998), Belgium, and a few other European countries as well (Baetens & Brewaeys, 2001), an unknown number of women choose self-insemination as a less costly, more autonomous, and more private alternative. The desire to use a known donor, to have access to medical information, to legally protect the mother/co-mother and child relationship, or to include the donor in the child's life are a few of the potentially competing priorities considered when deciding which of the insemination procedures to employ.

When one member of the lesbian couple bears or adopts a child, her partner is cast into the undefined and often "invisible" position of second or co-parent (McClellan, 2001). Although legal remedies are beginning to become available, most of these other mothers confront the ambivalence of their undefined role and its attendant emotional jeopardy without benefit of any legal, or even social, protections. Rather, the biological mother and the co-mother must act together to negotiate and "construct" definitions of their parenting roles, their kinship networks, and how they will interact with and within the existing institutionalized understandings of family relationships (Dalton & Bielby, 2000; Dunne, 2000; Hequembourg & Farrell, 1999; Wilson, 2000).

The lesbian stepparent is the least discussed of the parenting roles examined in this body of literature. Baptiste (1987) and Lynch (2000) describe the role as one that lacks acknowledgment and validation from either outside or inside the couple's relationship. Berger (2001) asserts that a lesbian stepparent experiences "triple stigmatization" by her identification as a sexual minority, a lesbian parent, and a member of a blended family. Before her involvement in the couple relationship, the new partner may not have considered herself a potential parent. She must undergo a personal redefinition—and, potentially, a joint reconsideration (with her new family) of earlier decisions about public disclosure of her own (and the family's) lesbian identity (Lynch & Murray, 2000)—as she, the couple, and the children simultaneously adapt to a new family structure. Hare and Richards (1993), exploring the roles of fathers and lesbian partners after a heterosexual dissolution, confirm these ambiguities in parental role and function that lesbian stepparents encounter. Adoption (single-parent or two-parent) and foster parenting, two avenues to parenthood that are strongly affected by law and social policy, are considered in the next section.

POLICIES, LAWS, AND ACCESS TO PARENTHOOD The legislative picture in relation to lesbians' ability to legally secure relationships with their child(ren) is, like legal recognition for their partnerships, both depressing and exciting given recent developments. Florida bans adoption by lesbians and gay men in all circumstances by state law. Two other states—Utah and Mississippi—also have laws that effectively ban these adoptions. Second-parent adoption is allowed in seven states and the District of Columbia, while four states (Colorado, Nebraska, Ohio, and Wisconsin) ban second-parent adoption. New Hampshire prohibited second-parent adoption until a recent statewide campaign led by a Republican legislator, a social worker, overturned the state law (McKay, personal communication). In all other states, including New Hampshire, adoption by same-gender second parents is left to the wisdom, biases, and sympathies of individual courts, judges, and social workers, making the process chancy at best.

Some local jurisdictions and individual courts make second-parent adoption relatively easy. However, whether a second-parent adoption is pursued in states without legal sanction or a "stepparent" adoption is sought in states with that option, the costs associated with the process may be prohibitive for some families. (In 2002 the process cost one of this chapter's authors more than $2,000.) The adopting partner must submit to an investigation and a home study before

---

INTERNATIONAL LAWS, THE HAGUE CONVENTION, AND LESBIAN FAMILIES

Recognition of lesbian and gay partnerships has also taken place in other countries. Most recently, Quebec became the second Canadian province, along with Nova Scotia, to fully recognize as legal the partnerships of lesbians and gays. Perhaps what is most significant about this is that Quebec has historically been one of the most conservative of the Canadian provinces and the one most influenced by the Catholic Church, a steadfast opponent to any recognition of lesbian or gay individuals, couples, or families.

In 2001 the Netherlands became the first country to grant lesbians and gays the right to marry. They are accorded the same rights, benefits, and protections as heterosexual couples, with the notable exception that lesbian and gay couples are not allowed to adopt internationally. While other European countries—among them Denmark (1989), Norway (1993), Sweden (1994), Iceland (1996), the Netherlands (1997), and Finland (2001)—had granted some form of domestic partnership benefits to same-gender couples previously, the right to marry in the Netherlands went much further. In addition to the granting of legal rights, churches are now empowered, if they choose, to marry same-gender couples on behalf of the state, just as they do heterosexual couples. In the other countries, same-gender partnerships are sanctioned by the state only as civil or domestic partnerships, without any church involvement.

European countries increased recognition of same-gender partnerships as part of a legislative strategy initiated by the European Union (EU). In a resolution passed in March 2000, member countries were called upon to make provisions for the recognition of lesbian and gay couples so that they would enjoy the same rights, responsibilities, benefits, and protections granted to heterosexual couples. While these changes are still controversial, other EU members are likely to follow the Netherlands' lead and grant lesbians and gays the right to marry.

Adoption, especially international or foreign adoption, is a common approach to parenthood for lesbian and gay couples. As noted earlier, the marriage legislation recently implemented in the Netherlands expressly prohibits international adoption by same-gender couples. This provision was included because the Netherlands has ratified the Hague Convention on Protection of Children and Cooperation in Respect of Intercountry Adoption (Hillis, 2001).

"CONTINUED"

Delegates from sixty-three countries from around the world—including representatives from both member and nonmember states to the Hague Convention for Private International Law—attended a conference at which the "Hague Convention" was developed. Intended to establish, by international agreement, minimum standards for intercountry adoptions and to promote the well-being of children in need of homes, the convention addressed three objectives: (1) to create legally binding minimum standards for conducting intercountry adoptions; (2) to agree to mechanisms for enforcing the standards; and (3) to strengthen the relationship between "sending countries" (those who send children) and "receiving countries" (those where the families live and the adoptions actually take place).

Representing a gigantic step toward establishing a global law to govern intercountry adoptions, the Hague Convention incorporated several changes to past policy. One change concerns the idea that the "best interest of the child" should be the most important criterion in adoption decision making. Hillis (2001) notes that pre–Hague Convention protocols placed the emphasis on matching a child according to the wishes of the adoptive parents. Under the convention, this emphasis is shifted to matching potential adoptive parents to the needs of the child. Another change is the expressed preference for an intercountry adoption over any in-country placement that is not permanent, including foster care. This represents a significant shift in public policy that encouraged "sending countries" to permit adoption only when they had depleted the supply of permanent or temporary child care arrangements.

Only a few countries have ratified the Hague Convention, and its impact on the ability of lesbians and gays to adopt is not yet clear. Given the "best interest of the child" mandate, coupled with a research record that clearly demonstrates that lesbians and gays can be successful parents, an argument could be made that lesbians and gays would make suitable adoptive parents. Hillis (2001) states: "A best interest test need not, and should not, give any weight to the potential adoptive parents' sexual orientation." However, according to the convention, lesbian and gay couples interested in adopting must reside in a country that does not forbid adoption by lesbians and gays. At the moment, Bulgaria and Romania are two "sending states" that forbid adoption by lesbians, gays, unmarried heterosexual partners, or single parents. Social workers interested in promoting adoption by lesbian and gay couples should pay close attention as the ratification and implementation processes of the Hague Convention unfold.

---

the court action. Legal representation is recommended, especially if local courts do not have a consistent record of permitting such adoptions. The second parent, legally regarded before the adoption as an "unrelated" partner, is treated as a stepparent even if the children were conceived and born into a relationship where the decision to have children was planned and mutual. One of the most significant features of the civil union legislation in Vermont and Quebec is that lesbian second parents no longer need to adopt children born to their partners through artificial insemination when the partnership has been legitimated by a civil union. In this instance, both partners' names are placed on the birth certificate, just as in the case of heterosexual parents.

LESBIANS AND THEIR CHILDREN

AND BABY MAKES THREE The presence or arrival of children alters the dynamics of any couple's relationship. Unlike other couples, lesbians confront that adjustment in a climate of concern that their relationship and social attitudes about homosexuality will prove harmful to the children.

Issues affecting couples and families that are formed after a heterosexual dissolution are quite similar to those experienced by heterosexual stepparent families (Erera & Fredriksen, 1999; Lynch, 2000), with some notable exceptions. Both have experienced the loss or disruption of a previous family unit and changes to their residential and nonresidential household membership, with all of the concomitant adjustments in family rules, roles, relationships, and expectations that such changes often entail. The lesbian parent/stepparent dyad is additionally faced with concerns evolving out of their sexual identity and the attendant stigma and discrimination of public disapproval. Yet researchers have found higher levels of relationship satisfaction among lesbian couples with children than among those without children (Koepke, Hare, & Moran, 1992), as well as positive family functioning "characterized by balanced levels of family cohesion and family organization" (Levy, 1992, p. 23) and access to strong social supports (Levy, 1989).

Lesbian couples express a strong child-centered focus in their family formation and demonstrate high degrees of flexibility and adaptability in responding to individual needs, a response quite different from the couple-centered focus described in heterosexual reconstituted families (Lynch, 2000). Children in the custody of divorced lesbian mothers have more frequent contact with their fathers than children in the custody of heterosexual moms, and lesbian mothers are supportive of that involvement (Hare and Richards, 1993). Not surprisingly, partnered lesbian mothers report greater economic and emotional resources than lesbian mothers living alone (Kirkpatrick, 1987).

Among couples and families formed from within a lesbian identity, researchers have primarily addressed questions about relationship quality and characteristics after the addition of a child to the couple dyad. McCandlish (1987) found that partners experienced the sense of "becoming a parent" very differently and that these reactions were magnified in interactions with respective families of origin and friendship networks. The child's arrival brought changes in roles, need-meeting capabilities, and sexual intimacy, resulting in increased conflict yet improved problem-resolution strategies between partners. Bonding and attachment with the child occurred equally for both partners, though more strongly for the nonbiological parent after the child had passed early infancy. These findings have been supported by research with other lesbian-parent families as well (Dalton & Bielby, 2000; Donaldson, 2000; Wilson, 2000).

In 1986 Gartrell et al. (1996) initiated a 25-year longitudinal study of 84 lesbian-parent families created following donor insemination. Findings have now been reported on three waves of interviews with the mothers and co-mothers—before birth, when the children reached age 2 (Gartrell et al., 1999), and again at age 5 (Gartrell et al., 2000). These couples carefully planned for and reached their decisions to become parents with the support of close friendship networks and extended family. The arrival of children was stressful to the couple relationship and one-third of the couples had "divorced" by the third interview, a rate comparable to that among heterosexual couples with children. Among those who remained together, 94% indicated that the presence of children diminished the time and energy available for each other, but many also felt that having a child had strengthened their relationship (Gartrell et al., 2000).

Researchers have focused on the division of labor between partners in child care, household maintenance, and outside wage earning following a donor insemination birth (Chan, Brooks, Raboy, & Patterson, 1998a; Dundas & Kaufman, 2000; Gartrell et al., 1999; Patterson, 1995; Sullivan, 1996). All have concluded that lesbian parents share more equally in child care and household maintenance than do heterosexual-parent couples. In some families, more "traditional" patterns in which one parent, typically the biological mother, provided more child care while the remaining co-parent engaged in more outside employment, were also present. The equitable distribution of child care and shared decision making evident in most families studied, however, was beneficial to the positive family adjustment and relationship satisfaction of both parents and children. Bialeschki and Pearce (1997) found that values of equity and flexibility around household and child care responsibilities also carried over into how partners were able to support one another in pursuing leisure interests.

REDEFINING RELATIONSHIPS WITH FAMILIES OF ORIGIN Families of origin are a source of both support and conflict to lesbian parents and their children. Custody challenges from related third parties (e.g., grandparents, aunts) have been well documented (Stein, 1996). Alternately, some lesbian mothers report a primary reliance upon families of origin for social and emotional support in their parenting role (Hare, 1994; Lewin, 1993). The experience of support or conflict is strongly linked to the lesbian mother's decision to disclose or conceal her sexual orientation.

Parental reaction to a child's revelation of homosexuality is oftentimes one of guilt and failure (Strommen,1990). Disclosure can precipitate a conflict for family members between their conceptions of homosexuality and the familiar family role of the now "new" gay member. In reaction, family members may engage in actions ranging from tolerant acceptance to overt rejection (Baptiste, 1987; Hare, 1994; Strommen, 1990). For lesbian parents, their partners, and their children, these reactions can have complex and far-reaching implications. Because family-of-origin members progress at different rates from awareness to integration of the disclosure, difficulties and awkwardness in interactions with their daughter and her partner are likely to occur. Though expressing acceptance, family members may inadvertently act in ways that diminish the status or ignore the boundaries of the parent couple. As with heterosexual couples, both families of origin and the couple must attend to the continual and evolving process of recognition, definition, and acceptance of the new family unit. For the lesbian couple and extended family, stigma and lack of social sanction confound this process.

"I HAVE TWO MOMS": HOW THE KIDS RESPOND   Researchers concerned about the effects of growing up in a lesbian-parent family have focused their investigations on the sexual identity development, psychological adjustment, and social relationships of children raised in such homes. Others have focused on concerns expressed by lesbian mothers about their children and on the involvement of fathers, partners, and other adults in the children's lives. Of specific concern to parents of children conceived through donor insemination, questions related to disclosure about the donor and explanations about conception have been addressed as well.

A relatively large body of research comparing the children of heterosexual and lesbian divorced parents has been generated in response to negative assumptions expressed in judicial opinions, legislative initiatives, and public policies (Patterson, 2000). Findings are highly consistent and may be summarized as follows. Gender identity, gender role behavior, and the sexual preferences of children of lesbian parents are unaffected by the parents' sexual orientation. No differences have been found between children of lesbian parents and children of heterosexual parents in behavior problems, self-concept, self-esteem, intelligence, moral development, or any other area of personal adjustment that researchers have examined. Children of lesbian parents have normal peer relationships and satisfactory relationships with adults of both genders. Adolescents may have greater difficulty than younger or older children upon learning about their mother's lesbian identity, but these reactions tend to change and become more positive over time. Readers interested in obtaining detailed information about these findings are referred to the original research reports or to one of a few recently published review articles (Allen & Burrell, 1996; Flaks, Ficher, Masterpasqua, & Joseph, 1995; Gershon, Tschann, & Jemerin, 1999; Golombok & Tasker, 1996; Gottman, 1989; Green et al., 1986; Hare, 1994; Lewis, 1980; O'Connell, 1993; Parks, 1998; Patterson, 1992, 2000; Tasker & Golombok, 1995; Wright & Schmitz, 2001).

The development, adjustment, and social relationships of children conceived via donor insemination and being raised in lesbian (versus heterosexual) two-parent (versus single-parent) households have also received the attention of researchers. Whether originating in the United States (Chan et al., 1998a; Chan, Raboy, and Patterson, 1998b; Gartrell et al., 1996, 1999, 2000; Patterson, 1995; Patterson, Hurt, & Mason, 1998; Sullivan, 1996), Canada (Dundas & Kaufman, 2000), Belgium (Baetens & Brewaeys, 2001; Brewaeys & van-Hall, 1997) or England (Golombok, Tasker, & Murray, 1997), the results are similar. Children raised in lesbian families are well adjusted and healthy; no adverse effects of lesbian motherhood on child development have been identified (Brewaeys, 2001;

Brewaeys & van-Hall, 1997). Differences between these children and those raised in heterosexual families are attributed to family process variables (e.g., egalitarian division of labor and child care) and parent gender and are unrelated to parental sexual orientation (Patterson, 2000).

Two additional areas may be of particular interest or concern to some lesbian parents—whether, when, and how to disclose donor identity (Barrett, 1997) and exposure of their children to sex education (Mitchell, 1998) and sexual(ity) decision making (Costello, 1997). Among respondents to the few studies identified, parents valued open, honest, and age-appropriate discussions of sex, reproduction, and sexuality. Parents assumed their children would grow up to be heterosexual, expressed a willingness to actively foster a sexual identity different from their own, and asserted that they would accept their children regardless of the sexual identity they eventually adopted (Costello, 1997). Finally, disclosures about donor identity were determined on the basis of the needs and concerns of both parents and children (Barrett, 1997).

LESBIAN FAMILIES AND COMMUNITY Contrary to popular stereotypes that lesbians are socially isolated and lacking in social support (Peplau, 1993), research documents that these women receive extensive support from multiple sources (Ainslie & Feltey, 1991; Kurdek, 1988; Levy, 1989, 1992). Families of origin are one resource; families of creation, or close networks of mostly lesbian friends, are another.

Lesbians and lesbian parents who live in close proximity to other lesbians or maintain close affiliations based on a shared identity and values, including feminism, define these associations as community (D'Augelli & Garnets, 1995; Lockard, 1985). Many lesbian parents report a reliance on these communities and, in larger metropolitan areas, on the availability of "lesbian mother groups" for social and emotional support (Ainslie & Felty, 1991; Levy, 1989, 1992; McCandlish, 1987). Since the majority of lesbians are not mothers, however, most activities and organizations within lesbian communities are not primarily concerned with the needs of mothers and children (Baptiste, 1987). Some view the rejection of monogamy (Hall, 1978) and the exclusion of male children from lesbian-sponsored events, endorsed by some feminists, as exerting pressures that are antagonistic to lesbian mothers (Gartrell et al., 1999; Pearlman, 1987). Some lesbian parents are thus disillusioned by a lack of support and acceptance from lesbian social networks (Hare, 1994; Lott-Whitehead & Tully, 1993). They rely instead on families of origin, friends, and other associates for affirmation of their parenting role.

The absence of public rituals in lesbian family formation is another dimension of invisibility with which these women contend. Slater and Mencher (1991), in their exploration of the lesbian family life cycle, highlight the importance of ritual to punctuate "normal" family stages and progression. While these authors note that lesbian families may indeed develop personal family rituals, it is the public component that is critical to the sense of validation and legitimacy that such rituals are intended to bestow. Publicly recognized "markers" of family formation and progression help to delineate boundaries, roles, and responsibilities both within the family and between the family and the rest of the world.

LEGAL AND ECONOMIC PROTECTIONS FOR CHILDREN   While many reasons are cited for not sanctioning lesbian and gay families, the most common is the concern that the children will suffer from living in a "deviant" family—notwithstanding the empirical record, which clearly disproves this belief. In reality, harm is done to lesbian and gay families, especially the children, when their relationships are not legally recognized. Children who live with two parents, of which only one is legally recognized, are vulnerable financially, legally, and psychologically as a result of discrimination, not lesbian parenting. While the partnership endures, that vulnerability is less evident. In the event that the family breaks up or the legal/biological partner dies, however, the other parent has no rights and may not be allowed to continue to parent her child. If the child's biological grandparents or other relatives of the biological parent attempt to assume custody of the child, the remaining "other" parent is left to seek protection of her parental relationship from an often hostile judicial system. In such circumstances, the children are at risk of losing both parents.

Until recently, lesbian mothers were always at risk of fierce custody battles with angry fathers or paternal families seeking custody, in part as a reaction to learning that their former wife/partner/in-law was a lesbian. Such custody battles leave lesbian mothers at great risk of losing their children (Doolittle, 2000; Stein, 1996), although when the primary standard in determining custody is the best interest of the child rather than the lifestyle of the parent, the decision is usually favorable to the lesbian mother. Another complicating factor, however, is the inclination of the court to seek the child's preference in making custody decisions. Doolittle (2000) notes that often the custody battle takes place shortly after the child has learned that his or her mother is a lesbian. Children have many reactions to this news, especially when it is recent. As a result, some mothers have lost custody of their children because the children have sided with the father in his quest for sole custody. All of these situations create uncertainty and vulnerability for lesbian mothers, their partners, and their children. Public policy intends to protect the interests of minor children, but in the absence of a coherent policy, major obstacles to healthy child development in lesbian families are created.

Another vulnerability lurks in the future for children in lesbian families who were conceived through anonymous donor insemination. Currently, sperm banks assure both the donating party and the receiving party absolute confidentiality, promising that the names will never be shared regardless of the circumstances. Records are kept, however, and it is only a matter of time until someone—a donor, the mother, or more likely an adult child—demands to know the genetic legacy of the donor parent. One of this chapter's authors worked in adoption in the early 1960s when similar absolute guarantees of confidentiality were given to biological mothers and fathers, as well as to adoptive parents. Today open adoptions have become the norm; adult children and biological mothers routinely locate each other. Given the rapid developments in genetic research, it stands to reason that adult children who were conceived through donor insemination will, in the not so distant future, sue to obtain the genetic makeup of their biological fathers, thereby threatening the promised confidentiality.

IMPLICATIONS FOR PRACTICE

MICRO PRACTICE

Research suggests that lesbians are active consumers of counseling services (Jones & Gabriel, 1999). As a result, social workers, from those in private practice settings to those in public child welfare agencies, are likely to be providers of such services, even if they do not realize it because the lesbian is closeted. As many researchers have noted (Laird & Green 1996), direct-service interventions with lesbian families are very much the same as with any other family. Whether single-parent, two-parent, multigenerational, or blended, lesbian families share many commonalities and bring similar issues to therapy as different heterosexual family units do. The major difference is that lesbian families are forced to cope with stigma and discrimination, including the risk that when they seek services from a social worker or social service agency, they will not be met or accepted as a "real" family with all the attendant rights, responsibilities, problems, and capacities. Lesbian families cannot be helped if they are not accepted, if they must hide the true nature of their family, if they are not free to be who they are. Just as direct-service staff are responsible for providing sensitive and respectful care to all who seek their services, agency administrators are responsible for preparing all staff, through training, consciousness-raising, and other opportunities, to respond effectively and compassionately to the service needs of lesbian families.

To effectively fulfill these responsibilities, it is imperative that all social workers become aware of and address their own attitudes and biases that can affect their ability to work effectively with this population. Studies conducted in the 1980s revealed that social workers scored higher than other professional groups on measures of homophobia, and in 1997 Berkman and Zinberg found that 11% of a sample of heterosexual social workers scored in the "homophobic range" (as cited in Newman, Dannenfelser, & Benishek, 2002). While more-recent studies (Newman et al., 2002) attest to a growing acceptance of GLBT people among

MSW students (5.5% of 2,522 students expressed negative attitudes in 1999), these findings confirm that lesbian couples and families cannot assume a positive reception from those they turn to for help.

Lesbian couples and lesbian-parent families are highly diverse in their origins, structures, and functioning. Researchers have only begun to describe the characteristics and experiences of a limited number of these women and children. The research to date reveals lesbian parents and their children to be healthy, secure, and quite effective in negotiating the many challenges that accompany their stigmatized and minority status. Lesbian couples are confronted by an environment that disavows their unions, challenges their right and fitness to parent, and denies them basic civil and legal protections to individual and family security. Yet they have succeeded in creating nurturing, egalitarian families in which they are bearing and raising well-functioning, well-adjusted, and socially tolerant children.

Though "nontraditional" in structure, lesbian families face many "traditional" dilemmas in early family formation and ongoing function. Because of societal homophobia, they also confront several complications or variations on traditional family themes. These include deciding to parent, negotiating family roles and boundaries, and reconciling relationships with extended-family members and outside others. Whether in interactions with pediatricians (Perrin & Kulkin, 1996), teachers (Bliss & Harris, 1999; Maney & Cain, 1997), or other professionals (Clarke, 2000; Crawford, McLeod, Zamboni, & Jordan, 1999), lesbian parents and their children risk reactions ranging from invisibility to overt censure as they endeavor to simply lead their lives. As the evidence attests, they have responded to these challenges with ingenuity and resilience.

Each partner's "parenthood history" represents an important dimension of lesbian family assessment (Hare & Richards, 1993). The different avenues pursued in achieving parenthood affect the adjustment and function of individual family members. Stepparents are particularly vulnerable to ambiguity and ambivalence during family formation; co-parents are more vulnerable during pregnancy or at the time of family dissolution. Clinicians need to be aware of these differences, sensitive to the changing needs of individual members, and informed about the community resources and supports available as lesbian families negotiate the challenges of creating and living within this alternative family structure.

Social workers are well advised to acknowledge and honor the heterogeneity and the strengths of lesbian-parent families with whom they come into contact. Lesbians and their children approach clinical services about issues and circumstances unrelated to sexual orientation. It would be erroneous to assume that the problems presented are ipso facto a result of the family's nontraditional status. It would be as erroneous to ignore or minimize the parents' sexual orientation and the potential impact of stigma and homonegativity on the family's experience.

MACRO PRACTICE

For social workers who engage in community organizing, administration, or policy practice, this is the golden age of opportunities to improve the lives of lesbian families and accomplish other important social goals as well. As more states consider civil union, second-parent adoption, and other relevant legislation, individual social workers and the organizations that represent them can be highly influential in facilitating desired outcomes (Lopez, 1997). Working to overturn federal or state DOMAs (or keep them off the books where they do not exist), serving as expert witnesses in actions adverse to individual lesbian families, working to promote understanding of the advantages of intercountry adoption by lesbians and gays, or acting to promote legislation that recognizes the partnerships of lesbians and gay men and their right to form families—these are just a few of the organizing and policy practice activities in which social workers can engage to support this population.

Social workers who are administrators can also act by making their organizations open, accessible, and accepting of lesbian families, among both their clients and their employees. Administrators can arrange training and help staff come to grips with their own homophobia and heterosexism, using the same techniques that are used when introducing any other value-laden content into agency practice.

Policy practitioners have many opportunities to help lesbian families. One example illustrates the ways in which practitioners can help lesbian families while meeting other important social needs at the same time. Ryan (2000) and Brooks and Goldberg (2001) argue that (1) the desire expressed by lesbians and gays to have families and (2) the availability of thousands of children in the United States (and a million worldwide) who are in need of stable, loving homes are complementary forces. The needs of both could be met by encouraging lesbian and gay families to adopt or foster children who are in need of families. Recently there have been many federal, state, and local efforts to increase the supply of homes for these children. Yet lesbian and gay couples who want to adopt children have not been included in this outreach effort. Only a few local jurisdictions and private agencies have experimented with this obvious and potentially effective way of increasing the supply of available homes. Because of continuing homophobic and heterosexist concerns, however, these small experiments are often difficult to maintain. Social workers who are experts in policy could help introduce programs that would match the supply with the need, beginning with small, carefully documented and researched demonstration projects. Any effort would necessarily start with the creation of formal agency policy that recognizes the legitimacy of lesbian and gay families. Such initiatives would help legitimate lesbian and gay families while also meeting a critical social need to find homes for children who really need them.

The current state of lesbian families has features of the proverbial quandary "Is the glass half empty or half full?" The proliferation of research has greatly strengthened the empirical record, supporting the argument that lesbian families are like other families when measured in terms of outcomes for children, especially in preparing them for healthy adulthood. At the same time, those who make public policy, responding to intense public opinion, still fail to recognize these research findings. Yet lesbian families have received some limited recognition and sanctions, as outlined in this chapter. Given the pernicious power of homophobia and heterosexism, the depth of hostility expressed by some toward lesbians and gays, and the increasingly conservative times that have overlapped these public policy accomplishments, such progress is a truly remarkable achievement. But much remains to be done. Social workers have played, and will continue to play, many constructive roles in these social change efforts. The coming years will be an exciting time for lesbian families, who will, we hope, face far fewer obstacles as they gain even greater social and legal acceptance.

REFERENCES

Ainslie, J., & Feltey, K. M. (1991). Definitions and dynamics of motherhood and family in lesbian communities. *Marriage and Family Review*, 17(1–2), 63–85.

Allen, K. R., & Demo, D. H. (1995). The families of lesbians and gay men: A new frontier in family research. *Journal of Marriage and the Family*, 57, 111–127.

Allen, M., & Burrell, N. (1996). Comparing the impact of homosexual and heterosexual parents on children: Meta-analysis of existing research. *Journal of Homosexuality*, 32(2), 19–35.

Baetens, P., & Brewaeys, A. (2001). Lesbian couples requesting donor insemination: An update of the knowledge with regard to lesbian mother families. *Human Reproduction Update*, 7, 512–519.

Baptiste, D. A. (1987). The gay and lesbian stepparent family. In F. W. Bozett (Ed.), *Gay and lesbian parents* (pp. 112–137). New York: Praeger.

Barrett, S. E. (1997). Children of lesbian parents: The what, when, and how of talking about donor identity. *Women and Therapy*, 20(2), 43–55.

Berger, R. (2001). Gay stepfamilies: A triple-stigmatized group. In J. M. Lehmann (Ed.), *The gay and lesbian marriage and family reader: Analysis of problems and prospects for the 21st century* (pp. 171–194). Lincoln, NE: Gordian Knot Books.

Berger, R. M. (1990). Passing: Impact on the quality of same-sex couple relationships. *Social Work*, 35, 328–332.

Bialeschki, M. D., & Pearce, K. D. (1997). "I don't want a lifestyle, I want a life": The effect of role negotiations on the leisure of lesbian mothers. *Journal of Leisure Research*, 29(1), 113.

Bliss, G. K., & Harris, M. B. (1999). Teachers' views of students with gay or lesbian parents. *Journal of Gay, Lesbian, and Bisexual Identity*, 4, 149–171.

Bolte, A. (2001). Do wedding dresses come in lavender? The prospects and implications of same-sex marriage. In J. M. Lehmann (Ed.), *The gay and lesbian marriage and family reader: Analysis of problems and prospects for the 21st century* (pp. 25–46). Lincoln, NE: Gordian Knot Books..

Bradford, J., Ryan, C., & Rothblum, E. D. (1994). National lesbian health care survey: Implications for mental health care. *Journal of Consulting and Clinical Psychology*, 62, 228–242.

Brewaeys, A. (2001). Review: Parent-child relationships and child development in donor insemination families. *Human Reproduction Update*, 7, 38–46.

Brewaeys, A., & van-Hall, E. V. (1997). Lesbian motherhood: The impact on child development and family functioning. *Journal of Psychosomatic Obstetrics and Gynecology*, 18, 1–16.

Brooks, D., & Goldberg, S. (2001). Gay and lesbian adoptive and foster care placements: Can they meet the needs of waiting children? *Social Work*, 46, 147–157.

Caron, S. L., & Ulin, M. (1997). Closeting and the quality of lesbian relationships. *Families in Society*, 78, 413–419.

Chan, R. W., Brooks, R. C., Raboy, B., & Patterson, C. J. (1998a). Division of labor among lesbian and heterosexual parents: Associations with children's adjustment. *Journal of Family Psychology*, 12(3), 402.

Chan, R. W., Raboy, B., & Patterson, C. J. (1998b). Psychosocial adjustment among children conceived via donor insemination by lesbian and heterosexual mothers. *Child Development*, 69, 443–457.

Clarke, V. (2000). "Stereotype, attack, and stigmatize those who disagree": Employing scientific rhetoric in debates about lesbian and gay parenting. *Feminism and Psychology*, 10, 152–159.

Costello, C. Y. (1997). Conceiving identity: Bisexual, lesbian, and gay parents consider their children's sexual orientations. *Journal of Sociology and Social Welfare*, 24(3), 63–89.

Crawford, I., McLeod, A., Zamboni, B. D., & Jordan, M. B. (1999). Psychologists' attitudes toward gay and lesbian parenting. *Professional Psychology: Research and Practice*, 30, 394–401.

Dalton, S. E., & Bielby, D. D. (2000). "That's our kind of constellation": Lesbian mothers negotiate institutionalized understandings of gender within the family. *Gender and Society*, 14(1), 36–61.

D'Augelli, A. R., & Garnets, L. D. (1995). Lesbian, gay, and bisexual communities. In A. R. D'Augelli, & C. J. Patterson (Eds.), *Lesbian, gay, and bisexual identities over the lifespan* (pp. 293–320). New York: Oxford University Press.

Day, N. E., & Schoenrade, P. (1997). Staying in the closet versus coming out: Relationships between communication about sexual orientation and work attitudes. *Personnel Psychology*, 50(1), 147.

Dean, L., Meyer, I., Robinson, K., Sell, R. L., Sember, R., Silenzio, V., Bowen, D. J., Bradford, J., Rothblum, E., Scout, M., White, J., Dunn, P., Lawrence, A., Wolfe, D., & Xavier, J. (2000). Lesbian, gay, bisexual, and transgender health: Findings and concerns. *Journal of the Gay and Lesbian Medical Association*, 4(3), 101–151.

D'Emilio, J., Turner, W. B., & Vaid, U. (Eds.). (2000). *Creating change*. New York: St Martin's.

Dew, B. J., & Myers, J. E. (2000). Gay and lesbian parents: No longer a paradox. *Adultspan Journal*, 2, 44.

Donaldson, C. (2000). Midlife lesbian parenting. *Journal of Gay and Lesbian Social Services*, 11(2/3), 119.

Doolittle, K. L. (2000). Don't ask, you may not want to know: Custody preferences of children of gay and lesbian parents. *Southern California Law Review*, 73(3), 677–703.

Dundas, S., & Kaufman, M. (2000). The Toronto Lesbian Family Study. *Journal of Homosexuality*, 40, 65.

Dunne, G.A. (2000). Opting into motherhood: Lesbians blurring the boundaries and transforming the meaning of parenthood and kinship. *Gender and Society, 14*, 11.

Eldridge, N.S., & Gilbert, L.A. (1990). Correlates of relationship satisfaction in lesbian couples. *Psychology of Women Quarterly, 14*, 43–62.

Erera, P.I. & Fredriksen, K. (1999). Lesbian stepfamilies: A unique family structure. *Families in Society, 80*, 263.

Flaks, D.K., Ficher, I., Masterpasqua, F., & Joseph, G. (1995). Lesbians choosing motherhood: A comparative study of lesbian and heterosexual parents and their children. Special issue: Sexual orientation and human development. *Developmental Psychology, 31*, 105–114.

Franke, R., & Leary, M.R. (1991). Disclosure of sexual orientation by lesbians and gay men: A comparison of private and public processes. *Journal of Social and Clinical Psychology, 10*, 262–269.

Friedman, L. (1997). Rural lesbian mothers and their families. *Journal of Gay and Lesbian Social Services, 7*, 73.

Gartrell, N., Banks, A., Hamilton, J., Reed, N., Bishop, H., & Rodas, C. (1999). The National Lesbian Family Study. 2. Interviews with mothers of toddlers. *American Journal of Orthopsychiatry, 69*, 362–369.

Gartrell, N., Banks, A., Reed, N., Hamilton, J., Rodas, C., & Deck, A. (2000). The National Lesbian Family Study. 3. Interviews with mothers of five-year-olds. *American Journal of Orthopsychiatry, 70*, 542–548.

Gartrell, N., Hamilton, J., Banks, A., Mosbacher, D., Reed, N., Sparks, C.H., & Bishop, H. (1996). The National Lesbian Family Study. 1. Interviews with prospective mothers. *American Journal of Orthopsychiatry, 66*, 272.

Gershon, T.D., Tschann, J.M., & Jemerin, J.M. (1999). Stigmatization, self-esteem, and coping among the adolescent children of lesbian mothers. *Journal of Adolescent Health, 24*, 437–445.

Golombok, S., & Tasker, F. (1996). Do parents influence the sexual orientation of their children? Findings from a longitudinal study of lesbian families. *Developmental Psychology, 32*, 3–11.

Golombok, S., Tasker, F., & Murray, C. (1997). Children raised in fatherless families from infancy: Family relationships and the socioemotional development of children of lesbian and single heterosexual mothers. *Journal of Child Psychology and Psychiatry, 38*, 783–791.

Gottman, J.S. (1989). Children of gay and lesbian parents. *Marriage and Family Review, 14*, 177–196.

Green, R., Mandel, J.B., Hotvedt, M.E., Gray, J., & Smith, L. (1986). Lesbian mothers and their children: A comparison with solo parent heterosexual mothers and their children. *Archives of Sexual Behavior, 15*, 167–184.

Hall, M. (1978). Lesbian families: Cultural and clinical issues. *Social Work, 23*, 380–385.

Hare, J. (1994). Concerns and issues faced by families headed by a lesbian couple. *Families in Society, 75*, 27.

Hare, J., & Richards, L. (1993). Children raised by lesbian couples: Does context of birth affect father and partner involvement? *Family Relations, 42*, 249–255.

Hartman, A. (1996). Social policy as a context for lesbian and gay families. In J. Laird and R.J. Green (Eds.), *Lesbians and gays in couples and families: A handbook for therapists* (pp. 69–85). San Francisco: Jossey-Bass.

Hequembourg, A.L., & Farrell, M.P. (1999). Lesbian motherhood: Negotiating marginal-mainstream identities. *Gender and Society, 13*, 540–557.

Hillis, L. (2001). Intercountry adoption under the Hague Convention: Still an attractive option for homosexuals seeking to adopt? *Indiana Journal of Global Legal Studies, 6,* 237.

Jones, M.A., & Gabriel, M.A. (1999). Utilization of psychotherapy by lesbians, gay men, and bisexuals: Findings from a nationwide survey. *American Journal of Orthopsychiatry, 69,* 209–219.

Kirkpatrick, M. (1987). Clinical implications of lesbian mother studies. *Journal of Homosexuality, 14,* 201.

Koepke, L., Hare, J., & Moran, P.B. (1992). Relationship quality in a sample of lesbian couples with children and child-free lesbian couples. *Family Relations, 41,* 224–229.

Krestan, J.A., & Bepko, C.S. (1980). The problem of fusion in the lesbian relationship. *Family Process, 19,* 276–289.

Kurdek, L.A. (1988). Perceived social support in gays and lesbians in cohabitating relationships. *Journal of Personality and Social Psychology, 54,* 504–509.

——. (2001). Differences between heterosexual-nonparent couples and gay, lesbian, and heterosexual-parent couples. *Journal of Family Issues, 22,* 727.

Kurdek, L.A., & Schmitt, P. (1986). Perceived emotional support from family and friends in members of homosexual, married, and heterosexual cohabiting couples. *Journal of Homosexuality, 14*(3/4), 57–67.

Laird, J. (1993). Lesbian and gay families. In F. Walsh (Ed.), *Normal family processes* (2d ed.) (pp. 282–328). New York: Guilford.

Laird, J., and Green, R.J. (1996). *Lesbians and gays in couples and families: A handbook for therapists.* San Francisco: Jossey-Bass.

Levy, E. (1989). Lesbian motherhood: Identity and social support. *Affilia, 4*(4), 40–53.

——. (1992). Strengthening the coping resources of lesbian families. *Families in Society, 73,* 23.

Lewin, E. (1993). *Lesbian mothers: Accounts of gender in American culture.* Ithaca, NY: Cornell University Press.

——. (2001). Weddings without marriage: Making sense of lesbian and gay commitments rituals. In M. Bernstein and R. Reimann (Eds.), *Queer families, queer politics: Challenging culture and the state* (pp. 44–67). New York: Columbia University Press.

Lewin, E., & Lyons, T.A. (1982). Everything in its place: The coexistence of lesbianism and motherhood. In W. Paul, J.D. Weinrich, J.C. Gonsiorek, & M.E. Hotvedt (Eds.), *Homosexuality: Social, psychological, and biological issues* (pp. 249–273). Beverly Hills: Sage.

Lewis, K.G. (1980). Children of lesbians: Their point of view. *Social Work, 25,* 198–203.

Lockard, D. (1985). The lesbian community: An anthropological approach. *Journal of Homosexuality, 11,* 83.

López, R. (1997). One view of the domestic partnership debate. *Journal of Gay and Lesbian Social Services, 6,* 83.

Lott-Whitehead, L., & Tully, C.T. (1993). The family lives of lesbian mothers. *Smith College Studies in Social Work, 63,* 265–280.

Lynch, J.M. (2000). Considerations of family structure and gender composition: The lesbian and gay stepfamily. *Journal of Homosexuality, 40,* 81.

Lynch, J.M., & Murray, K. (2000). For the love of the children: The coming out process for lesbian and gay parents and stepparents. *Journal of Homosexuality, 39,* 1–24.

Maney, D.W., & Cain, R.E. (1997). Preservice elementary teachers' attitudes toward gay and lesbian parenting. *Journal of School Health, 67,* 236.

Matthews, A.K., Tartaro, J., & Hughes, T.L. (2003). A comparative study of lesbian and heterosexual women in committed relationships. *Journal of Lesbian Studies, 7*(1), 101–114.

McCandlish, B. (1987). Against all odds: Lesbian mother and family dynamics. In F. W. Bozett (Ed.), *Gay and lesbian parents* (pp. 23–36). New York: Praeger.

McClellan, D. L. (2001). The "other mother" and second parent adoption. *Journal of Gay and Lesbian Social Services, 13*, 1–21.

Mitchell, V. (1998). The birds, the bees ... and the sperm banks: How lesbian mothers talk with their children about sex and reproduction. *American Journal of Orthopsychchiatry, 68*, 400–409.

Morris, J. F., Waldo, C. R., & Rothblum, E. D. (2001). A model of predictors and outcomes of outness among lesbian and bisexual women. *American Journal of Orthopsychiatry, 71*, 61–71.

Newman, B. S., Dannenfelser, P. L., & Benishek, L. (2002). Assessing beginning social work and counseling students' acceptance of lesbians and gay men. *Journal of Social Work Education, 38*, 273–288.

O'Connell, A. (1993). Voices from the heart: The developmental impact of a mother's lesbianism on her adolescent children. *Smith College Studies in Social Work, 63*, 281–299.

Parks, C. A. (1998). Lesbian parenthood: A review of the literature. *American Journal of Orthopsychiatry, 68*, 376.

Patterson, C. J. (1992). Children of lesbian and gay parents. *Child Development, 63*, 1025–1042.

———. (1995). Families of the lesbian baby boom: Parents' division of labor and children's adjustment. *Developmental Psychology, 31*, 115–123.

———. (2000). Family relationships of lesbians and gay men. *Journal of Marriage and the Family, 62*, 1052–1069.

Patterson, C. J., Hurt, S., & Mason, C. D. (1998). Families of the lesbian baby boom: Children's contact with grandparents and other adults. *American Journal of Orthopsychiatry, 68*, 390–399.

Pearlman, S. (1987). The saga of continuing clash in lesbian community, or will an army of ex-lovers fail? In the Boston Lesbian Psychologies Collective (Eds.), *Lesbian psychologies: Explorations and challenges* (pp. 313–326). Urbana/Chicago: University of Illinois Press.

Peplau, L. A. (1993). Lesbian and gay relationships. In L. D. Garnets & D.C. Kimmel (Eds.), *Psychological perspectives on lesbian and gay male experiences* (pp. 395–419). New York: Columbia University Press.

Peplau, L. A., Cochron, S., Rook, K., & Padesky, C. (1978). Loving women: Attachment and autonomy in lesbian relationships. *Journal of Social Issues, 34*(3), 7–27.

Perrin, E. C. (2002). Technical report: Coparent or second-parent adoption by same-sex parents. *Pediatrics, 109*, 341.

Perrin, E. C., & Kulkin, H. (1996). Pediatric care for children whose parents are gay or lesbian. *Pediatrics, 97*, 629.

Radonsky, V. E., & Borders, L. D. (1995). Factors influencing lesbians' direct disclosure of their sexual orientation. *Journal of Gay and Lesbian Psychotherapy, 2*(3), 17–37.

Rose, S., & Zand, D. (2000). Lesbian dating and courtship from young adulthood to midlife. *Journal of Gay and Lesbian Social Services, 11*, 77–104.

Roth, S. (1985). Psychotherapy with lesbian couples: Individual issues, female socialization, and the social context. *Journal of Marital and Family Therapy, 11*, 273–286.

Ryan, S. D. (2000). Examining social workers' placement recommendations of children with gay and lesbian adoptive parents. *Families in Society, 81*, 517.

Sarantakos, S. (1996). Same-sex couples: Problems and prospects. *Journal of Family Studies, 2*(2), 147.

Schneider, M. S. (1986). The relationships of cohabiting lesbian and heterosexual couples: A comparison. *Psychology of Women Quarterly, 10*, 234–239.

Schreurs, K. M. G., & Buunk, B. P. (1996). Closeness, autonomy, equity, and relationship satisfaction in lesbian couples. *Psychology of Women Quarterly, 20*, 577–592.

Sell, R. L. (1997). Defining and measuring sexual orientation: A review. *Archives of Sexual Behavior, 26*, 643.

Sell, R. L., & Becker, J. B. (2001). Sexual orientation data collection and progress toward Healthy People 2010. *American Journal of Public Health, 91*, 876–882.

Siegenthaler, A. L., & Bigner, J. J. (2000). The value of children to lesbian and non-lesbian mothers. *Journal of Homosexuality, 39*(2), 73–91.

Slater, S., & Mencher, J. (1991). The lesbian family life cycle: A contextual approach. *American Journal of Orthopsychiatry, 61*, 372–382.

Solarz, A. L. (1999). *Lesbian health: Current assessment and directions for the future.* Washington DC: National Academy Press.

Stein, T. J. (1996). Child custody and visitation: The rights of lesbian and gay parents. *Social Services Review, 70*, 435–450.

Strommen, E. F. (1990). Hidden branches and growing pains: Homosexuality and the family tree. *Marriage and Family Review, 14*(3/4), 9–34.

Sullivan, A. (1995). *Virtually normal: An argument about homosexuality.* New York: Knopf.

Sullivan, M. (1996). Rozzie and Harriet? Gender and family patterns of lesbian coparents. *Gender and Society, 10*, 747–767.

Tasker, F., & Golombok, S. (1995). Adults raised as children in lesbian families. *American Journal of Orthopsychiatry, 65*, 203–215.

——. (1998). The role of co-mothers in planned lesbian-led families. *Journal of Lesbian Studies, 2*(4), 49–68.

Vaid, U. (1995). *Virtual equality: The mainstreaming of gay and lesbian liberation.* New York: Doubleday.

Van Voorhis, R., & McClain, L. (1997). Accepting a lesbian mother. *Families in Society, 78*, 642.

Van Voorhis, R., & Wagner, M. (2001). Coverage of gay and lesbian subject matter in social work journals. *Journal of Social Work Education, 37*, 147–159.

Weinstock, J. S. (2000). Lesbian friendships at midlife: Patterns and possibilities for the 21st century. *Journal of Gay and Lesbian Social Services, 11*(2/3), 1–32.

Weston, K. (1991). *Families we choose: Lesbians, gays, kinship.* New York: Columbia University Press.

Wilson, C. M. (2000). The creation of motherhood: Exploring the experiences of lesbian co-mothers. *Journal of Feminist Family Therapy, 12*, 21–44.

Wright, J. M., & Schmitz, C. L. (2001). *Evaluating gender roles in sons growing up in lesbian families.* Paper presented at the Fifth Annual Conference of the Society for Social Work and Research, Atlanta.

11

BISEXUAL RELATIONSHIPS AND FAMILIES

Daphne L. McClellan

What is new is not bisexuality, but rather the widening of our awareness and acceptance of human capacities for sexual love. Today the recognition of bisexuality in oneself and in others is part of the whole mid-20th century movement to accord to each individual, regardless of race, class, nationality, age or sex, the right to be a person who is unique and who has a social identity that is worthy of dignity and respect.... Even a superficial look at other societies and some groups in our own society should be enough to convince us that a very large number of human beings, probably a majority—are bisexual in their potential capacity for love.... We will fail to evolve in our understanding of human sexuality if we continue to see homosexuals merely as "heterosexuals-in-reverse," ignoring the vast diversity actually represented by society's many varied expressions of love between people.

—MARGARET MEAD, 1975

WHAT DEFINES a bisexual person? What is a bisexual relationship? And what is a bisexual family? Each of these questions draws us further and further into uncharted territory. Usually sexuality is presented as a dichotomy, either one is heterosexual (the socially preferred and "normal" state) or one is homosexual. Even when homosexuality is presented as acceptable or morally neutral, heterosexuality and homosexuality are often regarded as discrete categories.

This chapter will answer important questions for social workers who serve bisexual people: How is a person defined as bisexual, and what does that really mean? Can a bisexual person be monogamous? What are some critical issues that people in bisexual relationships face? Is there such a thing as a bisexual family? What about children and child-rearing in bisexual families? What social supports exist for bisexual people? And finally, what are effective practice suggestions for social workers in this area?

REVIEW OF LITERATURE AND DEFINITIONS

The quickly growing body of literature on bisexuality can be divided into two types: social science research and anthologies of personal stories. As early as 1948 Kinsey and his colleagues published their finding that human sexual behavior exists on a continuum. They created a seven-point scale, still in use today, which shows the extremes at either end as exclusively heterosexual (o) or exclusively homosexual (6). All others (1–5) display some degree of bisexuality. Kinsey, Pomeroy, and Martin (1948) point out that while homosexuality and heterosexuality may be discrete categories, bisexuality covers many gradations in between. They break down the intervening five categories by describing them as "1. predominantly heterosexual, only incidentally homosexual, 2. predominantly heterosexual, but more than incidentally homosexual, 3. equally heterosexual and homosexual, 4. predominantly homosexual, but more than incidentally heterosexual, and 5. predominantly homosexual, but incidentally heterosexual" (p. 638). This portion of their studies, "the heterosexual-homosexual balance," included both overt sexual relations and psychosexual reactions. In their study of males, Kinsey et al. found that 50% were exclusively heterosexual and 4% were exclusively homosexual throughout their adult lives, leaving 46% who had engaged in sexual activities with members of both sexes or who sexually reacted to members of both sexes during their adulthood. In a subsequent study of women, Kinsey, Pomeroy, Martin, and Gebhard (1953) found that about 70% of women were exclusively heterosexual, 2% were exclusively homosexual, and about 28% had had sexual responses to both men and women.

More recently, Klein (1993) expanded on Kinsey's continuum by retaining a seven-point scale but introducing seven variables and several different points in time. While Kinsey's scale relies on only behaviors and psychological reactions for placement on the continuum, Klein's grid also includes self-identification, emotional preferences, and social preferences as variables. The resulting grid allows an individual to acknowledge the fluidity of sexual experience and preference over time. By considering a variety of factors and different points in time, an individual can often see a mixture of heterosexual and homosexual attractions, behaviors, and fantasies that might most appropriately be labeled bisexual. As Kinsey et al. (1948) observed more than fifty years ago, there is a wide variety of sexual expression in the bisexual middle.

The small body of social science research on bisexuality continues to burgeon as more is observed and written about bisexual identity formation (Fox, 1995), bisexual people in society (Klein, 1993), biphobia (Ochs, 1999a), and bisexual politics (Hutchins, 1996; Jeffreys, 1999). Firestein (1996) describes a paradigm shift that replaces the illness model with an affirmative model and goes beyond dichotomy to a multiplicity of sexual orientations and expressions.

Equally fascinating is the body of literature by bisexuals describing their personal histories (Hutchins & Kaahumanu, 1991; Orndorff, 1999; Rose et al., 1996). Despite the fact that a person has had sexual experiences with both men and women, that person may not necessarily self-identify as bisexual. Instead, he or she may identify as heterosexual or gay/lesbian. In fact, a person who is married and sexually active with a member of the opposite sex, who has never had sexual relations with a member of the same sex, may self-identify as gay/lesbian on the basis of attractions and fantasies. Conversely, it is common for men who have regular sexual relations with other men to self-identify as heterosexual if they are never the submissive partner in the sexual experience (Klein, 1993). Therefore, writings by people who self-identify as bisexual are important lenses through which we may understand the complexities of a bisexual identity.

Heterosexuality and homosexuality are not the only normal outcomes of sexual identity development, nor are they exclusive. Fox (1996) states:

> Bisexual identity development has not been conceptualized as a linear process with a fixed outcome, but rather as a complex and open-ended process. In fact, bisexuals, homosexuals, and heterosexuals are not three totally distinct groups. Research indicates that there is significant overlap in membership in these categories for many individuals in terms of both past and present sexual and emotional attractions and behavior.
>
> (P. 33)

The definitions of bisexuality are various. Smiley (1997) suggests that the most useful definition of bisexuality for mental health counselors consolidates a variety of perspectives:

> Bisexuality is a sexual orientation in which an individual experiences a combination of sexual and affectional attractions to members of both sexes; engages to varying degrees in sexual activities with both sexes; and self-identifies as bisexual in a way that is consonant with personal, social, political, and lifestyle preferences.
>
> (P. 375)

For the purposes of this chapter, a bisexual person will be broadly defined as one who is sexually attracted to both men and women, regardless of his or her behavior.

THE RELATIONSHIPS OF BISEXUAL PEOPLE

When we consider the relationships of bisexual people, the focus is not on how they feel in isolation or how they might self-identify; rather, it is on how a bisexual person relates to another person. Immediately, the dichotomous categories present themselves. If our bisexual woman begins an affectional/sexual relationship with a man, others typically perceive it as a heterosexual relationship. If that same woman is involved in a similar relationship with another woman, it is described as a lesbian relationship. The same is true for men. If a man becomes involved with a woman, it is considered a heterosexual relationship, and if with another man, the relationship is labeled gay. What, then, is a bisexual relationship? A bisexual relationship is any relationship in which at least one of the parties is bisexual. Even though it may look to the outside world like a heterosexual or a gay/lesbian relationship, it is not.

Why does it matter? Perhaps a person is bisexual only in the absence of a relationship. Or maybe a person is bisexual when dating a variety of people. But, what happens when that person makes a commitment to a life partner to be in a monogamous[1] relationship? Is that person still bisexual? Is the relationship still a bisexual one?

MONOGAMY

To be truly invisible is to be a bisexual person in a monogamous relationship. Once the choice of a partner has been made, friends, family members, and acquaintances may assume that now the individual has "decided" and acknowledged his or her true identity. This is especially true if the relationship is sealed with a wedding or a commitment ceremony. Of course, each person must be free to self-identify, and some who make such commitments may choose to identify with their chosen partner as either heterosexual or gay/lesbian. However, many who choose a committed relationship will still identify as bisexual, even if they share that identity only selectively.

One of the myths about bisexuals is that they cannot be monogamous. Rust (1996) found that 16.4% of bisexual respondents were in monogamous relationships, compared to 28% of lesbian and gay respondents. Rust further found that 29.5% of bisexual women and 15.4 % of bisexual men in her study indicated that ideally they would like to have a lifetime committed monogamous relationship with one partner. While more than 70% of the bisexual people in her study did not desire monogamous relationships, Rust maintains, "Monogamy might be less popular among bisexuals than among lesbians and gay men, but it is certainly a realistic option" (p. 136).

Though many bisexual relationships may have less of an emphasis on monogamy, this does not necessarily mean that the individuals involved are "cheating" on their partners. Frequently people in bisexual relationships have come to an understanding about the meaning of fidelity that allows for relationships outside of their primary union.

POLYAMORY

In addressing the cultural idealization of monogamy, Rust (1996) points out that it is "based on the assumption that the monogamous relationship should fulfill all the partner's sexual and romantic needs and the greater part of their emotional needs" (p. 131). She observes that some people of all orientations have found that they need more than one person in their lives to meet these needs. To describe a relationship that is not exclusive in the traditional sense of monogamy, Rust uses the positive term *polyamory* rather than the more negative *nonmonogamy*.

Why are many bisexual people polyamorous? Like some heterosexual and some gay/lesbian people, some bisexual people acknowledge that one partner cannot meet all of their sexual, emotional, and romantic needs. For others, it is specifically because they are bisexual. Because they are attracted to both men and women, they find that the differences between men and women are so significant that they cannot be happy relating intimately with just one or the other. They must have both kinds of relationships in their lives.

Polyamorous relationships must be defined by the people involved in them. Good communication is essential. This is one place where a counselor can be very helpful to a couple. The two people involved in the relationship must be honest about their needs and their vision of the primary relationship, as well as other relationships that might be formed. The couple must agree on what will be retained exclusively for the primary relationship and what other relationships may involve.

SERIAL MONOGAMY AND MULTIPLE PARTNERS

Bisexual relationships are even more varied than monogamous or polyamorous. Other common forms are serial monogamy and multiple partners (threesomes or more). The bisexual person who engages in serial monogamy may not even have an awareness of himself or herself as bisexual when a commitment to an original partner is made. Sometimes it happens that during the course of a relationship, one becomes aware of attractions to persons of the other sex. For many this may be an awareness of same-sex attractedness during a heterosexual marriage.

Awareness that one is attracted to members of the same sex does not have to translate into any change in the committed relationship. A married heterosexual person may become attracted to another person of the opposite sex during the course of his or her marriage. In fact, it is almost certain to happen at some point. However, this does not mean that he or she must act upon that attraction.

When a person who is heterosexually married finds himself or herself attracted to someone of the same sex, it may result in nothing more than a personal insight that helps the individual understand himself or herself better. Or it may result in a new sexual identity, a renaming of oneself as bisexual, gay, or lesbian. If the original heterosexual relationship ends and one partner becomes involved in a relationship with a person of the same sex, it could be a case of bisexuality as a transition from a heterosexual identity to a lesbian or gay identity. However, for others, leaving a heterosexual marriage and becoming involved with a partner of the same sex is not a choice of identity as gay or lesbian but rather an awakening to one's bisexuality and a desire to explore another side of oneself. If the second long-term relationship is with a person of the same sex, then the expression of bisexuality may be serial monogamy. This means that while in a relationship, the person is monogamous, regardless of the sex of the mate. When not partnered, however, the individual may date men and/or women.

Another possible relationship type for some bisexual people is the multiple-partner relationship, or threesome. A woman might live with her husband and her female lover. All three people might or might not be sexually involved with each other. The number might be more than three, but in these types of relationships each member is equal and is considered a primary member of the relationship.

OTHER RELATIONSHIP ISSUES

As described, relationships of bisexual people can become very complicated (as can the relationships of heterosexual or gay/lesbian people), but even the most uncomplicated monogamous relationships are affected by the fact that a person is bisexual. The bisexual individual must decide whether or not to share his or her identity with the partner. This can be a difficult decision because of the stereotypes associated with bisexuality. Upon learning of a loved one's bisexual identity, the partner or prospective partner may feel that a committed monogamous relationship is impossible and therefore may want to end the marriage or involvement. Once the couple works out an understanding of bisexuality within their relationship, there is still the daily decision of whether to come out to others. This decision must be made with the knowledge that he or she would likely face intolerance and discrimination. Such a response is very similar to what gay and lesbian people experience. However, gay and lesbian people often have access to a supportive gay and lesbian community. Bisexual communities are not as readily accessible and visible. It is also true that some heterosexual and some gay and lesbian people alike view bisexual people with suspicion. They may believe that bisexual people are not being honest about their sexual identity, are trying to have the "best of both worlds," or are out to steal their partners. As a result, bisexual individuals may be more "out" or less so about their personal identity, depending upon the company in which they find themselves.

Previous relationship histories can inform and complicate the current relationship for a bisexual person. The divorce rate for first marriages in the United

States is approximately 50 percent. As a society we have become used to dealing with ex-spouses, and there is even some protocol for it. However, the ways in which former same-sex partners relate to one another are less well known. There is some evidence, particularly among lesbians, that ex-partners frequently remain very close friends (Becker, 1988).

In our heterosexist society, it often takes a very tolerant and understanding partner to deal with a bisexual mate. There may be fallout from former partners who not only feel hurt that the relationship ended but also feel betrayed that their former mate has "turned" gay or lesbian or straight. This may be especially true if the issue of bisexuality was never discussed.

At the other end of the spectrum, but equally difficult for some new partners to deal with, is the potential for a continued positive relationship between the members of the former couple. A bisexual person is somewhere in the middle of the sexuality scale, capable of receiving sexual, emotional, and romantic gratification from both men and women. Therefore, maintaining vestiges of former relationships while moving on to a new primary relationship may be the most completely satisfying way of relating to both the old partner and the new one.

Another major issue in bisexual relationships is the threat of HIV/AIDS. Stokes, Taywaditep, Vanable, and McKirnan (1996) found that about a quarter of the men in their study engaged in unprotected intercourse with both men and women, exposing themselves and their partners to risk. A result of the AIDS pandemic has been less promiscuous sex and increased monogamy among the bisexual population (Klein, 1993). However, since some bisexual people do not share their sexual identity with their partners or spouses, the assumption that a partner is monogamous and/or exclusively heterosexual increases the risk for the uninformed partner.

Communication, of course, is key to any successful relationship. There is no real model for a successful bisexual relationship. In order for needs and expectations to be met, they must be clearly and repeatedly delineated and discussed by all involved. Otherwise, great opportunity exists for misunderstanding and disappointment. Relationship counseling can be very helpful in this regard, but it is imperative that social workers be familiar with different sexual orientations and preferences, and nonjudgmental about a variety of relationships.

BISEXUAL FAMILIES

The word *family* is a loaded term for many sexual minority people because a number of gay, lesbian, bisexual, and transgender individuals have been disowned or otherwise "kicked out" by their families when their sexual identity became known. Therefore, in the GLBT community one often talks about one's "family of origin," meaning the family one was born into or grew up in. One might also talk about one's "chosen family," meaning the family that we form as adults (Mallon, 1998). This family of choice may or may not be intergenerational and may include one's partner, former partners, and special friends.

BECOMING A PARENT

It is commonplace to refer to two people in a relationship as a couple. And in heterosexual society, when that couple decides to add a child, it is often referred to as "starting a family." Some childless couples dispute this terminology, arguing that a couple *is* a family. What is a bisexual family? For our purposes, a bisexual family is a family with a bisexual adult member.

When a bisexual person is a parent, family issues come to the forefront. Many bisexual people become parents with opposite-sex partners. For those who are single or are in same-sex partnerships, however, the first question may be, "How do I become a parent?" Bisexual people who are in relationships with a person of the same sex have the same issues as lesbian and gay couples who wish to have children. How does one become a parent? Essentially, the answers are the same for each group. A bisexual woman who is single or partnered with another woman can become pregnant several ways. She (or her partner) might have sex with a man, use alternative insemination techniques, or in cases of infertility, use in vitro fertilization. Minimal involvement of a man is required. Or she could adopt as a single person. In each case the biological mother or the adoptive mother is the legal parent of the child. While most states will allow single people to adopt, and most will even allow bisexual, gay, and lesbian people to adopt, most states will not allow a same-sex couple to adopt a child together. However, a child being parented by two same-sex parents (who has no other legal parent) may be adopted by the nonlegal parent (the one who did not give birth or adopt) in about half of the states in the United States. This is referred to as a second-parent adoption.

Options for bisexual men who are single or who are partnered with other men are more limited. Their opportunities for adoption are similar to those of bisexual women. However, if a man wants to "father" a child, he must rely on a woman. Unless a friend or relative volunteers to carry a child for him, the reproductive technologies available (i.e., surrogacy) can be extraordinarily expensive.

THE OPPOSITE-SEX-HEADED HOUSEHOLD

Once a child is born or adopted, one has a family that looks like either a heterosexual family or a gay or lesbian family. An opposite-sex bisexual family with a child is going to appear for all intents and purposes to be a heterosexual family. That is the family that people expect. That is the family that school and government forms are designed to accommodate. Laws regarding parental rights, child support, and inheritance encourage that model of family. Therefore, it might be that the primary problem such a family has to deal with is invisibility.

If one or both parents are bisexual and want to claim that as an important part of their identities, then the issue may well be recognition. It will not be hard for this family to be included in the heterosexual community. But if the family wishes to become involved with the GLBT community, it will probably have to make a concerted effort and may have to assert the right to be included; otherwise its invisibility makes it easily ignored or overlooked. In recent years many organizations that once described themselves only as gay and/or lesbian have added *bisexual* and *transgender* to their names. Other organizations have gone with the more generic, all-encompassing term *queer*. Even though these organizations have changed their names, however, some have been slow to actually reach out to bisexual and transgender people. Nor have they necessarily made changes within their organizations to be more accommodating to the issues that these additional groups may bring to the table.

THE SAME-SEX-HEADED HOUSEHOLD

Bisexual families with same-sex partners as parents often present as lesbian-headed or gay-headed households. The issues for these families will be more complex, as there are many in society who do not believe that gay and lesbian people should be parents. As discussed earlier in this book, the social policies of the United States are not designed for same-sex families. In some states a couple who have been together since before their child's conception, who planned to have a family together, and who both contribute to the parenting and fiscal support of the family may not both be allowed to be legal parents of the child. Few states allow a same-sex couple to adopt a child. Three states—Florida, Utah, and Mississippi—specifically prohibit gay and lesbian couples and/or individuals from adopting, and only about half of all states have permitted second-parent adoptions[2] (Human Rights Campaign Foundation, 2002; McClellan, 1997).

Though children today live in a multitude of family structures, most schools are unprepared for the two-mother or two-father household. The school's pre-printed forms often do not accommodate the reality of the child's family. The school personnel are neither educated about GLBT people nor do they protect children from the constant barrage of gay slurs that are part of most schoolyard conversation.

As a result, bisexual parents and other parents in same-sex relationships must make special efforts to ensure the safety and security of their children. They must execute legal documents—guardianships, wills, and parenting agreements—that protect their children's rights and their rights as parents. They must go to the schools, speak to the teachers and administrators, educate them about their family and families like theirs. They must be vigilant on behalf of their children. And then, at some point around middle school, many parents find that they must step back and allow their child to be the one to choose how "out" to be about his or her family. This too can be a difficult experience for parents as the child tries to fit in with his or her peers and avoid appearing to be different in some way.

EFFECT ON THE CHILDREN

At some point when sexuality is being discussed, the "out" parent may want to explain his or her sexual identity to the child. This will probably happen sooner in a same-sex-headed household, because the child will be aware at a younger age that the family is different. Children reared in GLBT households are more likely to have accepting attitudes toward people with a sexual minority status and are more likely to consider their own sexual orientation rather than just assume that they are heterosexual (O'Connell, 1999; Tasker & Golombok, 1997).

Historically, a number of concerns have been expressed regarding children reared by same-sex parents. Recent research has addressed such topics as the child's being raised to be homosexual (Bailey, Bobrow, Wolfe, & Mikachi, 1995; Patterson, 1992), the child's being sexually abused by the parents (Bigner, 1996; Patterson, 1992), or the child's suffering from gender confusion (Gottman, 1990; Johnson & O'Connor, 2001; Patterson, 1992, 1994). However, the rather definitive body of work regarding children raised in gay- and lesbian-headed families indicates that these concerns are unfounded (Appleby & Anastas, 1998; Falk, 1993; Green & Bozett, 1991; Patterson, 1995; Turner, Scadden, & Harris, 1990). Children reared in heterosexual-headed households and those reared in gay/lesbian-headed households show few, if any, significant developmental differences. There has been little research focused on children raised by bisexual parents (Appleby & Anastas, 1998). One might assume that since there are few significant developmental differences between children raised by heterosexual parents and those raised by gay/lesbian parents, the same would be true for children raised by bisexual parents, but as yet there is no empirical evidence to confirm that assumption.

SEPARATION AND DIVORCE

A significant number of couples separate and divorce whether they are legally married or not, whether they are heterosexual couples, bisexual couples, gay couples, or lesbian couples. When children are involved, the breakup often has long-term repercussions. Child custody may be the primary issue in a bisexual family with opposite-sex parents. This is particularly true if the bisexual parent subsequently becomes involved in a same-sex relationship. Many judges exhibit prejudice in such situations. Often the heterosexual parent will be assumed to be the best custodial parent for a child simply because he or she is heterosexual. The fear of losing custody of one's children has kept many bisexual, gay, and lesbian parents in abusive or otherwise unhappy marriages.

Fortunately, case law is changing, and the courts have made some favorable decisions for bisexual, lesbian, and gay parents in recent years. Some judges have stated in their opinions that homosexuality of the parent was inconsequential in determining the best interests of the child. In a few jurisdictions gay and lesbian couples are being permitted to adopt children as a couple instead of one member of the couple adopting as an individual. In April 2000 the New Jersey Supreme Court ruled that the former partner of a lesbian mother was entitled to visitation with the twins she had co-parented since their birth (Johnson & O'Connor, 2001). Another significant sign of change is that second-parent adoptions have been granted in about half of the states in the United States, as well as in Canada and England (Arnup, 1997; McClellan, 1997).

Children of divorce with opposite-sex parents face additional issues when one parent becomes involved in a same-sex relationship. Children are socialized to heterosexism at an early age. In addition to the usual trauma of divorce, the child in such a situation must reconcile the image of the parent with the very negative image of gay, lesbian, or bisexual people. Young children adapt to this change more easily than older, latency-age children do. It may take considerable time for an older child to understand and accept this new view of his or her parent.

When a bisexual relationship of same-sex parents ends, child custody may again become the primary concern. In this case it is likely that only one of the parents is the legal parent of the child. Or perhaps, if there are multiple children, each adult is the legal parent of different children. In any case, there may be significant fear of losing involvement with the children. When a legal, heterosexual parent loses custody of a child, he or she normally has significant visitation rights. However, when a nonlegal parent of a child separates from the child's legal parent, there is usually no legal right to maintain contact with that child. On the other hand, a legal parent who has been raising a child with a nonlegal parent and has been dependent on that person for a home and financial support may find himself or herself in significant financial distress as a single parent. Just as the nonlegal parent has no parental rights, in the absence of a parenting agreement the nonlegal parent often has no legal obligation to provide support.

Not all separations between bisexual parents and their partners result in child custody disputes. The majority of opposite-sex and same-sex parents who separate come to a mutual understanding and agreement regarding the welfare of their children (Becker, 1988). Parenting books for same-sex parents discourage separating couples from taking their custody cases to court, since the authors recognize that the courts are not designed to deal with such families (Clunis & Green, 1995). And yet many couples find it difficult to be objective and fair at this juncture in their relationship. Social workers acting as mediators in these circumstances can help couples understand the needs of their children so they may put their children's welfare first.

SOCIAL SUPPORTS

Social support for a bisexual individual, relationship, or family may be difficult to obtain. As previously discussed, the presumed dichotomy of sexual orientations leads to the invisibility of bisexual people. Just as a person who has any percentage of African or African American heritage is defined in American society as black, any person who has engaged in sex with a person of the same sex is defined by many as gay or lesbian, not bisexual. All of one's heterosexual contacts can be negated by one same-sex encounter. Certain behavior may be overlooked. A single youthful experience may be considered experimentation, or homosexual contacts resulting from long-term deprivation of opposite-sex companionship may be considered situational and acceptable. Once again, however, that person is not assumed to be bisexual; rather he or she continues to be labeled "heterosexual."

The reaction of the heterosexual majority to the person who identifies as bisexual is a reaction to perceived deviance. By withholding love, group membership, and societal approval, the group subscribes to a goal to get the individual to claim a more acceptable identity. Bisexual people, often described as "fence-sitters" who can't make up their minds, are told they do not exist. They are often viewed as heterosexuals who are dallying with forbidden sexual practices or as gays or lesbians who are trying to pass as heterosexual and avoid the negative repercussions of their true identity.

Interestingly, the gay and lesbian community reacts similarly to the person who identifies as bisexual (Ault, 1996; Weinburg, Williams, & Pryor, 1994). If the bisexual person was formerly in a same-sex relationship and is now dating an opposite-sex person, he or she may experience a withdrawal of approval, ostracism, and ridicule by gay and lesbian friends. This reaction dumbfounds many bisexual people who expected the gay and lesbian community, which has experienced so much intolerance itself, to be more accepting of sexual difference.

There may be a number of reasons for this negative reaction, in both the micro and the macro spheres. At the micro, or more personal, level, some gay and lesbian individuals may perceive their friends as abandoning them and choosing an easier, more socially acceptable life. Others might be frightened that this could happen in their own relationships, that a same-sex partner might leave for an opposite-sex relationship.

At the macro, or community level, bisexual people pose a challenge to various political positions articulated in the gay and lesbian community (Rust, 1995). In recent years the gay and lesbian community has been successful in gaining many civil rights victories. That effort has required the support of both liberal and conservative policymakers. In order to gain social understanding and acceptance of the reality of homosexuality, the gay and lesbian community has placed much emphasis on the fact that a number of people are "born gay," that sexual orientation is an immutable trait and should not therefore be cause for discrimination. Those who do not agree with homosexual sexual expression contend that homosexuality is not immutable but is a choice. They suggest conversion therapy to cure gay and lesbian people of their homosexual tendencies. Though no credible evidence exists that these programs are legitimate or successful (Appleby & Anastas, 1998), the unacknowledged existence of bisexual people, who are sexually oriented to both men and women, can unwittingly support the conservative position that homosexuality is a choice. The inclusion of bisexual people in the category "gay and lesbian" renders them invisible and allows civil rights to be denied to all on the basis that there should be no "special rights" for "immoral behavior." Lorri Jean, the executive director of the National Gay and Lesbian Task Force (NGLTF), agrees that it is not bisexuality that hurts the cause of the gay and lesbian community but the invisibility of bisexual people.

> The community is afraid that they will use the example of the bisexual as proof that people can be converted. To me, that is a perfect example of where the invisibility of bisexuality hurts us because as long as we act as if the only legitimate sexual orientations are homosexual or heterosexual, it leaves us wide open to those kind of challenges when people change the gender of their partners.
>
> (PENN, 2001, P. 48)

Though the bisexual person may have difficulty in finding social support from both the heterosexual and the gay and lesbian communities, increasing social support is in fact available. Support groups, either social or therapeutic, are important resources (Hayes, 2001), and support groups for bisexual people exist in many of the major metropolitan areas around the country.

Additionally, any bisexual person with Internet access is only moments away from bisexual-oriented chat rooms and list discussions. Ochs (1999b) recommends three Web sites as a starting point: www.biresource.org, www.bi.org, and www.bisexual.org. Firestein (1996) recommends Ochs's *Bisexual Resource Guide* (1999b), which is updated every few years, as the most complete listing of national and international groups and resources. The resource guide may be obtained through the biresource Web site above. In addition to Internet sources, bisexual people seeking community can seek out local GLBT resource centers or hotlines.

Even though the gay and lesbian community is not always welcoming to bisexual people, that is changing in some places. In an effort to live up to their more inclusive names, some organizations are adding support and social groups for bisexuals to their offerings. If such resources are not yet available, bisexual clients might be encouraged to call the organizations and request services. A telephone call from an interested person could be the catalyst needed to get something started.

GUIDELINES FOR PRACTICE

The role of broker is important to the social work profession. Describing a broker as a "social worker who links client systems with existing resources," Kirst-Ashman and Hull (1997) further state: "It is also the social work profession's responsibility to work to ensure that those resources treat client systems in a humane and effective way" (p. 22).

In order to provide useful services to bisexual people and their families, service providers need to be educated about bisexuality and issues related to it. Social workers work in a variety of settings. Not only can they broker relationships between clients and service providers, but knowledgeable social workers can also assist in assuring that the service providers are as effective as possible with GLBT clients.

HEALTH CARE

Many social workers are employed in health care settings, where they might be influential in facilitating change. Health care professionals should not assume that everyone is heterosexual. Patient information forms should allow adequate room and prompts for patients to provide all information that would be truly helpful to the patient's health care provider.

In addition to not assuming that a person is heterosexual, one should not assume that married and committed people are monogamous. Health care professionals should educate all of their patients about the risk of HIV/AIDS and safe-sex practices. Then those who personally need the information will have it, and those who do not need it will be informed and can pass it along to others.

In addition to asking patients for the name of their next of kin, providers should ask them whom they would like to make medical decisions for them if they become unable to make them for themselves. Health care professionals should have forms available for medical power of attorney, so that they can provide them to patients who may not have made arrangements for their person of choice to make medical decisions for them.

Pediatric offices should not make assumptions about a child's parents. When a new patient comes in for a first visit, forms and prompts should be provided so that the true nature of the child's family can be presented. This information should be received nonjudgmentally. When two parents are present, the health care provider should make every effort to address his or her remarks and questions to both parents rather than exclusively to the one who may have the legal relationship with the child.

CHILD WELFARE

Social workers work with children in many settings: child welfare agencies, Head Start, residential treatment facilities, mental health centers, and so on. They also work with others who provide services to children. The opportunities for collaboration and education are great. For instance, people who run child care facilities are certainly aware that there are many kinds of families. The children served at any given facility may include children raised in two-parent families with both biological parents, in two-parent stepfamilies, in single-parent families, or by their grandparents. Children may be living in foster care or in adoptive families. Despite the wide variety of families they encounter, many child care workers may have never considered that a child may be from a bisexual-, gay-, or lesbian-headed household. Social workers in these settings can help them to broaden their view.

Young children do not understand or need to know specific sexual information. Such information should be shared when it is age appropriate. However, young children do understand the concept of family. The best way for those working with children to meet the needs of bisexual families is to make sure that they are inclusive of all family types in their play and in their projects. There are a number of books on the market for young children that describe a wide variety of families. These are ideal for storytime. They ensure that any child can find a family that resembles his or hers in the story.

If art projects require that a child draw his or her family, then the worker should not cast doubt on anyone the child includes in the picture. If gifts are being made for Mother's Day or Father's Day, the child or the parent should be asked how many gifts are needed. One should assume neither that there is only one mother and one father in the family nor that there is both a mother and a father in the family.

Finally, workers should make sure that they leave ample opportunity for the family picture to be made clear. Forms should be open-ended and provide enough spaces for all the people who might be in parenting roles. When these small adjustments are made, both the children and the parents will feel welcome and included.

SCHOOLS

The issues for school personnel are similar to those already expressed, with the goal being welcoming and including all children no matter what kind of family they may come from. Once again, the teacher or the school social worker should make an effort to see that each child is able to see himself or herself in the families that are presented in language arts. When gifts are made at school for family members, each child should have the opportunity to make enough for all the people who should be included.

One challenge in schools today is hate speech. The favorite slurs on the playground are normally anti-gay. While one cannot always control what a child says or hears, school personnel should make a strong statement about hate speech in the classrooms, halls, and on the grounds of the school. When remarks are overheard, adults should comment on them and let those present know that they are unacceptable. Many times young children make and repeat these anti-gay remarks without even knowing what they mean, but the child from the sexual minority household who hears them often does know what they mean, and he or she may apply the remark to his or her own family members.

Finally, the school administration should be sensitive to the forms used, ensuring that they are inclusive of all types of families. It is important for the schools to work hand in hand with families to achieve their educational purpose. If they do not know who the family members really are, it is not possible to achieve their goals.

CLINICAL PRACTICE

In order to work effectively with a bisexual client, a social worker must first look inward, examining personal attitudes and prejudices that may inhibit a therapeutic relationship (Smiley, 1997; Wolf, 1992). Second, the social worker must be careful to place the client's sexual identity in proper perspective (Horowitz & Newcomb, 1999), neither ignoring the issue nor acting as though everything is related to it. An axiom of social work is "start where the client is." An effective clinician must listen carefully to the presenting problem, which may be more or less related to sexual identity issues.

To start where the bisexual client "is," social workers must apprise themselves of the issues that bisexuals face in our society today. While this book is a good starting point, a thorough education would involve seeking out some of the many sources listed in the reference section at the end of each chapter. Visiting one's local gay, lesbian, bisexual, and transgender community center would also be very useful, as it would inform the worker of local resources and issues. While many communities may not have an actual physical GLBT center, the nearest city will often have a hotline to call for local information.

In order to effectively serve this special population, social workers need to educate themselves about bisexual people, gather information about available resources, and maintain an open, nonjudgmental attitude. Once a social worker understands the challenge of bridging the gap between the gay and heterosexual communities, he or she can work with the client on developing the necessary social supports.

Because confusion regarding sexual orientation can be an ongoing issue for the client, the clinician must be careful to provide the information and space necessary for the client to explore the labels that make the most inherent sense for his or her life. While it is not necessary that everyone label himself or herself, that is often the issue that prompts a client to seek help. Matteson (1996) states that the most useful intervention might be simple acknowledgment by the clinician that some people are attracted to both men and women. Bisexual people can experience biphobia or homophobia in the same way that heterosexual people can. Acceptance on the part of the clinician will go a long way toward allowing the client to truly identify his or her own path. On the basis of their study of bisexual men, Stokes, Damon, and McKirnan (1997) suggest that the clinician should "adopt a flexible bisexual schema that allows for myriad variations in identification, behavior, and self-acceptance" (p. 12).

As stated earlier in this chapter, questions of monogamy versus nonmonogamy in bisexual relationships require clear communication and understanding on the part of each participant in the relationship. The clinician can serve an important function as an objective listener and mediator for these discussions, helping those involved reach clarity and agreement. Smiley (1997) suggests that in addition to couple counseling, group therapy can be an effective method to help the spouses of bisexual persons.

POLICY PRACTICE

The role of the social worker is never fulfilled until advocacy and policy practice have been addressed. Certainly there is plenty of opportunity for advocacy and policy practice with this population. Informed social work practitioners can advocate for bisexual people by helping them to be visible. Social workers are employed in all kinds of settings: health care institutions, schools, mental health facilities, corrections, homes for the elderly, industry, higher education, and so on. In each of these environments bisexual people are largely invisible and are left out of discussions that might be pertinent to their lives. By making sure that bisexuality is included when issues of sexuality are discussed, the social worker can be a very effective advocate.

In the policy arena, the social worker can work toward social policies that acknowledge a variety of family forms and offer the rewards of our society to all, not just to a select few. Issues such as same-sex marriage; nondiscrimination in employment, housing, and public accommodations; and gay and lesbian adoption are on the agenda of almost every legislature in the country. These issues need support. Social workers who are educated about GLBT issues can fulfill their ethical obligations (NASW, 1999) to engage in policy practice by offering expert testimony, writing letters to newspaper editors and elected officials, and otherwise supporting efforts to make sure that bisexual, gay, lesbian, and transgender people can enjoy the same rights and privileges as others in our society.

CONCLUSION

Bisexual men and women face some unique challenges that can be well served by the social work profession. They are not significantly different from other people. Bisexual people wrestle with many of the same concerns as anyone else. They also confront some special concerns, as discussed earlier in this chapter. Sometimes the most difficult issues that they, like other sexual minority individuals, face come not from within themselves but from without—from the misunderstanding and injustice in society. Social workers, who are uniquely trained to work at the micro, mezzo, and macro levels of an issue, can be tremendously effective with the bisexual client.

NOTES

1. *Monogamous* is used in this chapter to denote a commitment to one partner and sexual exclusivity with that one partner.
2. States where second-parent adoption is permitted statewide include: CT, IL, MA, NJ, NY, and VT, as well as the District of Columbia. States where second-parent adoptions have been granted in only some counties include: AL, AK, CA, CO, DE, HI, IN, IA, LA, MD, MI, MN, NV, NH, NM, OH, OR, RI, TX, and WA (Human Rights Campaign Foundation, 2002). This information changes quickly. For the most current information, please refer to the Human Rights Campaign Web site (www.hrc.org) and follow the links to Families.

REFERENCES

Appleby, G., & Anastas, J. (1998). *Not just a passing phase: Social work with gay, lesbian, and bisexual people.* New York: Columbia University Press.

Arnup, K. (Ed.). (1997). *Lesbian parenting: Living with pride and prejudice.* Charlottetown, P.E.I., Canada: Gynergy Books.

Ault, A. (1996). Ambiguous identity in an unambiguous sex/gender structure: The case of bisexual women. *Sociological Quarterly, 37*(3), 449–463.

Bailey, J. M., Bobrow, D., Wolfe, M., & Mikachi, S. (1995). Sexual orientation of adult sons of gay fathers. *Developmental Psychology, 31*(1), 124–129.

Becker, C. (1988). *Unbroken ties: Lesbian ex-lovers.* Boston: Alyson.

Bigner, J. J. (1996). Working with gay fathers: Developmental, postdivorce parenting, and therapeutic issues. In J. Laird & R. J. Green (Eds.), *Lesbians and gays in couples and families: A handbook for therapists* (pp. 370–403). San Francisco: Jossey-Bass.

Buunk, B., & van Driel, B. (1989). *Variant lifestyles and relationships.* Newbury Park, CA: Sage.

Clunis, M., & Green, D. (1995). *The lesbian parenting book: A guide to creating families and raising children.* Seattle: Seal Press.

Falk, P. J. (1993). Lesbian mothers: Psychological assumptions in family law. In L. D. Garnets & D. C. Kimmel (Eds.), *Psychological perspectives on lesbian and gay male experiences* (pp. 420–436). New York: Columbia University Press.

Firestein, B. (Ed.). (1996). *Bisexuality: The psychology and politics of an invisible minority*. Thousand Oaks, CA: Sage.

Fox, R. (1995). Bisexual identities. In A. D'Augelli & C. Patterson (Eds.), *Lesbian, gay, and bisexual identities over the lifespan: Psychological perspectives* (pp. 48–86). New York: Oxford University Press.

———. (1996). Bisexuality in perspective: A review of theory and research. In B. Firestein (Ed.), *Bisexuality: The psychology and politics of an invisible minority* (pp. 3–50). Thousand Oaks, CA: Sage.

Geller, T. (Ed.). (1990). *Bisexuality: A reader and sourcebook*. Ojai, CA: Times Change Press.

Gottman, J. S. (1990). Children of gay and lesbian parents. *Marriage and Family Review*, 13(3–4), 177–196.

Green, G. D., & Bozett, F. W. (1991). Lesbian mothers and gay fathers. In J. Gonsiorek & J. Weinrich (Eds.), *Homosexuality: Research implications for public policy* (pp. 197–214). Newbury Park, CA: Sage.

Hayes, B. G. (2001). Working with the bisexual client: How far have we progressed? *Journal of Humanistic Counseling, Education, and Development*, 40(1), 11–21.

Horowitz, J. L., & Newcomb, M. D. (1999). Bisexuality, no homosexuality: Counseling issues and treatment approaches. *Journal of College Counseling*, 2(2), 148–164.

Human Rights Campaign Foundation. (2002).*The state of the family: Laws and legislation affecting gay, lesbian, bisexual, and transgender families*. Washington, DC: Human Rights Campaign Foundation.

Hutchins, L. (1996). Bisexuality: Politics and community. In B. Firestein (Ed.), *Bisexuality: The psychology and politics of an invisible minority* (pp. 240–259). Thousand Oaks, CA: Sage.

Hutchins, L., & Kaahumanu, L. (1991). *Bi any other name: Bisexual people speak out*. Boston: Alyson.

Jeffreys, S. (1999). Bisexual politics: A superior form of feminism? *Women's Studies International Forum*, 22(3), 273–286.

Johnson, S., & O'Connor, E. (2001). *For lesbian parents: Your guide to helping your family grow up happy, healthy, and proud*. New York: Guilford.

Kinsey, A., Pomeroy, W., & Martin, C. (1948). *Sexual behavior in the human male*. Philadelphia: W. B. Saunders.

Kinsey, A., Pomeroy, W., Martin, C., & Gebhard, P. (1953). *Sexual behavior in the human female*. Philadelphia: W. B. Saunders.

Kirst-Ashman, K., & Hull, G. (1997). *Generalist practice with organizations and communities*. Chicago: Nelson-Hall.

Klein, F. (1993). *The bisexual option*. Binghamton, NY: Harrington Park.

Mallon, G. (Ed.). (1998). *Foundations of social work practice with lesbian and gay persons*. Binghamton, N.Y.: Haworth.

Matteson, D. R. (1996). Counseling and psychotherapy with bisexual and exploring clients. In Firestein, B. (Ed.), *Bisexuality: The psychology and politics of an invisible minority* (pp. 185–213). Thousand Oaks, CA: Sage.

McClellan, D. (1997). *Second parent adoption in lesbian families: Legalizing the reality of the child*. Doctoral dissertation, Brandeis University, Waltham, MA (UMI No. 9733746).

Mead, M. (1975, January). Bisexuality: What's it all about? *Redbook*, 29–31.

National Association of Social Workers (NASW). (1999). *Code of ethics*. Washington, D.C.: NASW Press.

Ochs, R. (1999a). Resources for bisexual women. In K. Orndorff (Ed.), *Bi lives: Bisexual women tell their stories* (pp. 248–251). Tucson, AZ: See Sharp Press.

——(Ed.). (1999b). *Bisexual resource guide 2000*. Cambridge, MA: Bisexual Resource Center.

O'Connell, A. (1999). Voices from the heart: The developmental impact of a mother's lesbianism on her adolescent children. In J. Laird (Ed.), *Lesbians and lesbian families: Reflections on theory and practice* (pp. 261–280). New York: Columbia University Press.

Orndorff, K. (Ed.). (1999). *Bi lives: Bisexual women tell their stories*. Tucson, AZ: See Sharp Press.

Patterson, C. (1992). Children of lesbian and gay parents. *Child Development, 63*, 1025–1042.

——. (1994). Children of the lesbian baby boom: Behavioral adjustment, self-concepts, and sex role identity. In Greene & Herek (Eds.), *Lesbian and gay psychology* (pp. 156–175). Thousand Oaks, CA: Sage.

——. (1995). Lesbian mothers, gay fathers, and their children. In A. D'Augelli and C. Patterson (Eds.), *Lesbian, gay, and bisexual identities over the lifespan* (pp. 262–290). New York: Oxford University Press.

Patterson, C., & D'Augelli, A. (Eds.). (1998). *Lesbian, gay, and bisexual identities in families: Psychological perspectives*. New York: Oxford University Press.

Penn, D. (2001). Bisexual visibility. *Lesbian News, 27*(3), 48.

Rose, S., Stevens, C., Parr, Z., Gollain, F., Behr, A., Lano, K., et al. (Eds.). (1996). *Bisexual horizons: Politics, histories, lives*. London: Lawrence and Wishart.

Rust, P. (1995). *Bisexuality and the challenge to lesbian politics: Sex, loyalty, and revolution*. New York: NYU Press.

——. (1996). Monogamy and polyamory: Relationship issues for bisexuals. In B. Firestein (Ed.), *Bisexuality: The psychology and politics of an invisible minority* (pp. 127–148). Thousand Oaks, CA: Sage.

Smiley, E. B. (1997). Counseling bisexual clients. *Journal of Mental Health Counseling, 19*(4), 373–382.

Stokes, J. P., Damon, W., & McKirnan, D. J. (1997). Predictors of movement toward homosexuality: A longitudinal study of bisexual men [Electronic version]. *Journal of Sex Research, 34*(3), 1–15.

Stokes, J. P., Taywaditep, K., Vanable, P., & McKirnan, D. J. (1996). Bisexual men, sexual behavior, and HIV/AIDS. In Firestein, B. (Ed.), *Bisexuality: The psychology and politics of an invisible minority* (pp. 149–168). Thousand Oaks, CA: Sage.

Tasker, F. L., & Golombok, S. (1997). *Growing up in a lesbian family: Effects on child development*. New York: Guilford.

Turner, P. H., Scadden, L., & Harris, M. B. (1990). Parenting in gay and lesbian families. *Journal of Gay and Lesbian Psychotherapy, 1*(3), 55–66.

van Wormer, K, Wells, J., & Boes, M. (2000). *Social work with lesbians, gays, and bisexuals: A strengths perspective*. Needham Heights, MA: Allyn and Bacon.

Weinburg, M. S., Williams, C. J., & Pryor, D. W. (1994). *Dual attraction: Understanding bixexuality*. New York: Oxford University Press.

Wolf, T. J. (1992). Bisexuality: A counseling perspective. In S. H. Dworkin & F. J. Gutierrez (Eds.), *Counseling gay men and lesbians: Journey to the end of the rainbow* (pp. 175–187). Alexandria, VA: American Counseling Association.

12

TRANSGENDER EMERGENCE WITHIN FAMILIES

Arlene Istar Lev

Through the transgression of loving someone who is differently gendered ... it is
possible for someone who does not appear to be a gender outlaw to become one.
—PAT CALIFIA, 1997

GENDER-VARIANT EXPERIENCE is not simply an internal psychological process
that needs to be navigated by transgender and transsexual people; it is also a
relational and systemic dynamic that intimately involves family, friends, loved
ones, and all social relationships. Social workers share with their professional colleagues in other disciplines a long history of negligence regarding advocacy and
clinical treatment of transgender people. However, social work—which professes
to maintain therapeutic focus on the needs of "persons in environment" (Germain & Bloom, 1999)—has been particularly remiss in addressing the emotional
issues faced by families with gender-variant members.

The bulk of contemporary research on gender-variant people has maintained
a pathologizing medical model perspective, ignoring or minimizing the influence of family systems, social environment, and biopyschosocial development.
Family members have been viewed as outside the assessment process, as well as
the clinical treatment process. The Harry Benjamin International Gender Dysphoria Association (HBIGDA) lists "educating family members" as one of the
tasks in its *Standards of Care* for mental health professionals working with transgender people, but little direction is given about how to assist families in moving
through the transition. Indeed, the clinical philosophy of most gender specialists
has been to view family members as extraneous to the process of evaluation and
treatment. The literature offers very little hope that marriage to a gender-variant

---

Some of the material presented in this chapter has been adapted from the 2004 book *Transgender
Emergence: Counseling Gender-Variant People and Their Families* (Binghamton, NY: Haworth).

person could be emotionally fulfilling or that marriages and families can mature through gender transitions.

The perspective of the model presented here is that *gender variance is a normal expression of human diversity* and that much of what gender-variant people experience is caused by societal oppression and is the result of the experience of being stigmatized, both socially and clinically. Gender-variant people are born into families, live in families, and seek support and refuge in families. The acceptance or rejection they experience from their families is a core issue in their ability to integrate their gender identity into their lives in productive and meaningful ways. Supportive systems-based psychotherapy for gender-variant people *and* their families will assist in the development and maintenance of healthy, stable families and consequently will yield greater success for gender-variant members of those families, particularly those engaged in sex reassignment.

Gender-variant people are embedded in a complex matrix of familial and societal relations, and their unique relationship to their sex and gender identities affects family members in numerous ways. Parents struggle to understand the issues facing gender-variant children and youth, and children often need to address the concerns of parents who are facing gender transitions. Spouses of transgender and transsexual people — husbands, wives, partners, and lovers — are often thrown into emotional chaos following the disclosure of a desire to transition; this is as true for gay, lesbian, and bisexual spouses as it is for heterosexuals. Brothers, sisters, aunts, uncles, adult children, and grandparents — all struggle with trying to make sense of and come to terms with transgender identity and/or transsexual sex changes in their loved ones. Families of infants born with an intersex condition are faced with immediate decisions about irreversible surgical procedures with little information to guide them. Until very recently, family members have had to manage these emotional upheavals in their family life cycle with little actual "help" from the helping professions.

RESEARCH ON FAMILY MEMBERS

The social work and marriage and family literature has been mostly silent on issues related to transgenderism within families. A social work/psychology literature search reveals very few articles on transgenderism (Chong, 1990; Cullen, 1997; Gainor, 2000; Oles, 1977; Peo, 1988; Wicks, 1977), and rarely are family issues acknowledged. Within the literature, one exception is Ma's article (1997) describing the use of structural family therapy with transsexuals. This is in some measure surprising, given the careful consideration to issues of gender and ethnicity in the growing fields of lesbian and gay family and lifespan development studies; however, discussion regarding *transgender* family development is still in its infancy.

Research on transgender people has focused on two groups: those who seek transsexual surgery in gender clinics and those who are active in cross-dressing clubs (Bullough, 2000). The treatment of transsexuals by the gender clinics has been critiqued by many transgender activists (Denny, 1996). Those who seek treatment from clinics may not be representative of the broader population of transgender people, in that fewer natal females, people of color, and people without access to medical insurance or money request medical services as a solution to their gender issues.

The one area that has received clinical and research attention is examining the adjustment of wives of cross-dressing males—referred to in the literature as "transvestites"—and, to a lesser extent, the wives of male-to-female (MTF) transsexuals and the partners of gender-variant females. Wives of cross-dressers have been viewed as having numerous psychological problems, including low self-esteem, masochistic behavior, dependency, affective disorders, and borderline personalities (Feinbloom, 1976; Stoller, 1967a; Wise, 1985; Wise, Dupkin, & Meyer, 1981). Other researchers have examined nonclinical samples of wives of cross-dressers (Brown, 1994; Doctor, 1988) and have found fewer psychological problems, but still note high levels of substance abuse, obesity, and what Brown and Collier (1989) note as a high level of "acceptable suffering" that these wives endured. Wise (1985) identifies various coping styles for wives of cross-dressers, including rage and rejection, dysthymia and passivity, extracting punishment, alcoholism, hopes of cure, and acceptance and enjoyment.

It is not surprising that the literature reports that wives of cross-dressers exhibit mental health problems, since historically the cross-dressers themselves were also perceived as having severe mental health problems, although generally transsexuals have been viewed as having more-severe pathologies than cross-dressers (Hartmann, Becker, & Rueffer-Hesse, 1997; Steiner; 1985a; Walinder, Lundström, & Thuwe, 1978). With the exception of Lothstein (1983), however, female-to-male (FTM) transsexuals and their "lesbian" partners have been viewed as lacking any major mental health problems and as maintaining long-term, stable partnerships (Fleming, MacGowan, & Costos, 1985; Kockott & Fahrner, 1987; Pauly, 1974; Steiner, 1985b; Steiner & Bernstein, 1981).

Many other types of gender-variant people have not been as visible to the researchers. Female cross-dressing has historically been deemed nonexistent (Doctor, 1988; Ettner & Brown, 1999; Steiner, 1985a; Stoller, 1982), and all FTMs were assumed to be sexually attracted to females (Blanchard, Clemmensen, & Steiner, 1987; Steiner, 1985b). In recent years extensive writing on female masculinity has attested to the diversity of sexual and gender expression among butch, transgender, and transsexual persons (Cromwell, 1999; Devor, 1989, 1997a, 1997b, 1998; J. Green, 1998; Halberstam, 1998; Rubin, 1992). The existence of FTMs who are gay post-transition is a newly emerging identity within the clinical literature (Blanchard et al., 1987; Clare & Tully, 1989; Coleman & Bockting, 1988; Coleman, Bockting, & Gooren, 1993; Devor, 1998; Dickey & Stephens, 1995; Rosario, 1996). Male cross-dressers were historically all assumed to be heterosexual (Steiner, 1985b), although this too has proved inaccurate (Bullough & Bullough, 1997). Additionally, researchers and clinicians are recognizing that many transgender people are identifying as bigendered, gender-blended, or mixed-gendered, and are seeking not complete sex reassignment but rather the freedom to express gender fluidity, or gender ambiguity, or mixed-gender presentations (Bockting & Coleman, 1992; Cole, Denny, Eyler, & Samons, 2000; Devor, 1989; Ekins & King; 1999; Gagné, Tewksbury, & McGaughey, 1997; McKain, 1996; Sell, 2001).

Research and theory addressing the treatment of children and adolescents experiencing gender-variant behaviors is abundant, and the bulk of it focuses on attempts to "cure" or fix the cross-gender behavior that is believed to be caused, in part, by psychopathological parenting (Coates, 1990; Coates, Friedman, & Wolfe, 1991; Lothstein, 1992; Rekers & Kilgus, 1995; Stoller, 1966, 1967b, 1968b; Zucker, 1990; Zucker & Bradley, 1995). There has been increasing criticism regarding the diagnosing and treatment of children with gender identity disorders (Bartlett & Vesey, 2000; Burke, 1996; Mallon, 1999), and although the parents are believed to be at fault for the child's cross-gender behavior, treatments are directed not at the parents but rather toward the child. Despite the fact that homosexuality is no longer considered a mental illness, the treatment strategies directed at children who are gender-variant have focused on eliminating cross-gender behavior in young children (usually boys) as a way to forestall adult homosexuality and transsexualism. Interestingly, cross-gender behavior in children and adolescents has been linked *not* to adult transgenderism but to homosexuality (Bailey & Zucker, 1995; R. Green, 1987; Zuger, 1984). Therapists sometimes invoke religious and moral reasoning as justification to treat "pre-homosexual" children (Lundy & Rekers, 1995a, 1995b). Green and Schiavi (1995) defend parents' right to insist on these treatments, "even if their only motivation is to prevent homosexuality" (p. 2007). They also state: "There is no convincing data that anything the therapist does can modify the direction of sexual orientation" (p. 2014).

Researchers and clinicians who believe that atypical gender identities are a sign of mental illness want not only to protect children who exhibit cross-gender behavior but also to protect children growing up in homes with transgender parents, in fear that such an environment will cause disturbances in the children's gender identity. In one study, as many as 30% of people seeking services for gender issues were parents (Valentine, 1998). Yet the research in this area is scant. The studies that have been done show that children being raised in homes by a transgender or transsexual parent do not exhibit any mental health problems or gender identity disturbances as a result (Ettner, 2000; R. Green, 1978, 1998). The research on children raised in gay and lesbian homes—families where gender expression may also be less conventional — is far more extensive (Bailey, Bobrow, Wolfe, & Mikach, 1995; Flaks, Ficher, Masterpasqua, & Joseph, 1995; Patterson, 1996) and also does not show any negative effects on the children, although these children may exhibit less rigid gender expressions and a greater sense of openness to dating members of the same sex (Stacey & Biblarz, 2001).

Finally, families of children born with an intersexed condition and adults who partner with intersex people have been ignored in the clinical literature. This is a complex area involving ethical questions about conducting early genital surgery on newborn babies so that they more accurately conform to the standard male or female sex assignment. Proper gender identity development was believed to rest on the appearance of the genitalia, although this is currently being questioned (Diamond & Sigmundson, 1997). Families with intersex members are coping with a diversity of issues, including questions regarding their gender identity and expression, and the effects of shame, betrayal, and stigma. Activists and research-ers are voicing criticism of these early pediatric surgeries (Chase, 1999a, 1999b; Dreger, 1999; Ford, 2001; Kessler, 1998; Kipnis & Diamond, 1998; Schober, 1999; Wilson & Reiner, 1999) and are advocating for changes in treatment protocols, including the halting of infant sex surgeries and the inclusion of trained therapists on the treatment team (Groveman, 2001; ISNA, 1994; Lightfoot-Klein, Chase, Hammon, & Goldman, 2000; Lev, in press; Meyer-Bahlburg, 1994; Schober, 1999; Wilson & Reiner, 1999).

Clearly, family members are affected by gender variance in numerous and profound ways. It is necessary to consider the psychosocial needs of parents, spouses, children, and extended-family members of those who are transgender, transsexual, gender-variant, or intersexed. This family work should not be thought of only as adjunctive to working with gender-variant people but should be part of the training of all therapists, as a potential developmental life cycle issue that all families might face.

FAMILY EMERGENCE

The professional literature on transgenderism is so pathologizing that it is dif-ficult at first to conceive of a model of transsexual or transgender life cycle development that is not embedded in psychopathology. The medical model of treatment has been challenged in recent years, and newer paradigms are being developed (Bockting & Coleman, 1992; Bolin, 1997; Lewins, 1995; Rachlin, 1997; Raj, 2002), including this writer's model of transgender emergence (Lev, 2004). Life cycle development for families is another newly emerging area (Carter & McGoldrick, 1999). A few clinicians have noted that families of transgender peo-ple move through a stage process that is as predictable as the one Kubler-Ross outlined in her work with patients addressing issues of death and dying (Kelley,

FIGURE 12.1 TRANSGENDER EMERGENCE—A DEVELOPMENTAL MODEL

Transgender emergence describes an adaptive stage model for transgender men and women who are coming to terms with their own gender variance and moving from an experience of denial and self-hatred to one of self-respect and gender congruence. The process of developing a gender identity is a normative process that everyone experiences, but for gender-variant people the process is complicated by cultural expectations that are dissonant with their core sense of self. These stages are not meant to "label" people or to define transgender maturity. They describe what clinicians may witness when clients seek help for "gender dysphoria." Many transgender people negotiate these stages without professional assistance.

I. Awareness. In this first stage, gender-variant people are often in great distress; the therapeutic task is the normalization of the experiences involved in emerging transgender.

II. Seeking information—Reaching out. In the second stage, gender-variant people seek to gain education and support about transgenderism; the therapeutic task is to facilitate linkages and encourage outreach.

III. Disclosure to significant others. The third stage involves the disclosure of transgenderism to significant others—spouses, partners, family members, and friends; the therapeutic task involves supporting the transgender person's integration in the family system.

IV. Exploration—Identity and self-labeling. The fourth stage involves the exploration of various (transgender) identities; the therapeutic task is to support the articulation of and comfort with one's gendered identity.

V. Exploration—Transition issues/possible body modification. The fifth stage involves exploring options for transition regarding identity, presentation, and body modification; the therapeutic task is the resolution of the decisions and advocacy toward their manifestation.

VI. Integration—Acceptance and post-transition issues. In the sixth stage the gender-variant person is able to integrate and synthesize (transgender) identity; the therapeutic task is to support the person's adaptation to transition-related issues.

1991; Rosenfeld & Emerson, 1998). Transgender emergence views the process of identity development in transgender people as a normative, healthy process of self-actualization (figure 12.1). The family emergence model (figure 12.2) depicts a developmental process that involves the whole family system.

Family emergence involves a complex interaction of both developmental and interpersonal transactions. As has been noted by most developmental theorists, although developmental stage processes are predictable, they are rarely linear. They often "resemble ... a kaleidoscopic journey in which individuals react and respond independent of one another and in different stages, depending on the circumstances" (Cole et al., 2000, p. 185). The process of family emergence is affected by many variables, including racial, ethnic, and cultural differences,

FIGURE 12.2 FAMILY EMERGENCE STAGES

Stage 1: Discovery and Disclosure   The first stage for most family members involves the discovery and/or disclosure of gender variance in a loved one. They are often shocked by this revelation and experience betrayal and confusion. Even if they are aware of the gender issues, the realization of the importance of these issues can be emotionally devastating.

Stage 2: Turmoil   The second stage for family members is often one of chaos and turmoil. They may become withdrawn or they may become emotionally volatile. It is usually a time of intense stress and conflict within families, who are struggling to accept the reality of gender variance.

Stage 3: Negotiation   The third stage is a time of negotiation for family members. Spouses and partners realize that the gender issues will not vanish and that they need to adjust to them in some manner. Partners and families begin to engage in a process of compromise, determining what they are comfortable living with regarding transition issues and what limits the family can set on the gender expression.

Stage 4: Finding Balance   Balance does not necessarily infer transition; neither does it infer permanent resolution of the gender issues. It means that transgenderism is no longer a secret, that the family is no longer in turmoil, and that they have negotiated the larger issues of transgenderism. The family has learned that there is a difference between secrecy and privacy, and they are now ready to integrate the transgender person—as a transgender person—back into the normative life of the family.

class access to money, age, legal marital status, religious upbringing, and current spiritual identification. Family emergence is an adaptive process, and unlike the developmental experience of gender-variant people, which emerges from an intrinsic need for biopsychosocial authenticity, family members are often unwilling participants on this journey.

STAGE 1: DISCOVERY AND DISCLOSURE

The first stage for family members involves the discovery and disclosure of the gender transgression, which is often met with shock and betrayal. Disclosure can include revealing a history of cross-dressing behavior or the sharing of increasing discomfort regarding cross-gender feelings that have been hidden or minimized. It can also refer to the disclosure that the person has a transsexual history and is now living postoperatively. Discovery can take place accidentally, which may evoke feelings of betrayal, anger, fear, and potentially shame. For heterosexual female spouses, research has shown that disclosure and discovery can raise questions about what other secrets their partner is hiding, how it will affect the children, and how they can protect their family from what others might think. Other questions may arise about the husband's sexual orientation and how this will affect their sexual relationships (Brown, 1994; Doctor, 1988; Weinberg & Bullough, 1988).

The female partners of transmen rarely experience the shock of disclosure the way wives of cross-dressers do; their partners' masculinity is commonly more publicly visible and integrated into their gender expression, since masculinity in females is somewhat more socially acceptable than femininity in males. Yet they too may experience shock and betrayal that their butch partner desires to live as a man, and this can evoke issues similar to those faced by wives of cross-dressing males: desire to protect the children, concerns about sexuality and sexual orientation, and fears about the effect it will have on their social relationships, particularly their acceptance within the lesbian community (see figure 12.2).

Children with a transgender parent might experience concerns about whether gender issues can be inherited and how a parent's gender transition might affect their peer relationships. It is important to remember that young children in particular may not be as "surprised" by gender transitions as adults; after all, they may not yet realize that this is "unusual." Brown and Rounsley (1996) state: "It helps to recognize that children grow up with fairy tales and cartoons in which transformation occurs all the time.... Children accept transformation as normal, everyday fare" (p. 191).

Children who are gender-variant themselves often express their discomfort regarding normative gender roles or express dissonance in their sexed body at remarkably young ages (Mallon, 1999; Wilson, 1998). When they disclose to their parents, or when their parents discover or recognize their atypical gender behavior, it is often a tumultuous time for the family. Parents often believe their children's behavior is their fault, and clinicians have not hesitated to reinforce fears that they are the cause of severe psychopathologies within the family matrix (Coates, 1990; Rekers & Kilgus, 1995; Zucker & Bradley, 1995). Sadly, the discovery and disclosure of gender variance in families is rarely met with compassion and support; more commonly, the response to disclosure is emotionality and turmoil.

STAGE 2. TURMOIL

Although some spouses, partners, children, and parents accept gender variance, and even sexual reassignment, with grace, ease, and support, it is more common for these family members to have initial responses that are intense and emotionally labile. Family members may experience a wide range of symptomatology that is often seen in other survivors of post-traumatic stress (Bass & Davis, 1988; Briere, 1989; Cole, 2000; van der Kolk, McFarlane, & Weisaeth, 1996). Herman (1992) has suggested that trauma survivors experience a "dialectic of trauma" — labile moods that alternate from expressively frozen to intensely dramatic emotionality, as the person relives his or her trauma and then dissociates from it.

Symptomatology in family members can include insomnia, withdrawal, depression, anxiety, suicidality, sexual dysfunction, substance abuse, mood instability, self-mutilation, emotional numbing, weight loss or gain, and work or school difficulties.

Spouses report feelings of betrayal, shame, personal responsibility, blame, revenge, and concern about how to protect their families, while wives of transsexuals have expressed fears of abandonment, disbelief, rage, depression, anxiety, confusion, low self-esteem, sexual difficulties, and physical health problems (Gurvich, 1991). Spouses may react by neglecting their own needs, suppressing their ambivalence and conflicted feelings, or feeling guilty of transgression because they are involved with a transgender person (Califia, 1997; Cole, 1998; Miller, 1996; Roberts, 1995). Therapists would be wise to assess for suicidality, depression, and the level of risk taking and danger in all family members. It is also important to recognize the possibility of domestic violence in families engaged in transition issues and to understand that transgender people may become the target for the family's discontent and turmoil (Blanchard, Steiner, Clemmensen, & Dickey, 1989; Lev & Lev, 1999). Families often reach out for services during this stage, and therapists who are ignorant about transgenderism can increase the level of turmoil in a family by expressing a sense of hopelessness about the family's ability to navigate through the storm.

STAGE 3: NEGOTIATION

The next stage for families is negotiating acceptable boundaries regarding how they will process the gender issues and the resulting impact on their relationships. When a partner discloses a desire for complete sex transition and surgery and is insistent that this must happen quickly, the intensity and turbulence created in the relationship are usually more difficult to overcome. It is sometimes hard for the transgender person to realize that although he or she has always struggled with these issues, it is still a new and complex situation for others to assimilate. Transgender people who are as yet unsure of their goals or who are willing to move slowly through a transition process while their partners emotionally "catch up" are more often able to successfully negotiate their transition while remaining in their intimate relationship.

The process of limit setting and boundary marking is necessary in gender/sex transitions, and it helps in the acceptance of transgenderism within families. Some of the issues that may need to be negotiated in relationships include frequency of cross-dressing or "outings," how to leave or enter the home when dressed, public appearance, disclosure to significant others, how much money can be spent on clothing or medical treatments, revealing the gender issues to the children, health risks of hormone treatments, name-changing and the use of proper pronouns, and sexual accommodation including cross-dressing or cross-gender play in the bedroom. Timing of transition-related issues becomes an important focus during the negotiation stage.

Negotiating gender variance in children and youth is extremely complicated, since young people are often considered unable to fully understand the consequences of their decisions and parents ultimately have the legal power to make decisions for their children. Children often act out their gender issues or learn to repress them, and the parents either insist that the child conform or allow him or her to experiment (Miller, 1996). Sometimes temporary accommodations can be made, such as cross-dressing at home, wearing unisex clothing, changing a name to a more gender-neutral one, or exploring cross-gender identity while on vacation. With older children, parents are faced with more-permanent decisions involving cross-living and medical treatments. Negotiation can involve professionals, school systems, and, in some cases, legal questions of the parent's right to allow children their own gender expression (GenderPAC, 2000). Gender issues can become the focus of power and control between parent and child with the additional influence, and potential intrusion, of public institutions. Transyouth, like LGB youth, are probably more vulnerable to "opting out" of these power struggles by running away, suicidality, substance abuse, self-harm, and self-mutilation, as they attempt to deal with gender dysphoria and body dysmorphia that increases with puberty (see Mallon 1999 and chapters 4 and 8 of this volume).

STAGE 4: FINDING BALANCE

The stage of finding balance does not mean that the gender issues are resolved, nor does it necessarily mean that the transgender person has transitioned. In some cases, it might mean a significant shifting of family roles, relationships, and even dwellings. Not all families "make it" through the process of sex reassignment or gender reassessment intact. However, families can successfully negotiate these processes whether or not marriages survive, which is especially important for children of transgender parents, for the children will need to retain healthy relationships with both parents.

Balance means that transgenderism is no longer a secret, that the family is no longer in turmoil, and that the family has integrated the transgender person—as a transgender person—back into the normative life of the family. Every family comes to its own unique resolution, which may include complete sex reassignment or full-time cross-living, or may involve setting boundaries about cross-dressing. Most important, the transgender person is no longer stigmatized within the family but is accepted for who he or she is and treated with respect and dignity. Conversely, family members are allowed to experience a range of emotions regarding having a transgender family member.

Balance might mean living with private cross-dressing, or it might mean living with a spouse who is transitioning. It may also mean living with the uncertainty of not knowing the trajectory of the transsexual process and learning to live with the "unknown." Sometimes the post-surgical or post-transition stage can be very difficult for a family and may include a kind of "postpartum depression" period; this does not mean that transition is unsuccessful any more than a postpartum depression following a birth infers unsuccessful parenting.

Transgenderism is commonly rooted in lies, secrecy, and family secrets. Keeping secrets, as family therapists have long noted, is an act of self-preservation, a way to manage pain (Imber-Black, 1998; Lerner, 1994). Secrecy has been detrimental to the family life of transgender people. At the balance stage, family members know the difference between secrecy and privacy. Each family will negotiate its own unique balance of revealing information, but members will no longer be sworn to a painful secrecy (even with themselves). Families that are able to move through their betrayal and lost trust regarding gender variance are often able to find contentment and satisfaction in their daily family lives.

HOPE FOR FAMILIES

Therapy has offered little hope for families of transgender people, and many clinicians have viewed family life as an impediment to a successful transition. Developing affirmative social work practices for gender-variant people and their families presumes that families struggling with gender issues can survive and thrive, and practitioners should adopt a strengths-based perspective. Stability of relationships is often used as a criterion to determine post-surgical success (Doctor, 1988; Green & Fleming, 1990; Meyer & Reter, 1979; Pfäefflin & Junge, 1998), and research has shown that partner involvement is related to positive outcome for transition (Blanchard & Steiner, 1983). The literature has particularly noted the longevity and stability of relationships between FTMs and their female partners (Fleming et al., 1985; Huxley, Kenna, & Brandon, 1981a, 1981b; Kockott & Fahrner, 1987; Lothstein, 1983; Pauly, 1974; Steiner, 1985b; Steiner & Bernstein, 1981). Yet little has been written about how to assist families in coping with the stress of gender transition and its impact on marital satisfaction. For that matter, gender clinics have traditionally viewed legal marriage as an obstruction to be resolved before moving ahead with medical treatment (Clemmensen, 1990; Randell, 1971).

Families must be seen as potential support for those who are struggling with gender dysphoria, and marriages and families must be honored and respected. Social workers should assume that marriages and family life can survive gender exploration and transition. Concerns about spousal rejection and fears of losing custody of their children (Lewins, 1995) have forced many gender-variant people to avoid facing their gender issues. Some transsexuals have used heterosexual marriages as a way to hide from or purge these issues (Anderson, 1998).

Relationship commitment, marriage vows, and parenting responsibilities can serve as a boundary marker for some transsexuals. Sometimes having a spouse say, "I can go this far and no farther" can force the transgender person to make a decision about whether or not the relationship will take precedence over the gender issue. Among transgender and transsexual activists, delaying or avoiding a transition process for the sake of maintaining a family has often been viewed in a negative manner. Transition is often regarded as "either/or," and if families do not demonstrate complete support, they are viewed as blocking the self-actualization of the transgender person. This view must be reframed so that families have time to "catch up" and work through their issues before the relationship is deemed unsalvageable. Family members need time to adjust to the changes. They deserve the time to work through difficult and often mind-boggling new conceptions of intimacy, identity, sexuality, and the meaning of gender before deciding on the viability of the relationship. Research has shown that the later in a marriage a woman finds out that her husband is a cross-dresser, the more difficulty she has accepting it (Brown & Collier, 1989; Weinberg & Bullough, 1988). This finding reinforces the need to help gender-dysphoric males to disclose earlier in their relationships; later disclosure just increases the sense of betrayal. Even if a marriage does end, a strengths-based perspective would encourage this process to happen with mutual support and conscious decision making, particularly when children are involved.

On a macro level, transgender and transsexual people have not fared well in custody battles. Transgender people have few legal protections, and in most jurisdictions a transgender person is likely to lose custody of his or her children. Clinicians have cautioned against the severing of parental contact solely on the basis of sex reassignment, but the courts have yet to respond to these concerns (R. Green, 1998). Ettner (2000) identifies the maturity and healthy functioning of the parental relationship as the most salient issue for children who have a parent who is transitioning. Even in very troubled families that are coping with divorce, remarriage, and post-transition difficulties, systemic interventions can assist in the healthy restructuring of family relationships (Sales, 1995). All family members need assistance in processing gender transitions, and Lesser (1999) documents the importance of a nonjudgmental, empathic stance to assist aging parents in accepting transsexual transitions. Support groups can be helpful for family members, serving as spaces where they will meet others who are struggling with similar issues, lessening their sense of uniqueness and isolation.

Families who have children who are gender-variant (intersexed or transgender) will need support and education about their child's medical and emotional needs. This is an area in which social workers can gather resources and serve as advocates. Parents may need assistance in grieving about their assumptions and hopes as to who their child would become, and they will need to develop skills to address extended-family members and school officials. Di Ceglie (1998) outlines treatment aims for working with transgender youth, including fostering recognition and nonjudgmental acceptance of their gender identity; breaking the cycle of secrecy; allowing mourning processes to occur; and enabling the child or adolescent and the family to tolerate uncertainty in the area of gender identity development. Parents need reassurance that their children's gender issues are not their fault. They also need assistance in incorporating their child's needs into the daily flow of family life so that the child does not become the focal point of family "pathology."

In families with gender-variant children, adolescence and puberty bring many decisions regarding the child's future gender identity. The issue of hormonal treatment for gender-variant youths raises ethical questions about adolescents' right to self-determination and their ability to offer informed consent (Swann & Herbert, 1999). Hormonal treatments can be used to temporarily halt puberty, which can "buy time" for the adolescent to mature sufficiently to make informed decisions. Without treatment, puberty will take its course, and sexual development will occur that could seriously affect the person's ability to successfully "pass" as an adult in the chosen gender (Gooren & Delamarre-van de Waal, 1996). Research has shown that with proper psychosocial evaluation and support, these hormonal treatments and early sex reassignments can be effective with the successful transition and adaptation by the youth (Cohen-Kettenis & van Goozen, 1997; Cohen-Kettenis, van Goozen, & Cohen, 1998). On a macro level, medical facilities and gender clinics in the United States need to learn to assess children and youth with gender issues without pathologizing them. Treatment modalities currently consist of a "wait until you grow up" philosophy, leaving young people without support and vulnerable to illegal procurement of hormones (Swann & Herbert, 1999). Educational systems need to become sensitized to the issues that gender-variant children and youth face: macro-level interventions include teacher training on trans issues and the creation of safe environments for children. Gender-variant youth are very sensitive to social environments that separate boys from girls, and they often feel like an outsider, not knowing which group to join.

Clinically, it is difficult to ascertain the meaning behind gender-variant behavior in children and youth, which exacerbates the ethical dilemmas involved in both offering and withholding medical treatments (Gooren & Delamarre-van de Waal, 1996). Gender-variant behavior can be indicative of a number of things, including the societal shifting of traditional social roles. The expression of cross-gender behavior may be transient, part of the child's emergent identity, indicative of future homosexual or bisexual sexual orientation (the most common outcome), or the nascent expression of transgender or transsexual identity. Regardless of the meaning of the behavior, however, parents have a right and an obligation to protect their children from outside harm (which might include bullies in school as well as overzealous psychologists or physicians who want to "fix" them). It is the responsibility of parents to raise children with an intact and secure sense of their own worth, regardless of their gender identity or expression. This can be a heavy burden, requiring therapeutic support, education, and social advocacy to assist the child and the family in their emotional adaptation.

Emerging as a transgender person is a developmental hurdle. For gender-variant people living within the social matrix called family, the entire family is also moving through a transition. Family members of transgender people are navigating difficult terrain. Therapists can have a great deal of influence in helping families survive transition. The most salient issue for therapists to recognize is that families of gender-variant people—those who are lesbian, gay, and bisexual, as well as those who are heterosexual—are in desperate need of advocacy and therapeutic support. Clinicians must recognize that transition can be a normative life cycle issue that families can weather with love and tenderness.

REFERENCES

Anderson, B. (1998). Therapeutic issues in working with transgender clients. In D. Denny (Ed.), *Current concepts in transgender identity* (pp. 215–226). New York: Garland.

Bailey, J. M., Bobrow, D., Wolfe, M., & Mikach, S. (1995). Sexual orientation of adult sons of gay fathers. *Developmental Psychology, 31*, 124–129.

Bailey, J. M., & Zucker, K. J. (1995). Childhood sex-typed behavior and sexual orientation: A conceptual analysis and quantitative review. *Developmental Psychology, 31*(1), 43–55.

Bartlett, N. H., & Vesey, P. L. (2000). Is gender identity disorder in children a mental disorder? *Sex Roles: A Journal of Research*. Retrieved May 13, 2002, from http://www.findarticles.com/cf_0/m2294/2000_Dec/75959827/print.jhtml.

Bass, E., & Davis, L. (1988). *The courage to heal: A guide for women survivors of child sexual abuse*. New York: Harper and Row.

Blanchard, R., Clemmensen, L. H., & Steiner, B. W. (1983). Gender reorientation and psychosocial adjustment in male-to-female transsexuals. *Archives of Sexual Behavior, 12*(6), 503–509.

———. (1987). Heterosexual and homosexual gender dysphoria. *Archives of Sexual Behavior, 16*(2), 139–152.

Blanchard, R., & Steiner, B. W. (1983). Gender reorientation, psychological adjustment, and involvement with female partners in female-to-male transsexuals. *Archives of Sexual Behavior, 12*(2), 149–157.

Blanchard, R., Steiner, B. W., Clemmensen, L. H., & Dickey, R. (1989). Prediction of regrets in postoperative transsexuals. *Canadian Journal of Psychiatry, 34*, 43–45.

Bockting, W. O., & Coleman, E. (1992). A comprehensive approach to the treatment of gender dysphoria. In W. O. Bockting & E. Coleman (Eds.), *Gender dysphoria: Interdisciplinary approaches in clinical management* (pp. 131–155). Binghamton, NY: Haworth.

Bolin, A. (1997). Transforming, tranvestism, and transsexualism: Polarity, politics, and gender. In B. Bullough, V. L. Bullough, & J. Elias (Eds.), *Gender blending* (pp. 25–31). Amherst, NY: Prometheus.

Briere, J. (1989). *Therapy for adults molested as children*. New York: Springer.

Brown, G. R. (1994). Women in relationships with cross-dressing men: A descriptive study from a nonclinical setting. *Archives of Sexual Behavior, 23*(5), 515–530.

——. (1998). Women in the closet: Relationships with transgendered men. In D. Denny (Ed.), *Current concepts in transgender identity* (pp. 353–37). New York: Garland.

Brown, G. R., & Collier, L. (1989). Transvestites' women revisited: A nonpatient sample. *Archives of Sexual Behavior*, 18(1), 73–83.

Brown, M. L., & Rounsley, C. A. (1996). *True selves understand transsexualism: For families, friends, coworkers, and helping professionals*. San Francisco: Jossey-Bass.

Bullough., B., & Bullough, V. (1997). Are transvestites necessarily heterosexual? *Archives of Sexual Behavior*, 26(1), 1–12.

Bullough, V. L. (2000). Transgenderism and the concept of gender. *International Journal of Transgenderism*, 4(3). Retrieved May 13, 2002, from http://www.symposion.com/ijt/gilbert/bullough.htm.

Burke, P. (1996). *Gender shock: Exploding the myths of male and female*. New York: Anchor Books/Doubleday.

Califia, P. (1997). *Sex changes: The politics of transgenderism*. San Francisco: Cleis.

Carter, B., & McGoldrick, M. (Eds.). (1999). *The expanded family life cycle: Individual family and social perspectives* (3d ed.). Boston: Allyn and Bacon.

Chase, C. (1999a). Rethinking treatment for ambiguous genitalia. *Pediatric Nursing*, 25(4), 451–455.

——. (1999b). Surgical progress is not the answer to intersexuality. In A. D. Dreger (Ed.), *Intersex in the age of ethics* (pp. 147–160). Hagerstown, MD: University Publishing Group.

Chong, J. M. L. (1990). Social assessment of transsexuals who apply for sex reassignment therapy. *Social Work in Health Care* 14(3): 87–105.

Clare, D., & Tully, B. (1989). Transhomosexuality, or the dissociation of sexual orientation and sex object choice. *Archives of Sexual Behavior*, 18, 531–536.

Clemmensen, L. H. (1990). The "real-life" test for surgical candidates. In R. Blanchard & B. W. Steiner (Eds.), *Clinical management of gender identity disorders in children and adults* (pp. 121–135). Washington, DC: American Psychiatric Association.

Coates, S. (1990). Ontogenesis of boyhood gender identity disorder. *Journal of the American Academy of Psychoanalysis*, 18(3), 414–438.

Coates, S., Friedman, R. C., & Wolfe, S. (1991). The etiology of boyhood gender identity disorder: A model for integrating temperament, development, and psychodynamics. *Psychoanalytic Dialogues*, 1(4), 481–523.

Cohen-Kettenis, P., & van Goozen, S. (1997). Sex reassignment of adolescent transsexuals: A follow-up study. *Journal of American Academy of Child and Adolescent Psychiatry*, 36(2), 263–271.

Cohen-Kettenis, P., van Goozen, S., & Cohen, L. (1998). Transsexualism during adolescence. In D. Di Ceglie (Ed.), *A stranger in my own body: Atypical gender identity development and mental health* (pp.118–125). London: Karnac.

Cole, S. S. (1998). The female experience of the femme: A transgender challenge. In D. Denny (Ed.), *Current concepts in transgender identity* (pp. 373–390). New York: Garland.

——. (2000). *A transgendered dilemma: The forgotten journey of the partners and families*. Paper presented at the XVI Harry Benjamin International Gender Dysphoria Association Symposium, August 17–21, 1999, London. Abstract at *International Journal of Transgenderism*, 4(1). Retrieved May 13, 2002, from http://www.symposion.com/ijt/greenpresidental/green10.htm.

Cole, S. S., Denny, D., Eyler, A. E., & Samons, S. L. (2000). Issues of transgender. In L. T. Szuchman & F. Muscarella (Eds.), *Psychological perspectives of human sexuality* (pp. 149–195). New York: John Wiley.

Coleman, E., & Bockting, W. (1988). Heterosexual prior to sex reassignment, homosexual afterward: A case study of a female-to-male transsexual. *Journal of Psychology and Human Sexuality, 12,* 69–82.

Coleman, E., Bockting, W., & Gooren, L. (1993). Homosexual and bisexual identity in sex-reassigned female-to-male transsexuals. *Archives of Sexual Behavior, 22,* 37–50.

Cook-Daniels, L. (1998, June). *Trans-positioned.* (First published in *Circles* magazine.) Retrieved May 13, 2002, from http://hometown.aol.com/marcellecd/Transpositioned. html.

Corbett, S. (2001, October 14). When Debbie met Christina, who then became Chris. *New York Times Magazine,* 84–87.

Cromwell, J. (1999). *Transmen and FTMs: Identities, bodies, genders, and sexualities.* Urbana: University of Illinois Press.

Cullen, J. (1997). Transgenderism and social work: An experiential journey. *Social Worker,* 65(3), 46–54.

Denny, D. (1996). In search of the "true" transsexual. *Chrysalis: The Journal of Transgressive Gender Identities,* 2(3), 39–48.

Devor, H. (1989). *Gender blending: Confronting the limits of duality.* Bloomington: Indiana University Press.

——. (1997a). *FTM: Female-to-male transsexuals in society.* Bloomington: Indiana University Press.

——. (1997b). More than manly women: How female-to-male transsexuals reject lesbian identities. In B. Bullough, V. L. Bullough, & J. Elias (Eds.), *Gender blending* (pp. 87–102). Amherst, NY: Prometheus.

——. (1998). Sexual orientation identities, attractions, and practices of female-to-male transsexuals. In D. Denny (Ed.), *Current concepts in transgender identity* (pp. 249–275). New York: Garland.

Diamond, M., & Sigmundson, H. K. (1997). Management of intersexuality: Guidelines for dealing with individuals with ambiguous genitalia. *Archives of Pediatrics and Adolescent Medicine.* Retrieved May 13, 2002, from http://www.afn.org/~sfcommed/apam.htm.

Di Ceglie, D. (1998). Reflections on the nature of the "atypical gender identity organization." In D. Di Ceglie (Ed.), *A stranger in my own body: Atypical gender identity development and mental health* (pp. 9–25). London: Karnac.

Dickey, R., & Stephens, J. (1995). Female to male transsexualism, heterosexual type: Two cases. *Archives of Sexual Behavior,* 24(4), 439–445.

Doctor, R. F. (1988). *Transvestites and transsexuals: Toward a theory of cross-gender behavior.* New York: Plenum.

Dreger, A. D. (Ed.). (1999). *Intersex in the age of ethics.* Hagerstown, MD: University Publishing Group.

Ekins, R., & King, D. (1999). Towards a sociology of transgendered bodies. *Sociological Review,* 47, 580–602.

Ettner, R., & Brown, R. (1999). Gender loving care: A guide to counseling gender-variant clients. New York: Norton.

Ettner, R. I., & White, T. J. H. (2000). *Children of a parent undergoing a gender transition: Disclosure, risk, and protective factors.* Paper presented at the XVI Harry Benjamin International Gender Dysphoria Association Symposium, August 17–21, 1999, London. *International Journal of Transgenderism,* 4(3). Retrieved May 13, 2002, from http://www.symposion.com/ijt/greenpresidental/abstracts.htm.

Feinbloom, D. (1976). *Transvestites and transsexuals.* New York: Dell.

Flaks, D. K., Ficher, I., Masterpasqua, F., & Joseph, G. (1995). Lesbians choosing motherhood: A comparative study of lesbian and heterosexual parents and their children.
Developmental Psychology, 31, 105–114.

Fleming, M., MacGowan, B., & Costos, D. (1985). The dyadic adjustment of female-to-
male transsexuals. *Archives of Sexual Behavior, 14*(1), 47–55.

Ford, K. K. (2001). "First, do no harm": The fiction of legal parental consent to genital-
normalizing surgery on intersexed infants. *Yale Law and Policy Review, 19,* 467–
489.

Gagné, P., Tewksbury, R., & McGaughey, D. (1997). Coming out and crossing over:
Identity formation and proclamation in a transgender community. *Gender and Society,
11*(4), 478–508.

Gainor, K. A. (2000). Including transgender issues in lesbian, gay, and bisexual psychology: Implications for clinical practice and training. In B. Greene and G. L. Croom
(Eds.), *Education, research, and practice in lesbian, gay, bisexual, and transgendered
psychology: A resource manual* (pp.131–160). Thousand Oaks, CA: Sage.

GenderPAC. (2000, August 29). Ohio court removes child from parents because of her
gender. *National News.* Retrieved May 13, 2002, from http://www.gpac.org/archive/
action/?cmd = view&archive = action&msgnum = 0009.

Germain, C. B., & Bloom, M. (1999). *Human behavior in the social environment: An ecological view* (2d ed.). New York: Columbia University Press.

Gooren, L. J. G., & Delemarre-van de Waal, H. (1996). Memo on the feasibility of
endocrine interventions in juvenile transsexuals. *Journal of Psychology and Human
Sexuality, 8*(4), 69–74.

Green, J. (1998). FTM: An emerging voice. In D. Denny (Ed.), *Current concepts in transgender identity* (pp. 145–161). New York: Garland.

Green, R. (1978). Sexual identity of 37 children raised by homosexual or transsexual parents. *American Journal of Psychiatry, 135*(6), 692–697.

——. (1987). *The "sissy boy syndrome" and the development of homosexuality.* New
Haven, CT: Yale University Press.

——. (1998). Transsexuals' children. *International Journal of Transgenderism, 2*(4).
Retrieved May 13, 2002 from http://www.symposion.com/ijt/ijtc0601.htm.

Green, R., & Fleming, D. (1990). Transsexual surgery follow-up: Status in the 1990s
Annual Review of Sex Research, 7, 351–369.

Green, R., & Schiavi, R. C. (1995). Sexual and gender identity disorders. In G. O. Gabbard
(Ed.), *Treatments of psychiatric disorders* (2d ed.) (pp. 1837–2079). Washington, DC:
American Psychiatric Press.

Groveman, S. (2001). Ethics primer for clinical management of intersex. *Kaiser Permanent
Ethics Rounds, 10*(1), 3–5. Retrieved May 13, 2002, from http://www.isna.org/articles/
kaiserethicsrounds.pdf.

Gurvich, S. E. (1991). The transsexual husband: The wife's experience. (Doctoral dissertation, Texas Woman's University, 1991). *Dissertation Abstracts International 52–08A,*
3089–3248.

Halberstam, J. (1998). *Female masculinity.* Durham, NC: Duke University Press.

Hartmann, U., Becker, H., & Rueffer-Hesse, C. (1997). Self and gender: Narcissistic
pathology and personality factors in gender dysphoric patients. Preliminary results of
a prospective study. *International Journal of Transgenderism, 1*(1). Retrieved May 13,
2002, from http://www.symposion.com/ijt/ijtc0103.htm.

Herman, J. L. (1992). *Trauma and recovery: The aftermath of violence—from domestic
abuse to political terror.* New York: Basic Books.

Huxley, P. J., Kenna, J. C., & Brandon, S. (1981a). Partnership in transsexualism: Part I— Pair and non-paired groups. *Archives of Sexual Behavior, 10*(2), 133–141.

———. (1981b). Partnership in transsexualism: Part II—The nature of the partnership. *Archives of Sexual Behavior, 10*(2), 143–160.

Imber-Black, E. (1998). *The secret life of families: Truth-telling, privacy, and reconciliation in a tell-all society*. New York: Bantam.

Intersex Society of North America (ISNA). (1994). *Recommendations for treatment of intersex infants and children.* Retrieved May 13, 2002, from http://www.isna.org/recommendations.html.

Israel, G. E., & Tarver, D. E. (1997). *Transgender care: Recommended guidelines, practical information, and personal accounts.* Philadelphia: Temple University Press.

Kelley, T. (1991). Stages of resolution with spouses. In J. Dixon & D. Dixon (Eds.), *Wives, partners, and others* (pp.126–133). Waltham, MA: International Foundation for Gender Education.

Kessler, S. J. (1998). *Lessons from the intersexed.* New Brunswick, NJ: Rutgers University Press.

Kipnis, K., & Diamond, M. (1998). Pediatric ethics and the surgical assignment of sex. *Journal of Clinical Ethics, 9*(4), 398–410.

Kockott, G., & Fahrner, E-M. (1987). Transsexuals who have not undergone surgery: Follow-up study. *Archives of Sexual Behavior, 16*(6), 511–522.

Lerner, H. (1994). *The dance of deception: Pretending and truth-telling in women's lives.* New York: HarperCollins.

Lesser, J. G. (1999). When your son becomes your daughter: A mother's adjustment to a transgender child. *Families in Society: The Journal of Contemporary Human Services, 80*(2), 182–190.

Lev, A. I. (2004). *Transgender emergence: Therapeutic guidelines for working with gender-variant people and their families.* (Haworth Marriage and the Family.) Binghamton, NY: Haworth.

———. (In press, 2006). Intersexuality in the family: An unacknowledged trauma. *Journal of Gay and Lesbian Psychotherapy, 10*(1). Ed. Vernon A. Rosario & Jack Drescher.

Lev, A. I., & Lev, S. S. (1999). Sexual assault in the lesbian, gay, bisexual, and transgendered communities. In Joan C. McClennen and J. Gunther (Eds.), *A professional guide to understanding gay and lesbian domestic violence: Understanding practice interventions* (pp. 35–62). Lewiston, NY: Edwin Mellen.

Lewins, F. (1995). *Transsexualism in society: A sociology of male-to-female transsexuals.* South Melbourne: Macmillan Education Australia.

Lightfoot-Klein, H., Chase, C., Hammon, T., & Goldman, R. (2000). Genital surgery on children below the age of consent. In L. T. Szuchman & F. Muscarella (Eds.), *Psychological perspectives of human sexuality* (pp. 440–479). New York: John Wiley.

Lothstein, L. (1983). *Female to male transsexualism: Historical, clinical, and theoretical issues.* Boston: Routledge and Kegan Paul.

———. (1992). Clinical management of gender dysphoria in young boys: Genital mutilation and *DSM-IV* implications. In W. O. Bockting & E. Coleman (Eds.), *Gender dysphoria: Interdisciplinary approaches in clinical management* (pp. 87–106). Binghamton, NY: Haworth.

Lundy, M. S., & Rekers, G. A. (1995a). Homosexuality: Development, risks, parental values, and controversies. In G. A. Rekers (Ed.), *Handbook of child and adolescent sexual problems* (pp. 290–312). New York: Lexington Books.

——. (1995b). Homosexuality: Presentation, evaluation, and clinical decision making. In G. A. Rekers (Ed.), *Handbook of child and adolescent sexual problems* (pp. 313–340). New York: Lexington Books.

Ma, J. L. C. (1997) A systems approach to the social difficulties of transsexuals in Hong Kong. *Journal of Family Therapy*, 19(1), 71–88.

Mallon, G. P. (1999). *Social services with transgendered youth*. Binghamton, NY: Haworth.

McKain, T. L. (1996). Acknowledging mixed-sex people. *Journal of Sex and Marital Therapy*, 22(4), 265–279.

Meyer, J. K., & Reter, D. (1979). Sex reassignment: Follow-up. *Archives of General Psychiatry*, 36(9), 1010–1015.

Meyer-Bahlburg, H. (1994). Intersexuality and the diagnosis of gender identity disorder. *Archives of Sexual Behavior*, 23(1), 21–40.

Miller, N. (1996). *Counseling in genderland: A guide for you and your transgendered client*. Boston: Different Path Press.

Nicolosi, J. (1991). Reparative therapy of male homosexuality: A new clinical approach. Northvale, NJ: Jason Aronson.

Oles, M. N. (1977). The transsexual client: A discussion of transsexualism and issues in psychotherapy. *American Journal of Orthopsychiatry*, 46(1), 66–74.

Patterson, C. J. (1996). Lesbian mothers and their children: Findings from the Bay Area Families Study. In J. Laird & R-J. Green (Eds.), *Lesbians and gays in couples and families: A handbook for therapists* (pp. 420–437). San Francisco: Jossey-Bass.

Pauly, I. (1974). Female transsexualism I and II. *Archives of Sexual Behavior*, 3, 487–526.

Peo, R. (1988). Transvestism. *Journal of Social Work and Human Sexuality*, 7(1), 57–75.

Pfäefflin, F., & Junge, A. (1998). Sex reassignment: Thirty years of international follow-up studies after sex reassignment surgery—A comprehensive review, 1961–1991. (Translated from German by R. B. Jacobson and A. B. Meier.) *International Journal of Transgenderism* electronic book collection, Symposion books. Available at http://symposion.com/ijt/pfaefflin/1000.htm.

Rachlin, K. (1997, June). *Partners in the journey: Psychotherapy and six stages of gender revelation*. Presented at the Second Congress on Sex and Gender, King of Prussia, PA.

Raj, R. (2002). Towards a transpositive therapeutic model: Developing clinical sensitivity and cultural competence in the effective support of transsexual and transgendered clients. *International Journal of Transgenderism*, 6(2). Available at http://www.symposion.com/ijt/ijtvoo6noo2 04.htm.

Randell, J. (1971). Indications for sex reassignment surgery. *Archives of Sexual Behavior*, 1(2), 153–161.

Rekers, G. A., & Kilgus, M. D. (1995). Differential diagnosis and rationale for treatment of gender identity disorders and transvestism. In G. A. Rekers (Ed.), *Handbook of child and adolescent sexual problems* (pp. 255–271). New York: Lexington Books.

Roberts, J. (1995). *Coping with crossdressing: Tools and strategies for partners in committed relationships* (3d ed.). King of Prussia, PA: Creative Design Services.

Rosario, V. A. (1996). Trans (homo) sexuality? Double inversion, psychiatric confusion, and hetero-hegemony. In B. Beemyn & M. Eliason (Eds.), *Queer studies: A lesbian, gay, bisexual, and transgender anthology* (pp. 35–55). New York: New York University Press.

Rosenfeld, C., & Emerson, S. (1998). A process model of supportive therapy for families of transgender individuals. In D. Denny (Ed.), *Current concepts in transgender identity* (pp. 391–400). New York: Garland.

Rubin, G. (1992). Of catamites and kings: Reflections on butch gender and boundaries. In J. Nestle (Ed.), *The persistent desire: A femme-butch reader*. Los Angeles: Alyson.

Sales, J. (1995). Children of a transsexual father: A successful intervention. *European Child and Adolescent Psychiatry*, 4(2), 136–139.

Schober, J.M. (1999). Long-term outcomes and changing attitudes to intersexuality. *British Journal of Urology International*, 83 Supplement(3), 39–50.

Sell, I. (2001). Not man, not woman: Psychospiritual characteristics of a western third gender. *Journal of Transpersonal Psychology*, 33(1), 16–36.

Stacey, J., & Biblarz, T.J. (2001). (How) does the sexual orientation of parents matter? *American Sociological Review*, 66, 159–183.

Steiner, B. (1985a). The management of patients with gender disorders. In B. Steiner (Ed.), *Gender dysphoria: Development, research, management* (pp. 325–350). New York: Plenum.

——. (1985b). Transsexual, transvestites, and their partners. In B. Steiner (Ed.), *Gender dysphoria: Development, research, management* (pp. 351–364). New York: Plenum.

Steiner, B.W., & Bernstein, S.M. (1981). Female-to-male transsexuals and their partners. *Canadian Journal of Psychiatry*, 26, 178–182.

Stoller, R.J. (1966). The mother's contribution to infantile transvestic behavior. *International Journal of Psychoanalysis*, 47, 384–395.

——. (1967a). Transvestites' women. *American Journal of Psychiatry*, 124, 89–95.

——. (1967b), "It's only a phase": Femininity in boys. *Journal of the American Medical Association*, 201, 314–315.

——. (1968). Male childhood transsexualism. *Journal of American Academy of Child Psychiatry*, 7, 193–209.

——. (1982). Transvestism in women. *Archives of Sexual Behavior*, 11(2), 99–115.

Swann, S., & Herbert, S.E. (1999). Ethical issues in the mental health treatment of gender dysphoric adolescents. In G.P. Mallon (Ed), *Social services with transgendered youth* (pp. 19–34). Binghamton, NY: Haworth.

Valentine, D. (1998). *Gender Identity Project: Report on intake statistics, 1989–April 1997*. New York: Lesbian and Gay Community Services Center.

van der Kolk, B.A., McFarlane, A.C., & Weisaeth, L. (Eds.). (1996). *Traumatic stress: The effects of overwhelming experience on mind, body, and society*. New York: Guilford.

Walinder, J.B., Lundström, B., & Thuwe, L. (1978). Prognostic factors in the assessment of male transsexuals for sex reassignment. *British Journal of Psychiatry*, 132, 16–20.

Weinberg, T., & Bullough, V.L. (1988). Alienation, self-image, and the importance of support groups for wives of TV's. *Journal of Sex Research*, 24, 262–268.

——. (1991). Women married to transvestites: Problems with adjustment. In J. Dixon & D. Dixon (Eds.), *Wives, partners, and others: Living with cross-dressing* (pp. 114–125). Waltham, MA: International Foundation for Gender Education.

Wicks, L.K. (1977). Transsexualism: A social work approach. *Health and Social Work*, 2(1), 179–193.

Wilson. B.E., & Reiner, W.G. (1999). Management of intersex: A shifting paradigm. In A.D. Dreger (Ed.), *Intersex in the age of ethics* (pp. 119–136). Hagerstown, MD: University Publishing Group.

Wilson, P. (1998). Development and mental health: The issue of difference in atypical gender identity development. In D. Di Ceglie (Ed.), *A stranger in my own body: Atypical gender identity development and mental health* (pp. 1–8). London: Karnac.

Wise, T.N. (1985). Coping with a transvestic mate: Clinical implications. *Journal of Sex and Marital Therapy*, 11(4), 293–300.

Wise, T. N., Dupkin, C., & Meyer, J. K. (1981). Partners of distressed transvestites. *American Journal of Psychiatry, 138*, 1221–1224.

Zucker, K. J. (1990). Treatment of gender identity disorder in children. In R. Blanchard & B. W. Steiner (Eds.), *Clinical management of gender identity disorders in children and adults* (pp. 24–45). Washington, DC: American Psychiatric Association.

Zucker, K., & Bradley, S. (1995). *Gender identity disorder and psychosexual problems in children and adolescents.* New York: Guilford.

Zuger, B. (1984). Early effeminate behaviors in boys: Outcome and significance for homosexuality. *Journal of Nervous and Mental Disease, 32*, 449–463.

13

LESBIAN, GAY, BISEXUAL, AND TRANSGENDER AGING

Elise M. Fullmer

Youth sees itself as immune to the threat of aging. I can remember the day when I would use the phrase "over the hill" to describe an old woman. The implications of the phrase, and my complicity in those implications, never crossed my mind. Now, from experience, I understand that someone "over the hill" is metaphorically out of sight. In my youthful complacency, I was banishing old age from my awareness by that phrase. Now that I am old, I have become increasingly curious about why I needed to reassure myself in this way.

—BABA COOPER, 1988

WHEN STUDYING gay, lesbian, bisexual, and transgender (GLBT) aging, it is important to recognize that people in our society who are consistently oppressed are likely to experience some aspects of the world differently than their less vulnerable counterparts do. This is not to say that these experiences are necessarily bad or good, worse or better, or always different in every respect. Instead we must recognize that these GLBT experiences are a valid part of the aging process, deserve to be heard in their own right, and must be recognized as an important and legitimate area of inquiry into human experience and behavior as it relates to the aging process.

In a world that assumes and privileges youth, heterosexuality, and gender-normative behaviors, GLBT older people can become invisible. The stereotypes that surround being old and the stereotypes about being GLBT may at times

---

This chapter is dedicated to the memory of Dr. Lynette J. Eastland. Her keen sense of humor, understanding, and appreciation of the value of storytelling, personal experience, and diversity, and her advocacy for vulnerable people enriched the lives of the many people who knew her.

contradict one another, but they influence a person's life nonetheless (Fullmer, Shenk, & Eastland, 1999). Older GLBT people are subjected to age-related stereotypes, like any other older person, and they also encounter GLBT-related biases; the resulting prejudice and discrimination make them vulnerable to oppression. Thus older GLBT people can be differentially challenged to meet the demands of the aging process.

It is important to acknowledge the divisions among GLBT people. Sexual orientation is always mitigated by age, gender, race, and in particular, class. Research on GLBT older people has had a role in socially constructing the identities of those people who were studied. The processes of research, and the resulting comparisons between groups, are political in nature and serve political agendas. Indeed, some would argue that most methods of investigation serve to highlight how people are different in order to structure political arguments and to further political agendas (Kitzinger, 1987). Yet the essence of being human is being allowed to "fit" and to be accepted, regardless of similarities or differences with others. A basic tenet of social work is that age, gender, and class are strong cultural symbols that tend to prevent people from being fully accepting of others who are "different" or who deviate from norms that an empowered majority holds to be acceptable. Yet most people who are GLBT can identify common threads of experience that have shaped their lives. Research and discussion regarding older GLBT people must recognize both the similarities and the differences among this population.

This chapter takes the middle ground in attempting to address the above issues. There is practical value in understanding significant differences between groups, particularly when these understandings help us to articulate the uniqueness of various peoples, to combat negative stereotypes, and to foster public debate and further political agendas that combat oppression and discrimination. Still, a fundamental rule of social and behavioral sciences applies: differences between groups are always much greater than differences between individuals. People must be recognized for their individual uniqueness as well as for their group identification.

The way older GLBT people view their lives in the present is influenced by the social environment and the cohort differences they experienced in the past. The purpose of this chapter, therefore, is to make connections between history, research, and social culture as they influence the biological, psychological, and social environments of older GLBT people. To accomplish this task, literature on cohort differences as reflected in historical events will be reviewed. Theories of the aging process of GLBT people will also be discussed. Finally, the relevance of that information to the practice of micro-, mezzo-, and macro-level social work is summarized.

HISTORICAL UNDERPINNINGS: COHORT DIFFERENCES
AND SEXUAL ORIENTATION

Advocating for the rights of GLBT people is not a new notion, particularly if a more global rather than a national perspective is taken. As early as the late 1800s, an active movement existed in Germany and other parts of Europe. People like Emma Goldman were speaking out about issues of sexual orientation in Europe and also in the United States. In the United States, however, a new wave of the GLBT movement began around the time of heightened activity of the women's movement and the Civil Rights Movement (Adam, 1987).

Each GLBT person experienced the social movement for GLBT rights differently, and these experiences should be considered in the larger social context of thinking about sexual orientation in general. The intent of this section is to present a brief overview of historical markers in the United States so as to provide insight into the experiences of people who are at midlife and older. The focus will be on the 1920s and beyond, times that represent the developmental years for the majority of elder GLBT people. (A more in-depth review of the history of GLBTs can be found in chapter 2 of this volume.) It should also be noted that factors such as personal developmental processes — including time of identifying as GLBT, geographic location, socioeconomic status, ethnicity, and religious affiliation have an impact upon one's experience of historical events as well. People living during the same time period likely experienced these events differently.

Furthermore, there is a paucity of information that specifically addresses aging among bisexuals and transgender people or that discusses the effects of race, ethnicity, and socioeconomic status on GLBT people generally. Neither bisexual nor transgender people are singled out in the literature; it is assumed that their experiences parallel those of lesbians and gay men. When bisexual and transgender people are specifically discussed, the focus is usually on youth.

THE EARLY YEARS

One of the first highly publicized books of fiction to be published in the United States was *The Well of Loneliness* (Hall, 1928), which is widely regarded as "the touchstone novel in discussions of lesbian history" (Newton, 1989) and in discussions of bisexual and transgender history as well. For several decades, this book was read by many people who were exploring their sexual identity, and so it has strong symbolic and social significance (Newton, 1989). For example, *The Well of Loneliness* was a voice for the idea that "sexual deviance" is something inborn, something that cannot necessarily be cured or changed. It gave a voice to people who felt out of place in their own physical body. This idea is in direct contrast to the idea that sexual orientation is a choice on the part of the "sexual deviant" to be sinful and immoral. The medicalization and restructuring of thinking about sexual orientation still permeate discussions about GLBT civil rights.

As the title suggests, the picture of lesbians and bisexual and transgender people painted in *The Well of Loneliness* is a depressing one. The book tells the story of a "mannish" woman, Stephen, who falls in love with a "feminine" (and presumably bisexual) woman named Mary. The two women become intimately involved, but after a conflicted relationship, Mary leaves Stephen for a man (who, by the way, initially fancied Stephen). The book implies that Stephen is a "misfit" or "freak of nature" who, as some cross between half man and half woman, will never really find a place in society at which to be content. Some of the themes of this book, however, were repeated for both men and women through the succeeding decades in books, plays, and movies. These themes have helped to shape the ways GLBT people think about themselves and about the world in general (Russo, 1985).

When it was published, and for many years thereafter, *The Well of Loneliness* was controversial. In the early 1970s the book still was held in the "private reserve" section of many libraries. For people under eighteen years of age, adult permission was required to check out this book. In many libraries across the country, this book was one of only a few references under "Homosexuality." Anyone looking for information on that topic would likely find the book listed; *The Well of Loneliness* had a profound influence on many people of both genders who were exploring their sexual identity.

WORLD WAR AND THE INFUSION OF NEW IDEAS

World War I (WWI) (1914–1918) and World War II (WWII) (1939–1945) marked changes in the traditional roles of women and men regarding definitions of gender. Most historians agree, however, that during WWII fundamental changes in how women viewed their role in society took place. These changes also significantly influenced the GLBT communities by creating a shift in thinking about the social meanings of gender. Rosie the Riveter (a fictional poster girl for WWII) became a popular symbol of the government, encouraging women to "step up to the plate" and work at the jobs that men had once filled. For the first time in history, women were being asked to take on roles traditionally assigned to men. Women played sports, worked in factories, flew planes, and drove buses. Rosie the Riveter forever changed how women and men thought about gender. This period in history opened doors for both men and women to rethink their lives relative to gender.

Many people serving in the armed forces in Europe, both men and women, were able to witness firsthand an active homophile movement overseas. They brought these impressions of a homosexual identity back with them to the United States, and their experiences helped provide the basis for eventual efforts to organize for GLBT rights. As noted in a preface to an article by Allan Berube (1989), the editors write:

> World War II has increasingly been recognized as a turning point in American life. Allan Berube's research reveals the war to have had a major impact on homosexual identity as well. ... The military's wartime adoption of a policy designed to manage homosexuality, together with the individual lesbian and gay soldier's strategies for coping with the resulting public stigma, made homosexuality of increasing concern to federal institutions and strengthened the homosexual component of the veteran's identity.
>
> (P. 383)

BACK TO THE "GOOD OLD DAYS" AND BACK IN THE CLOSET

After WWII, there was a drive to return to prewar conditions—that is, for women to focus on home, family, and men. Men returning from the war were expected to return to their "rightful" places of employment. The 1950s were characterized by the force of this social pressure for both men and women to return to traditional gender roles. In popular culture, television series such as *Father Knows Best* and *Leave It to Beaver* epitomized the symbolic nature of this social culture (Russo, 1987). Although these symbols did not reflect the lives of the majority of people, particularly the lower socioeconomic groups, a working husband with a wife at home caring for children was touted as the American ideal, and many women and men, including GLBT women and men, subscribed to that ideal. For GLBT people, this effort most often took the form of trying to appear "normal." This is an important point, since it was in this atmosphere of secrecy that many of the older GLBT people of today lived during their earlier years.

The anti-Communist campaign led by Senator Joseph McCarthy was of particular importance to GLBT people during the 1950s. Adam (1987) writes about this period:

> As early as 1945, the U.S. Chamber of Commerce conducted an active anticommunist campaign. Deeply alarmed by Soviet power in Eastern Europe and later by the 1949 revolution in China, the chamber's program directors drew together big businessmen, the Roman Catholic church hierarchy, federal agencies, and veterans' groups, all of whom held an apocalyptic view of Communism and an unremitting zeal to defeat the Soviet Union and its American supporters.... McCarthyism drew upon a wistful nostalgia for a golden age of small farmers and businessmen and [was] also an expression of a strong resentment and hatred toward a world which makes no sense in terms of older ideas.... On the face of it, there is no reason homosexuality should have been mixed into the anticommunist furor, but in McCarthyism as in other reactionary ideologies, psychosymbolic connections

between gender and power assigned a place to homosexuality. For the authoritarian mind, male homosexuality signified the surrender of masculinity and the "slide" into "feminine" traits of weakness, duplicity, and seductiveness.

(PP. 57–58)

During the McCarthy era, GLBT people were pursued as Communists, destroyers of society, sex murderers, and the like (Adam, 1987). It was in this climate of fear that many older GLBT people came of age. Despite these challenges, many GLBT people worked to gain civil rights. Probably the two most notable attempts were the Mattachine Society and the Daughters of Bilitis.

ACCOMMODATION OR SOCIAL CHANGE

Like so many other social movements, the homophile movement of the 1950s followed gains made by the Civil Rights Movement. Despite the hostile environment of the time, the Mattachine Society was formed in Los Angeles in 1951, followed by the Daughters of Bilitis in San Francisco in 1955. The Mattachine Society was initially created on the premise of a communist ideal of equity. In the climate of the 1950s, however, the organization eventually made the decision to take a less pro-communist stance and moved toward a lower-profile, accommodationist position. This organization fought for lesbian and gay civil rights with the idea that "homosexuals" could fit in, or accommodate to the prevailing social and cultural norms (Adam, 1987). The Daughters of Bilitis was accommodationist too, as is reflected by its organizational goals: to create public discussion, educate the "variant," and participate in research studies (Adam, 1987). Adam notes: "After the McCarthy terror, accommodation seemed the only realistic choice. Like other minorities facing a seemingly unmerciful oppressor, the homophiles sought to placate the enemy by being law-abiding and deferential and by lying low" (p. 64).

The concept of accommodation is an important one in understanding the adaptation of GLBT people during this time. Many GLBT people who are now old may still feel that they need to conform to a heterosexual norm in order to survive. Some of these feelings are reflected in the research on older GLBT people and will be discussed in the next section. Despite the supportive positions held by the American Psychological Association and the National Association of Social Workers, GLBT people are still viewed by some mental health "professionals" as deviant and mentally ill.

Another important event during this time was the "outing" of Christine Jorgensen, a male-to-female transsexual who transitioned (in Europe) in 1957. After being outed by the press when she returned from Europe after her operation, she traveled in the United States as an actress and a spokeswoman for transgender issues. Generally, however, the press viewed Jorgensen as "odd" at best and as a "circus sideshow" at worst. This portrayal was one reason why gay and lesbian homophile organizations attempted to distance themselves from transgender issues.

HOMOSEXUALITY AS A MENTAL ILLNESS

In 1969, when the police raided a New York City gay bar called the Stonewall Inn, a new era in the fight for GLBT rights began. GLBT people at the bar fought back by shouting, throwing stones and other objects at police, and generally resisting the raid. The gay liberation movement that drew its energy from the Stonewall riots was much less accommodating than its predecessors had been. Rather than adapt to the prevailing norms, GLBT activists sought to both change these norms and seek civil rights. Transgender people in particular were very instrumental in both the Stonewall riots and the preceding social movement, but as the movement gained momentum and political clout, transgender people were again relegated to second-class citizenship. Some gay men and lesbians viewed transgender people as an embarrassment or, at the least, as representatives of an orientation that was politically difficult to explain. A belief that the political inclusion of transgender people would undermine civil rights for lesbians and gay men was prevalent. It was not uncommon, for example, for some lesbian feminists to exclude male-to-female transsexuals who wished to participate in the lesbian feminist movement; these lesbians viewed MTFs as "fundamentally male" and so were suspicious of their intent. Bisexual people were also very much a part of this early movement. Many lesbians and gay men, however, challenged the concept of a bisexual identity, suggesting that bisexuals were people who simply could not accept their same-sex sexual orientation. This dichotomous thinking about sexual orientation still permeates arguments within the lesbian and gay communities.

D'Emilio (1989) discusses two important aspects of politics for GLBT civil rights after the Stonewall Rebellion. The first was that "coming out" became a political statement and a political strategy for fighting both internalized and external homophobia. This strategy, in light of the above-mentioned thinking about transgender and bisexual people, created a social and political rift between many gay men and lesbians and their bisexual and transgender peers. A second consequence of Stonewall was that a lesbian movement emerged.

One of the most significant strides made by gays and lesbians during this time was the successful campaign in 1973 to remove homosexuality from the category of mental illness in the *Diagnostic and Statistical Manual of Mental Disorders*, published by the American Psychiatric Association (Hall, 1985). Over a period of time it had been proposed that homosexuality is only one variation in normal sexual/emotional development (Kinsey, Pomeroy, & Martin, 1948). In 1957 Hooker conducted pivotal research comparing the physiological health and well-being of heterosexual and gay men and found no differences between them. These and subsequent studies helped to make the case for removing homosexuality from the *DSM*. Nevertheless, it is important to remember that older GLBT people have spent much of their lives in a society that defined homosexuality as a mental illness. It is also noteworthy that the *DSM* still includes a diagnostic category for people who are not comfortable with their sexual orientation or who are transgender, effectively leaving many people still classified as mentally ill on the basis of their sexual orientation or gender expression.

COHORT DIFFERENCES AMONG OLDER GLBT PEOPLE

Coming out is a critical issue in the process of identifying as GLBT, and some people do not go through this process early in life. For this reason, two GLBT people of the same age could have experienced these historical events very differently. For example, a forty-year-old gay man who identified as homosexual during the Stonewall Rebellion likely experienced coming out differently than did another forty-year-old gay man who was married to a woman at that time and who would come out later in his life (for an examination of coming out in later life, see Jensen, 1999).

Geographic location, race, socioeconomic status, and the availability of role models and support networks also likely influenced GLBT people's experiences of historical events. It is easy to understand how growing up and coming out in New York City or San Francisco would be qualitatively different from doing so in a conservative small town.

THE BEGINNINGS OF LESBIAN AND GAY GERONTOLOGY

Until the 1980s, gerontologists and others who were writing about the process of aging largely ignored GLBT issues. Among the few exceptions, two articles in particular deserve mention. Both articles were published as book chapters in *Positively Gay*, an anthology edited by Berzon (1970) and revised by Berzon and Leighton in 1979. *The Older Lesbian*, by Martin and Lyon (founders of the Daughters of Bilitis), discussed the place of role-playing and secrecy in the relationships of older lesbians and introduced the term "lace curtain lesbians" to describe lesbians who lived in relationships with other women but refused to acknowledge their same-sex sexual orientation. "Adjustment to Aging Among Gay Men," by Kimmel (1979), refuted stereotypes of older gay men that labeled them lonely, friendless, and without support, suggesting instead that there is great diversity in the lives of such men. The article pointed out that societal attitudes, rather than something inherent in being an aging gay male, create problems for gay men as they age.

One of the most notable articles on gay male gerontology, by Kelly (1977), also refuted stereotypes of gay males as lonely and secluded. It is particularly significant because it was the first to be published in a major mainstream journal of gerontology. As the large number of citations of this article in the gerontological literature within the next several years illustrates, Kelly's work was pivotal in bringing GLBT gerontology to the forefront.

Another important study on gay aging was carried out by a social worker named Berger (1982). In a survey conducted in the Midwest, he studied the life experiences of 112 gay men who were 40 years of age and older. Berger found that men who socialized intergenerationally tended to be better adjusted than their counterparts who did not. The men in Berger's study were relatively more positive about their lives than subjects reported on in subsequent studies (for example, Lee, 1987, 1988). More important, Berger discussed what he called "mastery of stigma," an idea that continues to influence writings on GLBT aging. Mastery of stigma hypothesizes that gay and lesbian people cope better with the stigma of being elderly because they have had to deal with the stigma of being gay all their lives. When a person has been able to deal positively with the stigma of being GLBT, he or she is likely to be able to deal positively with the stigma of aging as well. Berger's study also found that some of the men experienced a positive benefit from being retired. Since they were no longer in the workforce, they no longer had to face the threat of job discrimination on the basis of sexual orientation.

Legal and social systems do not allow for the variations of family that characterize the lives of GLBT people (for additional discussion about the effects of discrimination, see Vacha, 1985). It should be noted that Berger's subjects tended to be relatively well off financially, involved in their community, and largely white, all variables that likely influenced his findings.

Berger argued that the problems of older gay men come primarily from society rather than from the attitudes of the men themselves. One example of these issues for GLBT people is prejudice and personal and institutional discrimination in health care, as illustrated by some nursing homes, hospitals, and medical practitioners. Same-sex couples may be denied to right to live together in retirement settings or to make medical decisions for their partners. Doctors and other medical professionals may deny intersexed and other transgender persons the medical treatment they need because of blatant bias against them. Medical mistreatment, in particular, is a common theme in writings on transgender people.

An interesting study of men over 50 living in Canada (Lee, 1988) reported findings different from those of Berger's study. Lee found that older gay men tended to be somewhat cynical about their younger counterparts and resented, to some degree, their "in your face" gay liberationist stance toward the world. Lee suggested that for some older men, the pressure to come out is a disruption of privacy rather than a liberating experience. Lee also discussed the relative invisibility of older gay men in the GLBT community in Canada, a phenomenon that has also been noted in the United States by other researchers on GLBT aging (see, for example, Adelman, 1986; Berger, 1982; Cooper, 1988; Fullmer, 1999; Kehoe, 1989). The men in Lee's study were not as well off economically as the men in Berger's study, and they were somewhat less positive about their life circumstances.

One important study on the aging of both women and men began as a dissertation (Adelman, 1986). Perhaps the most important finding was a confirmation of Berger's previous work. People who had adjusted well to being gay or lesbian tended to have fewer psychosomatic complaints than people who had not adjusted well to their sexual orientation. Like Berger, Adelman found a connection between adjustment to being gay (or lesbian) and adjustment to aging.

Another study that dealt exclusively with women surveyed 100 lesbians who were 60 years of age or older (Kehoe, 1989). Kehoe pointed out that her research findings were limited because her subjects were white, well-educated women. She found that the women were more likely to be celibate than the men in previous studies and that they tended to have relatively good self-esteem.

More recently Fullmer et al. (1999) examined identity development among older GLBT people and used the concept of competing stereotypes to discuss the invisibility of older GLBT people both within and outside the GLBT communities. The primary tenet was that a popular stereotype about older people is that they are not sexual. Likewise, a popular stereotype about GLBT people is that their identity is primarily sexual. These competing stereotypes can inhibit a person's ability to consciously recognize older people who are GLBT. One can see this dynamic at work when visiting a nursing home. It is not likely to occur to visitors who are interacting with the residents that an older person may be GLBT. This recognition is unlikely to occur, in part, because of the effect of competing stereotypes.

Donovan (2001) wrote one of the few articles specifically addressing transgender aging, a short first-person account of being older and transgender. She tells her story of coming of age in the 1950s and 1960s. She had difficulties in finding employment and maintaining a steady income apart from public assistance throughout her life. Her stories of direct and harsh abuse from the medical establishment, including one incident in which a doctor called in other medical workers and forcibly "held up her dress" for others to see her male genitals, are disturbing. An important point that Donovan makes is that transgender people are often denied the opportunity to be gainfully employed in their youth, and they suffer the financial consequences of that later in life.

In another article on GLBT aging, Jones (2001) discussed the problems and challenges of aging for GLBT elders. The author pointed out that issues faced by GLBT elders are essentially the same as for other aging people. GLBT people, however, face additional problems and challenges. He identified ageism, loneliness, and health status as the three primary problems of aging people in general. Issues specific to GLBT people include a highly sexualized culture that privileges youth, particularly in the gay male community. The author also pointed out that AIDS has left some gay men with fewer friends who can offer support in old age. Finally Jones reiterated the need for health care providers to develop sensitivity to GLBT issues and the necessity for advance planning for one's later years.

In summary, the research on GLBT aging has some consistent characteristics with respect to its implications for older GLBT people. People who are GLBT are not legitimated and are seen as inferior to heterosexuals. For this reason, health care and social services for older people are not designed to deal with the particular needs of older GLBT people. Simple actions such as visiting a life partner in the hospital may be complicated by hospital rules that allow only bio-logical family members to visit and do not allow partners to participate in health care decision making.

Older GLBT people can feel invisible, even within the GLBT communities. An older person who comes out late in life may find it difficult to meet people of the same age and to develop relationships because of a youth-oriented culture both within and outside the GLBT communities. Research suggests, however, that despite the previously noted issues, many GLBT people are comfortable with their lives and have developed strong social support networks. For some, being GLBT may actually enhance their ability to adjust to the process of aging.

IDENTITY DEVELOPMENT, AGING, AND PSYCHOLOGICAL HEALTH

> Early psychiatrists considered us not damned, but sick. In *A General Introduction to Psychoanalysis*, Freud wrote, "... Perverted sexuality is nothing else but infantile sexuality... ." And Carl Jung, one of the first major theorists to diverge from Freud, added his vote to the psychiatric consensus of the day. He wrote in the early twen-ties, "The more homosexual a man is, the more prone he is to disloyalty and to the seduction of boys."
>
> (HALL, 1985)

Current theories of GLBT identity development are rooted in the develop-mental theories proposed by Sigmund Freud. This is problematic, because Freud and many of his successors, such as Lionel Oversey, Irving Bieber, and Charles Socarides, viewed (or currently view) homosexuality as a form of "arrested" de-velopment (LeVay, 1996). Since Freud was one of the first scholars to propose a developmental theory and many current developmental theories grew out of his work, these theories must be carefully scrutinized when applied to GLBT people. The underlying observations and resulting assumptions of many developmental theories have been criticized for a lack of sampling from disenfranchised groups in these scholars' studies and for an inherent assumption that heterosexuality represents "normal" developmental attainment. Nevertheless, some general developmental theories, and specific theories of GLBT identities, help to enhance understanding of the life issues that people face as they age. This section will outline the progression of identity development theories and their impact on characterizations of GLBT mental health.

It is important to remember, as one reads these theories, that GLBT identities can and often do develop later in life (see, for example, Adelman, 1986; Berger, 1982; Fullmer, 1995; Jensen, 1999; Morrow, 1996). This phenomenon can create unique issues and problems for older people. Jeanne Adleman (1993) describes her experience as follows:

> I surely did not think of myself as "coming out" when I decided shortly after my fifty-sixth birthday that I wanted to begin acting on the feelings of attraction to girls, then women, I'd been aware of since adolescence. What I told myself and others in 1975 was that I was "expanding my sexuality." This fit completely with the superficial understandings I'd gleaned at fifteen or sixteen from the psychology shelves in the public library, where I read all the books from Adler to Freud before I stopped. Everybody, I "understood," is born with potential to be bisexual, but the mature choice is to polarize with the opposite sex, and anyone who doesn't is immature. At sixteen I would know the dozen or so girls in my all-female high school that made themselves visible as lesbians. I found them exciting but I was more interested in becoming mature. Besides, I wasn't sexually attracted only to girls. This superficial understanding was still with me at fifty-six. I believed that what differentiated lesbians from heterosexuals, provided all were feminists, was that lesbians were sexual exclusively with other women.

(PP. 6–7)

ERIKSON'S STAGES OF DEVELOPMENT

Eric Erikson (1968) is best known for his work expanding on Freud's ideas about development and extending development into old age. While Freud saw development as occurring primarily during infancy through young adulthood, Erikson theorized that psychosocial development is a lifelong process characterized by many transitions. For this reason, Erikson's theory is important in discussions of aging.

Like Freud, Erikson believed that with each stage of development, people experience a psychosocial crisis. Each stage requires mastery of a developmental task. Mastery of each task is dependent upon mastery of previous stages. The stage and crisis applicable to late adulthood is "ego integrity versus despair." Older adults who successfully transcend this crisis achieve a state of ego integrity—the ability to look back over one's life, to be able to integrate the experiences that one has had, and ultimately to accept these experiences, bad and good, as important aspects of self. Those who do not successfully achieve this transition experience a state of despair. In short, to see value and worth in these experiences and to accept them as part of oneself is the essence of this stage of development. This stage also includes the ability to accept one's own death. Someone in a state of despair may have many unresolved regrets about life, may view his or her life as valueless, and may even fear dying because of these unresolved issues.

The implication for the older GLBT person is that the ability to accept one's life and see value in it, as a GLBT person, is an important part of the aging process. It should be noted, however, that a literal application of this theory to any given person could have negative consequences. For example, how is a determination made as to whether a person sees enough value in life to pass the test of ego integrity? Is a person in despair if he or she sees some value in life but still feels anger about prejudice and discrimination, perhaps even feeling somewhat depressed? The point here is that simple definitions will likely not do when developmental theories are applied to people who have been consistently disenfranchised in society. Perhaps the most important question is the degree to which individuals' beliefs about life hamper or strengthen their lives in the present moment.

ROBERT BUTLER AND PERSONAL MEANING

Robert Butler (1963) expanded on Erikson's theory of development, believing that older adults spend more time searching for personal meaning and reviewing their lives, attempting to make sense of them. The concept of life review is central to Butler's thinking; it is essentially a task of late adulthood that allows people to reinterpret past experiences and thus resolve conflicts. Life review may be a conscious or not-so-conscious event, but Butler believed that all older people go through the process nonetheless.

For older GLBT people, the ability to reinterpret and pass on to future generations what they have learned from a lifetime of prejudice and discrimination and to be able to reminisce in a way that allows them to make sense of their lives (and therefore to achieve ego integrity) are important developmental experiences. The process of reminiscing must occur in an environment that is safe and where positive regard for the person's story is forthcoming. This may be a difficult project for people who are alone, who have a limited support network, or who have little or no contact with affirming aging services.

Social construction theory proposes that our social reality is created through social interaction. Social reality, then, is the process of people coming to a common understanding of the world. Integrating Butler's ideas of reminiscence with social construction theory suggests that GLBT people could use reminiscence to reconstruct their identities in a positive way that thwarts negative social attitudes. It is from this perspective that Friend (1991) proposed his theory for successful aging among GLBT people.

RICHARD A. FRIEND AND SUCCESSFUL AGING

Friend (1991) discussed options for lesbians and gays in managing the socially constructed negative identity of "homosexuality." He suggested that some gay and lesbian people internalize negative discourse (internalized homophobia), while others "reconstruct its meaning in positive and affirmative ways" (p. 100). He also proposed a middle range along the continuum: lesbian and gay people who "accommodate heterosexism by marginally accepting some aspects of homosexuality, but still believing that heterosexuality is inherently better" (p. 104). From the above, Friend proposed three different styles of identity formation.

STEREOTYPIC OLDER LESBIAN AND GAY PEOPLE The people who belong to the group of stereotypic older lesbians and gays may experience self-loathing, guilt, and low self-esteem as a result of internalized homophobia and may not associate or identify with other members of the gay and lesbian community.

PASSING OLDER LESBIAN AND GAY PEOPLE The people who belong to the group of passing older lesbians and gays are at the midpoint of the continuum. "They believe the heterosexist sentiments with which they were raised, while also acknowledging and marginally accepting their homosexuality" (p. 105). These individuals typically manage conflict by disassociating themselves from any outward appearance of being gay or lesbian; for example, they may marry heterosexually in order to hide their orientation.

AFFIRMATIVE OLDER LESBIAN AND GAY PEOPLE The people who belong to the group of affirmative older lesbians and gays reconstruct the negative social labels of a heterosexist society into something positive. This group tends to be better adjusted and to have better self-esteem than the others. Rather than accommodating the negative social labels about lesbians and gays, they may actively attempt to change these perceptions.

Friend proposed his theory for lesbians and gay men, but it can easily be applied to bisexual and transgender people as well. Friend's categories of identity development support the previously reviewed literature on GLBT aging, helping to explain why some older GLBT people are found to be aging well, while others are not,. The theory makes a solid case for promoting strong and affirming networks within the GLBT communities and combating negative stereotypes where they exist.

MICRO AND MEZZO ISSUES FOR GLBT OLDER PEOPLE

GLBT people can and do experience difficulties that require intervention. This section will discuss psychosocial issues and concerns facing GLBT older clients, including alcoholism, grief, health care concerns, legal issues, the behaviors and attitudes of health care professionals, and definitions of family.

It is important to remember that social rather than personal issues are often the greatest barriers to problem solving for GLBT people. Certain aspects of problematic interpersonal situations may be an adaptive response to a hostile environment. Work with GLBT older people, then, does not take place in a vacuum; older GLBT clients must be viewed as part of larger family and social systems. Social workers can function as resource builders, linkers, and mediators for older GLBT clients. To be effective in these roles, however, practitioners must develop an understanding of GLBT individuals, communities, and resources. These resources vary from one community to the next; it will be necessary for practitioners to be creative in order to develop supports where none exist. Each section will discuss potential resources for addressing psychosocial issues among GLBTs.

SUBSTANCE ABUSE

Substance abuse is one issue that aging GLBT people may face. It is estimated that between 10% and 18% of the older population suffers from alcoholism. Alcoholism is the second most common reason, just behind depression, for older adult admissions to inpatient psychiatric facilities (Hutchison, 1999). Many older adults in the GLBT community experienced their early socialization in places such as bars, an environment that could encourage the development of a pattern of drinking. For some GLBT people, alcohol and/or other drugs serve as an anesthetic, easing their experience of a hostile social environment.

GRIEF

As Teitelman (1995) points out, one of the most problematic issues for older GLBT people is that they cannot openly grieve when a partner dies. Social services for this population are lacking and exist, if at all, only in larger cities. The norm in most areas across the country is to structure services for elderly people on the assumption that they are heterosexual. Practitioners need to recognize and validate GLBT clients' grief and help them negotiate any identity development issues that are related to the grieving process.

HOUSING

Finding and maintaining housing can be difficult for GLBT older people. For example, public retirement housing often prohibits "unrelated adults" from living together, while nursing homes and private retirement centers make the assumption that residents are heterosexual and structure living arrangements, activities, and social events accordingly.

Many GLBT people are coming up with creative ways to deal with housing issues. For example, developers are establishing new retirement communities specifically targeting GLBT populations. Recently, the first federally funded nursing home for GLBT people was created in Florida. Some GLBT people have pooled resources to purchase communal retirement housing. Such living alternatives for GLBT people, however, are often available to only the most economically advantaged people. For this reason, it is important to integrate GLBT people into mainstream aging services as well.

HEALTH CARE AND HOSPITALIZATION

GLBT older people encounter a number of organizational policies that complicate their access to health care services. Most organizations do not allow GLBT people to include their partners on health insurance policies. Many hospitals have policies stating that only immediate family members are allowed to make decisions about the care of seriously ill patients. Some hospitals require that only immediate family be allowed visitation. *Immediate family* is typically defined by hospitals as a husband, a wife, or a biological family member. This definition excludes partners and other family of choice for GLBT people. While these policies are changing in some hospitals or are not strictly enforced, the implications of their enforcement can be devastating. GLBT people can be separated indefinitely from their partners and other family of choice, and important life-and-death decisions may be left to people who are emotionally disconnected from the hospitalized person. Social workers must work within their organizations to advocate for policies that would better serve GLBT patients.

LEGAL ISSUES: WILLS, INHERITANCE, AND POWER OF ATTORNEY

One significant role that social workers can play is to assist GLBT people with legal planning. Some older gays and lesbians may be unaware of the legal problems that they may face in retirement, housing, inheritance, and hospitalization. With forethought, GLBT people can prepare for such issues, exploring them before a crisis situation arises, so that a plan is in place for care, treatment, and preferred place of hospitalization. Examples of the types of pre-planning that may be appropriate are creating a living will, which specifically states who should make decisions and under what circumstances, and taking steps to financially protect assets, such as writing a will or naming a partner as beneficiary on life insurance policies. Practitioners need to be aware of attorneys in their area who can competently and compassionately deal with the legal issues faced by older GLBT people and refer clients to them as needed.

THE FAMILIES OF GLBT PEOPLE

The process of establishing and ultimately recognizing forms of family among older GLBT people is complicated by oppression. Services for older GLBT people are still in their infancy. Few if any positive role models for coupling, aging, or creating alternatives to traditional family structures have been available until very recently. At present, there are some services that have been developed specifically for GLBT people, including communal living arrangements, nursing homes, and organizations for older GLBT people that promote socialization. In general, however, GLBT people may be the only representative of a different sexual orientation or gender expression in their family of origin, and they may have had to resolve their identity issues in isolation from others like themselves. Furthermore, heterosexual models of family have most likely predominated; therefore, GLBT people have had to be creative in establishing their own social networks. Often these social networks, particularly for the oldest GLBT people, have been close-knit and shrouded in secrecy (see, for example, Adelman, 1986; Clunis & Green, 1988).

Contrary to public perceptions, many GLBT people do actively participate as members of their family of origin. When biological families are supportive, they can be an important resource for older GLBT people. Clunis and Green (1988) suggest that this support from biological family may be particularly important for racial and ethnic minorities who need protection from a hostile mainstream society. Older GLBT people are caregivers to parents and other family members and are themselves aunts, uncles, parents, and grandparents and so they may fulfill diverse roles in their families of origin (Kimmel, 1992).

PROVIDING SERVICES TO GLBTS: THERAPY, SUPPORT GROUPS, AND GLBT AGING CENTERS

One of the most important issues at any level of intervention is the attitude of the social work professional. Any bias or stereotypes on his or her part will affect the relationships with GLBT clients. Negative stereotypes internalized by GLBT people affect self-esteem and functioning as well as the person's ability to act on his or her own behalf (Friend, 1991). Negative stereotypes also work at larger systems levels to keep GLBT people oppressed. In order for practitioners to avoid reinforcing internalized or external negative beliefs, it is important that they examine their own attitudes about GLBT people and work to eliminate biases where they exist (Fullmer, 1995). For example, Decker (1985), in discussing therapeutic issues related to same-sex relationships, notes that if therapists are to be authentic and create a constructive helping relationship with older GLBT people, they must have a basic belief in the worth of the people and a belief that a troubled GLBT relationship (or individual) can make changes for the better. Decker also observes that the training and knowledge base of clinicians is very important. Clinicians must have a thorough grounding in the principles of family systems and an understanding of atypical socialization and stigmatization related to identity formation and the process of coming out.

Organizations focused specifically on GLBT client needs also can benefit this population. One of the first groups formed to meet the needs of aging GLBT people was Senior Action in a Gay Environment (SAGE) in New York City. This organization offers a variety of services, including outreach to homebound GLBT people and other services directed at an aging population. Though similar organizations have been formed in other large metropolitan areas, SAGE remains a model for services to GLBT older people. It is not economically feasible, however, for GLBT people to develop aging services for the entire GLBT population. It is for this reason, therefore, that integrating GLBT people into national, state, and local aging services is imperative. Such integration is particularly important for GLBT people who live in smaller towns and rural areas where specialized supports are not likely to exist.

IMPLICATIONS FOR SOCIAL WORK PRACTICE

Both GLBT people and older adults require respect and honesty. Stereotypes about being old and about being GLBT serve to make older GLBT people invisible in a world where heterosexuality is assumed and GLBT issues are synonymous with sexuality. GLBT older people must have a voice within their larger communities. Discriminatory organizational policies of social service agencies, hospitals, insurance companies, educational institutions, and employers must be changed to include GLBT persons. It is not realistic to expect that aging services for GLBT people will be developed exclusively within GLBT communities. Limited resources and social and economic justice dictate that GLBT people have a right to share the existing resources. For this to occur, however, organizations must become more sensitive to GLBT issues. Social workers can play a fundamental part in creating more-sensitive service environments. On a larger scale, GLBT people must be included in local, state, and national policies and recognized therein as a vulnerable group whose civil rights must be constitutionally protected. Until the legal status of GLBT people is changed, little real equity in service provision and other resources can be achieved. Until then, older GLBT people will continue to be denied the basic supports and opportunities they need if they are to achieve psychological security and well-being. Recent policy events in San Francisco, California, granting GLBT people the legal right to marry provide a glimmer of hope that these changes will indeed be eventually made.

REFERENCES

Adam, B. D. (1987). *The rise of a gay and lesbian movement*. Boston: G. K. Hall.

Adelman, M. (1986). *Long time passing: Lives of older lesbians*. London: Alyson..

Adleman, J. (1993). To find a place. In J. Adleman, R. Berger, M. Boyd, V. Doublex, M. Freedman, W. S. Hubbard, M. Kight, A. Kochman, M. K. Robinson-Meyer, & S. M. Raphael (Eds.), *Lambda gray: A practical emotional and spiritual guide for gays and lesbians who are growing older* (pp. 1–16). Van Nuys, CA: Newcastle.

Berger, R. M. (1982). *Gay and gray: The older homosexual man*. Urbana: University of Illinois Press.

Berube, A. (1989 [1981]). Marching to a different drummer: Lesbian and gay GIs in World War II. In M. B. Duberman, M. Vicinus, and G. Chauncey Jr. (Eds.), *Hidden from history: Reclaiming the gay and lesbian past* (pp. 383–394). Dresden, TN: New American Library.

Berzon, B., & Leighton, R. (Eds.). (1979). *Positively gay: New approaches to gay life*. Millbrae, CA: Celestial Arts.

Butler, R. N. (1963). The life review: An interpretation of reminiscence in the aged. *Psychiatry, 26*, 65–70.

Clunis, D. M., & Green, G. D. (1988). *Lesbian couples*. Seattle: Seal.

Cooper, B. (1988). *Over the hill: Reflections on ageism between women*. Santa Cruz, CA: Crossing Press.

Decker, B. (1985). Counseling gay and lesbian couples. In R. Schoenberg & R. S. Goldberg (Eds.), *Homosexuality and social work* (pp. 39–52). New York: Haworth.

D'Emilio, J. (1989). Gay politics and community in San Francisco since World War II. In M. B. Duberman, M. Vicinus, and G. Chauncey Jr. (Eds.), *Hidden from history: Reclaiming the gay and lesbian past* (pp. 456– 473). Dresden, TN: New American Library.

Donovan, T. (2001). Being transgender and older: A first-person account. *Journal of Gay and Lesbian Social Services, 13*(4), 19–22.

Erikson, E. H. (1968). *Identity, youth, and crisis*. New York: Norton.

Faderman, L. (1981). *Surpassing the love of men*. New York: Morrow.

Foucault, M. (1978). *The history of sexuality*. Vol. 1, *An introduction*. New York: Vintage.

Fullmer, E. M. (1995). Challenging biases against families of older gays and lesbians. In G. C. Smith, S. S. Tobin, E. A. Robertson-Tchabo, & P. W. Power (Eds.), *Strengthening aging families: Diversity in practice and policy* (pp. 80–119). Thousand Oaks, CA: Sage.

——. (1999). Working an extra step: Recovery and aging of an ethnic minority lesbian. In L. S. Eastland, S. L. Herndon, & J. R. Barr (Eds.), *Communication in recovery: Perspectives on twelve-step groups* (pp. 129–141). Kresskill, NJ: Hampton.

Fullmer, E. M., Shenk, D., & Eastland, L. (1999). Negating identity: A feminist analysis of the social invisibility of older lesbians. *Journal of Women and Aging, 11*(2–3), 131–148.

Friend, R. A. (1991). Older lesbian and gay people: A theory of successful aging. In J. A. Lee (Ed.), *Gay midlife and maturity* (pp. 99–118). New York: Haworth.

Gilligan, C. (1982). *In a different voice: Psychological theory and women's development*. Cambridge, MA: Harvard University Press.

Hall, M. (1985). *The lavender couch: A consumer's guide to psychotherapy for lesbians and gay men*. Boston: Alyson.

Hooker, E. (1957). The adjustment of the male overt homosexual. *Journal of Projective Techniques, 21*, 18–31.

Hutchison, E.D. (1999). *Dimensions of human behavior: The changing life course.* Thousand Oaks, CA: Pine Forge.

Jensen, K.L. (1999). *Lesbian epiphanies: Women coming out in later life.* Binghamton, NY: Harrington Park.

Jones, B.E. (2001). Is having the luck of growing old in the gay, lesbian, bisexual, transgender community good or bad luck? *Journal of Gay and Lesbian Social Services,* 13(4), 13–14.

Kehoe, M. (1989). *Lesbians over sixty speak for themselves.* New York: Harrington Park.

Kelly, J. (1977). The aging male homosexual: Myth and reality. *Gerontologist,* 17, 328–332.

Kimmel, D.C. (1979). Adjustment to aging among gay men. In B. Berzon and R. Leighton (Eds.), *Positively gay: New approaches to gay life.* Millbrae, CA: Celestial Arts.

——. (1992). The families of older gay men and lesbians. *Generations,* 17(3), 37–38.

Kinsey, A.C., Pomeroy, W.B., & Martin, C.E. (1948/1998). *Sexual behavior in the human male.* Philadelphia: W. B. Saunders; Bloomington: Indiana University Press.

Kitzinger, C. (1987). *The social construction of lesbianism.* London: Sage.

Lee, J.A. (1987). What can gay aging studies contribute to theories of aging? *Journal of Homosexuality,* 13(4), 43–71.

——. (1988). Invisible lives of Canada's gray gays. In V. Marshall (Ed.), *Aging in Canada* (pp. 138–155). Toronto: Fitzhenry and Whiteside.

LeVay, S. (1996). *Queer science: The use and abuse of research into homosexuality.* Boston: MIT Press.

Martin, D., & Lyon, P. (1970). The older lesbian. In B. Berzon (Ed.), *Positively gay: New approaches to gay life* (pp. 34–42). Los Angeles: Media Mix.

Morrow, D.F. (1996). Coming out issues for adult lesbians: A group intervention. *Social Work,* 41(6), 647–656.

——. (2001). Older gays and lesbians: Surviving a generation of hate and violence. *Journal of Gay and Lesbian Social Services,* 13(1/2), 151–169.

Newton, E. (1989). The mythic mannish lesbian: Radcliffe Hall and the new women. In M.B. Duberman, M. Vicinus, & G. Chauncey Jr. (Eds.), *Hidden from history: Reclaiming the gay and lesbian past* (pp. 281–293). Dresden, TN: New American Library.

Russo, V. (1987). *The celluloid closet.* New York: Harper and Row.

Shenk, D., & Fullmer, E. (1996). Significant relationships among older women: Cultural and personal constructions of lesbianism. *Journal of Women and Aging,* 8(3/4), 75–89.

Teitelman, J.L. (1995). Homosexuality. In G.L. Maddox (Ed.), *The encyclopedia of aging: A comprehensive resource in gerontology and geriatrics* (2d ed.) (p. 270). New York: Springer.

Vacha, K. (1985). *Quiet fire: Memoirs of older gay men.* Santa Cruz, CA: Crossing Press.

PART FOUR

SOCIETY AND CULTURE

14

HEALTH CONCERNS FOR LESBIANS, GAY MEN, AND BISEXUALS

Caitlin Ryan and Elisabeth Gruskin

I have become convinced that our right to be different is in a deep sense, the most precious right we human beings have, and the one most likely, if we hold on to it, to ensure the human race a future. We need to treasure human differences.... . We need to cherish the unique achievements of various groups, to protect the beliefs and ideas and abilities that seem to grow more easily in one culture than in another. We may need them for our survival, certainly, we shall need some of them, one of these days, and we don't know which we shall need the most or where they may come to birth.

—LILLIAN SMITH, CIVIL RIGHTS ADVOCATE AND AUTHOR, KILLERS OF THE DREAM
(QUOTED IN CLIFF, 1978)

AS DO heterosexuals, gay men, lesbians, and bisexuals (GLBs) experience a range of health and mental health issues that are mediated by age, class, ethnicity, gender, income, and access to care. Until the AIDS epidemic, they were invisible within the American health system. Homophobia, misinformation, and inappropriate care have characterized most provider interactions. Since the emergence of the lesbian and gay health movement in the 1970s, and largely as an outcome of the AIDS epidemic, provider awareness has greatly increased. Agencies, in general, have become more responsive to the needs of GLB patients and clients, and the body of available research to guide practice and appropriate policies has grown substantially, particularly as it relates to gay men and HIV/AIDS. However, stigma continues to shape and inform the lives of gay men, lesbians, and bisexuals across the life course, affecting various cohorts and subgroups differently. And the health consequences of stigma—from internalized homophobia that contributes to depression, anxiety, and substance abuse to external forces of poverty, racism, and sexual prejudice that increase risk for HIV infection (Diaz, Ayala, Bein, Heine, & Marin, 2001)—affect the lives of gay men, lesbians, and bisexuals in multiple ways. This chapter will review the current literature on health issues of GLB people and provide recommendations for care from a life course perspective, using a life model of practice as a theoretical framework.

IMPACT OF CULTURAL COHORTS ON HEALTH

In the late 1980s, the anthropologist Gilbert Herdt (1992) identified four overlapping but distinct non-heterosexual cohorts of twentieth-century Americans, each with different life experiences that affected identity, behavior, and life events (table 14.1). Although the terms *homosexual* and *gay and lesbian* are often used interchangeably, they are actually very different cultural constructs that have emerged in the context of different social and historical periods, and they have different life course outcomes. The concept of community or even of nonheterosexual identity is radically different for the two earliest cohorts of nonheterosexual people in the twentieth century than for the most recent two. For lesbians and gay men—the third cohort—who came of age during and after the radicalism of the 1960s, cultural identity development involved coming out and social activism, founding GLB institutions to share and transmit a new culture, and leaving or exiting cultural heterosexuality, generally at various stages of early and middle adulthood. This process has enabled them to live openly gay lives in the context of a shared community, disclosing their sexual identities with family, coworkers, and others when it felt safe to do so—a radical departure from the experiences of *homosexual* adults, many of whom did not "come out" to parents, family members, and others who figured prominently in their lives.

TABLE 14.1 Gay Identity Cohorts, Twentieth Century

EVOLUTION OF GAY IDENTITY (HERDT, 1992)				
TIMEFRAME	COHORT	COMMUNITY	IDENTITY	LIFE STYLE
1910	1 - Came of age after WWI	no	no	hiding/lived as heterosexual
1940	2 - Came of age during/after WWII	secret	homosexual	secrecy/bars
1969	3 - Came of age after Stonewall/Gay Activism	yes	lesbian/gay	passing/coming out
1983	4 - Came of age in the era of AIDS	yes	queer	living "out"

Source: Ryan and Bradford (1998)

A NEW COHORT—LESBIAN AND GAY YOUTH

In their study of GLB youth in Chicago, Herdt and Boxer (1993) documented the emergence of a new lesbian and gay cohort with the potential to come out during adolescence and to experience developmental events on-time as GLB youth rather than off-time as adults experiencing a second adolescence after coming out in later life. Coming out during adolescence enables youth to share their lives with their families across the life course, to incorporate their families into their lives rather than having to compartmentalize their social, emotional, and sexual lives, as did earlier generations of GLB adults who came out at older ages. As D'Augelli (1998) points out, these cultural transitions have major implications for both the individual and his or her family and social network. These identities also have critical implications for behavior, stressors, health risks, and protective factors, as well as for health outcomes.

Gay, lesbian, and bisexual youth experience the same health and mental health concerns as their heterosexual peers, with the additional issue of having to deal with the health and social effects of stigma. Coping with stigma from an early age can increase risk, particularly in youth with underlying vulnerabilities engendered by dysfunctional or addicted parents, emotional deprivation, physical and sexual abuse, and severe stress. Dealing with stigma in adolescence can also foster problem-solving skills that people do not generally develop until later in life. Although little is known about resiliency and coping skills in GLB adolescents, many youth perceive being gay as a source of strength that helps them deal with other challenging issues (Anderson, 1998). At the same time, studies show high rates of chronic stress (Rosario, Rotheram-Borus, & Reid, 1996), substance use (DuRant, Krowchuk, & Sinal, 1998; Garofalo, Wolf, Kessel, Palfrey, & DuRant, 1998), sexually transmitted diseases (STDs) (Garofalo et al., 1998), victimization (D'Augelli & Hershberger, 1993; D'Augelli, Pilkington, & Hershberger, 2002; Garofalo et al., 1998), and suicidal thoughts and attempts (D'Augelli & Hershberger, 1993; D'Augelli, Hershberger, & Pilkington, 1998; D'Augelli et al., 2002; Garofalo et al., 1998) among a substantial proportion of GLB youth. Moreover, gay and bisexual youth, particularly youth of color, are at high risk for HIV infection.

Although researchers have documented a substantial decrease in the age of psychosexual milestones and self-identification as lesbian, gay, or bisexual, beginning with studies in the late 1980s, this information has rarely been included in provider training materials and professional literature (Ryan, 2000). Most studies have focused on gay male youth; only a handful have targeted lesbian adolescents, and although many youth identify as bisexual, to date no studies have been published on bisexual identity during adolescence (Ryan & Futterman, 1998). The importance of understanding bisexual identity in youth is highlighted by the findings of several studies that bisexual youth are more likely to have negative experiences and outcomes than their lesbian and gay (or heterosexual) peers. For example, Hunter (1996) found greater negative perceptions about sexuality among bisexual teens, while Hershberger, Pilkington, and D'Augelli (1997) reported greater likelihood of multiple suicide attempts among bisexual youth compared with their lesbian and gay peers. In an analysis of data from school-based surveys in Massachusetts from 1995 to 1999, Goodenow, Netherland, and Szalacha (2002) found that bisexually experienced male youth reported significantly higher levels of sexual risk and injection drug use than heterosexual or gay-identified peers. This result led the researchers to conclude that "there might be a constellation of especially high risk behaviors and experiences among youth with bisexual experience" and that many of the higher-risk results attributed to gay or sexual minority youth may actually be related to bisexual behavior (Goodenow et al., 2002, p. 207).

VICTIMIZATION

Victimization is normative in the lives of GLB youth. Research has shown that the more open youth are about their sexual orientation (and the more gender atypical), the more likely they are to be victimized (D'Augelli et al., 2002). School-based studies show significantly higher rates of victimization for GLB youth compared with their heterosexual peers. In the Massachusetts Youth Risk Behavior Study, GLB youth were more than four times as likely to have been threatened with a weapon at school, more than three times as likely to have been in a fight that required medical attention, and nearly five times as likely as heterosexual youth to have missed school because they were afraid (Garofalo et al., 1998). Youth who were more frequent victims were aware of same-sex feelings, identified as GLB, and came out to others at younger ages (D'Augelli, in press). Many GLB and questioning youth know of others who are victimized, which sends a powerful message to pass as heterosexual and to hide. Although hiding may protect closeted youth from harassment, it isolates them from access to a supportive community and available resources. Moreover, among adults hiding is also associated with negative health and mental health outcomes, including substance abuse, suicide, depression, and high-risk behaviors (Gonsiorek & Rudolph, 1991; Meyer, 1995).

Watching as other youth are victimized affects an adolescent's feelings of vulnerability and personal safety. In one multicity study, one in three youth feared verbal abuse and one in five feared physical abuse at school (D'Augelli, in press). Those who feared victimization reported more symptoms of psychological distress, while those who were victimized in high school had more symptoms of post-traumatic stress. Not all youth who are targets of anti-gay victimization are gay. Six percent of youth in the Seattle school survey who were targets of anti-gay abuse were heterosexual (Reis & Saewyc, 1999); they were victimized because they were *perceived* to be gay. Anti-gay harassment can have a profound effect on school climate, instilling fear and dread in many young people and promoting an atmosphere of intolerance. For many youth, the anxiety of trying to avoid detection and victimization at school can also affect academic performance and career options by contributing to school avoidance and dropping out.

The earlier age of initial awareness, self-identification as lesbian or gay, and coming out has increased conflict related to sexual orientation and gender identity in school and community settings. This is exacerbated by the lack of training of school personnel and the lack of school or agency policies to address the needs of GLB youth and to provide protection from harassment and abuse. Only recently have some individual agencies, several states, and a number of school districts begun to implement policies and staff training related to sexual and, in some cases, gender identity to enhance services and care for youth.

SEXUAL HEALTH AND STDS

Understanding emerging sexuality and learning about intimacy and sexual decision making are important tasks for all adolescents. However, obtaining accurate information about sexual health is much more difficult for non-heterosexual teens, since health promotion literature for youth and families rarely mentions GLB youth (Ryan & Futterman, 1998). Teens who fear that others will assume they are gay are unlikely to ask questions about GLB health. Moreover, accurate information about sexuality, safer-sex practices, and STDs transmitted between same-sex partners is generally not available in mainstream health settings.

By twelfth grade, a majority of students report that they have had sexual intercourse. Youth who have unprotected sex are at risk for a range of sexually transmitted diseases, nearly two-thirds of which occur in youth and young adults under age 25 (Zenilman, 1988). One-fourth of the 12 million new STD cases each year (3 million new infections) occur among adolescents, who are at greater risk than adults because they are more likely to engage in unprotected sex and other high-risk sexual behaviors. Moreover, adolescent girls and young women are more susceptible to cervical infections (Eng & Butler, 1996). Health consequences range from mild acute infections to serious long-term complications such as cervical, liver, anal, and other cancers and reproductive health problems. Like their heterosexual peers, sexually active GLB youth are at risk for STDs and HIV infection. However, their risk is heightened by the need for secrecy, the lack of accurate information, and the lack of supportive environments for socializing that do not promote risky sexual behavior.

Research on adults indicates that most lesbians have been sexually active with male partners. The risk for most STDs is substantially lower for women who have sex only with other women, and lesbians who have exclusively same-sex partners are the least likely to contract bacterial STDs (White & Levinson, 1993). Although research evidence is limited, it has been reported that some STDs can be transmitted between women, including human papillomavirus, bacterial vaginosis, and trichomoniasis. Herpes and chlamydia have also been found in lesbians who have not had sex with men, but rates appear to be lower than among heterosexual women (Marazzo, Stine, Handsfield, & Koutsky, 1996). Cases of female-to-female transmission of HIV infection are extremely rare, although at least two instances have been reported (Chu, Buehler, Fleming, & Berkelman, 1990). Sexually active lesbians also report having sex with gay and bisexual male peers, which increases their risk for a range of STDs and HIV infection. Moreover, providers have consistently documented unplanned pregnancy as a concern for lesbian youth (Ryan & Futterman, 1998). In one study of sexual orientation, sexual behavior, and pregnancy among American Indian youth, lesbian and bisexual girls reported more frequent intercourse, compared with heterosexual youth, and one in four had been pregnant at least once (Saewyc, Skay, Bearinger, Blum, & Resnick, 1998). Sexually active gay and bisexual male youth are at risk for a range of STDs, including urethritis, anogenital conditions, oropharyngeal conditions, gastrointestinal disease, hepatitis, herpes, and HIV. Hepatitis A and B are readily transmitted sexually, while hepatitis C is transmitted primarily through contact with blood and less often through sexual contact.

HIV/AIDS

Adolescents are also at high risk for HIV infection. One in four HIV-infected people is under age 22, and prevalence among adolescents has increased significantly, particularly among young men who have sex with men (MSM). In a multicity study of HIV prevalence and risk behaviors in young men (ages 15–22) who have sex with men, 7.2% of the young men were infected (Valleroy et al., 2000). HIV prevalence was higher among youth who reported anal sex, injection drug use, having an STD, or running away from home. Rates among youth of color were alarmingly high, with about 1 in 7 African American (14.1%) and mixed-race youths (13.4%) infected, compared with 1 in 14 Latinos (6.9%) and 1 in 30 white youths (3.3%). Because many of the 15-to-22-year-olds were probably recently infected or are likely to become infected in the near future, HIV education and prevention are critical, especially for youth of color. School-based HIV-prevention education is especially important, because health maintenance behaviors are developed during adolescence and young adulthood. However, GLB youth are significantly less likely than heterosexual youth to receive HIV-prevention instruction (Blake et al., 2001). In a statewide study in Massachusetts, only one in five schools throughout the state provided gay-sensitive HIV instruction that addressed the needs of GLB youth. In schools where gay-sensitive HIV instruction was provided, GLB youth were less likely to have been sexually active during the past three months, had fewer sexual partners, and were less likely to use alcohol and drugs that were GLB students in schools with no, low, or minimally sensitive instruction (Blake et al., 2001). GLB youth are exposed to many misconceptions and cultural stereotypes about homosexuality during childhood and adolescence. As a result, many have inaccurate and naive perceptions about their risk for various sexually transmitted diseases and pregnancy.

Today's GLB youth are growing up in the context of the AIDS epidemic, and they have been socialized into a culture in which premature death and chronic illness have become normalized. Many gay youth report feeling that HIV infection is inevitable, and they fear that even if they try to protect themselves they will not be able to do so (Ryan & Futterman, 1998). The HIV epidemic has a substantial impact on their development and their sense of the future, which has important implications for prevention, risk reduction, and self-care. In a study of adolescent development in an ethnically diverse sample of GLB youth, Herdt and Boxer (1993) found that GLB youth had a very limited sense of future time and could not conceive of themselves beyond age 35, unlike heterosexual adolescents, who could readily imagine themselves at age 50 and had a sense of who they would be and what they would be doing at midlife. This finding also reflects the lack of intergenerational contact and the invisibility of older GLB adults in mainstream and GLBT community life.

SUBSTANCE ABUSE

Most studies of GLB youth show higher rates of alcohol use, drug use, and cigarette smoking compared with their heterosexual peers. GLB youth in school-based studies were more likely than heterosexual youth to use alcohol and other drugs, such as steroids, marijuana, and cocaine (DuRant et al., 1998; Garofalo et al., 1998), to engage in high-risk or heavy drug use (Reis & Saewyc, 1999), to have smoked cigarettes during the past thirty days (DuRant et al., 1998; Garofalo et al., 1998), and to have used smokeless tobacco (Garofalo et al., 1998). Although these state and local school studies are representative of students in general, they include a very small proportion of lesbian- and gay-identified youth and a larger, but still small, group of bisexual youth. It is therefore difficult to know how widespread substance use may be among all GLB youth, especially since some other community studies show rates that are comparable to adolescents in general (e.g., Herdt & Boxer, 1993; Lock & Steiner, 1999).

Lesbian and gay youth use alcohol and drugs for many of the same reasons as their heterosexual peers: to experiment and assert independence, to relieve tension, to increase feelings of self-esteem and adequacy, and to self-medicate for underlying depression or other mood disorders (Ryan & Futterman, 1998). However, they become more vulnerable as a result of social isolation and the need to hide their sexual identity. So they may use alcohol and drugs to deal with stigma and shame, to deny same-sex feelings, or to defend against harassment or anti-gay violence. Since adolescent experimentation with substances may become habitual, education and early intervention are especially important. Some GLB adults report starting alcohol and drug use during adolescence to reduce tension during social and sexual interactions. However, substance use during or before sexual activity can affect judgment, increasing risk for HIV infection, and using injection drugs and sharing needles is another route for HIV transmission.

MENTAL HEALTH CONCERNS

Gay, lesbian, and bisexual youth experience a range of mental health concerns that affect adolescents in general. However, they are also at risk for stress and mental health problems related to stigma. Most GLB youth grow up to lead satisfying, productive lives, but some are more vulnerable. Some youth experience preexisting vulnerabilities, such as dysfunctional or addicted parents, abuse and neglect, severe stress, and underlying emotional disorders, making it difficult to manage the stress associated with integrating their sexual identity.

Chronic stress is a concern for many GLB youth, particularly those who are worried about disclosure and harassment. In a study of stressful life events for gay and bisexual youth of color, emotional distress increased with the amount of gay-related stress, such as coming out to parents, relatives, and friends; having their sexual identity discovered; and being ridiculed because of their sexual orientation (Rosario et al., 1996). Gay-related stress was associated with increasing depression. Youth with higher self-esteem reported less emotional distress, including depression and anxiety.

Suicide is a significant concern for all adolescents; it is the third leading cause of death among youth ages 15–24 and the fourth leading cause of death among children ages 10–14 (Hoyert, Kochanek, & Murphy, 1999). Far more youth attempt suicide than actually complete it. However, because past suicide attempts are powerful predictors for completed suicide, they must be taken seriously. Between 6% and 13% of adolescents have reported at least one suicide attempt (Garland & Ziegler, 1993). No one knows how many lesbian, gay, and bisexual youth actually commit suicide, but a range of studies has found rates of suicide attempts and suicidal thoughts to be consistently very high.

In school-based studies, GLB youth were more than three times as likely to have attempted suicide during the past twelve months (Garofalo et al., 1998; Reis & Saewyc, 1999) and were nearly twice as likely to have developed a suicide plan—a serious indicator of suicide intent (Reis & Saewyc, 1999). Studies of gay and bisexual suicide attempters show they were more likely to have self-identified as gay or bisexual and to have come out to others at younger ages (Hershberger & D'Augelli, 1995; Remafedi, Farrow, & Deisher, 1991), to have friends and relatives who attempted or committed suicide (Hershberger & D'Augelli, 1995; Remafedi et al., 1991), and to have been rejected because of their sexual orientation

(Schneider, Farberow, & Kruks, 1989). Gay and bisexual youth of color who attempted suicide were more likely to have dropped out of school, to have been ejected from their homes, and to have experienced more gay-related stress than those who had not attempted suicide (Hershberger & D'Augelli, 1995). Family problems, conflict with sexual identity, and pressure to conform to gender norms and behavior are also associated with suicide attempts.

GLBT youth are developing a vibrant new culture using Internet Web sites, social and recreational organizations for GLBT youth, Gay-Straight Alliance (GSA) groups in schools, and mainstream resources that support sexual minority youth. These community supports are making a substantial difference in providing opportunities for youth to integrate their sexual identity into other aspects of their lives, promoting empowerment and normative development. As these community supports increase and GLB youth become more visible in school and community settings, we anticipate that many of the stressors that youth currently experience will decrease, reducing their vulnerability, changing health outcomes, and making it much easier to integrate sexual orientation and other aspects of identity.

ACCESS TO CARE

Adolescents are the most uninsured and underserved of all age groups and are the least likely to use primary care services (Klein, Slap, Elster, & Cohn, 1993). At the same time, they have many unmet health and mental health needs; this is particularly true for youth of color, who are less likely than their white peers to receive the care that is needed. Adolescents with disabling health and mental health conditions face additional barriers to care and are more likely to live in poverty and to be covered by public health plans, primarily Medicaid. GLB youth, as part of these and other affected groups, face additional barriers to care, including providers' lack of training in adolescent development and sexuality in general, and misinformation and negative bias in dealing with homosexuality in particular.

These attitudes have been consistently reported among a range of providers over a period of years; surprisingly, however, they persist, even as public attitudes about homosexuality have become more accepting. In a 1996 survey of pediatricians, more than one-third felt uncomfortable caring for a gay or lesbian teen, and nearly as many were uncomfortable working with a child whose parents were lesbian or gay (Perrin, 1997). A recent survey of directors of family medicine training in medical schools found that nearly half were unaware of any education related to homosexuality during four years of medical school. Those who were aware of such curricula reported an average of 2.5 hours of instruction (Tesar & Rovi, 1998). Another survey of pediatricians found that the majority had reservations about addressing sexual orientation with patients and did not include sexual orientation in sexual histories. Not surprisingly, those who took sexual histories and included them with younger adolescents were more likely to identify youth who were questioning their sexual identity and discussed these concerns with their physicians. Most pediatricians surveyed wanted more information about gay health issues, and almost half requested further training, although nearly all were unfamiliar with community resources for GLB youth (East & Boekeloo, 1996).

Biased care and a need for training have been consistently reported by workers in other disciplines as well, including mental health and school-based providers (e.g., Ryan & Futterman, 1998). In a national survey of high school counselors, nurses, psychologists, and social workers conducted by the American Psychological Association's Healthy LGB Students Project, nearly all school-based providers reported a lack of capacity to provide services for GLB youth (American Psychological Association, 2001). A disturbing 90% to 97% of providers said they lacked the training, knowledge, or skills to care for GLB youth, while 77% to 89% lacked appropriate materials to provide services.

Persistent lack of training, misinformation, and negative bias have direct implications for delivery of health and mental health care, especially for GLB youth who are developing help-seeking and self-care behaviors and communication patterns with providers that must serve them throughout their lives. In a series of focus groups with GLB youth in seven cities in preparation for a federal government conference on the primary care needs of GLB youth, adolescents talked about their care-related needs and experiences. Although nine out of ten adolescents reported needing health care during the past five years, only two-thirds were able to obtain care. Only one in three felt they could talk openly with providers. Four-fifths were sexually active, but only half of their providers had discussed STDs and sexual activity with them, and only 55% of providers had discussed HIV. Nearly two-thirds (61%) had been tested for HIV, but testing had been suggested by only 16% of providers. And more than three-quarters acknowledged that providers assumed they were heterosexual (Ryan & Futterman, 1998).

HEALTH EFFECTS OF STIGMA

The social, behavioral, and health effects of stigma affect lesbians, gay men, and bisexuals throughout the life course. Because longitudinal research on developmental concerns and aging does not include questions on sexual orientation, we rarely consider the cumulative effects of internalized homophobia and negative life events on health and well-being. Yet for adolescents these experiences shape behavior (including risk and protective factors) and subsequent experiences. Interactions with health and mental health providers affect trust and willingness to disclose. Formative experiences with families and key adults affect self-esteem, self-care, and risk taking. Among the most important resiliency factors for Latino gay men is the presence of a gay role model during childhood (Diaz & Ayala,

TABLE 14.2 Lesbian and Gay Health Concerns

	LGB YOUTH	YOUNG ADULTS	MIDDLE-AGED ADULTS (40–60)	OLDER ADULTS (60+)
SOCIAL EFFECTS OF DISCRIMINATION	DISCRIMINATION In education In residential treatment, group homes, health care, access to care and social services Rejection by family and peers Restriction of life choices (education, occupation)	DISCRIMINATION In education, employment, housing In health care and access to care In child custody and adoption In income In lack of spousal and survivor benefits	DISCRIMINATION In education, employment, housing In health care and access to care In child custody and adoption In income In lack of spousal and survivor benefits	DISCRIMINATION In employment, housing In residential programs, health care, access to care and social services In lack of spousal and survivor benefits In nursing homes and long-term care Social invisibility
HEALTH EFFECTS OF DISCRIMINATION	ANTI-GAY VIOLENCE AND PSYCHOLOGICAL TRAUMA Highest risk—gay/lesbian youth and young adults Assault, murder, rape, physical abuse, threats, intimidation, verbal abuse	ANTI-GAY VIOLENCE AND PSYCHOLOGICAL TRAUMA Highest risk—gay/lesbian youth and young adults Assault, murder, rape, physical abuse, threats, intimidation, verbal abuse	ANTI-GAY VIOLENCE AND PSYCHOLOGICAL TRAUMA Assault, murder, rape, physical abuse, threats, intimidation, verbal abuse	ANTI-GAY VIOLENCE AND PSYCHOLOGICAL TRAUMA Frequency of violence drops Psychological impact remains Fear of disclosure Vulnerability and vigilance Monitoring of social interactions Health Effects of Discrimination
RELATED DISORDERS AND DISEASES	MENTAL HEALTH CONCERNS Stress related to hiding sexual identity, fear, anxiety Depression Substance abuse Risk for suicide Cigarette smoking	MENTAL HEALTH CONCERNS Stress related to hiding sexual identity, fear, anxiety Depression Substance abuse Risk for suicide Cigarette smoking	MENTAL HEALTH CONCERNS Stress related to hiding sexual identity Depression and anxiety AIDS-related bereavement Alcohol use Drug use Cigarette smoking	MENTAL HEALTH CONCERNS Stress related to hiding sexual identity Isolation (death of partner, loss of support system) AIDS-related bereavement Alcohol use Drug use Cigarette smoking

TABLE 14.2 Lesbian and Gay Health Concerns (continued)

LGB YOUTH		YOUNG ADULTS		MIDDLE-AGED ADULTS (40–60)		OLDER ADULTS (60+)	
MALE	FEMALE	MALE	FEMALE	MALE	FEMALE	MALE	FEMALE
Hepatitis	Pregnancy	Delay in seeking help	Delay in seeking help	Anal cancer	Breast cancer	Cardiovascular disease	Breast cancer
HIV	HIV	Eating disorders	Lack of gynecological care	Cardiovascular disease	Cardiovascular disease	Cerebrovascular disease	Cardiovascular disease
STDs	STDs	Hepatitis	Lack of preventive care	Chronic liver disease	Delay in help seeking	Chronic liver disease	Cerebrovascular disease
		HIV	Poor access to care	Delay in seeking help	Gynecological cancers	Liver cancer	Gynecological cancers
		STDs	Pregnancy	Lung cancer	Lack of preventive care	Lung cancer	Lung cancer
		Lack of preventive care	HIV	Hepatitis	Lack of gynecological care	HIV	Neurocognitive impairment
			STDs	Lack of preventive care	Lung cancer	Neurocognitive impairment	Poor access to care
				HIV	Poor access to care	Poor access to care	
				STDs	STDs		

Source: Ryan, C. (1994). Lesbian and gay health concerns. In C. Ryan and R. Bogard. What every lesbian and gay American needs to know about health care reform. Washington, DC: Human Rights Campaign Foundation.

2001). Predictably, family acceptance is also the most important protective factor in preventing HIV infection.[1]

The life model of social work practice considers the impact of an ever-changing environment on the individual and is concerned with goodness of fit between the person and the environment. This model has particular salience for gay men, lesbians, and bisexuals who must interact with an environment that changes continually in terms of adversity, availability of resources, and level of sexual prejudice. A life course perspective will enable practitioners to consider the cumulative impact of environmental stressors on the health and well-being of GLB people (table 14.2). Adverse experiences during childhood and adolescence increase vulnerability during adulthood. Moreover, many diseases that manifest in adulthood and older age are rooted in conditions and behaviors developed at an earlier life stage.

YOUNG ADULTS

Gay men, lesbians, and bisexuals in their mid-twenties and thirties have greater access to lesbian and gay health and mental health resources and social support than any other generation, in contrast to adolescents, who are the most under-served of any age group. Young adults are more likely to be open about their sexual identity in a wide range of settings (e.g., family, peer networks, and work-place) than are other age groups, and they are more likely to have integrated their sexual identity into various aspects of their lives. Studies show that lesbians and gay men who have integrated a positive identity are better adjusted (Miranda & Storms, 1989), more connected to a supportive lesbian/gay community, and less apt to suffer from depression (Meyer, 1995) than gay people who are in conflict with their identity. Ironically, at the same time that coming out enhances psychological adjustment and increases access to appropriate care, it places lesbians and gay men at greater risk for discrimination, victimization, and violence. The most frequent targets of anti-gay violence are those who are most open, particularly lesbian and gay youth and young adults.

VICTIMIZATION

Bias-related crime and victimization are common occurrences for lesbians and gay men. In one study, half of all respondents reported experiencing anti-gay crime or attempted crime as a result of their sexual orientation (Herek, Gillis, Cogan, & Glunt, 1997). More than one in 14 females (6.8%) and one in 12 males (8%) had witnessed the murder of a loved one because of his or her sexual identity. Although bisexuals are included in this and other studies, little research has been done on their specific needs and experiences; not only have they been largely invisible within lesbian and gay communities, but some research indicates that they are perceived differently and are not as stigmatized as lesbians and gay men. For example, Mohr and Rochlen (1999) found that heterosexual men viewed bisexuality as being more moral and tolerable than male homosexuality.

In a range of studies, men are victims more frequently than women, and gay men are more likely than bisexuals to be victims. Such crimes also precipitate post-traumatic stress and psychiatric symptoms. Herek and colleagues found that GLB people who had experienced a bias-related crime during the past five years showed higher levels of psychological distress, including depressive symptoms, post-traumatic stress, anger, and anxiety. They were also less likely to report positive attitudes toward the world and benevolence toward others, and more likely to feel vulnerable and not positive about themselves. In a national survey of lesbians, Descamps and colleagues found that those who experienced hate crimes reported significantly more stress and drug use than those who had experienced non-bias-related assault (Descamps, Rothblum, Bradford, & Ryan, 2000). In an analysis of a national probability sample, Mays and Cochran (2001) reported that GLB respondents who reported any lifetime or day-to-day discrimination were more likely to have a psychiatric disorder than those who had not had such experiences. An understanding of the negative sequelae of victimization is especially important in understanding behavior, health risks, and emotional distress, not only among youth and young adults but throughout the life course. Many early experiences of victimization continue to shape behavior, relationships, and attitudes about self-care as an individual ages.

SEXUALLY TRANSMITTED DISEASES AND HIV

Young adults are also at high risk for STDs and HIV infection. Nationwide, more than four in five cases of sexually transmitted diseases are reported in adolescents and young adults. STDs also increase susceptibility for HIV infection. In gay and bisexual men, STDs that inflame the urethra or rectum increase risk for HIV infection, while increasing the amount of virus present in the ejaculate or lesions of HIV-positive men. In women, many STDs have no symptoms and thus remain untreated for a longer period of time. For example, chlamydia is asymptomatic in three-fourths of infected women, while approximately half of gonorrhea infections in women have no symptoms. This is especially salient since 79% of reported cases of chlamydia occur in young women. Moreover, in young women the cervix is much more vulnerable to STDs, particularly chlamydia and gonococcus.

Contrary to what many health care providers may believe, a substantial proportion of lesbians and gay men have both male and female partners, which has important implications for prevention, screening, and treatment. At the same time, providers readily assume that heterosexuality is ubiquitous, and many GLB clients find themselves in the position of educating their providers about their health and mental health needs.

A high proportion of men with same-sex partners, particularly men of color, do not identify as gay or bisexual. In one study of more than 8,000 men of color, as many as 24% of African American men and 15% of Latino men who identified as heterosexual had same-sex partners (Centers for Disease Control and Prevention, 2000). However, behaviorally bisexual men are often unlikely to disclose their sexual identity to female partners (Kalichman, Roffman, Picciano, & Bolan, 1998). Moreover, they report lower intention of condom use, have weaker perceived norms for practicing safer sex (Heckman et al., 1995), and have higher rates of engagement in risky sexual behavior than homosexual men do (Doll & Beeker, 1996).

A study of STD prevalence and treatment among women who have sex with women underscores the need for more-accurate information for this population. A common perception among lesbians and their providers is that women who have sex with women are at low or no risk for STDs. However, 21% of a sample of women who have female partners reported having been diagnosed with an STD (Bauer & Welles, 2001). Of women who did not have male partners, 13% reported a history of STDs, including chlamydia, genital warts, trichomoniasis, and pelvic inflammatory disease. However, only 10% of these women reported regular testing for STDs, with older women least likely to get tested. Lesbians were only 27% as likely to get tested as women who identified as heterosexual or bisexual. Lack of appropriate screening or treatment for sexual health needs can manifest in later life as serious health concerns, such as gynecological or liver cancers.

AIDS

The AIDS epidemic has had a devastating impact on GLB communities since it was first characterized in 1981. Although losses were greatest early on among gay and bisexual men in their late thirties and forties, the long incubation period for disease progression has ultimately been reflected in increasing diagnoses and deaths among young adults. Moreover, men who have sex with men (MSM) continue to represent the largest number of reported AIDS cases each year. In 2000, more than half of HIV infections among young men were attributed to same-sex contact (Centers for Disease Control and Prevention, 2002). Data from the Young Men's Study show extremely high rates of infection in young men ages 23–29 who have sex with men (Valleroy et al., 2000), particularly among young men of color, that mirror rates of HIV infection in sub-Saharan countries (table 14.3).

Recent studies indicate a resurgence of high-risk sexual behavior and related sexually transmitted infections among gay and bisexual men, and some link treat-

TABLE 14.3 HIV Infection in Young Men Who Have Sex with Men

ETHNIC GROUP	YOUTH AGES 15–22 1994–1998 (7 U.S. CITIES) PREVALENCE	YOUNG ADULTS AGES 23–29 1998–2000 (6 U.S. CITIES) PREVALENCE
Whites	3.3%	7%
Latinos	6.9%	14%
African Americans	14.1%	32%
Mixed Race	13.4%	10%

Source: Valleroy et al. (2000).

ment advances and the normativity of HIV/AIDS in the lives of gay men with these increases. For example, a study of unprotected anal intercourse using a probability sample of gay men found that rates of unprotected anal sex increased from 38% in 1992 to 51% by 1998, which suggests that prevention efforts are diminishing (Ekstrand, Stall, Paul, Osmond, & Coates, 1999). A national probability study of men who have sex with men—the Urban Men's Health Study—was launched in the late 1990s to document AIDS-related behaviors and health experiences of urban men with same-sex partners. An alarming 17% of men were HIV-positive (nearly one in five men), and rates were highest among African Americans and men who were poorer and who used drugs, indicating that the epidemic among men with same-sex partners continues at a very high rate (Catania et al., 2001).

IMPACT OF THE EPIDEMIC

The AIDS epidemic has had a profound impact on GLB communities at all levels, affecting (1) individual behavior and emotional well-being, (2) social norms, friendship networks, and intimate relationships, (3) community institutions, allocation of resources, and advocacy focus, and (4) social and public policy, societal perceptions and attitudes about lesbians and gay men, and GLB community relationships with mainstream society (Paul, Hays, & Coates, 1995). The epidemic has affected each age cohort, in both similar and different ways. Middle-aged lesbians and gay men were most affected initially—some losing half or nearly all of their social and support networks. The highest proportion of gay and bisexual men with AIDS are young adults, under age forty, who have grown up with the epidemic and who became sexually active against a backdrop of potential infection.

For young adults, the threat of HIV infection shapes sexual behavior, dating, and choices about maintaining relationships, once they are established. HIV status has become a social marker, with social, emotional, and sexual decisions made according to a person's status. Concerns about health have become paramount for those with HIV, and an ongoing issue in decision making for those who are negative. Discrimination has increased substantially as a result of the AIDS epidemic, and among the general public AIDS remains linked with homosexuals (rather than heterosexuals or bisexuals), providing a vehicle for those who hold negative beliefs to express underlying sexual prejudice and anti-gay attitudes (Herek & Capitanio, 1999). Social support networks have become more vital for persons with HIV/AIDS, and caring for friends and loved ones is a daily experience for large numbers of gay men and lesbians, including young adults who have had little involvement with serious illness and death. Caring for people with AIDS is highly stressful, and many caretakers lack adequate resources and support. A national- and city-based probability survey found that more than half (54%) of gay men living in major cities had provided care for a lover, friend, or relative with AIDS (Turner, Catania, & Gagnon, 1994). Access to a peer support system is especially important for GLB people who have conflicted or nonexistent family relationships. In another study, close male friends (45%) or partners (42%) served as caregivers for gay men with AIDS, while fewer than one in ten (8%) caretakers were parents or siblings (McCann & Wadsworth, 1992). Survivor guilt is a common experience for GLB people who have lost many friends and loved ones. Individual, group, and community bereavement is expressed in myriad ways, from individual loss and psychological reactions to the lack of institutional memory resulting from the loss of two generations of leaders and apathy and infighting at a community level. Loss is compounded, as many GLB adults have experienced multiple losses, including chronic bereavement over a period of several years. Martin (1988) found that level of psychological distress, including symptoms of post-traumatic stress, sleep problems, and sedative and recreational drug use increased with the number of AIDS-related bereavements.

At the same time, the AIDS epidemic has provided an unprecedented opportunity for scores of Americans who did not realize that they already knew closeted lesbians and gay men to identify with their humanity in observing the mobilization of an extraordinary grassroots social service response. Individual social workers and other providers were at the forefront of building a community service network that rapidly implemented social and health services, AIDS-prevention and education initiatives, and public policies on blood donation, safer sex, infection control, and education in the absence of government response. This occurred initially through the existing lesbian and gay health network developed by early organizations such as the National Lesbian and Gay Health Foundation, together with other lesbian and gay volunteers in major urban areas, and later in suburban and rural communities. Many grassroots groups launched advocacy efforts that ultimately had a direct impact on shaping local, state, and federal policies, including new policies to expedite drug development and to include underserved groups in clinical trials for drug development. At an individual and community level, gay men and lesbians created rituals to cope with the ongoing loss and serious social ramifications of the AIDS epidemic, including discrimination and prejudice. Individual memorial services reflecting an individual's personality, creativity, and life experiences, the Names Quilt, and candlelight vigils helped contextualize these losses and provide a framework for coping and bereavement.

IMPACT OF CULTURE AND ETHNICITY

Cross-cultural literature has consistently pointed out that men and women from all ethnic groups in cultures within and outside of the United States engage in same-sex behavior without identifying as homosexual or GLB. In the context of each culture, they construct a range of identities to provide a cultural framework for desires and behaviors. Understanding these distinctions is essential to understanding risk and health outcomes and to developing appropriate health prevention and health promotion strategies.

Social worker and developmental psychologist Rafael Diaz (1998) has developed an important model to address these issues in his work on culture, sexuality, and risk behavior among Latino gay men. One of his central premises is that risky behavior is both natural and meaningful in the social and cultural context of men who have been socialized to hide and compartmentalize their sexuality to avoid shaming their families and to support cultural values and norms that privilege masculinity (machismo) while enforcing sexual silence about homosexuality. Diaz contends that Latino homosexuals are very different from white gay men on a wide range of issues related to HIV prevention. They represent a different cultural cohort with different interpretations of gender and sexual culture. These differences include the meaning of same-sex behavior and what constitutes homosexuality, the degree of identification with the gay community, sources of social support, and the processes involved in forming dual minority identities of ethnicity and sexuality. Diaz's primary critique of dominant AIDS-prevention models is that they do not reflect the cultural realities of the lives of gay men of color, so they will not be successful in promoting behavior change. Latino gay men are raised with strong family values in a culture with highly defined gender roles, where masculinity is expressed through behaviors such as risk taking, sexual prowess (especially penetration), and multiple partners, and where sexual intercourse is defined as active (masculine) and passive (feminine). Homosexuality is perceived as a gender problem, and gay men are perceived as not being "real men," so they are more vulnerable to cultural messages of machismo. Homosexuality is also shameful, so it is not openly discussed, and Latino gay men generally separate their sexual, social, and family lives to avoid hurting or embarrassing their families.

These early social and cultural messages are internalized and eroticized, affecting attraction, sexual behavior, and risk in adolescents and adults. Other experiences that promote risk include poverty and racism, which undermine the ability to self-regulate risk for HIV infection. In one of his studies, Diaz (1998) found that only 10% of the Latino gay and bisexual men studied felt they had no chance of becoming infected. He interprets this fatalism as a meaningful response to significant experiences with racism, poverty, and homophobia that erodes the ability to exercise control. Racism in the gay community affects the ability of gay men of color to find support and to more fully integrate their multiple identities. Diaz calls for intervention at the macro and mezzo levels to change oppressive social forces that shape individual risk behaviors, by recontextualizing HIV prevention to include strategies that counter racism, poverty, sexism, homophobia, and AIDS stigma. In addition, prevention interventions should help men understand the social forces that promote risk, critically analyze how and why those forces affect their ability to protect themselves against HIV infection, and respond strategically in ways that result in health and well-being rather than in risk and disease.

SUBSTANCE ABUSE

Alcohol and recreational drug use are common among young adults, generally tapering off in heterosexuals with the responsibilities of marriage and child-rearing. Recent population-based studies indicate that lesbian and bisexual women are at higher risk for alcohol abuse than are heterosexuals (Cochran & Mays, 2000; Diamant, Wold, Spritzer, & Gelberg, 2000; Gruskin, Hart, Gordon, & Ackerson, 2001; Nawyn, Richman, Rospenda, & Hughes, 2000; Valanis et al., 2000). In a study of more than 8,000 female members of a large HMO, lesbian and bisexual women were more likely to report heavy drinking and cigarette smoking than their heterosexual counterparts were (Gruskin et al., 2001). They were also more likely to use twelve-step programs or support groups. Highest rates of drinking were reported by lesbians and bisexual women in the youngest age group, 20–34 years. Women with same-sex partners in the 1996 National Household Survey of Drug Abuse were also more likely to be classified with alcohol or drug dependence than their heterosexual peers (Cochran & Mays, 2000).

Studies of gay men show comparable rates of alcohol use but higher rates of drug use, overall, than among heterosexual men (Stall & Wiley, 1988; Stall, Paul, et al., 2001). In the Urban Men's Health Study, Stall, Pollack, and colleagues (2001) found that one-fourth of young gay men (ages 18–29) used multiple illicit drugs and reported high-risk sexual behaviors (one-half had engaged in unprotected anal intercourse during the past year, while one-third reported unprotected receptive anal intercourse). Drug use is normative among a segment of gay men and some lesbians, and for many gay men, in particular, drug use is linked with sexuality and sexual behavior, which increases risk for STDs and HIV.

Reported rates of cigarette smoking are also high among GLB adults, with highest rates among young and middle-aged adults (Gruskin et al., 2001). In one of the few studies of smoking among gay men, Stall, Greenwood, Acree, Paul, and Coates (1999) found that 48% reported smoking, far higher than the 28% prevalence estimate for men in general. Smoking was associated with heavy drinking, frequent gay bar attendance, greater AIDS-related losses, and HIV infection.

MENTAL HEALTH

Studies of lesbians and gay men frequently report high rates of depression and anxiety. This is not surprising given the level of stress that most GLB people routinely experience. Moreover, depressive symptoms are a common feature of the coming out process (Hershberger & D'Augelli, 2000). In population-based surveys, lesbians and gay men report more-frequent use of mental health services than heterosexuals do (e.g., Cochran, Sullivan, & Mays, 2001), a finding also reported in other studies. Some would suggest that the use of mental health services is more accepted in GLB communities, particularly since they are often used to cope with stigma and lack of general support. Other studies, including more recent population-based studies of adults, indicate higher rates of suicide symptoms among GLBs than among heterosexuals (e.g., Cochran & Mays, 2000).

Only a few studies have explored the experiences of GLB adults of color. In a study of sexuality and risk among Latino gay men, many men reported high levels of psychological distress (Diaz et al., 2001). At the same time, experiences of social discrimination, including racism, homophobia, and poverty, were strong predictors of psychological symptoms. Men who were socially isolated, had low self-esteem, and were HIV-positive reported more symptoms; those who identified as high risk reported more experiences of homophobia, racism, and poverty than their "low risk" counterparts. Many used alcohol and drugs to cope not only with homophobic messages but also with the anger and frustration caused by poverty, racism, and other forms of social discrimination and abuse (Diaz & Ayala, 2001). Researchers also found a strong association between recent suicidal ideation and social discrimination (homophobia, racism, and poverty) in childhood and adulthood.

ACCESS TO HEALTH INSURANCE

Although we may not consider the health and mental health effects of unsupportive environments (poorness of fit), GLB people who experience heterosexism in the workplace exhibit higher levels of psychological distress and health-related problems (Waldo & Kemp, 1997). They also report lower health satisfaction, which is associated with more-frequent absenteeism and work withdrawal behaviors. Unsupportive and hostile work environments also increase stress, a correlate of many health problems and a common health concern in the lives of many lesbians and gay men. Concerns about the level of workplace support and the impact of disclosure on career development also affect the vocational choices, income level, and availability of benefits for many lesbians and gay men. In a study of sexual orientation and stress in the workplace, nearly half of the lesbians and gay men surveyed said that sexual orientation had influenced their choice of career (Woods, 1993). In the National Lesbian Health Care Survey, as in many other studies of lesbians, income level is significantly lower than educational attainment: 85% reported having some college, or a college or graduate degree, but 87% earned less than $30,000 per year, suggesting that many women may forgo income for more-supportive work environments (Bradford, Ryan, & Rothblum, 1994).

By selecting more-tolerant occupations or work settings such as the arts, however, lesbians and gay men reduce their income and benefits along with reducing stress. Although gay people in the arts are able to be more open about their sexual identity, salaries are substantially lower than those of other careers, and jobs frequently lack health insurance coverage, pensions, or retirement plans. Lack of third-party coverage restricts access to care and limits options for health prevention and promotion, particularly health care utilization (Cochran et al., 2001; Rankow & Tessaro, 1998). In a population-based survey of Los Angeles County, 30% of heterosexuals, 37% of lesbians, and 52% of bisexuals were uninsured (Diamant et al., 2000). In the Urban Men's Health Study, 16% of men who have sex with men in three large cities did not have health insurance (Stall, Paul, et al., 2001), and those without health insurance were less likely to receive antiretroviral treatment, a critical concern for persons with HIV/AIDS (Stall, Pollack, et al., 2000).

EXPERIENCES WITH PROVIDERS

GLB patients and clients have consistently reported inappropriate and discriminatory care from health and mental health providers. Even though the level of training and cultural competency has significantly increased during the past two decades, many providers are still uninformed about health and mental health needs of GLB patients and clients, and some continue to provide biased and inappropriate care. In a national survey of physician attitudes toward lesbian and gay patients, nine out of ten lesbian and gay physicians reported observing antigay bias in patient care (Schatz & O'Hanlan, 1994). More than two-thirds knew of patients who had received poor care or who were denied care because of their sexual orientation. And although nearly all agreed that physician knowledge of a patient's sexual orientation is important to ensure that specific medical needs are addressed, two-thirds believed that patients who come out to providers will receive inferior care.

In a survey of second-year medical students in the Midwest, 28% reported that homosexuality was immoral, 29% believed that homosexuals endangered the institution of the family, and 15% admitted feeling more negative about homosexuals as a result of the AIDS epidemic (Klamen, Grossman, & Kopacz, 1999). In a study of nursing students, more than half believed that the GLB "lifestyle" is in conflict with their religious beliefs, while 8% to 12% said they despised GLB persons and thought they should be punished (Eliason, 1998). And in a probability study of licensed clinical social workers and counselors in Virginia, only about one in five (more than half of whom were GLB providers) had received specific training on lesbian mental health issues (Ryan, Bradford, & Honnold, 1999). Heterosexual providers were much more likely to perceive lesbian identity as having only a sexual component rather than multiple dimensions of emotional, affectional, and spiritual aspects. Predictably, GLB providers were much better informed about lesbians' experiences, needs, and concerns than their heterosexual peers were.

Comfort and confidence in providers' ability to make available appropriate care is a basic expectation in seeking health and mental health services. Yet this remains an ongoing concern for many GLB patients and clients, who are still reluctant to disclose their sexual orientation for fear of compromised care. In a study of lesbians in Northern California, women who were open with their providers about their sexual orientation were more satisfied with care and used preventive services more often than those who did not come out to their providers (Gruskin, 1995). In another study, women who were open about their sexual identity with providers were more likely to have had Pap smears within the past two years (Diamant, Schuster, & Lever, 2000).

REPRODUCTIVE HEALTH AND FAMILIES

Many young and middle-aged GLB adults are also parents or are considering parenthood through donor insemination, surrogacy, adoption, or foster care. Increasingly, lesbians and gay men are choosing to parent after they come out, and finally parenting is being perceived as an option by GLB youth. According to several estimates, one in three lesbians is a mother, with higher rates for lesbians of color. In the National Lesbian Health Care Survey, another one in three wanted to parent, but social barriers and homophobia prevented them from having children (Bradford et al., 1994). Data from the Women's Health Initiative, a study of women over fifty, indicate that 35% of lesbians and 81% of bisexual women have been pregnant (Valanis et al., 2000). In a study of gay men and parenting, more than half wanted to raise children. Parenting also increased their sense of self-worth and well-being; gay fathers had higher self-esteem and lower internalized homophobia than non-fathers (Sbordone, 1993). Although parenting is a right for all people, lesbians report discrimination from health providers in fertility treatment and insemination, and in many states lesbians and gay men are prevented from adopting children by laws and discriminatory practices. Lack of partner benefits is also a barrier to supporting and sustaining families, particularly families with children.

MIDDLE-AGED ADULTS

Middle age is often identified as the period between ages 40 and 60 or 65, although the gerontologist Bernice Neugarten (1968) describes it as more a state of mind than a fixed number of years. The tasks of mid-adulthood involve caring for younger and older generations, with responsibility for helping to maintain, develop, and transmit culture, particularly to younger generations. Middle-aged men and women live in a society that may be oriented toward youth but is controlled by the middle-aged (Livson, 1981). This has unique implications for gay culture, which has historically been preoccupied with youth. Midlife is also a time of creativity and generativity, with increased concern for personal legacy and what one will leave behind. This generativity is expressed in many ways by GLB adults, including parenting, mentoring, community involvement, advocacy, volunteerism in GLB organizations, and career choices—many lesbians and gay men, in particular, work in health and human services, public service, and teaching. For many, these strivings extend an earlier commitment to developing lesbian and gay community institutions and to challenging long-standing prejudices and sources of discrimination, including laws that preclude or forbid adoption, equal employment, survivor benefits, and marriage.

Lesbians and gay men at midlife are part of the first generation to live openly gay lives as middle-aged people. This was not possible for older homosexuals, who lived much of their lives in the closet. Herdt's concept of gay cohorts provides an important framework for understanding the experiences of midlife GLB adults who represent the far end of the boomer generation. Middle-aged or older lesbians and gay men were reared with pervasive concepts of deviance and mental illness. They were isolated from one another during their youth, and most thought they were "the only one." Even in attempting to connect with others through homophile organizations or, later, lesbian and gay social groups as young adults, most lived separate lives of secrecy and compartmentalization. Many were married as young adults and came out in later life. And even after the dramatic social changes of the last twenty years, lesbians and gay men over age 50 experience and express their sexual identity in a variety of ways that may enhance or reduce their visibility and access to an organized community. One result of reduced visibility is a limited amount of data on lesbian and gay aging, in particular on the health and mental health of midlife and older GLB adults. For example, little information is available on the needs and experiences of older bisexual women and men, who become increasingly invisible as they age.

A characteristic feature of aging—shortened future time and growing awareness of mortality—seems less salient for GLB adults who have been heavily affected as younger adults by loss and early death as a result of the AIDS epidemic. Although more research has focused on gay male aging, little has addressed midlife gay men or lesbians. Lack of preventive care (a common finding in studies of lesbians and gay men) means that treatable conditions such as hypertension, diabetes, substance abuse, and early-stage cancers may not be identified. Many young adults who contract an infectious disease are unaware of the long-term complications if it is inaccurately diagnosed or left untreated. Hepatitis B, a common infectious disease in gay men, can be prevented with a vaccine, but patient education is generally poor. One out of five gay men infected with hepatitis B is at risk for developing chronic active hepatitis, which can become life-threatening in later years, leading to chronic liver disease, cirrhosis, liver cancer, and premature death (Ryan & Bogard, 1994). Undetected gynecological cancers in lesbians, which could be identified through routine screening, ultimately become life-threatening. Yet among participants in the National Lesbian Health Care Survey, Bradford and Ryan (1988) found that one in 20 lesbians over age 55 had never had a Pap smear and one in six had never self-examined her breasts.

HEALTH CONCERNS AND AGING

In one of the few studies of health concerns of middle-aged lesbians (ages 40 to 60), a majority considered their health to be excellent or good, similar to women in general (Ryan & Bradford, 1991). The most common health concerns were weight, arthritis, back trouble, and allergies. Although high proportions reported a past history of emotional distress and/or drug use, at the time of the survey relatively few reported significant difficulty with these concerns. Among lesbians with serious health problems, most were receiving care. However, many reported a range of health concerns for which they were not receiving care, and lack of appropriate services or health insurance represented a barrier to care for many women. For example, 9% did not receive gynecological care, and 8% did not receive care for other health needs. More than one in three lesbians reported having no health insurance. Lesbian and bisexual women in the Women's Health Initiative, a national study of postmenopausal women over 50, were less likely than heterosexual women to have health insurance and more likely to be smokers, to use alcohol, to report other risk factors for reproductive cancer and cardiovascular disease, and to score lower on measures of mental health and social support (Valanis et al., 2000).

One of the few published studies of older lesbians and gay men, particularly midlife adults, is a community survey in Chicago of adults over 50, with a median age of 51 (Herdt, Beeler, & Rawls, 1997). Not surprisingly, older lesbians and gay men were more likely to have been married than their younger counterparts (e.g., 29% of younger midlife men, compared with 40% of older men) and were less likely to have come out to their parents and other important individuals in their lives. Far more lesbians (79%) had partners, compared with gay men (46%), and nearly half reported being verbally harassed as a result of their sexual orientation, with nearly one in five (18%) experiencing employment discrimination and about one in eight (13%) men being physically attacked because they were gay. Lesbians tended to feel more positive about aging than gay men did, who seemed to feel more negative about their bodies and the future. Men who had been married experienced additional challenges with integrating a new sexual identity during adulthood, adapting to GLB culture, and finding a supportive community.

CANCER

A great deal of attention has been paid to the perception that lesbians may be at higher risk than heterosexual women for breast cancer, in particular. This assertion has been widely disseminated, and many lesbians believe that lesbians have a one in three chance of developing breast cancer. Even though community advocates consistently report these figures, no studies have documented a higher prevalence of breast cancer among lesbians than among women in general. Instead, a range of lesbian health studies has shown higher prevalence of behavioral risk factors for breast and gynecological cancers among lesbian and bisexual women than among heterosexual women. A recent analysis of seven lesbian health surveys conducted from 1987 to 1996 showed that compared with heterosexual women, lesbians were more likely to be overweight, to consume alcohol, and to have higher rates of problem drinking. They were also less likely to receive routine screenings such as mammograms and gynecological exams that lead to early cancer detection, and less likely to have given birth and/or to use oral contraceptives, which protect against endometrial and ovarian cancer (Cochran et al., 2001).

For lesbians with cancer, their partners, and loved ones, the persistent insensitivity to their needs and concerns, their invisibility as patients and family members, and the lack of provider awareness and understanding have been painful and difficult barriers to surmount. Breast cancer, in particular, is primarily a disease of older women. But for middle-aged and older lesbians, many of whom have lived much of their lives in the closet and who have not been out to their providers, a diagnosis can be profoundly isolating. Services are geared to heterosexuals, and few providers consider that not all their patients are straight. In the mid-1980s, the first feminist cancer project was developed in Berkeley, California, to provide information and support for women with cancer. In 1990, three weeks before she died of breast cancer, Mary-Helen Mautner wrote a plan for the first lesbian cancer project, and the Mautner Project for Lesbians with Cancer was formed. The Mautner Project soon moved beyond volunteer support and education to help found the National Breast Cancer Coalition in 1994. It stimulated development of lesbian cancer projects in many cities around the country and served as a focal point for lesbian health advocacy on a broad range of health concerns, including promoting provider training, services, and research.

OLDER GLB ADULTS

Less is known about older lesbians and gay men than any other age group. Most have been invisible, living within friendship networks and partnerships that have become increasingly restricted as friends and partners die. The first community services program for lesbian and gay seniors, Senior Action in a Gay Environment (SAGE), was developed in New York City in 1978. Only recently have similar programs been developed in a number of other communities. Research on lesbian and gay aging is quite sparse, with more data on gay men and very little on the experiences of bisexuals or GLB people of color. As a group, older lesbians and gay men report high levels of life satisfaction and are less likely to use mental health services than are younger GLB adults.

All of the studies on lesbian and gay aging describe strong friendship networks, and most respondents comment on the importance of their friends. In fact, strong, well-developed friendship networks, often extending over many decades, may be one of the predictors of successful aging among gay men and lesbians. Studies of lesbian and gay aging show considerable variability in how individuals express and integrate their sexual identity, but most older gays are active and selectively engaged in interests that have particular salience for them. These may include involvement with the lesbian and gay community, mainstream groups, family, and friendship networks. Some studies have suggested that older GLB adults are able to better adapt to the challenges and uncertainties of aging as a result of having had to cope with the stresses of managing a stigmatized identity and an unaccepting social environment for most of their lives (Quam & Whitford, 1992).

One of the few large studies of older GLB adults (with an average age of 68) shows that most identified as lesbian or gay (only 8% were bisexual) and almost two-thirds (63%) lived alone, while 29% lived with partners (Grossman, D'Augelli, & O'Connell, 2001). Eighty-four percent reported good to excellent mental health; those with lower incomes and more experiences with victimization reported lower levels of mental health. As with married heterosexuals, GLB adults who lived with domestic partners rated their mental health significantly more positively and reported higher levels of self-esteem. Similarly, individuals with higher income, more people in their support networks, and fewer instances of victimization reported higher self-esteem. Loneliness was a concern for many older adults, with 27% lacking companionship and 13% feeling isolated. Most reported low levels of internalized homophobia, with men reporting significantly higher levels than women. Older participants reported more homophobia. As with younger adults, suicidality was reported by a number of participants. Thirteen percent had attempted suicide at some point in their lives, and 10% sometimes or often considered suicide. Nearly one in five (17%) said they would prefer being heterosexual, and 9% had used counseling to try to change their sexual orientation.

Three-fourths of older adults in the study reported having good to excellent health, which was also linked to living with a partner, having higher income, having more people in their support network, and experiencing less victimization. Only 9% could be classified as problem drinkers, and this included significantly more men than women. Participants averaged 6.3 people in their support networks, generally close friends, partners, other relatives, and acquaintances. Bisexuals had significantly more heterosexuals in their networks than did lesbians or gay men.

Nearly two-thirds (63%) of seniors experienced verbal abuse as a result of their sexual orientation during their lifetimes, while nearly one-third (29%) had been victims of violence, 16% had been physically assaulted (12% with a weapon), 20% had experienced employment discrimination, and 7% reported housing discrimination (table 14.4). These rates of victimization are surprisingly high since many of the instances had occurred years earlier when homosexuals were largely invisible and most of the respondents were closeted.

AIDS affects GLB older adults in a variety of ways. Nearly all adults in this study had lost a friend to AIDS, and almost half had lost three or more friends. More than one in ten people with AIDS is over age 50, accounting for nearly 85,000 men and women. In the Urban Men's Health Study—a representative study of gay men in four cities—nearly one in five (19%) older men who have sex with men reported having HIV infection. Most affected were African Americans (30%) and men who were less closeted (21%).

On average, men and women in the Grossman study were born in 1929 and were middle-aged at the time of the Stonewall riots, which marked the beginning of the modern gay movement in the United States. They were 44 when the American Psychiatric Association removed homosexuality as a mental illness from the *Diagnostic and Statistical Manual*, 52 when the first cases of AIDS were reported in 1981, and 69 when Ellen DeGeneres came out to a national audience on her television show *Ellen* in 1997 (Grossman et al., 2001). These events empowered many older GLB adults to come out for the first time, and their ensuing experiences enabled many older lesbians and gay men to construct positive gay identities (Friend, 1990) and to participate openly in emergent GLBT culture.

TABLE 14.4 Victimization Experiences of LGB Youth and Seniors

EVENT	LGB YOUTH (15–21)*	LGB SENIORS (60–91)**
Verbal abuse	80%	63%
Threats of attack	44%	29%
Objects thrown	33%	11%
Physical assault	17%	16%
Assault with a weapon	10%	12%
Employment discrimination	—	20%
Housing discrimination	—	7%

Sources: *D'Angelli & Hershberger (1993) (14-city study); **Grossman, D'Angelli, & O'Connell (2001) (19-city study).

For many older lesbians and gay men, these events were also radically different than their life experiences had been, and entering this new world required guidance and support.

At the same time, aging as a lesbian or a gay man is not without challenges; chief among them are legal and institutional structures that place many barriers between gay people and their significant others. After retirement, income drops significantly. For older lesbians and gay men who have experienced lifelong income disadvantages, including lack of employee or survivor benefits and tax or inheritance rights, and who may have worked in marginalized, lower-income jobs to avoid having to hide their identity, the ability to pay for care is a primary concern. Chronic disease, which is often disabling, can limit mobility and independence, requiring home care, support services, and institutionalization. Like their heterosexual peers, older lesbians and gay men are at risk for heart attacks, cancer, and strokes. Most older GLB people fear institutionalization, particularly those who are not open about their sexual orientation. Discrimination in health care, housing, and long-term care are key issues (Quam & Whitford, 1992). However, few services even consider that clients might be lesbian or gay, much less have a life partner of 40 or 50 years' duration.

A concern for many older lesbians and gay men is the fear of being alone in old age. Several retirement communities for lesbian and gay seniors are under development in Florida, Boston, New York, and San Francisco, as well as other cities. San Francisco's program, Openhouse, is a nonprofit, intergenerational community organization that will include low-, moderate-, and upper-income seniors and is open to all people, with a special focus on GLBT adults. Such integrated communities will bring the generations together routinely for the first time. One of the great challenges for gay people has been connecting with one another across generations, a difficulty that has prevented many GLB youth and young adults from having role models for successful aging across the life course. These social and cultural barriers have also prevented older adults from having

opportunities for living with and sharing integrated lives with younger generations of GLBT youth and adults.

PRACTICE WITH GLB CLIENTS

Health is a basic human right, yet access to quality care and to respectful and
sensitive providers is beyond the reach of too many GLB clients. Social workers
can play a vital role in negotiating the health and mental health system on behalf
of their clients and, for lesbians, gay men, and bisexuals, helping to educate and
inform providers about the role of stigma in increasing risk, which also serves as a
barrier to care. Many studies show higher prevalence of risk behaviors in gay men,
lesbians, and bisexuals, compared with their heterosexual peers. These behaviors
include substance use, cigarette smoking, and unprotected sexual intercourse, as
well as higher rates of psychological symptoms such as depression and suicidal
ideation and attempts.

Social workers are trained to consider these behaviors and health indicators
in the context of social forces that increase vulnerability and risk, such as racism,
poverty, and homophobia. For many gay men of color, for example, risky behavior is meaningful in the cultural context of hiding their sexual identity to protect
their families from embarrassment and shame. Lacking safe, supervised settings
in which to socialize, to connect with a larger gay community, and to meet other
gay peers—settings that are routinely available to heterosexual youth—many gay
youth learn about their sexuality in high-risk environments where they are vulnerable to exploitation and risky sexual encounters. Fear of rejection and hu-
miliation, which prevents patients from coming out to their providers and from
accurate screening for STDs and other health concerns, is also a rational reaction
to sexual prejudice.

In general, risk behavior is viewed in terms of individual deficits in knowledge,
motivation, or skills, rather than as culturally determined behavior that is quite
rational and logical within a given cultural context. In facilitating health services
for clients, social workers are often involved with interpreting the reality of clients' lives for other health providers, just as they interpret medical jargon and
ensure that clients understand medical procedures and instructions for follow-
up care. Many gay men, lesbians, and bisexuals are invisible within the health
care system, and part of the social worker's role is helping organizations become
responsive to their needs. Workers can do this by promoting in-service training
on GLB health and mental health issues that includes routine updates, such as
circulating recent research articles and information on new interventions and
practice approaches with GLB clients and patients. Surprisingly, many agencies
still lack policies on serving GLB clients and patients, and few make an effort to
recruit GLB staff to help increase awareness of these issues within the agency

and to signal a supportive environment to clients. Agencies should sensitize staff members to the needs of GLB clients, include GLB organizations in routine outreach activities to signal that gay clients are welcome, and include GLB patients in a description of target populations and in agency brochures with other client populations.

Basic steps in helping GLB patients and clients, and making environments more sensitive to their needs, include the following:

- Develop an agency policy on serving GLB clients and patients
- Provide staff training with regular updates
- Recruit openly GLB staff
- Adapt agency forms to reflect the reality of GLB lives (e.g., change the word *spouse* to *partner*; add the word *partnered* or *domestic partner* to *marital status*; add space to list two mothers or two fathers in questions about parents, etc.)
- Include flyers and posters on GLBT issues in waiting rooms and on bulletin boards, and place books on bookshelves to signal to clients a concern about their issues
- Ask clients to identify their support systems, which may include a partner and close friends, and incorporate them into treatment plans, care, and decision making. This recognizes that many GLB individuals create a family of choice to provide support, particularly in the absence of support from their families of origin.
- Discuss and help clients obtain important legal documents (such as a medical power of attorney) that enable partners or close friends to make medical decisions in the event of incapacitation

Although large numbers of providers continue to assume that their clients and patients are heterosexual—particularly adolescents and older adults, GLB people, whether open about their sexual identity or not, are present in caseloads and practices, and they warrant respect and appropriate care. An understanding of their histories and social and cultural backgrounds will help sensitize providers to their needs. Research and advocacy related to the needs and experiences of GLB adolescents and adults have focused on problems and risks, generally overlooking the strength and resiliency needed to survive in an oppressive and unaccepting environment. In spite of the many challenges, stressors, and discriminatory events experienced throughout their lives, most gay men, lesbians, and bisexuals live healthy, productive lives. Society can learn much from their resiliency, adaptive abilities, and strengths. In addressing health-related concerns, providers should use a strengths perspective to maximize and build on these resources.

REFERENCES

American Psychological Association (2001). Needs assessment survey study: Evaluation and training needs of school staff relevant to prevent risk behaviors and promoting healthy behaviors among lesbian, gay, and bisexual you and those youth desiring or engaging in same-sex sexual behaviors. Paper presented at the Healthy Lesbian, Gay, and Bisexual Student Project Meeting. Washington, DC: Author.

Anderson, A. L. (1998). Strengths of gay male youth: An untold story. *Child and Adolescent Social Work Journal, 15,* 55–71.

Bauer, G. R., & Welles, S. L. (2001). Beyond assumptions of negligible risk: Sexually transmitted diseases and women who have sex with women. *American Journal of Public Health, 91*(8), 1282–1286.

Blake, S. M., Ledsky, R., Lehman, T., Goodenow, C., Sawyer, R., & Hack, T. (2001). Preventing sexual risk behaviors among gay, lesbian, and bisexual adolescents: The benefits of gay-sensitive HIV instruction in schools. *American Journal of Public Health, 91,* 940–946.

Bradford, J., & Ryan, C. (1988). *The National Lesbian Health Care Survey: Final report.* Washington, DC: National Lesbian and Gay Health Foundation.

Bradford, J., Ryan, C., & Rothblum, E. (1994). National Lesbian Health Care Survey: Implications for mental health care. *Journal of Consulting and Clinical Psychology, 62*(2), 228–242.

Catania, J. A., Osmond, D., Stall, R. D., Pollack, L., Paul, J. P., Blower, S., Binson, D., Canchola, J. A., Mills, T. C., Fisher, L., Choi, K. H., Porco, T., Turner, C., Blair, J., Henne, J., Bye, L., & Coates, T. J. (2001). The continuing HIV epidemic among men who have sex with men. *American Journal of Public Health, 91,* 907–914.

Centers for Disease Control and Prevention. (2000). HIV/AIDS among racial/ethnic minority men who have sex with men, United States, 1989–1998. *Morbidity and Mortality Weekly Report, 40*(1).

——. (2002). Need for sustained HIV prevention among men who have sex with men. *Fact Sheets.*

Chu, S. Y., Buehler, J. W., Fleming, P. L., & Berkelman, R. L. (1990). Epidemiology of reported cases of AIDS in lesbians, United States 1980–89. *American Journal of Public Health, 80*(11), 1380–1381.

Cliff, M. (Ed.). (1978). *The winner names the age: A collection of writings by Lillian Smith.* New York: Norton.

Cochran, S. D., & Mays, V. M. (2000a). Lifetime prevalence of suicide symptoms and affective disorders among men reporting same-sex sexual partners: Results from NHANES III. *American Journal of Public Health 90,* 573–578.

——. (2000b). Relation between psychiatric syndromes and behaviorally defined sexual orientation in a sample of the U.S. population. *American Journal of Epidemiology, 151,* 516–523.

Cochran, S. D., Mays, V. M., Bowen, D., Gage, S., Bybee, D., Roberts, S. J., Goldstein, R. S., Robison, A., Rankow, E. J., & White, J. (2001). Cancer-related risk indicators and preventive screening behaviors among lesbians and bisexual women. *American Journal of Public Health 91,* 591–597.

Cochran, S. D., Sullivan, J. G., & Mays, V. M. (2001). *Prevalence of psychiatric disorders, psychological distress, and treatment utilization among lesbian, gay, and bisexual individuals in a sample of the U.S. population.* Manuscript submitted for publication.

D'Augelli, A. R. (1998). Developmental implications of victimization of lesbian, gay, and bisexual youths. In G. M Herek (Ed.), *Stigma and sexual orientation: Understanding prejudice against lesbians, gay men, and bisexuals* (pp. 187–210). Thousand Oaks, CA: Sage.

——. (in press). *Developmental and contextual factors and mental health among lesbian, gay, and bisexual youth.* In A. E. Omoto & H. M Kurtzman (Eds.), *Recent research on sexual orientation.* Washington, DC: APA Books.

D'Augelli, A. R., & Hershberger, S. L. (1993). Lesbian, gay, and bisexual youth in community settings: Personal challenges and mental health problems. *American Journal of Community Psychology, 21,* 421–448.

D'Augelli, A. R., Hershberger, S. L., & Pilkington, N. W. (1998). Lesbian, gay, and bisexual youth and their families: Disclosure of sexual orientation and its consequences. *American Journal of Orthopsychiatry, 68,* 361–371.

D'Augelli, A. R., Pilkington, N. W., & Hershberger, S. L. (2002). Incidence and mental health impact of sexual orientation victimization of lesbian, gay, and bisexual youth in high school. *School Psychology Quarterly, 17*(2), 148–167.

Descamps, M. J., Rothblum, E., Bradford, J., & Ryan, C. 2000. Mental health impact of child sexual abuse, rape, intimate partner violence, and hate crimes in the National Lesbian Health Care Survey. *Journal of Gay and Lesbian Social Services, 11,* 27–55.

Diamant, A. L., Schuster, M., & Lever, J. (2000). Receipt of preventive health care services by lesbians. *American Journal of Preventive Medicine, 19,* 141–148.

Diamant, A. L., Wold, C., Spritzer, K., & Gelberg, L. (2000). Health behaviors, health status, and access to and use of health care: A population-based study of lesbian, bisexual, and heterosexual women. *Archives of Family Medicine, 9,* 1043–1051.

Diaz, R. (1998). *Latino gay men and HIV: Culture, sexuality, and risk behavior.* New York: Routledge.

Diaz, R. M., & Ayala, G. (2001). *Social discrimination and health: The case of Latino gay men and HIV risk.* New York: Policy Institute, National Gay and Lesbian Task Force.

Diaz, R. M., Ayala, G., Bein, E., Heine, J., & Marin, B. V. (2001). The impact of homophobia, poverty, and racism on the mental health of gay and bisexual Latino men: Findings from three U.S. cities. *American Journal of Public Health, 91,* 927–932.

Doll, L. S., & Beeker, C. (1996). Male bisexual behavior and HIV risk in the United States: Synthesis of research with implications for behavioral interventions. *AIDS Education and Prevention, 8*(3), 205–225.

DuRant, R. H., Krowchuk, D. P., & Sinal, S. H. (1998). Victimization, use of violence, and drug use at school among male adolescents who engage in same-sex sexual behaviors. *Journal of Pediatrics, 133,* 113–118.

East, J., & Boekeloo, B. (1996). *Pediatricians' approach to the health care of sexual minority youth.* George Washington University Medical School, Washington, DC, unpublished data.

Ekstrand, M. L., Stall, R. D., Paul, J. P., Osmond, D. H., & Coates, T. J. (1999). Gay men report high rates of unprotected anal sex with partners of unknown or discordant HIV status. *AIDS, 13,* 1525–1533.

Eliason, M. (1998). Correlates of prejudice in nursing students. *Journal of Nursing Education, 37,* 27–29.

Eng, T. R., & Butler, W. T. (1996). *The hidden epidemic: Confronting sexually transmitted diseases.* Washington, DC: Institute of Medicine.

Farland, A. F., & Ziegler, E. (1993). Adolescent suicide prevention: Current research and social policy implications. *American Psychologist, 48,* 169–182.

Friend, R. A. (1990). Older lesbian and gay people: A theory of successful aging. *Journal of Homosexuality, 20,* 99–118.

Garofalo, R., Wolf, C., Kessel, S., Palfrey, J., & DuRant, R. H. (1998). The association between risk behaviors and sexual orientation among a school-based sample of adolescents. *Pediatrics, 101*(5), 895–902.

Gonsiorek, J., & Rudolph, J. R. (1991). Homosexual identity: Coming out and other developmental events. In J. Gonsiorek & J. R. Rudolph (Eds.), *Homosexuality: Research implications for public policy.* Newbury Park, CA: Sage.

Goodenow, C., Netherland, J., & Szalacha, L. (2002). AIDS-related risk among adolescent males who have sex with males, females, or both: Evidence from a statewide survey. *American Journal of Public Health*, 92, 203–210.

Grossman, A. H., D'Augelli, A. R., & O'Connell, T. S. (2001). Being lesbian, gay, bisexual, and 60 or older in North America. *Journal of Gay and Lesbian Social Services*, 13(4), 23–40.

Gruskin, E. (1995). *The Contra Costa lesbian/bisexual women's health study*. Unpublished master's thesis, University of California, Berkeley.

Gruskin, E. P., Hart, S., Gordon, N., & Ackerson, L. (2001). Patterns of cigarette smoking and alcohol use among lesbians and bisexual women enrolled in a large health maintenance organization. *American Journal of Public Health*, 91, 976–979.

Heckman, T. G., Kelly, J. A., Sikkema, K. J., Roffman, R. R., Solomon, L. J., Winnett, R. A., Stevenson, L. Y., Perry, M. J., Normal, A. D., & Desiderato, L. J. (1995). Differences in HIV risk characteristics between bisexual and exclusively gay men. *AIDS Education and Prevention*, 7(6), 504–512.

Herdt, G. (1992). "Coming out" as a rite of passage: A Chicago study. In Gil Herdt (Ed.), *Gay culture in America* (pp. 29–67). Boston: Beacon.

Herdt, G., Beeler, J., & Rawls, T. (1997). Life course diversity among older lesbians and gay men: A study in Chicago. *Journal of Gay, Lesbian, and Bisexual Identity*, 2(3/4), 231–246.

Herdt, G., & Boxer, A. (1993). *Children of Horizons: How gay and lesbian teens are leading a new way out of the closet*. Boston: Beacon.

Herek, G. M., & Capitanio, J. P. (1999). AIDS stigma and sexual prejudice. *American Behavioral Scientist*, 42, 1126–1143.

Herek, G. M., Gillis, J. R., Cogan, J. C., & Glunt, E. K. (1997). Hate crime victimization among lesbian, gay, and bisexual adults. *Journal of Interpersonal Violence*, 12, 195–215.

Hershberger, S. L., & D'Augelli, A. R. (1995). The impact of victimization on the mental health and suicidality of lesbian, gay, and bisexual youths. *Developmental Psychology*, 31, 65–74.

———. (2000). Issues in counseling lesbian, gay, and bisexual adolescents. In R. M. Perez, K. A. DeBord, & K. Bieschke (Eds.), *Handbook of counseling and psychotherapy with lesbian, gay, and bisexual clients* (pp. 225–248). Washington, DC: American Psychological Association.

Hershberger, S. L., Pilkington, N. W., & D'Augelli, A. R. (1997). Predictors of suicide attempts among gay, lesbian, and bisexual youth. *Journal of Adolescent Research*, 12, 477–497.

Hoyert, D. L., Kochanek, K. D., & Murphy, S. L. (1999). *Deaths: Final data for 1997. National Vital Statistics Reports*, 47(9). Hyattsville, MD: National Center for Health Statistics.

Kalichman, S. C., Roffman, R. A., Picciano, J. F., & Bolan, M. (1998). Risk for HIV infection among bisexual men seeking HIV-prevention services and risks posed to their female partners. *Health Psychology*, 17(4), 320–327.

Klamen, D. L., Grossman, L. S., & Kopacz, D. R. (1999). Medical student homophobia. *Journal of Homosexuality*, 37, 53–63.

Klein, J. D., Slap, G. B., Elster, A. B., & Cohn, S. E. (1993). Adolescents and access to health care. *Bulletin of the New York Academy of Medicine*, 70, 219.

Livson, F. B. (1981). Paths to psychological health in the middle years: Sex differences. In D. H. Eichorn, J. A. Clausen, N. Haan, M. P. Honzik, & P. H. Mussen (Eds.), *Present and past in middle life*. New York: Academic Press.

Lock, J., & Steiner, H. (1999). Gay, lesbian, and bisexual youth risks for emotional, physical, and social problems: Results from a community-based survey. *Journal of the American Academy of Child and Adolescent Psychiatry, 38,* 297–304.

Marazzo, J. M., Stine, K., Handsfield, H. H., & Koutsky, L. A. (1996). Epidemiology of STD and cervical neoplasia among lesbian and bisexual women. *Abstracts of the National Lesbian and Gay Health Association Conference, Seattle.*

Martin, J. (1988). Psychological consequences of AIDS-related bereavement among gay men. *Journal of Consulting and Clinical Psychology, 61*(1), 94–103.

Mays, V. M., & Cochran, S. D. (2001). Mental health correlates of perceived discrimination among lesbian, gay, and bisexual adults in the United States. *American Journal of Public Health 91,* 1869–1876.

McCann, K., & Wadsworth, E. (1992). The role of informal careers in supporting gay men who have HIV-related illness: What do they do and what are their needs? *AIDS Care, 4*(1), 25–34.

Meyer, I. (1995). Minority stress and mental health in gay men. *Journal of Health and Social Behavior, 36,* 38–56.

Miranda, J., & Storms, M. (1989). Psychological adjustment of lesbians and gay men. *Journal of Counseling and Development, 68*(1), 41–45.

Mohr, J., & Rochlen, A. (1999). Measuring attitudes regarding bisexuality in lesbian, gay male, and heterosexual populations. *Journal of Consulting and Clinical Psychology, 46*(3), 353–369.

Nawyn, S. J., Richman, J. A., Rospenda, K. M., & Hughes, T. (2000). Sexual identity and alcohol-related outcomes: Contributions of workplace harassment. *Journal of Substance Abuse, 11,* 289–304.

Neugarten, B. (1968). The awareness of middle age. In B. Neugarten (Ed.), *Middle age and aging: A reader in social psychology* (pp. 93–98). Chicago: University of Chicago Press.

Paul, J. P., Hays, R. B., & Coates, T. J. (1995). The impact of the HIV epidemic on U.S. gay male communities. In A. R. D'Augelli & C. J. Patterson (Eds.), *Lesbian, gay, and bisexual identities over the lifespan: Psychological perspectives* (pp. 347–397). New York: Oxford University Press.

Perrin, E. (1997). *Attitudes of pediatricians about psychosocial issues.* McLean, VA: Ambulatory Pediatric Association.

Quam, J. K., & Whitford, G. S. (1992). Adaptation and age-related expectations of older gay men and lesbian adults. *Gerontologist, 32*(30), 367–374.

Rankow, E. J., & Tessaro, I. (1998). Cervical cancer risk and Papanicolaou screening in a sample of lesbian and bisexual women. *Journal of Family Practice, 47,* 139–143.

Reis, B., & Saewyc, E. (1999). *Eighty-three thousand youth: Selected findings of eight population-based studies as they pertain to anti-gay harassment and the safety and well-being of sexual minority students.* Seattle: Safe Schools Coalition of Washington.

Remafedi, G., Farrow, J. A., & Deisher, R. W. (1991). Risk factors for attempted suicide in gay and bisexual youth. *Pediatrics, 87,* 869–875.

Rosario, M., Rotheram-Borus, M. J., & Reid, H. (1996). Gay-related stress and its correlates among gay and bisexual male adolescents of predominantly Black and Hispanic background. *Journal of Community Psychology, 24,* 136–159.

Ryan, C. (1994). Lesbian and gay health concerns. In C. Ryan & R. Bogard, *What every lesbian and gay American needs to know about health care reform.* Washington, DC: Human Rights Campaign Foundation.

———. (2000). *An analysis of the content and gaps in the scientific and professional literature on the health and mental health concerns of lesbian, gay, and bisexual youth.* Report prepared for the American Psychological Association, Healthy LGB Students Project.

Ryan, C., & Bogard, R. (1994). *What every lesbian and gay American needs to know about health care reform.* Washington, DC: Human Rights Campaign Foundation.

Ryan, C., & Bradford, J. (1991). Health issues of middle-aged lesbians. In B. Sang & A. Smith (Eds.), *Lesbians at the midlife* (pp. 147–163). San Francisco: Spinster's Ink.

———. (1998). Methodological issues in research with lesbians, gay men, and bisexuals. In J. Carmichael (Ed.), *Daring to find our names: The search for lesbigay library history.* Westport, CT: Greenwood, 1998.

Ryan, C., Bradford, J., & Honnold, J. (1999). Social workers' and counselors' understanding of lesbian needs. *Journal of Gay and Lesbian Social Services, 9*(4), 1–26.

Ryan, C., & Futterman, D. (1998). *Lesbian and gay youth: Care and counseling.* New York: Columbia University Press.

Saewyc, E. M., Skay, C. L., Bearinger, L. H., Blum, R. W., & Resnick, M. D. (1998). Sexual orientation, sexual behaviors, and pregnancy among American Indian adolescents. *Journal of Adolescent Health, 23,* 238–247.

Sbordone, A. (1993). *Gay men choosing fatherhood.* Unpublished doctoral dissertation, City University of New York.

Schatz, B., & O'Hanlan, K. (1994). *Anti-gay discrimination in medicine: Results of a national survey of lesbian, gay, and bisexual physicians.* San Francisco: American Association of Physicians for Human Rights.

Schneider, S. G., Farberow, N. L., & Kruks, G. N. (1989). Suicidal behavior in adolescent and young adult gay men. *Suicide and Life-Threatening Behavior, 19,* 381–394.

Stall, R., Paul, J. P., Greenwood, G., Pollack, L. M., Bein, E., Crosby, G. M., Mills, T. C., Binson, D., Coates, T. J., & Catania, J. A. (2001). Alcohol use, drug use, and alcohol-related problems among men who have sex with men: The Urban Men's Health Study. *Addiction, 96,* 1589–1601.

Stall, R., Pollack, L., Mills, T. C., Martin, J. N., Osmond, O., Paul, J., Binson, D., Coates, T. J., & Catania, J. A. (2001). Use of antiretroviral therapies among HIV-infected men who have sex with men: A household-based sample of four major American cities. *American Journal of Public Health, 91,* 767–773.

Stall, R., & Wiley, J. (1988). A comparison of drug and alcohol use habits of heterosexual and homosexual men. *Drug and Alcohol Dependence, 22*(1–2), 63–74.

Stall, R. D., Greenwood, G. L., Acree, M., Paul, J., & Coates, T. J. (1999). Cigarette smoking among gay and bisexual men. *American Journal of Public Health, 89*(12), 1875–1878.

Tesar, C. M., & Rovi, S. L. D. (1998). Survey of curriculum on homosexuality/bisexuality in departments of family medicine. *Family Medicine, 30*(4), 283–287.

Turner, H. A., Catania, J. A., & Gagnon, J. (1994). The prevalence of informal caregiving to persons with AIDS in the United States: Caregiver characteristics and their implications. *Social Science and Medicine, 38*(11), 1543–1552.

Valanis, B. G., Bowen, D. J., Bassford, T., Whitlock, E., Charney, P., & Carter, R. A. (2000). Sexual orientation and health: Comparisons in the Women's Health Initiative sample. *Archives of Family Medicine, 9,* 843–853.

Valleroy, L. A., MacKellar, D. A., Karon, J. M., Rosen, D. H., McFarland, W., Shehan, D. A., Stoyanoff, S. R., LaLota, M., Celentano, D. D., Koblin, B. A., Thiede, H., Katz,

M. H., Torian, L. V., & Janssen, R. S. (2000). HIV prevalence and associated risks in young men who have sex with men. *Journal of the American Medical Association, 284*(2), 198–204.

Waldo, C. R., & J. L. Kemp. (1997). Should I come out to my students? An empirical investigation. *Journal of Homosexuality, 34,* 79–94.

White, J., & Levinson, W. (1993). Primary care of lesbian patients. *Journal of General Internal Medicine, 8,* 41.

Woods, J. (1993). *The corporate closet.* New York: Free Press.

Zenilman, J. (1988). Sexually transmitted diseases in homosexual adolescents. *Journal of Adolescent Health, 9,* 129–138.

15

TRANSGENDER HEALTH ISSUES

Emilia Lombardi and S. Masen Davis

I was, as one social worker termed me, a difficult placement case.

—CHRISTINE BEATTY, "BRYANT PATCH"

TRANSGENDER GENERALLY refers to a population of individuals who do not conform to traditional Western notions of sex and gender. A study of transgender individuals in the United States found that approximately 60% had experienced some form of harassment and/or violence and 37% had experienced economic discrimination (Lombardi, Wilchins, Preisling, & Malouf, 2001). Further, transgender men and women will likely experience physical and mental health problems, both in accessing health care resources and in dealing with the results of stress. The purpose of this chapter is to introduce the diversity found among transgender individuals and to present the mental and physical health and health care issues that transgender men and women may experience.

THE DIVERSITY OF GENDER IDENTITY AND EXPRESSION

Whereas the bulk of Western societies believe that one's biological sex (specifically genitals) irrevocably determines one's social gender, behavior, and identity, transgender individuals disrupt the connection between biological sex and social gender and create alternative forms of gendered presentations and identities. Generally, transgender individuals vary across four dimensions: (1) biological sex—the actual biology of the individual, including male, female, and many interesexed conditions; (2) psychological identity—gender identity, or to what extent one identifies as a man, woman, or something else; (3) social presentation—how typically masculine or feminine one looks and acts; and (4) legal sex—the sex designation that is listed on various legal documents (driver's license, passport, birth certificate, and so on) (Lombardi, 2001). It is important to note that individuals will have their own way of identifying themselves; thus the terminology introduced in this chapter is used in the general sense only. Social workers will need to talk with their clients about how they themselves identify.

CROSS-DRESSING

Cross-dressing refers to the act of individuals of one gender wearing the clothes and accessories of another gender (most notable are men who for various reasons wear the clothing and take on the various social attributes of women). Many men who cross-dress do so as a performance act (female impersonation/drag) or as a form of personal self-expression; while generally not acknowledged in society, many women also cross-dress for performance and self-expression. Many people view cross-dressing as a sexual problem, believing that individuals who cross-dress do so in order to fulfill their sexual fantasies. Indeed, the American Psychiatric Association lists cross-dressing as transvestic fetishism in the *Diagnostic and Statistical Manual of Mental Disorders* (DSM IV-TR) (302.3 Transvestic Fetishism). Focusing on cross-dressing as a sexual paraphilia, however, blinds clinicians to the variety of forms of transgenderism that clients could express without perceiving it as a problem. The *DSM* classification itself may cause some bias in the minds of clinicians regardless of the actual status of their client (and the client's own view), leading the social worker to view any incidence of cross-dressing as a problem. It is important to note that cross-dressing in and of itself should be seen not as pathological behavior but as one important aspect of a person's life.

TRANSSEXUALISM

Transsexualism refers to individuals who seek to permanently change their social and legal gender (man to woman or woman to man) to better match their psychological gender identity. Hormones are usually used to change some secondary sex characteristics, while surgery is used to alter other physical aspects (most notably, but not limited to, one's genitals). In addition to the medical aspects of transitioning from one sex to another, individuals typically seek to change their social and legal identities in order to fully take on the social role of the gender with which they identify..

The incidence of transsexualism, as gauged by studies outside the United States and using different measures of prevalence, is approximately 1 per 20,000 to 50,000, with the ratio favoring male-to-female transsexualism about 2.3 to 2.5:1 (Weitze & Osburg, 1996). While prevalence rates have been shown to vary, the ratio of male-to-female (MTF) to female-to-male (FTM) transsexualism still appears to favor male-to-female transgender individuals. Bakker, van Kesteren, Gooren, and Bezemer (1993), for example, reported on the prevalence of transsexualism among people native to the Netherlands by counting the number of people who were seen by psychiatrists and psychologists and were subsequently treated with hormonal and sex reassignment therapy. They found prevalence rates of 1 per 11,900 MTF and 1 per 30,400 FTM; suggesting a ratio of 2.5 men to 1 woman. There are exceptions with respect to the ratio of MTF and FTM transsexuals, but these seem to be few. In Sweden it was reported that transsexuality is found equally in MTF and FTM samples (Landeb, Walinder, & Lustrom, 1996). However, this study, like much research on transsexuals, sampled people from gender clinics and mental health settings; this methodology will confound the prevalence downward, as many transsexuals do not (or cannot) access such services. The diversity among transgender people precludes an easy way of identifying a transgender population, but professionals must be aware of many issues when providing care for transgender individuals. Many people who self-identify in diverse ways may still have much in common with each other.

It is important to note that there are significant differences between transsexual men and women in addition to the degree of access to gender reassignment services. Transsexual men and women themselves can have very different needs with regard to types of care. The hormonal and surgical procedures used by male-to-female (MTF) individuals are not equivalent to those used by female-to-male (FTM) individuals. The genital surgeries available to FTM individuals tend to be much more expensive and not as aesthetically or functionally realistic as the genital surgeries available to MTF individuals. In addition, unlike estrogen, all forms of testosterone are scheduled drugs (schedule III), while forms of estrogen and progesterone are unscheduled (scheduled drugs refer to the list of drugs that the U.S. government identifies as requiring special control because of their potential abuse and/or harmful nature).

GENDER IDENTITY DISORDER: PRO AND CON

Like transvestic fetishism, gender identity disorder (GID) is listed in *DSM-IV-TR* as a sexual paraphilia. This classification tends to mirror popular stereotypes that transgender individuals (both those who cross-dress and those who are transitioning, or changing, from one sex/gender to another) do so for sexual reasons—that one becomes a woman to have sex with men (and vice versa). Nevertheless, being transgender should be seen as distinct from one's sexuality. The sexual identities and behaviors within the transgender population can vary as widely as in the non-transgender population. To confound transgenderism with sexual orientation will cause individuals to miss important distinctions between the two and therefore to limit their understanding of transgender lives. For example, there are transsexual women (male to female) who identify as lesbian and have women as partners; at the same time, there are transsexual men (female to male) who identify as gay men and have men as partners. The stereotype of married, cross-dressing men as being heterosexual will likely cause one to overlook their sexual activity with other men while cross-dressed.

Transgender individuals tend to be unanimous when it comes to differentiating between sexual orientation and gender identity; however, a debate exists concerning the medicalization of transsexualism and the inclusion of gender identity disorder in the DSM. While people agree that gender nonconformity in general should not be pathologized, the medical interventions sought by transsexuals place them in an awkward position. Opponents to the inclusion of gender identity disorder in the DSM believe that its inclusion perpetuates the stigmatization and discrimination of transsexual individuals (Wilchins, 1997). For example, the removal of homosexuality from the DSM in 1973 was a critical step toward the acceptance of homosexuality in American culture. Proponents of inclusion, such as Pauly (1992), argue against removing GID for the following reasons:

1. … Transsexualism is much rarer than homosexuality, thus it is more difficult to sustain an argument that these GID are simply a variation of the human condition.

2. … A homosexual individual need not present to the medical or psychiatric profession in order to pursue his/her lifestyle. The exception to this might be the individual who is conflicted about his/her sexual orientation. The individual with GID requires evaluation by the psychiatric profession, so that appropriate referrals for hormone treatment and/or SRS can be separated from those individuals for whom this recommendation would be contra-indicated. Time has taught us the tragedy of approving SRS for individuals who were not carefully evaluated by the mental health profession.

3. Another reason why homosexuality was deleted from DSM-III was because non-clinical samples of homosexuals demonstrated no more psychopathology than heterosexuals. Gender dysphoric individuals do have a significant incidence of mood disorders (Pauly, 1990 sic a) as well as Axis II pathology (Levine, 1989). This is further justification for retaining GID in DSM-IV.

4. Last, but not least, there is the very practical issue that unless a condition is classified as a disorder, the insurance carrier will not reimburse the individual for the cost of professional care… .

5. Perhaps the most significant reason for retaining GID in the diagnostic classification system is the extent to which research in this field has been facilitated by having standardized criteria available for correctly diagnosing individuals with GID.

(PP. 10-11)

Responding to Pauly's arguments regarding the rarity of transsexualism, substantial literature documents gender forms other than those of men and women found in other societies around the world and across time. Transsexualism is merely Western industrial societies' way to describe individuals who do not conform to traditional gender norms; since our society lacks any alternative to man or woman, individuals often seek to transition to one gender or the other as completely as possible. In societies with culturally relevant alternatives, such gender nonconformity takes other forms. The Hijras of India, for example, are biologically male but present themselves socially in a feminine manner. They consider themselves as neither men nor women and undergo a ritualized procedure to remove their penis and testicles (Nanda, 1990). Hijras view their identity and lives in religious rather than medical terms, but they still have lives somewhat similar to those of transsexual women in Western societies.

Transsexuals do require medical intervention in order to fully transition from one gender to another, but that does not in itself require a psychiatric diagnosis (especially given that the bulk of the treatment is physical in nature). Reducing transsexualism to a psychiatric disorder needlessly removes any discussion of the social and legal aspects of changing gender. There are many situations in a person's life that may require medical intervention but are not labeled as disorders, pregnancy being one example.

Some of the literature contradicts the presence of psychopathology among transsexual individuals. Recent studies have compared the level of psychopathology among transsexuals against that among other populations. Haraldsen and Dahl (2000) compared transsexuals with people who had personality disorders and with a nontranssexual, healthy control group. Transsexuals were found to be more similar to the control group than to those suffering from personality disorders. Miach, Berah, Butcher, and Rouse (2000) and Tsushima and Wedding (1979) reported similar findings, concluding that transsexual individuals were no more likely than nontranssexual individuals to suffer from psychopathologies. Future studies examining larger populations outside of clinical settings will likely find similar relationships.

The argument that the inclusion of GID in the *DSM* is necessary in order for individuals to have their care covered by insurance is problematic because of the nature of Western health care systems (public and private). The presence of GID in the *DSM* has had no effect upon the coverage of transsexual-related procedures by third-party payers. Many insurers explicitly exclude transsexual-related medical procedures from their plans, regardless of the inclusion of GID in the *DSM*. Medical treatments for transsexualism are usually excluded from insurance packages because sex reassignment procedures are viewed as cosmetic, cost-prohibitive, inappropriate for the treatment of a psychiatric disorder, and/or experimental. In addition, a large majority of people do not have private health insurance and are unable to benefit from its (albeit theoretical) coverage. Even in nations that have universal coverage, individuals with private insurance are more able to receive medical services than those who rely on governmental aid. The insurance argument for inclusion of GID in the *DSM* will likely benefit only a very small percentage of transsexual individuals (those with private health insurance that does not explicitly exclude transsexual-related medical procedures).

The existence of standardized criteria for correctly diagnosing individuals with GID is also questionable as an argument in support of inclusion in the *DSM*, especially considering (1) the discrimination that many experience when trying to access the system and (2) the knowledge that transsexual individuals actually have on the subject and their ability to memorize and restate the *DSM* and other publications in order to receive medical services. Researchers Kessler and McKenna (1985) described how many transsexuals are knowledgeable about the clinical criteria and use that knowledge to obtain hormones and other medical interventions needed for changing their physical form and their legal sex designation. The transsexuals in their study knew as much about the medical aspects of GID as their doctors and were able to follow the criteria to the letter. Often individuals will self-diagnose as transsexual and will be more concerned with accessing medical services than receiving mental health services.

In her study of gender clinics, Namaste (2000) found that factors other than those related to the diagnostic criteria for GID influenced the treatment of transsexual men and women. She argued that sexism, classism, racism, and heterosexism can affect the experiences of many transsexuals who access medical services. For example, clinicians were deeply concerned with the gendered appearance and behavior of their patients, requiring them to express extremes in gender and not merely an androgynous presentation. Many transsexual women experienced sexual harassment by male staff members, while transsexual men were expected to exhibit stereotypical expressions of masculinity. Namaste also found that many professionals would not treat transsexual women who engage in sex work, their reasoning being that "real" transsexuals are not prostitutes. Namaste suggested that such a subjective criterion represents the sexism inherent in the process of selection for SRS (professionals defining what a "proper" woman is). Thus the existence of standardized criteria must be seen as questionable with regard to the activities of both transsexuals and clinicians, as the actions of both may serve to undermine such criteria.

Other authors posit that GID should be removed from the *DSM* as a means by which to negate the identities and lives of transsexual men and women. Janice Raymond's book, *The Transsexual Empire* (1994), is a critique of medicalization of transsexualism that also does not allow for the identities of transsexual men and women to be seen as valid. She feels that transsexualism is the result of men's attempting to control the bodies of women. Similarly, Billings and Urban (1982) assert that sex change surgeries reaffirm traditional gender roles and prevent a radical change in society's gender norms. Both Raymond and Billings and Urban present a very negative view of the process of changing sex and, by default, repudiate the lives and identities of transsexual men and women. While both go to great lengths to cite clinicians and other researchers, and to bring feminist (Raymond) and critical (Billings and Urban) theories to bear on the issue, not once does either present the actual voices of transsexual men and women (many of whom would themselves be very critical of how the medical system treats transsexuals but would still be adamant in their identity and their need for hormones and surgical interventions). Those who question the medical aspects of transsexualism will still acknowledge the pressure to attain a specific gendered appearance in order to function in society. Few, if any, publications concerning transsexuals refer to the social and legal issues that transsexual men and women face. For example, legal sex designations cannot be changed without documentation of some type of medical intervention (such as surgery). In another example, a transsexual woman was asked to prove she had genital surgery (sex change) in order to use the women's restroom; she refused and was later fired (Buchanan, June 2002). The desire for hormonal and surgical interventions is not just in the minds of transsexuals; it also results from societal forces that insist that men and women look and act a certain way.

While the DSM lists the criteria for gender identity disorder, the Harry Benjamin International Gender Dysphoria Association (HBIGDA), not the American Psychiatric Association (APA), actually creates the standards of care for the treatment of GID. HBIGDA's stated purpose is to present a consensus about the management of gender identity disorders by psychiatrists, psychologists, physicians, and surgeons. The HBIGDA standards of care present the diagnostic criteria for GID, the tasks for mental health care providers, psychotherapeutic issues, and requirements for hormonal and surgical interventions.

CHALLENGES FACING TRANSGENDER POPULATIONS

HIV/AIDS

Increasing evidence demonstrates that the rate of HIV infection among transgender women is high and that the risk of infection may even surpass that for bisexual and gay men in California (Nemoto, Luke, Mamo, Ching, & Patria, 1999; San Francisco Department of Public Health, 1999; Simon & Reback, 1999; Sykes, 1999). Reported HIV sero-prevalence exceeds 20% and rises as high as 60% for African Americans. Many transgender women (i.e., male to female [MTF]) are at risk primarily because of risky sex, but the sharing of needles in the injection of hormones or intravenous drugs is also seen as a risk factor (Nemoto et al., 1999; San Francisco Department of Public Health, 1999; Sykes, 1999). These individuals may be difficult to target with traditional prevention campaigns, and they may fear discrimination should they seek services such as HIV/AIDS education and testing (Bockting, Robinson, & Rosser, 1998; Clements, Wilkinson, Kitano, & Marx, 1999). The insensitivity of health care professionals has been cited as a reason that these and other services are not accessed (JSI Research and Training Institute, 2000). Indeed, reports of insensitive behavior by health care providers (e.g., referring to transgender women as "he" and "him," and not acknowledging or respecting their identity) suggest that services are severely lacking in the provision of culturally sensitive interventions and potentially in the provision of HIV-disease-related health care (Bockting et al., 1998; Clements et al., 1999).

While HIV/AIDS rates appear to be lower for FTMs (a San Francisco Department of Public Health [1999] study of 123 FTMs found a 2% transmission rate), a qualitative needs assessment in Quebec, Canada (Namaste, 1999) suggests that FTMs are at risk for HIV. Namaste found that five factors contribute to this risk:

> 1) there is a lack of informational and educational materials about FTM bodies and sexualities; 2) many FTMs do not consider themselves to be at risk for HIV; 3) poor access to intramuscular needles, used to inject hormones, creates conditions which put FTMs at risk of HIV transmission; 4) low self esteem may prevent FTMs from adopting safe behaviors with regard to drug use and sexual activity; and 5) the administrative practices of social service agencies exclude FTM transsexuals.

SUBSTANCE USE ISSUES

Anecdotal evidence from individuals who work with transgender clients in Los Angeles generally conveys similar experiences and needs. The negative incidents experienced by transgender individuals could have negative consequences for their recovery. Overall, transgender individuals face many hurdles and have little or no support. They must navigate a system that is unable to comprehend, let alone support, them. For this reason, their substance use may not be treated effectively, and the likelihood of relapse is thereby increased.

Studies have found that the level of substance use among gay men and lesbians is higher, compared with that of the general population, and their substance use has been linked to their experiences of homophobia (McKirnan & Peterson, 1989a; Skinner, 1994). A study of gay, lesbian, and bisexual youth conducted by Savin-Williams (1994) linked substance use with the stress of experiencing verbal and physical abuse arising from their sexual orientation. Otis and Skinner (1996) also found a relationship between victimization and depression. Further, Mc-Kirnan and Peterson (1989b) pointed to a need to examine population specific stressors in order to understand the substance use of gay men and lesbians.

Much less is known about substance use among transgender people, but discrimination and violence experienced by transgender men and women will likely influence their substance use. Reback and Lombardi (1999) reported that alcohol, cocaine/crack, and methamphetamines were the drugs most commonly used by the transgender women in their study (no studies have examined substances used by transgender men). Some transgender people also use hormones and inject silicone obtained from illicit sources. The use of nonprescribed hormones and silicone is not illegal in the same way that the use of cocaine and methamphetamines is, but it is nevertheless a risk to one's health (Cabral et al., 1994; Chen, 1995; Lai, Chao, & Wong, 1994; Matsuba et al., 1994; Rapaport, Vinnik, & Zarem, 1996; Rollins, Reiber, Guinee, & Lie, 1997; Shoaib, Patten, & Calkins, 1994; Wassermann & Greenwald, 1995).

Focus groups of transgender individuals conducted in San Francisco found that having a street lifestyle, lack of education and job opportunities, and low self-esteem were all associated with drug and alcohol abuse (San Francisco Department of Public Health, 1997).

Savin-Williams (1994) found that in addition to using substances, "cross-gendered" youths are more likely to be abused because they do not meet the cultural ideals of gender-appropriate behaviors and roles. These transgender youth are at a very high risk of substance use and HIV infection (Kreiss & Patterson, 1997; Rodgers, 1995). Garnets, Herek, and Levy (1992) stated that experiences of violence and harassment can significantly affect the mental health of gay men and lesbians, which, in turn, can influence their substance use as well as their experience in substance use treatment. Experiences of violence and harassment can similarly affect transgender individuals. Israelstam (1986) found that many treatment programs did not have policies or programs in place to help gay and lesbian substance users. The same can surely be said for transgender substance users. Many substance use programs are not sensitive to the needs of transgender individuals, and many transgender men and women want programs that are trans-gender-specific and deal with the realities that they face (Bockting et al., 1998; San Francisco Department of Public Health, 1997). The Transgender Substance Abuse Treatment Policy Group of the San Francisco Lesbian, Gay, Bisexual, Transgender Substance Abuse Task Force (1995) reported that transgender clients of substance abuse treatment programs experienced the following: (1) verbal and physical abuse by other clients and staff; (2) requirements that they wear only clothes judged to be appropriate for their biological gender; and (3) requirements that they shower and sleep in areas judged to be appropriate for their biological gender.

HEALTH CARE ISSUES

In many instances the discrimination experienced by transgender /transsexual individuals ends in tragedy. When a car struck Tyra Hunter, eyewitnesses noted that the paramedics who responded to the accident withheld treatment when they discovered that she had male genitals; she subsequently died from her injuries. A court case found the paramedics and the emergency room staff to be at fault and awarded Tyra's mother $2.9 million (Fernandez, 1998). Leslie Feinberg, who is a masculine-identified lesbian (female biological sex, but identifies as a woman and has a masculine social presentation), detailed the discrimination she received when suffering from an undiagnosed case of bacterial endocarditis. The physician examining her ordered her out of the emergency room even though she had a temperature above 104 degrees (Feinberg, 2001). He remarked that her fever was a result of her being a very troubled person. Another example is presented in the documentary *Southern Comfort*, which follows the last year in the life of Robert Eads, an FTM transsexual who died of ovarian cancer when his attempts to find a medical provider failed because the doctors did not want to treat a transgender patient (Davis, 2000). Many other transgender/transsexual individuals face similar problems in accessing primary health care.

Health care service providers have found that getting transgender and transsexual individuals the services they need (e.g., primary health care, substance use treatment, and housing) can be difficult for several reasons. Many transsexual adults are denied insurance coverage because of their use of hormone treatment and a diagnosis of gender identity disorder. Some providers may not want to work with TG/TS clients (JSI Research and Training Institute, 2000). Lack of sensitivity on the part of health care providers themselves may adversely influence whether transsexual and transgender people will access treatment and remain in treatment (Clements et al., 1999; Moriarty, Thiagalingam, & Hill, 1998; Transgender Protocol Team, 1995). Transgender and transsexual people might resist seeking treatment because other TG/TS individuals reported past discriminatory treatment on the part of service providers. Focus groups in San Francisco and Minneapolis found evidence of discrimination against TG/TS men and women in HIV/AIDS programs and determined that many HIV/AIDS programs are not sensitive to the needs of TG/TS individuals (Bockting et al., 1998; Clements et al., 1999). Further, studies have found that some physicians believed transsexual women to be emotionally disturbed and a smaller group believed that they were morally wrong (Green, Stoller, & MacAndrew, 1966). There has been some improvement in physicians' attitudes over time (Franzini & Casinelli, 1986); however, bias within the psychiatric discipline will likely allow these attitudes to persist until the *DSM* and related materials are revised (Cermele, Daniels, & Anderson, 2001).

In the Washington, DC, Transgender Needs Assessment ($N = 263$), approximately one-third of the participants reported that caregiver insensitivity/hostility toward transgender people and their own fear that their transgender status would be revealed were barriers in accessing regular medial care (Xavier, 2000). In the case of transgender-related health care, 52% of the study's participants reported using hormones at some point in their life, and 36% currently used hormones. Of those currently taking hormones, only 34% reported that a doctor was monitoring their hormone therapy, and 58% acquired hormones from friends or on the street. What is most significant is that a vast majority of the sample (73%) reported that word of mouth was an important source of information concerning transgender care, followed by transgender social groups and LGBT newspapers, magazines, and newsletters. In the case of HIV, of those who reported being HIV-positive (25% of participants), only 8% reported barriers to receiving HIV/AIDS services.

Participants reported that the most common barrier to receiving care was provider insensitivity to transgender individuals. Overall, the majority stated the need for transgender-specific HIV education and prevention material (79.4%) and transgender-related health care information (78.2%), and half wished for transgender-sensitive HIV/AIDS testing (50.4%).

The Los Angeles Transgender Health Study (Reback, Simon, Bemis, & Gatson, 2001) reported that 64% of its sample (total N = 244 MTFs) had no health care coverage, 18% had MediCal/Medicare/Medicaid, and 17% had some form of private insurance. Further, 24% of the sample reported that they did not seek health care, and 8% did not have a regular source for health care. However, 30% reported having some type of surgery performed in order to change their gender presentation. The most common surgery was breast augmentation (21%). Further, 65% had plans for surgery to change their gender presentation, the most common again being breast augmentation (50%). In addition to surgery, 58% reported using hormones (estrogen), with 51% stating that they obtained hormones from street sources; only 38% reported doctors or a clinic as a source for hormones. Of those who injected their hormones in the past six months (44%), 72% obtained needles from nonmedical sources (street contacts, etc.). Finally, 33% reported having silicone or oil injected into their bodies in order to enhance their gender presentation. The results of the study show that even with regard to gender-related medical care, many transgender /transsexual women access services outside the health care system.

Even individuals with insurance may have trouble accessing primary and gender-specific health care. Only a few doctors and clinics make hormones and related procedures available to patients, and they may not accept Medicare or Medicaid. Very few insurance companies allow sex reassignment procedures under their plans, leaving even those who do have health insurance with few options in accessing gender-related medical care. Most transgender people will pay their medical expenses out of pocket, and many times they will have to search to find a doctor/clinic that will provide the care they need.

THERAPEUTIC AND CLINICAL ISSUES

DIAGNOSIS ISSUES

The mere existence of a nontraditional gender identity or presentation is insufficient for a diagnosis of gender identity disorder (GID) per *DSM-IV-TR*. In order to justify a diagnosis of GID, the client must meet the diagnostic criteria as outlined in *DSM-IV-TR* under "Gender Identity Disorder" and exhibit "clinically significant distress or impairment in social, occupational, or other important areas of functioning" (American Psychological Association, 2000, p. 576). As alternate gender identities and presentation become more accepted by the general society, it is increasingly likely that individuals will enter therapy to explore their gender in the absence of any significant psychopathology. However, a diagnosis may be necessary regardless of the functional status of the individual in order for him or her to access the medical services needed for legally changing one's gender.

If a GID diagnosis is appropriate for the client, that diagnosis should not be treated as a permanent status. Once the gender conflict has been resolved through self-acceptance of the client's gender identity (whatever that may be and through whatever interventions it may entail), the GID diagnosis is no longer indicated. As Israel and Tarver (1997) assert, "Once an individual has self identi-fied transition goals or has established a self-defined gender identity, she or he is no longer considered to be gender dysphoric" (p. 8).

ASSESSMENT

A number of resources are available to guide social workers through the assessment of individuals with gender identity concerns (American Psychiatric Association, 2000; Harry Benjamin International Gender Dysphoria Association, 2001; Israel & Tarver, 1997). A differential diagnosis may be indicated to examine the etiology of gender dysphoric feelings and/or behaviors and rule out existent psychopathology manifesting as gender confusion. In addition, it is recommended that clients be assessed for substance abuse and suicidal ideation, since some research suggests that transgender individuals are at risk for these underlying concerns (Clements-Nolle, Marx, Guzman, & Katz, 2001; Reback & Lombardi, 2001). Existing mental heath concerns may be grounded in a lifetime of difference, characterized by social rejection and stress related to the client's nontraditional gender presenta-tion and/or identity. Indeed, psychopathology, should it exist, may be the result of social stigmatization of cross-gender behaviors/identities, rather than the cause of the client's gender concerns per se. Thus the presence of mental health issues and/or substance abuse should not necessarily preclude the transition of a trans-sexual client, but should be explored to help the client understand what role, if any, other diagnoses play in the development of gender identity. If transition is the client's goal, then it is necessary to help the client address coexisting issues before and during transition. Depending on the client's needs, the social worker may need to advocate for the client when referring him or her to other resources, such as domestic violence shelters and rehabilitative housing.

DEVELOPMENTAL ISSUES

Like all populations, transsexual and transgender people may present with a vari-ety of mental health issues based on individual concerns, existing psychopathol-ogy, and environmental stressors. Each client will bring unique experiences to the client-therapist relationship; however, certain developmental issues may become evident during the gender definition and acceptance process, and the client may progress through three stages of development: (1) exploration, (2) acculturation, and (3) integration.

EXPLORATION Loosely defined, the exploration period is a time for transgender, transsexual, and questioning individuals to explore their gender identity, understand what that identity means to them, and determine how best to manifest it in their day-to-day lives. It is common for transgender clients to initiate contact with clinicians during the exploration process; however, the impetus for therapy may vary. Some clients enter therapy with confusion or ambivalence about their gender identity and seek professional assistance to "heal" or come to terms with their nontraditional gender behavior and/or identity. Other individuals may present with a solid transgender identity and enter therapy with the exclusive goal of securing needed permission and documentation for eventual hormonal and/or sex reassignment procedures. Still other clients may not present with any gender concerns at intake, but gender identity issues may arise while they are addressing interrelated concerns, or after they resolve other mental health issues, such as alcohol or drug abuse.

For clients in the process of questioning their gender, the therapeutic relationship can provide a safe, accepting space in which to try on various identities (male, female, in-between, and so on). Increasing numbers of transgender-identified individuals are choosing to live with an androgynous gender identity/presentation, inconsistent gender identities/presentations (identify/present as a woman at one point in time and as a man at others), or fully as a member of the "opposite" sex without medical intervention (the ease with which this is accomplished varies depending on many factors, among them physical characteristics, voice, and social environment). The decision to live in a gender identity that defies traditional notions of male and female (or even notions about the medical transition from one sex to another) should be respected as a viable alternative to transitioning to a new gender. In the clinical setting, gender-questioning clients may benefit from the opportunity to experiment with alternate pronouns and/or names, to discuss the wide range of gender possibilities, and to reflect on the meanings attributed to various genders in their life and culture. For clients with a solid gender identity and an intent to alter their body to match their gender identity, the developmental task may be to explore the available resources and alternatives, to understand the short-term and long-term implications of transitioning, to examine underlying beliefs about the role of gender identity in their life (e.g., transitioning will not solve all of the client's problems), and to solidify a support system before making a physical transition.

Transsexual clients seeking sex reassignment procedures are typically required to produce a letter from one or more clinicians before receiving hormonal or surgical treatment. The current edition of the Harry Benjamin Standards of

Care for the treatment of transsexuals recommends a minimum of three months in therapy before the onset of hormonal treatment and one year before surgery (Meyer et al., 2001). The gatekeeper role may interfere with the therapeutic relationship, and it is recommended that social workers discuss any policies regarding letters for sex reassignment surgery (e.g., minimum number of sessions, etc.) with their clients early in the therapeutic process. Israel and Tarver (1997) recommend that in order to avoid the dual relationship of therapist and gatekeeper, therapists split these roles between two clinical partners, with the primary therapist focusing on the clinical agenda and the secondary clinician/gatekeeper making recommendations for SRS. Thus the secondary clinician might meet the client, review the case notes, discuss progress with the primary therapist, and make the recommendation for hormonal or surgical treatment. Because many transsexuals and gender-questioning people know the diagnostic criteria for GID, this separation between the therapeutic and diagnostic roles may help to avoid situations in which clients use therapy as a medium through which to convince the social worker that sex reassignment procedures are indicated. It is not uncommon for transgender clients to be more familiar with gender identity issues and the *Standards of Care* than the social worker; in this situation, clients may feel compelled to provide information for the professional and to lobby aggressively for the paperwork needed to access medical procedures and other resources. It is recommended that social workers actively seek information about transgender issues and resources outside of the therapeutic relationship.

ACCULTURATION After the exploration process, some transsexual clients may begin to "transition," or take steps to live in a new social gender and/or physical sex. Many variables have been found to affect the psychological outcomes resulting from transition, including the client's age (Bollund & Kullgren, 1996), transition results (Bollund & Kullgren, 1996; Ross & Need, 1989), physical appearance (Bollund & Kullgren, 1996; Green & Fleming, 1990), birth sex (Bollund & Kullgren, 1996), family structure, work environment, and level of social support (Bollund & Kullgren, 1996; Ross & Need, 1989). The acculturation process will be influenced by the varied social and psychological differences of those undergoing the process. Notions of what it takes to be a man or a woman are variable and make the process different from one person to another.

Changing one's gender is often stressful, and learning to live in a new gender presentation may result in social, physical, psychological, and economic changes that pose a significant acculturation challenge to those transitioning from one gender to another (often resulting in symptomatology associated with adjustment disorder). Clients may need support as they deal with disclosure of their new gender path, social stigma related to transsexualism, internal changes brought on by the administration of cross-gender hormones (e.g., the onset of a second puberty or a change in sexual orientation), and external changes from their environment

RESOURCES

Brown, M. L., & Rounsley, C. A. (1996). True Selves: Understanding Transsexualism—for Families, Friends, Coworkers, and Helping Professionals. San Francisco: Jossey-Bass.

FTM Alliance of Los Angeles
   http://www.ftmalliance.org
FTM International
   http://www.ftm-intl.org/
GIDreform.org
   http://www.transgender.org/tg/gidr/
Harry Benjamin International Gender Dysphoria Association, Inc.
   http://www.hbigda.org/
International Foundation for Gender Education
   http://www.ifge.org/
International Journal of Transgenderism
   http://www.symposion.com/ijt/
Israel, G. E., & D. E. Tarver. (1997). Transgender Care. Philadelphia: Temple University Press.
Opinions, Support, Resources
   http://www.firelily.com/gender/resources/index.html
Trans Accessibility Project: Training Sessions
   http://www.queensu.ca/humanrights/tap/7training.htm
TransBoy Resource Network
   http://www.geocities.com/WestHollywood/Park/6484/
Transsexual Women's Resources
   http://www.annelawrence.com/

(e.g., different social expectations for the new gender). In addition to professional assistance, transsexual clients may benefit greatly from contact with other transsexuals who have successfully negotiated the transition process.

Several empirical studies on the outcome of transsexuals have found that the social and psychological adjustment of transsexuals is greatly affected by the ability to assimilate into their new gender role (Green & Fleming, 1990; Lundstrom, 1981; Rehman, Lazar, Benet, Schaefer, & Melman, 1999). Most adults who transition from one sex to the other have been socialized in the gender role of their birth. Even if they have internally identified as a member of the opposite sex (and resisted their birth gender), they are still likely to have received a certain level of birth gender socialization through schools, media, and family. Studying the outcomes of postoperative MTFs, Rehman et al. (1999) noted: "Living in a society that prepares males and females for very distinct and specific sex-role behaviors, the anatomical female is socialized from birth to function as a female in our society, while the male-to-female person has to acquire new sex-role behavior patterns later in life" (p. 5). Rehman et al. (1999) concluded that sex reassignment surgery alone did not prepare respondents to live life as women in society, and they recommended that a period of postoperative psychotherapy be indicated in the Harry Benjamin *Standards of Care*. Thus the adjustment process for transsexual adults may be perceived as an acculturation challenge wherein clients must learn to negotiate the cultural expectations of their new gender. Social workers can support the acculturation process by acting as cultural mediators, helping transsexuals to learn new strategies for negotiating social challenges (de Anda, 1984). The identification of role models may also help in the resocialization of transsexual men and women.

In addition to learning new cultural expectations, transsexuals must prepare to "come out" to their friends, family members, coworkers, and acquaintances. Unlike gay men and lesbians, transitioning transsexuals do not have the opportunity to become internally comfortable with their new identity before coming out to others. Soon after the beginning of hormonal treatment, physical and emotional changes demand that clients address the gender change in many, or all, relationships. Thus the social worker should be prepared to support the transsexual client in developing a plan to come out as transsexual in various aspects of life, including work, home, school, and general society. A number of resources are available on the Internet and in the library to assist clients in the coming out process. Changing something as essential as sex can be disruptive to the family system, and preparation for coming out may need to include contingency plans for dealing with possible estrangement from significant others, friends, and children. This is especially important for clients who are financially dependent on family members for their well-being. Depending on the clients' circumstances, it may be helpful to consult an attorney to understand laws and precedents regarding custody and marriage for transsexual persons in their home state.

Finally, social workers should be prepared to discuss sexual orientation and relationships with transitioning clients. It is important not to make assumptions about transsexuals' sexual orientation, because transsexuals span the full range of sexual orientations (homosexual, heterosexual, and bisexual) and clients may experience an unexpected change in their sexual orientation during the transition process. For example, a heterosexual male client may decide to transition from male to female. If, after transition, the client continues to be attracted to women, the previously heterosexual man may identify as a lesbian woman. In another example, a lesbian woman may begin to transition from female to male. During the transition, the client's sexual orientation may change, leading to identification as a gay man; thus the client who was a lesbian before transition becomes a gay man after transition. Sexual orientation depends largely on a stable gender identity, and when the gender identity of a client changes, an alteration in sexual orientation may follow. In addition to coming out as transsexual, clients may need to explore their new sexual orientation and examine what impact it may have on their relationships.

Although the common myth suggests that a sex change can occur overnight and depends on "the surgery," the actual transition process may take several years to complete, depending on the course of hormonal treatment and the level of surgical intervention. Because few insurance companies cover gender-related surgeries, the decision to undergo SRS is often based on socioeconomic status; thus individuals who do not choose surgeries should not be considered less committed to their gender identity than those who undergo full SRS. Further, many transsexuals live comfortably in their gender of choice without undergoing any sex reassignment surgeries, whereas other clients may feel "incomplete" until they finish multiple SRSs. Given this range of experiences, the end of the transition process is largely self-defined.

INTEGRATION   Once transsexual clients adjust to living in a new social gender, they face the task of integrating their multiple gender experiences and living in the long term as a member of their new sex. Transsexual clients may reenter therapy after a successful transition to address issues unrelated to their gender identity, to secure permission for further surgical intervention, or to address long-term adjustment issues. Social workers should not assume that being transsexual or transgender is a problem for the client, especially for those living long term. Presenting problems may have nothing to do with the client's gender identity, and the clinical focus should follow the client's agenda.

In the instance of long-term adjustment issues, social workers may help the client explore ways to integrate multiple gender experiences, to value his/her difference, and to address ongoing challenges. Common adjustment challenges in the post-transition period include forming intimate relationships, coming out as a lifetime task, self-acceptance as a nontraditional man or woman, family relationships, limitations of medical interventions, and coping with stigma in society.

CONCLUSION

Traditional gender norms within society create the context in which transgender men and women, and all the rest of us, live. Yet transgender men and women are more likely to have problems because our society does not readily allow individuals to transition from one gender to another, either temporarily or permanently. As a result, transgender and transsexual individuals require much in the way of support and guidance through their transition. They are likely to experience numerous problems socially, such as accessing health care and housing, and finding and sustaining employment. Experiences of discrimination, gender role socialization, family issues, and sexuality are just a few of the issues that transgender/transsexual men and women will bring to a therapeutic relationship.

What is needed is legislation allowing for the transition from one gender to another, as well as legal protection for those who do make the transition. Anti-discrimination legislation exists in some but not all jurisdictions, not at the federal level. Further, some areas allow for the legal recognition of gender change, while others do not. Such recognition also may not be consistent. For example, many transgender individuals are able to have legal sex designation changed on their driver's license (even before any type of surgery), yet if they are arrested they will be placed on the basis of whether they have a penis or a vagina (men's jail for transsexual women and vice versa). Current legislation is a mix of supportive and discriminatory laws that vary from context to context and place to place. The legislation needs to be changed in order for it to be more supportive and consistent for transgender individuals.

Many transgender people are distressed by experiences of discrimination and not having their gender identity seen as real. When providing treatment to transgender/transsexual individuals, it is important to see them as human, to respect their gender identity, and to help them through a very difficult process—not only for themselves but for their family, friends, coworkers, and the other people with whom they share their lives. The role of the social worker is to help the client through the difficult moments in life, not to act as a final arbitrator concerning people's gender.

REFERENCES

American Psychiatric Association. (1994). *Diagnostic and statistical manual of mental disorders (DSM-IV)* (4th ed.). Washington, DC: Author.

——. (2000). *Diagnostic and statistical manual of mental disorders (DSM-IV-TR)* (4th ed. rev.). Washington, DC: Author.

Bakker, A., van Kesteren, P. J., Gooren, L. J., & Bezemer, P. D. (1993). The prevalence of transsexualism in the Netherlands. *Acta Psychiatry Scandinavia*, 87, 237–238.

Beatty, C. (1993). Bryant Patch. In C. Beatty, *Misery loves company*. San Francisco: Glamazon.

Billings, D. B., & Urban, T. (1982). The socio-medical construction of transsexualism: An interpretation and critique. *Social Problems*, 29(3), 266–282.

Bockting, W. O., Robinson, B., & Rosser, B. (1998). Transgender HIV prevention: A qualitative needs assessment. *AIDS Care*, 10(4), 505–526.

Bollund, O., & Kullgren, G. (1996). Transsexualism—General outcome and prognostic factors: A five-year follow-up study of nineteen transsexuals in the process of changing sex. *Archives of Sexual Behavior*, 25, 303–316.

Brown, M., & Rounsley, C. (1996). *True selves: Understanding transsexualism—for families, friends, coworkers, and helping professionals*. San Francisco: Jossey-Bass.

Buchanan, Susy. (2002, June 6). *A privates matter: Did a teacher at Estrella Mountain Community College lose her job over what's under her skirt?* Available at http://phoenixnewtimes.com/issues/2002-06-06/news.html/1/index.html.

Cabral, A. R., Alcocer-Varela, J., Orozco-Topete, R., Reyes, E., Fernández-Domínguez, L., & Alarcón-Segovia, D. (1994). Clinical, histopathological, immunological, and fibroblast studies in 30 patients with subcutaneous injections of modelants including silicone and mineral oils. *Revista de Investigacion Clinica*, 46, 257–266.

Cermele, J. A., Daniels, S., & Anderson, K. L. (2001). Defining normal: Constructions of race and gender in the *DSM-IV* casebook. *Feminism and Psychology*, 11(2), 229–247.

Chen, T. H. (1995). Silicone injection granulomas of the breast: Treatment by subcutaneous mastectomy and immediate subpectoral breast implant. *British Journal of Plastic Surgery*, *48*, 71–76.

Clements, K., Wilkinson, W., Kitano, K., & Marx, R. (1999). Transgender and HIV risks, prevention, and care. *International Journal of Transgenderism*. Available at http://www. symposium.com/ijt.hiv_risk/clements.htm.

Clements-Nolle, K., Marx, R., Guzman, R., & Katz, M. (2001). HIV prevalence, rish behaviors, health care use, and mental health status of transgender persons: Implications for public health intervention. *American Journal of Public Health*, *91*(6), 915–921.

Davis, K. (2000). *Southern comfort*. New York: Q-Ball Productions.

de Anda, D. (1984). Bicultural socialization: Factors affecting the minority experience. *Social Work*, *29*(2), 101–107.

Feinberg, L. (2001). Trans health crisis: For us it's life or death. *American Journal of Public Health*, *91*(6), 897–900.

Fernandez, M. E. (1998, December 12). Death suit costs city $2.9 million; mother of transgendered man wins case. *Washington Post*, p. C1.

Franzini, L. R., & Casinelli, D. L. (1986). Health professionals' factual knowledge and changing attitudes toward transsexuals. *Social Science and Medicine*, *22*(5), 535–539.

Garnets, L., Herek, G. M., & Levy, B. (1992). Violence and victimization of lesbians and gay men: Mental health consequences. In G. M. Herek and K. T. Berrill (Eds.), *Hate crimes: Confronting violence against lesbians and gay men* (pp. 207–226). Newbury Park, CA: Sage.

Green, R., & Fleming, D. T. (1990). Transsexual surgery follow-up: Status in the 1990s. *Annual Review of Sex Research*, *1*, 163–174.

Green, R., Stoller, R. J., & MacAndrew, C. (1966). Attitudes toward sex transformation procedures. *Archives of General Psychiatry*, *15*(2), 178–182.

Haraldsen, I. R., & Dahl, A. A. (2000). Symptom profiles of gender dysphoric patients of transsexual type compared to patients with personality disorders and healthy adults. *Acta Psychiatrica Scandinavica*, *102*(4), 276–281.

Israel, G. E., & Tarver, D. E. (1997). *Transgender care*. Philadelphia: Temple University Press.

Israelstam, S. (1986). Alcohol and drug problems of gay males and lesbians: Therapy, counseling, and prevention issues. *Journal of Drug Issues*, *16*, 443–461.

JSI Research and Training Institute. (2000). *Access to health care for transgendered persons in Greater Boston*. Boston: GLBT Health Access Project.

Kessler, S. J., & McKenna, W. (1985). *Gender: An ethnomethodological approach*. Chicago: University of Chicago Press.

Kreiss, J. L., & Patterson, D. (1997). Psychosocial issues in primary care of lesbian, gay, bisexual, and transgender youth. *Journal of Pediatric Health Care*, *11*, 266–274.

Lai, Y. F., Chao, T. Y., & Wong, S. L. (1994). Acute pneumonitis after subcutaneous injections of silicone for augmentation mammaplasty. *Chest*, *106*, 1152–1155.

Landeb, M., Walinder, J., & Lustrom, B. (1996). Incidence and sex ratio of transsexualism in Sweden. *Acta Psychiatrica Scandinavica*, *93*, 261–263.

Levine, S. (1989). Gender identity disorders of childhood, adolescence, and adulthood. In H. Kaplan & B. Sadock (Eds.), *Comprehensive textbook of psychiatry* (5th ed.) (vol. 1, pp. 1061–1069). Baltimore: Williams and Wilkins.

Lombardi, E. L. (2001). Enhancing transgender health care. *American Journal of Public Health*, *91*, 869–872.

Lombardi, E. L., Wilchins, R. A., Priesing, D., & Malouf, D. (2001). Gender violence: Transgender experiences with violence and discrimination. *Journal of Homosexuality*, 42(1), 89–101.

Lundstrom, B. (1981). *Gender dysphoria: A social-psychiatric follow-up of 31 cases not accepted for sex reassignment.* Hisings Backa: University of Göteborg Press.

Matsuba, T., Sujiura, T., Irei, M., Kyan, Y., Kunishima, N., Uchima, H., Miyagi, S., Iwata, Y., & Matsuba, K. (1994). Acute pneumonitis presumed to be silicone embolism. *Internal Medicine*, 33, 481–483.

McKirnan, D. J., & Peterson, P. L. (1989a). Alcohol and drug use among homosexual men and women: Epidemiology and population characteristics. *Addictive Behaviors*, 14, 545–554.

——. (1989b). Psychosocial and cultural factors in alcohol and drug abuse: An analysis of a homosexual community. *Addictive Behaviors*, 14, 555–563.

Meyer III, W., Bockting, W., Cohen-Kettenis, P., Coleman, E., DiCeglie, D., Devor, H., Gooren, L., Hage, J. Joris, Kirk, S., Kuiper, B., Laub, D., Lawrence, A., Menard, Y., Patton, J., Schaefer, L., Webb, A., & Wheeler, C. (2001). *The Standards of Care for gender identity disorders.* (6th version. IJT 5.1). Available at http://www.symposion.com/ijt/soc_2001/index.htm.

Miach, P. P., Berah, E. F., Butcher, J. N., & Rouse, S. (2000). Utility of the MMPI-2 in assessing gender dysphoric patients. *Journal of Personality Assessment*, 75(2), 268–279.

Moriarty, H. J., Thiagalingam, A., & Hill, P. D. (1998). Audit of service to a minority client group: Male to female transsexuals. *International Journal of STD and AIDS*, 9(4), 238–240.

Namaste, V. K. (1999). HIV/AIDS and female to male transsexuals and transvestites: Results from a needs assessment in Quebec. *International Journal of Transgenderism*, 3,1 and 2. Available at http://www.symposion.com/ijt/hiv_risk/namaste.htm.

——. (2000). *Invisible lives: The erasure of transsexual and transgendered people.* Chicago: University of Chicago Press.

Nanda, S. (1990). *Neither man nor woman: The Hijras of India.* Belmont, CA: Wadsworth.

Nemoto, T., Luke, D., Mamo, L., Ching, A., & Patria, J. (1999). HIV risk behaviors among male-to-female transgenders in comparison with homosexual or bisexual males and heterosexual females. *AIDS Care*, 11(3), 297–312.

Pauly, I. B. (1990). Gender identity disorders: Evaluation and treatment. *Journal of Sex Education and Therapy*, 16(1), 2–24.

——. (1992). Terminology and classification of gender identity disorders. *Journal of Psychology and Human Sexuality*, 5(4), 1–14.

Rapaport, M. J., Vinnik, C., & Zarem, H. (1996). Injectable silicone: Cause of facial nodules, cellulitis, ulceration, and migration. *Aesthetic Plastic Surgery*, 20, 267–276.

Raymond, J. G. (1994). *The transsexual empire: The making of the she-male.* New York: Teachers College Press.

Reback, C. J., & Lombardi, E. L. (1999). A community-based harm reduction program for male-to-female transgenders at risk for HIV infection. *International Journal of Transgenderism.* Available at http://www.symposion.com/ijt/HIV_risk/reback.htm.

Reback, C. J., Simon, P. A., Bemis, C. C., & Gatson, B. (2001). *The Los Angeles Transgender Health Study: Community Report.* Report funded by the Universitywide AIDS Research Program. Los Angeles: Authors.

Rehman, J., Lazer, S., Benet, A. E., Schaefer, L. C., & Melman, A. (1999). The reported sex and surgery satisfactions of 28 postoperative male-to-female transsexual patients. *Archives of Sexual Behavior*, 28(1), 71–89.

Rodgers, L. L. (1995). Transgendered youth fact sheet. In Transgender Protocol Team, *Transgender protocol: Treatment services guidelines for substance abuse treatment providers* (pp. 7–8). San Francisco: Lesbian, Gay, Bisexual, Transgender Substance Abuse Task Force.

Rollins, C. E., Reiber, G., Guinee Jr., D. G., & Lie, J. T. (1997). Disseminated lipogranulomas and sudden death from self-administered mineral oil injection. *American Journal of Forensic Medicine and Pathology, 18*, 100–103.

Ross, M., & Need, J. (1989). Effects of adequacy of gender reassignment surgery on psychological adjustment: A follow-up of fourteen male-to-female patients. *Archives of Sexual Behavior, 18*, 145–153.

San Francisco Department of Public Health. (1999). *The Transgender Community Health Project: Descriptive results*. San Francisco: Author.

San Francisco Department of Public Health, AIDS Office. (1997). *HIV prevention and health service needs of the transgender community in San Francisco: Results from eleven focus groups*. San Francisco: Author.

Savin-Williams, R. C. (1994). Verbal and physical abuse as stressors in the lives of lesbian, gay male, and bisexual youths: Associations with school problems, running away, substance abuse, prostitution, and suicide. *Journal of Consulting and Clinical Psychology, 62*, 261–269.

Shoaib, B. O., Patten, B. M., & Calkins, D. S. (1994). Adjuvant breast disease: An evaluation of 100 symptomatic women with breast implants or silicone fluid injections. *Keio Journal of Medicine, 43*, 79–87.

Simon, P. A., & Reback, C. J. (1999). *Baseline characteristics of a cohort of male-to-female transgenders receiving services at four community-based prevention programs in Los Angeles County*. Poster presented at the Sixteenth Annual AIDS Investigators' Meeting and Second Annual Conference on AIDS Research in California, San Diego.

Skinner, W. F. (1994). The prevalence and demographic predictors of illicit and licit drug use among lesbians and gay men. *American Journal of Public Health, 84*, 1307–1310.

Sykes, D. L. (1999). Transgendered people: An "invisible" population. *California HIV/AIDS Update, 12*(1), 80–85.

Transgender Protocol Team. (1995). *Transgender protocol: Treatment services guidelines for substance abuse treatment providers*. San Francisco: Lesbian, Gay, Bisexual, Transgender Substance Abuse Task Force.

Tsushima, W. T., & Wedding, D. (1979). MMPI results of male candidates for transsexual surgery. *Journal of Personality Assessment, 43*(4), 385–387.

Wassermann, R. J., & Greenwald, D. P. (1995). Debilitating silicone granuloma of the penis and scrotum. *Annals of Plastic Surgery, 35*, 505–509.

Weitze, C., & Osburg, S. (1996). Transsexualism in Germany: Empirical data on epidemiology and application of the German Transsexuals' Act during its first ten years. *Archive of Sexual Behavior, 25*(4), 409–425.

Wilchins, R. A. (1997). *Read my lips: Sexual subversion and the end of gender*. Ithaca: Firebrand Books.

Xavier, J. (2000). *The Washington, DC, Transgender Needs Assessment Survey: Final report for Phase Two*. Washington, DC: Author.

16

VIOLENCE, HATE CRIMES, AND HATE LANGUAGE

Mary E. Swigonski

Hatred never dispels hate
Only love dispels hate
This is an ancient and inexhaustible law.

—THE DHAMMAPADA[1]

SOCIAL WORK practice with those who have experienced violence as a consequence of how others perceived their sexual orientation or gender expression (SOGE) is a daunting endeavor. As human beings, and as social workers, how do we begin to understand this violence and hate? As social workers, how do we most effectively help our clients who have been victims of anti-SOGE-related incidents? The epigraph that opens this chapter reminds us that the temptation to respond to violence and hate with hate is not the answer. This chapter takes that admonition seriously and explores its implications, incorporating the Buddha's four noble truths as an organizing structure (Hahn, 1998).

The discussion here begins by defining violence and examining direct and structural violence. The second section analyzes the causes of violence, particularly ways that differences are (mis)understood. The third section proposes justice, care, and human rights as a theoretical framework that embodies love to dispel hate and end violence. The fourth section places practice strategies to address hate and violence within a public health prevention model.

Social work practice must go beyond healing the wounds of violence, hate speech, and hate crimes. That work is necessary, but not sufficient. Healing past wounds through therapeutic interventions allows current practices and patterns of violence to persist and leaves the door open for future violence. Therefore the chapter includes strategies to heal the wounds of violence and to work toward ending current violence and preventing future SOGE-related violence.

THERE IS VIOLENCE: FACTS AND FACES OF VIOLENCE

There is violence. As social workers, we are dedicated to compassion, human rights, social justice, and empowerment, but we live and work in a world where individuals, groups, and social institutions use force to cause harm to others. Violence includes "acts of commission or omission, as well as societal conditions that inhibit the development of individuals, social groups, classes, and entire people, by obstructing fulfillment of basic human needs, and unfolding of constructive human energy and potential" (Gil, 1998, p. 61). Harm is inflicted through direct violence — overt, immediate, concrete acts perpetrated on particular, identifiable people (Opotow, 2001, p. 102). Harm is also inflicted through structural violence — ways of being that are normalized, that characterize how things are done, and that inflict harm on others.

Direct violence against individuals, communities, or property, enacted because of apparent sexual orientation or gender expression, is referred to in this chapter as hate crime. Hate speech is verbal direct violence. Structural violence is much more subtle and pernicious. Structural violence is often invisible and unnamed, even unnamable. The responsibility for structural violence is blurred and unclear, because harm is inflicted through patterns of unequal access to social and economic resources that are pervasively woven throughout the social structure and its social institutions (Opotow, 2001, p. 102). Structural violence is the other side of the coin of social privilege. Homophobia (the irrational fear of homosexuality and homosexuals) and heterosexism (the presumption of heterosexuality as the only normal form of sexual attraction and behavior, and the hegemonic imposition of heterosexuality as normative) are elements of structural violence.

Both direct and structural violence interact with economic exploitation, political marginalization, powerlessness, and cultural imperialism to form an interlocking system of domination and oppression of individuals and communities identified by their SOGE (as well as individuals and communities with other devalued social identities) (Young, 1990). Acts of violence, both direct and structural, abrogate the other person's dignity and humanity and inflict physical and moral harm.

VIOLENCE BASED ON PERCEPTIONS OF SEXUAL ORIENTATION OR GENDER EXPRESSION

DIRECT VIOLENCE Acts of violence based on perceptions of sexual orientation or gender expression are not new phenomena. Men were executed for sodomy as early as 1624 (Katz, 1976, 1992). Lesbians and gay men have been, and continue to be, subjected to institutional violence, including felony imprisonment and fines, clitoridectomy and castration, forced psychiatric treatment, dishonorable discharge from the military, and general social ostracism (Herek, 1989, p. 948). Harm based on perceptions of SOGE represents the most violent and culturally legitimate type of hate crime in the United States (Jenness & Broad, 1997, p. 49). Mason (2002), summarizing the results from large victimization surveys undertaken on homophobic violence in a number of English-speaking countries, found that:

* 70 to 80 percent of lesbians and gay men reported experiencing verbal abuse in public because of their sexuality
* 30 to 40 percent reported threats of violence
* 20 percent of gay men reported physical violence
* 10 to 12 percent of lesbians reported physical violence

For people whose sexual orientation or gender expression is outside narrowly defined societal norms, violence is a normative part of life. That is a fact, but it is not a tolerable fact.

HATE CRIMES Hate crimes are criminal offenses committed against a person, family, or property that are motivated, in whole or in part, by the offender's bias against a race, religion, dis/ability, ethnicity/national origin, gender, or sexual orientation or gender expression. Even if the offender was mistaken in the perception that the victim was a member of the group against which he or she was acting, the offense is still a hate crime because the offender was motivated, in whole or in part, by bias against the group (Federal Bureau of Investigation, 1996). Examples of hate-motivated acts include threatening phone calls, hate mail, physical assaults, and vandalism, as well as noncriminal actions that are motivated by bias, such as nonthreatening name-calling, using racial slurs, or disseminating anti-group leaflets (National Hate Crimes Documentation Network, 2001).

Analysis of the statistics published by the Federal Bureau of Investigation (1996) reveals several patterns that have remained consistent over time. Racial-bias crimes are the most commonly reported hate crimes, and those crimes are most often perpetrated against African Americans. Religious bias is the second most prevalent type of hate crime reported, and those are most often anti-Jewish in nature. Sexual orientation hate crimes are consistently the third most prevalent type of hate crime reported, and those are more often perpetrated against gay men.

Hate crime statistics provide important information, but they profoundly underrepresent the parameters of the problem. These statistics reflect those incidents that were reported to particular agencies and recorded by them. But only a small proportion of crimes are reported, and many jurisdictions do not collect these data. Community surveys indicate that a profoundly small percentage of SOGE-related violence is reported to the police, conservatively less than 20%. For example, in one sample of 2,259 lesbians and gay men living in or around Sacramento, California, hate crimes were about half as likely as non-bias crimes to be reported to the police (Herek, Gillis, & Cogan, 1999). Fort Lauderdale's anti-violence project, Gays United to Attack Repression and Discrimination (GUARD) reported statistics showing that only about 2% of all hate crimes are reported. Columbus's Stonewall Union Antiviolence Project reported that across the United States gay/lesbian anti-violence projects consistently document a 1:10 ratio between violence reports known to local police and those reported to gay/lesbian community advocates (Jenness & Broad, 1997).

Why are there such disparities in the reporting of crimes that are characteristically so heinous? Peel (1999) found that those who did not report the crime agreed with statements such as "It was not practical," "I was scared and did not feel safe," "It happened at work and I felt partly to blame." Many of the non-reporters in Peel's study cited concern about police homophobia as a substantial factor influencing their decision to not report the crime.

Hate crimes are more than numbers and statistics; they represent human harm and suffering. The effects of hate crimes are not only the direct impact on the immediate victims and their families and friends but also the indirect impact on those who might just as easily have been targets—those who are members of the same identity group (Hood & Rollins, 1995, p. 239).

From the descriptions of those who have reported their experiences of SOGE-related hate crimes, the pattern of this violence is beginning to emerge. Mason (2002) describes it as follows:

> The typical homophobic incident is said to be a random street assault perpetrated by a group of young males who [are] strangers to the victim. The victim is often alone or with one or two friends at the time. In cases of physical violence, incidents are more likely to occur at night and to take place in public places such as the street, car parks, parks and beaches. This picture appears to be consistent across nations.
>
> (P. 40)

However, there are distinctions between violence against lesbians and violence against gay men. Gay men report greater levels of physical assault from strangers, and lesbians report that the perpetrator is more likely to be known to them (although not always).

Several studies of violence against lesbians indicate that although much of the aggression does appear to involve random street-based attacks, a significant number of the incidents take place at home or work, involve ongoing campaigns of harassment, and are committed by one older man acting alone, who may be known to the woman (Mason, 2002, p. 40).

Violence and hate crimes emerge from a larger context that implicitly, and at times explicitly, sanctions them.

INDIRECT VIOLENCE SOGE-related violence is often officially sanctioned and condoned by government, religious, and social institutions. That means that the direct violence of hate crimes is supported by interlocking systems of indirect structural violence. In an array of issues, contemporary social institutions such as government, religion, family, and economic and social welfare entities promulgate and support policies and practices that overtly or covertly cause harm to those who stand outside the dominant forms of sexual orientation or gender expression. The policy analysis and work of the National Gay and Lesbian Task Force are particularly helpful in reconstructing the parameters of indirect violence that structures life in America for gay men, lesbians, bisexuals, two-spirited people, transgender people, and those who question their sexual orientation or gender expression (GLBT[2]Qs).

Civil rights laws ban discrimination based on sexual orientation *and* gender identity in four states—Minnesota (1993), Rhode Island (2001), New Mexico (2003), and California (2003)—and the District of Columbia, while ten states ban discrimination based on sexual orientation.[2] In the remaining thirty-six states, discriminating against an individual or group because of sexual orientation is quite legal (National Gay and Lesbian Task Force, 2004). Only 9.3% of transgender people are protected by any form of anti-discrimination laws. Sodomy laws, an invasion of the privacy of sexual expression between consenting adults, remained in effect in fifteen[3] states (National Gay and Lesbian Task Force, 2003) until the United States Supreme Court struck down all sodomy laws in the *Lawrence v. Texas* decision. The military is a significant source of both direct and structural violence in relationship to SOGE. Since the adoption of the "don't ask, don't tell" policy by the U.S. military, the Service Members Legal Defense Network has documented 968 incidents of anti-gay violence between February 1999 and February 2000, a 142% increase from the preceding year (National Gay and Lesbian Task Force, 2002).

The concept of family is a deeply complex issue for GLBT[2]Q people, complicated by SOGE-related structural violence. Many religious groups deny the veracity of same-sex relationships. Same-sex couples who choose to parent children can expect to experience difficulties in becoming foster parents, in adopting, and even in sustaining the custody of their own biological children (National Gay and Lesbian Task Force, 2002). Within the United States of America, same-sex marriage is possible only for residents of Massachusetts, and that only since May 17, 2004. However, since the passage of the federal Defense of Marriage Act in 1996, thirty-nine[4] states have passed legislation or constitutional amendments specifically banning the establishment or recognition of such marriages in their states (National Gay and Lesbian Task Force, 2002). Because same-sex marriage is not a possibility in any state except Massachusetts, domestic partnership benefits are the primary avenue for sharing economic benefits and legal protections. However, domestic partnership benefits are provided by individual employers, municipalities, or states, and the value of those benefits is subject to federal and state taxes (similar benefits available to married heterosexual couples are not taxable).

Health issues, particularly breast cancer and HIV/AIDS, remain significant areas of concern and discrimination with regard to diagnosis, treatment, access to ancillary services, and confidentiality. Similar issues arise regarding mental health services.

Discrimination in housing and employment on the basis of sexual orientation remains legal in many states; same-sex couples generally are denied the community recognition, legal protections, and economic benefits accorded to married heterosexual partners; sexual intimacy between same-sex partners remains illegal in many states. Sexual orientation and gender identity, an individual's most basic expressions of love and identity, remain sources of oppression and discrimination—of structural violence—across the array of social institutions. This constellation of denied protections and benefits creates a pattern of structural violence that subtly and perniciously denigrates relationships among lesbian, gay, bisexual, transgender, and two-spirited people, and those who are questioning their sexual orientation or gender expression. Through this denigration, their orientations to love and their ways of being in the world are rendered less than fully human, and as a consequence, they are rendered less than fully human.

FACES OF VIOLENCE Acts of violence, and inactions that condone violence, affect particular individuals, families, and groups, and they have consequences for those individuals, families, and groups. Survivors of SOGE-related violence are particularly susceptible to the aftereffects of violence. Many crime victims report experiencing depression, anxiety, and post-traumatic stress disorder symptoms, fears related to personal safety, and diminution of their sense of self-worth. SOGE-related hate crime survivors displayed less willingness to believe in the general benevolence of people and rated their own risk for future victimization somewhat higher than did others. They also were more likely than others to regard the world as unsafe, to view people as malevolent, to exhibit a relatively low sense of personal mastery, and to attribute their personal setbacks to sexual prejudice (Herek et al., 1999, p. 950). SOGE-related hate crimes symbolically represent an attack on the victims' identities and community, and so affect the victims' feelings about their orientation to love, gender expression, and their community. Survivors of SOGE-related hate crimes may perceive that their sexual orientation or gender expression places them at heightened risk for an array of negative experiences in a dangerous world over which they have little control.

One pernicious manifestation of structural violence is that GLBT²Qs may not be able to count on the support of their family or community if they have been victimized. Nontraditional sexual orientations and gender expressions are often developed in opposition to one's family's or ethnic group's expectations. Because of this disjunction from family and community experiences and expectations, these individuals are not likely to be taught strategies for coping with prejudice — at least, not by their families (Herek et al., 1999, p. 946).

Given this context of violence and its seeming ubiquity, it is important for social workers to begin to understand some of its root causes. Without at least a preliminary understanding of causes, and without a clear focus on goals, intervention efforts are likely to flail and to address symptoms rather than the root of problem.

CAUSES OF VIOLENCE: SOCIAL CONTEXTS AND IMPLICATIONS

The findings from the factor analysis in a study of anti-gay behavior identified four motivational themes underpinning acts of SOGE-related violence: peer dynamics, anti-gay ideology, thrill seeking, and perceived self-defense (Franklin, 2000). Perpetrators enact violence as a way of securing their place in a group, and as a response to particular other groups, especially those whose sexual orientation or gender expression is perceived as different. Perpetrators enact violence for fun and self-protection. Perpetrators enact violence against those who are different as a way to bond with others like themselves. Perpetrators enact violence as a means of self-protection—as protection from those who are different and therefore are seen as a threat to preferred ways of being. Violence has become a highly valued weapon in America's response to differences.

MISUNDERSTANDING DIFFERENCES

Violence is a reaction to those who are perceived as different. It may not be the fact of differences that is at issue, but the meanings that are attached to those differences. Differences have come to be understood as identifiers that delineate people as belonging to groups that must compete for scarce and differentially allocated resources and privileges. This competitively based meaning of differences understands them as "absolute otherness, mutual exclusion, categorical opposition … one group occupies the position of a norm, against which all others are measured" (Young, 1990, p. 169). But differences can mean more than that. Differences also hold the potential to signify specificity, variation, heterogeneity, wisdom, and excitement (Young, 1990).

Differences are treated with fear and violence when they threaten one's sense of security or identity (Young, 1990). Violence against those whose sexual orientation or gender expression is different is rooted in precisely these fears. The differences of GLBT²Qs transgress a border that appears to be defined by behaviors that can seen to be a matter of choice. If those differences are perceived as a threat, then one's sense of identity and security must be protected. At times this protection is built through exclusionary policies within social institutions, and at other times it is sought through interpersonal violence (Gil, 1998). While the focus of this chapter is on SOGE-related violence, it is important to remember that this manifestation of violence also interacts with other dimensions of violence, oppression, and domination such as sexism, racism, ableism, classism, ageism, and so on.

The specificity, variation, and heterogeneity of differences enable the division of the world into the categories of "us" and "them." Relationships between "us" and "them" can be a source of wisdom and excitement or one of conflict, violence, and oppression. Roy (2002) has analyzed the importance of "us" and "them" as social constructions. She notes that the sense of we-ness, of belonging engendered by the solidarity of "us," allows people to form relational bonds with others in their families, among their friends, on the job, and in their communities. She also points out that constructions of "us *and* them" have the potential to become "us *versus* them," forming the polarizations that lie at the core of hate and violence. "Us versus them" thinking conflates difference and deviance and sets those who are different—them—as deviant competitors for limited pools of power and resources. "Us versus them" thinking renders differences into points of separation, disjunction, and division. These patterns of thought distort differences to foreclose empathy (Young, 1990) and to minimize the deviance of perpetrating violence upon those who are different. Those who are different are less human, not fully human, maybe even not human, and so harming them seems less of a moral violation, perhaps not even a moral violation at all.

THOUGHT PATTERNS THAT SUPPORT DIFFERENCES AS DIVISIONS

Four thought patterns characterize "us versus them" thinking: absolutism, stereotyping, scapegoating, and dehumanizing (Roy, 2002). Each of these thought patterns will be briefly defined and used to illustrate how differences in sexual orientation or gender expression are rendered into deviance, and how people who embody those differences then become targets for hatred and violence.

Absolutism is a process whereby individuals and groups are able to see only two sides of an issue, and they then polarize those sides into right and wrong. Polarization forecloses the possibility of understanding differences as equally acceptable alternatives, or even as better or worse, greater or lesser. Polarizing an issue into right and wrong makes compromise impossible. In fact, in this mode of thought, unwillingness to negotiate is a virtue (Roy, 2002, p. 8).

Literal interpretations of Hebrew and Christian scriptures that are understood to proscribe same-sex behaviors are often taken as a justification for polarizing heterosexuality and homosexuality into a right/wrong relationship. Numerous contemporary scriptural scholars have called this interpretation into question (Boswell, 1980; Countryman, 1988; Goss, 1993; Hasbany, 1989; Horner, 1978; Mc-Neill, 1976; Scanzoni and Mollenkott, 1978; Swidler, 1993; Wilson, 1995). Nonetheless, this absolutist position retains its influence in rhetorical debates and in policy decisions, such as the U.S. military's "don't ask, don't tell" policy, and federal and state "defense of marriage" laws restricting marriage and its benefits to two people of opposite sexes.

Stereotyping is the act of creating categories run amok. It is quite normal to structure our reality with categories; it is in fact an important scientific endeavor. But stereotyping is categorization based on ignorance about the items or people in the category. Stereotyping reduces a category and those in it to only one or a few characteristics, on the basis of very limited experience with a few group members or exclusively on prejudices learned from others. Stereotypes lead to inappropriate conclusions about others and their community at the same time that those stereotypes exclude and ignore other characteristics and qualities (Roy, 2002).

Stereotyping reduces people to their sexual orientation, and further reduces sexual orientation to sexual acts. Stereotyping reduces variations in gender expression to deviance in sexual orientation, which is already reduced to sexual acts—so they are all seen as the same. Stereotyping obscures the array of sociocultural ways of being that nuance the art, music, friendships, families, spirituality, and sexual and affectional expressions of sexual orientation. Stereotyping renders invisible the array of patterns and styles embodied in gender expression—in ways of being, mannerisms, speech, clothing, style, attitude—some of which are syntonic with biological sexuality and others of which are defined independently of biological attributes. Stereotyping conflates sexual orientation and gender expression, which in reality are related but independent elements of one's way of being in the world. Stereotyping renders individuals and groups less than they are by obscuring the full array of their attributes and capabilities.

Prejudice is prejudgment of an individual or group (Roy, 2002). Prejudices are frequently formed before one has substantial direct experiences with the object of the prejudice, and they are often founded on inaccurate stereotypes. The extent to which prejudices are harmful is contingent on the power of the person or group that holds the prejudice. Prejudices are unfounded judgments; harm is a consequence of those unfounded judgments put into action. Homophobia and heterosexism are ubiquitous prejudices related to sexual orientation. Homophobia is the irrational fear and hatred of same-sex sexual orientation (Herek,

1990; Mason, 2002; Pharr, 1988). Heterosexism is the ideological system built on the assumption that heterosexuality is the only or the normative form of sexual orientation, which concurrently denigrates and stigmatizes non-heterosexuality (Herek, 1990; Mason, 2002; Pharr, 1988). The ubiquity of these prejudices is also indicative of their pernicious power. Virtually all children are raised with the presumption of heterosexuality. Children learn early in adolescence the depreciative meaning of words such as *dyke, butch, faggot, queen,* and *queer.*

Scapegoating is a process that unjustly places blame for a problem on another person or group (Roy, 2002). The advantage to those who scapegoat is that they avoid responsibility and punishment for the problem. An irony of scapegoating is that blame is placed on others who have less power than those who do the blaming, but in the process those who are blamed are made to appear as if they have more power (Roy, 2002). GLBT[2]Qs have been scapegoats for an array of social problems in America, particularly for moral decline and decay. Consider how the photography of Robert Mapplethorpe was publicized as the harbinger of the deterioration of our country's aesthetic values. Consider how GLBT activism for basic civil rights was reframed as irresponsible advocacy for "special rights" and how simply seeking those rights has allegedly led to the deterioration of the American nuclear family. And most recently, the pedophilia of some Roman Catholic priests has been attributed to an excess (i.e., more than none) of "homosexual" clerics.

Dehumanization denies the full humanity of others. It strips other persons of any connection they might have had to "us" (Roy, 2002). Roy notes that dehumanization is a prerequisite to acts of violence because it allows perpetrators to deny that their actions actually are hurting, or even killing, other human beings. Absolutism, prejudices, and scapegoating all intersect to form a pattern of valuation that diminishes the other, diminishes those whose sexual orientation or gender expression is outside of the heterosexual norm, so that those others become a "them" that is less than fully human. If you are not heterosexual, if your enactment of gender does not match the embodiment of sex that you were born with, then you are less than perfect—less than fully human—and so violence against you is more conscionable. Violence against you becomes an act of bonding among those who are more perfectly human, and an act of protection for the integrity of humanity.

Feminist analysis of violence related to SOGE reminds us that it is an expression of the interaction between regimes of sexuality and gender. This type of violence enforces and maintains the idea that non-heterosexual sexual orientations and gender expressions that deviate from those prescribed for one's biological sex are viewed as expressions of disordered sexual desire and gender identity (Mason, 2002; Pharr, 1988). One of the most common words used to insult targets of SOGE-based violence is the adjective *dirty* (Countryman, 1988; Mason, 2002). This disgust manifests in fear of contamination, a fear that one may be polluted through proximity to the sources. In invoking these connections, acts of violence assert the perversity and inhumanity of both homosexuality and women (Mason, 2002). The deprecation of SOGE as deviant is an essential strategy to sustain the current systems of power, privilege, and economic allocation (Pharr, 1988).

In order to challenge the absolutism, stereotyping, scapegoating, and dehumanizing that support the violence that sustains the current system of power, privilege, and economic allocation, we need to understand and engage with differences in new ways.

> Advocating the mere tolerance of difference ... is the grossest reformism. It is a total denial of the creative function of difference in our lives. Difference must be not merely tolerated, but seen as a fund of necessary polarities between which our creativity can spark ... divide and conquer must become define and empower.
>
> (LORDE, 1984, PP. 111–112)

We need to begin to define ways of being that celebrate differences and diversity as vital components of empowerment within a just and humane world.

POTENTIAL FOR ENDING VIOLENCE: JUSTICE AND HUMAN RIGHTS

There can be an end to violence. While this feels more like an assertion of hope than a statement of reality, it is important to be clear about the goals toward which we are working. It is a fundamental precept of social work practice that it is more powerful to focus on the goal, on what we want to achieve, than it is to focus exclusively on the problem (Miley, O'Melia, & DuBois, 2001). It is important to understand the problem, to know where you are. It is equally important to have a clear vision of the goal, of where you want to get to—if for no other reason than to know *where* you are going, so that you will be able to determine when you have arrived.

How best to describe a world in which violence based on perceptions of sexual orientation or gender expression no longer occurs—a world without violence? The opening epigraph to this chapter frames the assumption that undergirds this section: hatred and violence beget further hatred and violence; love is the means to the goal of ending violence. Justice and human rights are put forth in this section as theoretical conceptualizations to professionally enact and embody that love. This is proposed as an imperfect and preliminary theoretical foundation for praxis (a reciprocal, developmental interaction between theory and practice) toward the goals of ending violence and creating a world in which sexual orientation and gender expression are simply understood as ways of being that express elements of identity and that celebrate the particular other that one's heart/spirit is drawn to in love.

Justice concerns the degree to which a society contains and supports the institutional conditions necessary for the realization of the values that constitute the good life—a society that supports the self-development and self-determination of its constituent individuals and community groups (Young, 1990, 2000). Self-development includes one's ability to meet basic needs, to use satisfying skills, and to have one's particular cultural modes of expression and ways of life recognized. The division of labor and the distribution of resources are central issues related to self-development (Gil, 1998; Young, 1990). Self-development also raises questions about the institutional organization of power, status, cooperation, and communication in ways not reducible to resource distribution (Young, 2000). Self-determination means being able to participate in determining one's actions and the conditions of one's actions (Young, 1990). Individuals are optimally self-determining if they are able to pursue life in their own way. But self-determination is frequently restricted by other agents and by institutional relations, including those that award differential power to some agents while constraining the choices and actions of others (Young, 2000).

In a just society, self-development would include the ability to meet basic needs for love in ways that are consonant with one's sexual and affectional orientation without fear of judgment, recrimination, or violence. In a just society, self-development would include the ability to express one's gender with freedom and openness, without fear of judgment, recrimination, or violence. In a just society, self-development would include the ability to build and live within a culture that honors and celebrates an array of sexual and affectional orientations and gender expressions. In a just society, self-determination would be supported by social institutions (governmental, economic, family, religion, and social welfare) that would seek out, hear, and attend to the voices and needs of all of its diverse constituents.

Justice is a necessary goal to end violence. But unless individuals feel a sense of connection to those who have justice claims on them, those claims are not likely to matter very deeply; they are not likely to move anyone to action. Justice helps to explicate the "what" of a goal to end violence (Clement, 1996). Care helps to explicate the "who" of that goal—the sense of personal connection to claims for justice.

Care facilitates an awareness of human interconnectedness that strengthens individual moral and ethical obligations to just relationships with others. Feminist scholars caution that autonomy must underlie care (Clement, 1996; Gilligan, 1982; Ruddick, 1989; Willett, 2001). In order to be genuine, caring relationships need to take place between autonomous individuals and should serve to promote the autonomy of all those within the relationship. But care needs to extend beyond those people in interpersonal relationships. One way to extend the ethical obligations of care beyond immediate relationships is to include vulnerability within the analysis of care. At least to the extent that those who are distant are vulnerable to particular actions and choices, there is a special obligation to care for them. People beyond family and friends are also vulnerable to one's actions and choices. Care and compassion challenge one to consider the ways and the expanse of people whose lives directly or indirectly depend upon whether and how one chooses to come to their aid. Native American cultures teach that decision making should include care about the impact of one's decisions and actions for seven generations.

Care and compassion are important in responding to violence, because the more clearly, explicitly, and encompassingly connections to others are recognized, the more all of their claims for justice will matter on a human and personal level to each individual. This will make a difference in whether and how each person carries out obligations. Nationally and internationally, human rights documents stand as efforts to articulate and build consensus on how to operationalize the intersection of justice and care. Human rights are founded on the "recognition of the inherent dignity and the equal and inalienable right of all members of the human family" (United Nations, 1948, p. 1). Statements of human rights proclaim the dignity of all human beings, of collective membership in the interdependent human family—of the individual and collective responsibility to care for and about each other. Analyses of human rights (and their violations) stand as concrete exemplars of the global interdependence that describes the parameters of the people who are vulnerable to our actions and choices. Future generations, the poor and needy, those whose self-development and self-determination have been constrained by particular acts or by the policies and practices of social institutions, individuals and groups who are at risk of violence because of their sexual orientation or gender expression—all of their lives depend on whether or not each of us (or any of us) chooses to come to their aid (Clement, 1996).

Human rights documents articulate internationally affirmed paradigms of human interrelatedness, and of values and principles for ending violence. While human rights documents do not yet contain direct references to sexual orientation or gender expression, they do prohibit discrimination on grounds of sex. In 1993 the United Nations Commission on Human Rights declared that the prohibition against sex discrimination in the International Covenant on Civil and Political Rights included discrimination on the basis of sexual preference (People's Movement for Human Rights Education, 2002).

Justice and care as articulated in human rights documents offer a preliminary goal to end violence. Goals need to be achieved. The next section proposes a set of strategies for working for justice and care for persons whose SOGE stands outside the dominant pattern.

WAYS TO END VIOLENCE: PRAGMATICS OF PRACTICE

There is a way to end violence. In this section, social work practice interventions are highlighted to suggest ways to work to end violence using our hearts, brains, and hands (Rose, 1983). Violence requires a response. But a response may not be adequate.

> For many survivors of violence, no response can ever be adequate. For some victims of violence and their families, closure is often not possible, and the suggestion of closure would be an insult to lives that are irreconcilably ruptured... . Even to speak, to grope for words to describe the horrific event, is to pretend to negate their unspeakable quality and effects. Yet silence is also an unacceptable offense.
>
> (MINOW, 1998, P. 5)

Justice, care, and human rights can serve as a framework for developing and deepening praxis to redress and end violence. Organizations working against SOGE-related violence have taken a lead in this work by documenting instances of violence that abrogate the human rights of lesbians, gay men, bisexuals, and transgender people, and identifying and drawing public attention to the harm that these acts inflict. They are developing proposals for anti–hate crime legislation and social policy reform; educating and training law enforcement agencies and personnel; and providing services such as hotlines, service centers, and support groups for victims of bias-motivated violence (Jenness & Broad, 1997). Social service agencies can form coalitions with anti-violence organizations.

Social workers can stand as allies for SOGE justice and human rights on three levels, comparable to the three levels of public health prevention (Albee & Ryan, 1998; Caplan & Caplan, 2000). Tertiary prevention seeks to reduce the rate of residual disability/violence and to reduce its effects and consequences by working to heal the wounds of violence through therapeutic goals. Secondary prevention seeks to reduce the prevalence of violence in the population, working to end the current violence through short- and medium-range sociopolitical goals. Primary prevention seeks to reduce the frequency of new events of violence through identification of the root cause of the problem, so that future violence is prevented through long-range sociopolitical goals. Strategies for responding to SOGE-related violence at each of these three levels are highlighted below.

TERTIARY PREVENTION TO HEAL THE WOUNDS
OF SOGE-RELATED VIOLENCE

Those who have survived SOGE-related hate crimes may well experience their sexual orientation or gender expression as increasing their risk for an array of negative experiences in a dangerous world where they have little control. Assisting victims/survivors to redefine and regain a balanced worldview that recognizes danger without a sense of overwhelming vulnerability or powerlessness is an important short-term goal for social work practitioners (Herek et al., 1999). Social work practice begins with relationship development and assessment. Within those processes, the client and social worker together determine if there is a need for crisis intervention and perhaps support in addressing additional existential issues on a longer-term basis.

The Medical Crisis Intervention Model (Koocher, Curtiss, Patton, & Pollin, 2001; Pollin, 1995) is readily adaptable for work with survivors of SOGE-related violence. The discussion below indicates how that model can be applied to work with these survivors. This crisis model is a focused, short-term approach to crisis intervention. It builds on the observation that crisis—in this case, the aftermath of SOGE-related violence—carries with it many rapid and stressful life changes that in turn generate considerable emotional distress. Because of those changes many survivors are likely to experience physical, interpersonal, emotional, and spiritual changes that manifest as symptoms but that are more accurately understood as normal consequences of the trauma (Koocher et al., 2001).

The first meeting with the client is essentially a consultation. Together, the social worker and the survivor focus on identifying the goals that are important to help the survivor to cope with the aftermath of the experience of SOGE-related violence. The session might begin with Suzanne Pharr's (1988) question "Tell me, what has it been like for you?" The power of that question emerges from the openness that it conveys to hearing the survivor's narrative and from the potential it creates for framing the stress as a normal reaction. The survivor is invited to recount the nature of the experiences preceding, during, and following the episode(s) of violence. The session should also explore what the survivor knows about any additional follow-up that will be necessary (both medical and legal), who provided the information, and how the survivor and family members communicate with any other professionals and institutional representatives involved. It is also important to explore attributions of meaning and beliefs about the experience, including any feelings of guilt or shame. Life changes and stresses associated with surviving an act of violence need to be addressed, as do coping strategies that have been useful during this process and in the past. The survivor's pattern of outness, and the effect of any publicity on life-partner relationship, family relationships, work relationships, and employment need to be carefully examined and addressed.

On the basis of what the social worker and client discern from the first session(s), goals for coping with the stress of the violent episode and its aftermath are identified, and steps are planned to work toward those goals. Subsequent sessions focus on the goals identified in the first session and on eight primary fears that commonly affect those confronted with crisis: loss of control, loss of self-image, dependency, stigma, abandonment, fear of expressing anger, isolation, and fear of death (Pollin, 1995). Survivors of SOGE-related violence will also need to address the fear of the loss of safety. The survivor is encouraged to acknowledge each fear as it emerges, to recognize it as an issue that can be addressed, and to strategize how to cope with the challenges it presents.

The relevance and appropriateness of forgiveness—of self, family, friends, and, perhaps, of the perpetrator—also need to be considered with the survivor. The immediacy of crisis intervention services to the experience of violence may render the discussion of forgiveness untimely. But follow-up work might include analysis of the reasons for, costs of, and benefits to forgiveness.

In terms of intervention strategies and tasks, the survivor might be invited to keep a journal or to complete homework assignments developed in collaboration with the social worker. Social support systems and improved communication with significant others, family, friends, coworkers, and other involved professionals are all possible elements for intervention (Koocher et al., 2001). The final session is used to review progress and plan for the future.

SECONDARY PREVENTION TO END CURRENT VIOLENCE: SOCIOPOLITICAL GOALS

Secondary prevention efforts are designed to reduce the prevalence—to end current SOGE-related violence. SOGE anti-violence organizations have been particularly active at this level of violence prevention, including the following array of programs and strategies (Jenness & Broad, 1997, pp. 78–101):

* Discovering and documenting violence through hotlines that collect reports and surveys that are used to produce epidemiological reports of anti-gay and -lesbian violence
* Publicizing the epidemic of SOGE-related violence to law enforcement agencies, government officials, members of the GLBT^{2}Q communities, and the general population, including highlighting the underreporting of undetected hate-motivated violence against GLBT^{2}Qs
* Creating crisis intervention and victim assistance programs that include support groups, walk-in counseling, and referrals to ancillary support services
* Providing assistance in obtaining restraining orders and advocating within the criminal justice system
* Conceptualizing educational campaigns as anti-violence activism to publicize the nature and extent of violence while offering proposals designed to prevent and respond to the violence
* Organizing street patrols to provide surveillance and intervention

Each of these actions, independently and together, addresses the goal of ending SOGE-related violence.

PRIMARY PREVENTION TO PREVENT FUTURE VIOLENCE

Work toward primary prevention focuses on the prevention of future episodes of SOGE-related violence. Primary prevention strategies pursue political objectives to create a climate conducive to justice, caring, and human rights. This work addresses the long-term goal of social transformation, of changing the social, economic, cultural, and political structures. It proceeds as a profound embodiment of praxis on two interacting and interdependent levels—consciousness and concrete behavior (Gil, 1998).

Critical consciousness is for creating visions of ways of being and living that support social justice, care, and human rights, and establishing social institutions consonant with those values. The development of critical consciousness needs to address such issues as images of social reality; taken-for-granted ideas, beliefs, and assumptions; perceptions of personal and group needs and interests; and personal and group values and ideologies, which reciprocally interact with perceptions and provision of needs and interests (Gil, 1998).

Critical consciousness is necessary but not sufficient. Praxis requires reflection and action. Concurrent with the development of critical consciousness, concrete, action-based strategies are needed to implement a long-range vision of the essential attributes of a society constructed on a foundation of social justice, care, and human rights—a society that supports an array of orientations to love and gender expression. Gil (1998) discusses a range of action-based strategies that have contributed to substantive social transformations and that can be readily adopted in work to prevent violence and to create a culture of justice, care, and human rights. Those strategies include the work of activists to create social movements; the development of social structures and interpersonal interactions to spread critical consciousness; the development of a politics of common human needs; efforts to transform individual consciousness concerning people and nature; changes in personal actions, social relations, and lifestyle; the creation and expansion of just and caring social, economic, political, and cultural institutions within established social orders; and the creation of societies in which human rights, including civil and political rights, are constitutionally guaranteed for each individual and group and are particularly protected for those who have experienced oppression or domination (Gil, 1998). This list, while long, complex, and more than the practice of any one social worker can embody, offers points of departure in praxis toward justice, care, and human rights.

CONCLUSION

Violence squelches the jouissance that nurtures the spirit of life. Work to end SOGE-related violence begins with each person as a human being and as a social worker. It begins by acknowledging the fact of violence. It proceeds by understand-ing what it means to live in fear because others abhor a fundamental characteristic of one's self. It builds toward the goal of a just, caring society that embodies human rights. It develops in coalitions and alliances with those already engaged in work to heal the wounds of violence, and in developing and implementing strategies to end current violence and prevent future violence through teaching, research, and interpersonal and political action. As social workers, we can dedicate ourselves to act with care for justice and human rights, to heal the wounds of violence, and to end violence—especially violence that is perpetrated because of who we love or how we embody particular aspects of our humanity. This is a call for radical trans-formation on the personal, interpersonal, cultural, political, and socio-institutional levels. It is a call to honor and celebrate diversity. It is a call to work with care for justice—for a future to be possible for each of us.

NOTES

1. Byrom, T. (1993). *The Dhammapada: The sayings of the Buddha* (Boston: Shambhala Press).
2. Wisconsin (1982), Massachusetts (1989), Connecticut and Hawaii (1991), New Jersey, and Vermont (1992), New Hampshire (1997), Nevada (1999), Maryland (2001), New York (2002).
3. Alabama, Florida, Idaho, Indiana, Kansas, Louisiana, Massachusetts, Mississippi, Missouri, North Carolina, Oklahoma, South Carolina, Texas, Utah, Virginia.
4. Only Connecticut, Delaware, District of Columbia, Massachusetts, Missouri, New Jersey, New Mexico, New York, Rhode Island, Vermont, Wisconsin, and Wyoming have yet to pass such laws.

REFERENCES

Albee, G., & Ryan, K. (1998). An overview of primary prevention. *Journal of Mental Health, 7*(5), 441–450.

Boswell, J. (1980). *Christianity, social tolerance, and homosexuality: Gay people in Western Europe from the beginning of the Christian era to the fourteenth century.* Chicago: University of Chicago Press.

Byrom, T. (1993). *The Dhammapada: The sayings of the Buddha.* Boston: Shambhala Publications.

Caplan, G., & Caplan, R. (2000). Principles of community psychiatry. *Community Mental Health Journal, 36*(1), 7–24.

Clement, G. (1996). *Care, autonomy, and justice: Feminism and the ethic of care.* Boulder, CO: Westview.

Countryman, L. W. (1988). *Dirt, greed, and sex.* London: SCM Press.

Federal Bureau of Investigation. (1996). *Training guide for hate crime data collection uni-form crime reporting.* Washington, DC: Author.

Franklin, K. (2000). Anti-gay behaviors among young adults. *Journal of Interpersonal Violence, 15*(4), 339–363.

Gil, D. G. (1998). *Confronting injustice and oppression: Concepts and strategies for social workers.* New York: Columbia University Press.

Gilligan, C. (1982). *In a different voice: Psychological theory and women's development.* Cambridge, MA: Harvard University Press.

Goss, R. (1993). *Jesus acted up: A gay and lesbian manifesto.* New York: HarperCollins.

Hahn, T. N. (1998). *The heart of the Buddha's teaching: Transforming suffering into peace, joy, and liberation.* New York: Broadway Books.

Hasbany, R. (Ed.). (1989). *Homosexuality and religion.* New York: Harrington Park.

Herek, G. M. (1989). Hate crimes against lesbians and gay men: Issues for research and policy. *American Psychologist, 44*(6), 948–955.

———. (1990). The context of anti-gay violence: Notes on cultural and psychological heterosexism. *Journal of Interpersonal Violence, 5*(3), 316–333.

Herek, G. M., & Gillis, J. R. (1997). Hate crime victimization among lesbian, gay, and bisexual adults. *Journal of Interpersonal Violence, 12*(2), 195–216.

Herek, G. M., Gillis, J. R., & Cogan, J. C. (1999). Psychological sequelae of hate crime victimization among lesbian, gay, and bisexual adults. *Journal of Consulting and Clinical Psychology, 67*(6), 945–951.

Hood, J. C., & Rollins, S. (1995). Some didn't call it hate. *Violence Against Women, 1*(3), 228–241.

Horner, T. (1978). *Jonathan loved David: Homosexuality in biblical times.* Philadelphia: Westminster.

Jenness, V., & Broad, K. (1997). *Hate crimes: New social movements and the politics of violence.* New York: Aldine de Gruyter.

Katz, J. N. (1976/1992). *Gay American history: Lesbians and gay men in the U.S.A.* New York: Plume.

Koocher, G. P., Curtiss, E. K., Patton, K. E., & Pollin, I. S. (2001). Medical crisis counseling in a health maintenance organization: Preventive intervention. *Professional Psychology: Research and Practice, 32*(1), 52–58.

Lorde, A. (1984). *Sister Outsider: Essays and speeches.* Freedom, CA: Crossing Press.

Mason, G. (2002). *The spectacle of violence: Homophobia, gender, and knowledge.* London: Routledge.

McNeill, J. J. (1976). *The church and the homosexual.* Boston: Beacon.

Miley, K. K., O'Melia, M., & DuBois, B. (2001). *Generalist social work practice: An empowering approach.* Boston: Allyn and Bacon.

Minow, M. (1998). *Between vengeance and forgiveness: Facing history after genocide and mass violence.* Boston: Beacon.

National Gay and Lesbian Task Force. (2002). *Issues. National Gay and Lesbian Task Force.* Available at http://www.ngltf.org/issues/index.cfm [2002].

National Hate Crimes Documentation Network. (2001). *Hate crimes.* Available at http://www.lambda.org/ [2001].

Opotow, S. (2001). Social justice. In D. Christie, R. Wagner, & D. D. Winter (Eds.), *Peace, conflict, and violence: Peace psychology for the 21st century* (pp. 102–109). Upper Saddle River, NJ: Prentice Hall.

Peel, E. (1999). Violence against lesbians and gay men: Decision-making in reporting and not reporting crime. *Feminism and Psychology, 9*(2), 161–167.

People's Movement for Human Rights Education. (2002). *Human rights and sexual orientation.* Available at http://www.pdhre.org/rights/sexualorient.html [2002]. Pharr, S. (1988). *Homophobia: A weapon of sexism.* Little Rock, AR: Chardon.

Pollin, I. (1995). *Medical crisis counseling: Short-term therapy for long-term illness.* New York: Norton.

Rose, H. (1983). Hand, brain, heart: A feminist epistemology for the natural sciences. *Signs, 9*(1), 73–90.

Roy, J.M. (2002). *Love to hate: America's obsession with hatred and violence.* New York: Columbia University Press.

Ruddick, S. (1989). *Maternal thinking: Toward a politics of peace.* New York: Ballantine.

Scanzoni, L., & Mollenkott, V.R. (1978). *Is the homosexual my neighbor? Another Christian view.* New York: Harper and Row.

Swidler, A. (Ed.). (1993). *Homosexuality and world religions.* Valley Forge, PA: Trinity Press International.

United Nations. (1948). *Universal declaration of human rights.* United Nations. Available at http://www.unhchr.ch/udhr/lang/eng.htm [2002].

Willett, C. (2001). *The soul of justice: Social bonds and racial hubris.* Ithaca, NY: Cornell University Press.

Wilson, N. (1995). *Our tribe: Queer folks, God, Jesus, and the Bible.* San Francisco: HarperCollins.

Witten, T.M., & Eyler, A.E. (1999). Hate crimes and violence against the transgendered. *Peace Review, 11*(3), 461–469.

Young, I.M. (1990). *Justice and the politics of difference.* Princeton, NJ: Princeton University Press.

——. (2000). *Inclusion and democracy.* Oxford Political Theory. New York: Oxford University Press.

17

RELIGION AND SPIRITUALITY

Deana F. Morrow and Boo Tyson

I will take you as my people, and I will be your God.
—EXODUS 6:7A, HOLY BIBLE, NRSV, 1989

RELIGION AND spirituality are major constructs in virtually any culture. The influence that religion has on civic life, even here in the democratic, pluralistic culture of the United States, becomes obvious when one examines the roles that religious doctrine and biblical interpretation play in shaping civic debate and public policies regarding GLBT people. Try to think of one argument that exists against extending the full rights and benefits assumed by heterosexual people to GLBT people that is not rooted in a religiously based belief. Nearly impossible. Given the religious and cultural history of the United States, it is not surprising that these religiously based arguments, while rooted in Judeo-Christian tradition, are Christian in nature. Therefore this chapter will examine Scripture and theology within a Protestant Christian framework as they pertain to sexual orientation and gender expression in the United States.

This is not meant to imply that other religious perspectives, such as Catholicism, or other religions, such as Judaism and Islam, do not influence American culture or are not involved in the ongoing debate about human sexuality. There are certainly similarities and differences with regard to how these kinds of discussions happen, beyond a Protestant Christian framework. For the purposes of this chapter, however, it is important to understand that there exists within the civic culture in the United States an underlying Christian ethic that profoundly influences policy debates on social issues like race relations and gender equality. Today, that influence continues to exclude GLBT people from the mainstream of civic culture—not only through discrimination by withholding from GLBT people the same civil rights and benefits afforded to heterosexual people (e.g., access to spousal health insurance benefits or the legal sanction of relationships) but also through the loss of social freedom, such as the comfort to hold hands while on a walk in the park or to attend Christian worship as openly GLBT people. These kinds of exclusions may affect the spiritual and/or psychological well-being of GLBT people; therefore, such issues become an area of examination necessary in spiritual- and/or psychological-related counseling.

SPIRITUALITY AND RELIGION DEFINED

Spirituality may be defined as a deep sense of wholeness, connectedness, and openness to the infinite (Shafranske & Gorsuch, 1984). Faiver, Ingersoll, O'Brien, and McNally (2001) describe it as a "vital life force" that is deeply part of us, yet also that transcends us. They further describe spirituality as that which "connects us to other people, nature, and the source of life" (p. 2). Chittister (1998) defines it as "the magnet within us that draws us to God ... a composite of those practices, attitudes, and values designed to bring us to the height of spiritual development" (p. 19). Spirituality is intrinsic to our inner feelings and to the experience of what we have come to know as "higher power" (Van Hook, Hugen, & Aguilar, 2001).

In contrast, *religion* may be thought of as the social vehicle through which spirituality may be channeled (Faiver et al., 2001). Religion pertains to the outward ways in which faith is expressed, including rituals, dogmas, creeds, denominational identity, and ecclesiastical structures (Van Hook et al., 2001). Organized religion is among the most powerful and influential of all social institutions in the United States (Morrow, 2003). A social institution may be defined as a system of social relationships and cultural elements that represent standardized, authorized mechanisms for structuring behavior and social expectations among people (Appleby & Anastas, 1998). In many instances, religious doctrine fashions the principles from which people define and construct the moral code of their lives. And, as a social institution, religion significantly influences people's perceptions of what they consider to be socially and morally acceptable. The influence of religion in shaping cultural views about the moral acceptability of GLBT people has been—and continues to be—enormous.

HETEROSEXISM IN RELIGION

Heterosexism is defined as the belief in the superiority of a heterosexual orientation over other forms of sexual orientation (Morrow, 1996)—that is, being gay, lesbian, or bisexual is viewed as subordinate and inferior to having a heterosexual orientation. The social institution of religion has long been a tool for the perpetuation of heterosexism toward GLBT people (Davidson, 2000; Hilton, 1992; McNeill, 1993; Spong, 1991, 1998). The concept of family values as espoused by various religious groups in the United States generally excludes GLBT families. In addition, most religious groups deny the official sacrament of marriage to GLBT couples, as well as limit the pastoral freedom of their clergy to minister to their GLBT parishioners. Furthermore, many religions deny GLBT people the right to participate in both formal and informal leadership roles, such as becoming members of the clergy or assuming lay leadership positions.

CHRISTIANS AND HOMOSEXUALITY

In the United States, social issues and biblical interpretation have long been linked: slavery, prohibition, war, and women's rights are all part of an ongoing theological movement that finds itself, in the early years of the twenty-first century, beginning to openly debate the social acceptability of GLBT people. The Bible is considered sacred text within the Christian tradition and is a source often quoted as such. There are Christians who hold that the Bible is without error and therefore is to be interpreted literally. Other Christians hold Scripture to be sacred text and yet understand other factors (such as reason, tradition, and experience) to be a part of an ongoing process of biblical interpretation and divine revelation.

The manner in which one interprets biblical writings seems to be a critical factor in the religious acceptance of GLBT people. In a study of 785 clergy members, Taylor (2000) found that the belief that the Bible should be taken literally was the strongest predictor of negative attitudes toward lesbians and gays. One must remember as well that literal interpretation of Scripture passages has been used over time to support other cultural political issues, including slavery and the subordination of women to men (Spong, 1998). If one is to uphold a strictly literal interpretation of the Bible, one must recognize that it also condemns such activities as sexual intercourse during menstruation, masturbation, and birth control. In addition, biblical passages endorse such activities as prostitution, polygamy, concubinage, treating women as property, and offering young girls for marriage. Even though we do not hold to such traditions today, many religious people still claim that biblical passages condemning same-sex sexual activity that were written more than two thousand years ago are culturally relevant despite current scientific research indicating that variation in sexual orientation is natural and normal among humans and across species

WHAT DOES THE BIBLE SAY?

What the Bible says about homosexuality is largely dependent on how one interprets Scripture. The debate centers on whether Scripture should be taken literally or within the context of the cultural and historical period in which it was written. Generally, those who hold to a literal interpretation of the Bible argue that homosexuality is condemned. Those who defend a more contextual interpretation of the Bible tend to argue that the biblical writers did not have a scientific basis for understanding sexual orientation as being part of normative variation across a continuum, and their limited knowledge and the cultural biases of the time were reflected in their writings:

> None of the Gospel writers, nor the missionary Paul, nor the formulators of the tradition, possessed the psychological, sociological, and sexological knowledge that now inform our theological reflections about human sexuality. They knew nothing of sexual orientation or of the natural heterosexual-bisexual-homosexual continuum that exists in human life. They did not postulate that persons engaging in same-gender sex acts could have been expressing their natural sexuality.
> (JOHNSON, 2001, P. 213)

Even the term *homosexuality* was not coined until the nineteenth century; it does not appear in any of the original biblical manuscripts (Boswell, 1980; Gomes, 1996; McNeill, 1993; Nelson, 1992). The biblical writers did not address the concept of loving, committed same-sex relationships (Bennett, 1998; Nelson, 1992). What they did address instead pertained to both same-sex and heterosexual acts that violated ancient Hebrew purity codes, involved prostitution, and were considered exploitive behaviors that, in the case of their homosexual nature, were understood at the time to be beyond a person's "natural" inclinations (Creech, 1998; Nelson, 1992). Nelson describes our current scientific understanding of sexual orientation as "vastly different" from that of the biblical writers. Interestingly, neither the Ten Commandments nor the summary of the law in the Bible mentions the subjects of homosexuality, bisexuality, and transgenderism (Gomes, 1996). Nor did Jesus address these issues (Bennett, 1998; Nelson, 1992; Spong, 1988, 1991).

Homosexuality actually is not a primary preoccupation of Scripture (Nelson, 1992; Scroggs, 1983). Although there are more than 350 biblical admonishments pertaining to heterosexual sexuality, only 8 passages are held as negating same-sex behaviors (More Light Presbyterians of Charlotte, 2001; Nelson, 1992). It is those passages that are so often used to condemn and/or exclude GLBT people. Each of those passages will be noted in the following paragraphs (using the Holy Bible, New Revised Standard Version (NRSV), 1989) along with contextual theological perspectives for each.

1. Genesis 1:27–28: "So God created humankind in his image, in the image of God he created them; male and female he created them. God blessed them, and God

said to them, 'Be fruitful and multiply, and fill the earth and subdue it; and have dominion over the fish of the sea and over the birds of the air and over every living thing that moves upon the earth.'"

2. Genesis 2:21–24: "So the Lord God caused a deep sleep to fall upon the man, and he slept; then he took one of his ribs and closed up its place with flesh. And the rib that the Lord God had taken from the man he made into a woman and brought her to the man.... Therefore a man leaves his father and his mother and clings to his wife, and they become one flesh."

These Genesis passages reflect the presence of variation between the two creation accounts included in the biblical canon. Some interpretations of these passages suggest that they exemplify the divinely appointed order of intimate relationships to be male-female so that the propagation of the human species will continue. Since same-sex relationships do not result in the conception of children, they are therefore not legitimate. Similar interpretations of the Genesis 2 passage are used to support the idea that God created women to live in a subordinate role to men. Women were created secondarily by God and, therefore, are intended to be subordinate to men. However, there are legitimate theological arguments that claim the Bible to be a document written within a historical and cultural context that supported a strong patriarchal and heterocentric sociocultural system (Comstock, 1993). Same-sex relationships were not understood by biblical writers to be part of the broad continuum of sexual orientation. Women were not considered to be primary characters in the recounting of the story. It follows then that the texts written in such a context would exemplify women's being created as helpmates for men and heterosexual couples as having dominion over all things. Interestingly, verse 31 of chapter 1 in Genesis also states: "God saw everything that he [sic] had made, and indeed, it was very good." Another interpretation of that statement can be that all of creation—including those who are gay, lesbian, bisexual, heterosexual, and transgender—is created by God and is, therefore, good.

3. Genesis 19:1–28: The Sodom and Gomorrah Story. Excerpts: "The men of Sodom, both young and old ... surrounded the house, and they called to Lot, 'Where are the men who came to you tonight? Bring them [Lot's visiting angels] out to us, so that we may know them'" (verses 4–5). "'Look, I have two daughters who have not known a man; let me bring them out to you, and do to them as you please; only do nothing to these men [the angels], for they have come under the shelter of my roof'" (verse 8). "'For we [the angels] are about to destroy this place, because the outcry against its people has become great before the Lord, and the Lord has sent us to destroy it'" (verse 13). "The angels urged Lot, saying, 'Get up, take your wife and your two daughters who are here, or else you will be consumed in the punishment of the city'" (verse 15). "Then the Lord rained on Sodom and Gomorrah sulfur and fire from the Lord out of heaven" (verse 24).

Anti-GLBT interpretations of the Sodom story have suggested that the city was destroyed because of the evil of same-sex sexuality. This assertion is based on the crowd's request that the visitors be brought to them so that they may "know" them. There is, however, theological debate as to whether the original phrasing of the writing actually refers to physical sex acts (McNeill, 1993). No matter, if homosexual behavior was condemned, it was homosexual rape (Nelson, 1992; Schested, 1999). This understanding strengthens the argument that the so-called sin of Sodom was one of inhospitality and idolatry (Creech, 1998; Eastman, 1990; McNeill, 1993; Mollenkott & Scanzoni, 1978; Nelson, 1992). The citizens of the city had become hardened and inhospitable toward humankind, toward the stranger, and for that reason—not because of same-sex sexuality—God sent angels to destroy the city.

References made to Sodom and Gomorrah by other biblical writers appear to support a broader interpretation of this act of divine destruction as well. For example, in Isaiah 1, the nation of Judah is rebuked as being like Sodom and Gomorrah. The transgressions mentioned include rebellion against God, empty observance of religious rituals, and failure to "rescue the oppressed, defend the orphan, and plead for the widow" (verse 17) (Mollenkott & Scanzoni, 1978). The list does not reference or mention same-sex acts. Likewise, same-sex acts are not referenced when Amos cautions that Israel will be punished "for all your iniquities" (Amos 3:2) and will be overthrown as "when God overthrew Sodom and Gomorrah" (4:11). In Amos, the iniquities mentioned include those who "oppress the poor, who crush the needy," but there is no reference to homosexual acts (Schested, 1999). Boswell (1980) points out that even Jesus links the sin of Sodom to inhospitality when he says, "If anyone will not welcome you or listen to your words, shake off the dust from your feet as you leave that house or town. Truly I tell you, it will be more tolerable for the land of Sodom and Gomorrah on the day of judgment than for that town" (Matthew 10:14–15).

4. Leviticus 18:22: "You shall not lie with a male as with a woman; it is an abomination."

5. Leviticus 20:13: "If a man lies with a male as with a woman, both of them have committed an abomination; they shall be put to death; their blood is upon them."

These verses in Leviticus are part of a collection of passages known to reflect Hebrew purity and holiness codes that are often referred to as the Old Testament "Holiness Code." This code consists of a long list of culturally based rules for living. The word *abomination* is used to specify a considerable violation of ritual purity rather than to point to a moral or ethical breach (Schested, 1999). In addition to prohibiting male-to-male sexual contact, the code also included other prohibitions, such as round haircuts, tattoos, husbands having sex with their wives during menstruation, sowing fields with two different kinds of seed, and wearing clothing made of two different materials (Nelson, 1992; Mollenkott & Scanzoni, 1978; Sehested, 1999). While these prohibitions are, for the most part, no longer considered relevant, many religious leaders have held fast to the prohibition against same-sex acts, selectively retaining the prohibition against same-sex eros. This can be viewed as a cultural manifestation of heterosexism in society and the power of religion in its perpetuation.

It is important to note that no biblical passages, not even these two from Leviticus, address the concept of same-sex acts within mutually loving and caring relationships (Gomes, 1996; Nelson, 1992; Spong, 1988, 1991, 1998). Same-sex sexuality is framed within a context of exploitation rather than one of love and care. Yet there are affirmations of same-sex care and devotion found in biblical writings. The Old Testament stories of David and Jonathan (in Samuel II) and Ruth and Naomi (in Ruth) are examples of such affirmations, while the bond between Jesus and the "beloved disciple" is another example, from the New Testament (Boswell, 1980; Nelson, 1992). Rarely are these passages noted as such by religious leaders.

> 6. Romans 1: 26–28: "For this reason God gave them up to degrading passions. Their women exchanged natural intercourse for unnatural, and in the same way also the men, giving up natural intercourse with women, were consumed with passion for one another. Men committed shameless acts with men and received in their own persons the due penalty for their error. And since they did not see fit to acknowledge God, God gave them up to a debased mind and to things that should not be done."

Most books of the New Testament, including the Gospels, do not address same-sex acts. Paul is the only New Testament writer to do so (Eastman, 1990). This passage contains the only verse in the Bible that directly addresses woman-to-woman sexual behavior (Goss, 1993; Mollenkott & Scanzoni, 1978). In this passage from Romans, Paul suggests that same-sex acts are unnatural. This culturally based presumption is not surprising, given the limited scientific understanding of the natural variation in sexual orientation during the time of its writing. Paul has no thought about sexual orientation. He, like those of his time, would have considered any kind of same-sex sexuality as something beyond a person's natural inclinations rather than as a natural expression of a GLB orientation (Boswell, 1980; Goss, 1993). Gomes (1996) addresses the lack of sexual orientation knowledge among the biblical writers:

> The Biblical writers never contemplated a form of homosexuality in which loving, monogamous, and faithful persons sought to live out the implications of the gospel with as much fidelity to it as any heterosexual believer. All they knew of homosexuality was prostitution, pederasty, lasciviousness, and exploitation. These vices, as we

know, are not unknown among heterosexuals, and to define contemporary homosexuals only in these terms is a cultural slander of the highest order.

(P. 162)

The models of same-sex sexuality available to the biblical writers did not typically involve the ideals of mutuality and respect. Prostitution, adultery, and ped-
erasty characterize the same-sex practices known to them (Mollenkott & Scanzoni, 1978; Scroggs, 1983). What is surprising is the extent to which such obsolete
information continues to carry such social force today.

7. 1 Corinthians 6:9–10: "Do you not know that wrongdoers will not inherit the
kingdom of God? Do not be deceived! Fornicators, idolaters, adulterers, male prostitutes, sodomites, thieves, the greedy, drunkards, revilers, robbers—none of these
will inherit the kingdom of God."
8. Timothy 1:9–11: "This means understanding that the law is laid down not for
the innocent but for the lawless and disobedient, for the godless and sinful, for the
unholy and profane, for those who kill their father or mother, for murderers, fornicators, sodomites, slave traders, liars, perjurers, and whatever else is contrary to the
sound teaching that confirms to the glorious gospel of the blessed God, which he
entrusted to me."

The terms that are interpreted to mean "male prostitutes" and "sodomites" in
these Pauline texts are the key to the biblical interpretation that suggests these
passages clearly show divine disapproval of same-sex sexuality. Some interpretations of the 1 Corinthians 6:9–10 text suggest that those who engage in same-sex
sexual activity—or in any of the other "vices" listed in the text—are to be denied
God's kingdom. Scroggs (1983) agrees that this is indeed a "catalog of vices," a
form of item-listing that was used widely in Greco-Roman literature. However,
Scroggs is emphatic that "the users or creators of these lists do not carefully select
the individual items to fit the context with which they are dealing" (p. 102). He
maintains that the format of listing items and the length of the list itself, more
so than its contents per se, most signify its importance. For example, the first
catalog of vices found in 1 Corinthians 6:10 has four "vices" listed: immoral,
greedy, robbers, and idolaters. The second list, found in 1 Corinthians 6:11, has six
items—the original four from 6:10, with revilers and drunkards added. Paul appears to build to a "rhetorical climax" with the third list of ten vices, 1 Corinthians
6:9–10. Here, adulterers, thieves, "male prostitutes," and "sodomites" are added
to the six vices from 6:11 (Scroggs, 1983). The content of the list was probably less
noteworthy than its length.

It is also particularly important to take a more careful look at the variations in
the translations used to try to capture the meaning of the two Greek terms *malakos* and *arsenokoitai*, which are translated in the NRSV as "male prostitutes" and

"sodomites." The King James Version (KJV) translates the terms as "effeminate" and "abusers of themselves with mankind," respectively. In 1952, the Revised Standard Version (RSV) edition of the Bible collapsed these two terms into the one word *homosexuals*. The 1973 edition employs the term *sexual perverts*. The New International Version (NIV) uses *male prostitutes* and *homosexual offenders*, and the Jerusalem Bible uses *catamites* and *sodomites*. Mollenkott and Scanzoni (1978) define *catamites* as "youths kept especially for sexual purposes" (p. 67). These variations over time demonstrate the difficulty that translators have experienced in attempting to fit these two terms into the English language (McNeill, 1993; Mollenkott & Scanzoni, 1978).

Malakos (male prostitutes) literally means "soft" (McNeill, 1993; Mollenkott & Scanzoni, 1978; Scroggs, 1983). This term is also used in Matthew 11:8 and Luke 7:25 and has nothing to do with any kind of sexual behavior (McNeill, 1993; Mollenkott & Scanzoni, 1978). Scroggs (1983) states that *malakos* is "no technical term for homosexual" (p. 14). Mollenkott and Scanzoni conclude that it is likely that the King James translators intended to communicate the idea of self-indulgence in their use of "effeminate" for *malakos*, because the seventeenth-century dictionary defines *effeminate* as such. Whatever its original meaning, this word was never used in Greek to designate same-sex-identified people as a group or to reference same-sex sexual behavior in general (Boswell, 1980). In fact, Boswell states, *malakos* "occurs in writings contemporary with the Pauline epistles in reference to heterosexual persons or activity" (p. 107).

Arsenokoitai (sodomites) does have sexual overtones, but its precise meaning is not known, perhaps because of its sparse use (Boswell, 1980; McNeill, 1993; Scroggs, 1983). McNeill states that while there does not appear to be an understanding of homosexuality as an orientation, there were names for people who participated in same-sex sexual behavior. These names include *paiderastes, pallakos, kinaidos, arrenomanes,* and *paidophthoros,* but do not include the term *arsenokoitai,* used in 1 Corinthians 6:9–10 (McNeill, 1993). It is likely that this term was understood to mean "male prostitute" until sometime in the fourth century (Boswell, 1980).

In sum, Paul's writings express his limited scientific understanding that same-sex behaviors are unnatural rather than a natural part of the continuum of sexual orientation diversity that is known about today.

MAJOR JUDEO-CHRISTIAN RELIGIONS AND THEIR POSITIONS

While there is no "one" religious position on the morality of GLBT people, the conservative religious argument that GLBT people are "sick, sinful, and in need of repentance" is often heard in public debate. In reality, significant variation exists among Judeo-Christian religions on the issue of the morality of gayness/

lesbianism, bisexuality, and transgenderism. Religious groups that have adopted strong anti-gay positions, in particular, include the Roman Catholic Church, the Southern Baptist Convention, the Church of Jesus Christ of Latter-day Saints (Mormonism), and Orthodox Judaism (Bennett, 1998). In contrast, religious groups that have identified themselves as more accepting toward GLBT people include the United Church of Christ, the Episcopal Church, Unity, Quaker Friends Meetings, and Unitarian Universalists.

Interestingly, the historically African American Christian denominations of the National Baptist Convention, the Church of God in Christ, and the African Methodist Episcopal Church have chosen to espouse no official policy statements on sexual orientation or on transgenderism. Even absent official policy, however, traditional African American religious communities are commonly described as conservative—and even closed—to embracing GLBT concerns (Bennett, 1998; Boykin, 1996).

There are two major GLBT-focused Christian denominations in the United States: the Universal Fellowship of Metropolitan Community Churches and the Unity Fellowship Church Movement. Both denominations are racially diverse; however, the Metropolitan Community Churches tend to have a more predominantly Caucasian membership and the Unity Fellowship Church Movement a more predominantly African American membership. Both denominations offer significant support to GLBT people and their allies in a Westernized religious culture where few such supports exist. Both denominations have churches located throughout the United States, especially near larger urban areas.

Table 17.1 offers further information about major Judeo-Christian religious groups and their positions on homosexuality, their willingness to accept lesbians and gays as clergy, and their positions on holy unions (same-sex commitment ceremonies).

CONVERSION THERAPY

Conversion therapy, also known as reparative therapy, is a systematic means for attempting to change a person's sexual orientation from lesbian, gay, or bisexual to heterosexual. Such therapies often occur in a religious-based context—commonly those identified as conservative Christian. Techniques used to try to change a person's sexual orientation can include prayer, exorcism, religious-based guilt inducement, and even punishment-oriented forms of behavior modification (Ritter & O'Neill, 1989; Tozer & McClanahan, 1999; White, 1995).

Conversion therapy is still in use—even though homosexuality was removed as a mental illness from the *Diagnostic and Statistical Manual of Mental Disorders* in 1973 and even though the practice of conversion therapy is considered unethical by primary national associations of mental health professionals, including

TABLE 17.1 Major Judeo-Christian Religions' Positions on Homosexuality, Acceptance of Gay/Lesbian Clergy, and Endorsement of Holy Union Ceremonies

RELIGION	POSITION ON HOMOSEXUALITY	ACCEPTANCE OF GAY/LESBIAN CLERGY	SANCTIONS HOLY UNION CEREMONIES FOR GAY/LESBIAN COUPLES
Roman Catholic Church (61.2 million members, largely Caucasian)	A gay/lesbian orientation is unnatural and disordered. Gay/lesbian Catholics should remain celibate for life.	All Roman Catholic clergy must remain celibate, thus obscuring overt sexual orientation.	No
Southern Baptist Convention (15.7 million members, largely Caucasian)	Homosexuality is sinful, impure, degrading, shameful, unnatural, indecent, and perverted. The SBC purports to bar any congregation that acts to affirm, approve, or endorse homosexual behavior. The SBC insists that gays/lesbians remain celibate or, more commonly, change their sexual orientation through prayer and conversion therapy.	No	No
United Methodist Church (8.5 million members, largely Caucasian)	Does not condone the practice of homosexuality and considers it incompatible with Christian teaching. Gay/lesbian sexual practices are sin	No, if a "practicing" gay/lesbian Yes, if remain celibate	No
National Baptist Convention, USA, Inc. (8.2 million members, largely African American)	No official policy Unofficially does not condone homosexuality	Unofficially, no	Unofficially, no
Church of God in Christ (5.5 million members, largely African American)	No official policy Unofficially does not condone homosexuality	Unofficially, no	Unofficially, no
Evangelical Lutheran Church of America (5.2 million members, largely Caucasian)	Gays/lesbians are welcome to participate fully in the life of the congregations.	Yes, if remain celibate	No

Religious group	Position on homosexuality		
Church of Jesus Christ of Latter Day Saints (4–8 million members, largely Caucasian)	Homosexuality is perverse, immoral. Encourages conversion therapy. Discipline for "practicing" gays/lesbians can include probation, exclusion from sacraments, or excommunication.	No	No
Judaism (3.9 million members, largely Caucasian)			
(1) Orthodox Judaism	Sexual relations between same-gender people are sinful.	No	No
(2) Conservative Judaism	No longer considers homosexuality an abomination. Supports nondiscrimination policies for gays/lesbians in civil society	No	No
(3) Reform Judaism (the largest Jewish movement)	Homosexuality is not a sin. Advocates freedom from employment discrimination in civil society. Supports marriage rights for gays/lesbians	Yes	Permits, but does not officially sanction, holy unions
(4) Reconstructionist Judaism	Fully supportive of gays/lesbians	Yes	Officially sanctions holy unions
Presbyterian Church, U.S.A. (3.6 million members, largely Caucasian)	Homosexuality is sin. It is not God's wish for humanity. It is neither a state nor condition like race, but rather a result of living in a fallen world.	Only if celibate. All church leaders must be heterosexually married cr celibate.	No
African Methodist Episcopal Church (3.6 million members, largely African American membership)	No official policy. Unofficially does not condone homosexuality	Unofficially, no	Unofficially, no

Sources: Bennett (1998); Morrow (2003).

the National Association of Social Workers (NASW), the American Counseling Association, the American Psychological Association, and the American Medical Association (Haldeman, 1994; Tozer & McClanahan, 1999). The National Committee on Lesbian, Gay, and Bisexual Issues of the NASW has published a position statement on conversion therapy that reads in part:

> Conversion and reparative therapies are an infringement to the guiding principles inherent to social worker ethics and values.... [Such] techniques may cause considerable harm and anguish for a client while reinforcing the existing prejudice and homophobia that gay men and lesbians experience daily. The use of these therapies denies the viability of same-gender relationships as fulfilling and natural.... NASW discourages social workers from providing treatments designed to change sexual orientation or from referring clients to practitioners or programs that claim to do so.
>
> (NATIONAL COMMITTEE ON LESBIAN, GAY, AND BISEXUAL ISSUES, 1999)

The continued prevalence of religious-based conversion therapies attests to the prevailing power of heterosexism and homophobia and the influence of religious institutions in creating and sustaining these forms of oppression. Despite the claims made by many groups professing success with conversion therapies, there is no credible empirical support that these therapies are successful in actually changing sexual orientation (Haldeman, 1994; Mills, 1999; Tozer & McClanahan, 1999). While people may learn to temporarily change overt sexual behaviors, changing such outward behaviors does not equate to changing something as basic and intrinsic to the essence of one's being as sexual orientation. That is, changing behaviors does not equal changing one's orientation. There simply is no clear scientific support that reparative therapies are successful in changing this most natural and fundamental aspect of the self. What these therapies can do, however, is reinforce the internalization of gay-negative stereotypes and images; that, indeed, can do psychological harm to clients.

What, then, is the appropriate ethical response when clients request therapeutic assistance from social workers for changing their sexual orientation? Should workers simply refuse therapeutic intervention, given that conversion therapy practice is unethical? An initial response would be to assess the nature of the personal thoughts, feelings, and experiences that could have led the client to the point of seeking sexual orientation change. Affirmative practice would include helping the client understand the powerful forces of homophobia, internalized homophobia, and heterosexism—at micro and macro levels of social power and influence—and the ways in which these forces create and perpetuate the internalization of GLB-negative messages. Thus, initial intervention in such cases lies in helping clients understand the power of heterosexism in how they view sexual orientation in their own lives. Also, it would be appropriate to inform clients that conversion therapy is scientifically unproven and that its practice is considered unethical.

CRISIS IN THE CATHOLIC CHURCH

The dawn of the twenty-first century brought with it the "worst crisis in centuries" for the Catholic Church (France & Downey, 2002). A flurry of reports on incidences of Catholic priests sexually abusing children made headlines across the United States and around the world. As the news coverage unfolded, it became clear that cases of child sexual abuse by priests had, in many instances, been hidden by Catholic Church authorities over the years in order to avoid public scandal. In some of those cases, priests who were known sexual offenders were permitted to remain in the ministry—and were simply moved from one parish to another as allegations would unfold—rather than being relieved of their ministerial duties. There were also reports of hush money being paid to victims and their families in order to avoid negative publicity (Winters et al., 2002). In 2002 a number of adult survivors of sexual abuse by priests began to publicly acknowledge their victimization. As one story would unfold, numerous others would follow. Homophobia became a part of the picture when some in the media began equating the pedophilia crisis in the Catholic Church with the church's growing tolerance for admitting gay men to the priesthood (Byfield & Byfield, 2002). Pedophilia is a mental illness that involves a person engaging in sexual activity with prepubescent children (generally age 13 or younger). Pedophilia can occur across sexual orientations and is not specifically associated with gay people. Gays are no more likely to abuse children than are heterosexual people. Attaching the pedophilia crisis in the Catholic Church to gays in the priesthood is homophobia at its worst.

If, after this initial level of intervention, clients should continue to request intervention to change their sexual orientation, what would be the next appropriate step? Given the social work ethic of client self-determination (National Association of Social Workers, 1999), it would not be appropriate to pressure clients to embrace a sexual orientation identity that might, at that point, feel unacceptable to them. Yet it would be equally inappropriate to support the idea that a GLB identity can be changed to a heterosexual identity. Tozer and McClanahan (1999) suggest, in such situations, the value of asking clients to defer coming to terms with a particular sexual orientation label and to focus instead on exploring their unique personal experiences. If, despite these efforts, a client continues to insist on reparative therapy intervention, then the worker would need to proceed toward termination, as it would also be unethical to refer the client to those who offer conversion therapy. The worker might assure the client of a willingness to continue future work in exploring the client's sexual orientation and his or her feelings about that—but not in the form of conversion therapy—should the client so desire.

RELIGION AND SPIRITUALITY AMONG GLBT PEOPLE

Religious worship and spiritual connection with the divine are central to the human experience for many people. Most Americans have been reared in families that ascribe to some type of religious belief or faith tradition (Shuck & Liddle, 2001). GLBT people are no different. What may be particularly significant for many GLBT people, however, is the extent to which they have experienced psychological harm or woundedness because of religious heterosexism and homophobia.

Such woundedness is reflected in the sources of religious conflict reported by GLBT people, which include negative religious teachings about homosexuality, oppressive atmospheres for GLBT people in their faith communities, and the internalization of guilt and shame surrounding being GLBT (Kaufman & Raphael, 1996; Mahaffy, 1996; Nugent, 2001; Shuck & Liddle, 2001). As a result, many GLBT people feel unwelcome or marginalized in their religious communities. Many stop attending worship services. Others leave their current religious community and become involved with other faith traditions that are more affirming of GLBT people, such as Reconstructionist Judaism, Unity, the United Church of Christ, Unitarian Universalists, the Universal Fellowship of Metropolitan Community Churches, or the Unity Fellowship Church Movement. Still others reject corporate religion altogether.

Rodriguez and Ouellette (2000) propose four levels of religious identity that sexual minority people might engage in trying to resolve the conflict between their sexual orientation identities and their religious identities. This review will extrapolate from their work to also include bisexual and transgender people in the discussion of these categories. The first category is to *reject one's religious identity*. This can occur when GLBT people experience religion as oppressive and shaming because of their sexual orientation or gender identity. As a result, the option of embracing a non-affirming religious identity is rejected. The second category is to *reject one's sexual orientation or transgender identity*. Gay, lesbian, and bisexual people may seek to adopt a heterosexual identity. Some may seek religious-based conversion therapy to try and manifest this transformation. Transgender people may seek to adopt a gender identity that conforms to that which is expected for their biological sex. The intent here is to conform to the heterosexist social expectations of the religious community and larger social culture. From a clinical practice perspective, there is concern with the self-rejection inherent in this category, since self-rejection can place clients at clinical risk for depression, substance abuse, and suicide.

The third category is *compartmentalization*. In this category, one's sexual orientation or transgender identity is kept separate from one's religious identity. That is, a person's sexual orientation or transgender identity is kept hidden from his or her religious expression, especially in the public worship arena. This category is similar to the Cass model (Cass, 1979, 1984a, 1984b) stage of identity tolerance (see chapter 4), in which gay and lesbian people may take on two separate identities—openly gay or lesbian within a circle of trusted others and presumed heterosexual outside that circle of confidants.

The fourth category is *identity integration*. Here there is a blending, or integration, of one's sexual orientation or transgender identity with one's religious beliefs. At this point religious beliefs affirm and support, rather than shame and denigrate, GLBT people. This category is similar to the Cass model stage of identity synthesis, in which a person's sexual orientation identity is integrated throughout the scope of his or her daily life experiences. Avenues for developing identity integration can include attending GLBT-affirming religious services, reading GLBT-affirmative theology, and developing connections with other GLBT and GLBT-affirming people who share similar religious and spiritual values and beliefs.

In many communities—especially in larger urban areas—GLBT-affirmative worship services are available. For those who wish to maintain ties to lifelong religious denominations and at the same time challenge the heterosexism within those institutions, a number of faith-based advocacy groups are available: Dignity (Catholic), Integrity (Episcopalian), More Light (Presbyterian), Affirmation (Mormon, also United Methodist), Friends for Lesbian and Gay Concerns (Quaker), Seventh Day Adventist Kinship International (Seventh Day Adventist), the World Congress of Gay and Lesbian Jewish Organizations for Jews (Jewish), and Evangelicals Concerned (Evangelicals).

While some GLBT people nurture their spirituality through formal religious practices, others accomplish this outside formal religious institutions. The experience and representation of spirituality among GLBT people can be as broad and diverse as are GLBT people themselves.

Many GLBT people honor Native American spirituality, which includes respect for Berdache, or two-spirit, people—those who are believed to represent both a female and a male spirit (TaFoya, 1997; Wilson, 1996). They are honored as special and spiritually powerful because of this gender blending of maleness and femaleness (Johnson, 2000).

Feminist forms of spirituality have become important to many GLBT people as well. Feminist spirituality honors the feminine, or Goddess presence, in spiritual expression. Themes of finding one's own spiritual voice and liberating oneself from oppressive forces, such as patriarchal authority, are common (Flinders, 1998). Some women ascribe to womanist forms of spiritual expression. The womanist perspective honors the history of black women in the United States, including the ways they have helped maintain black culture even in the midst of oppressive systems such as slavery and Jim Crow laws (Hayes, 1995).

For some GLBT people, especially those in recovery from addiction, twelve-step programs and the connection of those programs to a "higher power" component become significant forms of spiritual sustenance (Johnson, 2000). Many communities have formed GLBT-specific twelve-step recovery groups to uniquely serve sexual minority populations.

SUGGESTIONS FOR PRACTICE

Religious-based trauma can be devastating for GLBT people. Those who perpetrate such trauma often do so with absolute conviction because of what they have learned from authority figures such as religious leaders. GLBT people encountering such religious-based trauma are at risk for internalizing those negative messages, and that internalization can place them at greater risk for low self-esteem, depression, substance abuse, and suicide. It can be very difficult for GLBT people to counter and cope with the social effects of fervent religious-based prejudice. Therefore, affirmative social work practice should include an assessment of clients' spirituality/religious perspectives in order to determine the extent to which religious oppression may affect them. Religious beliefs should also be considered an important component of understanding cultural diversity among GLBT clients (Shafranske & Maloney, 1996). The following suggestions may be useful for responding to religious and spirituality concerns expressed by GLBT clients:

1. *Evaluate for the possibility of religious trauma.* Explore the client's experiences with religion and spirituality and assess the extent to which those experiences have been affirmative or oppressive. If there is a history of religious oppression, explore with the client what happened and its impact on the client. Assess for low self-esteem and internalized homophobia. If psychological distress is present, assess for signs and symptoms of depression, substance abuse, and self-harm.

2. *Honor losses engendered by religious oppression.* Many GLBT people have encountered significant losses because of religious oppression. Some have been ostracized from their families, some from their churches and faith communities. Many have even been told their lives will be condemned for eternity unless they somehow change their sexual orientation and/or gender expression. Those clients who have followed traditional forms of religion may especially feel that they no longer have a spiritual home. Acknowledging those losses and validating their impact in the client's life are important. In addition, helping clients to develop knowledge about more-GLBT-affirmative forms of religious practice and spirituality can be empowering in helping them to find faith-based alternatives from which to choose.

3. *Address the impact of religion as a tool for social injustice toward GLBT people.* Many clients may never have examined the impact of the intersection of religion and sexual orientation/gender expression in their own lives. Allowing them safe space to critically evaluate religious doctrine as a mechanism for social control can be liberating. In doing so, however, it is important to honor client self-determination with regard to religious beliefs. For the worker to impose his or her personal religious values on the client would be inappropriate. Rather,

the goal is to help clients to critically evaluate (and reconstruct if they so desire) their own religious beliefs in response to an ethic of religious social justice for GLBT people.

4. *Develop a list of religious and spiritual resources to share with clients.* Clients who seek resources for religious and spiritual support may benefit from the following types of information: a list of GLBT-affirming local places of worship; a list of GLBT-affirming religious and spiritual groups such as those previously noted; a referral list of area GLBT-affirming clergy who are willing to discuss religion and spirituality; and, a reading list of GLBT-affirming theology and spirituality (e.g., Christ, 1998; Christ & Plaskow, 1992; Comstock, 1993; Eller, 1995; Lake, 2001; Johnson, 1992; McNeill, 1993; Roscoe, 1988; Scott, 1999; Spong, 1988, 1991, 1998; TaFoya, 1997; Thistlewhite, 1991; Van Dyke, 1992).

5. *Become an advocate for ending religious-based social injustice against GLBT people.* As educated and respected community professionals, social workers are well positioned to be voices for social justice and the full inclusion of GLBT people in communities of faith. Such advocacy also carries forth the social work profession's ethical mandate that social workers engage in social and political action that promotes respect for the diversity of all people (National Association of Social Workers, 1999).

SUMMARY

This chapter reviewed the impact of spirituality and religion on GLBT people. *Spirituality* was defined as a deep sense of wholeness, connectedness, and openness to the infinite (Shafranske & Gorsuch, 1984) and as a vital life force that is deeply part of us, yet also transcends us (Faiver, Ingersoll, O'Brien, & McNally, 2001). *Religion* was defined as the social vehicle through which spirituality may be channeled (Faiver et al., 2001). It pertains to the outward ways in which faith is expressed, including rituals, dogmas, creeds, denominational identity, and ecclesiastical structures (Van Hook, Hugen, & Aguilar, 2001).

The ways in which religion can be a vehicle for heterosexism were discussed, and the Bible verses commonly cited as condemning same-sex sexual behaviors were addressed from a sociocultural contextual perspective. The major Judeo-Christian religions and their positions on the morality and inclusion of GLBT people were reviewed.

Conversion therapy was discussed as a weapon of religious oppression. Conversion therapy, also known as reparative therapy, is a systematic means for attempting to change a person's sexual orientation from lesbian, gay, or bisexual to heterosexual. Conversion therapy practice is considered unethical by the National Association of Social Workers, as well as by other major human services professional associations. Additionally, there is no clear scientific support that conversion therapies are effective for actually changing sexual orientation.

Four areas of religious identity development (Rodriguez & Ouellette, 2000) for GLBT people were presented: (1) rejection of one's religious identity; (2) rejection of one's sexual orientation or transgender identity; (3) compartmentalization; and (4) identity integration. Avenues for religious and spiritual expression for GLBT people were reviewed, including GLBT-affirmative subdivisions of traditional denominations, specific GLBT-affirming denominations, Native American spirituality, feminist forms of spirituality, and twelve-step practices. And, finally, suggestions for GLBT-affirmative practice from a religious/spiritual standpoint were presented.

REFERENCES

Appleby, G. A., & Anastas, J. W. (1998). *Not just a passing phase: Social work with gay, lesbian, and bisexual people.* New York: Columbia University Press.

Bennett, L. (1998). *Mixed blessings: Organized religion and gay and lesbian Americans in 1998.* Washington, DC: Human Rights Campaign Fund.

Boswell, J. (1980). *Christianity, social tolerance, and homosexuality: Gay people in Western Europe from the beginning of the Christian era to the fourteenth century.* Chicago: University of Chicago Press.

Boykin, K. (1996). *One more river to cross: Black and gay in America.* New York: Doubleday.

Byfield, T., & Byfield, V. (2002). The Catholic problem isn't pedophiles but gays, and cleaning it up may mean breaking the law. *The Report, 29*(13), 58.

Cass, V. C. (1979). Homosexual identity formation: A theoretical model. *Journal of Homosexuality, 4*(3), 219–235.

———. (1984a). Homosexual identity: A concept in need of definition. *Journal of Homosexuality, 9*(2/3), 105–126.

———. (1984b). Homosexual identity formation: Testing a theoretical model. *Journal of Sex Research, 20*(2), 143–167.

Chittister, J. (1998). *Heart of flesh: A feminist spirituality for women and men.* Grand Rapids, MI: Eerdmans.

Christ, C. P. (Ed.). (1998). *Rebirth of the Goddess: Finding meaning in feminist spirituality.* New York: Routledge.

Christ, C. P., & Plaskow, J. (Eds.). (1992). *Womanspirit rising: A feminist reader in religion.* San Francisco: Harper.

Comstock, G. D. (1993). *Gay theology without apology.* Cleveland: Pilgrim Press.

Creech, J. (1998). *Response to the judicial charge.* Omaha, NE: First United Methodist Church.

Davidson, M. G. (2000). Religion and spirituality. In R. M. Perez & K. A. DeBord (Eds.), *Handbook of counseling and psychotherapy with lesbian, gay, and bisexual clients* (pp. 409–433). Washington, DC: American Psychological Association.

Eastman, D. E. (1990). *Homosexuality: Not a sin, not a sickness.* West Hollywood, CA: Universal Fellowship of Metropolitan Community Churches.

Eller, C. (1995). *Living in the lap of the Goddess: The feminist spirituality movement in America.* Boston: Beacon.

Faiver, C., Ingersoll, R. E., O'Brien, E., & McNally, C. (2001). *Explorations in counseling and spirituality*. Belmont, CA: Wadsworth/Thomson.

Flinders, C. L. (1998). *At the root of this longing: Reconciling a spiritual hunger and a feminist thirst*. San Francisco: Harper.

France, D., & Downey, S. (2002). Battle of the faithful. *Newsweek, 139*(24), 49.

Gomes, P. J. (1996). *The good book: Reading the Bible with heart and mind*. New York: William Morrow.

Haldeman, D. C. (1994). The practice and ethics of sexual orientation conversion therapy. *Journal of Consulting and Clinical Psychology, 62*(2), 221–227.

Hayes, D. L. (1995). *Hagar's daughters: Womanist ways of being in the world*. New York: Paulist Press.

Hilton, B. (1992). *Can homophobia be cured?* Nashville: Abingdon.

Holy Bible. New Revised Standard Version. (1989). Grand Rapids, MI: Zondervan Publishing House.

Johnson, T. (2000). *Gay spirituality: The role of gay identity in the transformation of human consciousness*. Los Angeles: Alyson Books.

Johnson, W. R. (2001). Protestantism and gay and lesbian freedom. In B. Berzon (Ed.), *Positively gay: New approaches to gay and lesbian life* (3d ed.) (pp. 210–232). Berkeley: Celestial Arts.

Kaufman, G., & Raphael, L. (1996). *Coming out of shame: Transforming gay and lesbian lives*. New York: Doubleday.

Lake, C. (Ed.). (2001). *Recreations: Religion and spirituality in the lives of queer people*. Ontario: Insomniac Group.

Mahaffy, K. A. (1996). Cognitive dissonance and its resolution: A study of lesbian Christians. *Journal for the Scientific Study of Religion, 35*(4), 392–402.

McNeill, J. J. (1993). *The church and the homosexual* (4th ed.). New York: Beacon.

Mills, K. I. (1999). Mission impossible: Why reparative therapy and ex-gay ministries fail. *Human Rights Campaign*. Retrieved February 5, 2002, from http://www.hrc.org/publications/exgay_ministries/change.asp.

Mollenkott, V. R., & Scanzoni, L. (1978). *Is the homosexual my neighbor? Another Christian view*. New York: Harper and Row.

Morrow, D. F. (1996). Heterosexism: Hidden discrimination in social work education. *Journal of Gay and Lesbian Social Services, 5*(4), 1–16.

———. (2003). Cast into the wilderness: The impact of institutionalized religion on lesbians. *Journal of Lesbian Studies, 7*(4), 109–123.

National Association of Social Workers. (1999). *Code of ethics of the National Association of Social Workers*. Washington, DC: Author.

National Committee on Lesbian, Gay, and Bisexual Issues, National Association of Social Workers. (1999). *Position statement on reparative and conversion therapies for lesbians and gay men*. Washington, DC: National Association of Social Workers.

Nelson, J. (1992). *Body theology*. Louisville: Westminster/John Knox.

Nugent, R. (2001). Catholicism: On the compatibility of sexuality and faith. In B. Berzon (Ed.), *Positively gay: New approaches to gay and lesbian life* (3d. ed.). Berkeley: Celestial Arts.

Ritter, K. Y., & O'Neill, C. W. (1989). Moving through loss: The spiritual journey of gay men and lesbian women. *Journal of Counseling and Development, 68*, 9–15.

Rodriguez, E. M., & Ouellette, S. C. (2000). Gay and lesbian Christians: Homosexuality and religious identity integration in the members and participants of a gay-positive church. *Journal for the Scientific Study of Religion, 39*(3), 333–348.

Roscoe, W. (Ed.). (1988). *Living the spirit: A gay American Indian anthology*. New York: St Martin's.

Scott, I. C. (1999). *God is a woman: The last taboo and hidden secrets at the millennium*. Columbus, OH: Greyden Press.

Scroggs, R. (1983). *The New Testament and homosexuality: Contextual background for contemporary debate*. Philadelphia: Fortress.

Sehested, K. (1999). Biblical fidelity and sexual orientation. In W. Wink (Ed.), *Homosexuality and Christian faith: Questions of conscience for the churches*. Minneapolis: Fortress.

Shafranske, E. P., & Gorsuch, R. L. (1984). Factors associated with the perception of spirituality in psychotherapy. *Journal of Transpersonal Psychology, 16*, 231–241.

Shafranske, E. P., & Maloney, H. N. (1996). Religion and the clinical practice of psychology: A case for inclusion. In E. P. Shafranske (Ed.), *Religion and the clinical practice of psychology*. Washington, DC: American Psychological Association.

Shuck, K. D., & Liddle, B. J. (2001). Religious conflicts experienced by lesbian, gay, and bisexual individuals. *Journal of Gay and Lesbian Psychotherapy, 5*(2), 63–82.

Spong, J. S. (1988). *Living in sin? A bishop rethinks sexuality*. Nashville: Abingdon.

———. (1991). *Rescuing the Bible from fundamentalism*. San Francisco: Harper and Row.

———. (1998). *Why Christianity must change or die*. San Francisco: Harper.

TaFoya, T. (1997). Native gay and lesbian issues: The two-spirited. In B. Green (Ed.), *Ethnic and cultural diversity among lesbians and gay men* (vol. 3, pp. 1–10). Thousand Oaks, CA: Sage.

Taylor, T. S. (2000). Is God good for you, good for your neighbor? The influence of religious orientation on demoralization and attitudes toward lesbians and gay men (Doctoral dissertation, 2000). *Dissertation Abstracts International, Section A: Humanities and Social Sciences, 60* (12-A), 4472.

Thistlewhite, S. (1991). *Sex, race, and God: Christian feminism in black and white*. New York: Crossroad.

Tozer, E. E., & McClanahan, M. K. (1999). Treating the purple menace: Ethical considerations of conversion therapy and affirmative alternatives. *Counseling Psychologist, 27*(5), 722–743.

Van Dyke, A. (1992). *The search for a woman-centered spirituality: The cutting edge— lesbian life and literature*. New York: New York University Press.

Van Hook, M., Hugen, B, & Aguilar, M. (2001). *Spirituality within religious traditions in social work practice*. Pacific Grove, CA: Brooks/Cole.

White, M. (1995). *Stranger at the gate: To be gay and Christian in America*. New York: Simon and Schuster.

Wilson, A. (1996). How we find ourselves: Identity development and two-spirit people. *Harvard Educational Review, 66*(2), 303–317.

Winters, R., Morrissey, S., Scully, S., Sieger, M., Crittle, S., Dale, S. S., et al. (2002). Can the church be saved? *Time, 159*(13), 20–39.

18

WORKPLACE ISSUES

Kristina M. Hash and Sherry D. Ceperich

To [pass the Employment Non-discrimination Act] is not to create a special right for gay men and lesbians, but to end discrimination against them, as we have done for others. … To do less is to close our eyes to this inequity in our laws, and to give a quiet nod to discrimination in the workplace in a country that prides itself on rewarding merit and hard work.

—SENATOR SUSAN COLLINS, R-MAINE, 4/24/02 (CITED IN CLYMER, 2002)

IMAGINE THAT you have just finished a master of social work degree and are applying for a position in a social service agency. Accepting the position would require you to move to another city and relocate your same-sex partner of six years. If you are offered and accept the position, one of the first issues you will face is whether or not to disclose your sexual orientation to your employer and coworkers.

If you decide to "come out" to your current or prospective employer and co-workers, there will be other issues for you to consider, including:

* Will you come out at the interview, after you have been offered the position, or after you have worked at the agency for a few months?
* Does the agency or the city have a nondiscrimination policy banning discrimination based on sexual orientation in the workplace?
* Does the agency provide domestic partner benefits, including health insurance?
* If your partner becomes ill, would the medical savings account apply to his/her bills? And would the agency's family leave policy allow you to take time off to care for your partner?
* Will your partner be included in other benefits, such as "family memberships" to the local health club?

* Can you comfortably put a photo of your partner on your desk?
* Will you feel at ease taking your partner to the agency picnic and other social gatherings?

If you are gay, lesbian, or bisexual, you might have already encountered this type of experience in the workplace, as these are issues that lesbian and gay couples across the country commonly face. Gay, lesbian, bisexual, and transgender people (GLBTs) exist as the minority group that remains unprotected in the workplace by the lack of a national nondiscrimination policy. Despite the push for addressing diversity in the workplace, and the institution of protections and benefits by a handful of jurisdictions and private companies, many employees must deal with special issues and often inequitable policies related to their sexual orientation. This chapter will examine these special issues, including identity management and the decision of whether to come out at work, homophobia and heterosexism, discrimination, and unsupportive benefits and policies. Social workers assisting with employment-related problems should be prepared to address these special issues and to intervene on the individual, group, organizational, and public policy levels. This chapter will provide examples of how social workers can effectively intervene at these levels, as well as how organizations can create supportive and inclusive environments for GLBT employees and consumers. Special issues concerning transgender employees and employees with HIV/AIDS will also be discussed. The chapter concludes with resources and further readings on the topic.

GOVERNMENT POLICIES AND THE LARGER SOCIETAL CONTEXT

The work world exists within a larger context of society as well as federal, state, and local legislation. Many Americans support civil rights for gay men and lesbians. A 2001 Gallup Poll found that 85% of Americans believe gay men and lesbians should have equal opportunity in employment. This percentage has been rising steadily in the past few decades, since 1977, when 56% held such an opinion. Similarly, the percentage of Americans who think gay men and lesbians should be discriminated against in the workplace has declined, from 33% in 1977 to 11% in 2001. Although state, local, and private policies have been implemented, progress toward the adoption of a national policy protecting the rights of GLBT employees has been slow. In a recent survey, 61% of Americans supported federal protection against job discrimination for gay men and lesbians. Interestingly, more than 40% thought that this legislative protection currently existed (Human Rights Campaign, 2001).

FEDERAL, STATE, AND LOCAL LEGISLATION

FEDERAL LEGISLATION

The passage of two federal policies has laid the foundation for national protective legislation for GLBTs. The Civil Rights Act of 1964 paved the way for equality in the workplace. Although it does not address sexual orientation or gender identity, Title VII of the act bans discrimination on the basis of race, color, sex, religion, and national origin in the workplace. In 1998 President Clinton signed an executive order (#11478) that added sexual orientation to the list of groups in the federal civilian workforce who are protected from discrimination (including women, persons of color, persons with disabilities, etc.). Clinton's order, however, did not allow for a gay or lesbian employee to appeal a discrimination case to the Equal Employment Opportunity Commission (Human Rights Campaign, 1998).

The most promising piece of legislation directed toward GLBT employees is the Employment Non-discrimination Act (ENDA). This proposed federal bill would prevent employers from making employment decisions on the basis of an individual's sexual orientation. The decisions to which it would apply include hiring, termination, promotion, and compensation. This bill would not extend to businesses with fewer than fifteen employees, religious organizations, or any branch of the armed forces, however (Human Rights Campaign, 2001). Despite support from many members of Congress, the bill failed in the Senate in 1996 and again in 2001. Although the passage of ENDA would mark a monumental step in the attainment of equal rights, a few concerns have been voiced about the bill. A concern of the Human Rights Campaign (2001) is that ENDA will not explicitly protect transgender individuals or provide for domestic partner benefits.

STATE AND LOCAL INITIATIVES

Although federal legislation that would protect GLBTs in the workplace does not exist, individual states and localities have taken the issue in hand by enacting their own protective legislation. Twelve states and the District of Columbia have enacted state-level legislation protecting gay men and lesbians against workplace discrimination in public and private employment settings: California, Connecticut, Hawaii, Maryland, Massachusetts, Minnesota, Nevada, New Hampshire, New Jersey, Rhode Island, Vermont, and Wisconsin. Similar legislation has been enacted by 140 cities and counties (Human Rights Campaign, 2001, 2002).

Minnesota is the only state to have attempted to enact statewide domestic partner benefits. Twelve local governments have attempted similar measures. Far fewer localities and states have enacted legislation protecting transgender people from workplace discrimination. Thirty-two cities and counties and the states of

Minnesota and Rhode Island stand as the forerunners in this effort (Human Rights Campaign, 2001). Discrimination on the basis of gender identity, then, is still legal in many areas.

THE MILITARY

The armed forces are one of the largest employers in the United States, and they have been a battleground for gay and lesbian rights. Formal concern about gays in the military dates back to World War II, which marked the first time military recruits were specifically asked about their sexual orientation. As a result, many men were not enlisted or were dismissed after admitting that they were gay (Miller, 1995). Under the Clinton administration, the 1990s saw a renewed concern over gays in the military. The policy known as "don't ask, don't tell" became the mantra for this issue. This does not mean that the ban was lifted. Recruits would not be asked about their sexual orientation, but they could be discharged if they admitted to being gay or lesbian or if evidence proved that they were engaging in "homosexual conduct" (Halley, 1999).

The apprehension about gays and lesbians serving in the military may be fueled by the belief that an openly gay soldier would make heterosexual soldiers uncomfortable sharing close quarters and would damage the morale and cohesion within units (Evans, 2001). Despite this opinion, polls have generally shown support for gay and lesbian soldiers. In 1999 public support of gays in the military climbed to an all-time high of 70% of Americans surveyed by a Gallup poll (Yang, 1999). Despite this public support, one in every 2,000 men and women in the service has been discharged on the basis of sexual orientation since 1990 (Evans, 2001).

PRIVATE AND PUBLIC-SECTOR EMPLOYERS

Comparatively, the corporate world is more progressive toward equal rights for GLBTs in the workplace1. By 2001, more than half of the Fortune 500 companies had enacted nondiscrimination policies that include sexual orientation. Almost 90% of the top 50 Fortune 500 companies have written such policies. Corporate America has also led the way in enacting domestic partner benefits, with 145 Fortune 500 companies offering such benefits to their employees in 2001. This is an increase from 1993, when only 8 Fortune 500 companies offered such benefits. More than 50% of top 50 Fortune 500 companies offer similar benefits. It appears that when one company institutes such a policy, its competitors typically follow. As of 2001, 20 private companies also provided their employees protection from discrimination on the basis of gender identity. Five of these were Fortune 500 companies. Large companies also have been the staunchest supporters of ENDA, including corporate giants like AT&T and General Mills (Human Rights Campaign, 2001).

Although not as progressive as private employers, public agencies also have instituted protections for GLBT employees. As of 2001, the employees of 10 state and 106 local government agencies were protected from discrimination on the basis of sexual orientation. Eight state and 105 local governments also provided health benefits to the domestic partners of their employees. More than 300 colleges and universities have implemented sexual orientation discrimination policies, although only about half offer domestic partner benefits (Human Rights Campaign, 2001).

GLBTS AND THE WORKPLACE ENVIRONMENT

Despite a push for diversity in workplaces nationwide, GLBT employees may not receive the same consideration as other oppressed populations, such as women, people of color, or those with disabilities. This is apparent in the lack of legal protection of GLBTs in the workplace. The disparate treatment may be because GLBT identities are stigmatized and considered immoral by many. It may also be because GLBT status is not always physically observable, and the population may lack the visibility of other workers who are members of oppressed groups. As compared to these other groups in the workplace, GLBTs must deal with special issues, including identity management, homophobia and heterosexism, and discrimination related to their sexual orientation or gender identity.

IDENTITY MANAGEMENT

Identity management and the decision to "come out" is not just an issue that GLBT people face with family and friends. For those who spend a great portion of their lives on the job, disclosure in the workplace is a significant concern. Since GLBTs are not a visible minority, many have the choice of whether or not to come out in the workplace. Disclosure can also be an ongoing issue, as individuals change jobs over the course of their lifetimes and gain new coworkers and bosses in their places of employment.

Clearly, there are benefits as well as sanctions in coming out in the workplace. With disclosure, employees risk discrimination. They may also face an "involuntary disclosure," when a coworker "outs" them to others in the workplace. Whether voluntary or involuntary, disclosure in the workplace can have negative consequences, including harassment or even termination (Badgett, 1996). Since income is dependent on one's job, termination can prove devastating for GLBT employees.

Disclosure can also have positive effects for an employee. A few studies suggest that disclosure can provide increased satisfaction in the workplace and with coworkers (Boatwright, Gilbert, Forrest, & Ketzenberger, 1996; Driscoll, Kelley,

& Fassinger, 1996; Ellis & Riggle, 1995). Being out in the workplace can also have positive rewards for the individual, including increased productivity and self-worth (Gore, 2000). When a worker is out at work, he or she may feel more comfortable and less guarded, which can allow more energy for focusing on work-related tasks.

The timing of disclosure in the workplace is a very personal decision. Employees may feel it is better to come out after they have proven themselves as positive contributors to the organization. Others may choose to come out during the interviewing process so that they are candid from the beginning (Rosabal, 1996). Disclosure may be easier in an environment where employees have coworkers or supervisors who are also GLBT.

Choosing not to come out in the workplace, or passing as heterosexual at work, has been shown to cause stress for GLBT employees. Zuckerman and Simons (1996) call this being in the "work closet," an environment in which workers do not talk about their sexual orientation. Winfeld and Spielman (2001) contend that workers' job performance can suffer if they live in fear of being discovered as GLBT. Employees who are in the closet will have to lead a "double life," and their work life will cause them to hide details about their personal lives, like their partner. This can mean censoring what is said to coworkers (like what they did over the weekend) and being afraid to display personal memorabilia (such as a photo of one's partner on the desk).

HOMOPHOBIA AND HETEROSEXISM

Homophobia is fear or hatred of lesbians and gay men. This fear or hatred can be extended to transgender and bisexual people in the forms of transphobia and biphobia. Homophobia (as well as biphobia and transphobia) can be acted out in the workplace through slighting remarks or avoidance of GLBT employees. GLBT employees may also experience sexual harassment by other employees or supervisors. Although the literature is quite scarce in this area, a study by Nawyn, Richman, Rospenda, and Hughes (2000) found that gay men experienced significantly more sexual harassment than heterosexual men. An earlier study by Schneider (1982) found that lesbians experienced more sexual harassment than heterosexual women. This type of harassment can include suggestive comments, inappropriate touching, or threats. Although same-sex sexual harassment is becoming more common in the workplace, many victims fail to come forward for fear of being outed. Unfortunately, victims seeking justice have found little recourse in the court system, as the Civil Rights Act of 1964 does not account for same-sex workplace harassment (Bull, 1997).

Heterosexism is an assumption that heterosexuality is the norm as well as more natural and superior to other sexual orientations. GLBT employees can experience heterosexism interpersonally, as coworkers may ask whether an individual is (heterosexually) married or why he or she is not married. Invitations can also list employees, children, and spouses as those invited to attend agency social events. Heterosexism can also exist in the form of organizational policies. For example, "transgender" or "other" is not often listed as a gender category on human resource forms.

Along with homophobic and heterosexist attitudes, there are many misconceptions about GLBT employees. One myth is that GLBT people are interested in only certain professions. Gay men, for example, are stereotyped as florists, dancers, and chefs. The truth is that GLBT people exist in every profession and in most workplaces. Some people believe that GLBT people are mentally ill and immoral and that they are particularly unfit to work with children (Winfeld & Spielman, 2001). Another misconception is that gay men and lesbians benefit from higher incomes and more discretionary income. This is known as "income inflation." In truth, there is great diversity in the incomes of GLBTs, and studies have shown that gay men make 4% to 7% less money than heterosexual men and lesbians make about the same as heterosexual women (Badgett, 1998).

DISCRIMINATION

Homophobia and heterosexism can also result in discriminatory actions in the workplace. GLBT employees often experience significant discrimination on the job. In studies by Friskopp & Silverstein (1995) and Woods (1994), many respondents perceived that their sexual orientation prevented their promotion or a raise. Some had been threatened at work. Ragins and Cornwell's (2001) study of 534 gay and lesbian employees found that the policies and practices of organizations had a great impact on gay and lesbian employees, as workers reported more discrimination in organizations that lacked supportive policies and those that did not have openly gay bosses and coworkers. Those who perceived more discrimination also had more negative attitudes about their jobs. According to Croteau (1996), even if a GLBT worker has not experienced discrimination directly, he or she may fear or expect to be discriminated against in the workplace.

GLBT employees may also face compounding discrimination based on gender, race, and/or age. Although nondiscrimination legislation protects these other statuses, there is no guarantee that employees will not experience some form of discrimination on the basis of other minority statuses.

When work-related benefits are considered, GLBT employees and their families are often discriminated against in the workplace. GLBTs do not always receive "equal pay for equal work." Although they may have equivalent salaries and individual benefits, domestic partners and children of partners of GLBT employees rarely receive the same benefits as heterosexual spouses and their children (McNaught, 1995). Winfeld and Spielman (2001) distinguish between "hard" and "soft" benefits in the workplace. Hard benefits are those that are typically more costly to employers, like health insurance and pensions. Soft benefits often cost less and include family leave, child care, and employee discounts. The authors suspect that employers more commonly award soft benefits to domestic partners.

SOCIAL WORK IN THE WORKPLACE: INDIVIDUAL, GROUP, AND SYSTEM-LEVEL INTERVENTIONS

When GLBT employees feel that they are not supported or welcomed in their workplace, it can negatively affect their mental health. It can also affect their job performance, as hiding their sexual orientation requires great energy—energy that could be better spent carrying out job-related tasks. As a result, GLBT employees may also feel less committed to the success of their employer (Powers & Ellis, 1995). Social workers can intervene with GLBTs in the workplace to help to improve the mental health of employees and their happiness in their job. Social workers can provide these interventions at the individual, group, and system levels.

OCCUPATIONAL SOCIAL WORK AS AN EMERGING FIELD OF PRACTICE

The involvement of social work in the work world dates back to the early 1900s, when social workers responded to the needs of workers in large industries in England. In the United States, the role of social workers evolved into staffing and personnel management, and away from counseling-type tasks during the 1930s. The 1940s and 1950s saw the inclusion of social workers in alcohol-abuse-prevention programs, and the 1970s and 1980s moved them back into a more broad-based counseling role within organizations. Today, occupational social workers (OSWs) are most commonly employed in Employee Assistance Programs (EAPs). These positions may be part of the organization or they may be services contracted out (Barak & Bargal, 2000).

Because of their professional commitment to social justice, social workers may be uniquely prepared to help diverse workers within organizations. OSWs as well as other social workers can work on behalf of GLBT employees through individual counseling, individual and group empowerment, education and training, and advocacy and policy development.

CAREER DEVELOPMENT AND COUNSELING WITH GLBTS

CAREER COUNSELING PRACTICE ISSUES

The career development literature is most likely to address lesbian issues, followed by issues of gay men, with much less discussion of specific issues of bisexual individuals, and virtually none focused on unique issues of transgender people. An important theme in the GLBT career literature has been the interaction of sexual identity and career development. For example, Boatwright and colleagues (1996) found that ten self-identified lesbians believed that the demanding process of their sexual identity development led to delays and disruptions in their work life, so that their career development was behind that of their heterosexual peers. Sexual identity formation, as described by Cass (1979), has been implicated in defining psychological and personal concerns related to coming out in the workplace. Cass proposed a model that begins with identity confusion and, through a series of six stages, culminates in identity synthesis, or being able to integrate one's sexual identity in all areas of one's life, including work.

Although the career intervention literature is based mostly on anecdotal and clinical observation information, it offers a number of ideas for providing GLBT-sensitive career services. Perhaps most important, social workers and other counselors need to create an environment where people feel safe to seek services, disclose their sexual identity, and explore specific career-related concerns (Croteau, Anderson, Distefano, & Kampa-Kokesch, 2000). This can be done by posting GLBT-friendly insignia and pamphlets, using inclusive language in all literature, hiring staff identified as GLBT, and actively working with GLBT organizations to promote career development. Career services may be particularly valuable for GLBT high school and college students who are preparing to enter the work world. Besner and Spungin (1998) note the importance of increasing the self-esteem of and communicating a safe environment for GLBT students.

In general, when working with GLBTs, it is advisable for career professionals to apply concepts of effective multicultural counseling in terms of knowledge, attitudes, and skills (Elliot, 1993; Morgan & Brown, 1991). It is important for some GLBT individuals to have GLBT role models during their process of career exploration, particularly because such role models may have been scarce in other social contexts because of the effects of invisibility (Fassinger, 1995). Career professionals can encourage individuals to cultivate these resources and refer clients to GLBT organizations that may have members willing to serve as role models. The issue of role modeling is delicate, however, because of the potential differing levels of being "out" that may exist for people.

With GLBT clients, career professionals can advocate for the careful use of career inventories, card sorts, and personality tests commonly used in career counseling. For example, Belz (1993) promoted adding new cards in a values card sort such as "being out on the job." For an analysis of how five major psychological inventories used in career counseling and personnel selection have been used and misused with gay and lesbian clients, see Pope (1992).

In a review chapter, Croteau et al. (2000) provide several ideas about what constitutes good career counseling practice with GLBT individuals:

▪ Recognize that sexual identity development influences career development. However, not all clients will want to explore this interaction, particularly early in their sexual identity development.

▪ Be aware of the multiple issues around sexual identity management and be able to help individuals explore management strategies. Issues include environmental variables, tension between fear of discrimination and personal integrity, as discussed by Griffin (1992), whether the client is partnered, and past experiences in being "out" in the workplace.

▪ Be able to assess and increase client awareness of how societal messages about sexual orientation and gender have influenced client career interests and choices.

▪ Explore one's own homophobic and heterosexist biases, however subtle, to try to overcome, or at least be aware of and manage, such attitudes.

▪ Place emphasis on understanding environmental influences on career development and choices, especially considering that many of the unique concerns are the result of societal oppression.

▪ Explore the special concerns of GLBT clients with multiple oppressed identities, such as clients of color, especially as related to coming out at work.

▪ Assist clients with developing skills for building affirmation in the workplace and with developing career-related networks within the GLBT community.

RELEVANCE OF TRADITIONAL CAREER THEORIES FOR GLBTS

Career theories that emphasize environmental influences on career development may be most applicable to GLBT clients' career concerns, given that many of their unique issues stem from experiences and fear of oppression. *Social cognitive career theory* (Lent, Brown, & Hackett, 1994) as applied to lesbians and gay men by Morrow, Gore, and Campbell (1996) can provide a framework for how environmental and contextual influences shape academic and career-related interests. This can occur through their impact on a client's belief in his or her ability to carry out actions to reach a specific goal (self-efficacy beliefs) and expectations about the outcomes of his or her performance (outcome expectations). For example, despite an aspiring teacher's strong self-efficacy belief in her ability to work well with children in a classroom, she may be affected by an environment in which many lesbian teachers feel their job security is jeopardized if they are "out," and consequently she may change her feelings and expectations about this occupation. Internal and external barriers to career choice and adjustment discussed in *women's career development models* may or may not apply to lesbians (Fassinger, 1996). For example, lesbians may or may not share the same multiple role issues as heterosexual women. A lesbian may manage the role of mother, but she is less likely to experience role overload as a result of lack of active involvement of a husband in child care and household responsibilities.

Mobley and Slaney (1996) examined *Holland's theory* (1992) for its relevance for lesbians and gay men, specifically how key concepts such as individual personality type, work environment type, and congruence between the types relate to Cass's (1979) sexual identity development model. Holland's concept of congruence may have different application for GLBTs, since they may feel forced to make incongruent career choices because of homophobia in society and the workplace. An attempt to integrate gay and lesbian identity development with Super's *life-span approach* (1990) is offered by Dunkle (1996). For example, fundamental to Super's theory is the idea that the self-concept, composed of self-esteem and several other linked components, is central to career development. Because difficulty in one component can decrease successful integration in another component, it is possible that GLBT clients could experience complications in the career development process if they have trouble integrating their sexual identity into their overall self-concept (Belz, 1993).

INDIVIDUAL AND GROUP EMPOWERMENT

Empowerment involves increasing the power of individuals or groups of individuals so that they can make changes in their lives and their environments (Gutierrez, 1995). Empowering GLBT employees must begin with a social worker educating himself or herself about issues relating to gay, lesbian, bisexual, and transgender people. With this knowledge, the social worker can partner with employees to make supportive changes in their lives and in the workplace.

On an individual level, these changes may include coming out in the workplace. Social workers can help employees realize their capacities to come out to employers and coworkers as well as to family and friends. They can also help increase the power of GLBT couples by providing information and referrals for legal and financial matters related to domestic partnerships.

Social workers can empower groups of GLBT workers by promoting their group consciousness and visibility. Sussal (1994) suggests that occupational social workers include GLBT people in organizations' statistical reports, to increase the visibility of this group of workers. This can be included in the demographic data kept on employees, as well as in agency reports. Social workers can also empower GLBT employees by facilitating the development of employee groups. Such groups can help provide an opportunity for networking and socialization and allow GLBT employees to discuss and plan action around issues that need to be addressed in their work environment (McNaught, 1995). Social workers can also raise awareness and create connections to the larger GLBT community by organizing special events related to Gay Pride Month (June) or HIV/AIDS fund-raising events.

EDUCATION AND TRAINING

Social workers can provide education to GLBT employees regarding local support services and make referrals to supportive professionals. It is a good idea to have a listing of "gay-friendly" professionals and services that can provide counseling, legal advice, health care, and other services.

Social workers can develop and provide staff training on GLBT issues. Winfeld and Spielman (2001) also suggest that before undertaking the development of a training program, the social worker should conduct a needs assessment. In this case, a questionnaire can be designed that can assess the sensitivity and knowledge level of employees regarding GLBT issues. It can also involve surveying GLBT employees on what they identify as sensitivity issues in their workplace. McNaught (1995) suggests topics to be covered in a formal workshop, including discussing and dispelling the myths surrounding homosexuality, the effects of homophobia (including jokes and slighting comments) on coworkers, and how employees can abolish unsupportive behaviors in the workplace (including ways to intervene in harmful situations).

Staff education can also be less formal. For example, Winfeld and Spielman (2001) suggest "brown-bag" meetings where diversity issues can be presented. In addition, flyers and information about local GLBT centers and services can be made visible and available in the workplace. Articles related to GLBT issues can also be included in an organization's newsletter.

ADVOCACY AND POLICY DEVELOPMENT

Social workers functioning in EAP or other roles are uniquely positioned to serve as advocates for GLBT rights in the workplace and the larger community. To effectively function in this role, social workers should keep up to date on local and national legislation that affects GLBT workers, so they can facilitate understanding of these issues among agency directors and other management (Poverney, 2000). They should also become involved in advocacy efforts to further the civil rights of GLBTs in the workplace and society, including the national ENDA and local nondiscrimination policies.

Social workers can also assess the workplace culture as it applies to GLBTs. This assessment may include looking at discriminatory policies and practices. With this knowledge, social workers can begin to work toward improving the workplace culture (Poverney, 2000), perhaps by changing current policies or drafting new policies that support GLBT workers, such as adding GLBTs to the organization's nondiscrimination policy or developing a domestic partner benefits program. This work can be led by a social worker, but it will also likely involve others in an organization, including fiscal and human resource personnel. In this way it becomes an effort by the entire organization.

DIVERSITY AND NONDISCRIMINATION POLICIES

Organizations should begin by developing a diversity and/or nondiscrimination policy that includes GLBTs as well as other minorities (Powers & Ellis, 1995). Not surprisingly, GLBT employees who worked in organizations with nondiscrimination policies were more satisfied with their jobs (Ellis & Riggle, 1995). The Hennepin County (Minnesota) Diversity and Non-discrimination Policy (n.d.) clearly expresses its value of diversity:

> Hennepin County values differences and recognizes similarities among employees, volunteers, union representatives, clients, customers, and vendors. It is the responsibility of all Hennepin County employees and volunteers to generate and maintain work environments in which employees, volunteers, union representatives, clients, customers, and vendors are respected, valued, and welcomed. Consistent with this policy, all Hennepin County employees and volunteers will foster environments that value diversity and support the elimination of discrimination in the workplace.
>
> (¶ 3–4)

As exemplified by Hennepin County, a diversity or nondiscrimination policy should also include an organization's value of diverse (including GLBT) consumers and an expectation that all consumers will be treated equally. The policy should also clearly state the types of behaviors that will not be tolerated. In its equal employment opportunity policy, Apple Computer "prohibits harassment of any kind, including sexual harassment, and slurs or jokes based on any protected class" (including women, persons of color, GLBTs, etc.) (Transgender Law and Policy Institute, 1998). The policy should also list actions that can be taken by employees who experience discrimination and sanctions that will result for employees who violate the policy. Of course, the key to an effective policy is visibility and enforcement. Powers and Ellis (1995) suggest that employers state the organization's diversity policy to potential applicants to ensure that they understand the position. An employer can also ask potential employees about their attitudes about and experiences with diverse coworkers and clients, including GLBTs.

DOMESTIC PARTNER BENEFITS

Contrary to popular belief, extending benefits to same-sex partners has not been shown to greatly increase costs to employers (Powers & Ellis, 1995). Domestic partner benefits should cover partners and the children of partners of GLBT employees. Of course, these benefits could also be drafted to include heterosexual couples who are not legally married. Spielman and Winfeld (1996) suggest that organizations state the specific criteria for a domestic partnership. For example, at the University of Chicago, *domestic partnership* is defined as "two individuals of the same gender who live together in a long-term relationship of indefinite duration." The employee and his/her partner are asked to sign a Statement of Domestic Partnership affirming that the partnership meets the criteria set forth by the university (University of Chicago, 2002). The Children's Hospital of Boston includes "same sex spousal equivalents" in its dual and family coverage for health, dental, and life insurance plans (Children's Hospital of Boston, n.d.).

Once an organization sets criteria for domestic partnerships, decisions about obtainable benefits must be made. "Hard benefits" include medical insurance, life insurance, and pension plans. Domestic partners and children should be included in major medical and dental plans and medical savings accounts, and COBRA benefits should be extended to partners and children when an employee leaves the organization. Partners and children of partners should be listed as legitimate beneficiaries on employee life insurance policies. Pension plans should ensure that partners receive payment in the event the employee dies. Partners and children of partners should also be included in "soft benefits," such as family and sick leave, employee discounts, and child care services.

INFORMAL POLICIES

Informal policies are those carried out by individuals or groups that are not necessarily shared by other employees or an organization's administration (Flynn, 1992). Jansson (1999) claims that informal policies develop in the absence of formal (written) policies or as a way for staff to establish their own operating procedures. This includes how employees treat GLBT coworkers and consumers. Social workers can intervene on behalf of GLBT employees and clients by being intolerant of homophobic or heterosexist behaviors and attitudes.

SPECIAL ISSUES

EMPLOYEES WITH HIV/AIDS

More than 400,000 people are living with HIV/AIDS in the United States. Of new adult infections among these PLWHA, roughly a third are attributed to men who have sex with men (MSM) (Centers for Disease Control, 2001). Many of those in the MSM transmission category are gay or bisexual men. With the advent of new medications, many PLWHA are living longer and many will work long after diagnosis.

Workers with HIV/AIDS may experience special issues and have unique needs in the workplace. A PLWHA will face the issue of whether or not to disclose his/her HIV status to his/her employer (Fesko, 2001). Disclosure may also involve coworkers, so the individual must also deal with the attitudes of other employees toward him/her and the disease (Paul & Townsend, 1997). Since HIV/AIDS is still very stigmatized and many individuals still hold fears about people who have the disease, education of coworkers is crucial. As suggested by Paul and Townsend (1997), that education may involve a presentation by a medical professional, explaining the medical facts about HIV/AIDS, including information about its transmission, treatment, and illness progression.

Workers with HIV/AIDS will likely experience health-related challenges, including fatigue and other health problems that can affect their job performance. Sick leave can be a significant need, as workers may experience opportunistic infections or other complications of the disease. Similarly, medical costs will be a significant issue and may involve higher insurance premiums for the employer. Job performance may also be an issue, particularly if a job involves manual labor. In this case the employer may switch the employee to a different position within the organization. At some point it may be determined that the employee can no longer work (Paul & Townsend, 1997). An employer may consider various kinds of supportive accommodations for workers with HIV/AIDS, including a flexible work schedule, transfer to a less taxing position, and leaves of absence (Segal, 1993).

Workers with HIV/AIDS may also experience emotional difficulties through the course of the disease. As a result, the individual may need help with disclosure issues and adjustment to illness. Individual or family counseling may be warranted. Zuckerman and Simons (1996) propose developing an employee support group to care for the emotional needs of PLWHA as well as their coworkers. Financial difficulties may also arise, and an employee may need help with financing medication and medical treatments or housing assistance.

Several federal policies protect the rights of persons with HIV/AIDS in the workplace. The Americans with Disabilities Act (ADA) (1990) bans discrimination against job applicants based on disability and commands employers to make reasonable accommodations for the employee to perform the duties of the position. The Occupational Safety and Health Act (OSHA) (1970) ensures that employees are provided a safe working environment. This means that employers must ensure that the workplace environment does not exacerbate the illness of employees with HIV/AIDS. The Vocational Rehabilitation Act (1973) bars organizations that contract with or receive money from the federal government from discriminating in employment on the basis of disability. Federal employees with HIV/AIDS are protected by the Privacy Act of 1974, which gives employees the right to determine what information about them is kept by employers and who has access to the information. In addition, more than twenty states have included HIV/AIDS in their definition of *disability* in terms of anti-discrimination laws related to the workplace (Paul & Townsend, 1997).

Zuckerman and Simons (1996) suggest that workplace policies concerning HIV should address compliance with anti-discrimination policies as well as the Americans with Disabilities Act (ADA) (1990) and the Federal Rehabilitation Act (1973). The policies should also promote adherence to the Occupational Safety and Health Administration (OSHA) guidelines regarding infection control. Organizational policies should include preserving the confidentiality of medical records and other information about an employee's HIV status. Organizations should also document a plan on how discrimination in the workplace will be handled and how hiring, promotion, transfer, and firing of persons with HIV/AIDS will be conducted.

TRANSGENDER EMPLOYEES

Transgender people who identify as transsexuals are "individuals who strongly feel that they are, or ought to be, the opposite sex" (Brown & Rounsley, 1996, p. 6). Those who decide to live publicly as the other sex must go through a period of transition. "Transitioning" is the "process of making the change from living as a man to living as a woman or visa versa [sic]" (Walworth, 1998, p. 35). In "cross-living," which is often the beginning of the transition, an individual lives full-time in the preferred gender role for a period of at least a year. This process is typically recommended and required for persons who wish to pursue sex reassignment surgery. Cross-living involves dressing as the other sex, and it may also involve receiving male or female hormones and enacting a legal change of name. This is done during personal as well as work hours, so it will likely be noticed in the workplace (Walworth, 1998).

Before transitioning in the workplace, an employee will need to consider several issues, including how much he or she values his/her job and how much he or she is valued by his/her employer. Additionally, he or she will need to know if the employer has a nondiscrimination policy or would be tolerant of such a transition. He or she will also need to think about the physical transition, such as hormone treatments and possibly reassignment surgery, which brings up the issue of medical insurance. Hormones can cost more than $200 per month, and genital surgery can cost upwards of $25,000. A transgender employee will want to investigate whether any or all procedures will be covered by employee health insurance (Walworth, 1998).

Transitioning in the workplace can be frightening for individuals. Many cannot afford to lose their jobs, especially since therapy and medical procedures are very costly. Some may decide to stay in their present job, while others may choose to start over by changing employers or even changing careers. If they choose to stay in the present position, they can benefit from the stability of income. On the other hand, they may face discrimination or even harassment by their employer or co-workers. In some cases, they may even be terminated (Brown & Rounsley, 1996).

For those who wish to stay in their present job, the Human Rights Campaign (1999) offers suggestions for transitioning in the workplace. A beginning step is for the individual to prepare management and coworkers for his/her transition. This will involve educating staff and negotiating issues like timing of the transition and restroom use. The transgender individual may also consider writing a "transsexual

A TRANSSEXUAL TRANSITION LETTER (TO COWORKERS)

Through an intense process of self-discovery and psychotherapy, I have discovered myself to be a female-to-male transsexual. This process will lead to changes in my appearance at first and eventually a complete gender change through surgery. To determine if I am a candidate for surgery, by the Harry Benjamin Standards of Care [as adopted by the American Psychiatric Association], I must live full-time as a male for a continuous period of at least one year. I intend to do that within three to six months. During the coming months my appearance will slowly change as the hormones, which have been prescribed, take effect.

Initially I will be continuing to use the name which I currently use. Eventually I will drop my middle name, and have it legally changed. I will inform you of the name change and the dates of my transition to full-time living as soon as my therapist and physician determine I am ready. I will give you at least two weeks notice prior to this event.

Naturally, I will do everything to help you facilitate the company's accommodation of this. I wish this was not necessary, but unfortunately this is something I must do, not something I simply want to do.

The end result should be beneficial to [the organization] as well. Happy and healthy employees make better employees. My commitment to [the organization] shall, no doubt, be strengthened during this period of transition.

SOURCE: USED BY PERMISSION OF ALEX FOX, www.trans-man.org.

transition letter" describing his/her feelings and desire to transition as well as his/her expectations of coworkers' behavior. The HRC also advises that the individual be prepared for some level of harassment and possibly termination.

Those who choose to change employers will face the issue of disclosure. For example, providing references from employers who knew them as another gender can be problematic. One suggestion is to inform previous employers that they wish to have their name changed on workplace documentation. In addition, the individual can have his/her name changed on diplomas and other documents before applying for a new position. Another dilemma in applying for a new position is answering the question of whether he or she has ever been employed under a different name. This compounds the dilemma of whether or not to inform the new employer that he/she is a transgender person (Brown & Rounsley, 1996).

Employers can support transitioning employees in several ways. Walworth (1998) suggests that employers carefully plan the workplace transition process with the transgender employee. This may include a timeline of events and a discussion of possible problems. The employee's therapist and doctor and a human resources representative may also be involved in this planning process. To begin, employers should issue a statement to their employees expressing the organization's faith in the competence of the employee and continued faith that the employee's transition will not affect his/her competence. This statement should also include the organization's expectation that other employees will treat their coworker with respect. Coworkers will likely need help in adapting to the transition. Staff sensitivity training is often key to this adaptation, as coworkers will

Web Sites

American Civil Liberties Union (ACLU) (Gay and Lesbian Rights Project), http://www.aclu.org
Center for the Study of Sexual Minorities in the Military (CSSMM), http://www.gaymilitary.ucsb.edu/index.htm
GayWork.com, http://www.gaywork.com
GenderPac (Job Discrimination), http://www.gpac.org/
Human Rights Campaign (WorkNet), http://www.hrc.org
National AIDS Fund (Workplace Resource Center), http://www.aidsfund.org
National Gay and Lesbian Task Force (NGLTF), http://www.ngltf.org
Transgender at Work, http://www.tgender.net/taw/

Books and Publications

Gay Issues in the Workplace (1993), by Brian McNaught
Sexual Orientation in the Workplace: Gay Men, Lesbians, Bisexuals, and Heterosexuals Working Together (1996), by Amy J. Zuckerman and George I. Simons
Straight Talk About Gays in the Workplace (2001), by Liz Winfeld and Sue Spielman
Transsexual Workers: An Employer's Guide (1998), by Janis Walworth
Working with a Transsexual: A Guide for Coworkers (1999), by Janis Walworth

Videos

Gay Issues in the Workplace: Gay, Lesbian, and Bisexual Employees Speak for Themselves with Brian McNaught (1993), Brian McNaught, TRB Productions
Out at Work (1996), Kelly Anderson and Tami Gold, Frameline Productions

likely not be familiar with gender identity issues and may feel uncomfortable interacting with a transgender coworker. They will need to change the pronoun they use to address their coworker and perhaps become comfortable with a new first name, chosen by the transgender person, that is congruent with the new gender identity (Walworth, 1998).

Existing policies in the organization will need to be examined and potentially changed. In some cases, employers can make arrangements with insurance companies to provide needed services to their transgender employees. Organizational policies may need to be revised to include nondiscrimination on that basis of gender identity. Employers can also provide a flexible work schedule to support appointments with therapists and doctors and to allow sufficient time for recovery from surgical procedures (Walworth, 1998). Transgender employees may also gain support in gay, lesbian, and bisexual employee groups if the group is inclusive of these individuals.

Unlike gay men and lesbians and persons with HIV/AIDS, transgender employees have few legal protections in the workplace, as many nondiscrimination policies do not include this population among those covered by the policy. Transgender people have tried unsuccessfully to sue employers for discrimination based on sex (Title VII of the Civil Rights Act). It is also not specifically covered under the Americans with Disabilities Act (1990). Some transgender people, however, have been able to receive Social Security disability income when they have been fired from their jobs (Walworth, 1998).

CONCLUSION

The passage of ENDA would go a long way toward ensuring the rights of GLBT employees. Even if federal and local laws are enacted and enforced, homophobic and heterosexist attitudes and workplace cultures can be slow to change. Social workers can be instrumental in this change. They should begin by educating themselves about and acknowledging the special issues faced by GLBT employees, including identity management, homophobia and heterosexism, and discrimination. With an understanding of these issues, social workers can intervene with individuals, groups, organizations, and policies to promote the well-being and equality of GLBT employees. GLBT as well as other employees can join in this effort to advance social justice and improve workplace conditions. The result can and should be a workplace environment where GLBT employees and clients feel welcome, secure, and equal.

NOTE

1.   For a current list of states, localities, and organizations that have nondiscrimination policies and/or domestic partner benefits, visit the Human Rights Campaign (HRC) Web site at http//:www.hrc.org/worknet.

REFERENCES

Badgett, M. V. L. (1996). Employment and sexual orientation: Disclosure and discrimination in the workplace. *Journal of Gay and Lesbian Social Services, 4*(4), 29–52.

———. (1998). *Income inflation: The myth of affluence among gay, lesbian, and bisexual Americans.* Washington, DC: M. V. Lee Badgett and the NGLTF Policy Institute.

Barak, M. E. M., & Bargal, D. (2000). Human services in the context of work: Evolving and innovation roles for occupational social work. *Administration in Social Work, 23*(3/4), 1–11.

Belz, J. R. (1993). Sexual orientation as a factor in career development. *Career Development Quarterly, 41*, 197–200.

Besner, H. F., & Spungin, C. I. (1998). *Training for professionals who work with gays and lesbians in educational and workplace settings.* Washington, DC: Accelerated Development.

Boatwright, K. J., Gilbert, M. S., Forrest, L., & Ketzenberger, K. (1996). Impact of identity development upon career trajectory: Listening to the voices of lesbian women. *Journal of Vocational Behavior, 48*, 210–228.

Brown, M. L., & Rounsley, C. A. (1996). *True selves: Understanding transsexualism for families, friends, coworkers, and helping professionals.* San Francisco: Jossey-Bass.

Bull, C. (1997). Same-sex harassment: Gay men and lesbians being harassed are about to have their day in court. *Advocate, 747*, 30–33.

Cass, V. C. (1979). Homosexual identity formation: A theoretical model. *Journal of Homosexuality, 4*, 219–235.

Centers for Disease Control. (2001). *U.S. HIV and AIDS cases reported through June 2001: Midyear edition* (vol. 13, no. 3). Atlanta: National Center for HIV, STD, and TB Prevention.

Children's Hospital of Boston. (n.d.). *Benefits.* Retrieved August 14, 2002, from http://www.childrenshospital.org/jobs/benefits.html

Clymer, A. (2002, April 25). Senate panel moves to block bias against gays at work. *New York Times*, A26.

Croteau, J. M. (1996). Research on the work experiences of lesbian, gay, and bisexual people: An integrative review of methodology and findings. *Journal of Vocational Behavior, 48*, 195–209.

Croteau, J. M., Anderson, M. Z., Distefano, T. M., and Kampa-Kokesch, S. (2000). Lesbian, gay, and bisexual vocational psychology: Reviewing foundations and planning construction. In R. M. Perez, K. A. DeBord, & K. J. Bieschke (Eds.), *Handbook of counseling and psychotherapy with lesbian, gay, and bisexual clients* (pp. 383–408). Washington, DC: American Psychological Association.

Driscoll, J. M., Kelley, F. A., & Fassinger, R. E. (1996). Lesbian identity and disclosure in the workplace: Relation to occupational stress and satisfaction. *Journal of Vocational Behavior, 48*, 229–242.

Dunkle, J. H. (1996). Toward an integration of gay and lesbian identity development and Super's life-span approach. *Journal of Vocational Behavior, 48*, 149–159.

Elliot, J. E. (1993). Career development with lesbian and gay clients. *Career Development Quarterly, 41*, 210–226.

Ellis, A. L., & Riggle, E. D. B. (1995). The relation of job satisfaction and degree of openness about one's sexual orientation for lesbians and gay men. *Journal of Homosexuality, 30*(2), 75–85.

Evans, R. (2001). *U.S. military policies concerning homosexuals: Development, implementation, and outcomes*. Santa Barbara, CA: Center for the Study of Sexual Minorities in the Military.

Fassinger, R. E. (1995). From invisibility to integration: Lesbian identity in the workplace. *Career Development Quarterly, 44*, 149–167.

———. (1996). Notes from the margins: Integrating lesbian experience into the vocational psychology of women. *Journal of Vocational Behavior, 48*, 160–175.

Fesko, S. L. (2001). Disclosure of HIV status in the workplace: Considerations and strategies. *Health and Social Work, 26*(4), 235–244.

Flynn, J. P. (1992) *Social agency policy: Analysis and presentation for community practice.* Chicago: Nelson-Hall.

Friskopp, A., & Silverstein, S. (1995). *Straight jobs, gay lives: Gay and lesbian professionals, the Harvard Business School, and the American workplace.* New York: Touchstone/ Simon and Schuster.

Gore, S. (2000). The lesbian and gay workplace. In B. Greene and G. L. Croom (Eds.), *Education, research, and practice in lesbian, gay, bisexual and transgender psychology: A resource manual* (pp. 282–302). Thousand Oaks, CA: Sage.

Griffin, P. (1992). From hiding out to coming out: Empowering lesbian and gay educators. In K. M. Harbeck (Ed.), *Coming out of the classroom closet* (pp. 167–196). Binghamton, NY: Harrington Park.

Gutierrez, L. M. (1995). Working with women of color: An empowerment perspective. *Social Work, 35*(2), 149–153.

Halley, J. (1999). *Don't: A reader's guide to the military's anti-gay policy.* Durham, NC: Duke University Press.

Hennepin County (MN). (n.d.). Hennepin County diversity and non-discrimination policy (Appendix 7). Retrieved August 14, 2002, from http://www.hclib.org/extranet/IS_policy_guide/AP7.html.

Holland, J. L. (1992). *Making vocational choices: A theory of vocational personalities and work environments.* Odessa, FL: Psychological Assessment Resources.

Human Rights Campaign (1998, May 28). Human Rights Campaign commends Clinton executive order banning anti-gay job discrimination against federal workers. Human Rights Campaign News Release.

———. (1999, February). *Transgenderism and transition in the workplace.* Washington, DC: Human Rights Campaign Foundation.

———. (2001). *The state of the workplace for lesbian, gay, bisexual, and transgender Americans in 2001.* Washington, DC: Human Rights Campaign Foundation.

———. (2002). *The state of the workplace for lesbian, gay, bisexual, and transgender Americans: A semiannual snapshot.* Washington, DC: Human Rights Campaign.

Jansson, B. S. (1999). *Becoming an effective policy advocate: From policy practice to social justice* (3d ed.). Pacific Grove, CA: Brooks/Cole.

Lent, R. W., Brown, S. D., & Hackett, G. (1994). Toward a unifying social cognitive theory of career and academic interest, choice, and performance. *Journal of Vocational Behavior, 45*, 79–122.

McNaught, B. (1995). *Gay issues in the workplace.* New York: St. Martin's.

Miller, N. (1995). *Out of the past: Gay and lesbian history from 1869 to the present.* New York: Vintage.

Mobley, M., & Slaney, R. B. (1996). Holland's Theory: Its relevance for lesbian women and gay men. *Journal of Vocational Behavior, 48*, 125–135.

Morgan, K. S., & Brown, L. S. (1991). Lesbian career development, work behavior, and vocational counseling. *Counseling Psychologist*, 19(2), 273–291.

Morrow, S. L, Gore, P. A., & Campbell, B. W. (1996). The application of a sociocognitive framework for the career development of lesbian women and gay men. *Journal of Vocational Behavior, 48,* 136–148.

Nawyn, S. J., Richman, J. A., Rospenda, K. M., & Hughes, T. L. (2000). Sexual identity and alcohol-related outcomes: Contributions to workplace harassment. *Journal of Substance Abuse, 11*(3), 289–304.

Paul, R. J., & Townsend, J. B. (1997). AIDS in the workplace: Balancing employer and employee rights. *Review of Business, 18*(20), 9–14.

Pope, M. S. (1992). Bias in the interpretation of psychological tests. In S. Dworkin & F. Guitierrez (Eds.), *Counseling gay men and lesbians: Journey to the end of the rainbow* (pp. 272–292). Alexandria, VA: American Counseling Association.

Poverny, M. (2000). Employee assistance practice with sexual minorities. *Administration in Social Work, 23*(3/4), 69–91.

Powers, B., & Ellis, A. (1995). *A manager's guide to sexual orientation in the workplace.* New York: Routledge.

Ragins, B. R., & Cornwell, J. M. (2001). Pink triangles: Antecedents and consequences of perceived workplace discrimination against gay and lesbian employees. *Journal of Applied Psychology, 86*(6), 1244–1261.

Rosabal, G. S. (1996). Multicultural existence in the workplace: Including how I thrive as a Latina lesbian feminist. *Journal of Gay and Lesbian Social Services, 4*(4), 17–28.

Schneider, B. E. (1982). Consciousness about sexual harassment among heterosexual and lesbian women workers. *Journal of Social Issues, 38,* 75–98.

Segal, J. (1993). HIV: How high the risk? *HR Magazine, 38*(2), 93–97.

Spelman, S., & Winfeld, L. (1996). Domestic partner benefits: A bottom line discussion. *Journal of Gay and Lesbian Social Services, 4*(4), 53–78.

Super, D. E. (1990). A life-span, life-space approach to career development. In D. Brown, L. Brooks, & Associates (Eds.), *Career choice and development* (pp. 197–261). San Francisco: Jossey-Bass Management Series.

Sussal, C. M. (1994). Empowering gays and lesbians in the workplace. *Journal of Gay and Lesbian Social Services, 1*(1), 89–103.

Transgender Law and Policy Institute. (1998). *Apple supports gender identity and expression.* Retrieved August 14, 2002, from http://www.transgenderlaw.org/employer/apple. htm.

University of Chicago. (2002). *Domestic partnership FAQs.* Retrieved August 14, 2002, from http://hr.uchicago.edu/benefits/dpartnership-FAQs.html.

Walworth, J. (1998). *Transsexual workers: An employer's guide.* Westchester, CA: Author.

Winfeld, L., & Spielman, S. (2001). *Straight talk about gays in the workplace* (2d ed.). New York: Harrington Park.

Woods, J. D. (1994). *The corporate closet: The professional lives of gay men in America.* New York: Free Press.

Yang, A. (1999). *From wrongs to rights: Public opinion on gay and lesbian Americans moves toward equality, 1973 to 1999.* Washington, DC: Policy Institute of the National Gay and Lesbian Task Force.

Zuckerman, A. J., & Simons, G. (1996). *Sexual orientation in the workplace: Gay men, lesbians, bisexuals, and heterosexuals working together.* Thousand Oaks, CA: Sage.

19

SOCIAL WELFARE POLICY AND ADVOCACY

Lori Messinger

The petitioners are entitled to respect for their private lives. The State cannot demean their existence or control their destiny by making their private sexual conduct a crime.

—SUPREME COURT JUSTICE ANTHONY KENNEDY, WRITING ABOUT LESBIANS AND GAY MEN
IN THE MAJORITY OPINION, LAWRENCE V. TEXAS, JUNE 2003

PUBLIC POLICY is an arena always in flux. As you read this book, federal and state legislation is being developed, introduced, discussed, or voted on. Federal and state appeals courts are reviewing existing legislation, while lower-level courts are overseeing criminal prosecutions and settling disagreements between citizens. County commissions and city councils are instituting and reviewing ordinances and distributing funds. State and local social service organizations and public health agencies are devising policies that will shape their interactions with their employees and the public. Many of these policies and policy decisions will affect gay, lesbian, bisexual, and transgender people (GLBTs), either overtly, by naming one or more of these groups, or indirectly, influencing their lives by their absence from the policy. This chapter will provide an accurate, up-to-date review of federal and state social welfare policies affecting GLBTs at the time this book is published. Students of social welfare policy are reminded that they should always undertake the research necessary to determine the status of current legislation.

To aid in a full understanding of GLBT public policy issues, the chapter will begin with a discussion of the primary arguments in public policy regarding GLBTs, including the stated position of the National Association of Social Workers (NASW) on these issues. This will be followed by a review of those federal and state social welfare policies and laws that specifically target GLBT people, to the exclusion of others. This section will be followed by a review of existing mainstream social welfare policies and programs that do not specifically target

GLBT people but that affect them nonetheless. The chapter will conclude with a discussion of useful methods and resources for GLBT policy advocacy.

PRIMARY POLICY ARGUMENTS REGARDING GLBTS

A quick review of social welfare policy reveals four approaches to GLBTs: (1) *invisibility*: refusing to acknowledge the existence of GLBT people; (2) *illegality*: criminalizing same-sex erotic behaviors and behaviors that blur lines of gender; (3) *separation*: removing GLBT people from the public for the protection of a greater good; and (4) *rehabilitation*: establishing programs to "fix the brokenness" of GLBT citizens. Each of these policy responses is based upon competing conceptions of GLBT people. Proponents of the invisibility strategy might argue that GLBTs represent small natural aberrations in society, not significant enough to recognize in policies. Those who would support the illegality position would argue that the actions and behaviors of GLBT people are morally corrupt, destroying the fabric of American society. This argument might also support policies focused on the separation of GLBTs. The rehabilitation stance would rely on the argument that homosexuality, bisexuality, and transgenderism are forms of mental or physical illness that can be treated.

GLBT activists have fought against these conceptions of sexual orientation and gender expression for well over a century. Current activists argue that sexual orientation and gender expression are not indicative of illness, dangerousness, or aberration, but instead should be recognized as identity characteristics that signify an oppressed population. This population should be afforded equal rights (not special rights, as argued by its opponents) and should be recognized in traditional social welfare policies. Behaviors associated with GLBTs should not be criminalized or medicalized, but recognized as natural and normal for this group.

The National Association of Social Workers (NASW) has supported the position of the GLBT activists. Section 4.02 of the NASW *Code of Ethics* reads: "Social workers should not practice, condone, facilitate, or collaborate with any form of discrimination on the basis of ... sexual orientation." The *Code of Ethics* goes on to say, in section 6.04(d): "Social workers should act to prevent and eliminate domination of, exploitation of, and discrimination against any person, group, or class on the basis of ... sexual orientation" (NASW, 1999). Gender expression has not yet been recognized formally in the *Code of Ethics*, though NASW recognizes and fights discrimination based on gender expression (NASW, 2003). In addition to advocating for other activities concerning transgender expression, NASW advocates for education and support of parents of intersex children; development of and participation in coalitions to lobby for the civil rights of people of diverse gender expressions and identities; increased funding for education, treatment services, and research; the repeal of laws and discriminatory practices, especially in employment; and the adoption of laws to facilitate individuals' identifying with and expressing their gender choice in education, housing, inheritance, health and other types of insurance, child custody, property, and other areas (NASW, n.d.).

POLICIES DIRECTED AT GLBT PEOPLE

In the United States, a number of social welfare policies and laws target GLBT people or issues. These policies include sodomy laws, nondiscrimination laws, civil recognition of same-sex couples and transgender relationships, "defense of marriage" laws, anti-GLBT adoption and foster care policies, hate crimes laws, and laws affecting sexual education in schools. In this section, each of these policies, and its ramifications for GLBT people, will be critically reviewed.

SODOMY LAWS

State and federal sodomy laws have profoundly shaped the fight for GLBT rights. These laws, also known as Crimes Against Nature (CAN) laws, criminalized consensual and private intimacy—usually understood to encompass oral and anal sex acts. The National Gay and Lesbian Task Force (2003a) noted:

> In at least six states in 2001 (Indiana, Kansas, Louisiana, Mississippi, Oklahoma and South Carolina), individuals convicted under the sodomy law [were] required to register as sex offenders alongside rapists and child molesters. The effect of this classification [meant] that persons convicted under sodomy laws often [had to] distribute notices to neighborhood residents indicating where one (the "offender") [lived], or take out a classified ad in the local newspaper stating one's "sexual offender" status. One [could] also be denied employment in any profession that works with children. Louisiana already had a sex offender registry but passed a bill to add some additional offenses that would trigger the registration process. "Crimes Against Nature" was one of the added offenses.
>
> (P. 12)

While most CAN laws were designed to apply to both different-sex and same-sex partners, four states had laws targeting only sexual conduct between same-sex partners.

Regardless of whether the individual sodomy law focused specifically on same-sex sex acts, however, courts have used these CAN laws to justify anti-gay interpretations of the law (Cahill, Ellen, & Tobias, 2002, p. 75). Judges often believed that gay men, lesbians, and bisexuals should be seen as criminals, since their sexual orientations predispose them to commit sodomy. These laws have served as the

LAWRENCE V. TEXAS: A WATERSHED DECISION IN GLBT RIGHTS

The case of Lawrence v. Texas began in 1998. Police broke into the house of John Geddes Lawrence because of a report of a man brandishing a handgun. Instead they discovered Lawrence and Tyron Garner having consensual sex in the privacy of Lawrence's home. (A neighbor, angry with Lawrence, had made the false report.) Both men were arrested for breaking Texas's sodomy law, which outlawed same-sex sexual acts, and they were imprisoned overnight. The next day they both pleaded no contest. Each was fined $200 and forced to pay court costs. They appealed the conviction to the Court of Appeals for the Fourteenth District of Texas, challenging the constitutionality of the sodomy law under the equal protection (privacy) and due process clauses of the Fourteenth Amendment. Initially they won. The State of Texas appealed, and Lawrence lost when the court reheard the case en banc. So Lawrence and Garner, supported by New York–based Lambda Legal, appealed to Texas's highest appellate court, which declined to hear the case, and then to the U.S. Supreme Court (Lithwick, 2003; Human Rights Campaign, 2003).

The Supreme Court decision in Lawrence v. Texas overturned a prior decision in Bowers v. Hardwick (1986) and rendered unconstitutional sodomy laws in Texas and the twelve other states where such laws still existed. Writing in the majority opinion, Justice Anthony Kennedy acknowledged: "When homosexual conduct is made criminal by the law of the State, that declaration in and of itself is an invitation to subject homosexual persons to discrimination both in the public and in the private spheres." Kennedy's opinion, also quoted at the beginning of this chapter, issues a strongly worded call for the legal recognition of the right of privacy for gay and lesbian people and the acknowledgment of their dignity. The ruling will surely affect all legal and policy advocacy for GLBT rights for decades to come.

basis for many legal decisions against GLBT people and their families, in areas including child custody, foster parenting, adoption, employment, and housing. It therefore is difficult to overstate the positive effects of the June 2003 Supreme Court decision in *Lawrence v. Texas* that found sodomy laws unconstitutional.

NONDISCRIMINATION LAWS

One of the methods that activists have used to gain civil rights for GLBT people is the creation of nondiscrimination laws. At present, this fight is taking place on a state level; there is no federal nondiscrimination law or constitutional amendment addressing the overarching civil rights of GLBT people. A few courts have found that Title VII of the Civil Rights Act applies to certain kinds of discrimination based on gender nonconformity, seeing this as an extension of the protection against discrimination based on gender (Human Rights Campaign, 2002). In 1999 Democratic presidential hopeful Bill Bradley proposed amending the 1964 Civil Rights Act—which outlaws discrimination rooted in personal characteristics like race, gender, or religion in housing, employment, and lending—to include gay men and lesbians. African American, feminist, and GLBT leaders criticized the idea, fearing that the conservative Congress would use the opportunity to limit civil rights rather than to expand them (Barillas, 1999).

Over the last decade, activists in a variety of states have proposed new non-discrimination laws or suggested the addition of sexual orientation and/or gender expression to existing nondiscrimination laws, with varying results. Currently, the District of Columbia and fourteen states outlaw discrimination based on sexual orientation in employment, housing, and public accommodations (table 19.1). California, Minnesota, New Mexico, Rhode Island, and Washington, DC, have explicit statutory provisions against discrimination based on gender identity. Courts and administrative agencies in seven additional states (Connecticut, Florida, Illinois, Hawaii, Massachusetts, New Jersey, and New York) have interpreted their sex, disability, or sexual orientation discrimination statutes to prohibit certain forms of discrimination against transgender people (Human Rights Campaign, 2002). Kentucky and Pennsylvania have executive orders that protect public workers against discrimination based on sexual orientation and gender expression.

Anti-GLBT activists have responded to these nondiscrimination laws with state and local referenda that would restrict GLBT people from obtaining these protections, arguing that they amount to "special rights." State referenda have been introduced in Arizona, Colorado, Maine, Michigan, Missouri, Oregon, Nevada, and Washington, and local initiatives have been introduced in too many cities to name. Perhaps the most well-known state initiative is Amendment 2 in Colorado, which was designed to repeal existing state and local laws that would have protected GLBT people from discrimination and ban all future laws that would have recognized claims by GLBT people. "The Amendment was passed by voters in 1992, but was declared unconstitutional by the U.S. Supreme Court in 1994.... In the case, known as *Romer v Evans*, the Court ruled that Colorado's Amendment Two violated the equal protection clause of the Fourteenth Amendment to the US Constitution" (Barusch, 2002, pp. 353–354). In light of this ruling, anti-GLBT activists have rewritten their proposals so as to meet constitutional standards. Many are using the example of Issue 3, passed in Cincinnati in 1992, which struck down all "ordinances, regulations, rules, or policies which provided that homosexual, bisexual, or lesbian orientation, status, conduct or relationship constitutes, entitles, or otherwise provides a person with the basis to have any claim of minority or protected status, quota preference, or other preferential treatment" (Murdoch & Price, 2001, p. 484). The language of "protected status" and "preferential treatment," along with the narrow tailoring of the bill, allowed the Sixth Circuit Court to uphold the referendum as constitutional. The fights for and against these nondiscrimination policies are sure to continue.

RECOGNITION OF SAME-SEX RELATIONSHIPS

Perhaps the thorniest issue in the current GLBT political arena is the civil recognition of same-sex relationships. In 1996 the U.S. General Accounting Office

TABLE 19.1 GLBT-Related Policies: A State Analysis

STATE	NONDISCRIMINATION SEXUAL ORIENTATION (SO)	NONDISCRIMINATION GENDER EXPRESSION (GE)	HATE CRIMES SO	HATE CRIMES GE	DOMESTIC PARTNER BENEFITS	DOMA LAW/ CONSTITUTIONAL AMENDMENTS	RESTRICTIVE SEX EDUCATION POLICIES	SECOND-PARENT ADOPTION BY SAME-SEX PARENT
Alabama						-	-	S
Alaska	P					-		S
Arizona	P		+			-	-	
Arkansas					C			
California	+	+	+	+	+	-	-	+
Colorado	P					-		-
Connecticut	+	*	+		+			+
Delaware	P	+	+	+	+	-		S
District of Columbia	+	+	+	+	+			+
Florida	+	*	+			-	-	
Georgia						C		
Hawaii	+	*	+	+	**	-		S
Idaho						-		
Illinois	P	*	+					S
Indiana	P					-	-	S
Iowa			+			-		S
Kansas			+			-		
Kentucky	P	P	+			C		

Louisiana		+			C		S
Maine		+			-		S
Maryland	P	+		+			+
Massachusetts	*			+			S
Michigan	P	+		+	C		
Minnesota	+	+	+		-		S
Mississippi		+	+		C	-	
Missouri		+			C		
Montana	P	+			C		-
Nebraska		+			-		S
Nevada		+			-		+
New Hampshire	*	+					S
New Jersey	+	+			+		+
New Mexico	+ *	+	+		-		S
New York	+	+		+	+		+
North Carolina					-		
North Dakota					C	-	
Ohio					C		
Oklahoma		+			C	-	-
Oregon	P	+	+	+	C		S
Pennsylvania	P	+			-		+
Rhode Island	+	+		+			S
South Carolina					-	-	
South Dakota					-		S

TABLE 19.1 GLBT-Related Policies: A State Analysis (continued)

STATE	NONDISCRIMINATION SEXUAL ORIENTATION (SO)	NONDISCRIMINATION GENDER EXPRESSION (GE)	HATE CRIMES SO	HATE CRIMES GE	DOMESTIC PARTNER BENEFITS	DOMA LAW/ CONSTITUTIONAL AMENDMENTS	RESTRICTIVE SEX EDUCATION POLICIES	SECOND-PARENT ADOPTION BY SAME-SEX PARENT
Tennessee			+			-		
Texas			+			-	-	S
Utah						C	-	
Vermont	+		+	+	***	-		+
Virginia						-		
Washington	P		+		+	-		S
West Virginia						-		
Wisconsin	+		+					-
Wyoming								

Note: + = has a protective law or court decision; - = has a law or decision upholding discriminatory treatment; P = requires that there be no discrimination against public employees based on this category; * = not covered by law, determined instead by an extension of existing protective legislation to include gender expression; ** = Hawaii and California do not offer domestic partner benefits; instead, they offer some of the benefits afforded to spouses; *** = Vermont offers the option of civil unions to same-sex partners, thus according them all the rights of married couples; S = allows in some jurisdictions, but no statewide law or decision; C = state constitution bans recognition of same-sex relationships.

listed 1,049 ways in which marital relationships are given special treatment by the federal government (Cahill et al., 2002). There are also hundreds of rights, benefits, and responsibilities automatically conferred upon married couples that have implications at the local and state levels of government. In a report for the National Gay and Lesbian Task Force, Cahill, Ellen, and Tobias (2002) list some of the most important benefits of marriage:

* The ability to access coverage of partners under Medicare and Social Security.
* The ability to file joint tax returns.
* The ability to obtain death benefits when a partner dies.
* The ability to obtain health and retirement benefits from an employer.
* The right to sponsor his or her spouse for immigration to the U.S.
* The ability to take sick leave or bereavement leave to care for a partner or a partner's child.
* The right to make medical decisions for a partner who falls ill.
* Assumption that children born to a marriage are the children of both partners, regardless of biological relationship.
* Access to stepparent adoption of partner's children.
* The right to use the courts for divorce.
* The right to sue for wrongful death.
* The right to choose the method to dispose of a partner's remains when a partner has died.

(PP. 23–24)

Cahill et al. (2002) also find that children born to a marriage or adopted by their parent's opposite-sex partner obtain the following benefits:

* The right to live with a non-biological parent after a biological parent dies.
* Access to health benefits and the right to inherit death benefits from either parent.
* The right to Social Security benefits if either parent dies.
* The right to financial support and a continued relationship with both parents should their parents separate.

(PP. 23–24)

None of these benefits is automatically conferred on partners in same-sex relationships. It costs thousands of dollars to create legal contracts to achieve minimal protections for same-sex relationships, a price tag that puts this option out of reach for low-income couples. Moreover, many legal protections are conferred by law and cannot be secured by drafting documents or other private arrangements. Even heterosexual relatives suffer as a result of discriminatory marriage laws—for example, parents of a lesbian have no legal status as grandparents to any nonbiological children their daughter is raising (Cahill et al., 2002).

For these reasons, GLBT activists have been fighting for the recognition of same-sex relationships, proposing three different strategies: (1) domestic partnership, (2) marriage, and (3) civil unions.

DOMESTIC PARTNERSHIP

Same-sex and opposite-sex non-marital relationships are sometimes recognized as domestic partnerships (DP) in organizational and civil policies. The term *domestic partner* describes partners in amorous, committed, cohabiting relationships equivalent to a marriage, as opposed to a relationship between roommates or friends. Members of domestic partnerships sometimes qualify for some of the benefits usually associated with marriage. This is important because employee benefits typically constitute around 30 percent of a worker's compensation. Therefore domestic partner benefits are really an issue of equal pay for equal work.

Cahill et al. (2002) identify a variety of benefits associated with domestic partnership, including medical benefits, with dental and vision care; dependent life insurance; accidental death and dismemberment insurance; tuition assistance; long-term-care insurance; day care; flexible spending accounts; bereavement and sick leave; adoption assistance; relocation benefits; child resource and referral services; access to employer recreational facilities; participation in employee assistance programs; inclusion in employee discount policies; and survivor benefits from a partner's pension (pp. 39–40). Unfortunately, DP benefits do not indicate true economic equality. Domestic partner benefits are taxed as income—except on California state income taxes—whereas spousal benefits are not.

As of October 2002, eleven states and the District of Columbia extended benefits to domestic partners of some or all government employees (see table 19.1). Same-sex partners of state employees in Hawaii could also access benefits by registering as "reciprocal beneficiaries." These states were joined by at least 130 cities, local governments, and quasi-governmental agencies and more than 4,500 employers (Cahill et al., 2002). The Human Rights Campaign maintains on its Web site a current list of employers that offer DP benefits.

The number of employers with DP policies has grown with the passage of local equal benefits or "contractor" laws, which require that private companies wishing to do business with a governmental body provide employees' domestic partners with benefits comparable to those provided to spouses of employees. San Francisco was the first city to implement such a law, in 1997. As a result, more than two thousand employers and many insurance companies in San Francisco now offer domestic partner benefits. Other cities and counties that have implemented similar laws include Berkeley, Los Angeles, Oakland, and San Mateo County in California and Seattle and Tumwater in Washington (Cahill et al., 2002).

Legal challenges to DP laws have been pursued in at least fifteen localities, and five of these challenges have been successful. Opponents of DP laws have argued "first, that the jurisdiction had exceeded its state grant of power by regulating a state activity—such as marital status regulations—and, second, that domestic partners did not fit into state statutory definitions ... of who was entitled to benefits" (Cahill et al., 2002, pp. 41–43). Proponents of DP benefits laws respond that "including more family members in health care plans results in a decrease in the number of uninsured, an over-all improvement in public health, and decreased government expenditure" (p. 45). This argument would be moot, though, if same-sex partners were recognized as married in the eyes of the state.

SAME-SEX MARRIAGE

The debate about same-sex marriage has been raging in the United States since 1993, when the Hawaii Supreme Court ruled that it was discriminatory under the state constitution to deny three lesbian and gay couples the right to obtain a marriage license. Hawaii could deny the marriage licenses, they ruled, only if it could indicate a compelling reason to do so. In 1996 the trial court found that the state had failed to justify its denial with a compelling reason, and so the couples must be allowed to marry under civil law. An Alaska trial court also ruled in 1998 that marriage was a fundamental right that could not be denied same-sex couples (Cahill et al., 2002). Yet any movements in either state toward implementing same-sex marriage were curtailed by 1998 amendments to both state constitutions that limited marriage to a man and a woman—though Hawaii did create a limited domestic partnership law, as described in the previous section.

On November 18, 2003, the Massachusetts Supreme Court issued a ruling similar to the ones in Hawaii and Alaska, requiring the state to allow same-sex couples to marry. The court found in *Goodridge et al. v. Department of Public Health* that the guarantees of liberty and equality in the Massachusetts Constitution gave these couples the right to marry a person of their choice, regardless of gender. The justices also wrote that the state could not justify excluding gay and lesbian couples and their families from the institution of marriage and the hundreds of protections it provides. The seven plaintiff couples had been in committed relationships for between six and thirty-two years, and four of the couples are raising children (GLAD, 2003). Massachusetts state lawmakers, following the tradition of Hawaii and Alaska, moved to create an amendment to the state constitution to preclude the recognition of same-sex marriage. The amendment was passed by the legislature on March 29, 2004; to go into effect, "the amendment must be approved a second time by lawmakers during the 2005–2006 legislative session and by voters in November 2006" (Human Rights Campaign, 2004a). In the meantime, thousands of same-sex couples from Massachusetts and other states across the nation have been legally married.

Several months before the first couples were married in Massachusetts, officials in several states began licensing, solemnizing, and marrying same-sex couples. "On Feb. 12, 2004, the county clerk in San Francisco began issuing marriage licenses to same-sex couples, following a directive from Mayor Gavin Newsom.... . That first weekend, 2,340 couples were married, and over the following month, that number grew to more than 4,000" (Human Rights Campaign, 2004b). "Officials in [Portland, Oregon] began issuing marriage licenses to same-sex couples March 3, 2004, and continued doing so for six weeks, despite opponents' repeated attempts to force them to stop" (Human Rights Campaign, 2004c). Similar ceremonies were performed as acts of civil disobedience by mayors in New York and New Mexico.

The ultimate impact of these events remains unclear. "The California state Supreme Court ruled Aug. 12, 2004 that the city of San Francisco did not have the authority to issue marriage licenses to same-sex couples. It also ruled that the 4,037 marriage licenses that had been issued to same-sex couples were void and without any legal effect. The California Supreme Court did not rule on whether California marriage law, which excludes same-sex couples from marrying, violates the California constitution. Cases dealing with the constitutional issue are working their way through the trial court and may be decided by the California Supreme Court at a later date" (Human Rights Campaign, 2004b). In Oregon, the licenses were recognized as legal. On April 20, 2004, "an order from a Circuit Court judge ... brought the marriages to a temporary halt" (Human Rights Campaign, 2004c), and a constitutional amendment against same-sex marriage passed by Oregon voters in November 2004 put an end to same-sex marriages in the state, although it remains unclear how it will affect same-sex Oregon couples who had been legally married. In December 2004, legal challenges to recognize same-sex marriage rights were pending in Connecticut, Indiana, Maryland, New Jersey, and Washington.

CIVIL UNIONS

Another same-sex marriage lawsuit was the basis for the creation of "civil unions" in Vermont. In 1997 several gay and lesbian couples filed a lawsuit, known as *Baker v. State of Vermont*, after they were denied licenses to marry. Two years later, the Vermont Supreme Court decided that current law discriminated against homosexual couples and ordered the legislature to correct the problem, either by allowing same-sex marriage or by establishing a parallel "domestic partnership" status in which couples could register their relationships and enjoy the same civil rights as married couples. The state drafted a bill to establish "civil unions," which was signed into law by Governor Howard Dean (Barusch, 2002, pp. 335–336). It then took another year for the legislature's changes to related laws to go into effect, so that established benefits and programs could recognize members of these unions. At the moment, civil unions are unique to Vermont. Civil union bills have been introduced in a number of states, and an increasing number of elected officials and politicians, including Democratic presidential candidates for the 2004 election, expressed support for civil unions (Cahill et al., 2002).

THE "DEFENSE OF MARRIAGE" ACTS

Right-wing conservatives in Congress responded to the 1996 Hawaii Supreme Court decision by introducing the "Defense of Marriage Act" (DOMA). DOMA, which passed overwhelmingly in both houses of Congress in 1996, defined marriage as a union between a man and a woman for federal purposes. While it does not prohibit states from legalizing same-sex marriages, it denies federal benefits to same-sex couples who might someday win the right to marry legally in any state or overseas. Further, DOMA asserts that states do not have to recognize valid marriages entered into by same-sex couples in another jurisdiction (Cahill et al., 2002, p. 25).

Since the passage of the federal DOMA, its constitutionality has become a source of debate among legal scholars. Because states usually regulate the processes of marriage and divorce, it may be interpreted as unconstitutional for the federal government to develop a policy related to these areas. Also, although states may have different rules and processes for marriage and divorce, it is generally accepted, through the "full faith and credit clause" of the U.S. Constitution, that marriages in one state will be automatically recognized in another state. Cahill et al. (2002) explain:

> The "portability" of marriage and its benefits—which is directly threatened by DOMA—is key to its effectiveness as a family security package. Experts argue that DOMA would be unable to withstand the scrutiny of the United States Supreme Court. Nevertheless, it is unlikely that the law will be tested until one state permits the marriages of same-sex couples, another state or the federal government refuses to recognize those marriages, and the married couples challenge this discrimination.
>
> (PP. 26–27)

Ignoring these legal concerns, states have adopted state-level DOMAs as a way to keep from having to recognize same-sex marriages from another state or country. By February 2004, thirty-nine states had passed anti-same-sex marriage laws, most since the mid-1990s (see table 19.1).

States have also passed what are known as Super-DOMA laws, which have much greater breadth than previous DOMAs. Super-DOMAs aim to prohibit any kind of recognition of the relationships of same-sex couples.

Super-DOMA laws are designed to invalidate a range of measures protecting GLBT families, as well as prevent future advances. They may threaten employee-provided domestic partner benefits, joint and second-parent adoptions, recognition of contracts entered into by same-sex couples, health care decision making proxies, or indeed any policy or legal document that recognizes the existence of a same-sex partnership. In fact, the Pennsylvania Super-DOMA was used to back a court's ruling that a same-sex partner did not qualify for second-parent adoption, although the decision was reversed by the Pennsylvania Supreme Court.

(CAHILL ET AL., 2002, P. 31)

In the 2004 legislative session, as a reaction to the Massachusetts ruling requiring that marriage be available to same-sex couples, legislators in twenty-six states have introduced Super-DOMA laws or amendments that would ban any marriage-related rights and privileges for same-sex, and some unmarried opposite-sex, couples. Thirteen states passed these constitutional amendments in November 2004.

Also in 2004 there was a movement for a federal constitutional amendment, drafted by Republicans, to define marriage as strictly between a man and a woman. This federal marriage amendment would have been difficult to pass, requiring approval by two-thirds of the House and the Senate and ratification by three-fourths of the states to become part of the Constitution. Nonetheless, President Bush, Senate Majority Leader Bill Frist, and other Republicans have publicly supported the idea of such an amendment, and though it died in the Senate, it will be reintroduced in future sessions.

TRANSGENDER MARRIAGE ISSUES

Transgender persons who undergo sex reassignment surgeries encounter distinct problems with regard to marriage laws. In most states, a transgender person who has had sex reassignment surgery can marry a person of the "other sex," as the transgender person is legally recognized as being the post-surgical gender. Yet court cases have muddied the waters in the recognition of marriages by transgender people. In a 2002 case from Kansas, a transsexual woman (a male-to-female transsexual) had been married to a man who died without a will. The woman lost her claim to her husband's estate, which was awarded to his estranged son. The Kansas Supreme Court ruled that, despite the fact that the wife's birth certificate had been amended to state that she was female, she should be considered male and the same sex as her husband, thus making the marriage invalid (Cahill et al., 2002). The legal questions are further complicated by situations in which transgender people claim their gender identity and have sex reassignment surgery while legally married to people of the other sex, thus creating a same-sex couple who are legally recognized as married. No court has addressed this situation. "While there is the possibility that a court would determine that the marriage became invalid when the transition occurred, there is no precedent in U.S. law for involuntarily 'un-marrying' a couple against their will in such a fashion" (Cahill et al., p. 34).

FAMILY POLICIES AND GLBT PARENTS

The legal recognition of same-sex relationships is especially important for GLBT parents. The 2003 Census revealed a large number of same-sex couples raising children: 22.3% of male couples and 34.3% of female couples had children under eighteen years old in their household (Gay Demographics, 2003). Lesbian and gay people of color are more likely than their white counterparts to be parents. "While only 23% of the white women living with a same-sex partner had given birth to one or more children, 30% of Asian/Pacific Islander women, 43% of Hispanic women, and 60% of African American women in same-sex cohabiting relationships had given birth" (Cahill et al., 2002, p. 14) A survey of black GLBT people found that 40% of black lesbians and bisexual women, 15% of black gay and bisexual men, and 15% of black transgender people in 2000 had children. Therefore, family policies have a substantial impact on GLBT families. This section will review laws and policies concerning child custody, adoption, and foster care that directly target GLBT adults.

CHILD CUSTODY AND VISITATION Two specific family configurations are affected by court rulings in child custody cases: (1) separating opposite-sex couples where one of the partners is GLBT; and (2) separating same-sex couples. The threats of losing child custody and visitation are very real.

> A recent report suggests that approximately 30 percent of all lesbian and bisexual female parents, regardless of whether they first had children in a relationship with a heterosexual partner or with a partner of their own gender, have been threatened with loss of custody. Fathers, known sperm donors, female co-parents, grandparents and other relatives all have the potential of bringing custody challenges against lesbian mothers.
>
> (CAHILL ET AL., 2002, P. 74)

As with most policy areas, the courts treat sexual orientation and gender expression very differently. Therefore they will be discussed separately in this section.

When determining child custody in cases involving lesbian, gay, and bisexual parents, courts have used three approaches: "per se," "presumptive," and "nexus." The per se approach views being lesbian or gay [bisexual or transgender] as, in and of itself, a sufficient basis to deny custody to a parent. This approach was prevalent a decade ago, but now is rarely in use (Cahill et al., 2002). More common are the presumptive and nexus approaches. Using the presumptive approach, the court presumes a lesbian or gay parent to be unfit unless he or she can demonstrate that the child will not be exposed to any homosexual influences (Barusch, 2002). In some parts of the country, divorce courts routinely use this approach to impose non-cohabitation restrictions on divorcing parents, preventing them from having unmarried partners live with them or even stay overnight when children are present. Gay and lesbian parents have also been ordered by courts not to take their children to GLBT community events, while transgender parents are often prohibited from cross-dressing in front of their children (Cahill et al., 2002). These restrictions can inhibit the development of a trusting relationship between parent and child; they also perpetuate homophobia and transphobia in the legal system.

The most common approach of recent courts, however, is the nexus approach, wherein a connection between parenting and sexual orientation must be established before it can be discussed in the custody hearing. In 1996 roughly half of the states applied this approach (Barusch, 2002, p. 358). "The District of Columbia is currently the only jurisdiction in the country that has a statute explicitly guaranteeing that sexual orientation cannot, in and of itself, be a conclusive factor in determining custody or visitation" (Cahill et al., 2002, pp. 74–75).

For GLBT co-parents in same-sex couples, many of whom have no biological or legal ties to their children, custody and visitation decisions have been mixed. Cahill et al. (2002) write:

> Supreme Courts in Maryland, Massachusetts, New Jersey, Pennsylvania, Rhode Island and Wisconsin have all found that a co-parent who met specified standards had a legal right to seek visitation and/or custody of a child he or she had raised.... Unfortunately, there have also been numerous cases where the co-parent's relationship with the child was not recognized and the co-parent has been held to not have the standing to ask for visitation or custody.... In the hopes of reversing this trend and promoting greater respect for GLBT families, several GLBT organizations and individuals authored a set of ethical standards for child custody disputes in same-sex relationships.

(PP. 77–78)

These problems reveal the necessity of both parents in a same-sex couple having legal ties to their children, which is usually accomplished through adoption.

FOSTER CARE AND ADOPTION There are two types of adoption: primary and second-parent. Primary adoptions are those in which one or two individuals adopt a child to whom they are not biologically connected. A second-parent adoption is like a stepparent adoption, in which the legal—biological or adoptive—parent retains his or her parental rights, while consenting to the adoption of the child by his or her partner. This section will discuss foster care and both primary and second-parent adoption laws and practices in the United States.

GLBT persons can act as foster parents in all but two states: Arkansas, where the state Child Welfare Agency Review Board has banned gays and lesbians from foster parenting since 1999, and Utah, which prioritizes heterosexual married couples as foster parents (Cahill et al., 2002). Utah takes the same approach with primary adoptions by GLBT people, prioritizing heterosexuals as adoptive parents, and is one of three states (with Florida and Mississippi) that have anti-GLBT adoption policies. Florida prohibits "homosexual individuals" from adopting, while Mississippi denies adoption rights to same-sex couples. There are no laws explicitly denying transgender people the right to adopt, though they may face discrimination in court on the basis of their gender expression. Transgender people who are in same-sex relationships may encounter the same discriminatory treatment as other gay and lesbian potential parents. "Furthermore, an unfriendly judge might use the 'best interest of the child' standard that is a staple of family law as a way to deny both bisexual and transgender people access to adoption" (Cahill et al., 2002).

Many GLBT people choose to adopt children from foreign countries. These adoptions are governed by the Intercountry Adoption Act of 2000, the U.S. implementation of the Hague Convention on International Adoption, which provides structures and safeguards for international adoption (Joint Council on International Children's Services, 2003). In the United States, potential parents must obtain an "orphan's visa" from the U.S. Immigration and Naturalization Service (INS). Often, only one member of a same-sex couple will apply for the visa, though same-sex couples are able to be open with the INS, as a result of a case in 1993 in which the INS ruled that "the relationship a prospective adoptive parent has with another adult in the household is not a reason to deny an orphan's visa petition" (Freiberg, 1998, ¶ 22). International adoptions often allow GLBTs to adopt children who are younger and have fewer disabilities than those available for adoption in the United States.

The legal terrain for second-parent adoption is contested, with few clear laws and conflicting court decisions. By 2004, state and local courts in twenty-three states and the District of Columbia had approved second-parent adoptions involving a same-sex partner (see table 19.1) (Cahill et al., 2002). Second-parent adoption is feasible only if there is no "third parent," such as a biological father who has parented a child with a woman who is now part of a lesbian couple, who also is seen as a legal parent. If a state allows joint adoption but not second-parent adoption, the biological parent can relinquish his or her legal rights and both parents can jointly adopt the child. When neither second-parent nor joint adoptions are allowed, parents can draw up legal documents naming the nonbiological or nonlegal parent as guardian, able to make legal and medical decisions, in the absence of the legal parent. Yet ultimately, in this last case, the co-parent has no real legal tie to the child.

As is evident, current family policies leave GLBT families with tenuous legal standing. While these policies cause financial and practical harm to GLBT parents, it is the children of these families who stand to lose the most. Social workers must work toward the implementation of family policies that will strengthen and support these families.

HARASSMENT AND VIOLENCE

As members of an oppressed minority, GLBT people are often targets of hatred, which may be expressed in harassment, violence, and other hate crimes. This section will review current anti-harassment and hate crimes laws throughout the United States.

ANTI-HARASSMENT LAWS IN PRIMARY AND SECONDARY SCHOOLS One arena in which GLBT youth experience harassment and hate crimes is in school. A survey conducted by the Gay, Lesbian, and Straight Education Network (GLSEN) (2001) found that a majority of GLBT high school students felt unsafe in school because of their sexual orientation (68.6%), experienced verbal harassment (83.2%), and experienced sexual harassment (65.4%). To address these issues, laws in California, Minnesota, and New Jersey prohibit discrimination on the basis of sexual orientation and gender identity, while laws in Connecticut, Massachusetts, Maryland, New York, Vermont, and Wisconsin ban discrimination only against gay, lesbian, and bisexual students. Cahill et al. (2002) describe the differences among some of these statutes:

> Minnesota and New Jersey accomplish this through including the state's schools in the access to "public accommodations" section of their civil rights statute. In Minnesota, students in both public and private schools are protected against discrimination on the basis of both sexual orientation and gender identity. In New Jersey students are protected against sexual orientation discrimination in the state's public schools.... Five states promote nondiscrimination through their education statutes. By cross-referencing its hate crimes statute, California also prohibits discrimination on the basis of "gender."
>
> (P. 111)

These laws require administrators and teachers to intervene when harassment is occurring and to make schools safer for GLBT youth.

HATE CRIMES LEGISLATION Hate crimes legislation at the state and federal levels is designed to impose additional penalties for certain crimes that are based on animus toward some element of a person's identity, specifically an identity of a population that is oppressed. While all but five states have some sort of hate crimes legislation, only seven states have statutes against hate crimes that are based on prejudice toward gender expression, and twenty-nine states have statutes against hate crimes that are based on prejudice toward sexual orientation (see table 19.1) (Human Rights Campaign, 2002, 2003b).

The federal statute used to prosecute hate crimes does not include sexual orientation or gender expression as protected categories. However, three other federal laws related to hate crimes do include sexual orientation.

> The federal *Hate Crimes Statistics Act*, U.S.C. 524, which became law in 1990 and was reauthorized in 1996, authorizes the FBI to collect statistics on hate crimes on the basis of race, religion, ethnicity, sexual orientation and disability. The federal *Hate Crimes Sentencing Enhancement Act*, U.S.C. 994, which was passed as a part of the *Violent Crime Control and Law Enforcement Act* of 1994, directs the U.S. Sentencing Commission to provide sentencing enhancements of "not less than three offense levels for offenses that the finder of fact at trial determines beyond a reasonable doubt are hate crimes." ... The Hate Crimes Sentencing Enhancement Act is rarely enforced.
>
> (HUMAN RIGHTS CAMPAIGN, 2002, P. 29)

In 1998 another federal statute related to hate crimes was passed as part of the Higher Education Reauthorization Act. The Hate Crimes Right to Know Act "requires campus security authorities to collect and report hate crimes according to categories of prejudice, including sexual orientation bias. Campus security authorities are also required to develop programs and strategies to combat these crimes" (National Gay and Lesbian Task Force, 2003b). So while the current federal hate crimes law does not address crimes based on the sexual orientation or gender expression of the victim, other related laws pertaining to gathering statistics and sentencing do recognize these hate crimes.

To remedy this conflict, GLBT activists have been working with friendly politicians to pass federal hate crimes legislation that would include sexual orientation and gender expression. First introduced in 2001 as the Local Law Enforcement Enhancement Act (LLEEA), the statute would

* add gender, sexual orientation, and disability to the current hate crimes statute
* require only that the crime be connected to interstate travel or interstate commerce, and not to a federal right
* authorize the attorney general to make grants up to $100,000 and provide technical assistance to local law enforcement authorities
* allow federal prosecutors to bring federal charges only if the attorney general or his or her designee certifies that the local law enforcement authorities are unwill-

ing or unable to properly investigate or prosecute a hate crime (National Gay and Lesbian Task Force, 2003c).

In 2004 the bill was passed in the Senate, as part of a defense authorization bill, but it was stripped from the larger bill in conference committee. Advocates believe that with bipartisan support in the House and the Senate, the bill will eventually become law.

SEX EDUCATION POLICIES

Another area of policy that is specifically directed at issues of sexual orientation is sex education policies. (Gender expression is rarely recognized in part of the sex education curriculum and thus is often ignored in these policies.) Sex education policies are usually state and local concerns, though Congress has weighed in on the issue of appropriate sex education. While federal laws prohibit the federal government from requiring sex education programs or dictating the content of such programs, there are three sources of federal funds that support abstinence-focused education. The first is the Adolescent Family Life Act (AFLA), a grant program established in 1981 that awards funds to public and nonprofit organizations for the prevention of adolescent premarital sexual relations and adolescent pregnancy. Most of the recipients of these grants have been religious organizations, though they are precluded from using religious language and are required to respect the self-determination of teenagers.

The second policy that funds sex education is Section 510(b) of Title V of the Social Security Act, which provides abstinence-only matching funding to states through 1996 welfare reform legislation. This program requires, among other things, that recipients teach that a mutually faithful monogamous relationship in the context of marriage is the expected standard of human sexual activity, a standard that lesbian and gay people are unable to meet. The third federal program is the Special Projects of Regional and National Significance–Community-Based Abstinence Education (SPRANS-CBAE) grant program, approved in 2000, which prescribes a more strict abstinence education program, requires no state matching funds, and provides funding from the Maternal and Child Health Bureau directly to individual organizations. All three of these programs promote abstinence in sex education.

These three programs have been generously funded by Congress. In fiscal year 2002 federal appropriations for promoting abstinence-only sex education reached $102 million. President Bush proposed a $33 million increase in abstinence-only sex education for the fiscal year 2003 budget. All states but California receive the welfare reform abstinence education funds (Collins, Alagiri, & Summers, 2002, SIECUS, 2001).

The impact of these federal abstinence education policies, and their implicit or explicit condemnation of same-sex sexuality, is reflected in similar policies on the state level. Cahill et al. (2002) note:

> Six states (Alabama, Arizona, Mississippi, South Carolina, Texas, and Utah) have laws prohibiting the "promotion of homosexuality as an acceptable lifestyle" in sexual education courses. Another four (California, Florida, Indiana, and Louisiana) have laws which require the promotion of monogamous heterosexual marriage, while North Carolina and Oklahoma require a [consistent] correlation between homosexuality and the spread of HIV.
>
> (P. 126)

As a result of these laws, gay, lesbian, and bisexual students in these states do not see accurate or accepting images of themselves in sex education courses, nor do they receive appropriate or necessary safer-sex education about practices in which they may engage. This omission puts these children at increased emotional and physical risk. GLBT activists and their allies are organized in each of these states to overturn these laws and work for inclusive and appropriate sexual education.

SOCIAL WELFARE POLICIES THAT AFFECT GLBTS

Other than the policies mentioned above, most mainstream social welfare policies in areas such as public assistance, housing, employment, child welfare, health and mental health, services to the aging, criminal justice, and immigration do not explicitly mention sexual orientation and/or gender expression. However, these programs do have a profound impact on the lives of GLBT people and their families. This section will review current policies and programs in these areas and identify ways in which they discriminate or differentially affect GLBT people.

PUBLIC ASSISTANCE

Three aspects of the Personal Responsibility Work Opportunity Reconciliation Act (PRWORA)—specifically the subsection known as Temporary Assistance to Needy Families (TANF)—have adverse ramifications for GLBT people: the work requirement, the paternity identification requirement, and the marriage incentive programs. The work requirement, known by critics as "workfare," requires that recipients work or volunteer for twenty to thirty-five hours a week or receive a reduction in their benefit. This mandate can be an extra burden for GLBT people, who may experience discrimination and harassment at work sites for which there is often no legal recourse. Cahill and Jones (2001) report that a majority of transgender clients at New York City's Gender Identity Project have been verbally and physically harassed at workfare assignments and tend to drop off the welfare rolls as a result. Perhaps if there were a federal law prohibiting discrimination in employment on the basis of sexual orientation and gender expression, this requirement would not be as oppressive for GLBT people.

Another discriminatory requirement is the paternity program, which requires that recipient mothers identify the biological father of their child for the purpose of obtaining child support. (Single fathers, however, do not have to identify the maternity of their children [Cahill et al., 2002].) Lesbian individuals or couples who have been inseminated by an unknown donor cannot meet this obligation; lesbian parents who know the donor but who did not plan to have him take responsibility for the child face a different dilemma. Lesbians who cannot or will not comply with these regulations suffer a 25% decrease in cash assistance and risk termination of benefits (Cahill & Jones, 2001). This policy, then, imposes a heterosexual family structure on lesbian families and, in the case of lesbian co-parents, disregards the responsibilities of the nonbiological lesbian parent.

The marriage incentive program also forces the heterosexual paradigm on GLBT parents. Though the implementation of this policy differs in various states, many states offer cash incentives for recipients to marry or to attend pro-marriage counseling. Same-sex couples are not eligible for the cash incentives, since they cannot legally marry and attending pro-marriage counseling could be regarded as emotionally abusive to recipients who are not heterosexual.

Given the political volatility of TANF legislation, it is unlikely that any revisions to this legislation will be made to assist the GLBT people who receive these benefits. Politicians are more concerned with the larger issues of individual responsibility, public financing, and the establishment of a work ethic among low-income people. GLBT advocates do try to work with anti-poverty activists to reform these programs for all recipients.

HOUSING

Most GLBT families have no legal remedy if they encounter discrimination in purchasing or renting a dwelling. There is no federal law banning discrimination in housing that is based upon sexual orientation or gender expression, though ten states and the District of Columbia ban discrimination on the basis of sexual orientation (Cahill et al., 2002). The Department of Housing and Urban Development (HUD) does have a rule banning discrimination based on the sexual orientation of applicants who are applying for its subsidized rental properties. Two unrelated individuals may apply for an apartment together, and HUD rules prevent housing personnel from asking about the nature of the relationship between the pair who are applying for the apartment. However, since the household income eligibility requirements are so low, most couples would have too much income to qualify for such housing (Cahill, South, & Spade, 2000).

Homeless GLBT people face different dilemmas in accessing emergency shelter. No federal requirements for nondiscrimination in shelters based on sexual orientation or gender expression exist as part of any federal programs that fund emergency shelters. Consequently, partners in same-sex relationships are often separated from each other when they enter shelters and are subjected to discriminatory treatment by shelter staff. Transgender people may be forced to enter a shelter based upon their sex at birth, rather than their chosen gender, or they may be denied shelter altogether (Cahill et al., 2002). Further, in case management, relationships between GLBT people may be ignored and devalued. These factors can cause GLBT people to choose to live on the street rather than to access these services.

EMPLOYMENT

A cursory review of employment law reveals that most GLBT people have no protection from harassment and discrimination in the workplace. While there is no federal bill protecting GLBT people from discrimination in all employment settings, Executive Order No. 13087, issued by the Clinton administration in 1998, does ban discrimination based on sexual orientation in federal agencies (other than the military) but does not include employment protection for transgender people (Cahill et al., 2000, p. 77). In 2002 twelve states and the District of Columbia prohibited discrimination on the basis of sexual orientation in both the public and the private sectors, while nine states banned discrimination only in the public sector (Cahill et al., 2002, pp. 166–168). More than two hundred cities, towns, and counties have laws prohibiting discrimination based on sexual orientation, although they differ as to whether they apply to public and/or private agencies. Two states, along with thirty-three municipalities, explicitly ban discrimination in public agencies on the basis of gender identity (Cahill & Jones, 2001; Currah & Minter, 2000). This still leaves many GLBT people without protections.

To address this need, advocates introduced the federal Employment Non-discrimination Act (ENDA), which would bar employers from discriminating based on sexual orientation in hiring, firing, promotion, and compensation in private and public businesses. Though original versions had included gender expression, compromises among GLBT activists and politicians led to a bill focused only on sexual orientation. ENDA would not apply to the military, religious organizations, or businesses employing fewer than fifteen people. It specifically does not establish affirmative action for sexual minorities (Barusch, 2002). In 2002 ENDA made it to the floor of the full Senate, though it died in session. At the end of the 107th Congress, the bill had 44 cosponsors in the Senate and 191 in the House and was supported by more than 90 corporations. The bill was reintroduced in the 108th Congress (Herrschaft & Mills, 2003), and advocates continue to work for its passage.

CHILD WELFARE

In his book on gay and lesbian youth in foster care, Gerald Mallon (1998) found evidence of discriminatory and harassing treatment of GLBT youth by foster parents and residential care staff. Yet, in 2002, there was not one state foster care system that had an official policy prohibiting discrimination on the basis of sexual orientation or gender expression (Cahill et al., 2002). California almost became an exception with AB 2651, a bill establishing GLBT sensitivity training for foster parents and directing California's Department of Social Services to recruit GLBT adults to become foster parents for GLBT youth, which was passed by the state legislature. Unfortunately, the bill was vetoed by Governor Gray Davis. Without such legislation, GLBT youth will continue to experience discrimination and harassment by workers and volunteers who are insensitive regarding sexual orientation and gender expression.

HEALTH AND MENTAL HEALTH

The failure of the federal government to recognize the civil rights of GLBT people has had a profound influence on the design and impact of state and federal health and mental health care policies. Regulations regarding (1) health care decision making for a same-sex partner, (2) Medicaid and Medicare, (3) family medical leave, and (4) the institutionalization of GLBT youth all adversely affect the lives of GLBT people. This section will review each of these policy issues.

Being married automatically grants people the right to visit their partner in the hospital, to make health care decisions if their partner is incapacitated, and to supervise their partner's funeral arrangements if the partner dies. This is not the case for same-sex partners, who are regarded as unrelated persons who must secure a medical power of attorney form in order to make medical decisions and a financial power of attorney form in order to act as their partner's financial proxy and pay bills or sell assets (Cahill et al., 2002). The few exceptions could be Vermont couples who have had a civil union or some of those couples who have registered in communities that offer domestic partner registries, depending on the local regulations.

Unfortunately, domestic partner registries and civil unions do not have any standing with regard to federal insurance programs like Medicaid and Medicare; as a result, GLBT people in same-sex relationships suffer in their health care and economic well-being. For example, Medicaid regulations allow one member of a married heterosexual couple to remain in the couple's home for the rest of his or her life without jeopardizing his or her spouse's right to Medicaid coverage. Upon the survivor's death, the state may then take the home to recoup the costs of terminal care. Because same-sex relationships are not recognized, members of a same-sex couple could be forced to live separately from one another so that the ill partner could qualify for benefits, or they might have to spend down their savings and sell their home in order to qualify (Cahill et al., 2002). Another example of disparate treatment is the refusal of Medicaid and Medicare to cover hormone therapy or sex reassignment surgery for transsexuals, even though those procedures may be necessary for their mental health (Cahill et al., 2000).

The federal Family and Medical Leave Act (FMLA), passed in 1993, also discriminates against GLBT families. The FMLA provides up to twelve weeks of unpaid leave after the birth or adoption of a child, to facilitate recovery from a serious health condition, or to care for an immediate family member who is extremely sick. The definition of "family member" is a blood relation, child, or spouse, where "spouse means a husband or wife as defined or recognized under State law for purposes of marriage in the State where the employee resides, including common law marriage in States where it is recognized" (Cahill et al., 2002, p. 157). This construction of who is a qualifying family member puts members of same-sex relationships at a distinct disadvantage, making them more susceptible to termination if they miss work to care for a partner or a partner's child. Three states—California, Hawaii, and Vermont—include same-sex partners in their definition of family, allowing them to qualify for FMLA leave.

The final area of discrimination in mental health care policy to be discussed here affects GLBT youth. Cahill et al. (2002) found that despite the decision by the American Psychiatric Association to remove sexual orientation from its list of mental disorders, GLBT youth are often being inaccurately diagnosed with gender identity disorder, oppositional defiant disorder, and depression, and are being institutionalized by their parents for treatment of these "disorders." Since the law gives parents "broad legal control over the mental health treatment of their minor children" (p. 130), GLBT youth have little recourse. Courts are known to rely on the testimony of mental health practitioners associated with residential treatment facilities in their decisions. As a result, GLBT youth are inappropriately consigned to these facilities to "fix" their sexual orientation or gender identity, an approach that can have profound consequences for their long-term mental health.

POLICIES FOR THE AGING

Aging is another area of policy where the lack of recognition of same-sex relationships greatly affects the financial and social well-being of same-sex couples. Partners in same-sex couples are not eligible for survivor's benefits or spousal benefits. Cahill et al. (2002) point out:

> In 1998, 781,000 widows and widowers received an average of $442 a month in survivor benefits, a total of $4.1 billion dollars that year. If only 3 percent of the total population of seniors who survived their life partner are gay, lesbian, or bisexual same-sex partners, the failure to pay survivor benefits costs these seniors about $124 million a year.

(P. 138)

In same-sex couples where one partner has significantly more income than the other partner, the lower-paid partner also can suffer financially from not being eligible for the spousal benefit—a Social Security check that is worth 50% of the higher-paid partner's benefit, rather than his or her own check, which might be lower. Same-sex partners are also not provided any shelter from taxes when they are listed as beneficiaries of a deceased partner's pension or 401(k) retirement funds, often paying taxes as high as 20% on these monies.

Fortunately, there is a policy in the area of aging that provides some financial support for GLBT elders. The Older Americans Act (OAA), passed in 1965, provides funds for services to seniors and their caregivers. Part E of the OAA, also known as the National Family Caregiver Support Program, provides financial support for caregivers who include "an adult family member, or another individual, who is an informal provider of in-home and community care to an older individual" (Cahill et al., 2000, p. 40). This definition of caregivers allows the compensation of partners and friends who provide care to GLBT seniors to offset the financial costs.

CRIMINAL JUSTICE: DOMESTIC VIOLENCE LAWS

Domestic violence (DV) laws protect individuals from harassment, battery, rape, and physical harm by a person with whom they live or engage in an intimate relationship. Most DV laws are gender-neutral and apply to both men and women perpetrators, but there is often the assumption that the perpetrator and the victim are family members, housemates, or partners in a heterosexual relationship. As a result, GLBT victims of DV frequently have limited recourse.

In eighteen states, same-sex perpetrators can be prosecuted only if they reside with the victim. Three states—Delaware, Montana, and South Carolina—will not issue domestic violence protective orders, which require that the perpetrator refrain from contact with the victim, to a victim in a same-sex couple. Even the federal Violence Against Women Act (VAWA), which provides legal remedy for women abducted and transported across state lines by a partner, has no provision for men who are victims of a same-sex partner (Cahill et al., 2002). As a result, GLBT people in same-sex relationships are not afforded the same protections from partner violence as their heterosexual counterparts receive.

IMMIGRATION

Though there were once laws that excluded gay and lesbian people from immigrating to the United States, such legislation is no longer a part of U.S. immigration law. There are, however, other discriminatory policies in this area. For example, U.S. citizens are allowed to sponsor family members and spouses who are citizens of another country as they immigrate. This option is not available to citizens who are in same-sex relationships with people from other countries. As a result, foreign partners in same-sex couples either cannot enter the country or can enter only on a temporary basis, resulting in worry about deportation and employability. While foreign partners can obtain work visas and other visas, the legal fees can be too high for many (Cahill et al., 2002). Once again, the legal restrictions on recognizing same-sex relationships impose undue burdens on these couples.

WORKING FOR CHANGE: GLBT POLICY ADVOCACY

John D'Emilio (2002) discusses the most recent movement in GLBT advocacy as focusing on three distinct spheres: family, school, and work. He lists key issues in these areas for the current GLBT movement:

> The recognition of same-sex relationships either through domestic partnership arrangements, civil unions, or the legalization of same-sex marriage; the assertion of the right to parent, the quest for adoption, foster care, and custody policies, and the need to have the law recognize that some children have parents of the same gender; the proliferation of lesbian, gay, bisexual, and transgendered employee groups across the country and their efforts to achieve workplace equity; the local battles over school curricula, the rights of students to organize gay-straight alliance clubs, the need of gay-supportive counseling and other policies in order to make schools safer places for students of all sexual identities.
>
> (P. 97)

To pursue these (and other) policy goals, GLBT activists and their allies employ a variety of institutional and grassroots strategies. The next section will review these strategies, highlighting the ways that each strategy can be used and the national, state, and local organizations that utilize them. (Postal, Web, and e-mail addresses for each of these organizations are listed in table 19.2.) Social workers, who are called by the NASW *Code of Ethics* to support GLBT claims for social justice, should consider which of these strategies they might use.

INSTITUTIONAL STRATEGIES

In their book on effecting change in the political arena, Haynes and Mickelson (2003) identify many institutional strategies employed by social workers, including being involved in political action committees, joining political parties, running for office, conducting research, and filing lawsuits and friend-of-the-court briefs. GLBT rights advocates have utilized each of these methods.

Political action committees (PACs) are independent organizations that collect funds from members of a political interest group and dispense these funds to sup-

TABLE 19.2 GLBT Policy Resources

American Civil Liberties Union (ACLU) Lesbian and Gay
Rights Project
http://www.aclu.org
125 Broad St., 18th floor
New York, NY 10004
(212) 549-2627
lgbthiv@aclu.org

ANGLE—Access Now for Gay and Lesbian Equality
http://www.angleonline.org/
8721 Santa Monica Blvd., Suite 214
West Hollywood, CA 90069-4511

Gay and Lesbian Victory Fund
www.victoryfund.org
1705 DeSales St., NW, Suite 500
Washington, DC 20036
(202) VICTORY

Gay, Lesbian, and Straight Education Network (GLSEN)
http://www.glsen.org
121 W. Twenty-seventh St., Suite 804
New York, NY 10001-6207
(212) 727-0135
glsen@glsen.org

Gender Education and Advocacy (GEA)
http://www.gender.org

GenderPAC
http://www.gpac.org
1743 Connecticut Ave., NW, 4th floor
Washington, DC 20009-1108
(202) 462-6610
gpac@gpac.org

Lambda Legal Defense and Education Fund (LLDEF)
http://www.lambdalegal.org
120 Wall St., Suite 1500
New York, NY 10005
(212) 809-8585
lambdalegal@lambdalegal. org

Lesbian and Gay Immigration Rights Task Force
http://www.lgirtf.org
350 W. Thirty-first St., Suite 505
New York, NY 10001
(212) 714-2904
info@lgirtf.org

Log Cabin Republicans
http://www.lcr.org/
1607 Seventeenth St., NW
Washington, DC 20009
(202) 347-5306
info@lcr.org

National Center for Lesbian Rights (NCLR)
http://www.nclrights.org
870 Market St., Suite 570
San Francisco, CA 94102
(415) 392-6257
info@nclrights.org

National Gay and Lesbian Task Force (NGLTF)
http://www.ngltf.org/
1325 Massachusetts Ave., NW, Suite 600
Washington, DC 20005
(202) 393-5177
ngltf@ngltf.org

National Latina/o Lesbian, Gay, Bisexual,
and Transgender Organization
http://www.llego.org
1420 K St., NW, Suite 200
Washington, DC 20005
(202) 408-5380

National Stonewall Democrats
http://www.stonewall democrats.org/
P.O. Box 9330
Washington, DC 20005
(202) 625-1382
field@stonewalldemocrats.org

National Transgender Advocacy Coalition
http://www.ntac.org/
P.O. Box 76027
Washington, DC 20013
info@ntac.org

Parents, Families, and Friends of Lesbians
and Gays (PFLAG)
http://www.pflag.org
1726 M St., NW, Suite 400
Washington, DC 20036
(202) 467-8180
info@pflag.org

portive candidates for political offices. They also educate PAC members and politicians, research candidate positions on the issues, and provide formal collective endorsement for candidates. The most famous GLBT PAC is the Human Rights Campaign, which began as a PAC supporting candidates for federal office who were sympathetic on GLBT issues; the Human Rights Campaign now engages in all aspects of policy advocacy. Other national PACs include the Gay and Lesbian Victory Fund, which funds candidates for state and local offices; GenderPAC, an organization dedicated to ending oppression based on gender stereotypes by changing public attitudes, educating elected officials, and expanding legal rights; and ANGLE—Access Now for Gay and Lesbian Equality, a California-based PAC that raises funds for candidates in local, state, and national elections and advocates on policy issues of interest to GLBT people, especially in the areas of HIV/AIDS. Other states have GLBT-related PACs, such as Equality-NC PAC in North Carolina and the Gay and Lesbian Voters Political Action Committee in Pennsylvania. Social workers can volunteer with these PACs, attend their events, and contribute funds for candidates.

While PACs are nonpartisan organizations, there are also GLBT-specific organizations in each of the two major parties. The National Stonewall Democrats and the Log Cabin Republicans both advocate for GLBT issues within their parties, working for the inclusion of GLBT-related planks in party platforms and educating the GLBT community about the differences between the political parties. Though social workers cannot usually advocate for a political party as part of their employment, they are free and encouraged to be engaged in their political organizations as private citizens.

Social workers can also serve as candidates for office, working as advocates for GLBT issues from within. GLBT-friendly candidates are needed at all levels of government and on school boards. Social workers are in a unique position, having been educated about the needs and concerns of GLBT people, trained with the knowledge and skills necessary for government office, and possessed by a commitment to public service.

There are also a number of national advocacy groups that engage in and support GLBT-related issues. The Human Rights Campaign tracks changes in national and state policies, offers a wealth of educational materials on its Web site, and provides support for advocacy. The National Gay and Lesbian Task Force trains grassroots leaders across the United States, supports regional conferences on GLBT issues, and maintains a think tank, known as the NGLTF Policy Institute, to conduct research on GLBT policy issues. Another think tank, the Institute for Gay and Lesbian Strategic Studies, engages in academic and political research, collects data from other researchers, and disseminates findings for the purposes of GLBT advocacy. Gender Education and Advocacy (GEA) and the National Transgender Advocacy Coalition (NTAC) offer information services, educational materials, advocacy training, and technical assistance on the needs, issues, and concerns of gender-variant people. Social workers can join these organizations and use the resources they provide, along with other state and local advocacy groups, to work for changes in their communities and states, and in the entire country.

Finally, social workers can be involved with the legal system by working with national legal advocacy organizations supporting GLBT positions in legal cases. The Lambda Legal Defense Fund and the American Civil Liberties Union (ACLU) Lesbian and Gay Rights Project provide legal counsel and represent GLBT parties in cases of legal significance to the GLBT community. These organizations also file, and organize others to file, amicus curiae or "friend of the court" briefs—statements supporting one side of a legal case by a party who is not involved in the case but who believes the court's decision may affect its interest. These briefs are common in Supreme Court cases; for example, the National Association of Social Workers (NASW) and its Texas chapter—together with the American Psychological Association and the American Psychiatric Association—filed an amicus curiae brief supporting the petitioners in the *Lawrence v. Texas* case. Social workers can conduct research, provide expert testimony, and write these briefs.

GRASSROOTS STRATEGIES

Social workers do not need to work on a national stage to have an impact on GLBT issues in social welfare policy. In fact, perhaps the most successful venue for advocacy on these issues is the local community. One-on-one connection and public speaking in one's local community, where one is known and knows the culture and politics of one's neighbors, may be more effective than national activism. There are many ways for social workers, and their GLBT clients, to be involved in local advocacy, using a variety of approaches.

Local and regional GLBT groups often serve two functions: education and interpersonal support. More than 139 GLBT community centers and youth centers in thirty-six states provide service and support for GLBT people; many also offer education and training for advocacy concerning GLBT policy issues (National Association of Lesbian, Gay, Bisexual, and Transgender Community Centers, 2003). Local and regional chapters of Parents and Friends of Lesbians and Gays (PFLAG) and the Gay, Lesbian, and Straight Education Network (GLSEN) educate community members about GLBT issues and advocate for local changes. Community groups serving GLBT people of diverse racial and ethnic backgrounds provide support around GLBT issues as they affect their constituents. Local chapters of national religious GLBT groups like Integrity, Reconciling United Methodists, Rainbow Baptists, More Light Presbyterians, and the like advocate for secular and religious policy issues, often using newsletters or e-mail listservs to keep members updated on challenges and opportunities for change. Social workers can join these groups, refer their clients, or receive their newsletters or e-mails to stay up to date on local issues.

Social workers can work with state and local advocacy groups to lobby elected officials on GLBT policy issues, contacting officials and candidates through letters, e-mails, phone calls, and personal visits. The Human Rights Campaign (HRC) maintains a grassroots advocacy Web site with federal- and state-level updates on policy issues related to GLBT rights (http://www.hrc.org/actioncenter/grassroots.asp). HRC's online action center allows interested people to communicate directly—from their own computer—with state and federal elected officials. People can write their own message or use the prepared text, and the action center will send the e-mail to key decision makers. For particularly urgent action, it faxes the message or connects the writer by phone to them. Social workers can also testify and work with their clients to prepare them to testify at public hearings about GLBT-related policies.

Another area of involvement is to join the groups and individuals that are using protest and celebration strategies to bring media attention to GLBT issues. The eleven U.S. chapters of AIDS Coalition to Unleash Power (ACT-UP) frequently engage in confrontational "actions," demonstrations, and civil disobedience to raise the public's awareness of GLBT issues and to pressure elected officials to make better policy decisions, especially pertaining to HIV and AIDS. The GLBT Pride marches and rallies held across the United States represent additional advocacy strategies, fostering a sense of GLBT community and celebrating people's diverse identities, while educating the larger society about GLBT cultural and political concerns. These more-confrontational strategies complement the "friendly" grassroots strategies described above, furthering the movement for GLBT civil rights.

CONCLUSION

Many areas of social welfare policy discriminate against GLBT people—either actively, by treating them as different from and somehow less than other citizens, or passively, by ignoring the different ways in which sexual orientation or gender expression affects people's lived experiences. As social workers, we are called to use social work knowledge and skills to engage in advocacy, working against discrimination and for equality of all people, including gay men, lesbians, and bisexual and transgender people. Only through this advocacy can these policies be reformed and this country become a place where all people, regardless of their sexual orientation or gender expression, are valued and treated equitably.

REFERENCES

Barillas, C. (1999, September 21). Frank knocks Bradley on amending Civil Rights Act. *Data Lounge*. Retrieved July 21, 2003, from http://www.datalounge.com/datalounge/news/ record.html?record = 4673.

Barusch, A. S. (2002). *Foundations of social policy: Social justice, public programs, and the social work profession*. Itasca, IL: F. E. Peacock.

Cahill, S., Ellen, M., & Tobias, S. (2002). *Family policy: Issues affecting gay, lesbian, bisexual, and transgendered families*. New York: National Gay and Lesbian Task Force Policy Institute.

Cahill, S., & Jones, K. T. (2001). *Leaving our children behind: Welfare reform and the gay, lesbian, bisexual, and transgender community*. New York: National Gay and Lesbian Task Force Policy Institute.

Cahill, S., South, K., & Spade, J. (2000). *Outing age: Public policy issues affecting gay, lesbian, bisexual, and transgender elders*. New York: National Gay and Lesbian Task Force Policy Institute.

Collins, C., Alagiri, P., & Summers, T. (2002). *Abstinence only vs. comprehensive sex education: What are the arguments? What is the evidence?* San Francisco: AIDS Research Institute, University of California, San Francisco. Retrieved August 22, 2003, from http://ari.ucsf.edu/pdf/abstinence.pdf.

Currah, P., & Minter, S. (2000). *Transgender equality: A handbook for activists and policymakers*. New York: National Gay and Lesbian Task Force Policy Institute.

D'Emilio, J. (2002). *The world turned: Essays on gay history, politics, and culture*. Durham, NC: Duke University Press.

Freiberg, P. (1998). http://www.gay.ru/english/life/family/newroute.htm.

Gay and Lesbian Advocates and Defenders (GLAD). (2003). *Massachusetts' highest court hears landmark suit seeking civil marriage for lesbian and gay couples*. Retrieved July 21, 2003, from http://www.glad.org/.

Gay Demographics. (2003). *Percent of households with children under 18 years*. Retrieved August 14, 2003, from http://www.gaydemographics.org/USA/SF1_children.html.

Gay, Lesbian, and Straight Education Network (GLSEN). (2001). *The 2001 national school climate survey*. New York: Author. Retrieved August 14, 2003, from http://www.glsen.org/binary-data/GLSEN_ARTICLES/pdf_file/1029.pdf.

Haynes, K. S., & Mickelson, J. S. (2003). *Affecting change: Social workers in the political arena* (5th ed.). Boston: Allyn and Bacon.

Herrschaft, D., & Mills, K. I. (2003). *The state of the workplace for lesbian, gay, bisexual, and transgender Americans 2002*. Washington, DC: Human Rights Campaign.

Holland, J. (2003, July 20). U.S. awaiting court ruling on gay marriage in Mass. *Hearst Newspapers*. Retrieved July 21, 2003, from http://www.aacentral.com/news/article/0720gaymarriage20.html.

Human Rights Campaign. (2002). *The state of the family: Laws and legislation affecting gay, lesbian, bisexual, and transgender families*. Washington, DC: Author.

——. (2003a, June 26). *HRC lauds landmark Supreme Court ruling striking down state sodomy laws, recognizing right to privacy for GLBT Americans*. Retrieved July 23, 2003, from http://www.hrc.org/newsreleases/2003/030626sodomy.asp.

——. (2003b). *Statewide hate crimes laws*. Retrieved September 6, 2003, from http://www.hrc.org/stateaction/hatecrime.pdf.

——. (2004a). *Massachusetts Marriage/Relationship Recognition Law*. Retrieved December 3, 2004, from http://www.hrc.org/Template.cfm?Section=Home&CONTENTID=21686&TEMPLATE=/ContentManagement/ContentDisplay.cfm.

———. (2004b). *California Marriage/Relationship Recognition Law*. Retrieved December 3, 2004, from http://www.hrc.org/Template.cfm?Section=Center&Template=/TaggedPage/TaggedPageDisplay.cfm&TPLID=63&ContentID=17353.

Joint Council on International Children's Services. (2003). *Hague Convention*. Retrieved July 23, 2003, from http://www.jcics.org/haguetop.html.

Lithwick, D. (2003, March 26). *The Supreme Court tries sodomy … and discovers that Texas is confused about it too*. Retrieved July 23, 2003, from http://slate.msn.com/id/2080746/.

Mallon, G. (1998). *We don't exactly get the welcome wagon: The experiences of gay and lesbian adolescents in child welfare systems*. New York: Columbia University Press.

Murdoch, J., & Price, D. (2001). *Courting justice: Gay men and lesbians v. the Supreme Court*. New York: Basic Books.

National Association of Lesbian, Gay, Bisexual, and Transgender Community Centers. (2003). *International directory of lesbian, gay, bisexual, and transgender community centers and LGBT organizations* (48th ed.). Garden Grove, CA: Author.

National Association of Social Workers. (1999). *Code of ethics of the National Association of Social Workers*. Retrieved July 12, 2003, from https://www.socialworkers.org/pubs/code/code.asp.

———. (2003). *Social work speaks, sixth edition: NASW policy statements, 2003–2006*. Washington, DC: NASW Press.

———. (n.d.). *Social work speaks abstracts: Transgender and gender identity issues*. Retrieved July 12, 2003, from http://www.socialworkers.org/resources/abstracts/abstracts/transgender.asp.

National Gay and Lesbian Task Force. (2003a). *Capital gains and losses: A state by state review of gay, lesbian, bisexual, transgender, and HIV/AIDS-related legislation in 2001*. Washington, DC: Author.

———. (2003b). *The Local Law Enforcement Act: The appropriate next step in federal hate crimes law*. Retrieved July 12, 2003, from http://www.ngltf.org/downloads/fedhatecrimeslaw.pdf.

———. (2003c). *The Local Law Enforcement Enhancement Act: An important step in combating hate violence*. Retrieved July 12, 2003, from http://www.ngltf.org/downloads/locallawenfact.pdf.

SIECUS. (August/September 2001). *SIECUS reports supplement, 9*(6), 1–8. Retrieved August 22, 2003, from http://www.siecus.org/pubs/fact/FS_issues_answers.pdf.

20

TOWARD AFFIRMATIVE PRACTICE

Lori Messinger

THIS CHAPTER, as the last in this book, represents the culmination of this inquiry into social work practice with gay men, lesbians, and bisexual and transgender people (GLBTs). It offers a guide for affirmative practice with GLBTs — a short, readable overview of considerations for social workers who will work with GLBT clients and communities. Using the frameworks of cultural competence and empowerment practice, this chapter synthesizes all of the suggestions for practice offered in preceding chapters. The reader is reminded that much more information about working with GLBTs, including citations and additional resources, can be found in those preceding chapters. This chapter, though the last, can actually serve as a beginning for the reader, since learning is not a static endeavor but rather an ever-growing and -expanding process. Like all other social groups, GLBT individuals and communities, and the larger society in which they live, will change over time, and these changes will have implications for best practices. Social workers, then, should take the suggestions offered herein regarding practice with GLBT clients in casework, clinical, organizational, community, and policy settings and selectively apply them in practice. Through ongoing assessment of the appropriateness and efficacy of these practice models, social workers can continue to learn and refine their practice skills as they engage with GLBT clients during their careers.

AFFIRMATIVE PRACTICE

The rubric of affirmative practice is built upon the frameworks of cultural competence and empowerment practice. This section will provide an overview of both frameworks and describe how they inform affirmative practice with GLBT clients.

CULTURAL COMPETENCE

In 1989 the Georgetown University Child Development Center issued a monograph titled *Towards a Culturally Competent System of Care* (Cross, Bazron, Dennis, & Isaacs, 1989), outlining what would become known as the cultural competence model (Hernandez & Isaacs, 1998). According to this model, cultural competence is "a set of congruent behaviors, attitudes, and policies that come together in a system, agency, or among professionals, and enables that system, agency, or those professionals to work effectively in cross-cultural situations" (Cross et al., 1989, p. 13). Social workers, therefore, can learn the skills and acquire the knowledge necessary to engage in and facilitate culturally competent practice with populations who are different from themselves.

Green (1999) identifies several strategies that social workers can use to become more culturally competent. First, social workers must be aware of their self-limitations—that is, those cultural expectations and beliefs they possess as part of their own culture that might inhibit positive relationship building with the client. For example, if social workers grew up with the understanding that heterosexual relationships are the only morally good structure for a family, that belief might inhibit their work with same-sex couples and their families. Green is asking social workers to be aware of, and work to counter, their biases by adopting a perspective of openness to the client's differences. This openness and interest in the client's culture allow the social worker to learn from the client in a systematic way.

Social workers can also learn from outside resources: books, Internet sites, coursework and reading, professional consultation, cultural groups and professional organizations, and cultural events. Through the cultivation of these resources, social workers can develop a network of appropriate referrals for their clients. This is especially important for GLBT people, who may find it difficult to locate culturally appropriate and affirming resources. Through their work with clients and their pursuit of outside resources, social workers can recognize and work to create systems that value their clients' cultural integrity.

EMPOWERMENT PRACTICE

The concept of empowerment was popularized by Barbara Solomon (1976), a social work educator, in the mid-1970s to encourage better practice with people of color. Solomon believed that social workers should help clients develop the skills and capacities to meet their needs, support them in advocating for their issues, and work with them to change the system structures to be more responsive to the needs and styles of diverse client populations. Thus, empowerment practice includes micro-, mezzo-, and macro-level interventions.

In their review of empowerment frameworks, Browne and Mills (2001) identify four central concepts that are inherent in all empowerment theories (p. 24):

- Development of [clients'] attitudes, values, and beliefs around self-efficacy that extend from feelings of individual competency to the betterment of the community
- Validation of people's stories and the collective experience
- Knowledge and skills for critical thinking, access to information, and action based on critical analyses of structural forces that affect life and opportunity
- Individual-focused and social-justice-oriented strategies of intervention and action

Social workers practicing in the empowerment tradition can help clients and client communities to recognize their strengths and use these strengths to engage in advocacy.

Empowerment-based interventions are very important for GLBT persons, who may not be able to identify their own strengths, or the strengths within their communities, as they confront such issues as identity development, disclosure, social stigma, and discrimination. Empowerment strategies support GLBTs by helping them maintain a positive self-concept, advocate for their needs, and work for social justice in the larger society.

AFFIRMATIVE PRACTICE WITH GLBT INDIVIDUALS

In both clinical practice and casework, social workers employ a basic structure. First, a social worker builds rapport with a client, engaging and building trust. The social worker then conducts an assessment of the client in his or her environment, identifying the client's strengths, needs, and hopes for the future. This is followed by a treatment or case plan, wherein the social worker works with the client to identify goals and objectives and sets forth a plan to meet them. Finally, the social worker evaluates the effectiveness of the intervention and the client's progress, amending the treatment or case plan as needed. When the goals of the plan have been met, the social worker and the client will proceed to termination. This section will describe how social workers can use their knowledge, skills, and values to be culturally competent and empowering in their work with GLBT clients throughout these stages.

BUILDING RAPPORT

In building rapport with GLBT clients, it is important to recognize that social workers are not immune from the biases of the larger society. They must examine their own thoughts and feelings about sexual orientation and gender expression, about what is "normal" and "optimal" for themselves, and about the ways these attitudes affect their work with GLBT clients. This is true for all social workers, regardless of sexual orientation or gender expression—all have internalized to different degrees the homophobia, heterosexism, biphobia, and transphobia that shape current society.

Social workers should also consider how they present themselves to their GLBT clients. Are their offices welcoming, with GLBT-related books, symbols, and other information prominently displayed? Do they use words that are inclusive, such as *partner* (instead of *husband* or *wife*), *sexual orientation* (rather than *sexual preference*), *gay and lesbian* (instead of *homosexual*), and *transgender* (rather than *gender confused* or *disordered*)? Do they start where the client is, using terms that the client finds comfortable rather than their own words? These simple steps are a good way to build positive rapport with GLBT clients.

Heterosexual and gender-normative (non-transgender) social workers may encounter some mistrust and oppositional behaviors from their GLBT clients. This is common in working with members of oppressed populations who are frequently subjected to discrimination and prejudice in treatment and casework settings. Social workers can use this situation to explore the clients' feelings while also demonstrating their comfort with GLBTs and their knowledge about sexual orientation and gender expression.

GLBT social workers will need to consider whether they will disclose their own sexual orientation or gender identity to their GLBT clients. While such disclosure can build rapport, it may also provide a false illusion of friendship that can actually undermine the worker-client relationship. GLBT social workers should be aware that although they may share one characteristic with a GLBT client, there still may be many differences in experiences, perspectives, and concerns. GLBT social workers should remind themselves and their clients of these differences, recognizing commonalities as they arise but not assuming that there is some quick or deep understanding.

ASSESSMENT

In the assessment stage with GLBT clients, the social worker will need to consider some factors beyond the common categories of assessment. First, social workers should assess GLBT clients' knowledge about sexual orientation and/or gender expression. GLBTs are not always knowledgeable about GLBT history, culture, and communities. Second, GLBTs may be at different stages of their identity development when they present for treatment. Social workers must assess their stage of development. It is also necessary to understand the interplay between the client's stage of GLBT identity development and his or her life stage.

Third, assessment with GLBT clients should include their level of comfort with their sexual orientation and/or gender expression. For example, even a client who has self-identified as gay for many years may still be uncomfortable with his sexual orientation, feeling shame, anger, or confusion about it. Fourth, there should be a determination of the level of GLBT clients' disclosure about their sexual orientation and/or gender expression—whom they have told (i.e., parents, partners, children, coworkers, and friends), how much they have disclosed, and how they approach new situations (generally open versus generally closeted). All of these factors should be assessed and considered in case or treatment planning.

GLBT clients, like their social workers, have been socialized in a world that stigmatizes and discriminates against GLBT persons. Most of these clients will have internalized some of the beliefs that support this stigma and discrimination, and these will need to be addressed in treatment or case plans. Further, social workers should explore clients' experiences of stigma and discrimination and the various coping strategies clients have used to overcome them. The information gathered here can provide important insight into client functioning. Negative coping mechanisms, such as substance abuse, cutting and other self-mutilation, suicidal ideation, and depression, should be identified and addressed in planning. Positive coping strategies can serve as examples of resilience, and social workers can point to these strategies to highlight client strengths.

Like all other clients, GLBT people must be appreciated for other aspects of their identity—especially their race, ethnicity, and spiritual identity and/or religious affiliation. Each of these components must be understood as it relates to the clients' sexual orientation and/or gender expression. GLBT people of color living in the United States often experience multiple oppressions, as their race, ethnicity, class, and sexual orientation and/or gender expression intersect. Being GLBT can be an additional burden to a person of color, as sexual and gender diversity can sometimes cause distancing from one's family and community; thus social support networks are very important. A similar issue can arise for gay, lesbian, and bisexual people within their religious communities, since many mainline denominations have positions condemning same-sex eroticism. It is important to discover how GLBT clients define their spiritual lives, their level of connectedness to any particular group or congregation, and the importance of this aspect of their identity. Only in understanding the whole person's lived experience can the social worker be prepared to design a treatment or case plan that will suit the GLBT client.

PLANNING

Interventions with GLBT people should be client-centered and should not pathologize the clients' sexual and/or gender expression. Not all GLBT people who seek out a social worker are struggling with issues related to their identities. While it is important to take a client's sexual orientation and gender expression into account, that is not always related to the presenting or central problem. Include GLBT identity development, disclosure, management of stigma and discrimination, and issue-related advocacy only when those factors are pertinent.

A central task for most GLBT people as they develop their identities is disclosure—figuring out who to tell, when to tell, and how best to share the information. Client self-determination regarding disclosure should be a primary concern for social workers who are helping GLBT clients in structuring this process. Social workers can work with clients to make a plan for disclosure, providing them with access to materials about GLBT identities and helping them think through the costs and benefits of such a decision.

One theme that runs through the practice literature about GLBT people is the importance of narrative. Narrative, or storytelling, is an important part of how human beings create relationships and communities. This can be especially important to GLBT people, who may be challenged to re-create their own stories as they grow to embrace their sexual and gender identities. Social workers can help GLBT clients tell and retell their stories in ways that address any feelings of guilt and shame and empower them to meet their needs. This is especially important for victims of stigma-related violence, for they have to redefine and regain a worldview that balances the risk of violence with the sense of empowerment and safety.

Social workers can assist clients in the psychological tasks of managing stigma and discrimination while also providing them with the information and referrals necessary to advocate for justice. Social workers can combat stereotypes and misinformation with basic information on GLBT issues such as HIV/AIDS risk and prevention, sexual orientation, legal and religious issues, and transgender identity development processes,. As part of an intervention plan, social workers can help GLBT clients learn to access GLBT local and regional communities, improving social support networks, and perhaps, especially for GLBT youth, identifying role models.

AFFIRMATIVE PRACTICE WITH GLBT FAMILIES

Two kinds of GLBT families will be addressed in this section: (1) the fairly traditional families that include one or more GLBT members and (2) the nontraditional families established by GLBT adults. While both kinds of families may share many experiences, strengths, and needs, there are some distinct issues that social workers might need to address with each. These similarities and differences will be addressed below and suggestions offered for affirmative practice with each of these family types.

GLBT people often have to negotiate the disclosure of their sexual orientation and/or gender identity to their family of origin or, for those who come out later in life, to their partners and/or children. Some GLBTs use family therapy as a mechanism for negotiating this disclosure. Social workers should explore with the GLBT client at his or her level of knowledge and comfort, as well as the reasons for disclosure, and help the client devise a plan for disclosure to family members that is both age-appropriate and culturally appropriate.

In a family therapy setting, social workers are responsible for the well-being of the entire family. They will need to explore the implications of this disclosure for all family members, helping them to process their feelings, providing important information about sexual orientation and gender expression, and recommending referrals if necessary. Social workers can also help family members recognize and negotiate the impact of social attitudes and religious beliefs on their understandings of a family member's disclosure.

When working with "nontraditional GLBT families," social workers must allow the clients to define family as they will. Since some GLBT people have been rejected by their families of origin, they may create new "families of friends"— support networks that fill the role of family in their lives. Any and all members of these families should be invited to participate in family counseling sessions and included in case planning as appropriate.

GLBT families must be assessed regarding their stage of family development and their progress toward accepting a family member's sexual orientation and/or gender expression. The social worker can assist parents of GLBT teens who are in the process of coming out in understanding GLBT issues, especially related to the causes and innateness of orientation and gender identity. Social workers should also help these parents identify their teen's strengths and support the teen in progress through identity development.

When GLBT parents bring their children to a counseling session, it is important to recognize that GLBT issues may not be the most important issues with which the family is concerned. It is also important to understand how the GLBT parent or parents came to have children. Whether the children are adopted, are from a former marriage, or are the product of insemination by or of one of the partners can have a profound effect on relationships between the parents and between the parents and the children. A "parenthood history" will allow the social worker to understand and effectively intervene with the family.

Working with former partners of GLBT people can also be a part of family therapy or casework, especially if the adults are co-parents of children. In cases where one partner is in the process of coming out, the social worker must help the other partner cope with his or her anger, confusion, and other emotions as he or she adjusts to the new situation. Same-sex partners who are breaking up face different issues as they negotiate claims to property and child custody in a legal system that often does not recognize same-sex relationships. Social workers can help these partners negotiate in good faith and cope with the emotions that impede the necessary negotiations. Members of all of these kinds of families will need to work with one another to regain a sense of equilibrium and start again with new family arrangements.

AFFIRMATIVE PRACTICE IN ORGANIZATIONS

Social workers who want to make organizations more effective in their work with GLBT clients need to address four areas: program structures, environment, policies, and overall maintenance.

In evaluating the program structures of an organization, social workers should assess the delivery of services to GLBTs, identifying gaps in services for different subpopulations, such as youth, elderly, disabled people, and people of color. Organizations should target their services to GLBTs, seeking out needs and concerns unique to these populations. Forms should use appropriate inclusive language, and referral information should be maintained for GLBT-friendly agencies in the area. To ensure that staff members are educated about GLBT issues, hiring should include questions assessing applicants' knowledge and skills in working with GLBT people.

Social workers can also make a difference in their organizational environments by displaying GLBT-positive literature and symbols in the offices and waiting area. The posting of information about GLBT community events, groups, political issues, and other flyers in the waiting area can help inform GLBT clients. Front-line support staff can add to the welcoming environment by greeting GLBT clients warmly, addressing them by using the gender of their preference, and using appropriate terminology in all dealings with them.

To support the changes made in the structure and the environment, organizations should institute anti-discrimination policies and anti-harassment policies that are inclusive of the rights of GLBT employees, administrators, and clients. Other policies can be instituted around targeted hiring and diversity.

Finally, all of these interventions should be maintained through staff in-service training, the development of articles in agency newsletters addressing GLBT clients and their issues, the encouragement of staff members' involvement in GLBT client advocacy, the investigation of GLBT legal and political issues that affect GLBT clients, and agency support for advocacy with and on behalf of GLBT clients.

AFFIRMATIVE COMMUNITY PRACTICE

Community advocacy with GLBTs can take many forms. Social workers can educate members of the GLBT community about issues of specific concern, such as disclosure, transmission and treatment of HIV and AIDS, alcoholism and sub-

BECOMING AN ALLY

Washington and Evans (1991) define an ally as "a person who is a member of the dominant or majority group who works to end oppression in his or her personal and professional life through support of, and as an advocate for, the oppressed population" (p. 196). For heterosexual and gender-normative social workers, being an ally would mean working to support and advocate for the rights of GLBT people.

The Human Rights Campaign (HRC) (2003) has suggested the following description for "straight allies," who should strive to:

- be a friend
- be a listener
- be open-minded
- have his or her own opinions
- be willing to talk
- commit himself or herself to personal growth in spite of the discomfort it may sometimes cause
- recognize his or her personal boundaries
- recognize when to refer an individual to additional resources
- confront his or her own prejudices
- join others with a common purpose
- believe that all people, regardless of age, sex, race, gender, ability, religion, ethnicity, or sexual orientation, should be treated with dignity and respect
- engage in the process of developing a culture free of homophobia and heterosexism
- recognize his or her mistakes, but not use them as an excuse for inaction
- be responsible for empowering his or her role in a community, particularly as it relates to responding to homophobia
- recognize the legal powers and privileges that heterosexuals have and that GLBT people are denied
- support an ally program in his or her community, university, or workplace

By actively seeking to be an ally, all social workers can become part of the movement for social justice for all people, including GLBTs.

stance abuse, and basic information about sexual orientation and gender expression. Social workers can also educate the larger community about these GLBT issues and address any misinformation and myths that members may express. This education can serve as a first step for social workers to build a community of allies for GLBT equality.

Social workers can challenge the myths and misinformation of other professionals, especially those who work in the social services, health and mental health care, domestic violence, legal and judicial systems. By training personnel in these agencies, social workers can improve the delivery of services for GLBT people. These social service organizations can also be a part of establishing larger networks of GLBT-friendly agencies.

Another approach to education and raising community awareness is the creation of large-scale public events. By taking part in organizing or planning rallies, marches, and vigils, social workers can help GLBT people celebrate, educate, and commemorate their communities and the larger society. Social workers can train GLBT people in community assessment and organizing skills, so that they may be empowered to coordinate such events. Social workers working closely with GLBT people in community events must employ the same strategies as clinicians and caseworkers: using appropriate terminology, learning from GLBT perople what they need and want, and constantly assessing areas where the social workers themselves need to grow and learn.

AFFIRMATIVE POLICY PRACTICE

Social workers can engage in policy practice with GLBT people to address the policies and practices that oppress them. Gay men, lesbians, bisexuals, and transgender people, along with their families, friends, and allies, can make a difference in social policies. Social workers can help organize and educate these groups so that they can write letters to the editor, contact their legislators, speak out publicly, and perhaps even demonstrate for change.

The constitutional principles of due process and equal protection under the law, invoked in the recent Supreme Court majority opinion in *Lawrence v. Texas*, are the basis for many policy struggles throughout the United States that affect GLBT people: marriage, child custody, adoption, health and mental health care, insurance, retirement, violence and safety, employment, housing, and many other areas. Social workers can take advantage of opportunities to support GLBT advocates working for policy change by filing friend-of-the-court briefs, providing expert testimony to legislators and justices, writing or promoting legislation, providing input on rules for policy implementation, training staff to implement policies correctly, and evaluating the effects of these policies. The ultimate goal for all of these methods of social policy advocacy is social and economic justice for all people, including GLBTs.

CONCLUSION

The veil of American ignorance about sexual orientation and gender expression has lifted. As gay men, lesbians, bisexuals, and transgender people emerge in the media, in research literature, and in our communities, social workers can no longer ignore their presence. This book has provided important information for social workers who will work with GLBT clients—a category that is sure to include all social workers at some point during the course of their careers. It is the authors' hope that you, the reader, will take these recommendations for practice, evaluate their appropriateness for your clients, and apply them as they are useful. We also hope that you will continue in the learning process throughout your career, so that you may be able to meet the needs of your clients in an ever-changing society. In pursuit of social justice for gay men, lesbians, bisexuals, and transgender people, we must remain vigilant and committed to the service of our brothers and sisters in humanity.

REFERENCES

Browne, C., & Mills, C. (2001). Theoretical frameworks: Ecological model, strengths perspective, and empowerment theory. In R. Fong & S. B. C. L. Furuto (Eds.), *Culturally competent practice: Skills, interventions, and evaluations* (pp. 10–32). Needham Heights, MA: Allyn and Bacon.

Cross, T. L., Bazron, B. J., Dennis, K. W., & Isaacs, M. R. (Eds.). (1989). *Towards a culturally competent system of care. Vol. 1, A monograph on effective services for minority children who are severely emotionally disturbed.* Washington, DC: Georgetown University, Child Development Center, Child and Adolescent Service System Program, Technical Assistance Center.

Green, J. W. (1999). *Cultural awareness in the human services: A multi-ethnic approach* (3d ed.). Boston: Allyn and Bacon.

Hernandez, M., & Isaacs, M. R. (Eds.). (1998). *Promoting cultural competence in children's mental health services.* Baltimore: Paul H. Brookes Publishing.

Human Rights Campaign. (2003). *National coming out project: What is an ally?* Retrieved September 16, 2003, from http://www.hrc.org/ncop/allies/part1.asp.

Solomon, B. (1976). *Black empowerment.* New York: Columbia University Press.

Washington, J., & Evans, N. J. (1991). Becoming an ally. In N. J. Evans & V. A. Wall (Eds.), *Beyond tolerance: Gays, lesbians, and bisexuals on campus* (pp. 195–204). Alexandria, VA: American College Personnel Association.

APPENDIX A

WORDS AND SYMBOLS OF GLBT CULTURE

Patricia L. Greer and Deana F. Morrow

WORDS

androgyny Having both female and male characteristics, not distinguished from the other, such as in dress, appearance, or behavior

Benjamin Standards of Care Ethical guidelines for transgender people for biological changes (before surgery) that include a thorough psychological evaluation, one to two years of therapy, and living in the other identity for a year

bigender People who perceive that they are both male and female or androgynous, in their masculine and feminine traits

bisexual A sexual orientation where people may be intimately attracted to others of either sex

bull dyke A slang term for a lesbian who exhibits behavior associated with stereotypically masculine traits

butch A slang term for one who exhibits stereotypical or exaggerated masculine traits or appearance

civil union A legal commitment of two men or two women. Vermont is the only state offering legal civil unions for both residents and nonresidents

closet, in the Hiding one's sexual orientation to avoid dealing with internalized homophobia and/or external homophobia

coming out The process of first accepting oneself as gay or lesbian and then gradually revealing one's identity to others

commitment ceremony A public ceremony to commemorate the union of two gay men or lesbians in lieu of the legally recognized heterosexual marriage

conversion/reparative therapies Unethical practices of trying to change a gay or lesbian sexual orientation to heterosexual through negative reinforcements, electric shock treatments, and/or religiously based programs

cross-dresser A person who wears clothing usually associated with clothing usually associated with people of the other sex

Defense of Marriage Act (DOMA) A 1996 law exempting states from having to recognize a same-sex marriage performed in another state

disclosure Revealing one's sexual orientation to another person

disenfranchised grief Grief that is not validated because the relationship is not recognized as legitimate and/or legal

domestic partnership A term for the relationship that exists when two people reside together, are not married or related by blood, and take on the responsibilities of maintaining a commitment to each other

donor insemination Artificial insemination of a woman by an anonymous sperm donor

drag king/queen People who cross-dress in public, usually as performers, and may be heterosexual, gay, or lesbian

dyke A slang term for a lesbian who is noticeably masculine

Employment Non-discrimination Act (ENDA) A proposed federal law that would make job discrimination on the basis of sexual orientation illegal

fag A slang term referring to gay men

female impersonators *See* drag king/queen

femme A slang term for a lesbian who appears very feminine and consequently can "pass" easier as heterosexual

flamer A slang term for a gay male who appears very feminine

gay baiting Accusing someone of being gay even if the person is not; shaming someone into being disempowered

gay bashing Derogatory and hateful verbal attacks on gays and lesbians

gay liberation movement Originated with the Stonewall Inn riots in 1969—a social-political movement for gays and lesbians (later including bisexual and transgender people) to have equal rights in the United States

gender The behavioral, cultural, or psychological characteristics that are socially constructed to express femininity (associated with females) and masculinity (associated with males)

gender expression How a person outwardly manifests, or expresses, gender

gender identity An individual's personal sense of identity as masculine or feminine, or some combination thereof

gender roles Culturally defined masculine or feminine characteristics

GLBT Acronym for *gay, lesbian, bisexual, and transgender.* Sometimes "Q" is added to include those who are questioning their sexual orientation (GLTBQ)

hate crimes Crimes of violence committed against people strictly because of hatred of their minority status. The stigma and indifference toward GLBT people often prevents these crimes from being reported and/or prosecuted

heterocentric Actions and beliefs centered within a heterosexually oriented thought paradigm or perspective

heterosexism Belief in the superiority of heterosexuality over other forms of sexual orientation

heterosexual privilege Unearned social, cultural, and political advantages and dominance based on a heterosexual orientation

HIV/AIDS Acronyms for Human Immunodeficiency Virus and Acquired Immune Deficiency Syndrome

holy union A religious, sacred, and spiritual uniting of two people

homophobia Fear, hatred, and rejection of GLBT people or those presumed to be GLBT

homosexuality A sexual orientation in which people are intimately attracted to others of the same sex

internalized homophobia The personal internalization of anti-GLBT messages by GLBT people

intersexed or hermaphrodite individual A person having both male and female physical sex characteristics and reproductive organs that are not easily characterized as male or female. They are usually assigned as either male or female at birth and may be surgically altered to reflect the assigned sex.

Kinsey scale A self-categorized rating scale indicating the range of sexual orientation diversity in society, with o indicating predominantly heterosexual orientation and 6 reflecting a completely gay or lesbian orientation

lesbian Refers to homosexuality among women—when a woman is intimately attracted to another woman

lesbian culture The diverse social, business, and political communities of lesbians, often interrelated with feminist culture

MTF and FTM Acronyms for male to female (MTF) or female to male (FTM) for transgender people

oppression An unjust exercise of authority or power over another person. Any act that prevents a person from being fully human.

out When a person openly acknowledges their sexual orientation to others

outing When others disclose a GLBT person's sexual orientation and/or gender identity without the GLBT person's consent

passing When a GLB person seeks to pass as heterosexual. Also occurs when transsexual persons want to hide their birth sex.

queer Deviating from the expected or normal, something that is strange. A historically slang term for *gay* or *lesbian*. Many GLBTs now embrace the term as a form of activism for social justice

questioning The process of people exploring their sexual orientation, often occurring during the adolescent years

same-gender parenting When female couples or male couples are parents

same-gender relationships When two women or two men are in a relationship as a couple

same-gender sexual behavior Sexual behavior between two women or two men

sexism Attitudes, conditions, or behaviors that promote stereotyping of social roles based on gender and contribute to gender discrimination

sexual minority A term sometimes used by people who identify as being GLBT

sexual orientation A characteristic of people that describes whom they are attracted to for intimate, affectionate, and sexual needs—it can include people of the same sex or other sex

sex reassignment surgery (SRS) or gender reassignment surgery (GRS) The surgical procedures to change someone's sex, such as genital reconstruction, chest reconstruction, and cosmetic surgeries

Stonewall Inn Rebellion Occurred in 1969 when GLBT people rebelled against police officers who sought to arrest them because they were in a gay bar. This event marked the beginning of the gay rights movement.

swisher A slang term for a gay man who exhibits an exaggerated, effeminate style of walking

transgender People who have a gender identity different from the one typically accorded to their biological sex

transition The process and steps toward self-acceptance for transgender people, including the physical, psychological, and legal aspects of changing from one gender identity to another. *See also* Benjamin Standards of Care

transsexual (TS) This term is typically used to refer to a transgender person who is in the process of, or has undergone, sex reassignment procedures

SYMBOLS

Human Rights Campaign

This yellow equal sign in a blue box represents equal rights for gay, lesbian, bisexual, and transgender people.

Lambda

Lambda is currently used by gays and lesbians as a symbol identifying their sexual orientation. The ancient Greeks thought it meant unity, and the Romans thought it represented the light of knowledge to be shed on the darkness of ignorance.

Rainbow Flags

The rainbow flag, developed in 1978, is a highly recognized and frequently used symbol of gay pride, diversity, and freedom. The colors represent different aspects of gay and lesbian life: red for life, orange for healing, yellow for the sun, green for nature, blue for art, royal blue for harmony, and violet for spirit. There are many variations of the rainbow flag, two others of which are shown below.

Victory Over AIDS Flag

This flag recognizes people who have died from AIDS and shows a black stripe at the bottom of the rainbow flag. It is hoped that when the cure for AIDS is discovered, the black stripe will be removed from the flag and burned in a ceremony in Washington, D.C.

Pink Triangle

The pink triangle currently represents for gays and lesbians a badge of pride, solidarity, honor, and fighting back against institutional oppression, persecution, and denial of civil rights. It originated during World War II when the Nazis used it to mark male homosexuals, who were sent to prisons and later to concentration camps. Many homosexuals were sterilized by castration and/or put to death.

Gay Jewish Prisoners

A yellow Star of David under the superimposed pink triangle was designated for gay Jewish prisoners, known as the lowest of all Nazi concentration camp prisoners.

Black Triangle

The black triangle symbolizes lesbian and feminist pride, solidarity, and sisterhood. It originated from the Nazis' labeling of women who were not considered ideal women because they exhibited antisocial behavior. This group included feminists, women without children, lesbians, and prostitutes.

Bisexual Triangles

The interlocking bisexual triangles represent the middle ground in which bisexual persons live. The pink triangle represents the gay symbol, and the blue triangle represents heterosexuality.

GENDER SYMBOLS

Male and Female

Gay, Lesbian, and Feminist

The first symbol, two interlocking male symbols, stands for gay males.
The second symbol, two interlocking female symbols, indicates lesbians.
The third symbol, three interlocking female symbols, represents the sisterhood of women.

Bisexual

The bisexual gender symbol combines two sets of male and female symbols.

Transgender

The male and female symbols above, placed at opposite ends of the circle, represent balance between the two body parts and those who identify as intersexed or androgynous.

The version shown above merges the male and female symbols rather than interlocking them.

The circle in this symbol represents wholeness of society to include transgender people, with the male and female symbol connected to it. The arrow represents the misdirection of a society that ridicules transgender people.

MISCELLANEOUS SYMBOLS

Red Ribbon

A ribbon honoring those lost to AIDS, this symbol was designed to create awareness of HIV/AIDS transmissions, the needs of those with HIV/AIDS, and the need for funding of research and services. The color red signifies blood, passion, and love.

Labrys

A female symbol for lesbians and feminists, the labrys originated thousands of years ago among tribes of female Amazons and is associated with the harvest, peace, protection, and goddess worship.

APPENDIX B

GLBT RESOURCES

Patricia L. Greer and Deana F. Morrow

ADVOCACY/LEGAL RESOURCES

American Civil Liberties Union (ACLU)
125 Broad St., 18th floor
New York, NY 10004
http://www.aclu.org/

And Justice for All
P.O. Box 53079
Washington, DC 20009
(202) 547-0508
http://www.qrd.org/www/orgs/aja/contact.htm

Dedicated to achieving equality for everyone without regard to sexual orientation and to raising the visibility of heterosexuals in the gay, lesbian, bisexual, and transgender rights movement

Anti-Defamation League
Department of Campus Affairs
823 United Nations Plaza
New York, NY 10017
(212) 490-2525
http://www.adl.org/

To expose and combat the purveyors of hatred in our midst, responding to whatever new challenges may arise, in the form of anti-Semitism and other forms of bigotry, which in recent years have included attacks on immigrants, blacks, Hispanics, Asian Americans, gay men, and lesbians

Center for Democratic Renewal
P.O. Box 50469
Atlanta, GA 30302
(404) 221-0025
http://www.publiceye.org/cdr/cdr.html

Community-based coalition fighting hate-group activity. A national research institute based in Atlanta, Georgia, that fights racism through research and analysis, community empowerment, and changing public policy.

Center for Lesbian and Gay Law and Public Policy (CLGPP)
1023 Bainbridge St.
Philadelphia, PA
(215) 413-0509
Fax: (215) 592-1782
CLGLPP@aol.com

Citizens Against Homophobia
29 Clarendon St.
Boston, MA 02116
(617) 576-9866
ctznsAgnst@aol.com

Domestic Violence National Hotline:
(800) 799-SAFE, (800) 656-HOPE
TTY: (800) 787-3224
http://www.feminist.org/911/crisis.html

Staffed 24 hours a day by trained counselors who can provide crisis assistance and information about shelters, legal advocacy, health care centers, and counseling. Lists individual state hotlines. The Rape, Abuse, Incest National Network (RAINN) will automatically transfer you to the rape crisis center nearest you, anywhere in the nation. It can be used as a last resort if people cannot find a domestic violence shelter.

Equal Marriage
www.equalmarriage.ca
An advocacy organization for same-sex couples

Gay and Lesbian Alliance Against Defamation (GLAAD)
GLAAD/LA
GLAAD/NY
P.O. Box 931763
80 Varick St., Suite 3-E
Hollywood, CA 90093-1763
New York NY 10013
(213) 463-3632
(212) 966-1700
(213) 931-9429 (hotline)
www.glaad.org

M   the media (TV, radio, film, and news papers) to discourage bigotry and encourage realistic depiction of gay and lesbian people. Dedicated to promoting and ensuring fair, accurate, and inclusive representation of individuals and events in all media as a means of eliminating homophobia and discrimination based on gender identity and sexual orientation.

Gay and Lesbian National Hotline (GLNH)
Peer counselors available Monday–Friday 4 p.m.–midnight, Saturday noon–5 p.m. EST
National toll-free number: (888) THE-GLNH, (888) 843-4564
2261 Market St.
San Francisco, CA 94114
Administrative phone: (888) 415-3022
Fax: (415) 552-5498
www.glnh.org
glnh@glnh.org

A nonprofit, tax-exempt organization dedicated to meeting the needs of the gay and lesbian community by offering free and totally anonymous information, referrals, and peer counseling. Offers free and anonymous services by use of a toll-free telephone number. Callers will be able to speak directly to a trained volunteer who will be able to access a national database of referrals specific to the gay and lesbian community.

Gay and Lesbian Victims' Assistance 24-Hour Hotline
(800) 259-1536

Gay, Lesbian, and Straight Education Network
121 W. Twenty-seventh St., Suite 804
New York, NY 10001-6207
(212) 727-0135
glsen@glsen.org

A national advocacy organization dedicated to ending anti-gay bias in America's K–12 schools

GenderPAC
1743 Connecticut Ave., NW, 4th floor
Washington, DC 20009-1108
(202) 462-6610
gpac@gpac.org

A national organization working to end discrimination and violence caused by gender stereotypes, concerned with the way discrimination based on gender intersects with other kinds of discrimination, including that of race, class, ethnicity, and age

High Tech Gays (HTG)
P.O. Box 6777
San Jose, CA 95150
(408) 993-3830

This group is attempting to end discrimination in the Department of Defense's hiring and the granting of security clearances.

Human Rights Campaign (HRC)
919 Eighteenth St., NW, Suite 800
Washington, DC 20006
(202) 628-4160
TTY: (202) 216-1572
www.hrc@hrc.org

This organization believes in full equality for gay, lesbian, bisexual, and transgender Americans. The Human Rights Campaign is the largest national lesbian and gay political organization with members throughout the country. It effectively lobbies Congress, provides campaign support, and educates the public to ensure that lesbian, gay, bisexual, and transgender Americans can be open, honest, and safe at home, at work, and in the community.

LAMBDA GLBT Community Services AVP, Attn: GLNVAH
P.O. Box 31321
El Paso, TX 79931-0371
(915) 562-GAYS
Fax: (915) 533-6024
AVProject@aol.com

Lambda Legal Defense and Education Fund
120 Wall St., Suite 1500
New York, NY 10005-3904
(212) 809-8585
lambdalegal@lambdalegal.org

Lambda Legal Defense and Education Fund is a national organization committed to achieving full recognition of the civil rights of lesbians, gay men, and people with HIV/AIDS through impact litigation, education, and public policy work.

Lambda Letters Project
4577 Park Blvd., Suite 4
San Diego, CA 92116

Monthly letters on gay/lesbian/bisexual, AIDS/HIV, women, and people of color issues

Lesbian and Gay Immigration Rights Task Force
230 Park Ave., Suite 904
New York, NY 10169
(212) 818-9639
info@lgirtf.org

Log Cabin Republicans
1012 Fourteenth St., NW, Suite 703
Washington, DC 20005
(202) 347-5306
lcrnat@aol.com

The lobbying branch of the Log Cabin Federation

National Committee on Lesbian, Gay, and Bisexual Issues of the National Association of Social Workers (NASW)
750 First St., NE, Suite 700
Washington, DC 20002-4341
(202) 408-8600
http://www.naswdc.org/

National Gay and Lesbian Task Force (NGLTF)
1700 Kalorama Rd., NW
Washington, DC 20009-2624
(202) 332-6483
TTY: (202) 332-6219
ngltf@ngltf.org

Lobbies Congress to create new legislation for gay and lesbian rights. Provides information on pending bills that affect us as well as information to help you write letters to lobby your congresspeople.

National Institute Against Prejudice and Violence
31 S. Green St.
Baltimore, MD 21201
http://www.prejudiceinstitute.org/whoweare.html

A nonprofit institution involving the major disciplines of the social sciences and law. Organized around ten projects, including studi of the social and psychological effects of vic timization; the nature of violent attitudes and behavior; the nature of prejudice, conflict, and ethnoviolence as they are played out in college campus and workplace settings; and the role of the news media in communicating prejudice. This is a program of action research emphasizing the application of scientific knowledge in building programs of education, prevention, and response.

National Lesbian and Gay Law Association (NLGLA)
(508) 982-8290
http://www.nlgla.org/
nlgla@aol.com

A national association of lawyers, judges and other legal professionals, law students, and affiliated lesbian, gay, bisexual and transgender legal organizations

National Lesbian, Gay, and Bisexual Student Caucus
United States Student Association
815 Fifteenth St., NW, Suite 838
Washington, DC 20005
(202) 347-8772
Fax: (202) 393-5886

People for the American Way (PFAW)
2000 M St., NW, Suite 400
Washington, DC 20036
(202) 467-4999 or (800) 326-7329
pfaw@pfaw.org

Organizes and mobilizes Americans to fight for fairness, justice, civil rights, and the freedoms guaranteed by the Constitution

Southern Poverty Law Center
400 Washington Ave.
Montgomery, AL 36104
(334) 956-8200
K   Search: Southern Poverty Law Center in the Internet Explorer address bar
A nonprofit organization internationally known for its tolerance education program, its legal victories against white supremacist groups, its tracking of hate groups, and its sponsorship of the Civil Rights Memorial

Young Democrats of America, Gay, Lesbian, and Bisexual Caucus (GLB)
Caucus chair: Gary Perkins
2178 Lakemoore Dr., SW
Olympia, WA 98512
(206) 943-1808.
jmcderm@u.washington.edu

AGING/OLDER ADULT RESOURCES

Gay and Lesbian Association of Retiring Persons TM (GLARP)
10940 Wilshire Blvd., Suite 1600
Los Angeles, CA 90024
(310) 966-1500
www.gaylesbianretiring.org

A international nonprofit membership organization enhancing the aging experience of gays and lesbians

Lesbian and Gay Aging Issues Network (LGAIN)
http://www.asaging.org/networks/lgain/index.html

A constituent group that works to raise awareness about the special challenges that lesbian, gay, bisexual, and transgender (LGBT) elders face as they age, and about the unique barriers that these often invisible populations encounter in gaining access to housing, health care, long-term care, and social services. Includes a resource guide on LGBT aging issues. The full text of the guide, with links for purchasing many of the resources, is posted on the LGAIN home page at http://www.asaging.org/lgain; click on the "Recommended Resources" button.

BISEXUAL RESOURCES

BiNet USA
4201 Wilson Blvd., No. 110-311
Arlington, VA 22203
(202) 986-7186
BiNetUSA@aol.com

Bisexual Resource Center
P.O. Box 1026
Boston, MA 02117-1026
(617) 424-9595
www.brc@biresource.org

BISEXU-L
listserv@brownvm.brown.edu.

A mailing list for discussion of bisexual issues and bisexuality open to all orientations

ETHNIC/RACIAL-RELATED RESOURCES

Arab L/G/Bi Network and Arab Lesbian/Bi Women's Network
P.O. Box 460526
San Francisco, CA 94114
http://www.qrd.org/orgs/contacts/arab

Black, Gay, and Lesbian Leadership Forum/AIDS Prevention Team
1219 S. La Brea Ave.
Los Angeles, CA 90010
(213) 964-7830

Blackstripe
http://www.blackstripe.com/

Provides information for and about same-gender-loving, lesbian, gay, bisexual, and transgender people of African descent

Gay and Lesbian Arabic Society (GLAS)
Arabic Society
Box 4971
Washington, DC 20008
http://www.glas.org/

Gay and Lesbian Latinos Unidos
P.O. Box 85459
Los Angeles, CA 90072
(213) 660-9681

Gay Asian Pacific Support Network
P.O. Box 461104
Los Angeles, CA 90046
(213) 368-6488
www.gapsn.org

GLB People of Color (GLBPOC)
glbpoc-request@ferkel.uscb.edu

A mailing list for lesbian, gay, and bisexual people of color

LLEGÓ—National Latina/o Lesbian, Gay, Bisexual, and Transgender Organization
1420 K St., NW, Suite 400
Washington, DC 20005
(202) 408-5380
http://www.llego.org/

National Asian Pacific American Legal Consortium (NAPALC)
http://www.napalc.org/

Works to advance the legal and civil rights of Asian Pacific Americans through litigation, public education, and public policy. NAPALC focuses its expertise on anti-Asian violence prevention and education, voting rights, immigration, naturalization, affirmative action, language rights, and the census.

National Black, Lesbian, and Gay Leadership Forum
1714 Franklin St., Suite 100-140
Oakland, CA 94612
(510) 302-0930
www.nblglf.org

Native American Culture Resources for GLBT Communities
http://www.queertheory.com/cultures/ethnics/queer_native_americans.htm

Native American Health Center
(510) 261-2524
http://www.gayglobal.com/san_francisco/youth/natam.html

AIDS education and prevention for Native American youth. Information and referral (housing and food).

FAMILY RESOURCES

Children of Lesbians and Gays Everywhere
3543 Eighteenth St., Suite 1
San Francisco, CA 94110
(415) 861-KIDS
colage@colage.org

To foster the growth of daughters and sons of lesbian, gay, bisexual, and transgender parents of all racial, ethnic, and class backgrounds by providing education, support, and community on local and international levels, to advocate for their rights and those of our families, and to promote acceptance and awareness that love makes a family

Parents, Families, and Friends of Lesbians and Gays (PFLAG)
1726 M St., NW, Suite 400
Washington, DC 20036
(202) 467-8180
http://www.pflag.org/

PFLAG promotes the health and well-being of gay, lesbian, bisexual, and transgender people, their families, and friends through support, to cope with an adverse society; education, to enlighten an ill-informed public; and advocacy, to end discrimination and to secure equal civil rights. Provides opportunity for dialogue about sexual orientation and gender identity and acts to create a society that is healthy and respectful of human diversity.
http://www.bidstrup.com/parents.htm

Resources for the parents of gay, lesbian, bisexual, and transgender youth

Spouse Support Mailing List (SSML)
TO SUBSCRIBE: Send an e-mail message to listserv@home.ease.lsoft.com.

An Internet mailing list for straight spouses and their bisexual, gay, or lesbian partners who are trying to keep their marriages intact and for keeping the relationship positive for those couples that are separating and divorcing. Membership is confidential.

Straight Spouse Network (SSN)
Amity Pierce Buxton, Ph.D.
8215 Terrace Dr.
El Cerrito, CA 94530-3058
(510) 525-0200
http://www.ssnetwk.org/
dir@ssnetwk.org

In at least two million marriages, a spouse has come out or will disclose being, gay, lesbian, bisexual, or transgender. When this crisis occurs, the straight spouse and children go into their own closet. They need to know that they are not alone and that there is a safe place to find help. Professionals and the wider community need to become more aware of the impact on spouses and family members when a partner comes out. Addressing their unique needs will lessen isolation, aid healing, and increase understanding of everyone involved.

GAY MALE RESOURCES

Black Men's Exchange (BMX)
3288 Twenty-first St., Suite 50
San Francisco, CA 94110
(800) 274-3853
(310) 281-7742
http://www.qrd.org/orgs/contacts/black.mens.exchange

Gay and Married Men's Association. (GAMMA)
P.O. Box 28317
Washington, DC 20038
(703) 548-3238
FAX: (703) 425-6763

Gay Married Men
GAMMADC@aol.com

Gay Mormon Fathers (Gamofites)
400 Melrose Ave., Suite E
Seattle, WA 98102
http://www.gamofites.org/

A collection of information on books, pamphlets, magazines, and newsletters, as well as a selection of World Wide Web links of interest to gay Mormon fathers, their straight spouses and former spouses, children, and extended families

LESBIAN RESOURCES

Astraea National Lesbian Action Foundation
666 Broadway, Suite 520
New York, NY 10012-2317
http://www.astraea.org/

A national nonprofit public charity whose purp   is to advance the economic, political, educational, and cultural well-being of lesbians

Gatekeepers, Inc.
P.O. Box 25273
Richmond, VA 23260
g8kprs@aol.com

A nonprofit organization established to empower lesbians

Golden Threads
P.O. Box 65
Richford, VT 05476-0065
(802) 848-7037

To belong, an individual or one member of a couple must be 60 or over. OLOC provides support and networking and is an activist, specifically in regard to ageism.

Lesbian Herstory Educational Foundation (LHEF)
P.O. Box 1258
New York, NY 10116
(718) 768-DYKE (3953)
Fax: (718) 768-4663
pjthc@cunyvm.cuny.edu

Lesbians in Science (LIS)
A listserv for lesbians in industry, universities, government labs, etc. Send subscription requests to ZITA@JUNO.PHYSICS.WISC.EDU; send postings to LIS@JUNO.PHYSICS.WISC.EDU.

Lesbian Mothers Support Society (LMSS)
http://www.lesbian.org/moms/

Designed to help women who want to have babies through nontraditional means, specifically lesbians. Provides peer support to lesbian parents, their children, and lesbians considering parenthood.

Lesbian.org and WWWomen
A search directory for women online; have combined efforts in order to provide lesbians with the most comprehensive, up-to-date, and searchable database of lesbian links on the Internet

Mautner Project for Lesbians with Cancer
1707 L St., NW, Suite 500
Washington, DC 20036
(202) 332-5536
mautner@mautnerproject.org

National Center for Lesbian Rights
870 Market St., Suite 570
San Francisco, CA 94102
(415) 392-6257
http://www.nclrights.org/

NCLR is a progressive, feminist, multicultural legal center devoted to advancing the rights and safety of lesbians and their families. NCLR also recognizes the oppression and marginalization of other groups in our community, including gay men, bisexuals and transgender i   Through direct litigation and advocacy NCLR works to change discriminatory laws and to create new laws and policies benefiting lesbians and other oppressed members of the queer community.

Old Lesbians Organizing for Change (OLOC)
P.O. Box 980422
Houston, TX 77098
http://www.qrd.org/orgs/contacts/golden.
threads.and.oloc

SAPPHO
A forum and support group for lesbian and bisexual women. Membership is strictly limited to women. To subscribe, sappho-request@fiesta.intercon.com.

MEDICAL/HEALTH RESOURCES

AIDS National Hotlines
(800) 342-AIDS (2437)
Spanish: (800) 344-7432
TTY: (800) 243-7889

AIDS hotlines are an invaluable resource for basic HIV/AIDS information. You can talk to someone knowledgeable about HIV or AIDS and get referrals to various AIDS services in your city or state. Every state in the country has a hotline, and a few states also have numbers accessible for the hearing-impaired.

Deaf Queer
http://www.deafqueer.org/

A national nonprofit online resource center devoted to providing up-to-date Deaf Queer resource information to the community

Gay and Lesbian Medical Association
459 Fulton St., Suite 107
San Francisco, CA 94102

(415) 255-4547
info@glma.org

Gay and Lesbian Counseling Service
600 Washington St., Suite 219
Boston, MA 02111
(617) 542-5188
Outpatient organization of PRIDE Institute

Gay Council on Drinking Behavior
Whitman-Walker Clinic
2335 Eighteenth St., NW
Washington, DC 20009
(202) 332-5295
Outpatient organization of PRIDE Institute

GayHealth.com
Serving the gay, lesbian, bisexual, and transgender communities. Areas include news, sex, drugs, emotions, general health, image, food, fitness, society.

HIVandHepatitis.Com
http://www.hivandhepatitis.com/

Lesbian, Gay, and Bisexual People in Medicine
1890 Preston White Dr.
Reston, VA 22091
(703) 620-6600
Founded in 1976 to offer support to gay medical students

Montrose Counseling Center (MCC), located in Houston, Texas
www.neosoft.com/~mcc/
mcc@neosoft.com
MCC is a nonprofit organization providing services in the following areas: outpatient mental health, substance abuse treatment, HIV case management, hate crimes, same-sex intimate violence, and breast cancer awareness in lesbians. The primary target populations are gay, lesbian, bisexual, and transgender people, and those living with HIV disease.

National Association of People with AIDS
1413 K St., NW, 7th floor
Washington, DC 20005
(202) 898-0414
napwa@napwa.org

National Institute on Drug Abuse (NIDA)
(301) 443-1124
http://www.drugabuse.gov/NIDA
information@lists.nida.nih.gov

NIDA's mission is to lead the nation in bringing the power of science to bear on drug abuse and addiction. This charge has two critical components. The first is the strategic support and conduct of research across a broad range of disciplines. The second is to ensure the rapid and effective dissemination and use of the results of that research to significantly improve drug abuse and addiction prevention, treatment, and policy.

National Lesbian and Gay Health Association
1407 S St., NW
Washington, DC 20009
(202) 939-7880

National Minority AIDS Council
1931 Thirteenth St., NW
Washington, DC 20009
(202) 483-6622
info@nmac.org

PRIDE Institute
14400 Martin Dr.
Eden Prairie, MN 55344
(800) 547-7433
Inpatient alcoholism dependency rehabilitation facility specializing in treatment of lesbians and gays

Rainbow Alliance of the Deaf
P.O. Box 14182
Washington, DC 20044-4182
http://www.rad.org/

MILITARY RESOURCES

Gay, Lesbian, and Bisexual Veterans of America (GLBVA) Member Services
7716 W. Twenty-sixth St.
North Riverside, IL 60546
http://www.glbva.org/

Gay Military Page
http://www.gaymilitary.ucsb.edu/

GayVeterans.com
Call Servicemembers Legal Defense Network at (202) 328-FAIR (3247)

HuddleStone.com
www.HuddleStone.com
Helping the GLBT military community live healthier lives

Service Members Legal Defense Network (SLDN)
P.O. Box 65301
Washington, DC 20035-5301
(202) 328-3244
Fax: (202) 797-1635
www.SLDN@sldn.org

D   to ending witch hunts, death threats, imprisonment, lesbian-baiting, discharges, and other discriminatory actions against men and women in the military harmed by "don't ask, don't tell, don't pursue, don't harass," and related policies, through direct legal assistance, watchdog activities, policy work, outreach and education, and litigation support

MISCELLANEOUS/EDUCATIONAL RESOURCES

All Out Arts, Inc.
CSV Cultural Center
107 Suffolk St.
New York, NY 10002
(212) 477-9945
http://users.rcn.com/clgri//
clgri@interport.net

Dedicated to the belief that diversity enriches us all and that the LGBT community has a unique perspective of the world that should be expressed and celebrated through the arts. Supports community-based arts and artists. The long-term commitment is to create an Arts Complex in New York City to permanently house lesbian and gay creative expression.

Gay and Lesbian Community Services Center
Box 38777
1213 N. Highland Ave.
Los Angeles, CA 90038
(213) 464-7400

GayNet
majordomo@queernet.org.

Discussion and news network for gay, lesbian, and bisexual concerns

Gender Education and Advocacy
P.O. Box 65
Kensington, MD 20895
(301) 949-3822 (#8)

Hate Crime National Hotline
(800) 686-HATE
anywhere in the U.S.A
http://www.lambda.org/

Anti-Violence Project of the GLBT Hate Crime National Hotline
(800) 616-HATE
AVP@lambda.org

International Foundation for Gender Education
P.O. Box 540229
Waltham, MA 02454-0229
(781) 899-2212
info@ifge.org

Le Gambit
Box 35822
Dallas, TX 75235

LesBiGay subgroup of MENSA (an international organization for individuals who score in the top 2% of IQ tests)

Media Resources: Magazines, Television
http://www.qrd.org/media/
www.advocate.com
www.planetout.com

National Association of Lesbian, Gay, Bisexual, and Transgender Community Centers
208 W. Thirteenth St.
New York, NY 10011
(212) 620-7310
info@gaycenter.org

NetGALA—The Network of Gay and Lesbian Alumni Groups
P.O. Box 53188
Washington, DC 20009
http://www.qrd.org/www/orgs/netgala/
netgala@aol.com
netgalacnf@aol.com

NetGALA exists to facilitate interactions between its constituent alumni(ae) associations and to act as a resource of information pertaining to the organizing of gay and lesbian alumni(ae) associations.

The Other Queer Page
www.toqp.com.

The Other Queer Page, more than 1,350 sorted links and growing of the best of gay, lesbian, bisexual, and transgender resources available on the Web, ranging from coming out to getting involved in the fight for equal rights

Pridelinks.com/Organizations
General information on gay, lesbian, or queer

Pridenet.com
http://www.pridenet.com/main.html

To provide a "G-rated," intense resource center for gays and lesbians as well as a tremendous focus on transgender and bisexual resources

QueerAmerica
http://www.queer.com/queeramerica/

QueerNet
P.O. Box 14309
San Francisco, CA 94114
http://groups.queernet.org/
info@QueerNet.ORG

Provides hundreds of e-mail communities for the gay/lesbian/bisexual/transgender community

Queer Resources Directory
http://www.qrd.org/

General information and organizations on gay, lesbian, or queer

Ruralgay.com
http://www.ruralgay.com/

For gay rural folk to connect, with chat, personals, homepage links, forums, resource listings, and more

Sexuality Information and Education Council of the United States
130 W. Forty-second St., Suite 350
New York, NY 10036-7802
(212) 819-9770
siecus@siecus.org

RELIGIOUS RESOURCES

Affirmation (Mormon)
P.O. Box 46022
Los Angeles, CA 90046-0022
(323) 255-7251
http://www.affirmation.org/

Affirmation (United Methodist)
P.O. Box 1021
Evanston, IL 60204
(847) 733-9590
http://www.umaffirm.org/

Al-Fatiha Foundation (Muslim)
405 Park Ave., Suite 1500
New York, NY 10022
(212) 752-4242
http://www.al-fatiha.net/
gaymuslims@yahoo.com

American Gay and Lesbian Atheists, Inc.
P.O. Box 66711
Houston, TX 77266-6711
Dial-A-Gay-Atheist: (713) 880-4242
http://www.qrd.org/orgs/contacts/american.gay.and.lesbian.atheists

Anglican Institute for Affirmative Christian Studies
EACA2AIACS@aol.com

Association of Welcoming and Affirming Baptists
P.O. Box 2596
Attleboro Falls, MA 02763-0894
(508) 226-1945
Fax: (508) 226-1991
Mail@WABaptists.org

Brethren/Mennonite Council for Lesbian and Gay Concerns
P.O. Box 6300
Minneapolis, MN 55406
(612) 722-6906
http://www.webcom.com/bmc/welcome.html

Dignity/USA (Catholic)
1500 Massachusetts Ave., NW, Suite 11
Washington, DC 20005-1894
(800) 877-8797
www.dignityusa.org

Emergence International (Christian Scientist)
P.O. Box 26237
Phoenix, AZ 85068
(800) 280-6653

Evangelical Anglican Church in America
2401 Artesia Blvd., Suite 106-213
Redondo Beach, CA 90278
EACAOBIS1@aol.com

Evangelicals Concerned with Reconciliation
P.O. Box 19734
Seattle, WA 98109-6734
(206) 621-8960
http://www.ecwr.org/

Friends for Lesbian and Gay Concerns (Quaker)
143 Campbell Ave.
Ithaca, NY 14850
http://www.quaker.org/flgc/
jckelly@lightlink.com

Gay Buddhist Fellowship (GBF)
2215-R Market St., Suite 162
San Francisco, CA 94114
(415) 207-8113
(415) 974-9878
http://www.gaybuddhist.org/

Gay, Lesbian, and Affirming Disciples Alliance, Inc. (Disciples of Christ)
GLAD Alliance, Inc.
P.O. Box 44400
Indianapolis, IN 46244-0400
http://www.gladalliance.org/
W   for the full dignity and integrity of gay, lesbian, bisexual, and affirming people within the Christian Church (Disciples of Christ)

Integrity (Episcopalian)
1718 M St., NW
P.O. Box 148
Washington, DC 20036
(202) 462-9193
(800) 462-9498
http://www.integrityusa.org/

Interweave
Unitarian Universalists for Lesbian, Gay, Bisexual, and Transgender Concerns
167 Milk St., Suite 406
Boston, MA 02109-4339
http://www.qrd.org/www/orgs/uua/uu-interweave.html

Lutherans Concerned
P.O. Box 10197
Chicago, IL 60610
http://www.lcna.org/

More Light Presbyterians
369 Montezuma Ave., Suite 447
Santa Fe, NM 87501-2626
(505) 820-7082
http://www.mlp.org/

National Gay Pentecostal Alliance
P.O. Box 20428
Ferndale, MI 48220

Outspirit
http://www.outspirit.org/
Empowers the search of the lesbian, gay, bisexual, or transgender person in finding sacredness by bridging the similarities and the diversities of traditional religions and alternative spirituality. Supports all pathways by offering information, inspiration, involvement, and encouragement.

Religious Tolerance.Org
Ontario Consultants on Religious Tolerance (OCRT)
P.O. Box 514

Wellesley Island, NY 13640-0514
http://religioustolerance.org/
A multifaith agency of four volunteers who foll   four different religious beliefs (agnosticism, atheism, Christianity, and Wicca). This group is not affiliated with any religious organization. Purposes: to disseminate accurate religious information; expose religious fraud, hatred, and misinformation; and disseminate information on "hot" religious topics. Ethical systems from Asatru to Zorastrianism, including agnosticism, atheism, Buddhism, Christianity, Hinduism, humanism, Islam, Judaism, Native spirituality, New Age, neopaganism, Santeria, Wicca, and dozens of others.

SDA Kinship International
(Seventh-Day Adventist)
P.O. Box 7320
Laguna Niguel, CA 92607
(949) 248-1299
www.sdakinship.org

The Spirit Rainbow
704 Cocheco Court
Dover, NH 03820-4814
http://www.geocities.com/WestHollywood/Castro/2857/
nh.magi@gay.com
Religious laymen (or laypersons) who desire to help others. Affirms that it is a right, not only as created beings but by the First Amendment of the Constitution of the United States, to peaceably assemble for the freedom of religious expression.

Unitarian Universalist Association
25 Beacon St.
Boston, MA 02108
(617) 742-2100
http://www.uua.org/

United Church of Christ
700 Prospect Ave.
Cleveland, OH 44115
(216) 736-2100
Fax: (216) 736-2223
www.ucc.org

United Fellowship of Metropolitan Community Churches
8704 Santa Monica Blvd., 2d floor
West Hollywood, CA 90069
(310) 360-8640
http://www.ufmcc.com/

Unity Fellowship Church Movement (African American)
5148 W. Jefferson Blvd.
Los Angeles, CA 90016
(323) 938-8322

Whosoever
http://www.whosoever.org/

An online magazine for gay, lesbian, bisexual, and transgender Christians

World Congress of Gay and Lesbian Jewish Organizations
P.O. Box 23379
Washington, DC 20026-3379
(202) 452-7424
http://www.wcgljo.org/

TRANSGENDER RESOURCES

Renaissance Transgender Association, Inc.
987 Old Eagle School Rd., Suite 719
Wayne, PA 19087
(610) 975-9119
http://www.ren.org/

To provide the very best comprehensive educat   and caring support to transgender individuals and those close to them through offering a variety of carefully selected programs and resources focused on the factors affecting their lives

Susan's Place Transgender Resources
http://www.susans.org/

Information on activism, reassignment surgery, medical information, cross-dressing, spirituality, support groups, transitioning, articles, and chat rooms

TransGenderCare.com
http://www.transgendercare.com/default.asp

Specialists in the medical and psychological aspects of transgender health care. Contributors, editors, and health care advisors to TransGenderCare donate their time and expertise without compensation of any kind and do not conduct business, heath care practice, or any other enterprise through this noncommercial educational site.

Transgender Law and Policy Institute
http://www.transgenderlaw.org/

A nonprofit organization dedicated to engaging in effective advocacy for transgender people

in our society. TLPI brings experts together to work on law and policy initiatives designed to advance transgender equality.

Transgender Support Site
http://heartcorps.com/journeys/everything.htm

WORKPLACE/PROFESSIONAL RESOURCES

Council on Social Work Education
Commission on Sexual Orientation and Gender Expression
1725 Duke St., Suite 500
Alexandria, VA 22314-3457
(703) 683-8099
www.geocities.com/lgcommission/

P   the development of social work curriculum materials and faculty growth opportunities relevant to sexual orientation, gender expression, and the experiences of GLBT people

Gay America Business Directory
http://www.gabd.com/

Gay Financial Network (GFN)
http://www.gfn.com/

Provides the most comprehensive financial i   on everything from buying a home to making a stock trade

Gay, Lesbian, and Straight Teachers Network (GLSTN)
122 W. Twenty-sixth St., Suite 1100
New York, NY 10001
(212) 727-0135
http://www.glstn.org/respect/
glstn@glstn.org

Lesbian and Gay Labor Network
P.O. Box 1159, Peter Stuyvesant Station
New York, NY 10009
(212) 923-8690

National Lesbian and Gay Journalists Association (NLGJA)
1420 K St., NW, Suite 910
Washington, DC 20005
(202) 588-9888
Fax: (202) 588-1818
info@nlgja.org

An organization of journalists, online media professionals, and students that works from w   the journalism industry to foster fair and accurate coverage of lesbian, gay, bisexual, and transgender issues. NLGJA opposes workplace bias against all minorities and provides professional development for its members.

National Organization of Gay and Lesbian Scientists and Technical Professionals (NOGLSTP)

P.O. Box 91803
Pasadena, CA 91109
Phone or fax: (626) 791-7689
http://www.noglstp.org/

A national nonprofit educational organization of gay, lesbian, bisexual, and transgender people (and their advocates) employed or interested in scientific or high technology fields, and an affiliate of the American Association for the Advancement of Science. Goals include dialogue with professional organizations, disseminating information, improving members' employment and professional environment, opposing anti-queer discrimination and stereotypes, educating the queer, scientific, and general communities, and fostering intercity contacts among members.

Pride at Work

Lesbian and Gay Labor Network
P.O. Box 1159, Peter Stuyvesant Station
New York, NY 10009

Sociologists' Lesbian and Gay Caucus (SLGC)

P.O. Box 8425
Ann Arbor, MI 48107-8425

Graduate schools in sociology, the caucus has met for almost 20 years with the annual meetings of the American Sociological Association and the Society for the Study of Social Problems of the gay "climate" at the schools.

Sociologists' Lesbian, Gay, Bisexual, and Transgendered Caucus (SLGBTC)

P.O. Box 2133
Saint Cloud, MN 56302-2133
http://www.qrd.org/www/orgs/slgc/SLGC.html
Tracy Ore: tore@STCLOUDSTATE.EDU

YOUTH RESOURCES

Advocates for Youth

1025 Vermont Ave., NW, Suite 200
Washington, DC 20005
(202) 347-5700

www.youthresource.com
info@advocatesforyouth.org

Bridges Project of American Friends Service Committee (AFSC)

1501 Cherry St.
Philadelphia, PA 19102
(215) 281-7000, (215) 241-7133
BridgesPro@aol.com

Gay Youth Against Discrimination (GYAD)

http://www.geocities.com/njgts_kyd/gyad.html

An organization that urges kids across the country to participate in stopping homophobia in schools

National Advocacy Coalition on Youth and Sexual Orientation

1711 Connecticut Ave., NW, Suite 206
Washington, DC 20009
nacyso@aol.com

National Bisexual Youth Initiative

c/o Watergap Dr.
Fayetteville, NC 28314.
(910) 864-3769
http://www.biresource.org/byi.html

National Hotline for Gay, Lesbian, Bisexual, and Transgender Youth

(800) 347-TEEN (toll-free)`
http://www.geocities.com/WestHollywood/1590/

National Youth Advocacy Coalition

1638 R St., NW, Suite 300
Washington, DC 20009
(202) 319-7596
nyac@nyacyouth.org

Native American Gay, Lesbian, Bi, and Trans Youth

http://www.youthresource.com/

A project of Advocates for Youth

Oasis—A writing magazine for youth

http://www.oasismag.com/

OutProud, The National Coalition for Gay, Lesbian, Bisexual, and Transgender Youth

369-B Third St., Suite 362
San Rafael, CA 94901-3581
(415) 499-0993, (415) 460-5452
Fax: (415) 499-1013
http://www.outproud.org/
info@outproud.org

Publishes a database called QueerAmerica, used for referring queer youth (and adults) to local support resources. http://www.outproud. org/outproud/ and go to QueerAmerica.

Out Youth
(800) 96-YOUTH
Austin, TX

Queer Resources Directory
http://www.qrd.org/qrd/youth/
The "soc.support.youth.gay-lesbian-bi" Internet newsgroup
http://www.youth.org/ssyglb

TransBoy Resource Network
Internet resources for transgender, gender-bending, transsexual, intersex, and gender-questioning youth who were designated female at birth but identify as somewhere else on the gender spectrum
transboys@yahoo.com

Trevor Helpline/Hotline—national toll-free, 24 hours, seven days a week
(800) 850-8078
GLBT youth help line

Youth Suicide Problems
Gay/Bisexual Male Focus
http://www.virtualcity.com/youthsuicide/

Resource on gay and bisexual male suicide problems, related issues, and a little-known concept related to youth suicide

INDEX

ableism, 45, 371
absolutism, 371–72
abuse, 60, 134; anti-gay, 310–11; child,
    5, 142, 252, 397; fears of, 162, 310; in
    schools, 59, 311, 444; sexual, 252, 397;
    verbal, 46, 185, 365; of women, 29, 39
acceptance: in ethnic communities,
    154–55, 162, 182; family, 154–55, 157, 158,
    162, 168–69, 169; and identity, 90; and
    religion, 385, 386, 393, 394–95; of self,
    101, 153, 202–3, 206; and social work
    practice, 234–35
acculturation, 356–59
Acree, M., 326
action-based strategies, 380
ACT-UP (AIDS Coalition to Unleash
    Power), 32, 457
ADA. See Americans with Disabilities Act
Adam, B. D., 288–89, 289
Adams, Marge, 29
Addams, Jane, 9, 19
Adelman, M., 293
adjustment, 63; of children, 165, 166–67,
    208–9, 231; of families, 156, 158–63, 165,
    274; of heterosexual spouses, 164; and
    integration, 359; model of, 158–59, 160;
    of older adults, 293, 332; as process,
    157–58, 161; of transsexuals, 357, 358; of
    young adults, 319
Adleman, Jeanne, 294
Adler, Alfred, 295
Adolescent Family Life Act (AFLA), 446
adolescents, 12, 177–95; academic difficul-
    ties of, 133–34; and adolescence as
    transition, 177–78; advocacy for, 453; in
    affirmative practice, 188–89, 465, 466,
    467; and anti-harassment laws, 444;
    bisexual, 309–10; of color, 182, 309, 314,
    315–16; defined, 177; and depression,
    134, 184; development of, 178–79, 179,

181–82; and disclosure, 133–34, 179, 181,
    231, 309, 310, 314, 466; and family, 133,
    142, 186; fears of, 179–80, 310; health
    issues of, 187, 309, 310, 311, 315–16; and
    HIV/AIDS, 309, 313, 314; and identity,
    178–79; institutionalization of, 450, 451;
    isolation of, 63, 162, 181, 183–84; les-
    bian, 187, 309, 312; in lesbian families,
    167; mental health of, 134, 183, 184,
    314; peer pressure on, 133, 136, 178; and
    pregnancy, 187, 312; and relationships,
    187; risk factors for, 134, 177, 183–87,
    309; and role models, 178; in rural
    areas, 182–83; in school, 58–59, 59, 67,
    133–34, 181, 186–87, 315; self-destructive,
    180, 185; services for, 413; and sexual-
    ity, 63, 161–62, 178–79, 181–82, 187,
    311–12; sexually active, 311–12; as sexual
    minority, 178–79, 179; and STDs, 187,
    309, 311–12, 312; stress on, 133–34, 309,
    314; and substance abuse, 184–85, 309,
    313–14, 350, 351; and suicide, 134, 142,
    162, 185, 309, 314–15, 315; support for,
    133, 134, 142, 178, 315; transgender, 184,
    185, 272, 275; victimization of, 185–86,
    309, 310–11; violence against, 179, 180,
    185–86; working with, 187–91
adoption, 35, 250, 253, 451, 453; access
    to, 226–28; foreign, 58, 227–28, 443;
    for gay male couple, 210–11; joint,
    210–11, 443; laws against GLBT, 56,
    430, 440; legal assistance in, 210, 228;
    legal documents on, 443–44; and legal
    relationships, 435, 436; open, 234; pri-
    mary, 442–43; second-parent, 58, 210,
    216, 227–28, 432–34, 435, 442, 443–44;
    social policy on, 58, 429; state policies
    on, 432–34
adults, GLBT, 325–29. See also older
    adults, GLBT; young adults, GLBT